FLORIDA KEYS

JOSHUA LAWRENCE KINSER

Contents

FLORIDA KEYS

Big Cypress
National Preserve

Everglades
National Park

Gulf of Mexico

Big Torch
Key

Big Pine
Key

No Name
Key

Pigeon Key

Sugarloaf
Key

Little Torch
Key

Bahia Honda
State Park

Saddlebunch
Keys

Marquesas
Keys

Key West

Lower
Sugarloaf
Key

Fort Zachary Taylor
Historic State Park

Boca Chica
Key

Straits of Florida

© MOON.COM

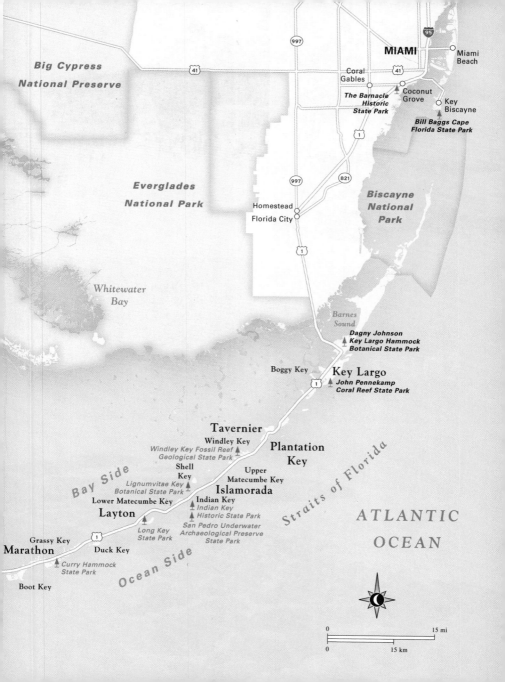

the Florida Keys

Even those who have never ventured south of New York City have probably heard of the Florida Keys. Stretching southwest from Miami between the Atlantic Ocean and the Gulf of Mexico, this diverse archipelago is, after all, legendary.

With its Mardi Gras vibe, much-publicized Hemingway connection, and ongoing "threat" to secede from the union, Key West is surely the most well-known island in the region. This unique place nurtures a strange blend of hardy natives, eccentric artists, and wide-eyed tourists. But the Keys hold more than just the country's southernmost city.

If you're driving from Miami or the Everglades—both vibrant areas worth a look before heading south—you'll first encounter enticing Key Largo, the slowly burgeoning getaway for southern Floridians. It's the kind of place where locals can dock their boats just steps from laid-back waterfront eateries. With fascinating underwater coral reefs that extend along the eastern shore, it's also the self-proclaimed "diving capital of the world."

South of Key Largo, the remaining Upper Keys accessible by the Overseas Highway (U.S. 1) compose Islamorada, an area long celebrated for its bountiful sportfishing. After crossing a lengthy bridge, you'll be in the heart of the Middle

Clockwise from top left: Miami Beach lifeguard stand; Clarence S. Higgs Memorial Beach; elkhorn coral at Molasses Reef off Key Largo; Duval Street in Key West; Southernmost Point Monument in Key West; aerial view of the Florida Keys.

Keys, a transitional space between the natural pleasures of the north and the unabashed revelry of the south. Centered on Marathon (which, like Islamorada, encompasses several keys), this region offers a number of wildlife-oriented activities, from bird-watching haunts to dolphin encounters.

For even more animal sightings, continue south to the Lower Keys, where wild creatures abound in the National Key Deer Refuge on and around Big Pine Key. Even farther south, you'll spy mammals of a different variety—the tourists who descend upon the streets of Key West. They're especially prevalent from October to April, when the weather is usually sunny and mild and offers a respite from colder places.

Even those who are intimately familiar with the Florida Keys only know a small percentage of them. The Overseas Highway—the only drivable link to the mainland—connects fewer than 50 of the more than 800 islands of this unforgettable chain. Venture out by boat to explore the more elusive ones, a trip that promises mystery, adventure, and an experience unlike anything else.

Clockwise from top left: Art Deco District in Miami; the Seven Mile Bridge between the Middle Keys and Lower Keys; a hand-painted sign in Key West; Fort Jefferson at Dry Tortugas National Park.

8 TOP EXPERIENCES

1 **Explore underwater:** Go snorkeling and diving amid shipwrecks, artificial reefs, and vibrant coral formations (pages 30, 109, 184, and 214).

2 **Have a wild time watching animals:** Get an up-close look at dolphins, key deer, alligators, and more (page 29).

3 **Savor local cuisine:** Feast on fresh seafood and key lime pie in the Keys, Cuban food in Miami, and fried gator tail in the Everglades (page 25).

>>>

4 **Find your perfect beach:** Whether you want to catch the sunrise, swim, fish, or watch turtles, there's a beach for you (page 27).

^
^
^

5 **Go for a paddle:** Experience the bountiful waters and amazing creatures of this region by kayak (pages 82, 115, 147, and 212).

6 **Party all night in Key West:** Do the "Duval crawl," stopping by every bar along Duval Street, from the Atlantic Ocean to the Gulf of Mexico (page 265). Key West has become a pilgrimage for LGBTQ folks (page 32).

7 **Take a picture at the Southernmost Point:** The southernmost point in the continental United States is a classic photo op—but be prepared for long lines (page 234).

∧
∧
∧

8 **Visit Ernest Hemingway's home:** Retrace the writer's steps and see the backyard studio where he wrote *To Have and Have Not* (page 238).

Planning Your Trip

Where to Go

Miami and the Everglades

While some travelers head directly to Key West by boat or plane, most pass through the gateway areas of Miami and the Everglades before driving south to the Florida Keys. If you have time, consider exploring this diverse region, where you can stroll amid Miami Beach's colorful **Art Deco District,** soak up some sunshine on the Magic City's stunning **beaches,** snorkel above the coral reefs of **Biscayne National Park,** take a guided canoe trip among the cypress trees of **Fakahatchee Strand Preserve State Park,** and visit the critters at the **Everglades Alligator Farm.**

Key Largo

From the mainland, most motorists take U.S. 1, also called the Overseas Highway, to reach the Florida Keys. The first island encountered is Key Largo, the largest of this unique archipelago. Here you'll find several outdoor diversions, including **Dolphin Cove** and **Dolphins Plus**—sister

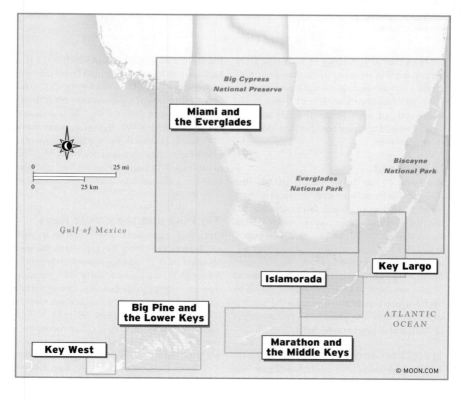

© MOON.COM

Islamorada marina

facilities that offer a range of activities, from natural dolphin swims to trainer-for-a-day programs. Outdoors enthusiasts will especially enjoy **John Pennekamp Coral Reef State Park,** where you can swim alongside sandy beaches, kayak among mangrove trees, or dive amid offshore coral reefs.

Islamorada

Southwest of Key Largo are the islands that make up Islamorada, an upscale resort area favored by anglers and scuba divers. Outdoor attractions dominate here: You can watch sea lion shows at **Theater of the Sea,** feed wild tarpon at **Robbie's of Islamorada,** and visit four different state parks, including **Indian Key Historic State Park** and **Lignumvitae Key Botanical State Park,** both of which are only accessible by boat. Sea lovers might also appreciate the **History of Diving Museum,** which houses a noteworthy collection of diving paraphernalia.

Marathon and the Middle Keys

After experiencing Islamorada, you'll pass into the Middle Keys, the heart of which is the laid-back town of Marathon. Animal lovers can swim with dolphins at the **Dolphin Research Center,** observe pelicans and raptors at **Curry Hammock State Park** and **Crane Point Museum and Nature Center,** or visit recovering sea turtles at **The Turtle Hospital.** For a quieter experience, visitors can relax on the area's lovely **beaches** or head south to isolated **Pigeon Key,** a historic base camp accessible by ferry or the **Old Seven Mile Bridge.**

Big Pine and the Lower Keys

Once you've crossed the **Seven Mile Bridge,** you'll enter the Lower Keys, perhaps the most tranquil part of this legendary archipelago. Although **Bahia Honda State Park** lures numerous visitors to its beaches, campgrounds, hiking trails, and warm waters that are ideal for both kayakers and snorkelers, you're likely to spy more wildlife in this region than fellow tourists. Among the plentiful offerings, recreationists will find wooded solitude in the **National Key Deer Refuge** on Big Pine Key, **fishing** charters on Summerland Key, and superb diving opportunities around Looe Key.

Key West

Celebrated for its breezy hotels, sunset celebrations, and festive atmosphere, especially along Duval Street, the Southernmost City will certainly keep you busy for days on end. Here you can relax on numerous beaches, tour historic homes, visit engaging museums and nature centers, view the entire city from atop the Key West Lighthouse, or take a ferry to the Dry Tortugas. At night you'll find no shortage of lively bars, and throughout the year, you can participate in an array of festivals and events.

Know Before You Go

Seasons

Although southern Florida is a year-round destination, some businesses, namely restaurants in Key West, close during September. In general, summer is the least crowded time to visit, perhaps because temperatures are fairly high from June to September, when the Atlantic hurricane season is at its peak.

Whereas spring and fall are comfortable in this subtropical region, winter is the high season in the Florida Keys, when the climate is much warmer than in the northern United States. In general, late December through April is often the busiest period as snowbirds descend upon the Keys; lodging rates are usually higher during this peak tourist season as well as during major events and holiday weekends. Accommodations often cost less during the midseason, which typically ranges from May to July and from late October to mid-December. Hotels, inns, and resorts can be at their cheapest during the low season, which, save for holidays and festivals, is normally late

the Overseas Highway

summer and early fall, between August and mid-October. Although the accommodations listings in this guide reflect southern Florida's wide range in rates, be advised that every establishment has its own seasonal schedule and therefore its own pricing policy, so be sure to check each place in question before making travel plans.

Your **activities** can also determine the timing of your trip. Swimmers and snorkelers might enjoy the slightly warmer waters of summer, but anglers must consider the varied fishing seasons before making plans. Blue marlins, for example, are prevalent from March to October while cobias are more common from November to April.

Hurricanes

Some out-of-towners are apprehensive about visiting the Florida Keys during the Atlantic hurricane season, which usually runs from June 1 to November 30. The truth is, however, that hurricanes are infrequent in this region, and many of the most popular events, such as Hemingway Days and Fantasy Fest, occur during this half of the year. Nevertheless, it's always a good idea to be prepared for the worst. If you do plan to visit the Florida Keys during hurricane season, stay apprised of weather updates and be prepared to evacuate if necessary. Although most radio and television stations provide weather updates, it's also possible to contact the **National Weather Service (NWS)** directly; there are offices in Key West (1315 White St., 305/295-1316, www.srh.noaa.gov/key) and Miami (11691 SW 17th St., 305/229-4522, www.srh.noaa.gov/mfl).

Transportation

DRIVING TO THE KEYS

Miami, the Everglades, and the Florida Keys constitute a fairly compact destination, especially given that one main highway—**the 110-mile Overseas Highway (U.S. 1)**—links much of this region. Though most visitors come by car, motorcycle, or RV, it's possible to reach southern Florida using other forms of transportation. For instance, you can travel by train or bus to Miami, take a flight to Miami International Airport, or arrive in Key West by plane or cruise ship.

lightning over Miami

If you choose not to drive to southern Florida, your best bet would still be to rent a car and hit the road as soon as possible. After all, taxis can get expensive, and it's infinitely easier to travel the Overseas Highway by car, as opposed to walking or biking. Just be prepared for the drive from Miami to Key West to take roughly 3.5-4 hours in the mid- and low seasons, and perhaps more than 5 hours during the high season. In the absence of traffic, it can take about an hour to drive from Miami to Key Largo, another half hour to reach Islamorada, roughly 45 minutes to hit the heart of Marathon, about a half hour to make it to Big Pine Key, and an additional 45 minutes to arrive in Key West.

SAILING TO THE KEYS

There are an abundance of marinas in the islands, and almost everywhere you look offshore you are likely to see sailboats anchored and moored in the surrounding waterways. The most popular and boat-friendly islands are Key West, Big Pine, Islamorada, Marathon, and Key Largo. These islands are where you will find the most available slips and resupply locations at marinas, as well as the most restaurants and attractions with docks that give sailors convenient access.

The water is shallow in this region, but usually very clear. The major danger is running aground on shallows and hitting reefs, rocks, and debris around the islands. Do your homework and plot your course diligently to avoid disaster. Steer clear of sailing during the height of hurricane season, which is generally July through November.

The Florida Keys are an exceptionally high-traffic area. You're likely to compete for space in waterways with other sailboats, large yachts, high-powered speedboats, tour boats, fishing vessels, commercial traffic, paddlers, Jet Skiers, swimmers, divers, snorkelers, and marinelife. It is vitally important to be on the lookout for obstacles and other people and animals while using the waterways in the Florida Keys.

Sailing will give you access to some of the best part of the Keys. With a sailboat you'll able to cruise through clear blue waters to some of the most beautiful reefs, wrecks, fishing spots, and secluded islands, where you can explore so much more of what the Keys has to offer than if you were bound to land only.

Reservations

No matter when you plan to travel to the Florida Keys, you should reserve your accommodations in advance. Resorts and B&Bs book up quickly during the high seasons of winter and spring, and many businesses close during September, which is in between seasons.

Annual Events

From December to February, several noteworthy art festivals are held in Miami and throughout the Keys (see page 336). Then July lures visitors to Key West for Hemingway Days, and many flock to the Southernmost City for Fantasy Fest in late October.

exploring Key West by bike

white ibises and egrets in the Everglades

The Best of the Florida Keys

First-time visitors to the Florida Keys should set aside at least a week to experience the best that these legendary islands—plus the gateway areas of Miami and the Everglades—have to offer.

Day 1: Miami

Most travelers reach the Florida Keys by vehicle, which means you'll likely begin your trip in the **Miami** area. For a taste of the city's multicultural vibe, head to **Little Havana,** where you can sample authentic Cuban food and browse aromatic cigar shops. Then venture east to **South Beach,** where you can tour the colorful **Art Deco District,** view impressive art and artifact collections at the **Jewish Museum of Florida—FIU** or the **World Erotic Art Museum,** and relax at the popular **Lummus Park Beach.**

After lunch at one of South Beach's savory cafés, head southwest to **Coconut Grove** and **Coral Gables,** both of which boast a variety of historic structures and shopping options. Savor a fine meal and perhaps stay the night at **The Biltmore Hotel,** a 1920s-era hotel in Coral Gables, where you can also play golf or enjoy a massage. If you'd rather experience Miami's nightlife, stay in one of the boutique hotels or world-class resorts in South Beach.

Day 2: The Everglades

Rise early and head to **Bill Baggs Cape Florida State Park,** where you can stroll along the beach, have breakfast at the Lighthouse Cafe, and take a guided tour of the 1825 **Cape Florida Lighthouse,** which provides panoramic views of Biscayne Bay. Afterward venture south to **Biscayne National Park,** where you can explore Boca Chita Key, Elliott Key, and other islands by kayak.

If you're an animal lover, stop by the **Everglades Alligator Farm** near Florida City, which features live alligator feedings and airboat rides in the Everglades. For a more intimate tour of this subtropical wilderness, take a canoe trip through **Everglades National Park,**

Big Cypress National Preserve, or Collier-Seminole State Park, all marvelous places to observe birds, alligators, and other native creatures.

To experience the region's heritage, head to the Miccosukee Indian Village on the Tamiami Trail or the Ah-Tah-Thi-Ki Museum on the Big Cypress Seminole Indian Reservation. After a day of sightseeing, unwind at the Miccosukee Resort & Gaming, where you'll find dining, entertainment, and lodging options.

Day 3: Key Largo

Venture south on U.S. 1 to the Florida Keys. In northern Key Largo, head to the tranquil Dagny Johnson Key Largo Hammock Botanical State Park, which lures hikers, bikers, and wildlife lovers daily. Farther south you'll encounter John Pennekamp Coral Reef State Park, where popular activities include kayaking, snorkeling, and scuba diving.

Afterward head to Dolphins Plus, where you can swim with dolphins and learn how to be a marine mammal trainer. Wildlife lovers will also

appreciate the Florida Keys Wild Bird Center, home to rehabilitating brown pelicans, turkey vultures, and great horned owls.

Following a day of outdoor diversions, relax at one of Key Largo's many waterfront restaurants, most of which offer ideal spots to watch the sunset. Throughout Key Largo you'll find a variety of eateries, bars, and hotels, including those at the Key Largo Resorts Marina, which also features the historic *African Queen*.

Day 4: Islamorada

Continue southwest to the islands of Islamorada. Here art lovers can explore paintings, sculptures, and other unique creations at The Rain Barrel on Plantation Key, while history buffs can learn about the ill-fated Overseas Railroad at Windley Key Fossil Reef Geological State Park. Farther southwest it's hard to miss the enormous sign for Theater of the Sea, which offers glass-bottom boat rides, entertaining marine mammal shows, and the chance to swim with the resident dolphins and sea lions. On Upper Matecumbe Key, you'll find the History of Diving Museum,

airboat ride at Everglades Alligator Farm

which houses an interesting collection of diving paraphernalia.

On Lower Matecumbe Key, **Robbie's of Islamorada** features boat rentals, fishing charters, and an open-air market. The marina also provides boat tours of two remote islands: **Indian Key Historic State Park,** once the site of a lucrative cargo-salvaging business, and **Lignumvitae Key Botanical State Park,** where you can tour a virgin tropical forest. While all the islands of Islamorada are worth visiting, Upper Matecumbe Key boasts most of the area's shops, spas, bars, restaurants, and accommodations.

Day 5: Marathon and the Middle Keys

Just past Layton in the **Middle Keys** is **Long Key State Park,** a tranquil place for canoeists, anglers, hikers, and snorkelers. Farther south, you can embrace other family-friendly diversions, such as flying high above the islands and coral reefs via **Island Hoppers Aerial Adventures,** frolicking with dolphins at the **Dolphin Research Center,** exploring the wooded islands of **Curry Hammock State Park,** and relaxing on **Sombrero Beach,** popular with swimmers, picnickers, and volleyball enthusiasts.

If you have time, take a walking tour of **The Turtle Hospital,** a rescue facility on Vaca Key. Then stop by the Pigeon Key Gift Shop, housed in a red train car, and purchase admission to **Pigeon Key,** an early 20th-century base camp for bridge workers. Admission includes a ferry ride to the island, which you can also access via the **Old Seven Mile Bridge.**

You'll find plenty of after-hours dining and lodging options in the Middle Keys. Though most lie on Vaca Key, Marathon's lengthiest island, you may prefer more isolated places, such as **Hawks Cay Resort** on Duck Key.

Day 6: Big Pine and the Lower Keys

After crossing the **Seven Mile Bridge,** you'll encounter the less populated **Lower Keys,** where **Bahia Honda State Park** lures kayakers,

snorkelers, anglers, and bikers daily. On **Big Pine Key,** you might be able to spot a tiny key deer in the **National Key Deer Refuge** or an alligator at the freshwater **Blue Hole.** While here, take a snorkeling or diving trip to **Looe Key Reef,** where you'll spy large coral formations, spiny lobster, and the remains of a shipwreck.

Where you choose to spend your evening depends on your budget. If you can't afford the high dining and lodging prices at the exclusive **Little Palm Island Resort & Spa,** consider some of the Lower Keys' more affordable options, from cottages on Big Pine Key to an RV park on Geiger Key.

Day 7: Key West

Head to **Key West** and survey its attractions aboard the **Conch Tour Train.** Then begin your self-guided tour on Duval Street in **Old Town,** where you can peruse art galleries, visit historical landmarks, and see colorful butterflies at **The Key West Butterfly & Nature Conservatory.** On nearby Whitehead Street, stroll among six-toed felines at the **Ernest Hemingway Home and Museum,** view the city from atop the **Key West Lighthouse,** and see John James Audubon's drawings at the **Audubon House & Tropical Gardens.**

Not far away, the impressive **Mel Fisher Maritime Museum** presents many of the treasures discovered in the famous *Atocha* shipwreck. Stroll to the nearby **Custom House Museum,** where you'll see portraits of famous Key West residents, and take a guided tour of the **Harry S. Truman Little White House.** If there's time, head to **Fort Zachary Taylor Historic State Park,** which offers guided tours of the 19th-century fort as well as the finest beach in town.

Be sure to experience the daily **Sunset Celebration** at **Mallory Square,** and enjoy the plethora of nearby shops, bars, and restaurants. While you'll find a variety of accommodations here, from low-key campgrounds to oceanfront resorts, consider staying in Old Town, which ensures easy access to Key West's most popular activities.

THE KEYS

Seafood

You'll find some of the best fresh seafood in the country in the Keys. You can walk a few feet along Duval Street, sit down at almost any restaurant, and marvel at the quality and variety of seafood on the menu. Try the catch-of-the-day selection at Chef Michael's (page 158) in Islamorada.

You can also catch your own supper, put it on ice, and take it to one of the many restaurants in the region that will prepare and cook your catch for a small fee. The service is called "catch and cook," and you'll see it advertised on menus all over the Keys. It's a memorable experience, and it's as fresh as fish gets.

Conch is a unique item on the region's menus. The conch, a large sea snail with an iconic spiraling shell (as seen on the official Key West flag), is more than just a simple mollusk in the Keys. Conch is served in a variety of ways: chowders, cold salads, stews, ceviche, gumbo, and best of all, as fried conch fritters. Try the fritters at Key Largo Conch House (page 122) in Key Largo.

Key Lime Pie

The iconic key lime pie is one of the most sought-after delicacies in the Keys. It's a simple pie dish made special by the juice of key limes, which only grow in this part of the world. Look for pies with a light-yellow color—that's the authentic stuff. When you a see a neon-green slice of key lime pie, run away as fast as you can. Try the pie at Mrs. Mac's Kitchen (page 123) in Key Largo or Kermit's Key West Key Lime Shoppe (page 276) in Key West.

Cocktails

The mojito was Hemingway's thirst-quencher of choice during his time in the Florida Keys, and today it is the most popular concoction in the region. The drink is prepared with crushed mint leaves, rum (with or without, it's spectacularly refreshing), simple syrup, lime juice, carbonated water, and ice squares, and is the perfect cure for the hot and humid weather. If you want something sweeter, but just as cold and refreshing, you'll find a long list of drinks that feature tropical fruits

key lime pie

and ice, the most popular being strawberry daiquiris and piña coladas. Quench your thirst at Sloppy Joe's Bar (page 283) in Key West.

MIAMI

Cuban Food

Make sure to feast on some Cuban food in Miami. Try Cuban chicken stew *(fricase de pollo)* and yummy fried plantains drizzled with honey. Caribe Cafe Restaurant (page 65) is a good place to start. For those with a sweet tooth, make sure to visit one of the many Cuban bakeries in Miami, which serve up churros, sweet breads, and guava-and-cream-cheese pastries called *pastelitos*. La Rosa Bakery (page 66) serves some of the best.

THE EVERGLADES

Alligator?

Alligator is mostly served as fried nuggets, but occasionally you'll see whole tail and other interesting preparations. If you're daring, try the fried gator tail at Coopertown Restaurant (page 86). And it's true…it pretty much tastes like chicken.

Key West Weekend

Luxury, history, and revelry combine on this whimsical island, a popular place for weekend getaways.

Friday

When planning your getaway, book a room at one of Key West's unique hotels, such as **Eden House** or the **Marquesa Hotel,** both of which offer deluxe accommodations and relaxing pool areas. For a stunning ocean view and access to a private beach, you might prefer a waterfront location like **Southernmost Beach Resort.** No matter where you decide to stay, though, reservations are highly recommended, especially on weekends during the high season.

After checking into your hotel and freshening up, take a stroll to **Mallory Square,** where artists, musicians, acrobats, and tourists converge daily to pay homage to Key West's gorgeous sunsets. To avoid the crowds, head to **The Westin Key West Resort & Marina,** where you can watch the sunset while sipping cocktails on the **Sunset Deck.**

Once the sun goes down, head inland for an early dinner, perhaps at **Michaels Restaurant** or **Café Solé,** two of Key West's best eateries. Afterward you can stroll along the quiet residential roads and make your way to **Duval Street,** a popular thoroughfare that's rife with lively late-night bars—plus curious shops and art galleries, some of which feature enticing window displays.

For a nightcap, stop by **Better Than Sex** on Simonton, a bordello-style lounge and restaurant that focuses exclusively on wine, beer, coffee, and decadent desserts. Often hosting live jazz, this relaxing, dimly lighted gem is usually open until midnight.

Saturday

Start the day with breakfast at the **Banana Cafe,** a popular French-style eatery that specializes in delectable crepes. Afterward, rent bicycles from **Eaton Bikes** on Margaret Street (or have them delivered to you) and tour Key West at your own pace. Be sure to ride up Whitehead Street, where you can visit such tranquil places as the

the historic and popular Duval Street in downtown Key West

Best Beaches

KEY LARGO

- **Cannon Beach** (page 104): This prized beach provides easy access to a swimming area and the remnants of an old Spanish shipwreck. Offshore activities include snorkeling, fishing, and kayaking.

ISLAMORADA

- **Anne's Beach** (page 145): Dedicated to local environmentalist Anne Eaton, this tranquil beach on the ocean side of Lower Matecumbe Key features a shallow swimming area and boardwalk access to secluded stretches of sand.

MARATHON AND THE MIDDLE KEYS

- **Long Key State Park** (page 173): Long Key State Park contains a narrow, grass-lined beach on the ocean side of U.S. 1. Only open to those staying in the state park campground, it tends to be more peaceful than the beaches farther south.

- **Curry Hammock State Park** (page 176): Little Crawl Key features a pleasant beach and playground area that is accessible to overnight campers and day-use visitors alike. Fishing, kayaking, picnicking, and beachcombing are popular activities here.

- **Coco Plum Beach** (page 181): With a long stretch of sandy shore, this dog-friendly beach on the Atlantic side of Marathon is a perfect spot to watch the sunset at the end of the day. It's also a sea turtle nesting area, and seeing cute baby turtles hatch and waddle their way to the waves for the first time is something you will likely remember for the rest of your life.

- **Sombrero Beach** (page 181): Located in the southern part of Marathon, this beautiful beach is one of the most popular in the Keys, particularly among locals. This curvy, palm-lined expanse of sand is also a preferred spot for nesting turtles from April to October.

BIG PINE AND THE LOWER KEYS

- **Sandspur Beach** (page 209): Arguably the most popular beach in the Florida Keys, this

beach view from the Fort Zachary Taylor Historic State Park in Key West

photogenic, sandy stretch includes swaying palm trees, turquoise waters, and white sand.

KEY WEST

- **Fort Zachary Taylor Historic State Park** (page 248): Praised by sunbathers, swimmers, snorkelers, and bird-watchers alike, the beach just south of Fort Zachary Taylor is surely the finest in Key West. The clear, deep waters nurture living coral and tropical fish.

- **Clarence S. Higgs Memorial Beach** (page 254): At the foot of White Street lies another popular beach, where sun worshippers can rent water-sports equipment or stroll on the adjacent swimming pier.

- **Smathers Beach** (page 254): On warm, sunny days, crowds flock to this lengthy beach alongside Roosevelt Boulevard, an ideal place to watch the sunrise.

- **Fort Jefferson Beach** (page 297): Only accessible via ferry or seaplane, this isolated beach is worth the trip. Besides its proximity to historic Fort Jefferson, it is terrific for swimming, snorkeling, and overnight camping.

Audubon House & Tropical Gardens and the **Ernest Hemingway Home and Museum,** both of which offer quiet spots to relax and gaze at the lush foliage. If you have time, stop by the **Key West Lighthouse,** which sits opposite the Hemingway Home, and climb the spiral staircase for an incredible view of the verdant city below.

Pedal over to Duval Street and stroll through **The Key West Butterfly & Nature Conservatory,** which features a glass-enclosed habitat filled with colorful birds and butterflies. Roughly 10 blocks away lies **Nancy Forrester's Secret Garden,** yet another peaceful spot to relish nature. For lunch, head to the **Schooner Wharf Bar,** where you can enjoy fresh seafood on a breezy upper deck overlooking the yachts and sailboats in the adjacent **Historic Seaport.**

Following lunch, you can either continue your biking tour through Key West or head to **Key West Eco Tours** or **Lazy Dog,** both of which offer guided kayaking trips. Rent a kayak, or take a tour and wind along mangrove creeks and get an up-close look at tropical fish, aquatic birds, and other marine wonders.

For another memorable adventure, spend the evening on a sunset cruise. Among those available, **Sunset Watersports Key West** offers a tropical buffet and a variety of beverages during the excursion. Enjoy the sunset views and have some fun on the lighted dance floor.

After the cruise, if you're not yet ready to call it a night, you'll find no shortage of distractions along Duval Street, from late-night dancing at the **Aqua Nightclub** to clothing-optional shenanigans at the rooftop **Garden of Eden.**

Sunday

If you have yet to return your bicycles to Eaton Bikes, a pickup can be arranged in the morning. After checking out of the hotel, stroll to **Martin's Key West,** a stylish German fusion restaurant on Duval, for brunch. Specialties include grilled bratwurst, seafood crepes, and eggs Benedict with lobster medallions. Following brunch, take a taxi or drive to **Fort Zachary Taylor Historic State Park,** where you can take some time to swim in the warm waters, snorkel amid colorful coral and parrotfish, and enjoy the best beach in town before heading back home.

Audubon House & Tropical Gardens

bikes on the beach in Key West

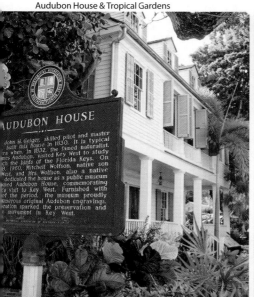

Animal Attractions

MIAMI

- Zoo Miami (page 54) is home to more than 1,000 different plant species and 500 different animal species, including endangered creatures like the tree kangaroo and Orinoco crocodile. At Miami Seaquarium (page 52) on Biscayne Bay, you can watch entertaining sea lions and killer whales, observe friendly manatees, and swim with dolphins. Situated between downtown Miami and South Beach, Jungle Island (page 46) has parrot shows, tiger and primate presentations, kangaroos interactions, and an Everglades habitat with alligators.

THE EVERGLADES

- You have several ways to get an up-close look at alligators, turtles, birds, and more in the Everglades. Go for a paddle or take a tram ride in Everglades National Park (page 83). Embark on a hike or drive down wildlife-filled Turner River Road in Big Cypress National Preserve (page 89). Or take an airboat ride through the swamps—Everglades Alligator Farm (page 75), Gator Park (page 86), Everglades Safari Park (page 86), and Billie Swamp Safari (page 91) are good options.

KEY LARGO

- Dolphins Plus (page 106) presents an array of year-round activities, from structured dolphin swims to trainer-for-a-day programs. The nonprofit Florida Keys Wild Bird Center (page 106) hosts a slew of native species, including woodpeckers, brown pelicans, laughing gulls, and great white herons.

ISLAMORADA

- At Theater of the Sea (page 142), you can swim with dolphins and sea lions and take a snorkeling cruise to an offshore coral reef. Several miles down U.S. 1, you can also feed visiting schools of tarpon at Robbie's of Islamorada (page 138).

MARATHON AND THE MIDDLE KEYS

- At Hawks Cay Resort on Duck Key, Dolphin

National Key Deer Refuge on Big Pine Key

Connection (page 173) allows visitors to interact with dolphins from the dock or in the water. In Marathon, the Dolphin Research Center (page 176) offers a variety of educational experiences, from brief dolphin dips to daylong research programs. Other animal diversions include the Crane Point Museum and Nature Center (page 177), where birds congregate alongside Florida Bay, and The Turtle Hospital (page 178), where guests can take a guided tour of a sea turtle rehabilitation area.

BIG PINE AND THE LOWER KEYS

- On Big Pine Key, you can search for diminutive key deer within the National Key Deer Refuge (page 207) or look for turtles and alligators at the Blue Hole (page 208).

KEY WEST

- The Key West Butterfly & Nature Conservancy (page 238) invites visitors into a vibrant, glass-enclosed habitat filled with colorful butterflies, birds, and flowering plants. In Mallory Square, the Key West Aquarium (page 238) presents daily shark feedings, plus the chance to observe tarpon, parrot fish, and sea turtles. The Florida Keys Eco-Discovery Center (page 249) contains a 2,500-gallon reef tank filled with living coral and tropical fish.

Underwater Adventure

The ocean waters along the eastern side of the Florida Keys constitute one of the finest—and most popular—underwater diving areas in the world. Stretching the length of the 220-mile archipelago and lying less than six miles offshore, the continental United States' only living coral barrier reef provides a thriving habitat for a wide array of fascinating marinelife, from sponges to kaleidoscopic fish, in waters ranging in depth from 5 to 70 feet.

Snorkelers and scuba divers—whether amateurs or aficionados—can easily spend five days exploring the shipwrecks, artificial reefs, and vibrant coral formations that are now protected within Florida Keys National Marine Sanctuary. If you plan to experience these underwater delights, there's no need to bring your own snorkeling gear and diving tanks; such equipment is available throughout the Keys.

No matter when you plan to travel to the Florida Keys, you should reserve your accommodations in advance. Wherever you decide to stay, you'll be within relatively easy driving distance of the region's varied diving outfitters and operators.

Key Largo

John Pennekamp Coral Reef State Park is America's first undersea park, and here you can take diving instruction, earn PADI Open Water certification, and participate in snorkeling or scuba-diving tours amid the offshore coral reefs east of Key Largo—such as **Key Largo Dry Rocks,** which contains the ever-popular *Christ of the Abyss* statue.

In addition to diving classes, Key Largo-area operators such as **Horizon Divers** also offer diving trips to various reefs and wrecks. Such underwater sights include the *Duane* and the *Bibb,* two U.S. Coast Guard cutters used in World War II; the **USS** *Spiegel Grove,* a 510-foot U.S. Navy transport ship purposely sunk

John Pennekamp Coral Reef State Park

The unique geography of the archipelago makes it an ideal destination for outdoors enthusiasts. The most sought-after diversions in the Conch Republic include diving, snorkeling, fishing, kayaking, biking, and hiking.

SPORTFISHING

- Anglers make a beeline for Islamorada (page 145), the self-proclaimed "sportfishing capital of the world." A plethora of full-service marinas, fishing charters, independent fishing guides, and boat rentals are available here. You're almost guaranteed to catch one of the region's many native species, from tarpon to red snapper.

KAYAKING

- In the Lower Keys (page 212), from Bahia Honda Key to Key West, kayakers will find countless waterways, plenty of mangrove islands, and even opportunities for paddling in the open ocean. You can rent kayaks and other watercraft such as stand-up paddleboards from the outfitter at Bahia Honda State Park.

BIKING

- Many hardy bikers have ventured from Key Largo to Key West, tackling U.S. 1 along the way. In addition, Key West (page 256) offers several ways to rent a bicycle and take a tour. It's simply a lovely town in which to while away an afternoon and absorb the sights on your own timetable.

HIKING

- Explore the hiking trails at Dagny Johnson Key Largo Hammock Botanical State Park (page 103) in Key Largo. The serene 2,421-acre preserve protects more than 80 different plant and animal species and has six miles of backcountry trails.

to create an artificial reef; and the sea caves of French Reef.

- EAT: Try Key Largo Conch House or Mrs. Mac's Kitchen.
- STAY: Spend the night at Amy Slate's Amoray Dive Resort in Key Largo or, for an unparalleled experience, Jules' Undersea Lodge, which offers submerged quarters in Key Largo Undersea Park. For great camping, stay at John Pennekamp Coral Reef State Park.

Islamorada and the Upper Keys

Through the Florida Keys Dive Center, based on the northern end of Plantation Key, you can take a diving class (if you haven't already) and see most of the nearby underwater attractions, including Conch Wall, home to a variety of conch, barrel sponges, and rare pillar coral. While down there, you might also spy green moray eels near Davis Reef, gorgonian coral along Crocker Wall, and the wrecked El Infante, a Spanish galleon that sank in a 1733 hurricane. You can also explore Alligator Reef, site of the shipwrecked USS Alligator, and the Eagle, a 287-foot freighter that became an artificial reef in the mid-1980s.

- EAT: Head to Morada Bay Beach Café for a special dinner under the stars, or, for something more casual, go to Lorelei Restaurant & Cabana Bar.
- STAY: Spend the night at Islander Resort or the Postcard Inn Beach Resort & Marina at Holiday Isle.

Marathon and the Middle Keys

Venture into the waters east of the Middle Keys. Tilden's Scuba Center, located in Marathon and open daily, provides classes, gear rentals, and Snuba diving, a patented form of deepwater snorkeling. Tilden's offers a number of snorkeling and scuba-diving excursions, even night dives.

Key West has a long history as a gay-friendly tropical getaway. With its exclusive hideaways, clothes-optional bars, and the outrageous Fantasy Fest, it's no wonder that more than 200,000 LGBTQ visitors travel to this island each year.

NIGHTLIFE

If you're looking for predominantly gay bars, the Aqua Nightclub (page 265) has karaoke, live piano, and drag shows. The Bourbon St. Pub (page 265) has a clothing-optional garden bar and male dancers. And 801 Bourbon Bar & Cabaret (page 265) features karaoke, drag queen bingo, and a twice-nightly drag show.

FESTIVALS AND EVENTS

Key West's grandest—and gayest—party of the year is Fantasy Fest (page 270), a 10-day event with parades, costumes, and plenty of drag queens. The gay festivities continue at Key West Pridefest (page 272), usually held in mid-June.

TOURS

For a gay lay-of-the-land, take the Gay Key West Trolley Tour (page 252), which features a plethora of gay bars, drag shows, and gay and lesbian accommodations. Climb aboard the rainbow-hued trolley and see all the gay and lesbian hot spots, hear about previous homosexual visitors, and learn about the contributions that gays and lesbians have made to the Florida Keys. The tour usually boards from the corner of Angela and Duval Streets.

ACCOMMODATIONS

The top gay-friendly places to stay include the Island House, Key West's largest gay male resort. Alexander's Guesthouse welcomes a gay and lesbian clientele to its stunning setting that includes tropical gardens, a relaxing spa, and a beautiful pool. The New Orleans House is the only all-male, gay guesthouse on Duval Street. See page 289 for more information on these accommodations.

INFORMATION AND SERVICES

Organizations like The Lodging Association of the Florida Keys and Key West (page 285) can help you choose the place that's right for you. For more gay-friendly establishments, consult with the Key West Business Guild (page 340), which is one of the oldest LGBT chamber of commerce organizations in the United States.

You're bound to see an assortment of underwater sites, including the spur-and-groove Sombrero Reef and the star, elkhorn, and brain coral of the Delta Shoals. In this area, you can also survey two shipwrecks: the *Adelaide Baker,* essentially the remains of a three-masted iron-rigged ship; and the *Thunderbolt,* a 188-foot vessel intentionally sunk in the mid-1980s and now home to coral, sponges, and angelfish.

- **EAT:** Check out Island Fish Co. Restaurant & Tiki Bar or Castaway Waterfront Restaurant & Sushi Bar.

- **STAY:** Spend the night at the Conch Key Cottages or camp at Long Key State Park.

Big Pine Key and the Lower Keys

To explore the offshore reefs and wrecks of the Lower Keys, consult the Looe Key Reef Resort & Dive Center on Ramrod Key, which offers scuba classes as well as three-hour snorkeling and diving trips to the spectacular, 33-acre Looe Key Reef. Named for the HMS *Looe,* which ran aground here in 1744, this spur-and-groove network now abounds with parrot fish, turtles, eagle rays, and whale sharks. Given its varying depths, the reef is ideal for both inexperienced snorkelers and advanced divers. Through the Dive Center, you can also survey the *Adolphus Busch,* a 213-foot freighter that was purposely sunk as an

beach at Bahia Honda State Park

artificial reef and is now home to a wide array of marine creatures, from eels to jewfish.

- **EAT:** Eat at the **Square Grouper Bar & Grill** or the **Geiger Key Marina Smokehouse Restaurant and Tiki Bar.**

- **STAY:** Camp at **Bahia Honda State Park** or stay at the **Big Pine Key Fishing Lodge.**

Key West

You'll find an array of vibrant coral reefs and engaging shipwrecks surrounding Key West. While first-timers can easily snorkel in the waters near **Fort Zachary Taylor Historic State Park,** situated on the southern end of the island, or **Dry Tortugas National Park,** which lies roughly 68 miles to the west, most of the underwater attractions in this area are only accessible with the help of professional diving charters. One such local operator, **Southpoint Divers,** provides gear rentals, diving classes, and guided trips to two intriguing wrecks: the 187-foot *Cayman Salvage Master* and the 522-foot **USNS** *General Hoyt S. Vandenberg,* a former World War II troop

transport ship and now the foundation for an artificial reef.

Several local operators also feature excursions to other wrecks, such as the weather-beaten *Joe's Tug,* a deepwater vessel that's home to an assortment of coral formations and marine creatures. Some of these companies even provide trips to the spur-and-groove networks of **Sand Key, Rock Key,** and the **Western Sambo Ecological Reserve.** Other nearby sites include **Kedge Ledge,** a patch reef that features coral-encrusted anchors from 18th-century schooners, and the **Ten-Fathom Ledge,** a network of caves and outcroppings that attract lobster, grouper, and sharks, among other inhabitants.

- **EAT:** While exploring Key West, eat at **Café Marquesa** or at **Michaels Restaurant,** and make sure to sample a slice of key lime pie from the **Key West Key Lime Pie Co.**

- **STAY:** Stay at the **Eden House,** the **Chelsea House Hotel,** or the **Ocean Key Resort & Spa.**

Miami and the Everglades

If you're driving to the Keys, you should spend

some time in one of the most fabulous gateway towns around: Miami.

While the Magic City's assortment of attractions, restaurants, and activities could consume a week or more, time and budget might dictate a shorter stay. If so, you should definitely visit the cultural microcosms of Little Havana and Little Haiti, take a self-guided walking tour of the pastel-hued Art Deco District, and soak in the ambience of infamous South Beach, a terrific place to shop for trendy apparel, dine alongside celebrities in sophisticated restaurants, and party the night away at one of numerous hip bars and dance clubs. Depending on your interests and the time of your visit, you might also catch a professional sporting event—this is, after all, the home of the Miami Dolphins, Miami

Highlights

Look for ★ to find recommended sights, activities, dining, and lodging.

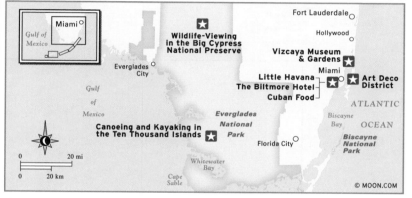

★ **Little Havana:** Home to many Cuban exiles and Cuban Americans, this neighborhood offers cigar shops, authentic markets and restaurants, live music, art galleries, and annual events like Calle Ocho, touted as the biggest Latino street party in the country (page 43).

★ **Art Deco District:** Colorful South Beach features an incredible collection of art deco-style buildings, which you can enjoy through a guided tour (page 44).

★ **Vizcaya Museum & Gardens:** Take a tour through this elaborate Italian villa replica, filled with antique furnishings and art objects from the 15th through 19th centuries (page 48).

★ **The Biltmore Hotel:** Since it opened in the 1920s, the oft-photographed jewel of Coral Gables has welcomed countless politicians and celebrities. Even if you choose not to stay, dine, or

play here, you have to see this architectural gem for yourself (page 50).

★ **Cuban Food:** You'll find plenty of tasty Cuban restaurants and coffeehouses in Miami, especially in South Beach, Coral Gables, and Little Havana (page 65).

★ **Canoeing and Kayaking in the Ten Thousand Islands:** This area of Everglades National Park offers fun open-water and mangrove paddling—and an excellent way to observe wildlife in the park (page 82).

★ **Wildlife-Viewing in the Big Cypress National Preserve:** Whether you explore by airboat, hike along the many trails, or drive down the wildlife-filled Turner River Road, you'll encounter wild animals, including great blue herons, American alligators, and, if you're lucky, the elusive Florida panther (page 89).

Miami and the Everglades

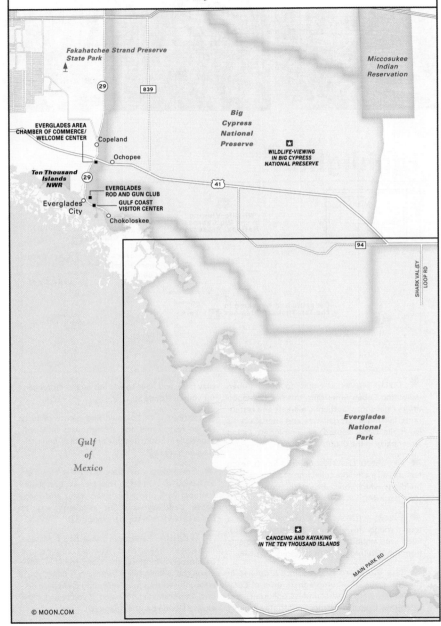

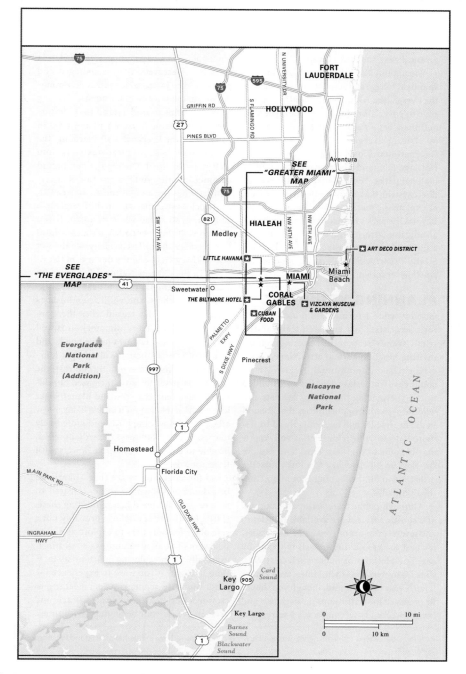

Marlins, Miami Heat, and Florida Panthers. Of course, you're also not far from the coral reefs of Biscayne National Park, a favorite spot for snorkelers and scuba divers.

You should also take time to explore the abundant foliage and serpentine waterways of the Everglades. Although it would be impossible to cover all of the Everglades, you can definitely get a taste of this "river of grass" by visiting Everglades National Park—an International Biosphere Reserve, a World Heritage Site, and one of America's largest national parks. You can hike amid this fragile ecosystem, bike along the designated roads, or explore the marshy wonderland by kayak. Beyond the park's borders, you can even visit an alligator farm, join an airboat tour, or take a guided canoe trip through Fakahatchee Strand Preserve State Park, all experiences you'll never forget.

PLANNING YOUR TIME

Given its wide assortment of museums, historic structures, art and architectural districts, trendy restaurants and nightclubs, inviting beaches, animal attractions, shopping enclaves, and annual events, Miami could easily entertain you for an extended visit. Experiencing the various habitats and wildlife-watching opportunities that abound in the Everglades will undoubtedly add a few more days to your trip. Even if you've primarily come to southern Florida to explore the Keys archipelago, try to allow yourself a little time to hit the highlights of Miami and the Everglades.

Although public transportation, taxicabs, and shuttle services are available in Miami, and several tours are offered in the Everglades, it's best to explore this sprawling region by car. The plethora of major surface streets, state highways, and federal interstates makes it fairly easy to get around, though you should be prepared for traffic jams on weekdays and holiday weekends. Of course, *when* you choose

to pass through the gateway areas of Miami and the Everglades will probably depend on several factors, including annual events, intended activities, or your plans for the Florida Keys. Hotel reservations are encouraged, and you should be prepared for pricey accommodations in the safer neighborhoods.

It also helps to understand that, despite the weather being fairly warm and mild in Miami and the Everglades all year long, the peak tourist season typically extends from November to April. During the hot, humid summer months, you'll often find that certain activities and establishments aren't available (such as airplane tours in the Everglades), so always call ahead when in doubt. If you plan to visit the Everglades, it's also helpful to remember the difference between the wet season (May-Oct.) and the dry season (Nov.-Apr.). In Big Cypress National Preserve and Everglades National Park, for example, hikers, bird-watchers, and wildlife enthusiasts might prefer the dry season when there are fewer mosquitoes, more migratory birds, and an abundance of creatures in the ponds and canals; of course, there are also larger tourist crowds at this time, too. By contrast, the wet season tends to cause increased humidity, elevated temperatures, and higher water levels, which means you'll be less likely to spy alligators and wading birds and more likely to encounter mosquitoes; you will, however, be able to enjoy the blooming flowers with fewer crowds.

As for safety, be aware that Miami can be a dangerous town, so always research an area or neighborhood before heading there. (Little Haiti, for example, is probably not a safe place for outsiders to explore at night.) Be aware of your surroundings at all times, especially when exploring non-touristy locations at night. If you want to experience the city's nightlife scene, consider heading to crowded, well-lit areas like South Beach, and keep an eye on your belongings at all times.

Previous: aerial view of Miami near South Beach; Miami Beach; barred owl in Fakahatchee Strand Preserve State Park.

While criminal activity is also a reality in the Everglades, the more pressing dangers involve the wildlife, so take care when exploring this vast wilderness and refrain from approaching any wild animals, no matter how docile those lounging alligators might appear to be.

For more information about this region, consult the **Greater Miami Convention & Visitors Bureau** (GMCVB, 701 Brickell Ave., Ste. 2700, Miami, 305/539-3000 or 800/933-8448, www.miamiandbeaches.com, 8:30am-5pm Mon.-Fri.) and the **Naples, Marco Island, Everglades Convention & Visitors Bureau** (2660 N. Horseshoe Dr., Naples, 239/225-1013 or 800/688-3600, www.paradisecoast.com, 8am-5pm Mon.-Fri.).

ORIENTATION

As big cities go, Miami isn't too hard to traverse by car or public transportation. Several major highways and interstates, such as U.S. 1, U.S. 27, U.S. 41, I-75, and I-95, link other Florida cities to Miami, and for the most part, all roads lead to the ocean. From downtown Miami, you can head north on I-95 or Biscayne Boulevard (U.S. 1) to reach North Miami, take U.S. 1 South or various surface streets to access Coconut Grove and Coral Gables, use I-195 or I-395 to cross Biscayne Bay toward Miami Beach, and hop on the Tamiami Trail (U.S. 41) to experience Little Havana and, farther west, the Everglades.

If you're planning to explore the Everglades, it's helpful to know how to reach the main towns. To reach Everglades City from Naples, head east for 32 miles on U.S. 41, turn south on CR-29, and continue roughly four miles. From downtown Miami, you can reach the same turnoff for Everglades City by taking I-95 North to SR-836 West (Dolphin Expy.), continuing west for about 10 miles, heading south on Florida's Turnpike (SR-821 S), merging onto the Tamiami Trail, and continuing west for roughly 65 miles. The gateway cities to the Florida Keys, Homestead and Florida City, are also easily accessible from the Miami area. Homestead lies about 26 miles southwest of downtown Miami via I-95 South and U.S. 1, and Florida City lies roughly 30 miles southwest of downtown Miami via I-95 South, U.S. 1, and Florida's Turnpike (SR-821 S). Tolls apply on certain portions of Florida's Turnpike.

Sights

DOWNTOWN MIAMI
Miami-Dade Cultural Plaza

Centered on a pleasant courtyard area where people often relax, eat, and read, the **Miami-Dade Cultural Plaza** (50 NW 2nd Ave., Miami) is a complex of separate buildings that feature engrossing exhibits.

Visitors to the area can peruse the various departments of the **Main Library** (101 W. Flagler St., Miami, 305/375-2665, www.mdpls.org, 9:30am-6pm Mon.-Sat., free), featuring a specialized Florida Department that contains an extensive collection of rare books, documents, and photographs about the Sunshine State, including Miami's history from pioneer days to the present.

Nearby you can learn about the city's pioneers at **HistoryMiami Museum** (101 W. Flagler St., Miami, 305/375-1492, www.historymiami.org, 10am-5pm Tues.-Sat., noon-5pm Sun., $10 adults, $8 seniors and students, $5 children 6-12, free for children under 6), which presents a permanent exhibit called *Tropical Dreams: A People's History of South Florida* as well as several temporary displays about the region's rich history that cover everything from infamous Prohibition-era gangsters to the drug wars of the 1980s to the experiences of Miami adolescents since World War II. The museum offers walking, boat, coach, bike, gallery, and eco-history tours with varying prices that

One Day in Miami

sphinx at Vizcaya Museum & Gardens

MORNING

Start your morning on **South Beach,** where you can enjoy breakfast with an ocean view at one of the neighborhood's swanky cafés. Spend some time relaxing on South Beach, which is famous for its beautiful landscape and stunning people-watching.

Take a stroll through **Lummus Park Beach,** which is shaded by palm trees and borders the ocean. Spend an hour or so touring the adjacent **Art Deco District,** taking in the impressive, colorful, and historical architecture that fills this vibrant neighborhood.

AFTERNOON

Head to **Little Havana,** where you can sample authentic Cuban food and bakeries, see cigars being rolled by hand, and watch the locals play dominoes at **Maximo Gomez Park,** also known as **Domino Park.**

For your next stop, head southwest to **Coconut Grove** and **Coral Gables,** home to several historical sites that are definitely worth seeing. At the top of the list is **Vizcaya Museum & Gardens.** Tour the spectacular gardens and wander through the mansion, where you'll get a firsthand look at what it's like to be rich and famous.

EVENING

For dinner and lodging, enjoy an upscale meal and stay the night at **The Biltmore Hotel,** Coral Gables's 1920s-era mansion. In the morning you can enjoy a massage on-site. If you're looking to party and dance the night away in one of Miami's full-throttle dance clubs, stay in one of the boutique hotels in South Beach.

give a more interactive glimpse into Miami's diverse history.

Bayfront Park

About five blocks east of the Miami-Dade Cultural Plaza, alongside Biscayne Bay, lies the 32-acre **Bayfront Park** (301 N. Biscayne Blvd., Miami, 305/358-7550, www. bayfrontparkmiami.com, 8am-11pm daily, no entrance fee though some activity and event fees apply), a well-landscaped municipal park that was created in the early 1920s and

Greater Miami

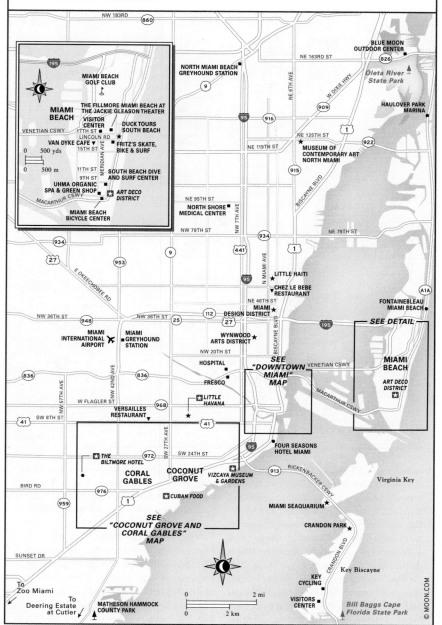

© MOON.COM

Downtown Miami

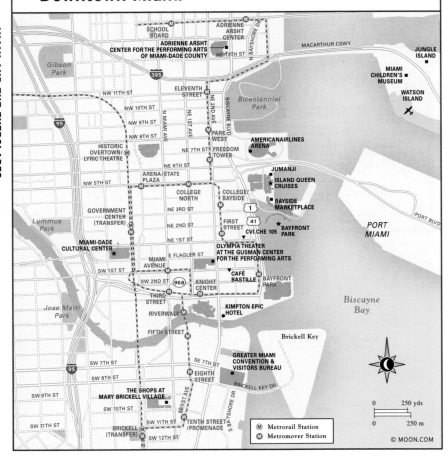

SCHOOL BOARD
ADRIENNE ARSHT CENTER
ADRIENNE ARSHT CENTER FOR THE PERFORMING ARTS OF MIAMI-DADE COUNTY
NE 13TH ST
MACARTHUR CSWY
JUNGLE ISLAND
Gibson Park
MIAMI CHILDREN'S MUSEUM
WATSON ISLAND
ELEVENTH STREET
NW 11TH ST
N BAYSHORE DR
BISCAYNE BLVD
Bicentennial Park
NW 10TH ST
NE 2ND AVE
NW 9TH ST
NE 1ST AVE
NW 8TH ST
N MIAMI AVE
PARK WEST
AMERICANAIRLINES ARENA
HISTORIC OVERTOWN LYRIC THEATRE
NE 7TH ST
FREEDOM TOWER
NE 6TH ST
JUMANJI
ISLAND QUEEN CRUISES
NW 5TH ST
ARENA/STATE PLAZA
COLLEGE NORTH
COLLEGE/BAYSIDE
BAYSIDE MARKETPLACE
NE 3RD ST
GOVERNMENT CENTER (TRANSFER)
NE 2ND ST
FIRST STREET
CVI.CHE 105
BAYFRONT PARK
Lummus Park
NE 1ST ST
PORT MIAMI
PORT BLVD
MIAMI-DADE CULTURAL CENTER
E FLAGLER ST
OLYMPIA THEATER AT THE GUSMAN CENTER FOR THE PERFORMING ARTS
SW 1ST ST
MIAMI AVENUE
SW 2ND ST
968
KNIGHT CENTER
CAFÉ BASTILLE
BAYFRONT PARK
Biscayne Bay
THIRD STREET
Jose Marti Park
RIVERWALK
KIMPTON EPIC HOTEL
FIFTH STREET
Brickell Key
SE 7TH ST
GREATER MIAMI CONVENTION & VISITORS BUREAU
SW 7TH ST
EIGHTH STREET
SW 8TH ST
BRICKELL KEY DR
S BAYSHORE DR
THE SHOPS AT MARY BRICKELL VILLAGE
SW 9TH ST
SE 1ST AVE
SW 10TH ST
TENTH STREET/PROMENADE
SW 11TH ST
SW 11TH ST
BRICKELL (TRANSFER)
SW 12TH ST

Ⓜ Metrorail Station
Ⓜ Metromover Station

0   250 yds
0   250 m

© MOON.COM

redesigned in the early 1980s by American sculptor Isamu Noguchi. Features include a sandy beach, a playground, a cascading fountain, a tropical rock garden and waterfall, and a variety of monuments and sculptures, including the Challenger Monument, a 100-foot-tall white metal pipe tower that is dedicated to the memory of the space shuttle *Challenger* astronauts. Home to two performance venues, the Klipsch Amphitheater and the Tina Hills Pavilion, Bayfront Park hosts numerous concerts, events, and other diversions, such as food trucks, trapeze lessons, and free yoga classes. The park offers both valet and self-parking; several public parking lots are also available in the area.

Pérez Art Museum Miami

Pérez Art Museum Miami (1103 Biscayne Blvd., Miami, 305/375-3000, www.pamm.org, 10am-9pm Thurs., 10am-6pm Fri.-Tues., $16 adults, $12 seniors, $12 students, $12 youth 7-18, free for children under 7 and active-duty U.S. military), located on the beautiful

Modern Art

After visiting the sights of South Beach, including the Art Deco District, art lovers should take a quick detour to North Miami and the Museum of Contemporary Art North Miami (MOCA, Joan Lehman Bldg., 770 NE 125th St., 305/893-6211, www. mocanomi.org, 10am-5pm Tues.-Fri., 11am-5pm Sat.-Sun., $10 adults, $3 seniors and students, free for children under 12, military veterans, city employees, and North Miami residents). Known worldwide for its ability to establish new trends in contemporary art, MOCA houses a permanent collection of roughly 600 pieces of cutting-edge sculptures, paintings, photographs, videos, and multimedia creations from emerging and established artists, such as photographer Melanie Schiff and sculptor Dennis Oppenheim.

In addition to its impressive collection, MOCA presents lectures, workshops, screenings, concerts, performances, and mind-bending temporary installations from the likes of Roy Lichtenstein, Keith Haring, and other innovators. Don't forget to visit the on-site gift shop, which is open during museum hours and houses one of the city's best selections of contemporary art books, imaginative jewelry, eye-popping designs, and other unique items. Just be advised that, given its currently limited space, MOCA must typically close during the installation of a new exhibition, so always call ahead before visiting.

Biscayne Bay, is a sight in and of itself. The stylish structure blends modern, industrial materials with lush, tropical foliage. Inside the museum, there are more than 500 pieces of multicultural artwork from the 20th and 21st centuries. PAMM presents the varied creations of contemporary artists like Cuban-born painter and sculptor Carlos Alfonzo, Dutch portrait photographer Rineke Dijkstra, and American sculptor and textile artist Ann Hamilton.

Wynwood Arts District

Miami is home to a thriving community of artists, designers, and collectors, and you'll find several arts districts here. One of the largest is the Wynwood Arts District (www. wynwoodmiami.com), which is roughly bordered by 20th Street, 6th Avenue, 36th Street, and 2nd Avenue. The district has well over 70 galleries, studios, stores, bars, and restaurants all within walking distance of one another. A highlight is the Miami Art Space (MAS, 244 NW 35th St., Miami, 305/438-9002, www. miamiartspace.com, 10am-4pm Mon.-Fri.), which contains contemporary art exhibits inside and out.

WYNWOOD WALLS

Within the Wynwood Arts District are the Wynwood Walls (on NW 2nd Ave., between NE 25th St. and NE 26th St.)—more than 80,000 square feet of old warehouse walls that have been transformed into modern murals. The street art represents a diverse range of styles from over 50 artists. It's a beautiful place to visit and a fun place for a photo shoot.

★ Little Havana

Home to many Cuban exiles and Cuban Americans since the 1960s, Little Havana (www.littlehavanaexperiences.com) lies just west of downtown Miami. A predominantly Latino neighborhood, La Pequeña Habana offers a plethora of cigar shops, quiet parks, authentic markets and restaurants, live music venues, art galleries, and annual events like Carnaval Miami, which takes place in March and features Calle Ocho, touted as the biggest Latino street party in the country. To experience the unique vibe of this ethnic enclave, simply stroll along the major streets, such as Calle Ocho (SW 8th St., Miami) and Cuban Memorial Boulevard (SW 13th Ave., Miami), and take note of various monuments such as a memorial plaque of Cuba, the bust of Cuban poet and revolutionary José Martí, and the black obelisk dedicated to those who perished during the Bay of Pigs Invasion. You'll also encounter places like Maximo Gomez Park (801 SW 15th Ave., Miami, 8am-8pm daily), named after a Cuban revolutionary who fought against Spanish oppression in the late 1800s. Affectionately known as Domino Park, this small meeting place is often filled with old-timers playing friendly (if competitive) rounds of chess or dominoes.

SOUTH BEACH
★ Art Deco District

East of downtown Miami is Miami Beach, an incorporated city and part of a barrier island that's linked to the mainland by four causeways: MacArthur (SR-A1A), Venetian, Julia Tuttle (I-195), and John F. Kennedy (SR-934). Surely the most famous portion of this island is the southern part, known as South Beach, where you'll encounter one of the most celebrated architectural districts in southern Florida. Officially listed in the National Register of Historic Places as the Miami Beach Architectural District, the colorful Art Deco District features an incredible collection of art deco-style buildings, roughly bounded by Alton Road, Dade Boulevard, the Atlantic Ocean, and 6th Street.

The best way to experience this historic neighborhood is with a walking, biking, or Segway tour, whether self-guided or otherwise. First-timers may especially appreciate the 90-minute walking tour (10:30am

Fri.-Wed., 10:30am and 6:30pm Thurs., $30 adults, $25 seniors, students, and military veterans) that the Miami Design Preservation League (MDPL, Art Deco Welcome Center, 1001 Ocean Dr., 2nd Fl., Miami Beach, 305/672-2014, www.mdpl.org) offers daily. Departing from the Art Deco Gift Shop (1001 Ocean Dr., Miami Beach, 305/531-3484, 9:30am-7pm daily), this guided stroll explores hotels, restaurants, and other commercial structures, providing an introduction to the art deco, Mediterranean Revival, and Miami Modern (MiMo) styles found within this important district. Reservations are not required for this tour.

No matter which tour you choose, you can easily reach South Beach by public bus or private vehicle. If you drive yourself, you'll find plenty of parking garages and metered street parking here ($2-plus hourly).

Museums and Memorials

Beyond its art deco splendor, South Beach contains several interesting museums and memorials. Near the southern end of the island is the spacious Jewish Museum of Florida—FIU (301 Washington Ave., Miami Beach, 305/672-5044, www.jmof.fiu.edu, 10am-5pm Tues.-Sun., $24 families, $12

neon lights in the Art Deco District

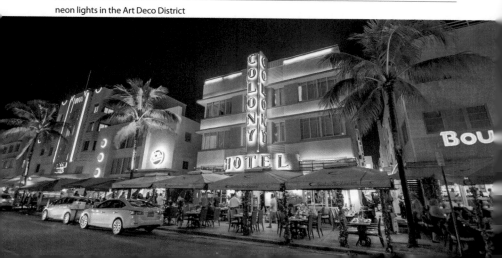

Little Haiti

Fly's Eye Dome

North of downtown Miami lies the city's traditional center of Haitian Creole and Francophone culture and the largest Haitian community outside of Haiti. Bordered by Little River to the north, Northeast 2nd Avenue to the east, Northeast 54th Street to the south, and North Miami Avenue to the west, this neighborhood has long been known as La Petite Haïti, or Little Haiti—and, traditionally, as Lemon City. Although crime exists here and the residents might look at you skeptically, this unique area is definitely worth visiting—if only in the daytime. Here you can gaze at multicolored building facades, listen to snippets of Creole, visit fascinating art and voodoo shops, and of course, enjoy spicy authentic cuisine at eateries like the long-standing **Chez Le Bebe Restaurant** (114 NE 54th St., Miami, 305/751-7639, www.chezlebebe.com, 8am-midnight daily, $4-12), where you'll find inexpensive delicacies like *tasso* (fried goat), *griot* (fried pork), and *mais* (grits). While eating, you might even learn a few Creole expressions, such as *souple* (please) and *mesi* (thank you), though the staff here isn't always so polite.

Near the southern part of Little Haiti is the trendy **Miami Design District** (305/722-7100, www.miamidesigndistrict.net), an 18-block stretch featuring more than 120 art galleries, restaurants, bars, and showrooms filled with designer fashions, furnishings, lighting fixtures, kitchen and bathroom products, wall and floor materials, and fine rugs. There's also an incredible version of the **Fly's Eye Dome** built by the Buckminster Fuller Institute. Situated between Northeast 37th Street, Biscayne Boulevard, Northeast 42nd Street, and North Miami Avenue, the stylish district is certainly worthy of a daylong stroll.

adults, $8 seniors, students, and children 18 and under), a complex that includes two former synagogues, one erected in 1929 and the other in 1936. Both synagogues are listed in the National Register of Historic Places, and together they boast an extensive collection of photographs, documents, and artifacts that illustrate the Jewish experience in the Sunshine State. Three informative films are also available: *Synagogue to Museum*, which presents Florida's Jewish history as well as the museum's history; *Jewish Settlement in Florida*, which explores four diverse Jewish families; and *L'Chaim: To Life*, which depicts Jewish traditions, including holiday cycles. Admission is free for all visitors on Saturday, though the on-site Bessie's Bistro is closed that day in observance of Shabbat. The entire museum complex is closed on Monday as well as on national and Jewish holidays.

The Wolfsonian–FIU (1001 Washington Ave., Miami Beach, 305/531-1001, www.wolfsonian.org, 10am-6pm Mon., Tues., Thurs., and Sat., 10am-9pm Fri., noon-6pm Sun., $12 adults, $8 seniors, students, and children 6-12, free for children under 6), a wheelchair-accessible design museum in the heart of the Art Deco District, houses an intriguing collection of roughly 120,000 objects from the modern era (1885-1945). Admission is always free for the students, faculty, and staff of Florida's state universities—and free for everyone else after 6pm on Friday.

Another art repository is the World Erotic Art Museum (WEAM) (1205 Washington Ave., Miami Beach, 305/532-9336 or 866/969-9326, www.weam.com, 11am-10pm Mon.-Thurs., 11am-midnight Fri.-Sun., $15 adults, $14 seniors over 60, $13.50 students 18 and over), which is two blocks north of The Wolfsonian. Home to the continent's largest collection of erotic art, the 12,000-square-foot museum includes everything from Lady Godiva depictions to Indonesian and Caribbean artifacts, plus erotic chessboards, pinup illustrations, gay photography, fetish artwork, and Picasso paintings, among other exhibits. Visitors to the WEAM will encounter 20 separate rooms, all part of a fascinating yet tasteful timeline of erotica, or the "art of love." The on-site gift shop contains an array of engaging erotic books, postcards, and posters. Not surprisingly, visitors must be 18 years or older to enter the museum.

Just south of Dade Boulevard is the Holocaust Memorial of the Greater Miami Jewish Federation (1933-1945 Meridian Ave., Miami Beach, 305/538-1663, www.holocaustmmb.org, 9:30am-10pm daily, free), erected to honor the six million Jews who perished during the Holocaust. Constructed over a four-year period and dedicated in February 1990, the memorial features a reflecting pool; a black granite wall presenting the history of the Holocaust (1933-1945) through text, pictures, and maps; and a narrow passage highlighting the most infamous death camps. From there visitors enter a large circular plaza paved in Jerusalem stone, surrounded by a high black granite wall and featuring a 42-foot-high bronze sculpture composed of nearly 100 anguished figures. This engaging yet heart-wrenching tour culminates with the Memorial Wall, an ever-growing etched list of names, representing a multitude of fallen children, parents, and grandparents.

Near the Holocaust Memorial is yet another art repository, the Bass Museum of Art (2100 Collins Ave., Miami Beach, 305/673-7530, www.bassmuseum.org, 10am-5pm Wed.-Sun., $10 adults, $5 seniors, students, and children 6-17, free for children under 6), which contains an enormous selection of European, Asian, North American, Latin American, and Caribbean paintings, sculptures, textiles, and photographs from the 15th through the 21st centuries, including the work of Peter Paul Rubens and Benjamin West. It has temporary art exhibits as well as a relatively new Egyptian gallery that includes an authentic mummy and sarcophagus. Free docent tours are available, and an on-site gift shop offers an intriguing selection of folk art, local jewelry, unique decorative items, educational toys, and art and photography books, plus a snack bar with free wireless Internet access.

Watson Island

En route from South Beach to downtown Miami via the MacArthur Causeway, you'll cross Watson Island in Biscayne Bay, which has two family-friendly attractions. At Jungle Island (1111 Parrot Jungle Trl., Miami, 305/400-7000, www.jungleisland.com, 10am-5pm daily, $49.49 adults, $37.34 children 3-10, free for children under 3) visitors can see parrot shows, view the antics of kangaroos and penguins, watch tiger and primate presentations, feed various birds, and wander

1: Bayfront Park 2: street murals lining the walls of the Wynwood Arts District

among the alligators in an Everglades habitat. Other activities include strolling through a lush greenhouse and relaxing on a private beach. With proper identification, all military personnel and veterans, firefighters, and law enforcement officers receive free admission year-round.

Across the road, the wheelchair-accessible **Miami Children's Museum** (MCM, 980 MacArthur Cswy., Miami, 305/373-5437, www.miamichildrensmuseum.org, 10am-6pm daily, $22 adults and children, $15 Florida residents, free for children under 1 and military personnel) lures visitors with an array of interactive exhibits that allow children to operate a crane and navigate a cruise ship at PortMiami, play in a music studio, steer a fire truck, explore the Everglades, peer inside a 900-gallon marine tank, and learn how to take better care of themselves and their pets. Other exhibits feature the inner workings of a bank, supermarket, and television studio.

COCONUT GROVE

★ Vizcaya Museum & Gardens

Situated southwest of downtown Miami, **Coconut Grove** is a popular shopping and dining destination that also boasts two winning attractions. When coming from the downtown area, the first one you'll encounter is the stunning **Vizcaya Museum & Gardens** (3251 S. Miami Ave., Miami, 305/250-9133, www.vizcaya.org, 9:30am-4:30pm Wed.-Mon., $22 adults, $16 seniors 62 and over, $15 students, $10 children 6-12, free for children under 6), an expansive property that served as the winter residence of American industrialist James Deering (vice president of an agricultural equipment company) from 1916 until his death in 1925. Construction on the Italian Renaissance-style mansion, which was intended to look like a 400-year-old estate that had been occupied and renovated by several familial generations, began in 1914 and continued until 1923. During this time, more than 1,000 European and Caribbean laborers and

craftsmen worked on the 180-acre complex that included the house, the formal gardens, a farm, and several service facilities. Hurricanes in 1926 and 1935 caused extensive damage to the house and surrounding grounds, and eventually most of the land was sold for development. In 1952, however, Deering's heirs sold the main house and formal gardens to the county and later donated the estate's substantial art collection and furnishings with the condition that Vizcaya be forever used as a public museum.

Today the house features 34 uniquely decorated rooms, with antique furnishings and art objects from the 15th through 19th centuries. Although the architectural design once permitted the free flow of breezes through the open courtyard, the house now features a glass-enclosed courtyard and a system for climate and humidity control to better preserve the building and its contents. The gardens, meanwhile, blend elements of French and Italian Renaissance designs, including fountains, statuary, and a central pool. Listed in the National Register of Historic Places since 1970, the museum welcomes visitors on narrated or self-guided tours of the opulent house, elaborate gardens, and impressive orchidarium. Audio tours ($5) are available, as are guidebooks ($3) in both English and Spanish. A café overlooks the swimming pool and serves sandwiches, salads, and desserts. A gift shop offers books, postcards, and jewelry. The facilities here are wheelchair-accessible, and the parking is free.

The Barnacle Historic State Park

Farther south, alongside Biscayne Bay, **The Barnacle Historic State Park** (3485 Main Hwy., Coconut Grove, 305/442-6866, www. floridastateparks.org/thebarnacle, 9am-5pm Wed. and Fri.-Mon., 9am-7pm Thurs., $2, free for children under 5) preserves the former home and grounds of Ralph Middleton

1: Venetian Pool **2:** The Biltmore Hotel **3:** Cape Florida Lighthouse at the southern end of Key Biscayne **4:** Vizcaya Museum & Gardens

Munroe, a sailboat designer, civic activist, naturalist, author, and photographer who was also one of Coconut Grove's most influential trailblazers. Built in 1891, the colorful, Caribbean-style house was inspired, especially throughout the interior, by sturdy hurricane-resistant boat designs. With a lower porch and upper balcony, the building also takes advantage of the peaceful bayside views. Although you're free to stroll through the home as well as the surrounding tropical hardwood hammock and nearby boathouse, 45-minute tours (10am, 11:30am, 1pm, and 2:30pm Fri.-Mon., $3 adults, $1 children 6-12, free for children under 6) are also available for an extra fee. The park is open on Wednesday and Thursday for group tours if arranged in advance. No matter the season, this park is an excellent place for picnics and bird-watching. Just remember that entrance fees must be placed in the honor box, and correct change is required.

CORAL GABLES
★ The Biltmore Hotel

Founded by George Merrick in the 1920s, the lovely community of **Coral Gables** is now home to the University of Miami and **The Biltmore Hotel** (1200 Anastasia Ave., Coral Gables, 855/311-6903, www.biltmorehotel. com), designed in 1924 by renowned architect Leonard Schultze and developer S. Fullerton Weaver as a monument to Italian, Moorish, and Spanish architectural styles. After opening in January of 1926, the jewel of Coral Gables welcomed countless movie stars, politicians, and other celebrities in its early years, including Judy Garland, Bing Crosby, Franklin D. Roosevelt, and Al Capone. World War II altered the property's fortunes, though, and from 1942 to 1968 The Biltmore served as a military hospital. After much lobbying by Coral Gables officials and residents, The Biltmore was acquired by the city in 1973 and remained vacant for a full decade until an extensive four-year restoration returned the resort to its former glory. Three years later, the hotel closed in the midst of the county's economic downturn, only to be bought and

fully restored by a private corporation. In 1996 the federal government finally declared The Biltmore a National Historic Landmark, ensuring its well-deserved preservation. Even if you choose not to stay overnight, play golf or tennis, dine in the Palme d'Or or Fontana restaurants, or enjoy a massage in the world-class spa, you simply must see this architectural gem for yourself.

Other Attractions

Several blocks north of The Biltmore Hotel is the **Coral Gables Merrick House and Gardens** (907 Coral Way, Coral Gables, 305/460-5361, www.coralgables.com, 1pm-3:45pm Wed. and Sun., $5 adults, $3 seniors and students, $1 children 6-12, free for children under 6), which was once the home of city planner George Merrick and is now listed in the National Register of Historic Places. Originally part of William and Sarah Gregory's 160-acre homestead, this property was acquired, sight unseen, by Reverend Solomon G. Merrick, who hoped to relocate his wife, Althea, and their children from the harsh climate of Massachusetts to the sunny Miami area. Solomon and his eldest son, George, preceded the rest of the family in order to cultivate the rocky, untamed land. By January 1900, Althea and the other children had arrived, and the immensely hard work continued. The Merrick men enlisted the help of Bahamian workers from Coconut Grove to replace the pine palmettos with grapefruit trees.

By 1906, the groves had begun to flourish, and the family had successfully expanded their small wooden cottage into a spacious New England-style home. George had aspirations of becoming a lawyer, but his father's death in 1911 forced him to return to Coral Gables, where he'd begun to envision a Mediterranean-style city with wide boulevards and lush landscaping. That vision became a reality when the City of Coral Gables was incorporated in 1925. Unfortunately, a 1926 hurricane stalled the city's momentum, and in an effort to save his new town, George

Coconut Grove and Coral Gables

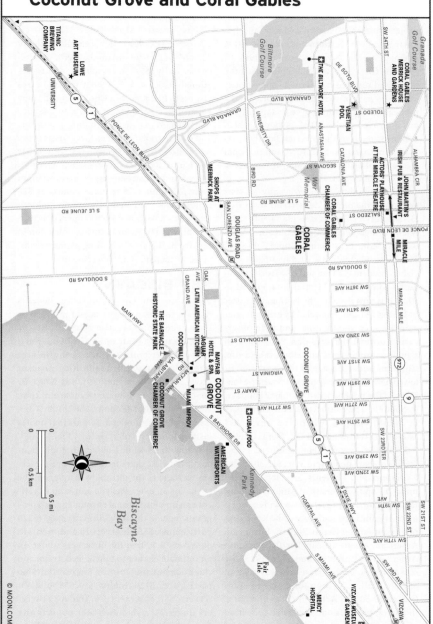

© MOON.COM

Biscayne Bay

Granada Golf Course

Biltmore Golf Course

TITANIC BREWING COMPANY

LOWE ART MUSEUM

UNIVERSITY

PONCE DE LEON BLVD

THE BILTMORE HOTEL

CORAL GABLES MERRICK HOUSE AND GARDENS

DE SOTO BLVD

GRANADA BLVD

SW 24TH ST

VENETIAN POOL

TOLEDO ST

UNIVERSITY DR

ANASTASIA AVE

CATALONIA ST

SEGOVIA AVE

ALHAMBRA CIR

JOHN MARTIN'S IRISH PUB & RESTAURANT

ACTORS' PLAYHOUSE AT THE MIRACLE THEATRE

SALZEDO ST

SHOPS AT MERRICK PARK

BIRD RD

War Memorial

S LE JEUNE RD

CORAL GABLES CHAMBER OF COMMERCE

PONCE DE LEON BLVD

MIRACLE MILE

S LE JEUNE RD

SAN LORENZO AVE

DOUGLAS ROAD

S DOUGLAS RD

CORAL GABLES

SW 36TH AVE

SW 34TH AVE

MIRACLE MILE

S DOUGLAS RD

OAK AVE

GRAND AVE

DOUGLAS ROAD

SW 32ND AVE

SW 31ST AVE

COCONUT GROVE

972

MAIN HWY

THE BARNACLE HISTORIC STATE PARK

COCOWALK

LATIN AMERICAN KITCHEN

JAGUAR

MAYFAIR HOTEL & SPA

MCDONALD ST

SW 29TH AVE

9

MCFARLANE RD

VIA ABITARE

MIAMI IMPROV

COCONUT GROVE CHAMBER OF COMMERCE

MARY ST

VIRGINIA ST

COCONUT GROVE

SW 27TH AVE

SW 25TH AVE

SW 23RD TER

S BAYSHORE DR

CUBAN FOOD

5

1

SW 22ND AVE

SW 21ST ST

AMERICAN WATERSPORTS

Kennedy Park

TIGERTAIL AVE

S DIXIE HWY

SW 19TH AVE

SW 22ND ST

SW 17TH AVE

Fair Isle

S MIAMI AVE

SW 3RD AVE

VIZCAYA

MERCY HOSPITAL

VIZCAYA MUSEUM & GARDENS

0   0.5 km

0   0.5 mi

lost all of his family's fortune except for the original house, where Althea continued to live with her daughter Ethel. In 1935 the house became an inn called Merrick Manor, and following Althea's death two years later, Ethel operated it until she passed away in 1961. In 1976 the City of Coral Gables purchased the house and restored it to its 1925 appearance. Today, as part of the admission price, visitors can take a 45-minute **tour** (1pm, 2pm, and 3pm Wed. and Sun.) of the house, which contains much of the Merrick family's artwork, photographs, furniture, and personal treasures, offering an outstanding look at the early days of Coral Gables.

On particularly hot days, many tourists venture to the nearby **Venetian Pool** (2701 De Soto Blvd., Coral Gables, 305/460-5306, www.coralgablesvenetianpool.com, 11am-6:30pm Mon.-Fri., 10am-4:30pm Sat.-Sun., $12 adults, $7 children 3-12, $4.50-5.50 Coral Gables residents), a tranquil coral rock lagoon designed by George Merrick and opened in 1923. It is now listed in the National Register of Historic Places. Encircled by brilliant bougainvillea, coconut palms, and twin observation towers, the Venetian Pool is worth a photo stop, even if you don't take a dip. Children under the age of three are not allowed here. Operating hours can vary seasonally and the pool is closed on major holidays.

South of The Biltmore lies the University of Miami campus, where the **Lowe Art Museum** (1301 Stanford Dr., Coral Gables, 305/284-3535, www6.miami.edu/lowe, 10am-4pm Tues.-Sat., noon-4pm Sun., $12.50 adults, $8 seniors and students, free for children under 12 and University of Miami students, faculty, and staff) features a wide assortment of paintings, sculptures, and photography representing Greco-Roman, European, American, Asian, African, Pacific, and Latin American cultures. Founded in 1952, the museum also encompasses the Myrna and Sheldon Palley Pavilion for Contemporary Glass and Studio Arts, which, as the name indicates, presents an impressive collection of contemporary glasswork, ceramics, and

fiber art. The museum is accessible via the University stop on the Metrorail and also has a metered parking lot.

The scenic **Matheson Hammock County Park** (9610 Old Cutler Rd., Miami, 305/665-5475, www.miamidade.gov, sunrise-sunset daily, $5-7 automobiles, $15 recreational vehicles, $13-17 boat trailers) lures visitors to Biscayne Bay, where they can enjoy a man-made pool, breezy beach, full-service marina and restaurant, picnic pavilions, and nature trails. Another lovely oasis is the **Fairchild Tropical Botanic Garden** (10901 Old Cutler Rd., Coral Gables, 305/667-1651, www.fairchildgarden.org, 9:30am-4:30pm daily, $25 adults, $18 seniors 65 and over, $12 children 6-17 and students, free for children under 6), an 83-acre property opened in 1938 that now nurtures an extensive collection of rare tropical plants, including palms, cycads, vines, succulents, and flowering trees.

KEY BISCAYNE

East of Coconut Grove and Coral Gables is **Key Biscayne,** a barrier island in Biscayne Bay, accessible via the **Rickenbacker Causeway.** En route to Key Biscayne you'll encounter Virginia Key, where the 38-acre **Miami Seaquarium** (4400 Rickenbacker Cswy., Key Biscayne, 305/361-5705 or 305/365-2501, www.miamiseaquarium.com, 10am-6pm daily, $48 adults, $38 children 3-9, free for children under 3, $8 parking) invites visitors to watch entertaining killer whales, dolphins, and sea lions, observe friendly manatees, and view shark feedings. There are several snack bars and gift shops throughout the park. For an extra fee, you can even experience an up-close animal encounter. Such programs include the **Dolphin Odyssey** ($220 participants, $58 observers 10 and over, $48 observers 3-9, free for observers under 3), an intimate chance to touch, feed, train, and ride a dolphin; the **Dolphin Encounter** ($160 participants, $120 children 5-9, $58 adult observers, $48 observers 3-9, free for observers under 3), a shallow-water opportunity to touch, feed, and play with the dolphins;

the Sea Trek Reef Encounter ($100 participants, $48 adult observers, $38 observers 3-9, free for observers under 3), a 20-minute underwater walking journey through a 300,000-gallon tropical reef; and the Seal Swim ($180-160 participants, $120-140 children 5-9, $48 adult observers, $38 observers 3-9, free for observers under 3), an occasion to swim alongside harbor seals in both shallow and deep water. Some programs have height and age restrictions.

Key Biscayne has two lovely recreation areas. Crandon Park (6747 Crandon Blvd., Key Biscayne, 305/365-2320, www.miamidade.gov, sunrise-sunset daily, $5-7 vehicles, activity fees apply) is a former coconut plantation that now features a golf course, marina, tennis courts, nature trails, kayak and cabana rentals, guided tram tours, an amusement area, and the Crandon Park Visitor and Nature Center (8am-5pm daily). Visitors can explore a variety of ecosystems, including coastal dunes, mangrove forests, tropical hardwood hammocks, and seagrass beds. Kayaking is an especially rewarding activity, as it affords you a leisurely, ecofriendly way to observe wading birds, raptors, sea turtles, and other marine creatures. Many visitors come for the gorgeous two-mile beach, which offers concession stands, picnic areas, several lifeguard towers, and plenty of parking. The beach, marina, tennis center, amusement area, nature center, gardens, and cabanas are all wheelchair-accessible.

At the southern end of Key Biscayne is Bill Baggs Cape Florida State Park (1200 S. Crandon Blvd., Key Biscayne, 786/582-2673, www.floridastateparks.org/capeflorida, 8am-sunset daily, $8 vehicles with 2-8 passengers and day-use boaters, $4 motorcycles and single-occupant vehicles, $2 pedestrians, bikers, and extra passengers), home to the 95-foot-tall Cape Florida Lighthouse, a whitewashed conical tower built in 1825, reconstructed in 1846, and now considered the oldest standing structure in Miami-Dade County. The photogenic lighthouse grounds, at the southern tip of Key Biscayne, are open from 9am to 5pm Thursday-Monday. You can watch a video presentation in the former cookhouse, view cultural displays about early island life in the lighthouse keeper's cottage, and visit the gift shop. Free guided tours of the lighthouse are offered at 10am and 1pm Thursday-Monday, though it's best to call the administrative offices (305/361-8779, 8:30am-4:30pm Mon.-Fri.) in advance, just in case a school group has reserved a tour. Be prepared to climb 109 steps in all, which can be a strenuous trek for some—though well worth the panoramic views, in spite of the cramped observation area. Unfortunately, and rather arbitrarily, children under eight are not allowed to reach the top.

The park also features a 1.25-mile beach, and popular activities here include biking, kayaking, sunbathing, swimming, shoreline fishing, and overnight boat camping. Other amenities include picnic pavilions ($100-165 daily), bicycle rentals ($9-60 hourly), beach chair rentals ($7), beach umbrella rentals ($10), kayak and hydro-bike rentals ($20-30 hourly), a primitive campground ($1-6 pp nightly), and two restaurants: the Boater's Grill (305/361-0080, www.lighthouserestaurants.com, 9am-sunset daily, $4-42) and the Lighthouse Cafe (305/361-8487, www.lighthouserestaurants.com, 9am-sunset daily, $2-38). Although leashed pets are allowed in the park, they are not permitted on the beach or playground, near the wetlands, within the lighthouse compound, or inside the restaurants.

SOUTHERN MIAMI

Miami's southern suburbs contain a few interesting attractions. Beside Biscayne Bay the 444-acre Deering Estate at Cutler (16701 SW 72nd Ave., Miami, 305/235-1668, www.deeringestate.com, 10am-4pm daily, $15 adults, $7 children 4-14, free for children under 4) invites visitors to take daily nature tours of several protected habitats, including pine rocklands, tropical hardwood hammocks, salt marshes, and mangrove forests. The property's 1920s-era, Mediterranean

Revival-style mansion, nicknamed the "Stone House," was once the home of Charles Deering—a wealthy Chicago industrialist, environmental preservationist, dedicated philanthropist, avid art collector, and amateur artist. (He was also the brother of James Deering, who owned the Vizcaya estate.) It now boasts a fine collection of antique furniture, chandeliers, and other furnishings, plus several pieces of artwork, such as family portraits as well as paintings like *Ash Wednesday Procession in Barcelona,* one of several works that Deering commissioned from Spanish artist Ramon Casas in the early 1900s. During your tour of the house, which is listed in the National Register of Historic Places, you'll also spy some of Deering's original volumes, such as classic novels by Cervantes, Chaucer, Dickens, Kipling, and Melville, plus a two-volume 1800 edition of Henry Fielding's *The History of Tom Jones.*

For a completely different experience, head west to **Zoo Miami** (12400 SW 152nd St., Miami, 305/251-0400, www.miamimetrozoo. com, 10am-5pm Mon.-Fri., 9:30am-5:30pm Sat. and Sun., $23 adults, $19 children 3-12, free for children under 3), home to more than 1,000 different plant species and 500 different animal species, including endangered creatures like the tree kangaroo and Orinoco crocodile. Visitors can stroll through a children's zoo, learn about the links between birds and dinosaurs in the American Bankers Family Aviary, explore the 27-acre *Amazon & Beyond* exhibit, and take a narrated **safari tram tour** (noon, 1:30pm, and 3pm daily, $6 pp) through the Asian or African habitat. All trams and the zoo's monorail system ($6.50 pp) are wheelchair-accessible, and visitors can rent both strollers ($8-10) and wheelchairs ($8-30).

Recreation

GARDENS AND BEACHES

The **Miami Beach Botanical Garden** (2000 Convention Center Dr., Miami Beach, 305/673-7256, www.mbgarden.org, 9am-5pm Tues.-Sun., free) is a 4.5-acre green space that invites visitors to relax amid vibrant orchids, tropical plants, and Japanese-style foliage. For a sandier landscape, consider visiting one of the many beaches that line the ocean side of this barrier island, including **Lummus Park Beach** (305/673-7779, sunrise-sunset daily, free), the main public beach in South Beach. Just east of the Art Deco District, this stretch of white sand extends alongside Ocean Drive between 5th and 15th Streets. Favored by teenagers, families, tourists, and celebrities alike, this oft-photographed beach is popular for swimming, sunbathing, and people-watching. Amenities include public restrooms, volleyball courts, beach chair rentals ($10 daily), umbrella rentals ($12 daily), and warm, clear ocean waters. If you're bringing the kids, keep in mind that topless sunbathing is common here.

BOAT TOURS

If you're a first-time visitor to the Miami area, consider taking a sightseeing boat tour of the city's coastline and lovely Biscayne Bay. One option is **Island Queen Cruises** (401 Biscayne Blvd., Miami, 305/379-5119 or 800/910-5119, www.islandqueencruises.com, times vary daily, $17-69 adults, $12-25 children), based out of the Bayside Marketplace and offering a variety of excursions, including party fishing cruises, dance cruises, and speedboat cruises past "Millionaire's Row." Another option is **Duck Tours South Beach** (1661 James Ave., Miami Beach, 305/673-2217,

1: fishing on the Rickenbacker Causeway with the Miami skyline in the background
2: AmericanAirlines Arena, home to the Miami Heat basketball team

www.ducktourssouthbeach.com, times vary daily, $37 adults, $30 seniors 65 and over, $20 children 4-12, $5 children under 4), featuring 90-minute narrated tours on amphibious vehicles that lead you past famous Miami landmarks before launching into Biscayne Bay. Duck Tours also has locations in downtown Miami and Fort Lauderdale.

GOLF

You'll find numerous golf courses in the Miami area, including the **Biltmore Golf Course** (1200 Anastasia Ave., Coral Gables, 305/460-5364, www.biltmorehotel.com, 10am-6pm Mon., 7am-6pm Tues.-Thurs., 6:30am-6pm Fri.-Sun., $50-200 pp with cart), a well-landscaped 18-hole course that surrounds the legendary Biltmore Hotel and features a clubhouse, bar, and restaurant. Created in 1925 by Scottish designer Donald Ross and restored in 2007 by architect Brian Silva, this course has lured numerous movie stars, athletes, and dignitaries over the years.

The **Miami Beach Golf Club** (2301 Alton Rd., Miami Beach, 305/532-3350, www. miamibeachgolfclub.com, 7am-7pm daily, $125-225 pp with cart) requires proper golf attire, offers rental shoes ($25 per pair) and clubs ($70 per set), and provides an on-site restaurant. Tee times can be reserved up to five days in advance. The **Miccosukee Golf & Country Club** (6401 Kendale Lakes Dr., Miami, 305/382-3930, www.miccosukee. com, 7am-8:30pm daily, $40-65 pp) is a picturesque course that features 27 challenging holes, a full-service golf shop, a sports bar, and an Olympic-size swimming pool.

HIKING

Although the Everglades offer more opportunities for long-distance hikers, the Miami area offers a few choice spots for a walk. On Key Biscayne you'll find several scenic nature trails on the west side of **Bill Baggs Cape Florida State Park** (1200 S. Crandon Blvd., Key Biscayne, 786/582-2673, www.floridastateparks.org/capeflorida,

8am-sunset daily, $8 vehicles with 2-8 passengers and day-use boaters, $4 motorcycles and single-occupant vehicles, $2 pedestrians, bikers, and extra passengers). You can also utilize the hiking trails at **Oleta River State Park** (3400 NE 163rd St., North Miami, 305/919-1844, www.floridastateparks.org/ oletariver, 8am-sunset daily, $6 vehicles with 2-8 passengers, $4 motorcycles and single-occupant vehicles, $2 pedestrians, bikers, and extra passengers), situated at the northern end of Biscayne Bay and considered Florida's largest urban park.

BIKING AND SKATING

You'll find no shortage of biking opportunities in the Miami area, especially in places like **Oleta River State Park** (3400 NE 163rd St., North Miami, 305/919-1844, www. floridastateparks.org/oletariver, 8am-sunset daily, $6 vehicles with 2-8 passengers, $4 motorcycles and single-occupant vehicles, $2 pedestrians, bikers, and extra passengers) at the northern end of Biscayne Bay, with miles of off-road biking trails ranging from novice to challenging.

Bicycles can be rented from several different outfitters, including the **Miami Beach Bicycle Center** (601 5th St., Miami Beach, 305/674-0150, www.bikemiamibeach.com, 10am-7pm Mon.-Sat., 10am-5pm Sun., starting at $5 hourly, $18 daily, $80 weekly), which provides a variety of cruisers, hybrids, mountain bikes, tandems, and other bicycles, plus the use of a lock, helmet, and basket with each rental. Farther south, **Key Cycling** (328 Crandon Blvd., Ste. 121, Key Biscayne, 305/361-0061, www.keycycling.com, 10am-7pm Mon.-Fri., 10am-6pm Sat., $24-50 daily, $80-200 weekly) features both mountain and hybrid options.

Another activity popular here is inline skating, especially in South Beach and along Biscayne Bay. If you haven't brought your own skates, stop by **Fritz's Skate, Bike & Surf** (1620 Washington Ave., Miami Beach, 305/532-1954, www.fritzsmiamibeach.

com, 10am-9pm daily), which has offered the largest selection of inline skates, skateboards, and bicycles in South Beach since 1989. With a $100 refundable deposit, you can rent skates for $10 hourly, $24 daily, and $69 weekly. Protective gear is included with all skate rentals, and lessons are available. Bicycle rentals cost the same as skate rentals and include a lock and a helmet, though a $200 deposit is required.

FISHING AND BOATING

As with the rest of southern Florida, fishing and boating are popular activities in the Miami area. If you're interested in deep-sea fishing, consider boarding the *Jumanji* (401 Biscayne Blvd., Miami, 786/486-7200, www.fishjumanji.com, rates vary), a 42-foot charter boat that offers year-round opportunities to snag a variety of fish, including kingfish, tuna, marlin, wahoo, swordfish, snapper, and grouper. Other available charter boats include the 41-foot *Old Hat* (305/773-0700, www.oldhat.com, rates vary) and the 57-foot *Spellbound* (305/785-0552, www.reeladventurecharters.com, $750-2,200 per half-day trip), both of which are located in the **Haulover Park Marina** (10800 Collins Ave., Miami Beach) and offer the chance to catch a variety of game fish, from amberjack to hammerhead shark.

If you bring your own boat to Miami, there's no shortage of boat ramps and marina slips. To rent a boat, head to Monty's Marina, where **American WaterSports** (2560 S. Bayshore Dr., Coconut Grove, 305/856-6559, www.americanwatersports.us, 10am-sunset daily) offers a range of powerboats ($250-400 for 2 hours, $600-850 for 8 hours).

CANOEING AND KAYAKING

The Miami area is surrounded by water—specifically, Biscayne Bay and beyond that the Atlantic Ocean. Canoeists and kayakers will find no shortage of opportunities to explore these shimmering waters. **EcoAdventures** (305/365-3018, www.miamidade.gov/ecoadventures) offers guided trips for paddling enthusiasts, including a leisurely canoe adventure ($35 pp) along the Coral Gables Waterway and a kayaking excursion ($45 pp) around Key Biscayne.

If you'd rather venture out on your own, you can easily rent a vessel from several helpful outfitters, including the **Blue Moon Outdoor Center** (3400 NE 163rd St., North Miami Beach, 305/957-3040, www.

Haulover Park

bluemoonoutdoor.com, 9am-sunset daily), which provides both kayaks ($25-35 for 90 min.) and paddleboards ($40 for 90 min.) in **Oleta River State Park.** Full-day rentals are also available ($75-90).

DIVING AND SNORKELING

Although most diving enthusiasts head straight to Biscayne National Park or Florida Keys National Marine Sanctuary, Miami also offers helpful outfitters and operators. One such company is the **South Beach Dive and Surf Center** (850 Washington Ave., Miami Beach, 305/531-6110, www.southbeachdivers.com, 9am-7pm Mon.-Sat., 10am-6pm Sun.), a PADI 5-Star facility whose courses include an introduction class ($250 pp), an open-water advanced class ($799 pp), and a digital underwater photography class ($295-395 pp)—plus snorkeling near Key Largo ($119 pp) and diving trips near Miami and Key Largo ($129-149 pp). **Diver's Paradise** (4000 Crandon Blvd., Key Biscayne, 305/361-3483, www.keydivers.com, 10:30am-4pm Mon.-Fri., 8am-2pm Sat.-Sun.) has been assisting area divers since 1979 and features daily diving and snorkeling trips ($65-75 pp) to area wrecks and coral reefs as well as diving classes and equipment rentals.

YOGA

The Miami area boasts several opportunities for yoga enthusiasts. One interesting option is the Tina Hills Pavilion in **Bayfront Park** (301 N. Biscayne Blvd., Miami, 305/358-7550, www.bayfrontparkmiami.com, sunrise-sunset daily, no entrance fee), where a certified yoga instructor offers free **yoga classes** (6pm Mon.-Thurs., 9am Sat.) for beginners as well as advanced participants. All students must be at least 18 years old, and registration is on a first-come, first-served basis, up to 40 participants. Everyone must bring his or her own yoga mat, water, and towel.

SPECTATOR SPORTS

Fans of spectator sports can't go wrong in Miami. From September to December, football fans can watch the **Miami Dolphins** (888/346-7849, www.miamidolphins.com, game times and ticket prices vary) take on other NFL teams at **Hard Rock Stadium** (347 Don Shula Dr., Miami Gardens, 305/943-8000, www.sunlifestadium.com), and from April to September, baseball lovers flock to **Marlins Park** (501 Marlins Way, Miami) to cheer on the **Miami Marlins** (305/480-1300 or 877/627-5467, www.mlb.com/marlins, game times and ticket prices vary). From October to April basketball fans can catch the **Miami Heat** (786/777-4328, www.nba.com/heat, game times and ticket prices vary) at **AmericanAirlines Arena** (601 Biscayne Blvd., Miami, 786/777-1000, www.aaarena.com). Even hockey fans will be happy in the Magic City, where the **Florida Panthers** (954/835-7825, http://panthers.nhl.com, game times and ticket prices vary) typically play between October and April at the **BB&T Center** (1 Panther Pkwy., Sunrise, 954/835-7000, www.thebbtcenter.com).

Entertainment and Events

NIGHTLIFE

Miami is celebrated around the world for many reasons, not the least of which is its sultry nightlife. After all, this is a town that lures the young, wealthy, and beautiful, many of whom celebrate to excess at the city's numerous bars and dance clubs, where 24-hour liquor licenses are not unheard of. If you, too, hope to live it up in the Magic City, you surely won't run out of options any time soon.

Nightclubs

For the quintessential Miami dance club experience, head to **Club Space** (34 NE 11th St., Miami, 305/375-0001 or 786/357-6456, www.clubspace.com, 10pm-4pm daily, cover varies), a multistory vintage warehouse that lures countless revelers nightly. Just be forewarned that drink prices and valet parking fees are high here, and you'll likely find it easier to breach the velvet ropes if you're attractive, well dressed, and female.

Of course, most night owls flock to neon-lit, gay-friendly South Beach, an area teeming with trendy bars, hot dance clubs, and outrageous cabaret shows. It's here that you'll find the biggest crowds, the longest lines, and the strictest door policies; if your hotel concierge can't add your name to the VIP list, your best bet is to arrive as early as possible. Among the most exclusive, most popular South Beach clubs is the **Mynt Lounge** (1921 Collins Ave., Miami Beach, 305/532-0727, www.myntlounge.com, noon-5am Thurs.-Sat., cover varies), which has hosted the likes of Paris Hilton, Jennifer Lopez, and Jamie Foxx.

Bars

At **John Martin's Irish Pub & Restaurant** (253 Miracle Mile, Coral Gables, 305/445-3777, www.johnmartins.com, 11:30am-midnight Mon.-Thurs., 11:30am-2am Fri.-Sat., 11am-midnight Sun., no cover), you can enjoy happy hour drink specials on weekdays (5pm-7pm Mon.-Fri.) and live entertainment on certain nights, as well as occasional events, such as an annual St. Patrick's Day celebration. This lively bar also offers full brunch, lunch, and dinner menus.

In South Beach, you can get refreshing daiquiris and other tasty drinks at **Wet Willie's** (760 Ocean Dr., 305/532-5650, www.wetwillies.com, 11am-2am daily, $5-15). They specialize in frozen drinks—exactly what you'll want on a hot Miami day. The 2nd-floor deck gives you an excellent view of South Beach.

Live Music

Jazid (1342 Washington Ave., Miami Beach, 305/673-9372, www.jazid.net, 10pm-5am daily, $10-20 cover) offers killer drink specials and some of the best live funk, soul, jazz, reggae, and world music in the city. It has two floors and was completely remodeled in 2019.

In the Wynwood Arts District, head to **Gramps** (176 NW 24th St., 305/699-2669, www.gramps.com, 11am-1am Sun.-Wed., 11am-3am Thurs.-Sat., $5-15 cover) for live rock, DJs, and comedy acts. The spacious patio is where most of the music happens, and the air-conditioned interior has an artsy bar with a young vibe.

For a laid-back atmosphere that will make you feel like you've stepped into a crowded bar in New Orleans, head midtown to the ever-popular **Lagniappe** (3425 NE 2nd Ave., 305/576-0108, www.lagniappehouse.com, 6pm-2am Sun.-Thurs., 6am-3am Fri.-Sat., $7-20 cover). The patio has lights strung around it and a stage in the back where bands play almost every night. Most of the talented musicians who perform here play folk, blues, rock, or jazz. It can feel as cozy and relaxed as a gathering in a neighbor's backyard—except this neighbor has the best barbecue and wine selection in the state. There's no liquor or cocktails, but if you like beer or wine, then you've discovered your next favorite chill-out space.

For additional nightlife ideas, consult periodicals like *The Miami Herald* (www.miamiherald.com), *Miami New Times* (www.miaminewtimes.com), *Ocean Drive* (www.oceandrive.com), and *South Beach Magazine* (www.southbeachmagazine.com).

THE ARTS

Cultural enthusiasts will find plenty of live performances in the Miami area. In the downtown performing arts district the **Adrienne Arsht Center for the Performing Arts of Miami-Dade County** (1300 Biscayne Blvd., Miami, 305/949-6722 or 786/468-2000, www.arshtcenter.org, showtimes and ticket prices vary) hosts an array of live entertainment, including intimate plays, Broadway musicals, one-act comedies and dramas, opera productions, contemporary dance performances, experimental multimedia shows, cabaret and comedy routines, family-friendly presentations, jazz and rock concerts, and even performances by the **Miami City Ballet** (305/929-7010, www.miamicityballet.org), **Florida Grand Opera** (800/741-1010, www.fgo.org), **New World Symphony** (305/673-3331, www.nws.edu), and **Miami Symphony Orchestra** (305/275-5666, www.themiso.org). To reach the center, you can use the Metrobus, Metrorail, or Metromover; if you plan to drive here, be prepared to pay for self-parking ($15) or valet parking ($25). Although you'll find several eateries in the downtown area, you can also enjoy a preshow meal at Prelude, the center's on-site restaurant.

Not far from Miami's Bayfront Park is the **Olympia Theater at the Gusman Center for the Performing Arts** (174 E. Flagler St., Miami, 305/374-2444, www.gusmancenter.org, showtimes and ticket prices vary). Erected in 1926 as a silent movie theater, this magnificently restored venue is now home to live performances, screenings, and community events, including shows hosted by the **Miami Lyric Opera** (www.miamilyricopera.org).

Other unique venues include **The Fillmore Miami Beach at the Jackie Gleason Theater** (1700 Washington Ave., Miami Beach, 305/673-7300, www.fillmoremb.com, showtimes and ticket prices vary), which features live concerts, comedy routines, and dance performances, and the recently restored **Actors' Playhouse at the Miracle Theatre** (280 Miracle Mile, Coral Gables, 305/444-9293, www.actorsplayhouse.org, showtimes and ticket prices vary), presenting main stage performances as well as a children's theater series. High school and college students between the ages of 13 and 22 can access various cultural events, festivals, and art exhibitions at affordable prices (typically $5 per ticket) by participating in **Culture Shock Miami** (305/375-1949, www.cultureshockmiami.com), a discounted ticketing program made possible through the **Miami-Dade County Department of Cultural Affairs** (111 NW 1st St., Ste. 625, Miami, 305/375-4634, www.miamidadearts.org).

FESTIVALS AND EVENTS
Art and Cultural Events

Miami honors its multifaceted culture with a wide array of annual festivals and events—too many, in fact, to list here. Given the city's passion for art, it's no wonder that many of Miami's most popular celebrations focus on architecture and other visual art disciplines. One of the biggest, the annual **Art Deco Weekend** (www.artdecoweekend.com, activity fees vary) lures more than 300,000 people to South Beach in mid-January. Begun in 1976 by the Miami Design Preservation League (305/672-2014, www.mdpl.org), this three-day event cultivates an appreciation for the legendary Art Deco District with an assortment of guided tours, film and lecture series, art and antiques sales, classic automobiles, live music, a fashion show, and other activities.

1: Adrienne Arsht Center for the Performing Arts of Miami-Dade County **2:** Bayside Marketplace in downtown Miami **3:** Miami skyline at night **4:** a variety of cigars for sale in Little Havana

Other area art festivals include the **Coconut Grove Arts Festival** (305/447-0401, www.cgaf.com, $5-15 pp daily), which attracts a multitude of painters, photographers, jewelry makers, and glass sculptors to the Coconut Grove area for a three-day weekend in mid-February, and the four-day **Art Basel Miami Beach** (www.artbasel.com, ticket prices vary), an extensive show in early December featuring an exclusive selection of more than 250 art galleries from North America, Latin America, Europe, Asia, and Africa. Art lovers will also appreciate the six-day **Art Miami** (305/515-8573, www.art-miami.com, one-day pass $65), the city's longest-running contemporary and modern art fair, usually held in early December in the Midtown Miami Arts District.

Miami also hosts several cinematic, musical, theatrical, and literary events. Among these are the 10-day **Miami International Film Festival** (305/237-3456, www.miamifilmfestival.com, showtimes and ticket prices vary) in early March; the 10-day **Miami Gay and Lesbian Film Festival** (305/751-6305, www.mglff.com, showtimes and ticket prices vary) in late April or early May; the **Mainly Mozart Festival** (786/468-2251, www.mainlymozart.com, $10-30 per concert, $215 per series), a six-concert chamber music series in May and June; the three-week **International Ballet Fest of Miami** (786/747-1877, www.internationalballetfestival.org, showtimes and ticket prices vary) from late August to mid-September; and the eight-day **Miami Book Fair International** (305/237-3258, www.miamibookfair.com, ticket prices vary) in mid-November.

Heritage Festivals

Residents and visitors can experience the city's intriguing cultural mosaic through such unique festivals as the monthlong **Carnaval Miami** (305/644-8888, www.carnavalmiami.com, entry fees vary), a celebration that takes place in Little Havana from early February to mid-March and features culinary and athletic competitions, live concerts, a domino tournament, and **Calle Ocho,** one of the largest Latino block parties in the country. Since 1976, the two-day **Miami/Bahamas Goombay Festival** (305/446-0643, www.goombayfestivalcoconutgrove.com, prices vary), which usually takes place in early June, has honored the Bahamian roots of Coconut Grove with authentic cuisine, live Caribbean and African music, and spirited festivities, including a vibrant parade of costumed dancers and musicians. Later in the year, typically on a Saturday in mid-November, thousands of spectators gather on Virginia Key for the free-to-watch **Miami International Dragon Boat Festival** (305/636-0902, www.miamidragon.com, entry fees apply), an energetic boat race that features several colorfully decorated, Hong Kong-style dragon boats.

Food and Sporting Events

The year wouldn't be complete without attending one of Miami's many culinary events or athletic competitions. For die-hard gourmands, it doesn't get much better than the **Food Network South Beach Wine & Food Festival** (877/762-3933, www.sobewff.com, event times and ticket prices vary), a star-studded, four-day event in late February that showcases the talents of the world's most renowned chefs, culinary personalities, and wine producers. Meanwhile, sports lovers and outdoors enthusiasts will appreciate such events as the five-day **Progressive Miami International Boat Show** (www.miamiboatshow.com, $25-40 daily, $100 for five-day pass, free for children under 13) in mid-February, held at the Miami Marine Stadium (3501 Rickenbacker Causeway, Miami).

Shopping

A mosaic of cultures and a hotbed of high fashion, the Miami area is indeed a shopper's paradise, offering a wide array of outdoor malls and shopping districts, even in suburbs like Aventura, Kendall, and other surrounding communities. Here are just some of the shopping areas available to residents and visitors.

DOWNTOWN MIAMI

Miami's downtown area offers a few intriguing options for shoppers, including the **Bayside Marketplace** (401 Biscayne Blvd., Miami, 305/577-3344, www.baysidemarketplace. com, 10am-10pm Mon.-Thurs., 10am-11pm Fri.-Sat., 11am-9pm Sun.). Situated alongside lovely Biscayne Bay, this popular outdoor mall features daily live entertainment, varied restaurants, and numerous shops ranging from Brookstone to Skechers—enough to fill a few hours, if not all day. Besides bicycle, Jet Ski, electric scooter, and wheelchair rentals, other helpful on-site amenities include ATM kiosks, taxi services, foreign currency exchange, sightseeing tours, and visitor information for local attractions.

In Miami's financial district you'll encounter another classy mall, **The Shops at Mary Brickell Village** (901 S. Miami Ave., Miami, 305/381-6130, www.marybrickellvillage. com, 10am-9pm Mon.-Sat., noon-6pm Sun.). Featuring three packed floors and an enormous parking structure, this neighborhood mall houses a plethora of boutiques, eateries, and other businesses, including wine and cigar shops, a fine seafood restaurant, a P. F. Chang's, a day spa, an LA Fitness gym, a Starbucks, and even a Publix grocery store.

LITTLE HAVANA

Miami's **Little Havana** (www.little havanaguide.com), the culturally rich neighborhood west of the city's downtown area, is home to several cigar shops, fruit stands, art galleries, antiques shops, and clothing boutiques. If you only have time for a quick visit, be sure to stop by the **Little Havana Cigar Factory** (1501 SW 8th St., Miami, 305/541-1103, www.littlehavanacigarfactory. com, 10am-6pm Sun.-Mon., 10am-7pm Tues.-Sat.), which offers a wide array of authentically fermented and matured cigars. Even if you're not a cigar aficionado, you're sure to appreciate the aroma.

SOUTH BEACH

The southern portion of Miami Beach, otherwise known as South Beach, is a magnet for high fashion. You'll find an incredible array of upscale clothing emporiums, jewelry boutiques, art galleries, beauty salons, and specialty stores on or near **Lincoln Road** (www.lincolnroad.org), which is home to **The Lincoln Road Outdoor Antique & Collectible Market of Miami Beach** (www. antiquecollectiblemarket.com, free) on various Sundays throughout the year. Nearby **Collins Avenue** and **Ocean Drive** offer their own share of shopping wonders, such as the **Effusion Gallery** (1130 Ocean Dr., Miami Beach, 305/538-3558, www.effusiongallery. com, 10am-11pm daily), showcasing a curious array of colorful art, from mixed-media clocks and whimsical mirrors to three-dimensional glass paintings and surreal celebrity portraits.

For more information about shopping opportunities in South Beach, consult *South Beach Magazine* (www. southbeachmagazine.com).

COCONUT GROVE

Coconut Grove is a family-friendly shopping enclave southwest of downtown Miami, ideal for a stroll in pleasant weather. One popular gathering place is **CocoWalk** (3015 Grand Ave., Coconut Grove, 305/444-0777, www. cocowalk.net, 10am-9pm Sun.-Thurs., 10am-11pm Fri.-Sat.), a Mediterranean-style open-air complex that features several shops and restaurants, from Victoria's Secret to The Cheesecake Factory, plus late-night bars like Fat Tuesday, known for its New Orleans-style daiquiris. Other amenities include covered parking, secure bicycle racks, ATM kiosks, and 24-hour security.

CORAL GABLES

The affluent, well-manicured village of Coral Gables features an array of sophisticated shopping options. The **Shops at Merrick Park** (358 San Lorenzo Ave., Coral Gables, 305/529-0200, www.shopsatmerrickpark. com, 10am-9pm Mon.-Sat., noon-6pm Sun.) is a cluster of fine shops and eateries centered on a lovely urban garden. Visitors can peruse shoes at Cole Haan, jewelry at Tiffany & Co., cookware at Williams-Sonoma, and stylish apparel at department stores like Nordstrom and Neiman Marcus. You can also visit **Equinox** (370 San Lorenzo Ave., 786/497-8200, www.equinox.com, 5:30am-11pm Mon.-Thurs., 5:30am-10pm Fri., 8am-8pm Sat.-Sun.) for a range of facials, body treatments, and massage therapies and afterward

enjoy a casual meal at the **Yard House** (320 San Lorenzo Ave., 305/447-9273, www. yardhouse.com, 11am-12:30am Sun.-Thurs., 11am-1:30am Fri.-Sat.), which boasts an incredible selection of draft beer.

Coral Gables offers more than just a high-class mall experience. In the quaint downtown area, several boutiques, salons, art galleries, outdoor cafés, and convenient parking lots make up the **Miracle Mile** (www.shopcoralgables.com), a four-block stretch between Douglas and Le Jeune Roads that comprises several surrounding streets. Of the many offerings here, you'll find classy menswear at **Jos. A. Bank** (336 Miracle Mile Way, Coral Gables, 305/441-0585, www. josbank.com, 10am-8:30pm Mon.-Fri., 9:30am-8:30pm Sat., 10:30am-6pm Sun.) and pricey hairstyling services, facials, and manicures at the **Avant-Garde Salon & Spa** (155 Miracle Mile, Coral Gables, 305/442-8136, www.avantgardesalonandspa.com, 10am-7pm Mon.-Tues. and Sat., 10am-8pm Wed.-Fri.).

Food

The varied cultural influences in Miami are present in the cuisine here, which ranges from Creole dishes in Miami's Little Haiti to *cubanos* (Cuban sandwiches) in Little Havana to fresh seafood and "Floribbean" cuisine throughout the city. For more information about eateries in the Miami area, consult the **Miami Dining Guide** (www.miami. diningguide.com).

DOWNTOWN MIAMI

If you love ceviche and small-plate seafood dishes with exotic flavors, head to the trendy **CVI.CHE 105** (105 NE 3rd Ave., Miami, 305/577-2217, www.ceviche105.com, 11:30am-10pm Mon.-Fri., noon-11pm Sat., noon-10pm Sun., $15-30). Helmed by award-winning chef

Juan Chipoco, this Peruvian fusion restaurant excels in blending the unique flavors of Peru and South America into delicious seafood ceviche samplers and larger traditional Peruvian entrees. Don't leave without trying the most popular dish on the menu, Ceviche Ganador, a mix of lime-soaked and lightly cooked corvina fish, shrimp, calamari, shellfish, and octopus, and topped with cilantro, sweet potato, corn, and red onion.

For breakfast, lunch, or dinner, enjoy an excellent French meal at **Café Bastille** (248 SE 1st St., Miami, 786/425-3575, 8am-10pm Mon.-Sat., 8am-5pm Sun., $10-25). Try their savory or sweet crepes, like the Paradis, a sweet crepe wrapped around strawberries, Nutella, and dulce de leche. Their lunch and dinner menus have a great selection of sandwiches and entrees that range from traditional French options like chicken fricassee to Italian pastas such as shrimp linguini. And in pure French fashion, they have an excellent selection of French wines and champagne. *Vive la France!*

LITTLE HAVANA

The Little Havana neighborhood is composed predominantly of Cuban Americans and Cuban exiles, which means you'll find plenty of authentic delicacies from *cafecito* (Cuban coffee without milk) and *cortadito* (Cuban coffee with steamed milk) to *cubanos,* the flattened, grilled sandwiches made with sliced ham, slow-roasted pork, Swiss cheese, and pickles, popularized by Cuban immigrants who settled in Miami in the early 1900s.

★ Cuban Food

For a romantic meal, head west from downtown via U.S. 41 toward **Casa Juancho** (2436 SW 8th St., Miami, 305/642-2452, www.casajuancho.com, noon-11pm Sun.-Tues., noon-midnight Wed.-Thurs., noon-1am Fri.-Sat., $24-36). The Spanish-style menu includes various steaks, paella dishes, and fish and shellfish entrées, such as *salmón con vieiras al albariño,* or fresh salmon and scallops in a reduced albariño wine and saffron sauce. Live music from accordionists and traditional guitarists often enhances the romantic atmosphere. Unlike other eateries in Little Havana, Casa Juancho requires dressy casual or business attire; hats, shorts, and T-shirts are not allowed, and reservations are recommended.

Farther west along U.S. 41, the ★ **Versailles Restaurant** (3555 SW 8th St., Miami, 305/444-0240, www.versaillesrestaurant.com, 8am-1am Mon.-Thurs., 8am-2:30am Fri.-Sat., 9am-1am Sun., $4-29) may sound—and even look—like a French restaurant, but it's actually been one of Miami's best Cuban-Caribbean restaurants since its opening in 1971. Given the frequent crowds here, it seems that the secret has long been out. Although its popularity makes parking at this restaurant rather difficult, it's a wonderful place to sample a traditional *cubano* or the fantastic garlic-roasted chicken. Take advantage of the restaurant's late hours, when parking is usually less of a hassle.

Caribe Cafe Restaurant (7173 W. Flagler St., 305/266-7170, www.caribecaferestaurant.com, 6am-midnight daily, $6-12) is in West Miami, very close to the airport and all of the

a strong Cuban coffee with a chicken empanada in Little Havana

Cuban Bakeries

Before you leave Miami, make sure you visit an authentic Cuban bakery. You can buy some of the best churros, sweet breads, and delicious, flaky, *pastelitos,* which are puff pastries baked with different sweet and savory fillings.

My number one pick is **La Rosa Bakery** (4259 W. Flagler St., Coral Gables, 305/443-2113, www.larosabakery.com, 7am-6pm daily, $1-5). It's a traditional bakery founded by five Cuban brothers. Get here early, because their guava and cream cheese *pastelitos* are usually gone before closing time, sometimes by as early as 2pm on weekends and holidays. The more-than-40-year-old bakery has a wide variety of meat- and fruit-filled goodies that are prepared using secret family recipes. There's definitely something special in these *pastelitos.*

In the neighborhood of Coral Way, **El Brazo Fuerte Bakery** (1697 SW 32nd Ave., Miami, 305/444-7720, www.ebfbakery.com, 6am-7pm Mon.-Sat., 6am-5:30pm Sun., $1-7) serves a mix of French and Cuban pastries that will make it difficult to leave without buying anything. The *pastelitos* are excellent, especially the coconut-filled ones. Again, get here early: This is considered one of the best bakeries in all of Miami, and it runs out of the good stuff before closing time.

In Little Havana, you can get a very cheap breakfast as well as tasty pastries at **Arahis Bakery** (745 SW 8th St., Miami, 305/854-8000, 5am-7pm Mon.-Fri., 5am-6pm Sat., 5am-2pm Sun., $1-7). The old-school atmosphere adds to the charm of the place.

If you're near Coral Gables, you can get all the popular Cuban pastries at **Lucerne Bakery** (7415 Coral Way, Coral Gables, 305/261-7791, 5am-6pm Mon.-Sat., 5am-3pm Sun., $1-7). Although the place is in a less-than-picturesque strip mall, this bakery is one of the best. The service is usually quick, which is good because the place gets super busy most days.

hotels there. The atmosphere is simple, but don't let it fool you: This place has some of the best Cuban food in all of Miami. Try the empanadas and fried plantains. The servings are generous, and they deliver, too.

Right in the heart of Little Havana, **El Exquisito Restaurant** (1510 SW 8th St., 305/643-0227, www.elexquisitomiami.com, 7am-11pm daily, $7-15) has a low-key, traditional vibe and Cuban art on the walls. The smells coming from this place are enough to make you run inside and grab a seat. For lunch, get the *pan con bistec* (steak sandwich), and at dinner order the *pargo entero frito* (whole fried snapper). Don't miss the Cuban coffee here—it's some of the best on the Calle Ocho.

Another great option is **El Cristo Restaurant** (1543 SW 8th St., 305/643-9992, 8am-10pm Sun.-Thurs., 8am-midnight Fri.-Sat., $6-12), which has been open since 1972. There's nothing fancy about this charming little restaurant, which is known for its low prices, large portions, and delicious Cuban

food. The pulled pork with rice, beans, and fried plantains is a favorite, and the mojitos are legendary—some say the best in all Miami.

SOUTH BEACH

Housed in an art deco-style dining car, the casual **11th Street Diner** (1065 Washington Ave., Miami Beach, 305/534-6373, www.eleventhstreetdiner.com, 7am-midnight Mon.-Tues., 24 hours Wed.-Sun., $4-19) serves traditional comfort food, from the Monte Cristo sandwich to Argentinian skirt steak—even in the wee hours.

The venerable **Joe's Stone Crab** (11 Washington Ave., Miami Beach, 305/673-0365, www.joesstonecrab.com, 6pm-10pm Tues.-Thurs. and Sun., 6pm-11pm Fri.-Sat., $6-40) may specialize in stone crabs and other locally caught seafood, but this popular eatery also features some amazing fried chicken—the dish most favored by former president Bill Clinton whenever he visits. Established in 1913, Joe's is one of the oldest restaurants in Miami.

Located in the Gale Hotel, **Dolce Italian Miami** (1690 Collins Ave., 786/975-2550, www.dolceitalianrestaurant.com, 7:30am-10pm Sun.-Thurs., 7:30am-11pm Fri.-Sat., $15-30) is one of the hottest Italian restaurants in Miami Beach. It's a classy, upscale place where you're likely to see people wearing suits, but the atmosphere is inviting with wood-paneled walls and comfy leather chairs and booths. The wine list is excellent and there are plenty of innovative cocktails to choose from. Try the arugula salad and the eggplant parmesan or roasted chicken with asparagus. Reservations are highly recommended.

COCONUT GROVE TO CORAL GABLES

For contemporary Latin American cuisine, head to the **Jaguar Latin American Kitchen** (3067 Grand Ave., Coconut Grove, 305/444-0216, www.jaguarspot.com, 11:30am-10pm Mon.-Thurs., 11:30am-11pm Fri., 11am-11pm Sat., 11am-10pm Sun., $9-33), a colorful eatery that offers a variety of ceviche, grilled meat, and seafood dishes. If you appreciate finely crafted beer, then you must visit the **Titanic Brewing Company** (5813 Ponce de Leon Blvd., Coral Gables, 305/668-1742, www.titanicbrewery.com, 11:30am-1am Sun.-Thurs., 11:30am-2am Fri.-Sat., $8-20), where you can pair a wonderful sampler tray of microbrews with any number of tasty dishes, including steamed mussels, crawfish and andouille bisque, shrimp wraps, or build-your-own burgers. The nautical decor and scrumptious desserts, from rum cake to key lime pie, only add to the fun. The kitchen shuts down two hours before closing time.

Accommodations

In general, staying overnight in the Miami area can be an expensive enterprise, especially if you'd prefer to stay in a safer, more tourist-friendly neighborhood like South Beach or Coral Gables. For more information about Miami's accommodations, consult **Miami Beach 411** (1521 Alton Rd., Ste. 233, Miami Beach, 305/754-2206 or 888/999-8931, www.miamibeach411.com).

DOWNTOWN MIAMI

While downtown Miami isn't known for the same swankiness that South Beach promises, a few premium options do exist in this part of the city. The **Four Seasons Hotel Miami** (1435 Brickell Ave., Miami, 305/358-3535, www.fourseasons.com/miami, rooms $290-650 d, suites $600-2,400) offers 221 stylish rooms and suites between the 20th and 29th floors of a 70-story tower made of glass and granite, overlooking beautiful Biscayne Bay. Besides a world-class spa and a magnificent pool, the hotel provides two amazing restaurants, a stylish lounge, and high-speed Internet access.

The Kimpton **EPIC Hotel** (270 Biscayne Blvd., Miami, 305/424-5226 or 866/760-3742, www.epichotel.com, rooms $180-450 d, suites $400-800) guarantees an equally high-class experience as the Four Seasons. In addition to its 411 luxurious rooms and suites, in-house spa, amazing pools, and marina services, EPIC is also one of the few pet-friendly lodgings in downtown Miami.

SOUTH BEACH

If you're looking for a hip, youthful vibe, then South Beach is definitely the place for you. In this famous Miami Beach neighborhood, you'll find several classic options, including the **Crowne Plaza South Beach** (1437 Collins Ave., Miami Beach, 305/672-4554 or 866/418-1269, www.zoceanhotelsouthbeach.com, suites $159-550), which features 79 roomy suites, a private glass-bottom pool, rooftop hot tubs, and the Front Porch Cafe. **The Betsy Hotel** (1440 Ocean Dr., Miami Beach, 305/531-6100 or 866/792-3879, www. thebetsyhotel.com, rooms $190-650 d, suites $450-800) is a historic property featuring 63 rooms and suites. Located beside the beach, this intimate hotel offers wireless Internet access, a full-range spa, two unique bars, and the BLT Steak, Laurent Tourondel's modern American steak house. Another winning option is the **Majestic Hotel South Beach** (660 Ocean Dr., Miami Beach, 305/455-3270 or 800/403-6274, www.majesticsouthbeach. com, $120-300 d), which is one of the most affordable lodgings in South Beach despite being only steps away from the neighborhood's world-famous beach.

Farther north lies one of the most well-known hotels in Miami Beach, if not all of Miami. The ★ **Fontainebleau Miami Beach** (4441 Collins Ave., Miami Beach, 305/535-3283 or 800/548-8886, www. fontainebleau.com, rooms $250-500 d, suites $400-3,000) has featured prominently in films like *The Bellboy* (1960) and *Goldfinger* (1964) and offers unparalleled luxury year-round. Following a $1 billion renovation and expansion, this enormous oceanfront resort now offers more than 1,500 airy, well-appointed rooms and suites, seven unique restaurants, three bars and nightclubs, a stylish pool area with private cabanas, a gym that overlooks the pool, and the 40,000-square-foot **Lapis Spa & Salon** (4441 Collins Ave., Miami Beach, 866/750-4772, www.fontainebleau.com, 9:30am-6:30pm Sun.-Fri., 9:30am-7:30pm Sat.).

COCONUT GROVE TO CORAL GABLES

Situated within an exclusive waterfront enclave of upscale restaurants, shopping, and nightlife, the stunning **Mayfair Hotel & Spa** (3000 Florida Ave., Coconut Grove, 305/441-0000 or 800/433-4555, www. mayfairhotelandspa.com, suites $200-500) contains a variety of luxurious suites, all of which have marble bathrooms, Roman soaking tubs, flat-screen plasma TVs, and wireless Internet access. In addition to its convenient proximity to Miami's beaches and downtown area, the Mayfair features a 4,500-square-foot spa that provides guests with first-class massages and body treatments.

If you do plan to stay in the Miami area before heading to the Keys—even for a night—you simply must consider ★ **The Biltmore**

Fontainebleau Miami Beach

Hotel (1200 Anastasia Ave., Coral Gables, 855/454-0196, www.biltmorehotel.com, rooms $200-400 d, suites $400-2,000), a historic 150-acre resort that features a vibrant, Mediterranean-style structure topped by a magnificent tower and encompassing 275 sumptuous rooms and suites. Other on-site amenities include a championship golf course, an incredible spa and fitness center, 10 tennis courts, a world-famous pool area, and several celebrated restaurants.

CAMPING

Miami may not be known for its camping options, but that doesn't mean you won't find at least one here: **Bill Baggs Cape Florida State Park** (1200 S. Crandon Blvd., Key Biscayne, 786/582-2673, www.floridastateparks.org/capeflorida, 8am-sunset daily, $8 vehicles with 2-8 passengers and day-use boaters, $4 motorcycles and single-occupant vehicles, $2 pedestrians, bikers, and extra passengers) offers boat camping. For a daily fee, boaters can anchor overnight in No Name Harbor ($20 daily), where during operating hours they'll have access to restrooms, coin-operated laundry machines, a rinse shower, a picnic shelter, a free pump-out service, and yummy meals at the Boater's Grill.

Information and Services

INFORMATION

Tourism and Government Offices

For brochures, maps, and other information about Miami, stop by the **Greater Miami Convention & Visitors Bureau** (GMCVB, 701 Brickell Ave., Ste. 2700, Miami, 305/539-3000 or 800/933-8448, www.miamiandbeaches.com, 8:30am-5pm Mon.-Fri.). You'll also find more localized tourism bureaus, such as the **Miami Beach Visitor and Convention Authority** (1701 Meridian Ave., Ste. 402A, Miami Beach, 305/673-7050, www.miamibeachvca.com, 9am-5pm Mon.-Fri.), the **Miami Beach Chamber of Commerce** (1920 Meridian Ave., Miami Beach, 305/674-1300, www.miamibeachchamber.com, 9am-5pm Mon.-Fri.), the **Miami Beach Latin Chamber of Commerce** (1620 Drexel Ave., Miami Beach, 305/674-1414, www.miamibeach.org, 9am-5:30pm Mon.-Fri.), the **Coconut Grove Chamber of Commerce** (2820 McFarlane Rd., Coconut Grove, 305/444-7270, www.coconutgrovechamber.com, 11am-4pm Tues.-Thurs.), the **Coral Gables Chamber of Commerce** (224 Catalonia Ave., Coral Gables, 305/446-1657, www.

coralgableschamber.org, 9am-5pm Mon.-Fri.), and the **Key Biscayne Chamber of Commerce & Visitors Center** (88 W. McIntyre St., Ste. 100, Key Biscayne, 305/361-5207, www.keybiscaynechamber.org, chamber 9am-5pm Mon.-Fri., visitors center 24 hours daily). If you're interested in gay-friendly activities, accommodations, shops, bars, and restaurants, consult www.miamigaytravel.com or the **Miami-Dade Gay & Lesbian Chamber of Commerce** (1130 Washington Ave., 1st Fl., Miami Beach, 305/673-4440, www.gaybizmiami.com), which oversees the **LGBT Visitor Center** (305/397-8914, www.gogaymiami.com, 9am-6pm Mon.-Fri., 11am-4pm Sat. and Sun.) at the same address. For government-related issues, consult the comprehensive websites of **Miami-Dade County** (www.miamidade.gov), the **City of Miami** (www.miamigov.com), the **City of Miami Beach** (www.miamibeachfl.gov), and the **City of Coral Gables** (www.coralgables.com).

Media

Miami offers a number of helpful periodicals, including *The Miami Herald* (www.miamiherald.com) and the *Miami New*

Times (www.miaminewtimes.com), which offer comprehensive listings of bars, restaurants, live music venues, art shows, current movies, and upcoming events. In addition, the monthly magazine *Ocean Drive* (www.oceandrive.com) offers a look at the latest trends in fashion, beauty, art, dining, travel, and entertainment.

You'll also have access to several radio stations, including **Y100** (www.y100.com), which offers an assortment of popular music, from rock to hip-hop. Major television stations in town include **CBSMiami** (http://miami.cbslocal.com), **WSVN 7NEWS** (www.wsvn.com), and **NBC 6 South Florida** (www.nbcmiami.com).

SERVICES
Money

For banking needs, stop by the **First Bank of Miami** (800/831-5763, www.1firstbank.com), which has three branches in the Miami area, including one in downtown Miami (50 NE 9th St., 305/358-0618) and another in Coral Gables (180 Aragon Ave., 305/444-1140).

Mail

For shipping, faxing, copying, and other business-related services, visit **The UPS Store** (www.theupsstore.com), with several locations in the Miami area, including one in downtown Miami (247 SW 8th St., 305/858-1221, 8am-7:30pm Mon.-Fri., 9:30am-3pm Sat.) and another in Coral Gables (1825 Ponce de Leon Blvd., 305/441-7161, 8am-6:30pm Mon.-Fri., 9am-5pm Sat.). **PostNet** (13550 SW 120th St., Ste. 406A, Miami, 786/409-2912, www.postnet.com, 9am-6:30pm Mon.-Fri., 10am-3:30pm Sat.) offers similar services in the Miami area. And of course, you'll find more than four dozen **post offices** (800/275-8777, www.usps.com) in the greater metropolitan area, including one in Coconut Grove (3191 Grand Ave., 305/529-6700, 9am-5pm

Mon.-Fri., 9am-10:30am Sat.) and another in Coral Gables (251 Valencia Ave., 305/443-2532, 8:30am-6pm Mon.-Fri., 8:30am-2pm Sat.).

Groceries and Supplies

For groceries, fresh seafood, and other supplies, head to **Fresco** (3401 NW 18th Ave., Miami, 305/634-4492, www.frescoymas.com, 7am-midnight daily). For pharmacy needs, stop by **Walgreens** (1 E. Flagler St., Miami, 305/371-5868, www.walgreens.com, 7am-7pm Mon.-Fri., 8am-6pm Sat., 9am-5pm Sun.). The **Publix** (800/242-1227, www.publix.com) chain has plenty of grocery stores in the Miami area, including one near Little Haiti (4870 Biscayne Blvd., Miami, 305/573-8601, 7am-11pm daily).

Laundry

Laundry facilities include **Sudsies Dry Cleaners & Laundry** (6786 Collins Ave., Miami Beach, 305/864-3279 or 888/898-7837, www.sudsies.com, 7am-7pm Mon.-Fri., 8am-6pm Sat.), which offers pickup and delivery (7am-7pm Mon.-Sat.).

Emergency Services

In case of an emergency that requires police, fire, or ambulance services, dial **911** from any cell or public phone. For medical assistance, consult one of several hospitals in the greater metropolitan area, such as **Mercy Hospital** (3663 S. Miami Ave., Miami, 305/854-4400, www.mercymiami.com), the **University of Miami Hospital** (1400 NW 12th Ave., Miami, 305/689-5000, www.umiamihealth.com), and the **North Shore Medical Center** (1100 NW 95th St., Miami, 305/835-6000, www.northshoremedical.com). For nonemergency assistance, contact the **Miami-Dade Police Department** (9105 NW 25th St., Doral, 305/471-1780, www.miamidade.gov/mdpd, 8am-5pm Mon.-Fri.), and for general county info, dial **311**.

Transportation

GETTING THERE
Air

To reach Miami by plane, you can fly directly into **Miami International Airport (MIA)** (2100 NW 42nd Ave., Miami, 305/876-7000, www.miami-airport.com), which is located about seven miles west of downtown Miami, or opt for **Fort Lauderdale-Hollywood International Airport (FLL)** (100 Terminal Dr., Fort Lauderdale, 866/435-9355, www.broward.org/airport), which lies roughly 25 miles north of downtown Miami. Both accommodate major air carriers, including **American Airlines** (800/433-7300, www.aa.com), **Air Canada** (888/247-2262, www.aircanada.com), **Caribbean Airlines** (800/920-4225, www.caribbean-airlines.com), **Virgin Atlantic** (800/862-8621, www.virginatlantic.com), and **Avianca** (800/284-2622, www.avianca.com). From either airport, you can rent a vehicle through such agencies as **Avis** (800/633-3469, www.avis.com), **Budget** (800/218-7992, www.budget.com), **Enterprise** (800/261-7331, www.enterprise.com), **Hertz** (800/654-3131, www.hertz.com), or **Thrifty** (800/847-4389, www.thrifty.com).

Bus or Train

Greyhound (800/231-2222, www.greyhound.com) offers bus service to several different stations, including the **Fort Lauderdale Greyhound Station** (515 NE 3rd St., Fort Lauderdale, 954/764-6551, 5:30am-1:30am daily), the **North Miami Beach Greyhound Station** (16000 NW 7th Ave., North Miami, 305/688-7277, 5am-11:30pm daily), the **Miami Greyhound Station** (4111 NW 27th St., Miami, 305/871-1810, 24 hours daily), and the **American Service Station** (10801 Caribbean Blvd., Cutler Bay, 305/278-9897, 24 hours daily).

You can also travel here by train. **Amtrak** (800/872-7245, www.amtrak.com) offers service via its Silver Service/Palmetto route. The three southernmost stations are **Fort Lauderdale** (FTL, 200 SW 21st Ter., Fort Lauderdale, 24 hours daily), **Hollywood** (HOL, 3001 Hollywood Blvd., Hollywood, 8am-6:20pm daily), and **Miami** (MIA, 8303 NW 37th Ave., Miami, 6:30am-9pm daily).

Transport from Airports and Stations

If you arrive in the Miami-Fort Lauderdale area by plane, bus, or train, you can easily rent a car or hire a taxicab or shuttle service to reach your destination. The lower arrivals level at Miami International Airport (MIA) is home to **SuperShuttle** (305/871-2000 or 954/764-1700, www.supershuttle.com), which offers one-way trips to destinations like downtown Miami ($17-26 pp), Coconut Grove ($17-27 pp), Coral Gables ($14-32 pp), South Beach ($22-29 pp), and Key Biscayne ($27-32 pp). Each additional passenger (in the same group) will run about $5-25 extra, depending on the destination. Most taxicabs, which you can also hire from the lower arrivals level at MIA, will run about $24 for a one-way trip to downtown Miami, Coconut Grove, and the University of Miami in Coral Gables. A trip to South Beach will cost roughly $34; to Key Biscayne is around $43.

From Fort Lauderdale-Hollywood International Airport (FLL), a taxicab ride to downtown Miami, South Beach, or Key Biscayne will run about $67-80. **GO Airport Shuttle** (954/561-8888 or 800/244-8252, www.go-airportshuttle.com) also offers shared ride service from FLL to destinations throughout Miami, including South Beach ($24 pp), downtown Miami ($30 pp), Coconut

Cruising Through Miami

cruising the coast

Miami is called the cruise capital of the world for a reason—nearly 5 million cruise ship passengers pass through PortMiami each year. If you're one of those passengers, you may only have a few hours on each end of your cruise to explore Miami. So what to do? PortMiami is located on Dodge Island, just off the coast from Bayside Marketplace and nestled between the mainland and South Beach, so cruisers are extremely close to many of the highlights of Miami.

Here are some suggestions if you only have a few hours:

- Stretch your legs at **Bayfront Park**, the closest highlight to PortMiami. You can reach it by walking west along Port Boulevard and crossing the bridge over Biscayne Bay, which also gives you an excellent view of downtown. On the other side of the bridge, **Bayside Marketplace** will be to your left (south). Walk through the marketplace and grab a bite at one of the waterfront cafes. Bayfront Park is just south of the marketplace. This is a wonderful introduction to Miami.

- Ride the free **Metromover** (from any of the stations adjacent to Biscayne Boulevard) to many places Downtown, such as the **Miami-Dade Cultural Plaza.** You'll find plenty of shopping, entertainment, and dining in downtown Miami.

- Take a taxi to **South Beach** and spend an hour or two at **Lummus Park Beach.** If you have time, explore the **Art Deco District.**

If you decide to venture out before your cruise, make sure you know the latest time you can board the ship. It's a bad day when you start your vacation watching your cruise ship sail away without you.

Grove ($34.50 pp), Coral Gables ($34.50 pp), and Key Biscayne ($34.50 pp). Cabs and shuttles are typically available 24 hours daily.

As an alternative, you can also use the **Tri-Rail** (954/783-6030 or 800/874-7245, www.tri-rail.com), a commuter train service operated by the **South Florida Regional Transportation Authority (SFRTA)** that links the Fort Lauderdale and Miami airports to several other communities in southern Florida, including Hollywood and West Palm Beach.

Car

Miami is accessible via several major roads, including I-75 from Tampa, Florida's Turnpike from Orlando, and I-95 from Jacksonville. No matter which route you take, be sure to call **511** for an up-to-the-minute traffic report.

Boat

PortMiami (1015 N. America Way, Miami, 305/347-5515, www.miamidade.gov/portmiami) claims to be the "cruise capital of the world," which means you can certainly arrive here by boat if you so choose.

GETTING AROUND

Car

The best way to travel through Miami is by car, truck, RV, or motorcycle—all of which offer easy access to the city's major thoroughfares. Given the sheer array of interstates, federal and state highways, county roads, and surface streets in the Miami area, traversing the city and its suburbs isn't too difficult a task, especially if you have a detailed map, such as the AAA Miami/Miami Beach foldout map, or access to an application like Google Maps on your cell phone. Although you can take surface streets pretty much everywhere, you'll probably save time by using major routes and highways. From downtown Miami, you can use I-95 or Biscayne Boulevard (U.S. 1) to reach North Miami, head south on the Dixie Highway (U.S. 1) to access Coconut Grove and Coral Gables, and take SR-913 to Key Biscayne. To reach Miami Beach, you can take I-195 East and head south on SR-A1A, and the Tamiami Trail (U.S. 41) offers relatively easy access to Little Havana and, farther west, the Everglades.

Public Transit

Miami has a convenient public transit system, including the **Metrobus** (305/891-3131, www.miamidade.gov/transit, $2-2.35 per ride, transfer fees may apply), which offers routes throughout southern Florida, even as far as Marathon in the Florida Keys. Each bus route

has its own schedule, so some routes (such as #3 in downtown Miami) run 24 hours daily while others have very limited timetables.

You can also travel through Miami using the city's light-rail system. The **Metrorail** (305/891-3131, www.miamidade.gov/transit, $2.25 per ride, $5 daily, $26 weekly, $113 monthly) features 23 stations, offering convenient access to stops such as the Civic Center and Coconut Grove. Another option is the **Metromover** (305/891-3131, www.miamidade.gov/transit), which provides free access to a number of stations in downtown Miami, including one near Bayfront Park and another near the Adrienne Arsht Center for the Performing Arts of Miami-Dade County. For both the Metrorail and the Metromover, trains typically operate between 5am and midnight every day.

For those who need to go a bit farther, the **South Florida Regional Transportation Authority (SFRTA)** offers the **Tri-Rail** (954/783-6030 or 800/874-7245, www.tri-rail.com), a commuter train service that links the Miami airport to Hollywood, Fort Lauderdale, West Palm Beach, and several spots in between. The southbound trains, which run from Mangonia Park in Palm Beach County to Miami International Airport, operate between 4am and 11pm on weekdays and between 5:50am and 11pm on weekends and holidays. The northbound trains operate between 4:18am and 1am on weekdays and between 5:20am and 11:45pm on weekends and holidays.

Taxi

Taxicab companies like **Flamingo Taxis** (305/599-9999, $2.50 per pickup, $2.50 per mile) can help you get around Miami at any time of day or night.

Bicycle or Boat

While you can certainly traverse Miami by bicycle, the sprawling nature of this region makes it challenging for novice riders. Still, it's a lovely, ecofriendly way to experience this subtropical city. Bicycles can be rented from several outfitters. The **Miami Beach Bicycle Center** (601 5th St., Miami Beach, 305/674-0150, www.bikemiamibeach.com, 10am-7pm Mon.-Sat., 10am-5pm Sun., starting at $5 hourly, $18 daily, $80 weekly) offers a variety of cruisers, hybrids, mountain bikes, tandems, and other bicycles, in addition to accessories and repairs.

Of course, you can also experience the Miami coast by boat. Having your own vessel makes navigating these waters even easier, and you'll find no shortage of boat ramps and marina slips in Miami. If you'd rather rent a boat, head to Monty's Marina, where **American WaterSports** (2560 S. Bayshore Dr., Coconut Grove, 305/856-6559, www.americanwatersports.us, 10am-sunset daily) offers a range of powerboats ($250-400 for 2 hours, $600-850 for 8 hours).

The Everglades

West of Miami lies a vast, legendary region of subtropical wetlands known as the Everglades. Part of southern Florida's massive watershed, this ever-evolving region has been shaped over the centuries by water, fire, storms, nonnative species, and human actions. Termed the "river of grass" by writer Marjory Stoneman Douglas in the late 1940s, the Everglades comprise a complex system of interdependent ecosystems, including sawgrass marshes, cypress swamps, mangrove forests, tropical hardwood hammocks, pine rocklands, coastal prairies, tidal mud flats, sloughs and estuaries, and the marine environment of Florida Bay. Despite prolonged damage caused by activities like water drainage, this mysterious landscape and its adjacent waters are preserved in part by two national parks, a national preserve, a wildlife refuge, and two state parks. As amazing as this region's natural resources are, there are cultural gems here, too, such as the Miccosukee Indian Village.

Constituting one of the largest tracts of wilderness in the United States, the Everglades are home to hundreds of bird, fish, reptile, amphibian, and mammal species. Whether you choose to explore the

cypress trees in Big Cypress National Preserve

Everglades by airboat, take a canoe trip through Everglades National Park, or simply stroll along the Big Cypress Bend Boardwalk in Fakahatchee Strand Preserve State Park, you're bound to encounter an array of curious birds and other wild animals, including great blue herons, American alligators, various snakes and turtles, and, for the lucky few, the elusive Florida panther.

The main thoroughfare through the Everglades is **U.S. 41,** also known as the **Tamiami Trail.** This highway cuts through the Everglades, beginning in downtown Miami and ending in Naples. The entire drive from Miami to Naples is 126 miles long and often takes about two hours to drive, depending on traffic in Miami.

When it comes to accommodations, for the most part the Everglades region offers quiet inns, chain hotels, and campgrounds—ideal for those on a budget. Of course, even here, you'll find a few resort-style choices, too.

HOMESTEAD AND FLORIDA CITY

The neighboring cities of **Homestead** and **Florida City** are at the southeastern entrance to the Everglades. These suburbs of Miami are surrounded by an agricultural area, home to myriad plant nurseries.

From Florida City you can head south 9.3 miles to the **Ernest F. Coe Visitor Center** (40001 State Road 9336, Homestead, 305/242-7700, www.nps.gov/ever, 9am-5pm daily, free), the main entrance to Everglades National Park, to view an introductory video to the Everglades and explore the options for your Everglades adventure. This entrance is primarily used to reach the Flamingo Visitor Center and an array of hiking trails into the wilderness.

Sights and Recreation
CORAL CASTLE MUSEUM
The **Coral Castle Museum** (28655 S. Dixie Hwy., Homestead, 305/248-6345, www.coralcastle.com, 9am-6pm Sun.-Thurs., 9am-7pm Fri.-Sat., $18 adults, $15 seniors 62 and

over, $8 children 7-12, free for children under 7) invites visitors to solve a long-standing mystery: How could a diminutive man like Edward Leedskalnin carve and sculpt 1,100 tons of coral all on his own? Erected secretly between 1923 and 1951, at a time when few modern construction conveniences existed, this strange sculpture garden has sparked countless debates over the years, and to this day, scientists and thinkers have yet to discern Edward's methods. Visitors can either take a guided tour or listen to a self-paced audio tour, available in English, Spanish, French, or German. The Coral Castle is part of the Historic Redland Tropical Trail, created to promote the agricultural heritage of the unique region between Miami and the Florida Keys.

EVERGLADES ALLIGATOR FARM
The Florida Everglades are home to a number of airboat tour operators, alligator exhibits, and live animal shows. Some places, like the **Everglades Alligator Farm** (40351 SW 192nd Ave., Homestead, 305/247-2628, www.everglades.com, 9am-5:30pm daily, $28 adults, $21 children 4-11, free for children under 4)—part of the Historic Redland Tropical Trail and situated about 40 miles southwest of Miami—offer all three. Beginning in 1982 as a mere airboat ride attraction, it is southern Florida's oldest alligator farm. Besides taking a narrated **airboat ride** (roughly 30 minutes long) along canals in the nearby Everglades, visitors can witness riveting **alligator feedings** (noon and 3pm daily), **alligator shows** (11am, 2pm, and 5pm daily), and **snake shows** (10am, 1pm, and 4pm daily); observe and perhaps even hold a baby alligator or two; and stroll among more than 2,000 alligators, caimans, native snakes, and specimens of three crocodile species: American, Nile, and Orinoco.

The on-site gift shop (9am-5:30pm daily) is also worth a quick visit, especially if you forgot to bring insect spray with you, which you'll need to deter mosquitoes. The last airboat departs at 5:25pm each day. Wearing

The Everglades

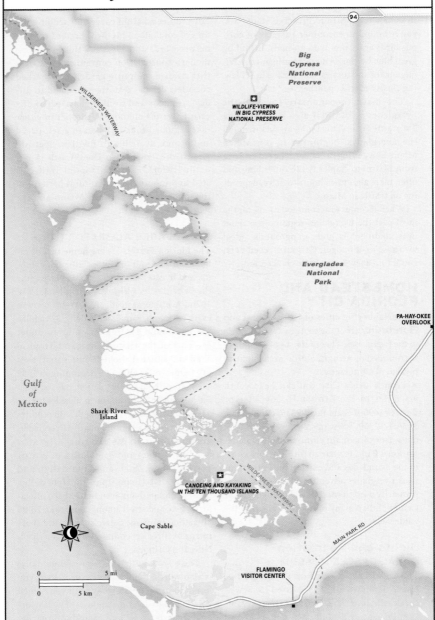

94

Big Cypress National Preserve

★ WILDLIFE-VIEWING IN BIG CYPRESS NATIONAL PRESERVE

WILDERNESS WATERWAY

Everglades National Park

PA-HAY-OKEE OVERLOOK

Gulf of Mexico

Shark River Island

★ CANOEING AND KAYAKING IN THE TEN THOUSAND ISLANDS

WILDERNESS WATERWAY

Cape Sable

MAIN PARK RD

FLAMINGO VISITOR CENTER

0   5 mi

0   5 km

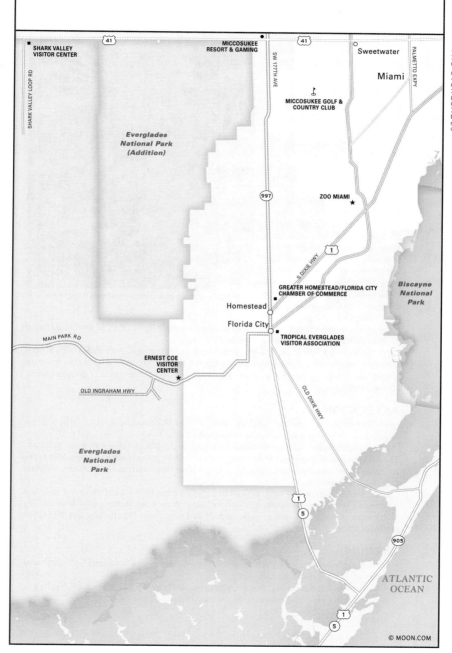

One Day in the Everglades

For this trip you'll definitely want strong bug spray, plenty of water, sunglasses, shoes you don't mind getting wet or muddy, comfortable clothes (preferably quick-dry, lightweight pants and a long-sleeved shirt), and a hat to protect you from the sun.

MORNING

From Miami, head west on U.S. 41 (the Tamiami Trail) to reach the Everglades.

Take a morning airboat ride through the swamps around **Everglades National Park.** It's a wonderful place to observe birds, alligators, and other native wildlife. One of the best airboat providers in the area is **The Original Coopertown Airboats Tour,** based in the small town of Coopertown along the Tamiami Trail. The tours are of-

Purple gallinules are found in Everglades National Park.

fered on a first-come, first-served basis. Be cautious around wildlife when adventuring around the Everglades, and do not feed the alligators!

For something a little more low-key, enjoy a tram tour through Shark Valley with **Shark Valley Tram Tours,** which leave from the **Shark Valley Visitor Center.** The tours are around two hours long, and it is a certainty that you will see an abundance of alligators, birds, and other wildlife.

AFTERNOON

Have lunch on the Tamiami Trail near Shark Valley at the **Miccosukee Restaurant,** a Native American restaurant that also serves American and Mexican fare.

After lunch, explore the region's cultural heritage at the **Miccosukee Indian Village.** You can view historical artifacts and photographs at the Miccosukee Indian Museum, and you're welcome to observe Miccosukee people as they create handicrafts such as baskets, wooden carvings, and beadwork.

Head farther west on the Tamiami Trail to **Big Cypress National Preserve.** Go for a hike on one of the preserve's trails or drive down Turner River Road, spotting wildlife and taking in the scenery. Residents of the preserve include wild hogs, great blue herons, and the elusive Florida panther.

EVENING

Head to Everglades City for a waterfront dinner at the **Everglades Rod and Gun Club** and stay the night in one of its cozy cottages.

Alternatively, head back east toward Miami, stopping by the **Miccosukee Resort & Gaming** for some entertainment and another option for food and lodging.

earplugs is strongly recommended, as air-boats can be very loud. The basic admission price includes an airboat ride, a visit to the alligator farm, and access to all animal shows; if you're only interested in the farm and the shows, then you can opt for a lower ticket price ($21 adults, $16 children 4-11, free for children under 4).

MONKEY JUNGLE

Situated between Miami and Homestead, not far from Zoo Miami, lies the family-owned **Monkey Jungle** (14805 SW 216th St., Miami, 305/235-1611, www.monkeyjungle. com, 9:30am-5pm daily but ticket office closes at 4pm, $30 adults, $28 seniors 65 and over, $24 children 3-9, free for children under 3), where, as the facility's slogan indicates, "humans are caged and monkeys run wild!" Home to nearly 400 primates, this 30-acre reserve features the natural, unrehearsed antics of 30 different species, including gibbons, guenons, spider monkeys, howler monkeys, gorillas, orangutans, endangered golden lion tamarins, and descendants of the original Java monkeys that animal behaviorist Joseph DuMond released into a dense southern Florida hammock in 1933.

FRUIT AND SPICE PARK

A 37-acre tropical botanical garden, the **Fruit and Spice Park** (24801 SW 187th Ave., Homestead, 305/247-5727, www. fruitandspicepark.org, 9am-5pm daily, $10 adults, $3 children 6-11, free for children under 6) hosts more than 500 varieties of plants, fruits, vegetables, spices, herbs, and nuts, including several varieties of mango, banana, and bamboo trees. Visitors can have a picnic on the premises or eat lunch at the on-site café. In addition, **guided tours** are conducted every day at 11am, 1:30pm, and 3pm, and various events regularly take place at the park, including the **Redland International Orchid Show** ($10 pp) in mid-May and the **Redland Summer Fruit Festival** ($10 pp, free for children under 12) in mid-June.

Shopping

Though most folks don't venture into the Everglades on a shopping quest, several spots are worth visiting. Drivers heading south of downtown Miami toward Homestead will encounter the nostalgic **Cauley Square Historic Village** (22400 Old Dixie Hwy., Miami, 305/258-3543 or 305/878-1410, www. cauleysquare.com, 11am-5pm Tues.-Sun.), part of the Historic Redland Tropical Trail. Here you can stroll along garden paths, enjoy tea and sandwiches at the on-site Victorian-style **Tea Room Restaurant** (305/258-0044, www.tearoommiami.com, 11am-4pm Tues.-Fri., 9am-6pm Sat.-Sun.), and browse a variety of quaint cottages housing a cornucopia of jewelry, candles, handmade crafts, antique furniture, and other specialty items. Also on the premises is **The Village Chalet** (305/258-8900 or 305/878-1410, www. cauleysquare.com/restaurants/village-chalet, 11am-9pm Wed.-Sun.), a cozy restaurant that features salads, sandwiches, steaks, seafood entrées, and pasta dishes, plus live rock and jazz on occasion.

The **Schnebly Redland's Winery & Brewery** (30205 SW 217th Ave., Homestead, 305/242-1224, www.schneblywinery.com, noon-5pm Mon.-Thurs., noon-11pm Fri.-Sat., 11am-5pm Sun.), also part of the Historic Redland Tropical Trail, invites visitors to sample handcrafted wine and beer among beautiful gardens filled with coral and waterfalls.

The area in and around Homestead, especially along Krome Avenue (SR-997/SW 177th Ave.), is also known for its bountiful nurseries, including the **Santa Barbara Nursery** (20425 SW 177th Ave., Miami, 305/256-7577, www.santa-barbaranursery.com, 7:30am-5:30pm Mon.-Sat., 9am-5pm Sun.), which offers a wide assortment of trees, plants, and flowers. In addition, the Historic Redland Tropical Trail features three other agricultural delights, including **Miami Tropical Bonsai** (14775 SW 232nd St., Miami, 305/258-0865, www.miamitropicalbonsai. com, 9am-4:30pm Mon.-Sat.), selling an assortment of bonsai trees and supplies, and **R.F. Orchids** (28100 SW 182nd Ave., Homestead, 305/245-4570, www.rforchids. com, 9am-5pm Tues.-Sun.), which provides an array of vibrant orchids. Closer to Florida City is the **Robert Is Here Fruit Stand and Farm** (19200 SW 344th St., Homestead, 305/246-1592, www.robertishere.com, 8am-7pm daily Nov.-Aug.). Established in 1960, this store offers a range of seasonal produce and products, from oranges and mangoes to preserves and salsas.

Food

Dining options include the popular chain restaurant **Sonny's Bar-B-Q** (33505 S. Dixie Hwy., Florida City, 305/245-8585, www. sonnysbbq.com, 11am-10pm daily, $12-22), which should satisfy your craving for barbecue beef, pork, and chicken, not to mention southern-style sweet tea.

On the adjacent street, **Capri Restaurant** (935 N. Krome Ave., Florida City, 305/247-1542, www.dinecapri.com, 11am-9pm Mon., 11am-10pm Tues.-Fri., 4pm-10pm Sat., $9-27), a family-owned operation since 1958, serves fine Italian cuisine, from traditional dishes like chicken marsala to unique concoctions such as shrimp casino, which features sautéed shrimp, onions, peppers, bacon, and garlic butter served over angel-hair pasta.

Accommodations

There are plenty of chain hotels and motels in the Homestead/Florida City area, including the standout **Best Western Gateway to the Everglades** (411 S. Krome Ave., Florida City, 305/246-5100, www.bestwestern.com, $70-120). Simple but a great value, the hotel includes a nice pool and a hot tub under a tiki hut and provides free breakfast—and you can be in the Everglades in minutes. It's only six miles from Everglades Alligator Farm and five miles to the Coral Castle Museum.

A unique place to stay, the **Hoosville Hostel** (20 SW 2nd Ave., Florida City, 305/363-4644, www.hoosvillehostel.com) in Florida City is especially wonderful for those who are social and enjoy meeting new people. This popular hostel has a variety of lodging options, from simple shared bunk rooms ($30) to private rooms (starting from $55) to a deluxe suite ($265). A full kitchen is shared and the garden courtyard, relaxing gazebo, and tropical pool make the stay memorable.

CAMPING

Between Miami and the Everglades, not far from the Monkey Jungle, lies the appropriately named **Miami Everglades Resort** (20675 SW 162nd Ave., Miami, 305/233-5300 or 800/917-4923, www.rvonthego.com). Here you'll find a slew of spacious RV and tent sites ($31-65 daily), some of which include patios and picnic tables, plus several air-conditioned cabins and lodges ($59-179 daily) that can also be rented by the week or month. Campers will enjoy an array of recreational facilities, including a heated pool and hot tub, a large playground, a paved walking and jogging track, bicycle rentals, horseshoes, and volleyball, basketball, and shuffleboard courts. Other amenities include shaded tiki huts, a recreation hall, a well-stocked camp store, a casual eatery, a propane filling station, modern restrooms, laundry facilities, wireless Internet access, and free U-pick avocados and mangoes.

Getting There

To reach Homestead from Miami, simply follow U.S. 1 west (N. Homestead Blvd.) for 37 miles, which takes around one hour. From Homestead, continue on U.S. 1 for 2 miles to Florida City, about a 10-minute drive.

EVERGLADES NATIONAL PARK

Between Miami and Naples stretches **Everglades National Park** (40001 SR-9336, Homestead, 305/242-7700, www.nps. gov/ever, park 24 hours daily, $30 vehicles, $25

1: Coral Castle Museum in Homestead
2: observation tower at Shark Valley Visitor Center in Everglades National Park 3: American alligator

motorcycles, $15 bicyclists and pedestrians, free for children under 17), the largest subtropical wilderness in America and the third-largest national park in the Lower 48 states.

Established in 1947 and since designated a World Heritage Site, an International Biosphere, and a Wetland of International Importance, this unique place protects more than 1.5 million acres and offers a plethora of outdoor diversions for recreationists, from hiking and canoeing trails to campgrounds to ample fishing and wildlife-viewing opportunities. There are **ranger-led programs** throughout the year, **narrated tram tours** in the Shark Valley area, and **airboat tours** and **paddling tours** through the Ten Thousand Islands region.

Sights
VISITORS CENTERS

This vast park has several helpful visitors centers, all of which offer educational displays and public restrooms, among other amenities. At the **Ernest F. Coe Visitor Center** (40001 SR-9336, Homestead, 305/242-7700, 9am-5pm daily), the main park entrance, you'll find an art exhibit, a bookstore, and walking trails. West of Miami, on the Tamiami Trail, the **Shark Valley Visitor Center** (36000 SW 8th St., Miami, 305/221-8776, 9am-5pm daily) features walking trails, bicycle rentals, guided tram tours, and an observation tower. Farther west along the Tamiami Trail, the **Gulf Coast Visitor Center** (815 Oyster Bar Ln., Everglades City, 239/695-3311, 8am-4:30pm daily mid-Nov.-mid-Apr., 9am-4:30pm daily mid-Apr.-mid-Nov.) provides boat tours and canoe rentals. The **Flamingo Visitor Center** (239/695-2945, 8am-4:30pm Mon.-Fri., 6am-5:30pm Sat.-Sun.) is the only visitors center situated deep within the park, roughly 38 miles south of the main park entrance. Here you can procure backcountry permits; rent canoes, kayaks, and bicycles; and access campground facilities, a marina store, a public boat ramp, and several hiking and canoeing trails.

Recreation

★ CANOEING AND KAYAKING

With its sawgrass marshes, cypress swamps, and mangrove forests, the Everglades provide ideal spots for paddlers, especially those who enjoy observing or photographing wild animals in their element.

You can rent **canoes** ($46 per day) and **kayaks** ($65 per day) through Everglades National Park at the Flamingo Visitor Center, where well-equipped, well-prepared paddlers can explore a labyrinth of water and mangroves in the **Ten Thousand Islands** area. Everglades National Park is America's only subtropical wilderness, a third of it given over to marine areas and shallow estuaries easily paddled by rookie or seasoned kayakers or canoers (in my experience, a kayak seems easier to navigate through these sometimes-tight quarters). The mangroves form canopied tunnels through the swamp, through which you pick in a peculiar way: Often the flat of your paddle is used to gently push off from the tangle of mangrove roots when it's too tight to actually dip the paddle into the water. In this way you pole through the tight spots, the nose of your craft sometimes hitching up in the roots, necessitating backward paddling to disengage. However, don't overestimate your abilities, and time your trip with the tides (a falling tide flows toward the Gulf of Mexico; a rising tide flows toward the visitors center). It can be easy to become disoriented in the mangroves, and a nautical chart is a necessity if you are embarking on longer excursions. You can pick up nautical charts at any visitors center in the park, including the Flamingo Visitor Center.

For the most adventurous at heart, consider traversing the **Wilderness Waterway,** a 99-mile canoe trail that winds from Flamingo Visitor Center to Everglades City at the northwest entrance of the national park. It's about an eight-day excursion, to be undertaken only after plenty of diligent preparation.

If you prefer to take a **guided paddling**

tour of the area, the NPS website offers a list of permitted guides that can take you paddling in the national park. A guide is recommended, but not necessary for experienced paddlers. Rangers at the Flamingo Visitor Center can provide more information on paddling the Wilderness Waterway.

WILDLIFE-VIEWING

No matter where you go in Everglades National Park, you're bound to see an array of wildlife, including white-tailed deer, alligators, crocodiles, turtles, snakes, herons, and egrets (as well as mosquitoes, unfortunately). If you're lucky, you might even spy an endangered creature like the Florida panther or West Indian manatee.

Canoeing and kayaking offer an excellent way to observe wildlife in the park. For those visitors who have little or no experience with those activities, **tram rides** and **airboat tours** provide a good opportunity to learn about the unique environment of the Everglades firsthand. Although some conservationists worry about the presence of airboats in the Everglades, citing reasons like noise pollution and wildlife disturbance, most airboat operators are exceedingly passionate and knowledgeable about this fragile landscape.

The **Shark Valley Tram Tours** (Shark Valley Loop Rd., 305/221-8455, www. sharkvalleytramtours.com, $25 adults, $19 seniors, $12.75 children 3-12, children under 3 free) are around two hours long and explore the wildlife and scenery of Shark Valley. It's a relaxing way to enjoy the Everglades and it is a certainty that you will see an abundance of alligators, birds, and other wildlife. From mid-December to April, tours depart hourly from 9am to 4pm; from May to mid-December, tours depart at 9:30am, 11am, 2pm, and 4pm.

There are three tour operators that are authorized to give airboat tours inside Everglades National Park, all found along the Tamiami Trail: **The Original Coopertown Airboats** (22700 SW 8th St., Miami, 305/226-6048, www.coopertownairboats.

com, 9am-5pm daily, $23 adults, $11 children 7-11, free for children under 7), **Gator Park** (24050 SW 8th St., Miami, 305/559-2255 or 800/559-2205, www.gatorpark.com, 9am-5pm daily, $20 adults, $15 children), and **Everglades Safari Park** (26700 SW 8th St., Miami, 305/226-6923 or 305/223-3804, www.evergladessafaripark.com, 9am-6pm daily, $28 adults, $15 children 5-11, free for children under 5).

HIKING AND BIKING

Everglades National Park has several hiking trails, some of which allow bicycles. These multipurpose trails include the 1.6-mile **Snake Bight Trail**, the 0.8-mile **Anhinga Trail** (near the Royal Palm Information Station), and the 2.6-mile **Rowdy Bend Trail**. When these three trails are combined with the main park road, they form a 12.6-mile, round-trip biking excursion from the Flamingo Visitor Center.

Bicycle rentals ($9 hourly) are available in the park through **Shark Valley Tram Tours** (305/221-8455, www.sharkvalleytramtours.com) and at the Flamingo Visitor Center. Pets are not allowed on any park trails.

FISHING AND BOATING

Roughly one-third of Everglades National Park is covered by water, so it's no wonder that fishing and boating have long been popular activities in this region. Anglers will find both saltwater and freshwater fishing opportunities here, especially by boat, which allows access to a multitude of channels, shallow flats, and mangrove keys, not to mention Florida Bay. Depending on the time of year, you're likely to find snapper, redfish, bass, bluegill, and other varieties in these waters. Just be aware that saltwater and freshwater fishing require separate Florida fishing licenses, and remember that collecting plants and animals, such as orchids and conchs, is forbidden in protected waters. For more info on fishing licenses, visit the **Florida Fish and Wildlife** website (www.myfwc.com/license).

Even if you don't like to fish, traversing the

Everglades by boat can be a rewarding experience—though it's only advisable for skilled boaters. There are innumerable obstacles in the Everglades, from seagrass banks to oyster reefs. It helps to know the draft of your vessel, be able to "read" the water for signs of shallow areas, and adhere to slow-speed zones at all times.

Camping

Naturally, Everglades National Park offers several camping options, including two front-country campgrounds (518/885-3639 or 877/444-6777): the **Long Pine Key Campground** ($20 daily), which provides 108 tent and RV sites on a first-come, first-served basis, plus restrooms, a dump station, a picnic area, and a fishing pond; and the **Flamingo Campground,** where reservations are strongly recommended for the 276 available tent and RV sites ($20-30 daily), 41 of which have electrical hookups. At the Flamingo Campground, which is situated alongside Florida Bay, campers can utilize cold showers, two dump stations, picnic tables, an amphitheater, and several nearby hiking and canoe trails. Everglades National Park also allows backcountry camping (free May-mid-Nov., $15 per permit, plus $2 pp daily mid-Nov.-Apr.), though a permit must be secured less than 24 hours in advance.

Getting There

To reach Everglades National Park from Miami, follow U.S. 1 to Florida City. Turn right onto East Palm Drive and follow it for 1.3 miles, then continue west on SR 9336 for 8 miles until you reach the entrance station near Pine Island and Parachute Key. The drive is 49 miles and, depending on Miami traffic, often takes about 1.5 hours.

BISCAYNE NATIONAL PARK

Water enthusiasts should venture to **Biscayne National Park** (9700 SW 328th St., Homestead, 305/230-1144 or 305/230-7275, www.nps.gov/bisc, water portion 24 hours daily, Convoy Point 7am-5:30pm daily, free admission though tour and rental rates apply), a stunning wonderland of aquamarine waters, peaceful islands, and living coral reefs, all within sight of downtown Miami.

To explore this 172,000-acre park, **Biscayne National Underwater Park Inc.** (305/230-1100, www.biscayneunderwater.com, 9am-5pm daily) offers canoe and kayak rentals as well as scuba-diving and snorkeling trips in Biscayne Bay, around the islands inside the park, and to the fascinating underwater coral reefs.

If you'd prefer a less active experience, **glass-bottom boat tours** ($45 pp) provide a glimpse of the coral reefs as well as frolicking dolphins and other marine creatures.

The bay's islands are also worth exploring but can only be accessed with a canoe, kayak, or boat. Once home to a thriving community of wreckers, sponge makers, and pineapple farmers, the park's largest island, **Elliott Key,** offers ample picnicking, swimming, hiking, camping, fishing, and wildlife-viewing opportunities. On **Boca Chita Key,** the park's most popular island, you can enjoy a relaxing picnic, stroll along a half-mile hiking trail, or tour the 65-foot ornamental lighthouse, which is open intermittently and affords a fantastic view of nearby islands, Biscayne Bay, and the Miami skyline. One way to reach Boca Chita is by doing the **Boca Chita Lighthouse Adventure** (305/230-1100, www.biscayneunderwater.com, Oct.-mid-Mar., $35 pp), a three-hour boat ride and island tour offered through Biscayne National Underwater Park Inc. from October to March.

Although the water portion of Biscayne National Park is open 24 hours daily, the keys have different operating hours; Adams Key, for instance, is a day-use area only. Also keep in mind that there are no bridges or ferries to the islands and, consequently, no RV camping facilities on the islands themselves.

For more information about tours and activities, consult the **Dante Fascell Visitor Center** (9700 SW 328th St., Homestead, 305/230-7275, 7am-5:30pm daily) near Convoy Point on the mainland.

Recreation
CANOEING AND KAYAKING

Biscayne National Underwater Park Inc. offers canoe and kayak rentals (rates vary) for those hoping to explore the islands and coral-rich waters of Biscayne National Park. You can explore the shallow bay or the mangroves that line the shore. For longer excursions, paddlers can cross the seven-mile-long bay to Boca Chita or Elliott Keys. Rays and a variety of fish and birds are often spotted in the shallows of Jones Lagoon, and Hurricane Creek is an excellent spot to paddle and snorkel amid the mangroves.

FISHING AND BOATING

Boating in Biscayne National Park is only advisable for skilled boaters—it's critical to understand the shifting tides. As with boating in the Everglades, it also helps to know the draft of your vessel, be able to "read" the water for signs of shallow areas, and adhere to slow-speed zones at all times.

Fishing is allowed in the park, where you can enjoy flats and deeper-water fishing offshore. Lobster collection is prohibited in the Biscayne Bay and Card Sound Lobster Sanctuary. A variety of fish can be caught in the area, including the popular bonefish and black grouper.

A great (and free!) fishing class is offered in the park one day every other month. You'll learn what tackle and equipment to use for a variety of fish found in the park, as well as information on how to identify a variety of fish species. Check the NPS website (www.nps.gov/bisc) for more info.

DIVING AND SNORKELING

Despite all of the outdoor activities available in the Everglades, diving and snorkeling aren't common there. That's not the case, however, in Biscayne National Park, which is accessible by boat from the coast near Homestead.

If you don't have a boat of your own, you can board a guided scuba-diving or snorkeling tour ($45-99 pp) through Biscayne National Underwater Park Inc., which offers excursions around Biscayne Bay and trips to the offshore coral reefs that are part of the national park.

Food

While exploring Biscayne National Park, you can eat at **La Playa Grill** (9698 SW 328th St., Homestead, 305/257-6918, www.laplayagrill.com, 11am-9pm Mon.-Fri., 11am-11pm Sat., 11am-10pm Sun., $10-20), which is located in the national park, about one mile east of the entrance station. It serves a variety of seafood dishes like whole fried snapper, lobster, conch fritters, coconut shrimp, and fish sandwiches. It also has Mexican, Asian, and American options like nachos, burgers, and chicken fried rice. The views of the bay are excellent.

Camping

Camping is possible on the islands of Biscayne National Park, which lies between Key Biscayne and Key Largo. **Tent camping** ($25 daily) is available on popular **Boca Chita Key,** featuring a grassy waterside camping area with picnic tables, grills, and toilets, and spacious **Elliott Key,** offering waterside and forested camping areas, picnic tables, grills, drinking water, and restrooms with cold showers. Group camping ($30 daily) is also available, and boaters are welcome to stay in either of the two harbors for a fee ($20 daily). RV camping isn't possible in the park, and any vessel still in the harbor after 5pm is presumed to be staying overnight and will be charged as such. The islands are only accessible by boat; if you don't have your own, you can easily arrange transportation through Biscayne National Underwater Park Inc. (rates vary).

Getting There

Biscayne Bay National Park is approximately 32 miles south of Miami. It often takes around one hour of driving to reach. By car, simply drive south on U.S. 1 for 22 miles. Turn left onto Tallahassee Road and go 9.5 miles. Turn left onto SW 328th Street and follow it for 4.1 miles until you reach the entrance of Biscayne National Park.

HEADING WEST ON THE TAMIAMI TRAIL

Heading west on the Tamiami Trail, you'll find a string of attractions—including the Miccosukee Indian Village, where you can learn about the rich heritage of the Miccosukee people—and airboat ride companies that will take you on exhilarating tours through the swamps of the glades.

Miccosukee Resort & Gaming

The enormous **Miccosukee Resort & Gaming** (500 SW 177th Ave., Miami, 305/222-4600 or 877/242-6464, www.miccosukee.com, $79-129) lies 24 miles west of Miami, at the intersection of Krome Avenue and the Tamiami Trail. It's operated by the Miccosukee Tribe of Indians of Florida, who separated from the native Seminole Indians in the 1950s and gained federal recognition in 1962. Here visitors can enjoy a 24-hour casino with an assortment of gaming options, including a high-stakes bingo hall, a 32-table poker room, and more than 1,900 video slot machines.

The hotel features 302 comfortable rooms and suites, all of which include wireless Internet access, premium cable television, 24-hour room service, and laundry service. The resort complex also includes a well-equipped fitness center, an indoor heated pool, a full-service European spa, a children's center, a teen arcade, a live entertainment venue, a lounge and martini bar, and five dining options.

Coopertown

Along the Tamiami Trail, eight miles west of the Miccosukee Resort, is Coopertown. The small town is mostly a string of airboat operators that include **The Original Coopertown Airboats** (22700 SW 8th St., Miami, 305/226-6048, www.coopertownairboats.com, 9am-5pm daily, $23 adults, $11 children 7-11, free for children under 7), which has been in operation since 1945 and now offers 40-minute narrated tours through a sawgrass marsh and an alligator hole. You'll see alligators as well as other wildlife and birds such as egrets, herons, and anhingas.

The **Coopertown Restaurant** (22700 SW 8th St., Miami, 305/226-6048, www.coopertownairboats.com, 9am-5pm daily, $8-30) is a convenient stop before taking a Coopertown airboat ride. Offering an authentic taste of the Everglades, this no-frills, country-style eatery serves standard fare as well as frog legs, catfish, and alligator tail.

Gator Park

Just a mile west from Coopertown along the Tamiami Trail is **Gator Park** (24050 SW 8th St., Miami, 305/559-2255 or 800/559-2205, www.gatorpark.com, 9am-5pm daily, $20 adults, $15 children), where you can experience an airboat ride (roughly 40 minutes) among the birds, snakes, alligators, sawgrass, and hammocks of the nearby Everglades, and observe a fascinating wildlife show, during which staff members capture alligators using a barehanded technique favored by the Native Americans of southern Florida. Also on the premises is a souvenir shop and a restaurant that serves hamburgers, hot dogs, and regional delicacies like alligator sausage, catfish, and frog legs. The last wildlife show usually occurs at 4:30pm daily, and the last airboat ride starts at 5pm.

Everglades Safari Park

Three miles west of Gator Park, the **Everglades Safari Park** (26700 SW 8th

St., Miami, 305/226-6923 or 305/223-3804, www.evergladessafaripark.com, 9am-6pm daily, $28 adults, $15 children 5-11, free for children under 5) offers an ecoadventure tour that includes a 30-minute narrated airboat ride; a show featuring alligators, crocodiles, turtles, and other wildlife; a stroll along the Jungle Trail boardwalk and elevated observation platform; a glimpse at a replica chickee (Seminole stilt house) village; and the chance to view more than 100 alligators on their very own island. The airboat tours depart every 30 minutes, and the last one leaves around 4pm. At both Everglades Safari Park and nearby Gator Park, you'll even be able to hold a baby alligator.

Miccosukee Indian Village

Head 9.4 miles west of Everglades Safari Park and you'll find a cultural gem: the Miccosukee Indian Village (MM 70 on U.S. 41, Miami, 305/480-1924, www.miccosukee. com, 9am-5pm daily, $15 adults, $8 children 6-12, free for children under 6). Here you can observe live alligator demonstrations, take an airboat ride into the Everglades, view historical artifacts and photographs at the Miccosukee Indian Museum, and taste authentic cuisine at the on-site restaurant. You're also welcome to observe Miccosukee people as they weave baskets, craft dolls, carve wood, and fashion colorful beadwork and patchwork, much of which you can purchase at the on-site gift shop. Two annual festivals here also highlight such handmade crafts: American Indian Day in late September and the Miccosukee Indian Arts Festival in late December.

FESTIVALS AND EVENTS

The Miccosukee Indian Arts Festival ($13 adults, $12 seniors, $9 children 7-12, free for children under 7) is held over the course of nine days, usually from late December to early January. You can experience Native American dances and musical performances, marvel at traditional costumes, enjoy authentic foods, browse genuine arts and crafts from various Native American tribes, observe alligator demonstrations, and perhaps even take an airboat ride into the Everglades. As a bonus, proceeds from the festival help to fund educational programs for Native American youth.

FOOD

Have breakfast or lunch at the Miccosukee Restaurant (305/894-2374, 10am-4pm Mon.-Fri., $7-15), a Native American restaurant that also serves American and Mexican fare. The breakfast options are standard American with omelets, waffles, eggs, and the like. Lunch options are more varied and include traditional Native American foods such as fry bread and an Indian stew that includes roasted beef with fry bread. They also have seafood dishes and gator bites.

BIG CYPRESS NATIONAL PRESERVE

North of Everglades National Park lies Big Cypress National Preserve (33100 E. Tamiami Trl., Ochopee, 239/695-2000, www. nps.gov/bicy, preserve 24 hours daily, free), a 720,000-acre region that protects the freshwater ecosystem of Big Cypress Swamp, an area that supports the marine estuaries along Florida's southwestern coast. Visitors can hike along the Florida National Scenic Trail, hunt for deer and turkey in the backcountry (permits required), experience one of several paddling trails, or join a ranger-led nature walk (late Nov.-mid-Apr.).

Sights and Recreation
VISITORS CENTERS

The Big Cypress Swamp Welcome Center (33000 E. Tamiami Trl., Ochopee, 239/695-4758, 9am-4:30pm daily) and the Oasis Visitor Center (52105 E. Tamiami Trl., Ochopee, 239/695-1201, 9am-4:30pm daily) both offer various exhibits, educational materials, an introductory film, a bookstore, and public restrooms.

BIG CYPRESS GALLERY

The **Big Cypress Gallery** (52388 Tamiami Trl., Ochopee, 239/695-2428, www.clydebutchersbigcypressgallery.com, 10am-5pm daily) is on the south side of the Tamiami Trail (U.S. 41), roughly 37 miles west of Krome Avenue and less than a mile east of the preserve's Oasis Visitor Center. Featuring the black-and-white landscape photography of Clyde and Niki Butcher, this art gallery and studio also offers two-hour **guided swamp walks** (7:30am, 11:30am, and 2:30pm Fri.-Mon., $125 pp for 2 people, $117 pp for 3 people, $95 pp for 4-10 people, special rates for more than 10 people) behind the on-site cottage. Hats, long pants, old sneakers, insect repellent, snacks, and a waterproof camera are recommended for such tours.

CANOEING AND KAYAKING

Everglades Rentals and Eco Adventures (The Ivey House, 107 Camellia St., Everglades City, 239/695-3299 or 877/567-0679, www.evergladesadventures.com, tours $59-188) offers spectacular three- or four-hour tours led by naturalist guides who have a clear passion for the abundant natural beauty of the Big Cypress Preserve. They offer paddling tours in the morning, afternoon, and at sunset. One trip launches at the old Turner River Canal, quickly passing into narrow mangrove tunnels, out into lagoons, past sawgrass prairies, and into Turner Lake. The company runs its tours November-April and offers a range of specialty tours for small groups, from photography workshops to night paddles. It also rents equipment if you prefer to explore the area on your own.

★ WILDLIFE-VIEWING

Home to tropical and temperate plant communities, Big Cypress nurtures a wide array of wildlife, including wild hogs, various birds, and the elusive Florida panther.

1: an airboat touring the Everglades **2:** kayaking in Biscayne Bay **3:** Boca Chita Lighthouse in Biscayne National Park **4:** Anhinga Trail in Everglades National Park

A great way to view wildlife from the safety of your car is to take a long drive down **Turner River Road** (3 miles east of the Big Cypress Welcome Center on U.S. 41). Expect to spend an hour or two driving the road, but you are able to turn around at any time.

Turner River Road is about 10 miles long, stretching between Highway 90 and Highway 93 (Alligator Alley). You can follow the length of the road, or make a **12-mile loop:** Start at H. P. Williams Roadside Park along Highway 90 and follow Turner River Road for about five miles; then turn left onto Wagon Wheel Road and follow for two miles; then turn left onto Birdon Road and follow for five miles back to Highway 90. All roads mentioned are gravel and are generally in good enough condition for all types of vehicles. It is best to explore this area during a dry period, as the canals can become full and occasionally flood the roadway.

Several hiking trails in the area also offer excellent opportunities for wildlife- and bird-watching, including the 0.8-mile **Kirby Storter Trail,** near Ochopee, and the 4.7-mile **Gator Hook Trail,** south of the Monroe Station along the Loop Road. The **Florida National Scenic Trail** runs north to south through the park and offers loops and long-distance hiking with campsites for those looking to backcountry camp in the preserve.

Touring the preserve by airboat is another good wildlife-viewing option. **Wooten's Everglades Airboat Tour** (32330 E. Tamiami Trl., Ochopee, 239/695-2781 or 800/282-2781, www.wootenseverglades.com, 9am-5pm daily, airboat rides $32.50 adults, $20 children 4-10, $7 children under 4) has been guiding airboat tours since 1953. Wooten's also features 35-minute swamp buggy rides ($27.50 adults, $20 children 4-10, $7 children under 4) and an animal sanctuary ($9 adults, $7 children 4-11, $5 children under 4). The airboat tours are 30 minutes.

HIKING

Long-distance hikers can enjoy three different sections of the **Florida National Scenic**

Trail in Big Cypress National Preserve. This path ultimately connects with Gulf Islands National Seashore, a park that includes parts of southern Mississippi and the Florida Panhandle. The longest section in Big Cypress extends for roughly 28 miles between the Oasis Visitor Center on U.S. 41 and the rest area at Mile Marker 63 on I-75; along the way it passes through a rugged, often overgrown habitat of pinelands, prairies, cypress swamps, and hardwood hammocks. Only experienced hikers should attempt this route. Make sure to bring enough drinking water with you, especially during the dry season (Nov.-Apr.). There are also plenty of shorter-distance trails in the park.

Camping

Eight campgrounds are available within Big Cypress National Preserve, two of which are seasonal (open Nov.-May) and six of which are open all year. While most of these are primitive campgrounds with no available drinking water, the year-round **Midway Campground** features a dump station, restrooms, drinking water, a day-use area, 10 tent sites ($24 daily), and 26 RV sites ($30 daily) with electrical hookups. For those looking for a more authentic wilderness experience, the **Gator Head** and **Pink Jeep** campgrounds cater exclusively to tent campers. The best camping season is between December and January when the weather is cooler and the mosquito population is tolerable.

Before camping in the reserve you'll need to go to a visitors center (or visit the National Park Service website at www.nps.gov/bicy) to see an informative 15-minute movie about the preserve, view a small wildlife exhibit, and pick up a permit ($10-30, depending on location) and literature about the preserve. You are required to watch the video and view the exhibit before obtaining your permit.

All campgrounds are available on a first-come, first-served basis. For more information about campground availability and potential closures, contact the **Oasis Visitor**

Center (52105 E. Tamiami Trl., Ochopee, 239/695-1201, 9am-4:30pm daily).

Getting There

From downtown Miami (SW 8th St.), follow U.S. 41 (Tamiami Trail) west for 74 miles to the preserve. The drive often takes about 1.5 hours, depending on traffic in and around Miami.

To reach Big Cypress Preserve from Naples, head east on U.S. 41 for 34 miles. The drive often takes about 45 minutes.

BIG CYPRESS SEMINOLE INDIAN RESERVATION

Located north of Big Cypress Preserve and Everglades National Park, the 2,200-acre Big Cypress Seminole Indian Reservation is home to couple of attractions worth checking out: the Ah-Tah-Thi-Ki Museum, where you can learn about the fascinating history and culture of this Native American tribe, and the Billie Swamp Safari, an adventure park that offers the unusual opportunity to stay overnight in a Seminole chickee lodge.

Ah-Tah-Thi-Ki Museum

You can better understand the Seminole native people by visiting the **Ah-Tah-Thi-Ki Museum** (34725 W. Boundary Rd., Clewiston, 877/902-1113, www.ahtahthiki. com, 9am-5pm daily, $10 adults, $7.50 seniors, students, and military personnel, $30 for family of two adults and up to 4 children ages 5-18, free for children under 5) on the Big Cypress Seminole Indian Reservation north of I-75. Featuring the country's largest display related to Florida Seminole culture, this spacious museum presents exhibits and artifacts that illustrate how the Seminole ancestors once lived in the Florida Everglades, from cooking customs to traditional Green Corn Ceremony dances. Besides perusing the exhibits, visitors can watch an orientation video, stroll along a one-mile boardwalk through a 60-acre cypress dome, experience a living village, and purchase authentic jewelry, carvings, beadwork, and patchwork clothing crafted by Seminole and Miccosukee tribes.

Billie Swamp Safari

Billie Swamp Safari (30000 Gator Tail Trl., Clewiston, 863/983-6101 or 800/467-2327, www.billieswamp.com, 7am-6pm daily) invites visitors to experience the Everglades by **airboat** (10am-4:30pm daily, $25 adults, $20 seniors, $15 children 4-12, free for children under 4) or **swamp buggy** (11am-5pm daily, $25 adults, $20 seniors, $15 children 4-12, free for children under 4), either of which offers you the chance to see native flora and fauna in an untamed landscape. The airboat ride is roughly 20 minutes long, and the swamp buggy tour takes an hour. You can also visit **animal exhibits** (11am-4pm daily) and watch a show about native and nonnative swamp critters (1:15pm and 3:15pm daily), as well as an up-close presentation about venomous snakes, nonvenomous snakes, and of course, alligators (12:15pm and 2:15pm daily).

The park offers a **day package** ($50 adults, $46 seniors 62 and over, $36 children 4-12, free for children under 4) that includes all-day access to airboats, swamp buggies, and animal shows. Another option is the **twilight swamp expedition** that features campfire storytelling and a one-hour swamp buggy tour (7pm daily, $43 adults, $38 seniors 62 and over, $31 children 4-12, free for children under 4). You can also opt for an **overnight stay** in a traditional-style Seminole chickee lodge ($40-120 daily). Both the twilight package and the overnight stay require advance reservations. Other combo packages are available, and you'll find both a gift shop (8:30am-6pm daily) and a restaurant, the **Swamp Water Café** (7am-6pm Sun.-Thurs., 7am-9pm Fri.-Sat., $4-21), on the premises. Children must be at least four years old to ride an airboat.

Camping

The year-round ★ **Big Cypress RV Resort** (30290 Josie Billie Hwy., Clewiston, 863/983-1330 or 800/437-4102, www.bigcypressrvresort.com) lies 18 miles north of I-75 on SR-833 and offers easy access to Billie Swamp Safari and the Ah-Tah-Thi-Ki Museum. Facilities here include tent sites ($35 daily), RV sites ($55-65 daily, $300-345 weekly, $680-865 monthly), and air-conditioned cabins ($99-180 daily)—all of which typically require reservations. All tent sites include water and electrical service, and RV sites feature water and electrical service as well as sewer access. Other amenities include a heated pool and hot tub, a general store, a clubhouse, an exercise room, a playground, a miniature golf course, basketball courts, a propane/dump station, and laundry facilities.

Getting There

From Miami, take I-95 North for 39 miles. Take I-75 North for 31.7 miles. Take exit 49 and continue on West State Road 84 for 19.4 miles until you arrive at the reservation. The drive will take 1.75 hours, depending on Miami traffic.

From Naples, take I-75 south for 55 miles. Take exit 49 and continue on West State Road 84 for 19.4 miles until you arrive at the reservation. The drive will take 1.5 hours.

EVERGLADES CITY AND CHOKOLOSKEE

Everglades City is a locus of ecotourism, with canoe tours, airboat rides, fishing guides, and other nature-based businesses capitalizing on the mystery and majesty of the million acres of mangrove jungle just to the south. It's significantly more rustic than swanky Naples to the north—there are no Ritz-Carltons or tux-clad waiters anywhere near—but Everglades City is a must for adventure seekers.

To the south of Everglades City is **Chokoloskee Island.** A very small island that is mostly residential, it's an excellent launching point for kayak trips into the Ten Thousand Islands.

Sights
MUSEUM OF THE EVERGLADES

For Native American history, specifically about the Calusa people, as well as tales of southwestern Florida's pioneers, head to the **Museum of the Everglades** (105 W. Broadway, Everglades City, 239/695-0008, www.evergladesmuseum.org, 9am-4pm Mon.-Sat., $2 suggested donation), which features both permanent and traveling displays of artifacts, sketches, photographs, and the like. The on-site Pauline Reeves Gallery presents monthly exhibits from local and regional painters, photographers, and artisans. The Museum of the Everglades is housed within an old laundry building that was built in 1927 by Barron Gift Collier, who had purchased the village in 1922 from the Storter family in order to create a company town that would serve as the new county seat and the engineering headquarters for the construction of the Tamiami Trail.

Faithfully restored to its 1920s-era appearance, the museum is listed in the National Register of Historic Places. During certain events, such as artists' receptions, you can take a guided walking tour (20 min.-1 hour) of the historic buildings near the museum, such as the landmark Everglades Rod and Gun Club, once known as the Allen House. Private tours can also be arranged. While admission and parking are free at this wheelchair-accessible museum, donations are gratefully accepted, even for the walking tours. No food, drink, or gum is allowed in the museum, and flash photography is prohibited in the galleries.

Recreation
CANOEING AND KAYAKING

From November to April **Everglades Rentals and Eco Adventures** (The Ivey House, 107 Camellia St., Everglades City, 239/695-3299 or 877/567-0679, www.evergladesadventures.com) provides both canoe ($30 per day) and kayak rentals ($50-65 per day) as well as guided kayaking trips ($59-188 pp) through mangrove tunnels, cypress swamps, and sawgrass prairies. **Everglades Area Tours** (238 Mamie St., Chokoloskee Island, 239/695-3633 or 800/860-1472, www.evergladesareatours.com) provides canoes ($45 per half day, $65 daily), recreational kayaks ($40-45 per half day, $60-65 daily), fishing kayaks ($45-55 per half day, $65-75 daily), and sea kayaks ($60-85 per half day, $80-105 daily).

The small coastal town of Everglades City offers airboat rides along the Barron River.

AIRBOAT TOURS

Several airboat tour operators are situated in Everglades City, including **Speedy's Airboat Tours** (621 Begonia St., Everglades City, 239/695-4448 or 800/998-4448, www. speedysairboattours.com, 9am-5pm daily, $40 adults, $25 children 3-10, free for children under 3), which offers a two-hour airboat tour through swamp, grassland, and mangrove; **Everglades City Airboat Tours** (907 Dupont St., Everglades City, 239/695-2400 or 877/222-6400, www.evergladescity-airboattours.com, 8:30am-5pm Mon.-Sat., $44 adults, $25 children under 11), with one-hour rides; and **Jungle Erv's Airboat Tours** (804 Collier Ave., Everglades City, 877/695-2820, www.jungleervairboatworld.com, 9am-5pm daily, $42 adults, $26.50 children 4-10, $7 children under 4), featuring a variety of airboat tours.

FISHING AND BOATING

Chokoloskee Charters (239/695-9107, www.chokoloskeecharters.com), helmed by Captain Charles Wright, provides guided light-tackle fishing and fly-fishing trips into the Everglades backcountry. The rates depend on the trip length and the number of anglers. For two people, a half-day trip costs $450, while a full-day trip costs $795. Four anglers can expect a rate of $650 per half day and $1,195 per day. All charters include the necessary bait, tackle, gear, coolers, licenses, insurance, and safety equipment.

Festivals and Events

For about four decades, Everglades City has hosted the annual **Everglades Seafood Festival** (239/695-2277, www. evergladesseafoodfestival.org, free admission though fees apply for some activities), a family-friendly event that usually occurs during the first weekend of February. Besides carnival rides, arts and crafts, and live music, attendees are treated to plenty of delicious food. Fresh seafood is the main event; highlights include fresh shrimp, catfish, lobster, stone crabs, and fish chowder.

Food

Everglades City features several options, including the **Island Cafe** (305 Collier Ave., Everglades City, 239/695-0003, 6am-9pm daily, $5-14), which prepares decent breakfast dishes, plus inexpensive sandwiches, burgers, and seafood.

At the **Everglades Rod and Gun Club** (200 Riverside Dr., Everglades City, 239/695-2101, 11am-2:30pm and 5pm-9:30pm Mon.-Sat., $12-25, cash only), set your sights on the conch fritters, gator nuggets, hush puppies, or blue crab claws. At **Triad Seafood Market and Cafe** (401 School Dr., Everglades City, 239/695-0722, www. triadmarketcafe.com, 10:30am-5pm daily, call for summer hours, $7-15), try the crab cake sandwiches, grouper sandwiches, fried shrimp platters, and homemade peanut butter pie. If you've worked up an appetite after a day of Everglades adventure, order up the all-you-can-eat stone crab.

The **Camellia Street Grill** (202 Camellia St., Everglades City, 239/695-2003, 11am-9pm daily, $10-20) is a fun and colorful place on the water in Everglades City, with Florida and fishing memorabilia decor and nice outdoor seating on the back deck. They have seafood platters and stone crabs, fish tacos, salads, and other usual choices. It's a casual place and the seafood is very fresh. Try the peanut butter pie for dessert.

On the island of Chokoloskee near Everglades City, the ★ **Havana Cafe** (191 Smallwood Dr., Chokoloskee, 239/695-2214, www.myhavanacafe.com, 7am-4pm daily, call for summer hours, $6-15) has the best breakfast and lunch in town. It specializes in Cuban cuisine and American eats with a bent toward fresh seafood and classic sweets. It's the best spot to grab an omelet and a cup of authentic Cuban-style *café con leche* as well as delicious Cuban sandwiches, fish platters, peel-and-eat shrimp, and key lime pie. There are a few tables inside, but the best seats are out on the back patio, which is surrounded by hibiscus and other tropicals. The place is as charming and upbeat as they come. Even if you're not hungry, stop in for a cup of Cuban coffee and some friendly banter with Carlos and Dulce Valdez, the owners of this excellent café.

Accommodations
$100-200

The landmark ★ **Everglades Rod and Gun Club** (200 Riverside Dr., Everglades City, 239/695-2101, cottages $100-170) is situated on the Barron River and borders Everglades National Park. Formerly known as the Allen House and converted to a private club in the 1920s, this historic building has hosted a number of famous guests over the years, including Ernest Hemingway, President Eisenhower, John Wayne, Jack Nicklaus, Mick Jagger, and Sean Connery. Inside, the hunting lodge-style decor includes dark, wood-paneled walls, old-fashioned furniture, and mounted tarpon, deer, and alligator trophies. Outside, the airy screened porch entices guests to relax in the white wicker furniture and watch passing boats in the adjacent river. Overnight guests can choose from one of several private air-conditioned cottages—essentially cozy, raised, modern-looking structures with small porches, hardwood floors, comfortable beds, and convenient bathrooms. If you stay here, you can enjoy access to an on-site restaurant and lounge, a convenient marina, and an outdoor pool with a picturesque waterfall.

OVER $200

The Ivey House (605 Buckner Ave. N., Everglades City, 239/695-3299 or 877/567-0679, www.iveyhouse.com, $89-279 d) is a family-owned and ecofriendly bed-and-breakfast that encompasses a variety of accommodations, including a lovely inn, a historic lodge, and a cozy cottage. Guests can also relax in a tropical pool, rent a canoe, join a guided kayaking trip, and enjoy free wireless Internet

access in certain areas. The facilities here are nonsmoking, and pets are not allowed.

CAMPING

Alongside the Barron River, you'll find relative luxury at **Everglades Isle** (803 Collier Ave., Everglades City, 239/695-2600, www.evergladesisle.com, $105-143 daily), an exclusive motor home retreat offering 61 landscaped and paved sites. Each site includes a social membership in the Lighthouse Club and the option of having your own wet slip at the on-site marina. Other amenities include a pool and hot tub, a movie theater, fitness center, restaurant and lounge, boat launch, spa treatment salons, golf cart rentals, satellite television, and wireless Internet access.

Getting There

From Miami, take I-95 North for 2.3 miles. Then take I-75 North for 117 miles to exit 105. The 125-mile drive takes about 2.5 hours.

To reach Everglades City from Naples, head east for 32 miles on U.S. 41, turn south on CR-29, and continue roughly four miles. The drive takes a half hour.

FAKAHATCHEE STRAND PRESERVE STATE PARK

Often called "the Amazon of North America," the linear swamp forest known as **Fakahatchee Strand Preserve State Park** (137 Coastline Dr., Copeland, 239/695-4593, www.floridastateparks.org/park/Fakahatchee-Strand, 8am-sunset daily, free) beckons bird-watchers and wildlife lovers. Situated along the Tamiami Trail, this lush state park lies roughly 80 miles west of Miami and immediately west of Carnestown on SR-29.

Sights and Recreation

Wander along the 2,000-foot-long **Big Cypress Bend Boardwalk,** located on the Everglades City side of the state park near the Weavers Station, or take guided swamp walks and canoe trips amid bald cypress trees, royal palm groves, and colorful orchids—home to alligators and varied birds (including egrets and anhingas), as well as other wildlife such as snakes, white-tailed deer, raccoons, endangered Florida panthers, and black bears.

Everglades Rentals & Eco Adventures (The Ivey House Inn, 107 Camellia St., Everglades City, 239/695-3299 or 877/567-0679, www.evergladesadventures.com, tours $59-188) offers spectacular three- or four-hour tours in the Fakahatchee Strand. They conduct paddling tours in the morning, afternoon, and at sunset. The company runs its tours November-April and offers a range of specialty tours for small groups, from photography workshops to night paddles. It also rents equipment if you prefer to go explore the area on your own.

Getting There

From Miami, follow U.S. 41 West for 79 miles. Turn right onto SR-29 in Ochopee and follow it for 2.5 miles. Turn right onto Janes Memorial Scenic Drive and follow it for 9.4 miles. The drive takes 2.5 hours.

From Naples, follow U.S. 41 South for 44.3 miles. Turn left onto SR-29 in Ochopee and follow it for 2.5 miles. Turn right onto Janes Memorial Scenic Drive and follow it for 9.4 miles. The drive takes 45 minutes.

COLLIER-SEMINOLE STATE PARK

Thirty-three miles west along the Tamiami Trail from Fakahatchee Strand is the 7,271-acre **Collier-Seminole State Park** (20200 E. Tamiami Trl., Naples, 239/394-3397, www.floridastateparks.org/park/Collier-Seminole, 8am-sunset daily, $5 vehicles with 2-8 passengers, $4 motorcycles and single-occupant vehicles, $2 pedestrians, bikers, and extra passengers), offering even more outdoor diversions. As a bonus, well-behaved pets on leashes are welcome here.

Sights and Recreation

Visitors can canoe through mangrove swamps,

hike or bike amid pine flatwoods, camp beneath majestic royal palm trees, fish in the Blackwater River, or simply take a stroll through the on-site nature center.

Wildlife-viewing opportunities abound. Along with alligators, snakes, and a variety of birds such as herons and egrets, you can find wildlife such as Florida panthers, bobcats, tortoises, gophers, and manatees. There are four nature trails in the park: the 0.9-mile **Royal Palm Nature Trail,** the 5.25-mile **Strand Swamp Trail,** the 3-mile **Flatwoods Trail,** and the 3.5-mile **Prairie Hammock Trail.**

For paddlers, the 13.5-mile **canoe trail** is an excellent way to experience the wildlife in the area. Paddlers can launch from the boat basin along the Blackwater River. Canoe rentals are available ($25/two hours, $60/day).

This bountiful park also offers picnic areas, playgrounds, a boat ramp, and guided tours along the nature trail and boardwalk.

Camping

Collier-Seminole State Park offers a 120-site, pet-friendly campground ($22 daily) and primitive camping for hikers and canoeists. Nestled among gumbo limbo trees and royal palms, the campground can accommodate tents as well as motor homes. Every site offers water and electrical service, and other amenities include an activity building as well as restrooms with showers. For reservations, contact **ReserveAmerica** (800/326-3521, www.reserveamerica.com).

Getting There

To reach the park from Miami, follow U.S. 41 West for 95 miles. The drive takes 1.75 hours.

To reach the park from Naples, follow U.S. 41 South for 17.2 miles. The drive takes about 25 minutes.

MARCO ISLAND

Along the coast of southwestern Florida lies a chain of islands and mangrove islets known as the Ten Thousand Islands region—though the islands actually number in the hundreds, not the thousands. The largest, northernmost island in this chain, **Marco Island** (www.marco-island-florida.com), is a popular locale for outdoors enthusiasts, especially anglers, boaters, kayakers, bird-watchers, and beachcombers. Marco Island features two public beaches, **Tigertail Beach** (Spinnaker Dr. and Hernando Dr., 8am-sunset daily, $8 parking) and **South Marco Beach** (Collier Blvd. and Swallow Ave., 8am-sunset daily, $8 parking). While South Marco offers no facilities, Tigertail features a concession stand, playground, butterfly garden, volleyball courts, public restrooms, and water-sports rentals.

Besides outdoor diversions, Marco Island also boasts several specialty shops and waterfront restaurants, including those at **The Esplanade Shoppes, Residences and Marina** (760 N. Collier Blvd., Marco Island, 239/394-7772, www.theesplanade.com, hours vary daily), an Italian-style village on Smokehouse Bay.

From Collier-Seminole State Park, the island is an 11-mile drive via San Marco Road, which takes about 20 minutes. From Naples, follow U.S. 41 for 8.2 miles, then turn right onto Collier Boulevard and follow for 8 miles until you reach Marco Island.

INFORMATION AND SERVICES
Tourism and Government Offices

For maps, brochures, and information about the Everglades, consult the **Naples, Marco Island, Everglades Convention & Visitors Bureau** (2660 N. Horseshoe Dr., Naples, 239/225-1013 or 800/688-3600, www.paradisecoast.com, 8am-5pm Mon.-Fri.), the **Everglades Area Chamber of Commerce Welcome Center** (32016 E. Tamiami Trl., Everglades City, 239/695-3941, www.evergladeschamber.org, 9am-4pm daily), **Everglades National Park** (40001 SR-9336, Homestead, 305/242-7700, www.nps.gov/ever, 9am-5pm daily), and the **Greater Homestead/Florida City Chamber of Commerce** (455 N. Flagler Ave., Homestead, 305/247-2332, www.chamberinaction.com, 10am-7pm Mon.-Fri., 10am-5pm Sat.).

The nonprofit **Tropical Everglades Visitor Association (TEVA)** (160 U.S. 1, Florida City, 305/245-9180, www.tropicaleverglades.com, 8am-5pm Mon.-Sat., 10am-2pm Sun.), which is part of the Historic Redland Tropical Trail, and the website www.florida-everglades.com are also helpful resources.

bird observation tower at the Tigertail Beach boardwalk on Marco Island

For government-related issues, you'll have to first figure out which county you need to contact. The Everglades, after all, constitute a large area—so large that it extends across three different counties: **Miami-Dade County** (www.miamidade.gov), **Monroe County** (www.monroecounty-fl.gov), and **Collier County** (www.colliergov.net).

Mail

If you need to purchase stamps or send packages while you're in the Everglades, you'll find a handful of **post offices** (800/275-8777, www.usps.com) in the area, including one in Everglades City (601 Collier Ave., 239/695-2174, 10am-noon and 1pm-3pm Mon.-Fri.).

Groceries and Supplies

Though the Everglades may seem to be filled with flyspeck towns and undeveloped hinterlands, there are several groceries and other helpful stores here. **Publix** (www.publix.com) has several branches in Homestead, including one within the **Homestead Towne Square** (891 N. Homestead Blvd., 305/242-1500, 7am-11pm Mon.-Sat., 7am-10pm Sun.). Even isolated Marco Island has a **Winn-Dixie** (625 N. Collier Blvd., 239/642-9126, www.winndixie.com, 7am-11pm daily), with a deli, bakery, fresh seafood, ATMs, and an on-site pharmacy (239/393-0843, 8am-8pm Mon.-Fri., 9am-6pm Sat., 10am-5pm Sun.).

Emergency Services

In case of an emergency that requires police, fire, or ambulance services, dial **911** from any cell or public phone. For nonemergency assistance, contact the **Miami-Dade Police Department** (9105 NW 25th St., Doral, 305/471-1780, www.miamidade.gov/mdpd, 8am-5pm Mon.-Fri.) or the **Collier County Sheriff's Office** (3319 E. Tamiami Trl., Bldg. J, Naples, 239/774-4434, www.colliersheriff.org, 8am-5pm Mon.-Fri.). If you're seeking medical assistance, consult one of several hospitals in southern Florida, including **Mercy Hospital** (3663 S. Miami Ave., Miami,

305/854-4400, www.mercymiami.com) or the **NCH Downtown Naples Hospital** (350 N. 7th St., Naples, 239/624-5000, www.nchmd.org).

GETTING THERE

Air

To reach the Everglades by plane, you can either fly major carriers into **Miami International Airport** (MIA, 2100 NW 42nd Ave., Miami, 305/876-7000, www.miami-airport.com) or commuter flights into **Naples Municipal Airport** (APF, 160 N. Aviation Dr., Naples, 239/643-0733, www.flynaples.com). From either one, you can rent a vehicle through such agencies as **Avis** (800/633-3469, www.avis.com), **Enterprise** (800/261-7331, www.enterprise.com), **Hertz** (800/654-3131, www.hertz.com), and **Thrifty** (800/847-4389, www.thrifty.com).

Bus or Train

You can reach southern Florida by bus or train and then rent a vehicle to reach the Everglades. **Greyhound** (800/231-2222, www.greyhound.com) offers service to several different stations, including the **Miami Greyhound Station** (4111 NW 27th St., Miami, 305/871-1810, 24 hours daily) and the **Central Park Bus Terminal** (2669 Davis Blvd., Ste. 1, Naples, 239/774-5660, 8am-11am and 1pm-3pm Mon.-Sat.).

Amtrak (800/872-7245, www.amtrak.com) offers service via its Silver Service/Palmetto route. The three southernmost stations are **Fort Lauderdale** (FTL, 200 SW 21st Ter., Fort Lauderdale, 24 hours daily), **Hollywood** (HOL, 3001 Hollywood Blvd., Hollywood, 8am-6:20pm daily), and **Miami** (MIA, 8303 NW 37th Ave., Miami, 6:30am-9pm daily).

Car

The Everglades region is accessible via several major roads, including I-75 from Tampa, U.S. 41 from Miami, and U.S. 1 from the Florida Keys. No matter how you get here, be sure to call 511 for an up-to-the-minute traffic report.

Boat

Many visitors arrive in southern Florida by boat—whether by cruise ship, ferry, or private vessel. **PortMiami** (1015 N. America Way, Miami, 305/347-5515, www.miamidade.gov/portmiami) is nicknamed the "cruise capital of the world." In addition, the Florida Keys offer their share of deepwater marinas, including the **Key West Bight Marina** (305/809-3983 or 305/809-3984, www.keywestbightmarina.com) at the northwest end of Grinnell Street in Key West, where the **Key West Express** (888/539-2628, www.keywestexpress.net) arrives from Fort Myers Beach almost every day and from Marco Island on certain days during December-April.

GETTING AROUND

Car

In lieu of a kayak or airboat, the most efficient way to travel through the Florida Everglades is by car, truck, RV, or motorcycle—all of which offer easy access to major highways as well as detours to places like Marco Island. Essentially, you can traverse the Everglades via two main routes, both of which offer access to Big Cypress National Preserve: **I-75**, also known as Alligator Alley or the Everglades Parkway, runs from Tampa to Fort Lauderdale; **U.S. 41**, more commonly called the Tamiami Trail, connects Naples to Miami.

Boat

You can also experience the Everglades by canoe, kayak, or airboat. Although having your own vessel makes navigating these waters even easier, you can rent one from several different outfitters, including **Everglades Rentals and Eco Adventures** (The Ivey House, 107 Camellia St., Everglades City, 239/695-3299 or 877/567-0679, www.evergladesadventures.com), which provides both canoe ($30 per day) and kayak rentals ($50-65 daily) from November to April.

Key Largo

With fascinating coral reefs, shipwrecks, and landmarks that extend along the Atlantic shoreline—part of the Florida Keys National Marine Sanctuary—Key Largo is the self-proclaimed "diving capital of the world."

Nestled between the Everglades and the continental United States' only living coral reefs, Key Largo has become a getaway town for southern Floridians and northern snowbirds alike, though it's still a quieter, more laid-back destination than Miami or even Key West. Here locals can dock their boats just steps from their favorite waterfront eateries or tiki bars, and visitors can stay at any number of intimate inns and posh resorts, some of which are linked to well-equipped marinas.

The area's biggest claim to fame is its wealth of outdoor diversions,

Look for ★ to find recommended sights, activities, dining, and lodging.

Highlights

★ **Dagny Johnson Key Largo Hammock Botanical State Park:** Wandering these backcountry trails offers a chance to spy endangered species like the Key Largo woodrat and American crocodile (page 103).

★ **John Pennekamp Coral Reef State Park:** The most popular state park in the Keys lures outdoors enthusiasts with its pleasant beaches, canoe and kayak rentals, snorkeling and diving excursions, and glass-bottom boat tours (page 104).

★ **Dolphin Attractions:** Pick from a variety of interactive programs, which include swims with the resident dolphins (page 106).

★ **Diving and Snorkeling amid Wrecks and Reefs:** Explore the underwater coral reefs of the Florida Keys National Marine Sanctuary (page 109).

★ **Canoeing and Kayaking:** These islands, patch reefs, tidal flats, and mangrove creeks are ideal places to observe wild dolphins, birds, and a gentle manatee or two (page 115).

★ **Key Largo Pirates Fest:** Celebrate Key Largo's curious past with this four-day event, featuring pirate costume contests, a pirate bazaar and thieves' market, and an underwater treasure hunt (page 119).

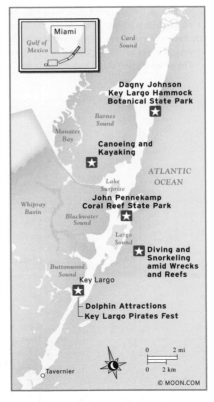

© MOON.COM

including sportfishing, paddling, and of course, snorkeling and scuba diving. No first-time visitor should skip John Pennekamp Coral Reef State Park, America's first undersea park and one of the jewels of Florida's state park system. Beyond informative marine exhibits in the visitors center, the park offers daily glass-bottom boat tours, snorkeling trips, and scuba-diving excursions. In addition, visitors can rent a canoe or kayak for a bird-watching adventure in the park's winding mangrove creeks.

Other enticing attractions in Key Largo include interactive dolphin programs, a wild bird center, and a wooded state park at the northern end of the island, not to mention the weathered old boat used in the Bogart-Hepburn film *The African Queen*. Of course, if you desire a taste of the zaniness that you'll encounter farther south, you might want to plan your vacation around the annual Key Largo Pirates Fest, a lively October event with pirate costume contests, a pirate bazaar and thieves market, and an underwater treasure hunt.

PLANNING YOUR TIME

Despite being the largest island in the Florida Keys, Key Largo has fewer overall diversions than, for instance, Key West—and not much in the way of museums, historical districts, or cultural attractions. Still, the interactive dolphin programs, diverse state parks, sight-seeing boat tours, and underwater coral reefs can keep you busy for at least three days. If you choose to pursue other outdoor activities like full-day fishing charters, kayaking excursions, and scuba-diving trips, you'll need to stay two or three days more.

Even with its large size and the spread-out nature of its attractions and lodgings, the island is easy to navigate by vehicle. Stretching from Mile Marker 110 to Mile Marker 91, Key Largo is easily traversed via the Overseas Highway (U.S. 1). Just be aware that much of the thoroughfare is divided by a wide median here, often making it necessary to use the center access roads to reach destinations on the opposite side of U.S. 1.

Given how popular Key Largo can be in winter and early spring, traffic congestion is often an issue from December to April, so be sure to give yourself plenty of time to get around, especially if you have tour reservations. During this peak season, you're also sure to encounter higher lodging rates and more crowded attractions. When planning a trip to Key Largo, you might also want to consider factors like annual events and fishing seasons. The weather is an equally important consideration. Although usually comfortable, the climate can be a little too chilly for sunbathing in January and rather hot and humid from June to September—an ideal time for water-related activities like snorkeling.

As for safety, while Key Largo is relatively crime-free, certain outdoor activities—such as kayaking or scuba diving—can be dangerous without proper instruction. It also helps to have a full understanding of any necessary guidelines or regulations before venturing out, especially if you're a first-timer.

For more information about Key Largo, consult the **Monroe County Tourist Development Council** (1201 White St., Ste. 102, Key West, 305/296-1552 or 800/352-5397, www.fla-keys.com, 9am-5pm Mon.-Fri.) and the **Key Largo Chamber of Commerce and Florida Keys Visitor Center** (106000 Overseas Hwy., Key Largo, 305/451-4747 or 800/822-1088, www.keylargo.org or www.keylargochamber.org, 9am-6pm daily).

Key Largo

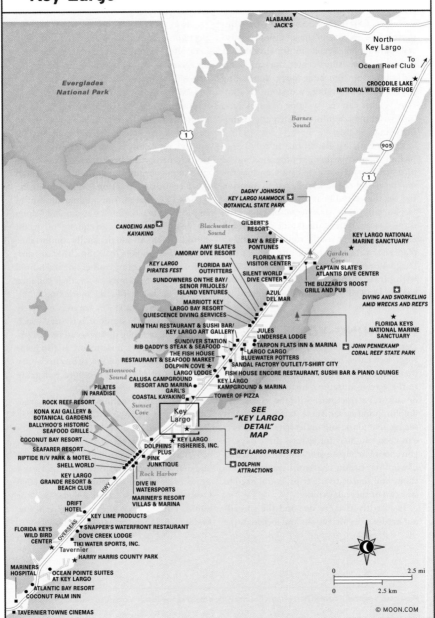

ALABAMA JACK'S ▼

North Key Largo

To Ocean Reef Club

CROCODILE LAKE ★
NATIONAL WILDLIFE REFUGE

Everglades National Park

Barnes Sound

DAGNY JOHNSON
KEY LARGO HAMMOCK
BOTANICAL STATE PARK

CANOEING AND KAYAKING

Blackwater Sound

GILBERT'S RESORT

KEY LARGO NATIONAL MARINE SANCTUARY ★

AMY SLATE'S
AMORAY DIVE RESORT

BAY & REEF
PONTUNES

KEY LARGO
PIRATES FEST

FLORIDA BAY
OUTFITTERS

FLORIDA KEYS
VISITOR CENTER

Garden Cove

SUNDOWNERS ON THE BAY /
SENOR FRIJOLES /
ISLAND VENTURES

SILENT WORLD
DIVE CENTER

CAPTAIN SLATE'S
ATLANTIS DIVE CENTER

THE BUZZARD'S ROOST
GRILL AND PUB

AZUL
DEL MAR

DIVING AND SNORKELING
AMID WRECKS AND REEFS

MARRIOTT KEY
LARGO BAY RESORT

QUIESCENCE DIVING SERVICES

FLORIDA KEYS
NATIONAL MARINE
SANCTUARY ★

NUM THAI RESTAURANT & SUSHI BAR /
KEY LARGO ART GALLERY

JULES
UNDERSEA LODGE

SUNDIVER STATION

RIB DADDY'S STEAK & SEAFOOD

TARPON FLATS INN & MARINA

LARGO CARGO

JOHN PENNEKAMP
CORAL REEF STATE PARK

THE FISH HOUSE
RESTAURANT & SEAFOOD MARKET

BLUEWATER POTTERS

DOLPHIN COVE ★

SANDAL FACTORY OUTLET / T-SHIRT CITY

LARGO LODGE

FISH HOUSE ENCORE RESTAURANT, SUSHI BAR & PIANO LOUNGE

CALUSA CAMPGROUND
RESORT AND MARINA

KEY LARGO
KAMPGROUND & MARINA

Buttonwood Sound

GARL'S

PILATES
IN PARADISE

COASTAL KAYAKING

TOWER OF PIZZA

ROCK REEF RESORT

Sunset Cove

Key Largo ★

SEE
"KEY LARGO
DETAIL"
MAP

KONA KAI GALLERY &
BOTANICAL GARDENS

BALLYHOO'S HISTORIC
SEAFOOD GRILLE

COCONUT BAY RESORT

SEAFARER RESORT

DOLPHINS
PLUS

KEY LARGO
FISHERIES, INC.

KEY LARGO PIRATES FEST

RIPTIDE R/V PARK & MOTEL

PINK
JUNKTIQUE

DOLPHIN
ATTRACTIONS

SHELL WORLD

Rock Harbor

KEY LARGO
GRANDE RESORT &
BEACH CLUB

DIVE IN
WATERSPORTS

MARINER'S RESORT
VILLAS & MARINA

DRIFT
HOTEL

KEY LIME PRODUCTS

FLORIDA KEYS
WILD BIRD
CENTER

SNAPPER'S WATERFRONT RESTAURANT

DOVE CREEK LODGE

TIKI WATER SPORTS, INC.

Tavernier

HARRY HARRIS COUNTY PARK

MARINERS
HOSPITAL

OCEAN POINTE SUITES
AT KEY LARGO

ATLANTIC BAY RESORT

COCONUT PALM INN

TAVERNIER TOWNE CINEMAS

0   2.5 mi

0   2.5 km

© MOON.COM

Key Largo Detail

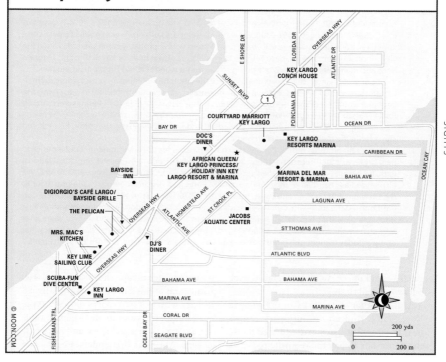

MOON.COM ©

Sights

★ DAGNY JOHNSON KEY LARGO HAMMOCK BOTANICAL STATE PARK

If you're driving to Key Largo, your first stop should be in the northern part of the island, north of the U.S. 1 turnoff and not far from Crocodile Lake National Wildlife Refuge, which is closed to the public. Here on the ocean side of the county road lies the tranquil **Dagny Johnson Key Largo Hammock Botanical State Park** (MM 106.0, CR-905, www.floridastateparks.org, sunrise-sunset daily, $2.50 pp). Spared from becoming a

condominium development in the early 1980s and named after a local environmental activist, this 2,421-acre preserve now protects 84 plant and animal species, plus one of the country's largest tracts of West Indian tropical hardwood hammock.

Hikers, bikers, bird-watchers, photographers, and other wildlife lovers can explore the park's more than six miles of backcountry trails, where you might spot mahogany mistletoe, semaphore cactus, Key Largo woodrats, varied butterflies, migratory birds, or an American crocodile. If you have the time, consider bringing a picnic lunch and relaxing at one of the designated tables near the butterfly

Who Is John Pennekamp?

Established in 1960, **John Pennekamp Coral Reef State Park** (MM 102.5, 102601 Overseas Hwy., 305/451-1202 or 305/451-6300, www.floridastateparks.org or www.pennekamppark.com) lures plenty of visitors every year. If you're one of them, you've probably come to snorkel amid the vibrant offshore coral reefs, peer at them from a glass-bottom boat, or kayak through seagrass beds and mangrove swamps. While doing so you might wonder about the name of the park.

This one-of-a-kind locale serves as a tribute to the late John D. Pennekamp, a longtime journalist, *Miami Herald* editor, and regional environmentalist who was instrumental in preserving the land that would eventually become Everglades National Park. Born in 1897, Pennekamp worked for 14 years at *The Cincinnati Post* before heading to southern Florida, where he joined the *Miami Herald* staff in 1925. First serving as a city editor and later as the associate editor, Pennekamp stayed with the *Herald* until his retirement in 1976.

Beyond his editorial duties, Pennekamp had a passion for the environment—and a desire to help preserve it for future generations. Subsequent to his efforts to establish Everglades National Park, he became a member of the Everglades National Park Commission from 1945 to 1947. He also served as chairman of the Florida Board of Parks and Historic Memorials, the precursor to the Division of Recreation and Parks, from 1953 to 1976. During the 1960s, Governor LeRoy Collins honored the journalist's unwavering dedication to conservation by naming America's first undersea park after him. When Pennekamp died in 1978 at the age of 81, only two years after retiring from the *Herald,* he left behind a legacy of appreciation for the natural world, a legacy that endures today through the more than one million annual visitors who venture inside the park.

garden—and of course, don't forget to pack out any and all trash.

Unlike other state parks in the Florida Keys, you'll find no on-duty park ranger near the front gate, so you're expected to use the honor box to pay the requisite park fee. Remember that motorized vehicles are prohibited in the park, as is the collection of any plants or animals. Moreover, you should keep to the paved roadways and designated trail unless you have a backcountry permit, which is available through the John Pennekamp Coral Reef State Park office (305/451-1202). Leashed, well-behaved pets are welcome in the picnic areas and on the self-guided nature trail; service animals are welcome throughout the park. The park's main, half-mile trail can accommodate bicycles and wheelchairs.

★ JOHN PENNEKAMP CORAL REEF STATE PARK

For nature lovers, one of the primary stops in Key Largo should be the incredible **John Pennekamp Coral Reef State Park** (MM 102.6, 102601 Overseas Hwy., 305/676-3777, www.floridastateparks.org or www.pennekamppark.com, 8am-sunset daily, $8 vehicles with 2-8 passengers plus $0.50 pp, $4.50 motorcycles and single-occupant vehicles, $2.50 pedestrians, bikers, and extra passengers), America's first undersea park—and the perfect spot for a wide range of outdoor activities, from sunbathing to bird-watching to sportfishing. Established in 1960 and situated on the ocean side of U.S. 1, this well-regarded park offers several picnic areas, pavilion rentals ($32-54 daily), a small campground ($42.70/night, with modern restrooms), a souvenir and gift shop, a boat ramp ($10 per vessel), and convenient access to two sandy beaches, including **Cannon Beach,** which features the remnants of an old Spanish shipwreck.

Visitors enjoy swimming in the relatively warm waters here, plus paddling through the mangrove swamps. You can even rent canoes and kayaks on-site (8am-3:45pm daily, $12-20 hourly). Also available are diving tours ($75

1: Cannon Beach **2:** *Christ of the Abyss* underwater sculpture at John Pennekamp Coral Reef State Park

pp) and glass-bottom boat tours ($24 adults, $17 children under 12) on the flagship *Spirit of Pennekamp*. Visitors can also opt for 2.5-hour snorkeling tours ($30 adults, $25 children under 18) or 4.5-hour snorkeling tours ($39 pp) amid the vibrant shallow-water coral reefs of Florida Keys National Marine Sanctuary—part of the only living coral reef system in the continental United States and a real treat for underwater explorers.

For nominal fees, the park also offers all necessary rental gear for snorkelers, including masks, snorkels, fins, and wetsuits, so there's typically no need to bring more than a swimsuit and a towel. While first-time snorkelers are common here, scuba divers must be certified to participate in the park's reef adventures; scuba instruction is offered through the park (305/451-6322 or 877/727-5348). All anglers must have a saltwater fishing license. Although this is definitely the spot for active visitors, individuals with disabilities are welcome aboard the glass-bottom boat tours and snorkeling trips, provided that they are able to get in and out of the water on their own or with the assistance of accompanying helpers.

For those who prefer a less up-close-and-personal underwater encounter, the park's visitors center (8am-5pm daily) features several natural history exhibits as well as a 30,000-gallon saltwater aquarium, housing many of the tropical fish, sea creatures, and other organisms you might see in the ocean. Do yourself a favor, though: Don't leave this park without venturing into the sometimes choppy waters of Florida Keys National Marine Sanctuary. The sight of all those kaleidoscopic fish—and perhaps a sand shark or two—is an experience you'll never forget.

★ DOLPHIN ATTRACTIONS

Together the sister facilities **Dolphins Plus Bayside** (MM 101.9, 101900 Overseas Hwy., 305/451-4060 or 877/365-2683, www.dolphinsplus.com, 8am-5pm daily, nonparticipating admission $10 adults, $5 children 7-17, free for children under 7) and **Dolphins Plus Oceanside** (31 Corrine Pl., 305/451-1993 or 866/860-7946, www.dolphinsplus.com, 8am-5pm daily, nonparticipating admission $10 adults, $5 children 7-17, free for children under 7) pursue marine mammal research, promote environmental awareness, and present year-round educational opportunities to the visiting public. At Dolphins Plus, visitors can meet the dolphins while standing in waist-high water through **shallow-water encounters** (9:30am, 12:30pm, and 2:30pm daily, $165 pp) or experience dorsal tows and belly rubs in **structured swims** (9:30am, 12:30pm, and 2:30pm daily, $210 pp).

Other activities include **painting with dolphins** ($125 pp) and the **behind-the-scenes tour** (11:15am-2:30pm daily, $20 pp) for participants 7 years of age or older, which offers a behind-the-scenes look at this fascinating marine mammal facility. Reservations are highly recommended for all programs.

FLORIDA KEYS WILD BIRD CENTER

While Key Largo is mainly known for its wide assortment of water-related activities, you should also consider taking a walk through the **Laura Quinn Wild Bird Sanctuary** (MM 93.6, 93600 Overseas Hwy., Tavernier, 305/852-4486, www.keepthemflying.org, sunrise-sunset daily, $10 pp donation requested), part of the nonprofit **Florida Keys Wild Bird Center,** founded in 1984 when veterinarian Bob Foley asked retired teacher Laura Quinn to assist with the rehabilitation of several wild birds that he had treated. Mainly operated by volunteers and comprising natural habitats as well as open-air enclosures, the 5.5-acre sanctuary allows visitors to stroll along a narrow shaded boardwalk where they can observe a variety of caged species, from cormorants to laughing gulls to great horned owls—most of whom have been injured as a result of human activities, such as mercury poisoning and fishing tackle entanglements, and are currently undergoing rehabilitation.

In the adjacent black and red mangrove

Just the Facts About Dolphins

wild bottlenose dolphins

The Atlantic bottlenose dolphin *(Tursiops truncatus)* inhabits temperate coastal waters throughout the world. Here are some interesting facts about these playful creatures:

- Active predators who feed on small, schooling fish, bottlenose dolphins can live into their 40s, grow to 10 feet in length, weigh up to 600 pounds, and reach sexual maturity between ages 5 and 12.

- Calves, born after a yearlong gestation period, can be three feet long and 30 pounds at birth, will typically nurse for two to four years, and begin to eat fish at a few months of age.

- The bottlenose, or rostrum, is used for touching and pushing while the small, cone-shaped teeth (dolphins typically have 88) are used for grasping and tearing food, not chewing.

- The blowhole on the top of each dolphin's head serves as a nostril, through which the dolphin typically breathes twice per minute.

- Dolphins can conveniently breathe and eat at the same time, and they can hold their breath for eight minutes if necessary.

- The blowhole, not the throat, produces their vocalizations, which they can manipulate to mimic other sounds, such as human laughter.

- The pectoral fins, containing all the bones of a land animal's forelimbs and located on the dolphin's sides, are used for steering, while the dorsal fin, made entirely of cartilage and located on the dolphin's back, is used for balance.

- The peduncle is the muscular area that powers the flukes, or two halves of the tail, allowing dolphins to swim up to 17 miles per hour.

- Dolphins can only swim forward, not backward, and they can shut down half of their brains while resting and still manage to swim, hunt, and communicate.

- Although Atlantic bottlenose dolphins have no sense of smell, they have excellent eyesight above and below the water, and they can also hear well, especially below the water, where they navigate, detect prey, and locate other objects by utilizing echolocation—a sonar-like system whereby high-pitched sounds are emitted, reflected off other surfaces, and interpreted by sensory receptors, typically the jowls.

- Dolphins appreciate eye contact, which is why they tend to be more motivated when you look at and speak to them directly.

wetlands and along the Florida Bay shoreline, you'll spot a slew of native birds, including brown pelicans, common egrets, and great white herons, most of whom are usually waiting for the afternoon feeding. Almost more curious, though, is the innumerable mass of makeshift wooden sponsor plaques affixed to the cages and boardwalk railing—a testament to all of the individuals and organizations who have helped to support the sanctuary and the separate hospital space (93997 Overseas Hwy., Tavernier) over the years.

After visiting the bird center, consider heading south to Mile Marker 92.6, where you can cross the highway via Burton Drive. From here continue on Burton to 1st Street, and take East Beach Road to **Harry Harris County Park** (MM 92.6, 305/852-7161, 7:30am-sunset daily, $5 non-county residents 16 or older Sat.-Sun. and holidays, free for children under 16 and Monroe County residents, $10 to launch a boat), a popular place on the weekends and the perfect spot to watch one of the Keys' sensational sunsets. Other amenities here include a sandy beach, a swimming area, a boat ramp, playground equipment, two baseball fields, numerous picnic tables and pavilions, barbecue grills, and public restrooms. Pets are allowed in the park, though not along the beach.

BOAT TOURS

Every day the **Coral Reef Park Company Inc.** (305/451-6300) operates three separate 2.5-hour glass-bottom boat tours ($24 adults, $17 children under 12) out of **John Pennekamp Coral Reef State Park** (MM 102.6, 102601 Overseas Hwy., 305/451-1202, www.floridastateparks.org or www.pennekamppark.com, 8am-sunset daily, $8 vehicles with 2-8 passengers plus $0.50 pp, $4.50 motorcycles and single-occupant vehicles, $2.50 pedestrians, bikers, and extra passengers). Such excursions are offered on the flagship *Spirit of Pennekamp*, a 65-foot, high-speed catamaran that's capable of whisking up to 130 passengers toward the coral formations and vibrant sealife of Florida Keys National Marine Sanctuary in the ocean waters east of Key Largo. Tours run

The Bogie Connection

Several famous people, from novelists to singers to presidents, are inextricably linked to the Florida Keys. Among them is Humphrey Bogart, whose 1948 film *Key Largo* was filmed on the northernmost island. This well-regarded crime drama, directed by John Huston, is not the only reminder of Bogart's connection to Key Largo. Over the years, Bogart has been such a legendary presence here that you'll even find pets named after him, such as Bogie, the beloved yellow-naped Amazon parrot at the Rock Reef Resort near Mile Marker 98. Even better, you can view the one and only *African Queen,* the actual vessel featured in the eponymous 1951 film starring Bogart and Katharine Hepburn. When not reserved for private rides, the small, weathered vessel is typically docked beside the aptly named *Bogie's Café,* a casual eatery at the Holiday Inn Key Largo Resort & Marina near Mile Marker 100.

at 9:15am, 12:15pm, and 3:15pm, and all tours require a minimum number of passengers to leave the marina; limited wheelchair accessibility is available on board.

Farther south you'll find other glass-bottom boat tours, such as the *Key Largo Princess* (MM 100, 305/481-4655 or 877/307-1147, www.keylargoprincess.com, $37 adults, $21.50 children, free for children under 2), a luxurious 70-foot, 129-passenger yacht that operates three daily two-hour excursions (10am, 1pm, and 4pm). Docked at the Holiday Inn Key Largo Resort & Marina (MM 100, 99701 Overseas Hwy., 305/451-2121, www.holidayinnkeylargo.com), the *Key Largo Princess* also offers private cocktail cruises (complete with underwater lights). If you choose one of the daytime excursions, try to get a seat on the sundeck, which affords you a panoramic offshore view of the Florida Keys and the multicolored ocean waters around you. Once you reach the living coral reef, you'll be able to observe varied coral specimens and kaleidoscopic fish through a 280-square-foot viewing window below your feet. Advance tickets can be purchased through their website.

Before heading out on the *Princess,* take note of the small weathered boat docked beside her. Built in 1912 for service in Africa, the *African Queen* was used until 1968 by the British East Africa Railway to ferry cargo passengers across Lake Albert. During that time, the *Queen* was featured in the eponymous 1951 John Huston film that also starred Humphrey Bogart and Katharine Hepburn. Feel free to take photographs of this famous vessel or step into Bogie's shoes and reserve an unforgettable ride (305/451-8080) aboard the *Queen* herself.

A little farther south, **Caribbean Watersports** (MM 97.5, Playa Largo Resort and Spa, 97450 Overseas Hwy., 305/852-4707, www.caribbeanwatersports.com, 9am-6:30pm daily) offers 2-hour champagne sunset cruises ($60 pp) and 2-hour "Enviro-Tours" ($65 adults, $45 children) across Florida Bay and into the Everglades. These personalized excursions, which can accommodate up to six passengers at a time, provide an intimate glimpse at the diverse ecosystems of southern Florida, from mangrove forests to shallow creeks and bays. Along the way, you may encounter any number of wild creatures, including bottlenose dolphins, laughing gulls, bald eagles, and endangered manatees.

Beaches and Recreation

BEACHES

Several resorts and hotels on Key Largo have human-made beaches that guests can enjoy. Two public beaches can be found in John Pennekamp Coral Reef State Park.

John Pennekamp Coral Reef State Park

John Pennekamp Coral Reef State Park (MM 102.6, 102601 Overseas Hwy., 305/451-1202 or 305/451-6300, www.floridastateparks.org or www.pennekamppark.com, 8am-sunset daily, $8 vehicles with 2-8 passengers plus $0.50 pp, $4.50 motorcycles and single-occupant vehicles, $2.50 pedestrians, bikers, and extra passengers) offers two sandy beaches. **Cannon Beach,** which features the remnants of an old Spanish shipwreck offshore, is the best spot in the park to snorkel. The shipwreck is about 100 feet offshore. **Far Beach** is an excellent spot to sit in the shade of the palms that line the shore and enjoy a little swimming or sunbathing. Swimming is only allowed within the designated area unless you are using a dive flag. The beach has a mat across the sand that makes it wheelchair accessible.

TOP EXPERIENCE

★ DIVING AND SNORKELING

In the ocean waters east of Key Largo is Florida Keys National Marine Sanctuary, a 220-mile-long coral reef ecosystem that stretches from the southern end of Key Biscayne to the Dry Tortugas—the only living coral reef system in the continental United States and the third-largest coral reef system in the world. If you're new to snorkeling and scuba diving, head first to **John Pennekamp Coral Reef State Park** (MM 102.6, 102601 Overseas Hwy., 305/451-1202, www.floridastateparks.org or www.pennekamppark.com, 8am-sunset daily, $8 vehicles with 2-8 passengers plus $0.50 pp, $4.50 motorcycles and single-occupant vehicles, $2.50 pedestrians, bikers, and extra passengers). Through the **Coral Reef Park Company Inc.** (305/451-6300) you can take diving instruction ($185-385 pp), earn PADI Open Water certification ($485 pp), and participate in 2.5-hour snorkeling trips ($30 adults, $25 children under 18, plus gear rentals), 4.5-hour snorkeling trips ($39 pp, plus gear rentals), or scuba-diving tours ($75 pp, plus $29 for gear rental) amid the vibrant coral reefs a few miles offshore.

You'll encounter amazing sealife like parrot fish, yellow cherubfish, brain and staghorn coral, spotted spiny lobster, and sea hermit crabs, plus formations such as **Grecian Rocks** and **Key Largo Dry Rocks,** which contains elkhorn coral, and the ever-popular, often-photographed *Christ of the Abyss* statue (also known as *Christ of the Deep*). Before heading out on a snorkeling or diving trip, consider stopping by the park's visitors center (8am-5pm daily) to see several saltwater aquariums housing many of the kaleidoscopic tropical fish, coral formations, and other sea creatures you might see while exploring the ocean.

There are numerous diving outfitters in Key Largo. **Amy Slate's Amoray Dive Resort** (MM 104, 104250 Overseas Hwy., 305/451-3595 or 800/426-6729, www.amoray.com) offers an array of diving classes, from a two-hour beginner's class ($75 pp) to a three-day PADI rescue diver class ($450 pp), plus twice-daily snorkeling excursions (8:30am and 1pm, $45-50 pp) and two-location diving trips (8:30am and 1pm daily, $85 pp with gear). In addition to diving classes, diving trips (and, in most cases, snorkeling excursions) to the reefs and wrecks that compose Florida Keys National Marine Sanctuary are offered by operators such as the well-regarded **Silent World Dive Center** (MM 106.5, 47 Garden Cove Dr., 305/451-3252, www.silentworld.com, 8:30am-5:30pm daily, trips 8:30am and 12:30pm daily, $79-109 pp), **Island Ventures** (MM 103, 51 Shoreland Dr., 305/451-2248, www.islandventure.com, trips 8am and 1pm daily, $45-85 pp), the **Key Largo Dive Center** (MM 100.6, 100670 Overseas Hwy., 305/451-5844, www.keylargodivecenter.com, 8am-5pm daily, trips 8:30am and 1:30pm daily, $99 pp, $495 per charter), and the **Sea Dwellers Dive Center** (MM 100, 99850 Overseas Hwy., 305/451-3640 or 800/451-3640, www.seadwellers.com, 8am-5pm daily, trips 8am and 1pm daily, $65-85 pp with gear). Underwater sights include the *Duane* and the *Bibb,* two U.S. Coast Guard cutters used in World War II, and the **USS** *Spiegel Grove,* a 510-foot Navy transport ship originally launched in November 1955, sunk in May 2002 to create an artificial reef, and shifted into an upright position

sea turtle near Key Largo in Florida Keys National Marine Sanctuary

Shipwreck Dives

While many snorkelers and scuba divers primarily come to the Florida Keys to explore the vibrant living coral reefs, others are more interested in the shipwrecks that pepper these offshore waters. Several were wrecked by the treacherous coral reefs that lure so many underwater enthusiasts today. Signifying the European colonial, American, and modern periods of the Keys' maritime history, nine of these shipwrecks now constitute the official Shipwreck Trail.

- *City of Washington:* Built in Pennsylvania in 1877, accidentally run aground in 1917, and now lying in 25 feet of water near Elbow Reef, this steel-hulled vessel was the first ship to assist the USS *Maine* following the explosion in Havana Harbor.

- *Benwood:* Constructed in England in 1910, this ship sunk in 1942 after colliding with another vessel; it now lies between French Reef and Dixie Shoals, in water that ranges in depth from 25 to 45 feet.

- *Duane:* Built in Philadelphia in 1936 and now lying in 120 feet of water one mile south of Molasses Reef, this U.S. Coast Guard cutter was used in World War II, decommissioned in 1985, and purposely sunk two years later as an artificial reef.

- *Eagle:* Constructed in Holland in 1962 as *Raila Dan,* this 268-foot freighter went through several incarnations before catching fire in 1985, after which it was renamed *Eagle Tire Company* and sunk as an artificial reef; it now lies on its starboard side (split in two by a 1998 hurricane) in 70-110 feet of water near Lower Matecumbe Key, three miles northeast of the Alligator Reef Light.

- *San Pedro:* This 287-ton, Dutch-built Spanish ship, which wrecked south of Indian Key during a 1733 hurricane, has undergone several salvaging attempts since its discovery in 1960 and now serves as the San Pedro Underwater Archaeological Preserve State Park.

- *Adelaide Baker:* Constructed in Maine in 1863 as the *F. W. Carver,* this three-masted, iron-rigged ship wrecked in 1889 while toting a cargo of milled timber and now lies in 20 feet of water four miles south of Duck Key.

- *Thunderbolt:* Built in West Virginia in 1942 to lay defensive coastal mines, and formerly known as *Randolph,* this 188-foot steel ship was intentionally sunk in 1986 and now lies, encrusted with coral and sponges, in 75-120 feet of water four miles south of Key Colony Beach.

- *North America:* Lying in 14 feet of water in the sand and grass flats north of Delta Shoals, this vessel is believed to be the *North America,* built in 1833 in Bath, Maine, and lost in 1842 while transporting dry goods and furniture.

- *Amesbury:* Originally constructed as a U.S. Navy destroyer escort in 1943 and locally known as "Alexander's Wreck," this vessel was being towed to deep water to be sunk when it grounded and broke up in a storm five miles west of Key West.

A spar buoy identifies each of these sites, which are all accessible by private boat or diving charter. Underwater conditions vary from site to site, meaning that you can expect both easy, shallow-water dives as well as deeper dives with swift currents. For more information, contact Florida Keys National Marine Sanctuary (305/852-7717 for the Key West office or 305/809-4700 for the Key Largo office, www.floridakeys.noaa.gov) or consult area diving operators, many of whom offer charters or private trips to these sites. To help protect these fragile structures—all of which are artificial reefs that now support tropical fish and other marine creatures—remember to control your buoyancy, avoid anchoring near the sites, and refrain from damaging or removing any and all artifacts that you see.

Protecting Florida's Coral Reefs

While visiting **John Pennekamp Coral Reef State Park** (MM 102.6, 102601 Overseas Hwy., 305/451-1202 or 305/451-6300, www.floridastateparks.org or www.pennekamppark.com), take a moment to stop by the on-site visitors center to learn more about the 2,900-square-mile Florida Keys National Marine Sanctuary, the fragile coral reef system that extends for 220 miles along the eastern side of the Florida Keys. The following boating and diving regulations are strictly enforced by state park officials:

- Always consult weather conditions ahead of time, as it's best not to go out in rough seas. Poor visibility, strong winds, and increased waves can hinder safe interaction with coral reefs.

- Be sure to maintain all equipment to avoid inadvertent discharges of oil and other toxic substances.

- Do not discharge any raw sewage into offshore waters; instead, use official pump-out facilities, available throughout the Keys.

- Do not litter in the ocean or abandon structures on the seabed, especially near the reefs; if you see such debris, please retrieve it and properly dispose of it on land.

- Use nautical and tidal charts to practice safe navigation, know your boat's draft, and be aware of the variations in surface water color: Deepwater areas, for instance, are typically blue; shallower areas are often green; brown usually indicates shallow coral reefs and seagrass beds; and white signifies sandbars and rubble areas.

- Stay in marked channels, and do not approach lighthouses, reef light towers, shoal markers, or yellow buoys, which usually indicate shallow reef and seagrass areas.

- Slow down to an idle speed in dive areas, and stay at least 100 feet from a red-and-white, diver-down flag.

- Be careful while navigating a boat around coral reefs and seagrass beds, and do not drop anchors on or near living coral; instead, use the white-and-blue mooring buoys or anchor in the sandy patches adjacent to the reef.

- Do not damage or remove markers and mooring buoys.

- If you run aground, immediately turn the engine off and, if possible, tilt the motor upward; wait until high tide to remove the vessel by walking or poling, and if necessary, call the **Florida Fish and Wildlife Conservation Commission (FWC)** (888/404-3922) for assistance. Be prepared to incur towing fees as well as fines for damaging the seagrass habitat.

- To avoid standing on the coral, use inflatable vests (if snorkeling) and practice proper buoyancy control (if diving).

by Hurricane Dennis in 2005. In this region, you might also see star coral, elkhorn coral, and other formations on **Molasses Reef,** the *Benwood* shipwreck south of **Dixie Shoals,** the sea caves of **French Reef,** and the *City of Washington* shipwreck near **Elbow Reef.**

You'll also find a number of diving operators in the **Key Largo Resorts Marina** (MM 100 OS U.S. 1, 527 Caribbean Dr., 305/453-7171, www.keylargomarina.com). Options here include **BlueWater Divers of Key Largo** (99701 Overseas Hwy., 305/453-9600, www.bluewaterdiver.net, trips 8:30am and 1pm daily, $50-90 pp), **Horizon Divers** (105800 Overseas Hwy., 305/453-3535 or 800/984-3483, www.horizondivers.com, 8am-6pm daily, $20-100 pp), the **Keys Diver & Snorkel Center**

a healthy reef in the Keys

- Avoid touching, kicking, defacing, or sitting on living coral formations.

- Do not collect historical resources (such as parts of shipwrecks), plant life, living coral, seashells, tropical fish, queen conch, sea stars, or other marine creatures near the reef.

- Do not engage in spearfishing or release exotic species near the reef.

- Don't feed fish, seabirds, or marine mammals. Avoid any wildlife disturbance.

You can assist in the welfare of such coral reefs even when you're not in the water. Choose seafood from fisheries that have the least negative impact on the ocean, and minimize your use of chemically enhanced pesticides and fertilizers, which may end up in offshore waters. Avoid purchasing coral jewelry and souvenirs, unless you know for certain that such decorative objects were not illegally harvested.

Be sure to report all damage to coral reefs to dive operators or conservation groups that monitor coral reef health, such as the **Coral Reef Conservation Program** (866/770-7335). For more information about area coral reefs, consult **Florida Keys National Marine Sanctuary** (305/852-7717 or 305/809-4700, www.floridakeys.noaa.gov). To learn how to protect these beautiful, complex, and surprisingly fragile formations, contact the **Project AWARE Foundation** (949/858-7657, www.projectaware.org) or the **Reef Relief Environmental Center & Headquarters** (631 Greene St., Key West, 305/294-3100, www.reefrelief.org), two nonprofit organizations dedicated to preserving living coral reef ecosystems around the world.

(MM 99.6, 99696 Overseas Hwy., 305/451-1177 or 888/289-2402, www.keysdiver.com, 8am-5pm daily, trips 7:15am and 11:30am daily, $45-120 pp), and **Ocean Divers** (522 Caribbean Dr., 305/451-1113 or 800/451-1113, www.oceandivers.com, 7:30am-5pm daily, trips 8am and 1pm daily, $85-90 pp). Other area operators that feature diving classes as well as diving excursions include

Captain Slate's Atlantis Dive Center (MM 90.7, 90791 Overseas Hwy., 305/451-3020 or 800/331-3483, www.captainslate.com, 7:30am-5pm daily, $20-195 pp), which hosts an annual Underwater Easter Egg Hunt; **Quiescence Diving Services** (MM 103.6, 103680 Overseas Hwy., 305/451-2440, www.keylargodiving.com, 8am-6pm daily, $55-119 pp with gear); and the **Scuba-Fun Dive**

Center (MM 99.2, 99222 Overseas Hwy., 305/394-5046 or 877/977-3483, www.scubafun.com, 8am-5:30pm daily, $45-85 pp), which is hard to miss thanks to the stunning Wyland Wall on its exterior.

Of course, many of these operators also offer snorkeling as an option. You can also enjoy snorkeling excursions to the reefs within John Pennekamp Coral Reef State Park by boarding the *Sundiver III,* operated by the **Sundiver Station Snorkel Shop** (MM 102.8, 102840 Overseas Hwy., 305/451-2220 or 800/654-7369, www.snorkelingisfun.com, trips 9am, noon, and 3pm daily, 5:30pm trips seasonally, $45 adults, $35 children under 13 and passengers, plus gear rentals); or the *Reef Roamer* (MM 99.7, 99751 Overseas Hwy., 305/453-0110, www.snorkelkeylargo.com, trips 9am, 12:30pm, and 5pm daily, $35-50 pp) and the *Morning Star* (MM 99.7, Key Largo Fisheries, 1313 Ocean Bay Dr., 305/451-7057, www.morningstarcharters.com, trip 9am-1pm daily, $75 pp with gear).

For more information about snorkeling and diving sites around Key Largo, consult the **Upper Keys Artificial Reef Foundation** (MM 106, 106000 Overseas Hwy., 305/451-1414, www.keylargowrecks.com), which has information about both shipwrecks and coral reefs in the surrounding waters. Another helpful resource is the local office of the **Florida Keys National Marine Sanctuary** (MM 95.2, 95230 Overseas Hwy., 305/852-7717, www.floridakeys.noaa.gov).

FISHING AND BOATING

Key Largo features a wide array of fishing charters and boat rentals. Probably the best place to start your search for a fishing charter is the **Key Largo Resorts Marina** (MM 100 OS U.S. 1, 527 Caribbean Dr., 305/453-7171, www.keylargomarina.com), hard to miss beside the Holiday Inn. Among the numerous options available is **Beaver Charters** (305/394-0679), which offers half-day charters ($600 per trip), full-day charters ($950 per trip), evening tarpon trips ($400 per trip), and swordfish excursions ($1,200 per trip). All

charters include bait, tackle, ice, and temporary fishing licenses.

In the same marina is the *Sailors Choice* party fishing boat (305/451-1802, www.sailorschoicefishingboat.com), a 65-foot vessel offering two daily trips (9am-1pm and 1:30pm-5:30pm, $25-45 pp) as well as special night trips (7:30pm-midnight) on Friday and Saturday, all of which you can book on their website. Passengers will likely catch snapper, grouper, wahoo, and other offshore fish, though every experience is unique. Also here is **Key Largo Fishing Adventures** (305/942-9982, www.keylargofishingadventures.com), featuring the 38-foot *Fin Razer* ($875 per half day, $1,300 daily), ideal for reef and offshore fishing, plus swordfish trips ($1,700 and up per trip) night or day.

Operating out of the Dove Creek Lodge, on the ocean side of U.S. 1 near Mile Marker 94.5, **Blackfoot Charters** (305/481-0111, www.blackfootfishing.com, $400 per night or half day, $550-600 daily) offers backcountry, flats, and canoe fishing in the Upper Keys, the Everglades, and Biscayne National Park. Captain Mike Makowski, a native of southern Florida, invites novice and veteran anglers alike to seek out bonefish, tarpon, permit, snook, redfish, and other seasonal species—while listening to his colorful tales of local history. Other area charters include **Rodeo Charters** (305/852-3829 or 305/522-2638, www.rodeocharters.com, rates vary), which has featured offshore, reef, wreck, and backcountry fishing since 1973; and **Tails Up Fishing Charters** (MM 104, 305/394-1383, www.tailsupfishing.com, $500 per half day, $700 daily), which targets redfish, bonefish, snook, and tarpon in the backcountry and flats.

If you'd rather purchase a vessel while you're in the Keys, consult **Tiki Water Sports, Inc.** (94381 Overseas Hwy., 305/852-9298, www.tikiwatersports.com, 8am-6pm Mon.-Thurs., 8am-4:30pm Fri., 11am-3pm Sat.-Sun.), a one-stop shop that sells sailboats, kayaks, pedal boats, and stand-up paddleboards (SUP); offers a wide array of marine supplies; and provides boat maintenance, repairs, and dry boat storage. You can also rent kayaks ($75 daily, $250-375 weekly) as well as sailboats ($200-300 daily, $500-1,000 weekly) during store hours.

★ CANOEING AND KAYAKING

With access to mangrove swamps, the Atlantic Ocean, Florida Bay, and of course, the wildlife-rich waterways of the Everglades, Key Largo provides an ideal landscape for canoeists and kayakers. Many first-timers head initially to **John Pennekamp Coral Reef State Park** (MM 102.6, 102601 Overseas Hwy., 305/451-1202, www.floridastateparks.org or www.pennekamppark.com, 8am-sunset daily, $8 vehicles with 2-8 passengers plus $0.50 pp, $4.50 motorcycles and single-occupant vehicles, $2.50 pedestrians, bikers, and extra passengers) in the northern part of Key Largo, where the **Coral Reef Park Company Inc.** (305/451-6300) offers canoe ($20 hourly) and kayak rentals ($12-17 hourly). No matter when you visit, it seems that you'll always spot a brightly colored kayak winding its way through the mangrove trees—the ideal mode of transport for those hoping to get an up-close, yet unobtrusive, look at area birds and other critters.

Of course, the Coral Reef Park Company isn't the only game in town. **Caribbean Watersports** (MM 97.5, Playa Largo Resort and Spa, 97450 Overseas Hwy., 305/852-4707, www.caribbeanwatersports.com, 9am-6:30pm daily) offers both kayak ($20-30 hourly, $30-45 for two hours) and paddleboat rentals ($30-40 hourly, $45-55 for two hours), while **Florida Bay Outfitters** (104050 Overseas Hwy., 305/451-3018, www.paddlefloridakeys.com, 8:30am-6pm daily) and **Garl's Coastal Kayaking** (305/393-3223, www.garlscoastalkayaking.com, trip times vary) both provide guided kayaking trips throughout the Upper Keys and the Everglades—and both typically offer pickup service to the launch point.

Florida Bay Outfitters features a wide array of trips, ranging from three-hour tours to Dusenberry Creek ($60 pp), where dolphin and manatee sightings are probable, to three-day kayak sailing excursions among the islands of Florida Bay ($495 pp, including meals and camping gear). Free pickups and drop-offs at participating resorts are offered for most trips, and reservations are necessary for all of them. Florida Bay Outfitters—one of Florida's largest paddle-sports retailers—also offers rental canoes, sea kayaks, pedal and sail kayaks, sit-on-tops, and rec boats ($30-100 per half day, $40-150 daily), plus three-hour instructional sessions ($75 pp with rental gear) focused on specific topics like kayaking basics, advanced skills, or rescue techniques.

Meanwhile, Garl's half-day Florida Bay trips ($75 pp) allow you to explore the mangrove islands near Key Largo; besides kayaking in a glass-bottom boat, you'll also have the opportunity to snorkel among a variety of marine creatures, from starfish to horseshoe crabs. For the Everglades trips ($95-125 per half day, $125-150 daily), Garl can transport passengers (when there's room in his Jeep) from Key Largo to Flamingo. Depending on the weather conditions and the type of trip, Garl guides paddlers on a combination of hikes to alligator holes, freshwater kayaking excursions amid mangroves and crocodiles, and saltwater kayaking tours at sunset. No matter which trip you choose, you should wear your swimsuit and bring your camera. Single and double kayaks are available, and reservations are required for all trips.

GOLF

At the exclusive **Ocean Reef Club** (35 Ocean Reef Dr., 305/367-5912 or 800/741-7333, www.oceanreef.com) on the northern end of Key Largo, guests staying in on-site vacation rentals or at the 144-room inn have access to two championship 18-hole courses. Both the Hammock Course, partially situated within a mangrove and tropical hardwood hammock, and the Dolphin Course, with fairways that wind past mahogany trees and coconut palms,

feature incredible vistas and challenging holes. Instructional sessions are also available. Unfortunately, you must either be staying or renting on the premises or be a social member of the Ocean Reef Club or a member's guest in order to access the golf courses, lodgings, and other areas of this private community. Guests of the Ocean Reef Club may reserve tee times by contacting the Membership Office (305/367-5921, rates vary seasonally).

HIKING AND BIKING

Although Key Largo is primarily a water lover's playground, there are certainly activities for landlubbers. Hikers can experience the winding self-guided nature trail through **Dagny Johnson Key Largo Hammock Botanical State Park** (MM 106, CR-905, www.floridastateparks.org, 8am-sunset daily, $2.50 pp). Of course, to really experience the woods of this serene 2,421-acre preserve, which protects more than 80 different plant and animal species, you should explore the six miles of backcountry trails, for which you'll need a backcountry permit, available through **John Pennekamp Coral Reef State Park** (MM 102.6, 102601 Overseas Hwy., 305/451-1202, www.floridastateparks.org or www.pennekamppark.com, 8am-sunset daily, $8 vehicles with 2-8 passengers plus $0.50 pp, $4.50 motorcycles and single-occupant vehicles, $2.50 pedestrians, bikers, and extra passengers). If you're a birding enthusiast, you'll especially appreciate Dagny Johnson State Park, where you're likely to spot a variety of species, from white-crowned pigeons to red-bellied woodpeckers to great blue herons. Rare sightings might include mangrove cuckoos, masked boobies, black vultures, and great horned owls. With its two beaches and three nature trails, nearby John Pennekamp also offers a treasure trove of species for avid bird-watchers.

Bikers, too, will enjoy the backcountry trails of Dagny Johnson State Park (provided you secure a permit). In addition, a 15.5-mile biking path, part of the **Florida Keys Overseas Heritage Trail,** runs past numerous businesses and parks in Key Largo between Mile Marker 106.5 and Mile Marker 91. Bicycles can be rented from the **Key Largo Bike Shop** (MM 100.1, 100109 Overseas Hwy., 305/395-1551, www.keylargobike.com, 8am-5pm daily, $18-60 daily), offering road bikes as well as hybrids. Weekly rates are also available, and helmets and locks are included with all rentals.

OTHER OUTDOOR ACTIVITIES

As an alternative to activities like fishing or snorkeling, consider taking flight. **Key Largo Parasail** (MM 104, 877/904-8865, www.keylargoparasail.com, 10am-5pm daily, $65-75 pp, $20 observers), weather permitting, welcomes people of all ages to fly 500 to 1,000 feet above the ocean. Boat trips leave from Sundowners at Mile Marker 104, on the bay side of U.S. 1. Single and tandem rides are available on a first-come, first-served basis. Farther south, **Caribbean Watersports** (MM 97, 97000 Overseas Hwy., 305/852-4707, www.caribbeanwatersports.com, 9am-6:30pm daily), based out of the Playa Largo Resort and Spa, has offered parasailing flights ($70 per flyer, $130 per tandem) for more than two decades. Caribbean Watersports also provides WaveRunner rentals ($75 per half hour, $120 hourly), for which certain riders (ages 14-21) must have Florida-approved boater certification, as well as stand-up paddleboard rentals ($30 hourly, $45 for two hours).

Another option for stand-up paddleboarding (SUP), a sport that's growing in popularity, is **PADDLE! the Florida Keys** (MM 90.7, 90773 Old Hwy., Tavernier, 305/434-5930, www.paddlethefloridakeys.com, 9am-5pm daily). In addition to renting paddleboards ($35 daily) and kayaks ($30-70 daily), it also offers two-hour ecotours via paddleboard or kayak ($49.50 pp). PADDLE! also sells a wide

1: sailboats near Key Largo **2:** wooden walkway through the mangrove forest at John Pennekamp Coral Reef State Park

array of paddleboards, kayaks, skateboards, clothing, and accessories.

Located in Key Largo Community Park at Mile Marker 99.6, on the ocean side of U.S. 1, the **Jacobs Aquatic Center (JAC)** (MM 99.7, 320 Laguna Ave., 305/453-7946, www.jacobsaquaticcenter.org, 10am-6pm daily Oct.-Apr., 10am-7pm daily May-Sept., day passes $25-30 families, $10-12 adults, $8-10 children 11-17, and $6-8 children 3-10) offers three different swimming pools, each of which has separate temperature controls. One pool, ideal for children, features a "spray" gym and a pirate ship with waterslides. Other amenities here include a multipurpose activity room, bathrooms with showers and lockers, and a wide array of activities and classes, including water aerobics, water polo, swimming lessons, Pilates, and scuba certification. Multiple-day passes and long-term rates are also available.

You might find an even greater release at **Pilates in Paradise** (MM 103.4, LivingFit Wellness Center, 103400 Overseas Hwy., Ste. 255, 305/453-0801, www.pilatesinparadise.net or www.livingfitwellnesscenter.net, 7am-7pm Mon.-Sat., prices vary), where depending on how long you'll be in the area, you can experience just one class or a series of them. Several options are available here, from a mat session that teaches breathing, stretching, and strengthening exercises to a Nia program that fosters a unified body-mind-spirit fitness and lifestyle practice.

Entertainment and Events

NIGHTLIFE

Key Largo isn't exactly a hotbed of nighttime activity. Still, you will find several after-hours diversions here, mostly in the form of live entertainment—or at the very least, people-watching and sunset-gazing opportunities—at area bars and restaurants. The **Caribbean Club** (MM 104, 104080 Overseas Hwy., 305/451-4466, www.caribbeanclubkl.com, 7am-4am daily), which has been locally owned and operated since 1963, is one such joint. Although it may look like a typical Keys-style bar, you'll soon notice that it's filled with locals. Don't let the motorcycles parked outside dissuade you; this is an amiable, dog-friendly place, noted for its cheap drinks and vittles, daily happy hour (4pm-6pm), and live music Thursday-Sunday nights. Besides, the bikers weren't the first tough guys to frequent the Caribbean Club. It was here that Humphrey Bogart and Lauren Bacall filmed their famous 1948 movie *Key Largo*, memorabilia from which now fills this famous watering hole. Just as in the days of Bogie, the club allows smoking inside, though the doors stay open to let in some fresh Florida air. So order a burger and a cocktail, and enjoy the laid-back atmosphere.

Several miles south, at Mile Marker 94.5, **Snapper's Waterfront Restaurant** (139 Seaside Ave., 305/852-5956, www.snapperskeylargo.com, noon-10pm Mon.-Sat., 10am-10pm Sun.) is another winning spot for nightly entertainment, from magic acts to blues, jazz, reggae, and classic rock performances. On the last Sunday of every month Snapper's hosts a "Turtle Club Party," a daylong event featuring live music, games, giveaways, and specials, plus free food for all Turtle Club members. Past parties have revolved around everything from crawfish boils to Mardi Gras.

In Key Largo—and really throughout the Florida Keys—most bars and some restaurants offer regular happy hours, complete with appetizer and drink specials. For more information about such watering holes, consult **Happy Hour Keys** (www.happyhourkeys.com). If in doubt about the accuracy of information on this third-party website, contact the bar or restaurant directly.

An Eye on Mailboxes

In the Keys, art often exists where you least expect to find it. Everywhere you turn, for example, you're liable to spy a clever, colorful mailbox inspired by this diverse place. From lighthouses and manatees on the Overseas Highway to fishing lures and mini bungalows on the side streets, these mailboxes are always photo-worthy, so keep a sharp lookout for them as you venture through the Florida Keys. If you decide you'd like a memorable mailbox of your own, contact an online company like BudgetMailboxes.com (866/505-6245, www.budgetmailboxes.com), which features everything from dolphins to brown pelicans—or better yet, ask the locals where they got theirs.

THE ARTS

Key Largo offers its own cultural diversions. Since 1978, The Key Players (305/453-0997, www.thekeyplayers.org, showtimes and ticket prices vary) has presented live theater in assorted venues across the Upper Keys. This nonprofit community troupe typically produces four shows each year, ranging from Broadway musicals to lesser-known comedies and dramas.

The Florida Keys Community Concert Band (305/451-4530, www.keyscommunityconcertband.org) was founded in 1992 by a small group of dedicated musicians and usually performs free family concerts at Islamorada's Founders Park (Nov.-Apr.). On occasion, it offers an extra concert in Key Largo's Murray E. Nelson Government and Cultural Center at Mile Marker 102. Check the band's online schedule for specific dates, and consult the Florida Keys Council of the Arts (1100 Simonton St., Key West, 305/295-4369, www.keysarts.com) for information about other cultural events in the Upper Keys.

If you enjoy arts of a more cinematic bent, you can always head to the Tavernier Cinema 5 (91298 Overseas Hwy., Tavernier, 305/853-7004, showtimes and ticket prices vary) at the southern end of Key Largo. Although this isn't the fanciest movie theater you'll ever encounter, you'll certainly be able to catch the latest flicks here, and it's rarely crowded.

FESTIVALS AND EVENTS

★ Key Largo Pirates Fest

For four fun-filled days in late October, the annual Key Largo Pirates Fest (305/394-3736, www.keylargopiratefestival.com, activity prices vary) invites visitors to celebrate the pirating lifestyle—in particular, the legend of the notorious African pirate Black Caesar, who allegedly prowled Florida's coastal waters in the 1700s. Before heading south to Key West for the annual Fantasy Fest extravaganza, which also takes place in late October, consider getting a taste of the island mayhem with this lively event. Festival activities include a pirate parade, pirate costume contests, a pirate bazaar and thieves market, an underwater treasure hunt, choreographed pirate shows, and various celebrations at area restaurants.

Other Area Festivals

Besides holiday gatherings like the St. Patrick's Day Parade and New Year's Eve fireworks display, Key Largo hosts several other annual events, including fishing tournaments and food festivals. In mid-January the 10-day Uncorked ... the Key Largo & Islamorada Food & Wine Festival (305/394-3736, www.floridakeysuncorked.com, activity prices vary) lures gourmands with wine tastings, wine classes, cooking demonstrations, and progressive wine dinners. During the last weekend of the month the Key Largo Stone Crab & Seafood Festival (305/451-4502, www.keylargoseafoodfestival.com, $5 adults, free for children under 12) features an array of fresh seafood, cooking demonstrations, fishing workshops, eating contests, arts-and-crafts vendors, live entertainment, and other distractions.

In late April, the eight-day **Key Largo Conch Republic Days** (305/394-3736, activity prices vary) honors the 1982 ceremonial secession of the Florida Keys from the United States with a lineup of zany activities at area restaurants, such as a Jimmy Buffett songwriting contest, a conch fritter eating contest, a key lime dessert cook-off, a coed stiletto strut, and an attempt at the world record for conch shell blowing.

If you're here in early or mid-December, consider watching the **Holiday Boat Parade**

(305/451-4502, www.keylargoboatparade.com, dates vary) on Blackwater Sound, near Mile Marker 104 on the bay side of U.S. 1. With a different theme each year, this lighted boat procession, which typically occurs on a Saturday evening, is a festive, family-friendly way to kick off the holiday season—whether you decide to participate in the parade, view from your boat, or observe the proceedings from shore. Each year, cash prizes are awarded in various categories, including best use of the selected theme.

Shopping

In general, travelers flock to Key Largo for its bountiful outdoor diversions, not its shopping opportunities. Beyond the Tradewinds Shopping Center and several diving emporiums, shoppers won't find as many options in this part of the Florida Keys as in, for instance, Key West. Nevertheless, several area stores are worth mentioning.

ART GALLERIES

Art aficionados will appreciate the **Key Largo Art Gallery** (MM 103.2, 103200 Overseas Hwy., Ste. 10, 305/451-0052, www.keylargoartgallery.com, 10am-5pm Tues.-Sat., 10am-1pm Sun.), with its occasional jewelry classes and a wide array of kaleidoscopic paintings from new artists as well as veterans like Jackie Campa and Teresa Kelley.

Stephen Frink Photographic (MM 100.7, 100750 Overseas Hwy., 305/451-3737 or 800/451-3737, www.stephenfrink.com or www.stephenfrinkphoto.com, 10am-5pm Mon., 8am-5pm Tues.-Sat.) displays the stunning images of one of the world's most widely published underwater photographers.

You'll find the tastefully displayed paintings from several world-renowned artists at **The Gallery at Kona Kai** (MM 97.8, 97802 Overseas Hwy., 305/852-7200, www.konakairesort.com, 9am-7pm daily or by appointment), an elegant gallery situated amid the lush foliage of the Kona Kai Resort. For more information about these and other art galleries, consult the **Florida Keys Council of the Arts** (1100 Simonton St., Key West, 305/295-4369, www.keysarts.com).

GIFT AND SOUVENIR SHOPS

Gifts and souvenirs can be found at a handful of interesting shops, including the **Florida Keys Gift Company** (MM 102.4, 102421 Overseas Hwy., 305/453-9229, 9am-7pm Mon.-Sat., 9am-6pm Sun.), a repository of tropical jewelry, clothing, and decor, plus regional products like the aromatic roasts of Baby's Coffee, a store in the Lower Keys. Nearby, **Largo Cargo** (MM 103.1, 103101 Overseas Hwy., 305/451-4242 or 800/795-8889, www.largocargo.com, 8:30am-8:30pm daily), which has been in operation since 1985, offers an assortment of tropical apparel, Panama Jack hats, Future Beach kayaks, island music, maps and books, collectible coins, fragrances, and glassware.

You can pick up seashells, seasonal outfits, and other souvenirs at the 20,000-square-foot **Shell World** (MM 97.6, 97600 Overseas Hwy., 305/852-8245, 9am-8pm daily), situated on the median of U.S. 1 and with a second location on the northern end of Key Largo (MM 106, 106040 Overseas Hwy., 305/451-9797,

9am-5pm daily). If you're short on beach staples like towels, sunglasses, hats, sandals, and other apparel—not to mention souvenirs—stop by the touristy **Sandal Factory Outlet/T-Shirt City** (MM 102.4, 102411 Overseas Hwy., 305/453-9644, 9am-8pm Mon.-Sat., 9am-6pm Sun.), which also has locations in Islamorada and Marathon.

FOOD AND CIGAR EMPORIUMS

If you have a hankering for regional treats, head to **Key Lime Products** (MM 95.2, 95231 Overseas Hwy., 305/853-0378 or 800/870-1780, www.keylimeproducts.com, 9am-5pm Mon.-Fri., 10am-6pm Sat.-Sun.), offering a wide assortment of tangy delights, from key lime iced tea to key lime thimble cookies to key lime shampoo. If you're staying in a room, suite, or cottage equipped with kitchen facilities, you might also want to partake of the fresh fish, crab, lobster, shrimp, and conch as well as the key lime pie and other delectables that **Key Largo Fisheries Inc.** (1313 Ocean Bay Dr., 305/451-3782 or 800/432-4358, www.keylargofisheries.com, 7:30am-5:30pm Mon.-Sat.) has been serving since 1972.

Cigar lovers will find shopping bliss in Key Largo. The **Island Smoke Shop** (MM 103.4, 103400 Overseas Hwy., 305/453-4014, www.islandsmokeshop.com, 10am-6pm daily) offers pipes, ashtrays, humidors, lighters, and over 1,200 brands and sizes of handmade premium cigars, including El Original maduros. Besides its vast inventory, it also boasts the largest walk-in humidor in southern Florida.

Food

SEAFOOD

Considering Key Largo's allure for anglers and other water lovers, it surely comes as no surprise that seafood restaurants abound on this island. **Alabama Jack's** (58000 Card Sound Rd., 305/248-8741, 11am-7pm daily, $8-24) has been family-owned since 1947, and its motto of "anything goes" could apply to the food as well as the country-western dancing on the weekends. Given the waterfront access, you can dock your boat and be eating in no time at all, and while the place doesn't have a complex menu, what the cooks do, they do well. (The conch fritters have been voted among the best in the Keys.) It's no wonder that locals flock to this beloved roadhouse on a regular basis.

Just past the junction of U.S. 1 and CR-905, **The Buzzard's Roost Grill and Pub** (MM 106.3, 21 Garden Cove Dr., 305/453-3746, www.buzzardsroostkeylargo.com, 11am-9pm Mon.-Thurs., 11am-10pm Fri.-Sat., 10:30am-9pm Sun., $9-34) offers an extensive menu, including many hook-and-cook options. Provided you catch a fish at its legal size and in its proper season, then clean and fillet it yourself, the staff will prepare it for you, whether you prefer your fish fried, grilled, blackened, or jerked. Not far from Buzzard's is **Shipwrecks Bar & Grill** (MM 106.3, 45 Garden Cove Dr., 305/453-3153, 11am-10pm daily, $5-15), a friendly, casual joint that earns rave reviews. Locals especially favor this hidden gem, which offers a daily happy hour (4pm-6pm), not to mention a wide array of draft and bottled beers, plus a menu that boasts everything from homemade coconut onion rings and pork sandwiches to seafood baskets and mahimahi quesadillas.

Farther south on U.S. 1 lies **Sundowners** (MM 103.9, 103900 Overseas Hwy., 305/451-4502, www.sundownerskeylargo.com, 11am-10pm daily, $9-40), one of the finest places to watch a sunset in the Upper Keys. Specializing in sandwiches, steaks, and of course, seafood, Sundowners features many local favorites, including conch chowder, Florida lobster tails, key lime pie, and pan-seared snapper with grapefruit beurre blanc. Not surprisingly, the Friday-night fish fry ($18 pp) is a popular draw.

Both a restaurant and a seafood market for more than 25 years, **The Fish House** (MM 102.4, 102401 Overseas Hwy., 305/451-4665, www.fishhouse.com, 11:30am-10pm daily, $9-40) presents a relaxed atmosphere and specializes in yellowtail snapper, mahimahi, and other fresh local seafood. After sampling the smoked fish or homemade chowders at The Fish House for lunch, consider a dinner at **The Fish House Encore** (MM 102.3, 102341 Overseas Hwy., 305/451-0650, www.fishhouse.com, 5pm-10pm Wed.-Mon., $12-33), a fine-dining eatery that features seafood, steaks, pasta dishes, and a raw bar, plus expertly prepared sushi—and, as with most Florida Keys restaurants, tangy key lime pie. Beyond the main dining room, Encore also serves dinner in the outdoor patio or the piano lounge. Reservations are recommended.

Whether it's for breakfast, lunch, or dinner, the airy, pet-friendly ★ **Key Largo Conch House** (MM 100.2, 100211 Overseas Hwy., 305/453-4844, www.keylargoconchhouse.com, 8am-10pm daily, $9-30) offers an amazing menu in a lovely wooded setting. Try the cracked conch Benedict for breakfast, the fish tacos for lunch, or the mahi key lime almandine for dinner. Additional specialties include the conch chowder, conch fritters, and the lobster and conch ceviche. If the weather is pleasant, dine on the porch or relax in the courtyard, which is surprisingly pleasurable despite the eatery's proximity to busy U.S. 1. Feel free to take advantage of the free wireless Internet access while you eat.

If you appreciate a lovely view, head south to the **Bayside Grille** (MM 99.5, 99530 Overseas Hwy., 305/451-3380, www.keylargo-baysidegrill.com, 11:30am-10pm daily, $8-32), a friendly, family-owned eatery situated beside Florida Bay, directly behind DiGiorgio's Café Largo. Both restaurants are, in fact, owned by the same family, though the Bayside Grille is a better spot for watching drifting sailboats, swaying palm trees, and incredible sunsets. The cuisine, meanwhile, is often delicious. Lunchtime offerings include blackened

Conch in the Keys

Eating conch during a Keys vacation has become a tradition, and for many it's a must-do item on their Keys bucket list. The question is: How will I choose to consume my lucky sea snail?

The most popular way to eat conch in the Keys is with the snail chopped up and served in a **conch fritter.** Despite the fancy name, fritters are really just hush puppies with a bit of conch meat in them. They are fried balls of cornmeal and flour, sometimes with vegetables added, and usually with some sort of sauce on top, often containing key lime juice. A fault of the fritter is that inside all of that fried dough, it's very difficult to get a fair taste of your sea snail that you've traveled so far to feast upon.

A better option is to order **cracked conch,** which you'll find on most seafood menus in the Keys. In this recipe, the conch is fried in a seasoned batter and often served with a sauce. **Conch chowder** is another island favorite. The traditional chowder in the Keys is the red chowder with blended tomatoes, bits of conch, herbs and spices, and potatoes. You'll also find **conch salads, conch ceviche, fried conch sandwiches,** and conch served nearly every other way imaginable.

Be sure to ask your waiter two things: if the conch is harvested in a sustainable manner, and if it's fresh. It's illegal to harvest conch in the Keys, and there's a lot of frozen and unsustainably harvested conch being sold to tourists because of this. There are restaurants, however, that get fresh, sustainably harvested conch from the Bahamas.

mahimahi, coconut shrimp baskets, and non-seafood dishes like barbecue ribs. The dinner menu is a bit more extensive, with everything from conch fritters to seafood enchiladas to filet mignon. The place prides itself on more than just fresh seafood, though—everything here is made on the premises daily, from the tuna salad to the grilled pineapple salsa. To enhance your experience, order a refreshing cocktail such as the Havana Margarita or a pineapple ginger mojito and watch the sun sink into the bay.

Established in 1976, ★ **Mrs. Mac's Kitchen** (MM 99.3, 99336 Overseas Hwy., 305/451-3722, www.mrsmacskitchen.com, 7am-9:30pm Mon.-Sat., $6-27) is an extremely popular and often crowded joint, filled with as many locals as tourists. If you're looking for a meal like Mom used to make—especially if Mom was a gourmet chef—then look no farther than this casual eatery. Featuring plenty of Keys favorites, the extensive menu includes everything from "Konk" chowder to relleno-style fish. The key lime pie here, a classic version with a graham cracker crust, is among the best you'll find in the Keys. The decor is a winner, too. Making use of the entire space, inside and out, Mrs. Mac's feels like a kid's clubhouse, with beer bottles along the rafters, license plates all over the walls and ceiling, overhead lamps cleverly fashioned from similar license plates, and small aluminum-can planes hanging everywhere. A second restaurant, the aptly named **Mrs. Mac's Kitchen II** (MM 99.0, 99020 Overseas Hwy., 305/451-6227), sits on the nearby median.

Nestled on the median, **Ballyhoo's Historic Seafood Grille** (MM 97.8, 97860 Overseas Hwy., 305/852-0822, www.ballyhoosrestaurant.com, 11am-10pm daily, $8-36) sits in a lovingly preserved Conch-style structure that started as a fishing camp and now serves an array of seafood, steaks, and sandwiches. Try the gumbo, the whole fried snapper, fresh fish prepared in any number of interesting ways, and, when in season, all-you-can-eat stone crabs.

Following its opening in 1989, **Snapper's Waterfront Restaurant** (MM 94.5, 139 Seaside Ave., 305/852-5956, www.snapperskeylargo.com, noon-10pm Mon.-Sat., 10am-10pm Sun., $9-28) quickly became one of Key Largo's busiest eateries—not to mention a hot spot for live nighttime entertainment. Try the seared tuna or the blue cheese-encrusted filet mignon.

AMERICAN AND EUROPEAN

The **Tower of Pizza** (MM 100.6, 100600 Overseas Hwy., 305/451-1461, www.towerofpizzakeylargo.com, 11am-11pm daily, $10-19) has never closed, not even for a hurricane. In addition to excellent pizza, this eat-in, take-out, and delivery joint offers other Italian fare, from minestrone to veal parmesan.

Bogie's Café (MM 99.7, 99701 Overseas Hwy., 305/451-2121, www.holidayinnkeylargo.com, 7am-9pm daily, $8-16) is part of the Holiday Inn complex and just steps from the historic *African Queen*. You can enjoy the American and continental-style dishes inside or in the garden patio, and the entire menu is also available at the hotel's tiki bar (11am-close daily).

The family-run **Doc's Diner** (MM 99.6, 99696 Overseas Hwy., 305/451-2895, www.docsdinerkeylargo.com, 6am-2pm daily, $5-9) is a local favorite for breakfast and lunch. If you're here with your family, try Doc's Feast, which offers a huge assortment of the joint's most popular breakfast foods, including ham steak, pancakes and French toast, creamy grits, warm biscuits, a dozen types of scrambled eggs, and more. For an equally casual meal, stop by the 1950s-style **DJ's Diner** (MM 99.4, 99411 Overseas Hwy., 305/451-2999, www.djsdiner.com, 7am-3pm daily, $5-14). Sample a breakfast burrito or a burger while gazing at celebrity photos on the walls.

For a taste of Europe, stop by **DiGiorgio's Café Largo** (MM 99.5, 99530 Overseas Hwy., 305/451-4885, www.keylargo-cafelargo.com, 4:30pm-11pm daily, $8-30), which serves a fantastic assortment of Italian dishes, from traditional fare like littleneck clams and linguini to Conch-style items such as the parmesan-crusted yellowtail. Established in 1992, this family-run restaurant also offers basic pizzas and subs for those in a hurry. The DiGiorgio family also owns the Bayside Grille, which lies between Café Largo and Florida Bay.

ASIAN AND LATIN AMERICAN

Two cuisines are better than one at the **Num Thai Restaurant & Sushi Bar** (MM 103.2, 103200 Overseas Hwy., 305/451-5955, 11:30am-3pm and 5pm-10pm Mon.-Fri., 5pm-10pm Sat.-Sun., $8-16), where you can sample a spicy tuna roll or some excellent pad thai all in the same night.

If you're in the mood for some killer Mexican food, head north to **Señor Frijoles** (MM 103.9, 103900 Overseas Hwy., 305/451-1592, www.senorfrijolesrestaurant.com, 11am-10pm daily, $12-22), which has been serving delicious south-of-the-border dishes and fantastic margaritas since 1981. One local favorite is the steak fajita burrito, filled with marinated beef tenderloin and served with citrus pico de gallo, frijoles, and a tasty chipotle sour cream—all wrapped in a large tortilla, topped with ranchero sauce, and covered with Monterey Jack cheese.

Sunrise Cuban Café and Market (MM 91.8, 91885 Overseas Hwy., Tavernier, 305/852-7216, http://sunrisecubancafe.com, 5am-9pm daily, $3-15) serves authentic Cuban food for breakfast, lunch, and dinner. The atmosphere is colorful and cheerful. Choose between soups, salads, sandwiches, and a wide variety of seafood, beef, chicken, and vegetarian entrees, or get the buffet and sample a little of everything. Their Cuban coffee is strong and delicious, in case you just need to stop in for a quick pick-me-up.

Accommodations

$100-200

Initially built as a fishing camp in 1903, **Gilbert's Resort** (MM 107.9, 107900 Overseas Hwy., 305/451-1133, www.gilbertsresort.com, rooms $170-270 d, suites $200-250) presents a laid-back atmosphere that's especially apparent in the on-site tiki bar, which offers live music and a full menu. The standard rooms provide two double beds, air-conditioners, small refrigerators, and cable television. Also available are bayside rooms with waterfront patios, as well as spacious family suites. Unlike at many establishments in the Upper Keys, pets are allowed here, though an extra charge applies.

Situated beside Florida Bay, ★ **Amy Slate's Amoray Dive Resort** (MM 104.2, 104250 Overseas Hwy., 305/451-3595 or 800/426-6729, www.amoray.com, rooms $120-299 d, apartments $109-269) caters to the diving or snorkeling enthusiast. Peppered with palm trees, this breezy property offers a wide variety of airy accommodations, with ceiling fans, tropical decor, free wireless Internet access, and in some cases, full kitchens. Even better, you can take a variety of scuba-diving classes on the premises, and while staying here, you'll be just steps away from the resort's two boats: the 45-foot *Amoray Diver* and the 26-foot *Just-In-Time*, both of which deliver guests to the reefs and wrecks of John Pennekamp Coral Reef State Park and Florida Keys National Marine Sanctuary.

For a blend of Victorian charm and Caribbean flair, reserve a room at the year-round ★ **Tarpon Flats Inn & Marina** (29 Shoreland Dr., 305/453-1313 or 866/546-0000, www.tarponflatsinn.com, $170-220 d). This well-appointed bed-and-breakfast offers lovely rooms and suites, with British colonial-style furnishings and intimate verandas that open onto stunning Largo Sound. Besides amenities like satellite television and kitchenettes, the inn's major claim to fame is its proximity to an assortment of natural pleasures and outdoor diversions. You'll find swimming, sailing, and kayaking opportunities right at your doorstep, and you'll be within

1: Mrs. Mac's Kitchen **2:** Amy Slate's Amoray Dive Resort **3:** Key Largo Conch House **4:** Rock Reef Resort

walking distance of several tiki bars and waterfront restaurants. You're also not far from the wonders of John Pennekamp Coral Reef State Park—not to mention the Everglades, which are just a 30-minute boat ride away.

If you're traveling with your cat or dog, the **Marina Del Mar Resort & Marina** (527 Caribbean Dr., 305/451-4107, www.marinadelmarkeylargo.com, rooms $190-260 d, studios $220-300) offers 76 pet-friendly rooms, studios, and apartments. Queen-size or king-size beds are provided, as well as cable television and free wireless Internet. Other amenities include a heated pool, tennis courts, and a free continental breakfast. The 56-unit pet-friendly **Bayside Inn** (MM 99.4, 99490 Overseas Hwy., 305/451-4450 or 800/242-5229, www.baysidekeylargo.com, rooms $100-275 d, suites $300-400) includes one-bedroom waterfront suites, bay-view rooms, and island-view rooms. Each contains a small refrigerator and a large flat-screen television, and the suites also have full kitchens. The property features a relaxing pool.

The Pelican (MM 99.3, 99340 Overseas Hwy., 305/451-3576 or 877/451-3576, www.pelicankeylargo.com, rooms $100-170 d, suites $170-230, cottages $130-160) offers 23 rooms, suites, and cottages, all of which are equipped with cable television, refrigerators, and air-conditioners. The hotel also provides free wireless Internet access. While staying here, take advantage of the bayfront beach, where gorgeous sunsets are common, or feel free to rest on one of the available hammocks. Anglers and boaters will also appreciate the on-site boat ramp and docks.

Just a little farther south lies one of the few smoke-free hotels in Key Largo, the weathered **Key Largo Inn** (MM 99.2, 99202 Overseas Hwy., 305/451-2478 or 866/488-3020, www.keylargoinn.com, $100-190 d), which features a two-story Caribbean-style building surrounded by a pool and a tropical courtyard. The rooms are clean but simple and contain extra-long queen-size beds; additional amenities include a complimentary breakfast and free wireless Internet access. The staff members here are usually amiable, helpful, and more than willing to offer solid recommendations for local restaurants and activities.

The ★ **Rock Reef Resort** (MM 97.8, 97850 Overseas Hwy., 305/852-2401 or 800/477-2343, www.rockreefresort.com, $89-180 d) is a year-round oasis beside Florida Bay that was once part of an old key lime grove. Operated since 1989 by on-site owners Linda and David Adams, this low-key resort offers a wide range of comfortable accommodations. The main hotel is a white two-story building that contains standard and deluxe rooms as well as efficiencies; beyond that lie the lush, spacious grounds, where shady palm trees and vibrant bougainvillea surround more intimate lodgings that include well-furnished apartments ($145-260 daily) and beachside cottages ($180-280 daily). With several hammocks among the trees, numerous lounge chairs on the beach, a fishing pier with docking facilities ($15 daily), a hot tub in the garden, a waterfront tiki hut, and a communal picnic and barbecue area, it's no wonder that the 21-unit resort is a popular option for wedding parties and family reunions. Other amenities include cable television, laundry services, wireless Internet access, and on-site parking. Those seeking romance and relaxation will also appreciate the no-pet and no-fireworks policies.

Offering suites, cottages, villas, and efficiencies—all with full kitchens—the lush, 2.5-acre **Coconut Bay Resort** (MM 97.7, 97702 Overseas Hwy., 305/852-5695 or 800/385-0986, www.bayharbourkeylargo.com, rooms $120-185 d, cottages $170-260, suites $260-350, villas $230-490) can accommodate any type of Upper Keys vacation. Every room has cable television, barbecue grills, and shady huts.

Perfect for divers, anglers, and snorkelers, the **Seafarer Resort** (MM 97.6, 97684 Overseas Hwy., 305/852-5349, www.seafarerresort.com, $100-200 d) features a private beach ideal for relaxing, watching a romantic sunset, or embarking upon a variety of water-related adventures. Here you can snorkel in the turquoise waters nearby, arrange a fishing trip with one of the many local guides, or enlist the help of the on-site dive center. With studio and standard rooms, as well as cottages ($150-230 daily), a family apartment ($150-230 daily), and a beach house ($140-230 daily), the resort can even accommodate large groups.

Farther south, the **Drift Hotel** (MM 95.3, 95320 Overseas Hwy., 305/852-8114, www.stoneledgeparadiseinn.com, $100-140 d) offers bright, modern lodgings alongside Florida Bay. As with most places in the Keys, the rooms range in size, with some providing full kitchens.

Situated on Florida Bay, the **Atlantic Bay Resort** (160 Sterling Rd., Tavernier, 305/852-5248 or 866/937-5650, www.atlanticbayresort.com, rooms $180-270 d, suites $300-1,000, cottages $300-700) features 500 feet of relaxing waterfront, plus 20 efficiencies, cottages, and suites, all of which have full kitchens. Guests can utilize the resort's boat ramp and dock.

OVER $200

Among the pricier lodging options that Key Largo offers is the **Azul del Mar** (MM 104.3, 104300 Overseas Hwy., 305/451-0337, www.azulkeylargo.com, suites $200-400), a small, quiet, adults-only boutique hotel that features six suites with ocean or garden views, various water sports and ecoadventures, and a rejuvenating beach beside Florida Bay. Each room here provides a king-size bed, a kitchenette, a large television, and wireless Internet access.

The **Marriott Key Largo Bay Resort** (103800 Overseas Hwy., 305/453-0000 or 888/731-9056, www.marriottkeylargo.com, rooms $250-400 d, suites $600-900) offers a complete resort experience with full watersports facilities, a full-service day spa, and access to the Keysgate championship 18-hole golf course only 25 minutes away. In addition, the property houses three separate eateries: the open-air Breezer's Bar and Grill (4pm-11pm daily), ideal for sunset-watching; Flipper's Poolside Tiki Bar (11am-sunset daily); and Gus' Grille (7am-11pm daily), featuring award-winning Floribbean cuisine. The rooms here range from standard accommodations with two double beds to a two-bedroom suite, and all include cable television, small refrigerators, and wireless Internet access.

Formerly an underwater research habitat, ★ **Jules' Undersea Lodge** (51 Shoreland Dr., 305/451-2353, www.jul.com, $675 per individual, $800 per couple) is now open to the public for a unique lodging experience. To enter the lodge, you must dive 21 feet beneath the sea, making this the perfect base camp for diving enthusiasts. The lodge consists of the same creature comforts you would expect above the sea: hot showers, a well-stocked kitchen, a common room for winding down after a long day of scuba diving, and two bedrooms with 42-inch windows, offering a fascinating glimpse of the ocean floor. If you decide to come with friends, you're in luck: Group economy packages are also available.

Near some of the best fishing and diving waters, the **Largo Resort** (MM 101.7, 101740 Overseas Hwy., 305/451-0424, www.largoresort.com, rooms $200-300 d, suite $240-350, bungalows $250-400) lies only a mile from John Pennekamp Coral Reef State Park. Located on three acres alongside Florida Bay, the waterfront suite, two bungalows, and three units here offer kitchenettes or full kitchens—making them especially economical for families.

Relish some quiet time near the poolside tiki bar at the **Courtyard Marriott Key Largo** (MM 99.7, 99751 Overseas Hwy., 305/451-3939 or 888/731-9092, www.marriott.com, rooms $180-320 d, suites $300-400), perhaps after returning from a dive or fishing adventure provided by one of the many guides in the adjacent marina. Every room features comfortable king-size or queen-size beds, cable television, and free Internet access. The king Jacuzzi suites also include wraparound balconies with spectacular views of the marina.

The 130 rooms at the **Holiday Inn Key Largo Resort & Marina** (99701 Overseas Hwy., 305/451-2121 or 888/465-4329, www. holidayinnkeylargo.com, $170-280 d) are all tropically themed, some with private balconies overlooking the oceanside marina and the on-site Bogie's Café. The rooms offer queen-size or king-size beds, plus cable television and free Internet access. Besides the immediately available water sports, the hotel features two freshwater pools as well as a poolside tiki bar.

If you're an experienced sailor who's come to the Keys without a boat of your own, the **Key Lime Sailing Club** (MM 99.3, 99306 Overseas Hwy., 305/451-3438, www. keylimesailingclub.com, cottages $185-395) has one at your disposal. For a smaller vessel, try one of the available kayaks, canoes, paddleboats, or rowboats. With a variety of cottages on-site, this hideaway has something for every occasion. Be aware, though, that each cottage charges a one-time cleaning fee ($50-100), the specific amount of which depends upon the size of the cottage.

Barely visible from the highway, the **Kona Kai Resort, Gallery & Botanic Gardens** (MM 97.8, 97802 Overseas Hwy., 305/852-7200 or 800/365-7829, www.konakairesort. com, rooms $219-439 d, suites $279-1,078) provides a lush, intimate setting with 11 guest rooms and suites. The grounds have been transformed into a beautiful botanic garden, offering a serene setting in which to relax and replenish. Guests can pamper themselves by tanning on one of the largest private beaches in Key Largo, swimming in the beachside pool, or napping in one of the shaded hammocks. The property also features an elegant art gallery.

To take advantage of the "diving capital of the world," head to the **Mariner's Resort Villas & Marina** (MM 97.5, 97501 Overseas Hwy., 305/853-1111 or 305/853-5000, www. keyscaribbean.com, villas $200-450), which features direct access to a beautiful marina. Luxury townhomes and villas offer a quiet escape in this gated resort. The grounds also promise plenty of adventure, with two freshwater pools—one of which is supposedly the largest pool in the Keys.

Perhaps one of the Hilton chain's prettiest properties is the **Hilton Baker's Cay Resort** (MM 97, 97000 Overseas Hwy., 305/852-5553 or 888/871-3437, www.bakerscay.com, rooms $190-300 d, suites $200-400), hidden away on

Kona Kai Resort, Gallery & Botanic Gardens

13 acres of lush forestland. Boasting all of the expected amenities of any complete resort, the Hilton Baker's Cay equally suits family vacations, with its impressive lineup of water sports, as well as romantic getaways, given the solitude offered by its sumptuous grounds. The rooms and suites all feature queen-size or king-size beds, cable television, free Internet access, and private balconies with either bayside or forest views. Other on-site amenities include a beachside watering hole, a swimming pool and adjacent bar, and Dry Rocks (7am-10pm Sun.-Thurs., 7am-10:30pm Fri.-Sat.), a restaurant offering panoramic views of Florida Bay.

For an intimate island-style boutique hotel, try the **MB at Key Largo** (147 Seaside Ave., 305/852-6200 or 800/401-0057, www.mbatkeylargo.com, rooms $140-290 d, suites $290-600). There are 21 comfortable choices including one-bedroom and two-bedroom suites with small refrigerators, cable television, free wireless Internet access, and lockers to store your fishing, boating, or diving equipment. The two-bedroom luxury suites each have a well-equipped gourmet kitchen, two full bathrooms, and a private screened patio. In addition to the comfortable accommodations at the **Ocean Pointe Suites at Key Largo** (500 Burton Dr., Tavernier, 305/853-3000 or 800/882-9464, www.providentresorts.com, suites $142-260), the resort specializes in arranging snorkeling, fishing, and ecotours as package deals. Spend the day at the private beach or the freshwater pool, and then grab a bite to eat at the on-site café and lounge.

The unique and pet-friendly **Coconut Palm Inn** (198 Harborview Dr., Tavernier, 305/852-3017 or 800/765-5397, www.coconutpalminn.com, rooms $160-260 d, suites $250-430) offers 20 rooms and suites, varying between standard rooms with garden views, patio rooms with bay views and screened porches, and suites with separate living areas, bay views, and balconies or decks. Here you'll also enjoy a sandy beach hidden amid a grove of coconut trees, some of which have hammocks hanging between them.

CAMPING

Key Largo offers several budget-friendly campgrounds ideal for families and outdoors enthusiasts. Near the northern end of Key Largo, **John Pennekamp Coral Reef State Park** (MM 102.6, 102601 Overseas Hwy., 305/451-6300, www.floridastateparks.org or www.pennekamppark.com, 8am-sunset daily, $8 vehicles with 2-8 passengers plus $0.50 pp, $4.50 motorcycles and single-occupant vehicles, $2.50 pedestrians, bikers, and extra passengers) offers a full-facility 47-site campground for both RVs and tents ($36 daily) with access to a dump station, wheelchair-accessible restrooms, and hot showers. Besides full hookups, each site features a picnic table and a grill. While this pet-friendly campground might not be as stunning as other state park campgrounds in the Florida Keys, it's a terrific home base for park activities from sunbathing to snorkeling. For reservations, contact **ReserveAmerica** (800/326-3521, www.reserveamerica.com) up to 11 months in advance.

Located on 40 acres alongside the Atlantic Ocean, the **Key Largo Kampground & Marina** (MM 101.5, 101551 Overseas Hwy., 305/451-1431 or 800/526-7688, www.keylargokampground.com, $50-130 daily, $335-865 weekly) presents a variety of campsites, from tent sites with no hookups to waterfront full-hookup sites ideal for RVs. Amenities here include laundry facilities, a general store for limited grocery needs, and a dock that offers boat owners easy access to the Atlantic Ocean.

The gated **Calusa Campground Resort and Marina** (MM 101.5, 325 Calusa St., 305/451-0232, www.calusacampground.com, $70-243 daily, $496-1,700 weekly, $1,300-3,081 monthly) features a relaxing pool, direct access to the marina, and three types of full-hookup RV sites: inland, canal, and bayfront. Other amenities include shady palm trees, picnic tables, and a small playground. The **Riptide RV Resort** (97680 Overseas Hwy., 305/852-8481, www.sunrvresorts. com, starting at $61 daily, $365 weekly, $1,453 monthly) offers 39 palm-shaded sites with oceanfront views, cement patios, full hookups, and free cable TV and Wi-Fi access.

Additional amenities include a dump station, laundry facilities, a bayside picnic pavilion, a private beach, a shuffleboard area, a small motel, and various communal activities, from bingo games and karaoke nights to barbecues and ice cream socials. Tents are welcome.

Information and Services

INFORMATION

For brochures, maps, and other information about Key Largo, stop by the **Key Largo Chamber of Commerce and Florida Keys Visitor Center** (MM 106, 106000 Overseas Hwy., 305/451-1414 or 800/822-1088, www. keylargochamber.org, 9am-6pm daily), a yellow two-story building on the bay side of U.S. 1, near Mile Marker 106; inside you'll spy an 18th-century British cannon, one of several found in an offshore patch reef. You can also consult the **Monroe County Tourist Development Council** (1201 White St., Ste. 102, Key West, 305/296-1552 or 800/352-5397, www.fla-keys.com, 9am-5pm Mon.-Fri.) for information about Key Largo and the rest of the Florida Keys. For government-related issues, contact the **Monroe County offices** (1100 Simonton St., Key West, 305/292-4537, www.monroecounty-fl.gov, 8am-5pm Mon.-Fri.).

For local news, consult *Florida Keys News* (www.flkeysnews.com), **The Weekly Newspapers** (www.keysweekly.com), and **KeysNews.com.** In addition, the dailies *Miami Herald* (www.miamiherald.com) and *The Key West Citizen* (www.keysnews.com) are available throughout the Keys.

Key Largo has several radio stations, including **Thunder Country** (WCTH-FM 100.3, www.thundercountry.com) and classic-rock station the **SUN** (WFKZ-FM 103.1, www. sun103.com).

SERVICES

Money

For banking needs, stop by **Capital Bank** (MM 103.3, 103330 Overseas Hwy., 305/451-2000 or 800/639-5111, www.capitalbank-us. com, 9am-4pm Mon.-Thurs., 9am-6pm Fri., 9am-noon Sat., extended drive-through hours) or the **First State Bank of the Florida Keys** (MM 97.6, 97670 Overseas Hwy., 305/852-2070 or 866/298-1858, www. keysbank.com, 8am-5pm Mon.-Thurs., 8am-6pm Fri., extended drive-through hours).

Mail

For shipping, faxing, copying, and other business-related services, visit **The UPS Store** (MM 101.4, 101425 Overseas Hwy., 305/453-4877, www.theupsstore.com, 8am-6pm Mon.-Fri., 9am-5pm Sat.). You'll also find two **post offices** (800/275-8777, www. usps.com) in the area: one in Key Largo (MM 100.1, 100100 Overseas Hwy., 305/451-3155, 8:30am-4:30pm Mon.-Fri., 10am-1pm Sat.) and one in Tavernier (MM 91.2, 91220 Overseas Hwy., 305/853-1052, 9am-4:30pm Mon.-Fri.).

Groceries and Supplies

Groceries and other supplies are found at **Winn-Dixie** (MM 105.3, 105300 Overseas Hwy., 305/451-0328, www.winndixie.com, 7am-10pm daily), which houses an on-site pharmacy (305/451-3591, 8am-8pm Mon.-Fri., 9am-6pm Sat., 10am-5pm Sun.). In the

Tradewinds Shopping Center is a **Publix** (MM 101.4, 101437 Overseas Hwy., 305/451-0808, www.publix.com, 7am-10pm daily), which, in addition to groceries and other services, includes an on-site pharmacy (305/451-5338, 9am-9pm Mon.-Fri., 9am-7pm Sat., 10am-5pm Sun.). **Walgreens** (MM 99.5, 99501 Overseas Hwy., 305/451-4385, www.walgreens.com, 7am-10pm daily) offers a pharmacy drive-through (9am-5pm daily) as well as a full liquor department.

Laundry

There are several coin-operated laundries in the area, including the **Waldorf Plaza Coin Laundry** (MM 99.6, 99607 Overseas Hwy., 305/451-4575, 8am-6pm daily).

Internet Access

For Internet access, head to the **Key Largo Branch Library** (MM 101.4, 101485 Overseas Hwy., 305/451-2396, www.keyslibraries.org, 9:30am-6pm Mon.-Fri., 10am-6pm Sat.) in the Tradewinds Shopping Center.

Emergency Services

In case of an emergency that requires police, fire, or ambulance services, dial **911** from any cell or public phone. Even in less critical situations, you can consult the **Key Largo Fire Rescue Department** (305/451-2700 or 305/451-2701, www.keylargofire.com), which operates two fire stations: one at 220 Reef Drive and the other at 1 East Drive. For nonemergency assistance, contact the **Monroe County Sheriff's Office** (Roth Bldg., 50 High Point Rd., Ste. 100, Tavernier, 305/853-3211, www.keysso.net, 8am-5pm Mon.-Fri.).

For medical assistance, consult the **Mariners Hospital** (MM 91.5, 91500 Overseas Hwy., Tavernier, 305/434-3000, www.baptisthealth.net). Foreign visitors seeking help with directions, medical concerns, business issues, law enforcement needs, or other problems can receive **multilingual tourist assistance** (800/771-5397) 24 hours daily.

Transportation

GETTING THERE

Air

Despite the presence of a private airport at the **Ocean Reef Club** (201 Ocean Reef Dr., 305/367-3690, www.oceanreef.com), Key Largo has no major airport of its own. To travel here by plane, you'll need to fly into **Fort Lauderdale-Hollywood International Airport** (FLL, 100 Terminal Dr., Fort Lauderdale, 866/435-9355, www.broward.org/airport), **Miami International Airport** (MIA, 2100 NW 42nd Ave., Miami, 305/876-7000, www.miami-airport.com), **Key West International Airport** (EYW, 3491 S. Roosevelt Blvd., Key West, 305/296-5439 or 305/296-7223, www.keywestinternationalairport.com), or **Florida Keys Marathon Airport** (MTH, 9400 Overseas Hwy., Marathon, 305/289-6060). From there you can rent a vehicle from agencies like **Avis** (800/633-3469, www.avis.com), **Budget** (800/218-7992, www.budget.com), or **Enterprise** (800/261-7331, www.enterprise.com) to reach Key Largo.

Bus or Train

The **Miami-Dade County Metrobus** (305/891-3131, www.miamidade.gov/transit) operates the **301 Dade-Monroe Express** between Florida City and Marathon (5:15am-10:40pm daily, $2.25 per one-way trip), with stops in Key Largo and Tavernier until 9:25pm and 9:40pm, respectively. **Greyhound** (800/231-2222, www.greyhound.com) offers limited bus service to Key Largo. **Amtrak** (800/872-7245, www.amtrak.com) provides train service only as far south as Miami, from where you can rent a car or hop a shuttle to reach the Florida Keys.

Transport from Airports and Stations

If you arrive in the Fort Lauderdale-Miami area via plane, bus, or train—or Key West via plane or bus—you can either rent a car or hire a shuttle service to reach Key Largo. Companies include **Keys Shuttle** (305/289-9997 or 888/765-9997, www.keysshuttle.com, $60-70 pp for shared ride, $275-325 for exclusive service), which provides service from the Miami and Fort Lauderdale airports, and **SuperShuttle** (305/871-2000 or 954/764-1700, www.supershuttle.com, $189 for up to 10 passengers), which provides nonstop van service for Key Largo visitors flying into Miami.

Car

To reach Key Largo from Miami, head south on U.S. 1 (Overseas Hwy.). If you're headed from the Everglades via I-75 (Everglades Pkwy.), drive south on U.S. 27, veer right onto SR-997 (Krome Ave.), and follow the signs to U.S. 1. From U.S. 41 (Tamiami Trl.) in the Everglades, head south on SR-997 and continue toward U.S. 1. If you are traveling during

the high season (Dec.-Apr.), be sure to call **511** for an up-to-the-minute traffic report.

GETTING AROUND

Car

The best way to travel through Key Largo is by car, truck, RV, or motorcycle—all of which offer easy access to U.S. 1 and other roads, such as CR-905, which traverses the northern part of Key Largo and accesses Dagny Johnson Key Largo Hammock Botanical State Park and the exclusive Ocean Reef Club.

Van Service

If you're staying in Key Largo and want to head to Key West for the day—and would rather leave your vehicle at the hotel, resort, or campground where you're staying—consider **Sea the Keys** (305/896-7013, www.keywestdaytrip.com, rates vary), a passenger van service that will pick you up from your hotel in the Upper Keys and drop you off in Key West around 11am. You'll be free to explore the city's restaurants, bars, museums, and other attractions before making the return trip around 7pm or 8pm.

Bicycle or Boat

While you can certainly traverse Key Largo

driving between Key Largo and the mainland

via bicycle, the sprawling nature of this region makes it challenging for novice riders. Nevertheless, it's a lovely, ecofriendly way to experience the northernmost island, and there's even a 15.5-mile biking path that runs past numerous businesses and parks between Mile Marker 106.5 and Mile Marker 91. Bicycles can be rented from places like the **Key Largo Bike Shop** (91946 Overseas Hwy., 305/395-1551, www.keylargobike.com, 8am-5pm daily, $18-60 daily), which offers road bikes as well as hybrids. Weekly rates are also available, and helmets and locks are included with all rentals.

Of course, you can also experience Key Largo via boat. Having your own vessel might make navigating these waters a bit easier, and you'll find no shortage of boat ramps and marina slips in Key Largo. If you'd rather rent a boat, contact **Atlantis Boat Rentals** (47 Shoreland Dr., 305/801-1897, www.atlantisboatrental.com, rates vary), which offers an assortment of vessels from fishing boats to luxury pontoon boats.

Islamorada

South of Key Largo, most of the remaining

Upper Keys have become part of Islamorada (eye-lah-more-AH-dah), an incorporated town long celebrated for its bountiful sportfishing opportunities.

Its name—derived from the Spanish phrase *islas moradas* (purple islands)—might refer, depending on the resident you ask, to the region's incredible violet-tinted sunsets or the brilliant flowers that blossom here, or even the purplish snail shells that once peppered the shores of these islands.

Regardless of its origin, however, this "Village of Islands," allegedly the first inhabited place in the Florida Keys, includes several keys that are accessible via the Overseas Highway—namely, Plantation Key

Highlights

Look for ★ to find recommended sights, activities, dining, and lodging.

★ **Indian Key Historic State Park:** This lovely offshore island lures hikers, swimmers, sunbathers, bird-watchers, snorkelers, scuba divers, and anglers (page 138).

★ **Lignumvitae Key Botanical State Park:** Escape to this offshore island to enjoy the kind of virgin tropical hardwood hammock that once thrived in the Upper Keys (page 140).

★ **History of Diving Museum:** This curious collection includes diving paraphernalia from around the world, plus treasures recovered from the ocean (page 141).

★ **Theater of the Sea:** Swim with dolphins and sea lions, enjoy a glass-bottom boat ride, and take a snorkeling cruise to an offshore coral reef (page 142).

★ **Fishing and Boating:** The self-proclaimed "sportfishing capital of the world" boasts full-service marinas, fishing charters, independent fishing guides, and boat rentals (page 145).

★ **Kayaking:** Islamorada offers a wealth of opportunities for kayakers, who can either rent watercraft or opt for a guided excursion amid backcountry waters and offshore islands (page 147).

★ **Spas and Yoga:** The Village of Islands is home to rejuvenating spas where you can enjoy refreshing facials, body treatments, massages, and beachside yoga (page 151).

(which includes part of the Tavernier community), Windley Key, Upper Matecumbe Key, and Lower Matecumbe Key. There is also a pair of remote state-park islands only reachable by boat that are definitely worth a visit: Indian Key Historic State Park, site of a 19th-century settlement, and Lignumvitae Key Botanical State Park, home to a virgin tropical hardwood hammock.

Islamorada, one of the wealthier areas in the Florida Keys, boasts several high-end art galleries, boutiques, and full-service spas as well as sophisticated restaurants and resorts, but it's the sportfishing that lures most people. The clear, warm waters around Islamorada teem with tarpon, trout, redfish, snapper, sailfish, and other sought-after species. It's a snap to rent a boat, hire a fishing guide, or charter a full crew, if you so desire.

If fishing is not your preference, you'll find several other distractions in the area, including a geological state park on Windley Key that has vestiges of Henry Flagler's ill-fated Overseas Railroad. You can watch entertaining dolphins and sea lions at a year-round marine mammal center; peruse one of the world's largest collections of diving helmets and artifacts; feed wild tarpon at Robbie's of Islamorada; and explore an underwater archaeological state park, which preserves the wreck of a Spanish treasure-fleet ship that sank here nearly three centuries ago.

PLANNING YOUR TIME

Though Islamorada comprises several islands between Mile Marker 91 and Mile Marker 72, with attractions and resorts stretching from Plantation Key to Lower Matecumbe Key, it's fairly simple to navigate this area by car via the Overseas Highway. In fact, the only main attractions that will require a boat ride are the underwater coral reefs and shipwrecks as well as the two island state parks of Indian Key and Lignumvitae Key.

In Islamorada you'll find a wide range of diversions, from marine mammal shows to day spas to a diving museum, so you could indeed spend a full weekend here—conceivably a whole week if you also plan to hire a fishing charter or visit the offshore state parks. As with other parts of the Keys, you may encounter traffic congestion, crowded restaurants and attractions, and higher lodging rates during the peak tourist season from December to April, so plan accordingly.

When scheduling a trip to Islamorada, you might also want to consider factors like annual events, fishing seasons, and climate. For instance, while the hot, humid summer months can be less popular among tourists, those who favor snorkeling and scuba diving might appreciate the warmer waters. No matter when you visit, however, it's important to understand the risks of outdoor activities like kayaking and scuba diving, which can be dangerous without proper instruction and preparation.

For more information about Islamorada, consult the **Monroe County Tourist Development Council** (1201 White St., Ste. 102, Key West, 305/296-1552 or 800/648-5510, www.fla-keys.com, 9am-5pm Mon.-Fri.) and the **Islamorada Chamber of Commerce** (MM 87.1, 87100 Overseas Hwy., Islamorada, 305/664-4503 or 800/322-5397, www.islamoradachamber.com, 9am-5pm Mon.-Fri., 9am-4pm Sat., 9am-3pm Sun.).

Previous: sunrise at Cheeca Lodge Resort; fishing boat near Islamorada; Lorelei Restaurant & Cabana Bar on the water.

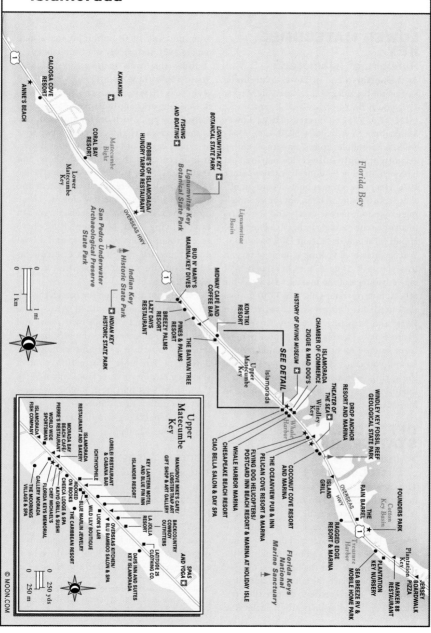

Islamorada

1

CALOOSA COVE RESORT

ANNE'S BEACH

KAYAKING

FISHING AND BOATING

LIGNUMVITAE KEY BOTANICAL STATE PARK

ROBBIE'S OF ISLAMORADA/ HUNGRY TARPON RESTAURANT

CORAL BAY RESORT

Lower Matecumbe Key

Matecumbe Bight

Lignumvitae Key Botanical State Park

OVERSEAS HWY

San Pedro Underwater Archaeological Preserve State Park

Lignumvitae Basin

Indian Key Historic State Park

INDIAN KEY HISTORIC STATE PARK

Florida Bay

BUD 'N' MARY'S MARINA/KEY DIVES

MIDWAY CAFE AND COFFEE BAR

LAZY DAYS RESTAURANT

BREEZY PALMS RESORT

PINES & PALMS RESORT

THE BANYAN TREE

KON TIKI RESORT

Upper Matecumbe Key

HISTORY OF DIVING MUSEUM

SEE DETAIL

Islamorada

ISLAMORADA CHAMBER OF COMMERCE

ZIGGIE & MAD DOG'S

THEATER OF THE SEA

Windley Key

Whale Harbor

DROP ANCHOR RESORT AND MARINA

WINDLEY KEY FOSSIL REEF GEOLOGICAL STATE PARK

Cotton Key Basin

CIAO BELLA SALON & DAY SPA

CHESAPEAKE BEACH RESORT

WHALE HARBOR MARINA

POSTCARD INN BEACH RESORT & MARINA AT HOLIDAY ISLE

FLYING DOG HELICOPTERS/

PELICAN COVE RESORT & MARINA

THE OCEANVIEW PUB & INN

COCONUT COVE RESORT AND MARINA

ISLAND GRILL

RAGGED EDGE RESORT & MARINA

THE RAIN BARREL

Florida Keys National Marine Sanctuary

Treasure Harbor

FOUNDERS PARK

SEA BREEZE RV & MOBILE HOME PARK

PLANTATION KEY NURSERY

MARKER 88 RESTAURANT

Plantation Key

JERSEY BOARDWALK

PLANTATION PIZZA

OVERSEAS HWY

0   1 mi
0   1 km

0   250 yds
0   250 m

Upper Matecumbe Key

ISLAMORADA FISH COMPANY

WORLD WIDE SPORTSMAN

PIERRE'S RESTAURANT

MORADA BAY BEACH CAFE

ISLAMORADA RESTAURANT AND BAKERY

LORELEI RESTAURANT & CABANA BAR

ICHTHYOPHILE

MANGROVE MIKE'S CAFE/ LOBSTER TRAP ART GIFT SHOP & ART GALLERY

KEY LANTERN MOTEL AND BLUE FIN INN

ISLANDER RESORT

THE MOORINGS VILLAGE & SPA

GALLERY MORADA

FLORIDA KEYS MEMORIAL

CHEF MICHAEL'S

KAIYO GRILL & SUSHI

CHEECA LODGE & SPA

ON BOOKS

HOOKED

THE CARIBBEAN RESORT

BLUE MARLIN JEWELRY

WILD LILY BOUTIQUE

LION'S LAIR

OVERSEAS KITCHEN/ BLU BAMBOO SALON & SPA

LA JOLLA RESORT

BACKCOUNTRY COWBOY OUTFITTERS

DAYS INN AND SUITES KEY ISLAMORADA

LATITUDE 25 CLOTHING CO.

SPAS AND YOGA

© MOON.COM

Sights

LOWER MATECUMBE KEY

Robbie's of Islamorada

At the northern end of Lower Matecumbe Key, on the bay side of U.S. 1 near Mile Marker 77.5, you'll find **Robbie's of Islamorada** (MM 77.5, 77522 Overseas Hwy., Lower Matecumbe Key, 305/664-8070 or 877/664-8498, www.robbies.com, 7am-sunset daily), a family-friendly full-service marina that has been offering outdoor distractions since 1976. Here you can rent boats, board an offshore sportfishing charter, opt for a snorkeling excursion, peruse crafts and souvenirs in an open-air market, and grab a bite in the Hungry Tarpon restaurant (305/664-0535). You can also feed visiting schools of tarpon from the dock ($1 pp, $3 per bucket of fish) or take advantage of the marina's status as the official tour operator (800/979-3370) for two remote islands: **Indian Key Historic State Park** and **Lignumvitae Key Botanical State Park.** The marina is typically open from sunrise to sunset year-round, which means you can expect later hours during the spring, summer, and fall months, following the daylight saving time change in mid-March.

OFFSHORE STATE PARKS

★ Indian Key Historic State Park

The earliest Upper Keys community is believed to have existed on this 11-acre island, which in 1830 became the site of John Jacob Housman's lucrative cargo-salvaging business. In 1836 it was designated the first county seat of Dade County, and in 1840 during the Second Seminole War the Seminole invaded the island, plundered the buildings, and allegedly killed several settlers, despite the presence of Fort Paulding on nearby Teatable Key.

From the early 1900s until it became a state park in 1971, Indian Key was uninhabited.

Today the lovely **Indian Key Historic State Park** (MM 78.5 OS U.S. 1, 77200 Overseas Hwy., Indian Key, www. floridastateparks.org/indiankey, 8am-sunset daily, $2.50 pp), which lies on the ocean side of the Overseas Highway, is only accessible by canoe, kayak, or boat, and it lures hikers, swimmers, sunbathers, bird-watchers, and anglers alike. The park offers an interpretive trail through a re-created street system and also features one of the few close-to-shore areas where snorkelers and scuba divers can explore living coral. Although visitors have access to an observation tower and a boat dock, there are no restrooms or picnic facilities on-site, and most facilities are not wheelchair-accessible.

Pets are not allowed on the island, though service animals are permitted. Also, if you head to the island via your own vessel and plan to dive or snorkel in the offshore waters, you must use a red-and-white diver-down flag. For more information, contact **Windley Key Fossil Reef Geological State Park** (MM 84.9 BS U.S. 1, 84900 Overseas Hwy., Windley Key, 305/664-2540, www. floridastateparks.org/windleykey, 9am-5pm Thurs.-Mon., $2.50 pp).

GETTING THERE

This park is only accessible by boat. You can rent a kayak or powerboat from **Robbie's of Islamorada** (MM 77.5, 77522 Overseas Hwy., Lower Matecumbe Key, 305/664-8070 or 877/664-8498, www.robbies.com, 7am-sunset daily), or opt for the most popular way of getting there, through Robbie's three-hour island heritage tour aboard the *Happy Cat*

1: view of Indian Key Historic State Park 2: brown pelicans waiting for fish at Robbie's of Islamorada marina

snorkeling catamaran (800/979-3370, www.robbies.com, 10am and 1:30pm daily, $36 adults, $29 children 6-12, free for children under 6). The tour includes transportation to and from Lignumvitae Key as well. The island is about 1,500 feet from Mile Marker 77; it takes about 20 minutes to paddle there at a very leisurely pace. Boaters can get there in about 2 minutes.

Make sure to take the time to get advice at Robbie's (or wherever you rent a boat from) about the surrounding water channels. This area has many extremely shallow flats that can damage both your boat and the ecosystem if you run aground. Kayaks and canoes can navigate the shallower flats easily, but a powered boat should stay in the deeper channels.

San Pedro Underwater Archaeological Preserve State Park

South of Indian Key lies **San Pedro Underwater Archaeological Preserve State Park** (www.floridastateparks.org/sanpedro, 8am-sunset daily, free), site of the *San Pedro*, a 287-ton Spanish ship that wrecked here during a hurricane on July 13, 1733. Discovered in 1960, the wreck site underwent major salvaging efforts over the subsequent decade, so today all that remains is a large pile of ballast stones. Later enhanced with seven replica cannons and an anchor, the site (which usually lies in 18 feet of water) now forms an artificial reef that is home to many tropical fish and is popular among snorkelers and scuba divers. Swimmers, kayakers, and boaters also favor this site. Listed in the National Register of Historic Places, San Pedro Underwater Archaeological Preserve State Park is also part of the Florida Keys National Marine Sanctuary Shipwreck Trail. For more information, contact **Windley Key Fossil Reef Geological State Park** (MM 84.9 BS U.S. 1, 84900 Overseas Hwy., Windley Key, 305/664-2540, www.floridastateparks.org/windleykey, 9am-5pm Thurs.-Mon., $2.50 pp).

GETTING THERE

The underwater archeological park is only accessible by boat. If you don't have a private vessel, you can rent a boat at one of the many boat rental companies on Islamorada. The park is approximately 1.25 nautical miles south of Indian Key, and the GPS coordinates are 24°51.802'N, 80°40.795'W. To prevent anchor damage, park officials ask that boaters tie up to the mooring buoys located at the site.

★ Lignumvitae Key Botanical State Park

Situated on the bay side of the Overseas Highway and only accessible by boat, canoe, or kayak, the wooded **Lignumvitae Key Botanical State Park** (MM 78.5 BS U.S. 1, 77200 Overseas Hwy., Lignumvitae Key, www.floridastateparks.org/lignumvitaekey, 9am-5pm Thurs.-Mon., $2.50 pp) features the kind of virgin tropical hardwood hammock that once thrived in the Upper Keys. Formerly known as Jenkinson Island, Lignumvitae (pronounced lig-num-VIE-tee, and meaning "tree of life") has been home to various individuals since at least the 1830s—including William J. Matheson, a wealthy Miami chemist who bought the island in 1919 and soon afterward built a caretaker's home, with a cistern for rainwater and a windmill for electricity. Today Matheson's former hideaway is now the park's visitors center.

You can take a one-hour, ranger-guided tour ($2 adults, free children 5 and under) amid the peaceful foliage or inside the Matheson house. The tours, which are offered twice daily (10am and 2pm) from Friday to Sunday, enable you to access trails through the preserve that would normally be off-limits to visitors.

Pets are not allowed in this remote park, though service animals are permitted. For more information, contact **Windley Key Fossil Reef Geological State Park** (MM 84.9 BS U.S. 1, 84900 Overseas Hwy., Windley Key, 305/664-2540, www.floridastateparks.org/windleykey, 9am-5pm Thurs.-Mon.).

Lignumvitae Key Christmas

Although the wooded **Lignumvitae Key Botanical State Park** (MM 78.5 BS U.S. 1, 77200 Overseas Hwy., Lignumvitae Key, www.floridastateparks.org/lignumvitaekey) is fun to explore all year long, visiting this island at Christmastime can be even more magical. On the first Saturday of December, the Lignumvitae Key Christmas is presented by the park staff and the Friends of the Islamorada Area State Parks for the benefit of the park. The event invites visitors to step back in time and experience the holiday traditions of the early 20th century. As part of this annual event, dulcimer players welcome arriving visitors, who can then take ranger-guided walking tours of the historic Matheson House, typically decorated for the holidays with tropical greenery, handmade ornaments, and other Keys-inspired decorations. Visitors can also take a guided tour of the nearby virgin hardwood hammock, enjoy free key limeade and homemade cookies, and paint holiday themes on sea beans, oyster shells, and sea grape leaves to create souvenir ornaments.

During the event, which usually runs from 9am to 3pm, guests can board the 43-foot *Happy Cat* catamaran at **Robbie's of Islamorada** (MM 77.5, 77522 Overseas Hwy., Lower Matecumbe Key, 305/664-8070 or 800/979-3370, www.robbies.com) to reach the island. Though it normally costs $2.50 per person to visit the park, the fee is slightly higher during this Christmas event— usually around $5 per adult, but it's free for children under 12. For more information, contact the **Windley Key Fossil Reef Geological State Park** (MM 84.9 BS U.S. 1, 84900 Overseas Hwy., Windley Key, 305/664-2540, www.floridastateparks.org/windleykey, 9am-5pm Thurs.-Mon., education center 8am-5pm Fri.-Sun.).

GETTING THERE

To reach the island, you can rent a kayak or powerboat from **Robbie's of Islamorada** (MM 77.5, 77522 Overseas Hwy., Lower Matecumbe Key, 305/664-8070 or 877/664-8498, www.robbies.com, 7am-sunset daily) or opt for a three-hour island heritage tour (800/979-3370, 9am daily, $37.50 adults, $20 children 6-12, free for children under 6) aboard the *Happy Cat* snorkeling catamaran, which includes transportation to and from both Lignumvitae Key and Indian Key. The island is one mile west of U.S. 1 at mile marker 78.5. It would take a paddler about 30 minutes to reach it at a leisurely pace. Boaters can get there in about 5 minutes.

You should be familiar with the water channels in the area before boating to the island because of the surrounding flats. Kayaks and canoes can often navigate through these flats, but if you're taking out a powerboat, you'll want to stay in the deeper channels. Kayaks can easily access the island by using the kayak ramp at the service dock.

UPPER MATECUMBE KEY
★ History of Diving Museum

Sea lovers will enjoy the interactive, educational **History of Diving Museum** (MM 82.9, 82990 Overseas Hwy., Upper Matecumbe Key, 305/664-9737, www.divingmuseum.org, 10am-5pm daily, $12 adults, $11 seniors and veterans, $6 children 5-11, free for children under 5 and active-duty U.S. military personnel), which sits on the bay side of Mile Marker 83 on Upper Matecumbe Key. Even non-divers might appreciate this well-designed attraction, which packs a lot of information and artifacts into a deceptively small space.

Following an orientation video, you'll be able to stroll amid a collection of diving paraphernalia, including diving machines, rare diving helmets, armored diving suits, vintage U.S. Navy diving gear, underwater photographs, old-fashioned scuba tanks, recovered coins, and other treasures relating to sea exploration. You'll even be able to test your ability to hold your breath, sit inside Halley's enormous diving bell, crank several hand-operated air pumps, view a reef aquarium from inside a diving helmet, and check out Captain Nemo's submarine and diving helmet from the Disney film 20,000 Leagues Under the Sea (1954).

Founded by Dr. Joseph A. Bauer Jr. and his wife, Dr. Sally E. Bauer, whose extensive personal collection forms the basis of these engrossing exhibits, the museum is intended to demonstrate "man's quest to explore under the sea" over the course of 4,000 years, from the ancient times of Gilgamesh to the modern days of recreational diving. Ask the museum staff about free monthly programs, which cover a range of topics from the 1733 Spanish galleon treasure fleet to life as a female Navy diver.

Florida Keys Memorial

While traveling across Upper Matecumbe Key, most people whiz right past the **Florida Keys Memorial** at Mile Marker 81.6 on the ocean side of U.S. 1. The memorial itself is fairly simple and nondescript, but still, if you have a moment, you ought to stop and take a look; it's free to do so. Dedicated in 1937 and now listed in the National Register of Historic Places, the memorial commemorates the fateful 1935 Labor Day Hurricane that took many lives, caused much property damage, and effectively destroyed the Overseas Railroad. The bronze plaque notes that the memorial is "dedicated to the memory of the civilians and war veterans whose lives were lost in the hurricane of September Second, 1935"—a sobering reminder of nature's power.

WINDLEY KEY

Windley Key Fossil Reef Geological State Park

Once two separate islands known as the Umbrella Keys, Windley Key is one of the highest islands in the Florida Keys archipelago. The Umbrella Keys were formed from Key Largo limestone (fossilized coral) over 125,000 years ago. In the mid-1800s,

the Russell family homesteaded the easterly Umbrella Key until it was sold to the Florida East Coast Railway in 1908. Soon afterward railroad workers filled in the gap between the two Umbrella Keys, forming the Windley Key of today. From 1908 until the completion of the Overseas Railroad in 1912, the three coral rock quarries on the eastern end of Windley Key were used to supply thousands of tons of limestone for the railbed and bridges that eventually stretched all the way to Key West.

Today the **Windley Key Fossil Reef Geological State Park** (MM 84.9 BS U.S. 1, 84900 Overseas Hwy., Windley Key, 305/664-2540, www.floridastateparks.org/windleykey, 9am-5pm Thurs.-Mon., education center 8am-5pm Thurs.-Mon., $2.50 pp, free for children under 6) invites visitors to walk along self-guided trails through three former quarries. Here you can view old mining equipment and walk along eight-foot-high quarry walls to see cross sections of the ancient coral. The Alison Fahrer Environmental Education Center features informative exhibits about the connection between the quarry complex and the ill-fated railroad, which came to an end with the Labor Day Hurricane of 1935. One-hour guided tours ($2 pp, free for children under 6) are available Friday-Sunday at 10am and 2pm, though reservations are suggested. Given the small size and limited nature of this park, it's best to visit when you can take full advantage of the education center and guided tours.

★ Theater of the Sea

Around Mile Marker 84.5 on Windley Key, you'll be hard-pressed to miss the enormous sign for **Theater of the Sea** (MM 84.7, 84721 Overseas Hwy., Windley Key, 305/664-2431, www.theaterofthesea.com, 9:30am-5pm daily, $39.95 ages 11 and over, $22.95 children 3-10, free for children under 3), the second-oldest marine mammal facility in the world. Established in 1946, this lush 17-acre animal park features entertaining dolphin, sea lion, and parrot shows every day of the year.

Such shows integrate lessons about anatomy, physiology, husbandry, natural history, and conservation into an informative, interactive, and often hilarious presentation. In addition to watching the varied shows, you can stroll amid habitats containing enormous sea turtles, alligators, tropical birds, reptiles, and other marine creatures—and perhaps catch a glimpse of a free-roaming iguana.

Some visitors choose to take a guided glass-bottom boat ride (11:30am, 2pm, and 4:30pm). Of course, many visitors come to Theater of the Sea to interact with the animals themselves. You can watch dolphins and sea lions paint colorful abstract pictures, learn the hand signals for natural behaviors like waving and kissing, and even swim with the resident dolphins, sea lions, and stingrays in the on-site lagoon.

The cost of admission includes access to the lagoon-side beach, the guided marinelife tour, the bottomless boat ride, snorkel gear, and the dolphin, sea lion, and parrot shows. Additional charges apply for special programs, such as swimming with the rays ($75 pp), meeting a sea lion or dolphin ($95 pp), swimming with a sea lion ($155 pp), wading with a dolphin ($190 pp), swimming with a dolphin ($199 pp), swimming with nurse sharks ($95 pp), meeting a sea turtle ($65 pp), and meeting an alligator ($65 pp). Reservations may be required for certain programs, and restrictions such as age and physical fitness may apply, so be sure to call ahead. Be aware, too, that the shows run continuously, so you can simply join the one in progress as soon as you arrive. Allow roughly three hours to experience everything except the adventure cruise and other special programs.

PLANTATION KEY

If you're driving to Islamorada from Key Largo, you'll first encounter **Plantation Key,** just west of Mile Marker 91 and across Tavernier Creek. Primarily a residential area that includes part of Tavernier, Plantation Key contains a handful of diversions, including several art galleries, the Tavernier Creek Marina, and **Founders Park** (MM 87, 87000 Overseas Hwy., Plantation Key, 305/853-1685, www.islamorada.fl.us, sunrise-sunset, $8 adults, $5 seniors 65 and over and children 3-17, free for children under 3 and residents), a 42-acre public park on the bay side of U.S. 1. Its many features include a large heated Olympic-style swimming pool and children's water park, a playground and skateboard park, an open-air amphitheater, a sandy beach, a dog park, and access to the Plantation Yacht Harbor Marina, which also offers a boat ramp (8am-6pm daily). In addition to family-friendly diversions like water-sports rentals, fitness and walking trails, tennis and basketball courts, and multiuse fields, Founders Park hosts events throughout the year, from the "Pops in the Park" concert series (Nov.-Apr.) to an annual Easter egg hunt. For a current schedule of events, contact the park directly. There's a fee for use of the pool and skate park (hours vary daily, $3 adults, $2 seniors 65 and over and children 3-17, free for children under 3).

Beaches and Recreation

BEACHES
Anne's Beach

On the ocean side of Lower Matecumbe Key is **Anne's Beach** (MM 73.5 OS U.S. 1, Lower Matecumbe Key, sunrise-sunset daily, free), a peaceful place to watch the sunrise or sunset, swim in the Atlantic Ocean, give kiteboarding a try, or spend some quiet time with your friends and loved ones. Dedicated to local environmentalist Anne Eaton, this pet-friendly beach features several covered picnic tables, plus a half-mile boardwalk that allows access to more secluded stretches of sand. Public restrooms and ample parking are also available.

★ FISHING AND BOATING

Anglers and boaters will find a treasure trove of options in the Islamorada area. Boasting one of the largest fishing fleets in Florida, it might just be, as residents claim, the "sportfishing capital of the world." Just consider all of the resorts that offer access to fishing charters and boat rentals, such as the **Ragged Edge Resort & Marina** (243 Treasure Harbor Rd., Plantation Key, 305/852-5389, www.ragged-edge.com) on Plantation Key and the slew of fishing-friendly resorts on Windley Key: **Smugglers Cove Resort & Marina** (MM 85.5, 85500 Overseas Hwy., Windley Key, 305/664-5564), the **Drop Anchor Resort and Marina** (MM 85 OS U.S. 1, 84959 Overseas Hwy., Windley Key, 305/664-4863, www.dropanchorresort.com), **Coconut Cove Resort and Marina** (MM 84.8, 84801 Overseas Hwy., Windley Key, 305/664-0123, www.coconutcove.net), **Pelican Cove Resort & Marina** (MM 84.4, 84457 Overseas Hwy., Windley Key, 305/664-4435, www.pelicancovehotel.com), and **Postcard Inn Beach Resort & Marina at Holiday Isle**

1: Founders Park **2:** Whale Harbor Marina **3:** Florida Keys Memorial for victims of a 1935 hurricane **4:** Anne's Beach

(MM 84, 84001 Overseas Hwy., Windley Key, 305/664-2321, www.holidayisle.com).

Farther south, on Upper Matecumbe Key, lies **Bud N' Mary's Marina** (MM 79.8, 79851 Overseas Hwy., Upper Matecumbe Key, 305/664-2461, www.budnmarys.com), which has been around since 1944 and now comprises more than 40 fishing captains and guides, making it home to the oldest and largest fishing fleet in the Florida Keys. Here anglers can find backcountry fishing expeditions ($450-500 per half day, $700-1,000 daily), offshore fishing charters ($650-2,000), and a 65-foot party fishing boat ($70 pp), the *Miss Islamorada,* plus a tackle and bait shop, boat storage, diving excursions, and an outdoor eatery. The many boats docked here include the 44-foot *Redfish* (305/360-1360, www.redfishsportfishing.com, hours and rates vary), operated by veteran Captain Merv Finch and featuring offshore trips in search of (depending on the season) mahimahi, sailfish, wahoo, snapper, grouper, marlin, tuna, permit, tilefish, amberjack, swordfish, and king mackerel.

You can also visit one of the non-resort marinas in the area, such as the **Tavernier Creek Marina** (MM 90.8, 90800 Overseas Hwy., Tavernier, 305/852-5854), which lies on the bay side of Plantation Key and boasts the largest dry-storage facility in the Florida Keys. On Upper Matecumbe Key are two more impressive fleets: one at the **Whale Harbor Marina** (MM 83.4, 83413 Overseas Hwy., Upper Matecumbe Key, 305/664-4511, ext. 201, www.whaleharbormarina.com, trips and rates vary) and the other at the **World Wide Sportsman Bayside Marina** (MM 81.5, 81576 Overseas Hwy., Upper Matecumbe Key, 305/664-4615, www.basspro.com, $450 half day, $600 full day). Many anglers head even farther south to **Robbie's of Islamorada** (MM 77.5, 77522 Overseas Hwy., Lower Matecumbe Key, 305/664-8070

Fishing Seasons

Fishing has been popular in the Keys since the early 20th century, when authors like Zane Grey and Ernest Hemingway explored these waters. Thanks to widely practiced catch-and-release efforts, fish are still plentiful. While fishing opportunities abound throughout the year, many anglers plan their trips around the region's varied fishing seasons.

You can choose from an assortment of fishing styles (flats, backcountry, light-tackle, deep-sea, wreck, reef, harbor, and bridge), but what you catch will depend on the time of year. Although most species are available year-round, some are only prevalent in certain months (and some are better for mounting than for eating). What you keep will be determined by species limits and seasonal restrictions, so be sure to consult local fishing guides beforehand. Also be advised that certain marine species, such as bonefish, are catch-and-release only, but others, including sturgeon, goliath grouper, and queen conch, are prohibited at all times. With that in mind, here are some of the more popular seasons:

- African pompano: year-round
- amberjack: August-May
- barracuda: year-round
- blackfin tuna: year-round
- black grouper: May-December
- blue marlin: March-October
- bonefish: April-December
- bonito: year-round
- cobia: November-April
- common snook: September-December
- hogfish: year-round
- king mackerel: December-August
- mahimahi: April-September
- permit: August-April
- redfish: year-round
- red grouper: May-December
- red snapper: June-July
- sailfish: October-August
- shark: year-round
- Spanish mackerel: year-round
- swordfish: year-round
- tarpon: year-round
- wahoo: year-round
- yellowfin tuna: year-round
- yellowtail snapper: year-round

or 877/664-8498, www.robbies.com, 7am-sunset daily), which offers an array of back-country, patch-reef, and offshore fishing opportunities (trips and rates vary). In addition, Robbie's provides boat rentals, including 18-foot Wagner skiffs ($195 per half day, $245 daily), 21- to 23-foot deck boats ($245 per half day, $295 daily), 18-foot Wagner center consoles ($195 half day, $245 full day), 24-foot Hurricane deck boats ($295 half day, $345 full day), and 21-foot center-console boats ($295 half day, $345 full day).

★ KAYAKING

While sportfishing is the most popular activity in Islamorada, kayakers also appreciate the bountiful waters surrounding this Village of Islands. After all, some attractions—such as Indian Key Historic State Park, San Pedro Underwater Archaeological Preserve State Park, and Lignumvitae Key Botanical State Park—are only accessible via kayak, canoe, or boat.

Even if you haven't lugged your own kayak with you, you're in luck. There are several kayaking outfitters in the region:

At **Backcountry Cowboy Outfitters** (MM 82.2, 82240 Overseas Hwy., Upper Matecumbe Key, 305/517-4177, www.backcountrycowboy.com, 9am-6pm Mon.-Sat., 10am-5pm Sun.) you can rent single or double kayaks for a half day ($50-65), a full day ($65-85), multiple days ($90-165), or an entire week ($165-195). Backcountry Cowboy also offers three different two-hour guided kayaking excursions: the backcountry nature tour ($45 adults, $22.50 children under 13), the sunset tour ($45 pp), and the Indian Key historical tour ($45 pp).

Based out of the local Days Inn, **A1A Watersports** (MM 85.9, 85970 Overseas Hwy., Upper Matecumbe Key, 305/664-8182, www.keyswatersports.com, 8am-5pm daily, $45-199) offers single and double kayaks for half-day, full-day, multiday, weekly, and monthly rentals, all of which include instruction, seat backs, paddles, life jackets, and a navigational chart. Local delivery and pickup is possible for multiday rentals. They also rent motorboats, pontoons, stand-up paddleboards, fishing gear, snorkeling equipment, and Jet Skis. A1A has several other locations in the Florida Keys, including the **La Siesta Resort and**

kayak rentals

Underwater Safety

Thousands of snorkelers and scuba divers flock to the Florida Keys every year. All underwater enthusiasts should take necessary precautions:

- Check weather conditions before venturing out; strong winds and rough seas can create unsafe conditions.

- If operating your own vessel, make sure you stay at least 300 feet from diver-down flags in open water and at least 100 feet from flags in rivers and inlets; if you cannot maintain such distance, slow down to an idle speed when passing other divers.

- Make sure you've had proper snorkeling and/or scuba-diving instruction.

- When in doubt about your abilities, don't hesitate to join a professional guide or tour.

- Always tell someone on land where you're planning to go and when you intend to return.

- If you plan to be in the water for a while, apply ample waterproof sunscreen or wear a shirt to avoid sunburn.

- Make sure your mask and flippers fit properly, and check that you have all necessary equipment, such as inflatable vests for snorkelers and weights and tanks for scuba divers.

- If you find it difficult to walk on the boat while wearing flippers, carry them into the water before putting them on.

- Never snorkel or dive without displaying a proper red-and-white diver-down flag on your vessel, and always remove said flag when all divers have returned to the boat.

- Always snorkel or dive with a buddy, and try to stay together.

- Plan your entry and exit points before jumping into the water.

- Swim into the current upon entering the water, and then ride the current back to your exit point.

- Don't touch any tempting sea creatures, as they may sting you.

- Look above the water every now and again to ensure that you haven't drifted too far away from the boat; try to stay within 300 feet of the diver-down flag when in open water and within 100 feet when in a river or inlet.

- If you have a diving emergency, dial 911 from your cell phone, or use a VHF radio to signal a "MAYDAY."

Marina (MM 80.2, 80241 Overseas Hwy., Tavernier, 305/664-2132) and **Casa Mar Village** (MM 90.7, 90775 Old Hwy., Fiesta Key, 305/434-5930).

Located at Robbie's of Islamorada, **Florida Keys Kayak** (MM 77.5, 77522 Overseas Hwy., Lower Matecumbe Key, 305/664-4878, www.kayakthefloridakeys.com, 9am-sunset daily) provides single and double kayaks ($40-55 per half day, $50-65 daily), stand-up paddleboards ($50 per half day), single and double Hobie pedal kayaks ($50-65 per half day, $60-75 daily), and canoes ($60 per half day). Free delivery is available to local resorts and residences, and earlier hours (such as sunrise) are possible with 24-hour notice. Florida Keys Kayak features three two-hour guided excursions: the backcountry tour ($45 pp), the sunset tour ($45 pp), and the Indian Key snorkeling tour ($45 pp).

North American diver-down flag

A helpful saying to remember is "Snorkel aware, dive with care!" For scuba divers, another helpful saying is "Dive ALIVE," with the letters in "ALIVE" standing for these tips:

- **Air:** Monitor your air supply; always surface with at least 500 PSI, and practice out-of-air procedures.

- **Lead Weights:** Wear only enough lead to achieve proper buoyancy, and know how to release your and your buddy's weight systems.

- **Inspection:** Inspect your gear before every dive trip, replace missing or worn gear, replace batteries in any electronics, and have regulators serviced annually.

- **Verification:** Verify your dive skills, and review your dive plan, signals, and lost-buddy procedures with your diving buddy.

- **Escape:** Always dive with surface-signaling devices. If you become entangled, remain calm and do what you can to free yourself. If you're lost on the surface, inflate your buoyancy compensation device (BCD), remain calm, maintain your position if possible, and try to attract others' attention.

For more safety tips, consult area diving operators or **Florida Keys National Marine Sanctuary** (305/852-7717 or 305/809-4700, www.floridakeys.noaa.gov).

DIVING AND SNORKELING

Whether you're a novice or an experienced underwater explorer, you should definitely reserve part of your trip for the waters east of Islamorada, an area filled with shallow coral reefs, curious wall formations, and shipwrecks. Through the **Conch Republic Divers** (Tavernier Creek Marina, MM 90.8, 90800 Overseas Hwy., Tavernier, 305/852-1655 or 800/274-3483, www.conchrepublicdivers. com) or the **Florida Keys Dive Center** (MM 90.45, 90451 Old Hwy., Tavernier, 305-852-4599 or 800/433-8946, www. floridakeysdivectr.com), both of which are based on the northern end of Plantation Key, you can take various diving classes, rent scuba-diving gear, and join twice-daily diving excursions (8am and 1pm, $84 pp) to explore many of the nearby underwater attractions.

Some of the sights you might encounter include the **Conch Wall,** noted for barrel sponges, rare pillar coral, and of course, conch; the **Davis Reef,** an ideal spot to observe green moray eels; the **Crocker Wall,** home to gorgonian coral and eagle rays; **Hens and Chickens,** an area that offers mounds of star and plate coral; and **Little Conch Reef,** adjacent to the wrecked *El Infante,* a Spanish galleon that sank in the 1733 hurricane. In these waters you'll also find the **Alligator Reef,** site of the shipwrecked USS *Alligator,* and the *Eagle,* a 287-foot freighter donated by the Eagle Tire Company as an artificial reef in 1985 and now teeming with countless fish.

Besides Conch Republic Divers and the Florida Keys Dive Center, several other diving operators are found in the area. These options, all of which provide instructional scuba-diving programs, include **Key Dives** (MM 79.8, 79851 Overseas Hwy., Upper Matecumbe Key, 305/664-2211 or 800/344-7352, www.keydives.com, 8am and 12:30pm daily, $85-350 pp), offering professional underwater tour guides for small groups of up to six divers. All three of the aforementioned dive operators also offer affordable daily snorkeling excursions ($35 pp).

You can also opt for a private two-hour snorkeling trip through the **Bay and Reef Company** (MM 81.8, 81801 Overseas Hwy., Upper Matecumbe Key, 305/393-1779 or 305/393-0994, www.bayandreef.com, $300 per group of 1-4 people, $100 hourly beyond the initial 2 hours, and $50 pp beyond the initial 4 people), which is based out of the Cheeca Lodge & Spa; or board the *Happy Cat* at **Robbie's of Islamorada** (MM 77.5, 77522 Overseas Hwy., Lower Matecumbe Key, 800/979-3370, www.robbies.com, 9am, noon, 3pm, and 6pm daily, $36 adults, $29 children 12 and under).

Snorkelers and scuba divers can also rent a kayak or boat from **Robbie's of Islamorada** (MM 77.5, 77522 Overseas Hwy., Lower Matecumbe Key, 305/664-8070 or 305/664-9814, www.robbies.com, 7am-sunset daily, rates vary) and head toward the **San Pedro Underwater Archaeological Preserve State Park** (305/664-2540, www.floridastateparks.org/sanpedro, 8am-sunset daily, free), south of Indian Key. Here underwater explorers will find the remains of the *San Pedro,* a 287-ton Spanish ship that wrecked during a 1733 hurricane. It now forms an artificial reef that is home to plenty of tropical fish.

HIKING AND BIKING

While Islamorada doesn't offer much for long-distance hikers, you can certainly enjoy a pleasant stroll through places like **Indian Key Historic State Park** (MM 78.5 OS U.S. 1, 77200 Overseas Hwy., Indian Key, www.floridastateparks.org/indiankey, 8am-sunset daily, $2.50 pp), which has an interpretive trail, and **Lignumvitae Key Botanical State Park** (MM 78.5 BS U.S. 1, 77200 Overseas Hwy., Lignumvitae Key, www.floridastateparks.org/lignumvitaekey, 9am-5pm Thurs.-Mon., $2.50 pp), featuring guided ranger walks ($2 pp). Both islands are only accessible by boat, and neither has a direct phone number. For more information about either island, contact **Windley Key Fossil Reef Geological State Park** (MM 84.9 BS U.S. 1, 84900 Overseas Hwy., Windley Key, 305/664-2540, www.floridastateparks.org/windleykey, 9am-5pm Thurs.-Mon., $2.50 pp).

Given Islamorada's sprawling nature and numerous bridges, bikers will undoubtedly appreciate the region even more—though care should always be taken on the Overseas Highway, and a proper helmet should be worn at all times. Between Mile Marker 91 and Mile Marker 71 you'll find 10 miles of actual biking paths, part of the **Florida Keys Overseas Heritage Trail.** Bicycles can be rented from **Backcountry Cowboy Outfitters** (82240 Overseas Hwy., Upper Matecumbe Key, 305/517-4177, www.backcountrycowboy.com, 10am-6pm Mon.-Sat., 10am-5pm Sun., $15-39 per half day, $20-55 daily, $35-80 for two days, $80-170 weekly), which offers one-speed, three-speed, hybrid, and road bicycles—plus helmets, combination locks, and copies of the state's bicycle laws. Local delivery is also available.

★ SPAS AND YOGA

Save for Key West, Islamorada is surely the best locale in the Florida Keys to seek pampering rejuvenation for the body, mind, and soul. The **Cheeca Lodge & Spa** (MM 81.8, 81801 Overseas Hwy., Upper Matecumbe Key, 305/664-4651, 800/327-2888, www.cheeca.com, spa 8am-8pm Mon.-Sat., 8:30am-5pm Sun., fitness center 6am-midnight daily, rates vary) features a 5,700-square-foot "oasis of relaxation and rejuvenation." Here resort guests age 18 or older can choose from an array of fitness classes, steam rooms, salt scrubs, skin and body treatments, refreshing facials, and massage therapies—in private treatment rooms, poolside cabanas, or an oceanside tiki hut.

Unlike the Cheeca Lodge, **The Moorings Village & Spa** (123 Beach Rd., Upper Matecumbe Key, 305/664-4708, www.themooringsvillage.com) allows nonguests to partake of the facials, massages, and beachside yoga lessons provided at the on-site **Island Body & Sol Spa** (305/664-3264, www.islandbodyandsolspa.com, 10am-5pm Mon.-Sat., by appointment daily, $50-190 per treatment).

Beyond such resort-type facilities, you'll find several day spas in the area, including the European-style **Ciao Bella Salon & Day Spa** (MM 82.9, 82913 Overseas Hwy., 305/664-4558, www.theislamoradaspa.com, 9am-5pm Tues.-Sat.). It specializes in hair care (rates vary), natural manicures and pedicures ($25-40 pp), clean waxing treatments (rates vary), and healing massages for men, women, and couples ($60-290 pp). Appointments are recommended, and a 24-hour cancellation notice is required.

Just down the road, the **Blu Bamboo Salon & Spa** (MM 82.2, 82205 Overseas Hwy., Upper Matecumbe Key, 305/664-9342, www.blubamboo.com, 9am-6pm Tues.-Sat.) encourages you to "indulge your senses and soothe your soul" with an array of facials ($60-150 pp), waxing services ($10-65 pp), hand treatments ($5-40 pp), foot treatments ($5-80 pp), and massages ($80-165 pp). Appointments are advisable, and the spa requires 24-hour notice to cancel.

Entertainment and Events

NIGHTLIFE

As with much of the Florida Keys region, most of the nightlife options in Islamorada consist of bars and restaurants that offer live entertainment or a chance to watch televised sports with like-minded folks. The **Island Grill** (MM 85.5, 85501 Overseas Hwy., Plantation Key, 305/664-8400, www.keysislandgrill.com, 7am-10pm Sun.-Thurs., 7am-11pm Fri.-Sat.) features nightly performers, from local funk and blues singers to magicians and rock 'n' roll bands. Just down the road, **The Oceanview Pub & Inn** (MM 84.5 BS U.S. 1, 84500 Overseas Hwy., Windley Key, 305/664-2556, www.theocean-view.com, 7am-2am daily) has the distinction of having secured the first liquor license in the Florida Keys. For well over

a decade, this long-standing watering hole has been co-owned by former NFL players Gary Dunn and Dennis Harrah, who have made extensive renovations but maintained the casual vibe that residents and local anglers have adored for years. Stop by for some cold beer and your favorite televised sporting event; if need be, you can always stay the night at the adjacent inn, which has an on-site pool.

The **Postcard Inn Beach Resort & Marina at Holiday Isle** (MM 84, 84001 Overseas Hwy., Windley Key, 305/664-2321, www.holidayisle.com) boasts several different bars, including the **Holiday Isle Tiki Bar** (noon-close Mon.-Fri., 11am-close Sat.-Sun.) where live rock and pop bands perform on the weekends (8pm-1am Fri.-Sat.). It also claims

Three Days Sailing the Upper Keys

DAY 1

Start your morning sail by cruising through Angel Fish Creek on the north side of Marathon, and then head to the Grecian Rock Reefs off the coast of John Pennekamp Coral Reef State Park. Spend midmorning to midafternoon snorkeling, swimming, diving, or just lounging on the boat and soaking up some rays. If you snorkel or dive, you'll be amazed by the beautiful coral formations and the remarkable variety of colorful tropical fish. At some point, make your way to the *Christ of the Abyss* statue, which welcomes you with open arms to the Upper Keys. In the afternoon, head to the anchorages at Rodriguez Key for the night, or sail to Key Largo and dock at the Marina Del Mar. If you choose to anchor at Rodriguez Key, consider taking your dinghy to the pier at Rock Harbor, where you'll find good seafood restaurants such as Island Grill and Ballyhoo's.

DAY 2

It would be easy to spend an entire week exploring the wrecks and reefs around John Pennekamp Coral Reef State Park. But if you only have three days to explore the area, you'll want to sail back into the protected Hawks Channel and sail southwest to Hens and Chickens Reef, off the coast of Windley Key. This is an excellent spot to snorkel. The inner reef is somewhat protected by the outer reef, so the water is usually fairly calm here, making it a relaxing place to snorkel; you are likely to find clear water and excellent views of the reef formations and fish. In the afternoon, pull anchor at the Hens and Chickens Reef and sail the 2.8 miles via Hawks Channel to Postcard Inn Beach Resort & Marina at Holiday Isle. Here you'll find one of the most beautiful beaches in all the Keys, snorkeling right off the beach, a relaxing swimming pool, and excellent restaurants within walking distance. The Holiday Isle Tiki Bar is nearby for drinks, and the Florida Keys Dolphin Research Center on Long Key is within a short drive if you want to spend a few minutes swimming with the dolphins there. Spend the evening at Holiday Isle.

DAY 3

Leave Holiday Isle early in the morning and sail the 6.2 miles via the Hawks Channel to Indian Key Historic State Park. At Indian Key you can tie up to one of the many moorings near the coast and spend the morning exploring the ruins of the settlement on the island or snorkeling and diving around one of the island's many reefs. You can also take a ranger-led or a self-guided tour of the island. In the early afternoon, set sail back the way you came, taking the Hawks Channel back to Rodriguez Key and Marina Del Mar.

to be the home of the first-ever rumrunner cocktail. Other on-site bars include Shulas 2 and Jaw's Raw Bar.

At the Lorelei Restaurant & Cabana Bar (MM 81.9, 81924 Overseas Hwy., Upper Matecumbe Key, 305/664-2692, www. loreleicabanabar.com, 7am-midnight daily) you can enjoy happy-hour specials every day (4pm-6pm) and live pop, rock, country, folk, or rhythm-and-blues every night (5pm-9pm)—not to mention waterfront dining, free wireless Internet access, and an ideal spot to watch a classic bayside sunset. A little farther

south, the Morada Bay Beach Café (MM 81.6, 81600 Overseas Hwy., Upper Matecumbe Key, 305/664-0604, www.moradabay.com, 11:30am-close daily) presents an array of activities, from happy hours to open jam sessions around a bonfire. Of course, the most popular event at Morada Bay is the well-publicized Full Moon Party (dates vary, $20-30 cover) each month. Essentially a large beach bash, this lively event consists of multiple bonfires, specialty drinks at the indoor and outdoor bars, a fireworks display, and a menagerie of live performers, including flamenco and jazz guitarists, electric reggae bands, stilt walkers, balloon artists, acrobats, and fire blowers.

THE ARTS

Islamorada offers a few options for those seeking an alternative to outdoor activities. Since 1978 **The Key Players** (305/453-0997, www.thekeyplayers.org, showtimes and ticket prices vary) has presented live comedies, dramas, and Broadway musicals in venues throughout the Upper Keys, such as the **Murray E. Nelson Government and Cultural Center** (MM 102, 102050 Overseas Hwy., Key Largo). The nonprofit community theater troupe typically produces four shows every year.

From November to April, the **Florida Keys Community Concert Band** (305/451-4530, www.keyscommunityconcertband.org), founded in 1992 by a small group of dedicated musicians, features "Pops in the Park," a free monthly concert series at the open-air Capital Bank Amphitheater in Founders Park, near Mile Marker 87 on Plantation Key. The performances are held on a Saturday afternoon (4pm-5pm) each month during the concert season, and attendees are welcome to bring chairs and blankets, as there are no seats on the lawn. Check the band's online schedule for specific dates.

Islamorada Community Entertainment (ICE, 305/395-6344, www.keysice. com, showtimes and ticket prices vary) helps to bring plays, operas, concerts, and film festivals to the Capital Bank Amphitheater in Founders Park and the Coral Shores High School Performing Arts Center (89901 Old Hwy., Tavernier) on Plantation Key. For information about other cultural events in the Upper Keys, consult the **Florida Keys Council of the Arts** (1100 Simonton St., Key West, 305/295-4369, www.keysarts.com).

If you're craving a bit of cinematic entertainment, head east of Plantation Key to what's technically the southern end of Key Largo, where you'll find the **Tavernier Cinema 5** (91298 Overseas Hwy., Tavernier,

305/853-7004, showtimes and ticket prices vary). It might not be the fanciest movie theater in southern Florida, but you'll be able to catch the latest flicks here.

FESTIVALS AND EVENTS

Besides numerous annual fishing competitions—such as the four-day **Islamorada Sailfish Tournament** (305/767-7875, www.islamoradasailfishtournament.com), which takes place in late November or early December—Islamorada hosts several popular events throughout the year. In mid-January art lovers spend the Saturday prior to Martin Luther King Jr. Day perusing the arts and crafts at **Art Under the Oaks** (305/360-8556, www.artundertheoaks.com, free admission), a long-standing community event that's taken place at the San Pedro Catholic Church (MM 89.5, 89500 Overseas Hwy., Tavernier, 305/852-5372, www.sanpedroparish.org) on Plantation Key for more than three decades. Beyond fine art and original crafts, you'll be treated to local musicians, specialty food booths, a raffle, and a self-guided nature walk. Parking is available on-site ($5) or at the nearby Coral Shores High School (89901 Old Hwy., Tavernier, free parking and shuttle service).

In late February, locals flock to Founders Park (MM 87, 87000 Overseas Hwy., Plantation Key) for the two-day **Gigantic Nautical Flea Market** (305/712-1818, www. giganticnauticalfleamarket.org, $5 adults), a popular event hosted by the Upper Keys Rotary Club. Here you'll find hundreds of vendors offering bargains on new and used boats, anchors and motors, other marine and dock equipment, diving and fishing gear, clothing, electronics, antiques, jewelry, sunglasses, and nautical arts and crafts. Each morning begins with a $5 all-you-can-eat pancake breakfast. Free parking as well as free shuttle service are available at Coral Shores High School on Plantation Key. While there's technically no admission fee to attend the flea market, the Rotary Club encourages all adults

to donate $5 to the event, which funds college scholarships for area youth.

Islamorada Community Entertainment (ICE, 305/395-6344, www.keysice.com, show dates and ticket prices vary) hosts several events throughout the year, including the annual **Bay Jam,** a premier one-day outdoor music festival that typically occurs in Founders Park in the spring, sometime between mid-March and early April. If you're here in early December, consider attending the full-day **Florida Keys Holiday Festival,** which takes place every year in Founders Park (MM 87, 87000 Overseas Hwy., Plantation Key) and features a holiday parade, an arts-and-crafts bazaar, and carolers singing around an enormous holiday tree. For more information about the holiday festival and other area events, contact the **Islamorada Chamber of Commerce** (MM 87, 87100 Overseas Hwy., Upper Matecumbe Key, 305/664-4503 or 800/322-5397, www.islamoradachamber.com, 9am-5pm Mon.-Fri., 9am-4pm Sat., 9am-3pm Sun.).

Shopping

Islamorada lures eager spenders with its assortment of art galleries, clothing boutiques, gift shops, and other unique emporiums.

ART GALLERIES

You'll find it hard to miss Betsy, the 30-foot-tall lobster sculpture that welcomes art lovers to **The Rain Barrel** (86700 Overseas Hwy., Plantation Key, 305/852-3084, www.keysdirectory.com/rainbarrel, 9am-5pm daily), a working village of artists situated in a lush, rustic setting on the bay side of U.S. 1. A popular stop for locals and tourists alike, this unusual complex features several eye-popping galleries, including the **Main Gallery** (305/852-3084), the barn-like structure marking the entrance; and the **Rain Barrel Sculpture Gallery** (305/852-8935, www.rainbarrelsculpture.com), situated at the rear of the property and offering bronze statues and stoneware items fashioned by gallery owners Dwayne and Cindy King. You'll also find **King's Treasure** (305/852-9797), which features Dwayne King's nautical-themed jewelry creations; the **Spectrum Studio of Glass Design** (800/488-7780), which presents Michael Robinson's delicate glass sculptures of tropical fish and other marinelife prevalent in the Florida Keys; and the **Nathan P. Hall Art Gallery** (305/852-3084), which showcases Hall's expressionistic landscapes of Maine, where he spends his summers, and the Keys, his winter home.

On Upper Matecumbe Key is the **Stacie Krupa Studio Gallery of Art** (MM 82.9, 82935 Overseas Hwy., Upper Matecumbe Key, 305/942-0614, www.staciekrupa.com, 10am-6pm daily), while the unique **Lobster Trap Art Gift Shop & Art Gallery** (82200 Overseas Hwy., Upper Matecumbe Key, 305/664-0001, www.lobstertrapart.com, 8am-6pm daily) features the vivid sea-inspired paintings of Nadine and Glenn Lahti and other local artists. Interestingly, all the wooden frames in this gallery have been crafted from old lobster traps that were once used throughout the Florida Keys; since 2003, the gallery has produced more than 10,000 of these handmade, customized frames. **Pasta Pantaleo Signature Gallery** (MM 81.6, 81599 Old Hwy., Upper Matecumbe Key, 305/619-9924, www.artbypasta.com, 10am-5pm daily) is home to the colorful paintings and wooden sculptures of marinelife artist Pasta Pantaleo.

For more information about these and other art galleries, consult the **Florida Keys**

1: Ciao Bella Salon & Day Spa **2:** Betsy, a giant lobster sculpture by Richard Blaze, greeting visitors at the Rain Barrel artists' village

Council of the Arts (1100 Simonton St., Key West, 305/295-4369, www.keysarts.com).

CLOTHING BOUTIQUES

Whether you're a serious clotheshorse or just in need of a casual outfit, you'll find a handful of clothing boutiques in Islamorada, including the Latitude 25 Clothing Co. (MM 82.7, 82748 Overseas Hwy., Upper Matecumbe Key, 305/664-4421 or 866/664-4421, www. floridakeysstore.net, 10am-5pm Mon.-Sat., 11am-4pm Sun.), which offers a wide array of women's and men's apparel, from Body Glove bikinis to Tommy Bahama shirts, plus shoes, accessories, sunscreen, pet toys, and tropical gifts. The Lion's Lair (MM 82.2, 82185 Overseas Hwy., Upper Matecumbe Key, 305/664-9921 or 800/220-1691, www. lionslairdesigns.com, 10am-6pm daily) features an assortment of ladies' swimwear and lingerie, and the one-of-a-kind Wild Lily Boutique (MM 81.9, 81933 Overseas Hwy., Upper Matecumbe Key, 305/741-7276, www. wildlilyboutique.com, 10am-6pm Mon.-Fri., 10am-4pm Sat., 10am-6pm Sun.) lures shoppers with its ever-changing collection of youthful apparel, creative jewelry, and island-style accessories.

GIFT AND BOOK SHOPS

For those who hope to bring a special souvenir home with them, Islamorada doesn't disappoint. You'll find a wide array of emporiums in the Village of Islands, all of which commemorate a particular aspect of this unique region. The Plantation Key Nursery (MM 88 OS U.S. 1, 87971 Overseas Hwy., Plantation Key, 305/852-9190, 9am-5pm daily) offers native plants and colorful accessories for garden

lovers, while Blue Marlin Jewelry (MM 81.5, 81549 Old Hwy., Upper Matecumbe Key, 305/664-8004 or 888/826-4424, www. bluemarlinjewelry.com, 9:30am-5:30pm Mon.-Sat., 11am-5pm Sun.) features nautical-inspired jewelry, from swordfish pendants to earrings made of salvaged treasure coins.

Hooked on Books (MM 81.9, 81909 Overseas Hwy., Upper Matecumbe Key, 305/517-2602, www.hookedon booksfloridakeys.com, 10am-5:30pm daily) provides a wealth of Florida-related selections, including regional travel guides, novels by Florida-based writers, and books about Florida Keys history, cuisine, activities, and wildlife.

On the bay side of the highway, the two-story Bass Pro Shops (MM 81.5, 81576 Overseas Hwy., Upper Matecumbe Key, 305/664-4615, www.basspro.com, 9am-9pm Mon.-Sat., 9am-7pm Sun.) looms large in a sprawling complex that includes the Bayside Marina and the Islamorada Fish Company. Inside this vast, well-designed store, you'll find casual clothes and shoes, inshore and offshore fishing gear, and souvenirs. You can peruse the displayed memorabilia, mounted fish, and engrossing aquariums; visit an elegant art gallery; step aboard the *Pilar,* the sister ship to Ernest Hemingway's famous fishing boat; and relax on the balcony of the Zane Grey Long Key Lounge. For something a bit more intimate, head to The Banyan Tree (81197 Overseas Hwy., Upper Matecumbe Key, 305/664-3433, www.banyantreegarden. com, 10am-5pm Mon.-Sat.), which features a plethora of antiques, linens, housewares, ceramics, home furnishings, garden fixtures, and exotic plants and flowers.

Food

PLANTATION KEY
American

Overlooking Florida Bay, the Marker 88 Restaurant (MM 88, 88000 Overseas Hwy., Plantation Key, 305/852-9315, www.marker88. info, 11am-10pm daily, $11-36) is a wonderful place to relax and relish dishes like cheeseburgers and broiled Florida lobster. Dine indoors or sit outside to enjoy a beautiful view of the ocean. Just across the road, you'll encounter the M.E.A.T. Eatery & Tap Room (88005 Overseas Hwy., Plantation Key, 305/852-3833, www.meateatery.com, 11am-9pm Sun.-Thurs., 11am-10pm Fri.-Sat.), a casual, friendly joint that serves all-American burgers, hot dogs, sausages, pulled pork sandwiches, and other treats, such as lobster mac-and-cheese, truffled bistro fries, homemade pork rinds, and Wisconsin beer cheese soup. The Tap Room also offers microbrewed sodas, organic wines, and specialty beers.

Italian

For fine Italian dining, visit the Old Tavernier Restaurant (MM 90.3, 90311 Overseas Hwy., Tavernier, 305/852-6012, www.oldtavernier.com, 4pm-10pm Sun.-Thurs., 4pm-11pm Fri. and Sat., $16-46) on Plantation Key, which provides both indoor and outdoor seating. Although the portions here aren't enormous, the quality is top-notch, especially if you enjoy sampling inspired dishes like scallops de Provence. If you have a hankering for more basic Italian cuisine, try Jersey Boardwalk Pizza (20 High Point Rd., Plantation Key, 305/853-3800, www.jerseyboardwalkpizza.com, 11am-9pm Sun.-Thurs., 11am-10pm Fri.-Sat., $4-17) for tasty pizzas, subs, salads, and pasta. If you'd prefer to stay in your hotel, Boardwalk will deliver to any location in Islamorada.

WINDLEY KEY
Seafood

Given Islamorada's focus on fishing and boating, the prevalence of seafood restaurants should be less than surprising. Seafood lovers should head first to the Island Grill (MM 85.5, 85501 Overseas Hwy., Windley Key, 305/664-8400, www.keysislandgrill.com, 7am-10pm Sun.-Thurs., 7am-11pm Fri.-Sat., $11-33), which features fried seafood platters, tuna nachos, peel-and-eat shrimp, a variety of sandwiches and salads, and lobster mac-and-cheese. Come for dinner, and you'll often be treated to live music from one of the local bands that perform here nightly.

American

A fun-loving spot is the Hog Heaven Sports Bar & Grill (MM 85.3, 85361 Overseas Hwy., Windley Key, 305/664-9669, www. hogheavensportsbar.com, 11am-3:30am daily, $7-19). Situated just opposite Windley Key Fossil Reef Geological State Park, this late-night joint features happy-hour specials, beachfront dining, and a range of vittles, from tuna melts to barbecue rib platters.

UPPER MATECUMBE KEY
Seafood

In the Whale Harbor Restaurants and Marina complex (MM 83.4, 83413 Overseas Hwy., Upper Matecumbe Key, www. whaleharborinn.com) on Upper Matecumbe Key, you'll find Wahoo's Bar & Grill (305/664-9888, www.wahoosbarandgrill. com, 11am-10pm daily, $12-26), an ideal spot to enjoy fresh seafood and waterfront views.

Mangrove Mike's Cafe (MM 82.2, 82200 Overseas Hwy., Upper Matecumbe Key, 305/664-8022, www.mangrovemikes.com, 6am-2pm daily, $6-22) offers more than just a meal. With breakfast and lunch you might also receive a history lesson about the Conchs. Still, the food is paramount here. Many locals believe Mike's has one of the best breakfast menus in the Keys. Among the most popular dishes is the Mangrove Oscar, a toasted English muffin with sautéed spinach, poached eggs, and your choice of blue crab, grilled shrimp, or grilled mahimahi, covered in a béarnaise sauce.

Occupying the building that once housed the well-regarded Chanticleer South, ★ **Chef Michael's** (MM 81.6, 81671 Overseas Hwy., Upper Matecumbe Key, 305/664-0640, www. foodtotalkabout.com, 5pm-10pm Mon.-Sat., 10am-2pm and 5pm-10pm Sun., $7-40) has quickly developed a reputation for fresh, top-quality seafood. The catch-of-the-day selection here may include hogfish, tuna, mahimahi, mangrove snapper, and swordfish, just to name a handful of the varieties available in the Florida Keys. Appropriately, the walls here are decorated with colorful, fish-focused art, and whether you eat in the dining room or sit on the shaded patio, you'll be treated to cloth napkins and white linen tablecloths, offering a small touch of class in this airy, island-style restaurant. Beyond its signature seafood dishes, such as broiled twin lobster tails in a coconut curry sauce, the menu offers options for meat lovers, such as grilled filet mignon with crispy fried spinach and "crazy taters." If possible, save room for dessert, which has ranged from seven-layer carrot cake to key lime pie.

While they may share the same beach, the ★ **Morada Bay Beach Café** (MM 81.6, 81600 Overseas Hwy., Upper Matecumbe Key, 305/664-0604, www.moradabay-restaurant.com, 11:30am-10pm daily, $11-33) and ★ **Pierre's Restaurant** (MM 81.6, 81600 Overseas Hwy., Upper Matecumbe Key, 305/664-3225, www.moradabay.com/pierres, 5pm-10pm Sun.-Thurs., 5pm-11pm Fri.-Sat., $34-40) offer far different dining experiences. With several colorful tables set upon the sand—in addition to its indoor and patio seating, of course—Morada Bay takes full advantage of its laid-back beachside setting.

Although this breezy eatery does many dishes well, from the island-style conch chowder to fresh salads and sandwiches, a highlight is the whole fried snapper served with cilantro rice. If you're not hungry enough for an entrée, try the tapas menu, which includes dishes like mahimahi fish tacos and crab cakes. The bar is open later than the dining areas, and if you're here at the right time, be sure to stick around for the Friday-night jam sessions and monthly Full Moon Parties.

Housed within a picturesque French colonial-style mansion, Pierre's provides one of the best fine-dining experiences in the Keys. With an interior that blends sailing motifs with exotic Moroccan-themed decor (which even pervades the restrooms), the 1st-floor lounge and 2nd-floor dining area are at once comfortable and elegant. Your meal will be especially memorable on the candlelit balcony that overlooks Florida Bay and the beach below, which is often lined with tiki torches. Pierre's features a small but eclectic menu, the star of which is the seafood curry served with half a lobster tail. Reservations are recommended here, though the dress code is decidedly casual. The wine list is on the pricey side.

The World Wide Sportsman complex (now part of the Bass Pro Shops chain) features the waterfront **Islamorada Fish Company** (MM 81.5, 81532 Overseas Hwy., Upper Matecumbe Key, 305/664-9271, www.fishcompany.com, 11am-10pm daily, $9-21). With 175 outdoor seats overlooking the beach, this exceptional eatery provides the perfect spot to watch the sunset or host a party. Serving classic Florida Keys cuisine, the Fish Company excels with its fried baskets and grilled platters.

For lighter fare, consider the adjacent Bass Pro Shops, which features the **Zane Grey Long Key Lounge** (MM 81.5, 81576 Overseas Hwy., Upper Matecumbe Key, 305/517-2190, www.basspro.com, 11am-10pm daily, $10-16) on its upper level. After returning from a long day of fishing, you can relax here on the open-air balcony that overlooks the marina, have a cocktail, and sample seafood treats like coconut shrimp and lobster salad.

Zane Grey: Author and Angler

While Ernest Hemingway is undoubtedly the most famous novelist to be linked to the Florida Keys, he is most certainly not the only one. As evidenced by places like the **Zane Grey Long Key Lounge** (MM 81.5, 81532 Overseas Hwy., Upper Matecumbe Key, 305/664-9271, www.basspro.com) in Islamorada's World Wide Sportsman complex, it's apparent that American novelist Zane Grey was also part of this archipelago's colorful history.

Born Pearl Zane Grey in 1872 in Zanesville, Ohio, Grey wrote his first novel in 1903. He discovered the Florida Keys in the early 1900s, when he began fishing the local waters of Long Key, Duck Key, and Grassy Key. In 1910 he stayed at the Long Key Fishing Camp, a luxurious fishing resort built in 1906 by Henry Flagler's East Coast Hotel Company on the ocean side of Long Key. Featuring a large wooden lodge, a store, post office, railroad station, roughly 30 small cottages, and a tunnel beneath the roadbed connecting the camp with the bayside docks, the resort attracted famous and wealthy sportfishing enthusiasts such as Andrew Mellon, William Hearst, Herbert Hoover, Franklin D. Roosevelt, and of course, Zane Grey, who became the Long Key Fishing Club's first president in 1917.

By the 1920s, Gray was earning half a million dollars per year from his writing career, and he owned several homes in California, fishing camps in Oregon and New Zealand, and a hunting lodge in Arizona. Although he traveled throughout the world, from California's Santa Catalina Island to Mexico to Tahiti, he always returned to Long Key, where he favored not only the marvelous fishing but also the quietude, which allowed him to write such Western classics as *Wild Horse Mesa* (1928) and *Code of the West* (1934).

Though Grey was best known for his novels about the American West, some fans still prefer his real-life fishing adventures, including *Tales of Fishes* (1919), in which he wrote about light-tackle fishing for sailfish and kingfish near Long Key and the surrounding islands, and *The Bonefish Brigade* (1922), in which he described his companions at the Long Key Fishing Camp and their obsessive quest for the elusive bonefish. In fact, such pioneering accounts helped to lure more wealthy sportfishing fans to the region at a time when most local residents were using spears and harpoons to snag their supper from the passes between the keys.

To reach the Long Key Fishing Camp, Grey and his fellow anglers would travel on the Key West Extension of the Florida East Coast Railway. While staying at the camp, he would dine on such delicacies as stone crab, grouper chowder, conch fritters, broiled king mackerel, coconut pudding, and key lime pie—cuisine that's still popular today. In fact, Grey loved the camp so much that after the terrible Labor Day Hurricane of 1935 destroyed the lodge, the buildings, and roughly 30 miles of Henry Flagler's railroad tracks, he honored the vacation spot in the foreword of a saltwater fishing book: "It is sad to think that Long Key, doomed by a hurricane, is gone forever," he wrote. "But the memory of that long white winding lonely shore of coral sand, and the green reef, and the blue Gulf Stream will live in memory, and in such fine books as this."

Four years after the storm that destroyed the Long Key Fishing Camp, Grey passed away in Altadena, California, having sold more than 27 million copies of his novels and nonfiction books. Since then that number has risen dramatically, and more than 110 movies have been made from his stories, including a silent D. W. Griffith short called *Fighting Blood* (1911) as well as the most recent version of *Riders of the Purple Sage* (1996), which starred Ed Harris and Amy Madigan. Although Grey's beloved Long Key Fishing Camp was eventually replaced by a state park, sportfishing is still popular in the Upper and Middle Keys—for the rich and the not-so-rich alike.

The **Lazy Days Restaurant** (MM 79.8, 79867 Overseas Hwy., Upper Matecumbe Key, 305/664-5256, www.lazydaysrestaurant.com, 11am-10pm Sun.-Thurs., 11am-11pm Fri.-Sat., $6-25), as the name suggests, provides a relaxing oceanfront dining experience where you can relish a fried oyster sandwich for lunch or jumbo stuffed shrimp for dinner.

American

Ziggie & Mad Dog's (MM 83, 83000 Overseas Hwy., Upper Matecumbe Key,

305/664-3391, www.ziggieandmaddogs.com, 5:30pm-10pm Mon.-Thurs., 5:30pm-11pm Fri.-Sat., $16-42) serves a variety of soups, salads, seafood dishes, steaks, and chops. One of several favorite dishes is the Thai coconut chicken.

For tasty, inexpensive breakfast, lunch, or dinner, try the **Lorelei Restaurant & Cabana Bar** (MM 81.9, 81924 Overseas Hwy., Upper Matecumbe Key, 305/664-2692, www.loreleicabanabar.com, 7am-midnight daily, $4-23). Between three-egg omelets, spinach salads, cracked conch sandwiches, and baby back ribs, there's surely something for everyone.

If you're staying at the exclusive Cheeca Lodge & Spa or looking for a fine-dining alternative, consider **Atlantic's Edge** (MM 81.8, 81801 Overseas Hwy., Upper Matecumbe Key, 305/517-4447, www.cheeca. com, 7am-10pm daily, $28-45). With indoor and outdoor seating—most of which offers remarkable ocean views—it can be a pleasant place for the discerning gourmand, especially if you don't mind the slightly elevated prices on both the menu and the wine list. Specialties include the black Angus filet mignon and the whole local snapper.

Open for breakfast and lunch, the **Islamorada Restaurant and Bakery** (MM 81.6, 81620 Overseas Hwy., Upper Matecumbe Key, 305/664-8363, www.bobsbunz.com, 6am-2pm daily, $2-8) is one of those places that locals would prefer to keep secret. Although the popular eatery offers a hundred different breakfast and lunch items, most people come for Bob's Bunz. Taste one, and you too will be hooked.

For excellent coffee, breakfast selections, and vegetarian dishes, make a trip to the **Midway Café and Coffee Bar** (MM 80.5, 80499 Overseas Hwy., Upper Matecumbe Key, 305/664-2622, 7am-3pm Mon.-Sat., 7am-2pm Sun., $5-14), which is equally worthwhile.

Greek

Craving some excellent Greek cuisine? Stop by the **Overseas Kitchen** (MM 82.2, 82205 Overseas Hwy., Upper Matecumbe Key, 305/664-0848, 11am-9pm Mon.-Fri., $4-17), where you'll be treated to inexpensive Mediterranean salads, hummus wraps, pita sandwiches, and heftier dishes such as the Greek-style rack of lamb. For those in a hurry, the café also offers carryout service and free delivery between Mile Marker 74 and Mile Marker 90.

Asian

The **Kaiyo Grill & Sushi** (MM 81.7, 81701 Overseas Hwy., Upper Matecumbe Key, 305/664-5556, www.kaiyokeys.com, 5pm-10pm Tues.-Sat., $13-36) considers itself a Florida-inspired Asian cuisine restaurant. Besides sushi, Kaiyo offers dinner entrées like seared scallops with bacon and caramelized shallots. Try the white chocolate macadamia pie for dessert.

LOWER MATECUMBE KEY

Seafood

Although open for both breakfast and lunch, the **Hungry Tarpon Restaurant** (MM 77.5, 77522 Overseas Hwy., Lower Matecumbe Key, 305/664-0535, www.hungrytarpon.com, 6:30am-9pm daily, $12-27) lures even more diners, especially locals, for the dinner menu. Based at Robbie's of Islamorada, the Tarpon serves favorites like pan-seared local snapper served with snap peas and green papaya slaw, or the broiled spiny lobster tail served with creamy mashed potatoes and charred asparagus with béarnaise sauce. Come down for Robbie's famous tarpon feedings and stay to feed yourself.

1: Morada Bay Beach Café **2:** Postcard Inn Beach Resort & Marina at Holiday Isle **3:** Pierre's Restaurant **4:** fishing pier at sunrise at the Cheeca Lodge & Spa

Accommodations

UNDER $100

Situated on a large grassy property alongside the Atlantic Ocean, the Ragged Edge Resort & Marina (243 Treasure Harbor Dr., Plantation Key, 305/852-5389, www.raggededge.com, $79-259 d) offers standard motel rooms with small refrigerators, efficiencies with kitchenettes, large studios with full kitchens and balconies or screened porches, and a deluxe two-bedroom suite with two bathrooms, a full kitchen, a balcony, and a large family room. Anglers will especially like this resort, which offers access to a full-service marina and a fishing pier. Clang the cowbell when you arrive and the manager will be with you shortly.

The La Jolla Resort (MM 82.2, 82216 Overseas Hwy., Upper Matecumbe Key, 305/664-9213 or 888/664-9213, www.lajollaresort.com, $99-399 d) provides both garden-facing rooms and bayfront rooms. Some offer only basic amenities while others sport well-equipped kitchens and porches with hammocks and barbecue grills. Free wireless Internet access is available throughout the property.

If you're looking for basic lodgings at an affordable price, consider the Sunset Inn (MM 82.2, 82200 Overseas Hwy., Upper Matecumbe Key, 305/664-3454, www.sunsetinnkeys.com, $60-80 d), which offers rooms with either one king-size bed or two double beds, plus efficiencies with full kitchens. Every room has cable television and small refrigerators. When not exploring Islamorada, take a dip in the on-site freshwater pool.

The Key Lantern Motel and Blue Fin Inn (MM 82.1, 82150 Overseas Hwy., Upper Matecumbe Key, 305/664-4572, www.keylantern.com, $60-90 d) offers perhaps the cheapest accommodations in the entire Florida Keys archipelago. Here you'll find basic rooms with kitchenettes and free wireless Internet access.

More difficult to categorize—at least where cost is concerned—is the Pines & Palms Resort (MM 80.4, 80401 Overseas Hwy., Upper Matecumbe Key, 800/624-0964, www.pinesandpalms.com, rooms and suites $99-299 d, cottages $119-499, houses and villas $399-629), which encompasses a variety of accommodations ranging from a budget-priced efficiency with a queen-size bed to an enormous three-bedroom villa featuring two king-size beds and a sofa bed. All rentals come with well-equipped kitchens and free wireless Internet access. The property also includes an oceanfront freshwater pool, a free boat ramp, and dockage at no extra charge.

$100-200

The Coconut Cove Resort and Marina (MM 84.8, 84801 Overseas Hwy., Windley Key, 305/664-0123, www.coconutcove.net, $105-285 d) presents three types of accommodations: the Captain's Cottages, each of which includes a single bed, a queen-size bed, and a kitchen; the General Quarters, which also boast luxurious hot tubs; and the Admiral's Accommodations, each containing two queen-size beds, a queen-size sleeper sofa, and a kitchen. In addition, the resort's friendly staff can help you arrange any kind of fishing excursion in the area.

The Drop Anchor Resort and Marina (MM 84.9, 84959 Overseas Hwy., Windley Key, 305/664-4863 or 888/664-4863, www.dropanchorresort.com, $140-350 d) on Windley Key has 18 individualized rooms, ranging from basic lodgings with a mini fridge and a coffeemaker to a two-bedroom suite with a full kitchen, living room, and dining area. This oceanfront hideaway also offers a nice private beach, a heated freshwater pool, a boat launch, and bulkhead docking.

The spacious ★ Postcard Inn Beach Resort & Marina at Holiday Isle (MM 84, 84001 Overseas Hwy., Windley Key,

305/664-2321 or 800/327-7070, www. holidayisle.com, $179-229 d) features a range of accommodations, from standard rooms with queen-size beds to oceanfront suites with kitchenettes. In this laid-back, palm-studded setting, guests can easily while away their vacation, relaxing by the pool or sunning themselves on the beach. If you have a little more energy, be sure to take advantage of the available personal watercraft rentals, sportfishing charters, scuba-diving trips, and snorkeling excursions. Pets up to 45 pounds are allowed with a small nonrefundable deposit. The resort also includes the on-site Italian restaurant, the Ciao Hound, and several tropical bars, including the multilevel Rumrunners, reminiscent of the Swiss Family Robinson's island home.

Formerly the Days Inn and Suites, the **Hadley House Resort** (MM 82.7, 82749 Overseas Hwy., Upper Matecumbe Key, 305/664-3681, www.hadleyhouseresort.com, rooms $120-250 d, suites $179-359) houses an array of accommodations, from courtyard efficiencies with two double beds and a kitchenette to a two-bedroom, 2,000-square-foot oceanfront suite ($379-529 daily) with two bathrooms and a full kitchen. The property also features a boat ramp, boat dockage for vessels up to 21 feet, personal watercraft and boat rentals, and an oceanside tiki bar.

The first thing you'll notice as you arrive at the **Kon Tiki Resort** (MM 81.2, 81200 Overseas Hwy., Upper Matecumbe Key, 305/664-4702, www.kontiki-resort.com, rooms $129-285 d, villas and houses $298-427) is the lush tropical landscape, featuring tempting hammocks, a barbecue grill and picnic area, and a heated freshwater pool alongside a private lagoon. Guests can dock and launch their boats on-site, and the 27 uniquely decorated rooms and villas provide enough options and amenities (from cable television to screened porches) to suit any vacationer.

Avid anglers can certainly plan a memorable fishing trip at **Bud N' Mary's Fishing Marina** (MM 79.8, 79851 Overseas Hwy.,

Upper Matecumbe Key, 305/664-2461 or 800/742-7945, www.budnmarys.com, $205-215 d), where in addition to lodgings you'll find a spacious marina housing a fleet of more than 40 fishing boats, plus a tackle shop and outdoor eatery. Beyond comfortable, standard rooms, the complex offers a penthouse with a full kitchen ($400 daily) and a three-bedroom beach house ($475 daily) with a full kitchen, a backyard, and access to a dock. In addition, Bud N' Mary's provides a houseboat rental with a queen-size bed and a small kitchenette.

The family-friendly **Breezy Palms Resort** (MM 80, 80015 Overseas Hwy., Upper Matecumbe Key, 305/664-2361 or 877/412-7339, www.breezypalms.com, $204-325 d) is a terrific home base for your Florida Keys adventures. Offering boat rentals and dockage, the resort can easily assist you in arranging your next fishing excursion. The accommodations range from a standard motel room with one bedroom, one bath, and a small refrigerator to a two-bedroom suite with king-size and queen-size beds, a sofa sleeper, a full kitchen, and a dining room.

Lined with hibiscus and bougainvillea, the **Coral Bay Resort** (MM 75.7, 75690 Overseas Hwy., Lower Matecumbe Key, 305/664-5568, www.coralbayresort.com, rooms $129-209 d, one-bedroom apartments $149-219, two-bedroom apartments $210-325, cottages $220-325) features everything from a standard bedroom with a small refrigerator to a comfortable cottage with four double beds, two bathrooms, and a well-equipped kitchen. Each unit includes cable television, as well as a cozy patio or covered porch.

Situated on a 10-acre estate, the **Caloosa Cove Resort** (MM 73.8, 73801 Overseas Hwy., Lower Matecumbe Key, 305/664-8811, www.caloosacove.com, $175-275 d) houses 30 rooms, including luxury efficiencies and one-bedroom suites, all with kitchen areas and private balconies. In addition, the resort features a full-service marina, a bait and tackle shop, boat rentals, tennis courts, a heated freshwater pool, and a large sandy beach.

OVER $200

Islamorada is home to some of the most up-scale, exclusive resorts in the entire Florida Keys archipelago.

The **Pelican Cove Resort & Marina** (MM 84.4, 84457 Overseas Hwy., Windley Key, 305/664-4435 or 800/445-4690, www.pelicancovehotel.com, $199-289 d) offers standard hotel rooms with mini refrigerators and private balconies, as well as efficiencies with full kitchens, plus a luxury suite ($339-399 daily). The entire resort features free wireless Internet access, and other amenities include a tennis court, an oceanfront hot tub, a freshwater pool, water-sports equipment, and an on-site restaurant, Wild and Lime.

The tranquil **Chesapeake Beach Resort** (MM 83.4, 83409 Overseas Hwy., Upper Matecumbe Key, 305/664-4662 or 800/338-3395, www.chesapeake-resort.com, rooms $179-340 d, villas $188-450) on Upper Matecumbe Key provides a quiet place to relax and replenish. This luxurious, well-landscaped property features a variety of accommodations, from tastefully furnished hotel rooms with garden views to premium ocean villa suites. In addition to the 6.5-acre tropical garden, the resort offers two heated oceanfront pools, a hot-water spa, tennis and shuffleboard courts, and a tiki-style observation deck, plus the ubiquitous kayaks, lounge chairs, and hammocks.

Situated on 25 lush acres, the **Islander Resort** (MM 82.1, 82100 Overseas Hwy., Upper Matecumbe Key, 305/664-2031, www.guyharveyoutpostislamorada.com, $260-400 d) provides full kitchens, screened lanais, free Internet access, and free continental breakfasts daily. Three lodging types are available here: courtyard rooms with a lanai and one double bed, ocean-view rooms with two double beds, and poolside rooms with a lanai and two double beds. The resort also features a lanai courtyard room where pets are allowed for a nonrefundable fee. Other amenities here include two heated pools, a hot tub, Tides Beachside Bar and Grill, and 1,300 feet of sandy beach, with a shallow snorkeling area.

If you're looking for all the comforts of a well-appointed oceanfront home, look no farther than **The Caribbean Resort** (117 S. Carroll St., Upper Matecumbe Key, 800/799-9175, www.thecaribbeanresort.com, one-bedroom homes $350-525 d, two-bedroom homes $450-750, three-bedroom homes $875-1,500), situated far enough from U.S. 1 that it's easy to forget about the traffic for a while, especially during the peak winter months. This sumptuous property contains an array of spacious homes, each with its own unique style. On-site amenities include lush gardens filled with tropical flowers and banana trees; a gorgeous pool and spa oasis, graced with waterfalls and arching coconut palms; and private sundecks, gazebos, tables, and lounge chairs scattered throughout the grounds.

Established in 1946, the lavish ★ **Cheeca Lodge & Spa** (MM 81.8, 81801 Overseas Hwy., Upper Matecumbe Key, 844/993-9713, www.cheeca.com, rooms $229-500 d, suites $269-899, two-bedroom suites $569-998, bungalows $329-597) has hosted an array of U.S. presidents and movie stars since its opening. Today the renovated resort provides guests with a relaxing, pampering, tropical playground where you can play tennis or golf, fish from the 525-foot-long pier, relax on the private beach, or seek rejuvenation in the incredible on-site spa. You may just feel like royalty in the spacious Caribbean-style rooms, suites, and adults-only bungalows, which include 42-inch televisions, wet bars, luxurious furniture, and marvelous views of the ocean, beach, lagoon, and resort. In fact, it's the varied views, as well as the shifting seasons, that determine the wide range in lodging rates. Besides the lovely surroundings, the amenities here include two fine restaurants, Atlantic's Edge and Nikai Sushi, and an adults-only pool.

Perhaps the best example of Islamorada's luxury and seclusion is ★ **The Moorings Village & Spa** (123 Beach Rd., Upper

Matecumbe Key, 305/664-4708, www. themooringsvillage.com, one-bedroom inland homes $300-800 daily, two-bedroom oceanfront bungalow $3,250-4,650 weekly, two-bedroom inland homes $3,950-5,700 weekly, one-bedroom oceanfront home $4,300-5,875 weekly, two-bedroom oceanfront homes $6,750-9,200 weekly), a serene, splendidly lush property on the ocean side of U.S. 1 near Mile Marker 81.6. Part of a coconut plantation in the 1930s, the verdant 18-acre resort offers 18 private homes and cottages (which greatly range in price depending on the season), from small, brightly painted Caribbean bungalows tucked amid the foliage to a three-bedroom French colonial plantation house ($7,800-10,600 weekly) directly beside the ocean. These self-sufficient residences, many of which lure the same guests year after year, contain televisions, telephones, well-equipped kitchens, luxurious beds, and sometimes, washers and dryers. All lodgings require a two-night or one-week minimum stay, and all are only a short stroll from a private Polynesian-style beach—complete with swaying palm trees, cushioned lounge chairs, relaxing hammocks, and complimentary kayaks. It's no wonder that the beach is often used as a backdrop in movies and catalog photo shoots.

Other on-site amenities include tennis courts, a stunning pool area, and the Island Body & Sol Spa (305/664-3264, www.

islandbodyandsolspa.com, $50-190 per treatment), which offers a selection of rejuvenating facials and massages. The family-owned resort also boasts two of the finest eateries in the Keys—the Morada Bay Beach Café, ideal for light lunches beside the beach, and Pierre's Restaurant, perfect for a romantic dinner. Both restaurants are on the bay side of the Overseas Highway, only a short drive from the Moorings.

CAMPING

Despite its plethora of accommodations, Islamorada has few options for campers, especially those hoping to stay awhile. The Sea Breeze RV & Mobile Home Park (87425 Old Hwy., Plantation Key, 305/852-3358, www.suncommunities.com), on the ocean side of U.S. 1, is one such option. Essentially a residential mobile home park, Sea Breeze offers several full-hookup RV lots, including some with oceanfront views, on a month-to-month basis (starting from $650 May-Oct., $900 Nov.-Apr.). The park is conveniently located across the street from Islamorada's Founders Park and only a few miles northeast of attractions like Windley Key Fossil Reef Geological State Park and Theater of the Sea. Other amenities include on-site laundry facilities, a boat ramp, a fish-cleaning station, cable television, phone service, boat dockage ($135 monthly), and dry-dock storage ($80 monthly).

Information and Services

INFORMATION

For brochures, maps, and other information about Islamorada, stop by the Islamorada Chamber of Commerce and Visitors Center (MM 83.2 BS U.S. 1, Upper Matecumbe Key, 305/664-4503 or 800/322-5397, www.islamoradachamber.com, 9am-5pm Mon.-Fri., 9am-4pm Sat., 9am-3pm Sun.) or consult the Monroe County Tourist

Development Council (1201 White St., Ste. 102, Key West, 305/296-1552 or 800/352-5397, www.monroecounty-fla.gov, 8am-5pm Mon.-Fri.). For government-related issues, contact the Islamorada Village Administration Center & Public Safety Headquarters (MM 86.8, 86800 Overseas Hwy., Plantation Key, 305/664-6400, www.islamorada.fl.us, 8am-5pm Mon.-Fri.) or the Monroe County offices (1100 Simonton St., Key West, 305/292-4459, www.monroecounty-fl.gov, 8am-5pm Mon.-Fri.).

For local news, consult *Fl Keys News* (www. flkeysnews.com), the Upper Keys *Free Press* (www.keysnews.com), and The Weekly Newspapers (www.keysweekly.com). The dailies *Miami Herald* (www.miamiherald.com) and *The Key West Citizen* (www.keysnews. com) are available throughout the Keys.

Islamorada has several radio stations, including the SUN (WAIL-FM 99.5, www. wail995.com), which offers a classic rock format.

SERVICES
Money
For banking needs, stop by the Capital Bank (MM 80.9, 80900 Overseas Hwy., Upper Matecumbe Key, 305/664-4483 or 800/639-5111, www.capitalbank-us.com, 9am-4pm Mon.-Thurs., 9am-6pm Fri., extended drive-through hours) or the First State Bank of the Florida Keys (MM 81.6, 81621 Overseas Hwy., Upper Matecumbe Key, 305/664-9070, www.keysbank.com, 8am-5pm Mon.- Fri., extended drive-through hours).

Mail
For shipping, faxing, copying, and other business-related services, visit PostNet (MM 88, 88005 Overseas Hwy., Plantation Key, 305/853-1101, www.postnet.com, 9am-5pm Mon.-Fri.). You can also package and ship items at the local post office (MM 82.8, 82801 Overseas Hwy., Upper Matecumbe Key, 305/664-4738 or 800/275-8777, www.usps. com, 8am-noon and 1pm-4:30pm Mon.-Fri., 9am-noon Sat.).

Groceries and Supplies
For groceries, baked goods, and other supplies, head to the Winn-Dixie (MM 92.1, 92100 Overseas Hwy., Tavernier, 305/852-5904, www.winndixie.com, 6am-midnight daily), which has an on-site pharmacy (305/852-5069, 8am-8pm Mon.-Fri., 9am-6pm Sat., 10am-5pm Sun.). A CVS (MM 82.8, 82894 Overseas Hwy., Upper Matecumbe Key, 305/664-2576, www.cvs.com, 8am-10pm Mon.-Sat., 8am-8pm Sun.) offers limited supplies as well as an on-site pharmacy (8am-8pm Mon.-Fri., 8am-7pm Sat., 9am-6pm Sun.).

Laundry
There are several coin-operated laundries in the area, including the Coral Reef Laundry (MM 90, 90071 Old Hwy., Tavernier, 305/509-7750, 8am-7pm daily) on Plantation Key.

Internet Access
You'll find useful services at the Islamorada Branch Library (MM 81.8, 81830 Overseas Hwy., Upper Matecumbe Key, 305/664-4645, www.keyslibraries.org, 9:30am-8pm Mon.-Tues., 9:30am-6pm Wed.-Fri., 10am-6pm Sat.).

Emergency Services
In case of an emergency that requires police, fire, or ambulance services, dial 911 from any cell or public phone. For nonemergency assistance, contact the Monroe County Sheriff's Office (MM 87, 87000 Overseas Hwy., Plantation Key, 305/853-7021, www. keysso.net, 8am-5pm Mon.-Fri.). For medical assistance, consult the Mariners Hospital (MM 91.5, 91500 Overseas Hwy., Tavernier, 305/434-3000, www.baptisthealth.net). Foreign visitors seeking help with directions, medical concerns, business issues, law enforcement needs, or other problems can receive multilingual tourist assistance (800/771-5397) 24 hours daily.

Transportation

GETTING THERE
Air

Despite the presence of a private airstrip at **TavernAero Park Airport** (MM 90 BS U.S. 1, 135 N. Airport Rd., Tavernier, www.tavernaero.com) on Plantation Key, Islamorada has no major airport of its own. To travel here by plane, you'll need to fly into **Fort Lauderdale-Hollywood International Airport (FLL)** (100 Terminal Dr., Fort Lauderdale, 866/435-9355, www.broward.org/airport), **Miami International Airport (MIA)** (2100 NW 42nd Ave., Miami, 305/876-7000 or 800/825-5642, www.miami-airport.com), **Key West International Airport (EYW)** (3491 S. Roosevelt Blvd., Key West, 305/809-5200 or 305/296-5439, www.keywestinternationalairport.com), or **Florida Keys Marathon Airport (MTH)** (9400 Overseas Hwy., Marathon, 305/289-6060). From there you can rent a vehicle from agencies like **Avis** (800/331-1212, www.avis.com), **Budget** (800/527-0700, www.budget.com), **Enterprise** (800/325-8007, www.enterprise.com), **Hertz** (800/654-3131, www.hertz.com), or **Thrifty** (800/367-2277, www.thrifty.com) to reach Islamorada.

Bus or Train

The **Miami-Dade County Metrobus** (305/891-3131, www.miamidade.gov/transit) operates the **301 Dade-Monroe Express** between Florida City and Marathon (5:15am-8:40pm daily, $2.35 per one-way trip), regularly stopping in Islamorada. In addition, **Greyhound** (800/231-2222, www.greyhound.com) offers bus service to the Burger King in Islamorada (82201 Overseas Hwy., Upper Matecumbe Key). **Amtrak** (800/872-7245, www.amtrak.com) only provides train service as far south as Miami, from where you must rent a car or hop a shuttle to reach the Florida Keys.

Transport from Airports and Stations

If you arrive in the Fort Lauderdale-Miami area via plane, bus, or train—or Key West via plane or bus—you can either rent a car or hire a shuttle service to reach Islamorada. Companies include **Keys Shuttle** (305/289-9997 or 888/765-9997, www.keysshuttle.com, $70-80 per shared ride, $300-350 for exclusive service), which provides service from the Miami and Fort Lauderdale airports, and **SuperShuttle** (305/871-2000 or 954/764-1700, www.supershuttle.com, $235 for up to 10 passengers), which only serves visitors flying into Miami.

Car

To reach Islamorada from Miami, head south on U.S. 1 (Overseas Hwy.) and continue through Key Largo toward your destination on the islands of Islamorada. If you're headed from the Everglades via I-75 (Everglades Pkwy.), drive south on U.S. 27, veer right onto S.R. 997 (Krome Ave.), and follow the signs to U.S. 1. From U.S. 41 (Tamiami Trl.) in the Everglades, head south on S.R. 997 and continue toward U.S. 1. If you are traveling during the peak season (Dec.-Apr.), be sure to call **511** for an up-to-the-minute traffic report.

GETTING AROUND
Car

The best way to travel through Islamorada is by car, truck, RV, or motorcycle—all of which offer easy access to U.S. 1 as well as the side roads.

Van Service or Tour Bus

While staying in Islamorada, if you want to head to Key West for the day—and would rather leave your vehicle at your hotel—consider boarding **Sea the Keys** (305/896-7013, www.keywestdaytrip.com, rates vary), a passenger van service that will pick you up from your hotel in the Upper Keys and drop you off in Key West around 11am. You'll be free to explore the city's restaurants, bars, museums, and other attractions before making the return trip around 9pm.

Taxi

Taxicab companies such as **Marty's Islamorada Taxi** (305/853-6505, $7 per pickup, $2.50 per mile) and **Spring's Island Taxi** (305/664-4331, www.springsislandtaxi. com, $7 per pickup, $3 per mile after initial two miles) can help you get around Islamorada.

Bicycle or Boat

While you can certainly traverse Islamorada via bicycle, the region's sprawling nature and numerous bridges make it challenging for novice riders. Nevertheless, it's a lovely, eco-friendly way to experience the Upper Keys. Between Mile Marker 91 and Mile Marker 71 are 10 miles of biking paths.

Bicycles can be rented from **Backcountry Cowboy Outfitters** (MM 82.2, 82240 Overseas Hwy., Upper Matecumbe Key, 305/517-4177, www.backcountrycowboy. com, 9am-6pm Mon.-Sat., 10am-5pm Sun., $15-39 per half day, $20-55 daily, $35-80 for two days, $80-170 weekly), which offers one-speed, three-speed, hybrid, and road bicycle rentals—plus helmets, combination locks, and copies of the state's bicycle laws.

You can also experience the islands of Islamorada by boat. In fact, certain locales, such as Indian Key Historic State Park, are only accessible by boat, canoe, or kayak. Having your own vessel might make navigating these waters a bit easier, and you'll find no shortage of boat ramps and marina slips in Islamorada. If you'd rather rent a boat, head to **Robbie's of Islamorada** (MM 77.5, 77522 Overseas Hwy., Lower Matecumbe Key, 305/664-8070 or 877/664-8498, www.robbies.com, 7am-sunset daily), which offers an array of vessels ($195-295 per half day, $245-345 daily) ranging 18-24 feet in length.

As an alternative, you can rent a kayak from **Backcountry Cowboy Outfitters** (MM 82.2, 82240 Overseas Hwy., Upper Matecumbe Key, 305/517-4177, www. backcountrycowboy.com, 9am-6pm Mon.-Sat., 10am-5pm Sun., $50-65 per half day, $65-85 daily, or $165-195 weekly).

Marathon and the Middle Keys

Seeking some peace and quiet? The Middle

Keys are idyllic, offering top-notch recreation and family-friendly activities without the crowds.

Beyond the bridges south of Islamorada and the minuscule community of Layton, the first major stop is Long Key State Park, the perfect place to escape the crowds at other islands. Hiking, canoeing, kayaking, snorkeling, and picnicking are favored pastimes here, and unlike other public beaches in the region, the narrow stretch of sand at Long Key is only available to overnight campers, making it decidedly more tranquil than the beaches of Key West.

After crossing the Long Key Viaduct, you'll be in the "Heart of the Keys," a transitional space between the outdoor pleasures of Key

Highlights

Look for ★ to find recommended sights, activities, dining, and lodging.

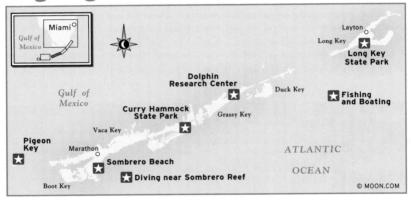

★ **Long Key State Park:** This tranquil park offers easy ocean access for swimmers, snorkelers, and anglers (page 173).

★ **Dolphin Research Center:** Once home to the aquatic stars of the 1963 film *Flipper,* this nonprofit marine mammal facility on Grassy Key offers a variety of educational experiences, including dolphin encounters (page 176).

★ **Curry Hammock State Park:** This family-friendly park features a campground, a 1.5-mile nature trail through a preserved hardwood hammock, and a pleasant beach and playground area (page 176).

★ **Pigeon Key:** Stroll among several picturesque buildings that served as the base camp for railroad workers in the early 20th century (page 179).

★ **Sombrero Beach:** This curvy, palm-lined expanse of sand is a preferred spot for swimmers, beachcombers, and, from April to October, nesting turtles (page 181).

★ **Fishing and Boating:** Full-service marinas, fishing charters, and boat rentals help anglers in search of permit, bonefish, and tarpon (page 181).

★ **Diving near Sombrero Reef:** Learn the ropes of scuba diving before venturing out to explore the elkhorn coral and tropical fish of this spur-and-groove reef formation, designated by a 142-foot tower (page 184).

Largo and the unabashed revelry of Key West. Family-friendly activities reign supreme in the Middle Keys, from up-close dolphin encounters on Duck Key to the playground and picnic areas of Sombrero Beach, popular among swimmers and windsurfers alike and the site of a spirited dragon boat festival each year. Past Duck Key you'll encounter the town of Marathon, an unassuming 13-mile-long community that stretches from Grassy Key to Knight's Key.

Besides casual seafood eateries and motel hideaways, this sleepy region offers several wildlife-oriented activities, from dolphin swims to bird-watching haunts. On Grassy Key, you'll find a nonprofit dolphin and sea lion center that offers tours and interactive programs; farther south lie the islands that make up a 260-acre state park that is especially popular with kayakers, who frequently spot manatees, raptors, herons, egrets, and other birds in the area.

Marathon also has relaxing spas, a public golf course, several campgrounds, a commuter airport, and numerous adventure outfitters and operators that assist visiting bikers, anglers, boaters, and scuba divers. A popular attraction among children is the Crane Point Museum and Nature Center, which encompasses a natural history museum, a bird center, a nature trail, and one of the oldest houses in the Florida Keys.

En route to the Lower Keys, you'll cross the Seven Mile Bridge—a long stretch across open water that's unnerving for some. Along the way, you'll pass tiny Pigeon Key, a historic early 20th-century work camp situated beside the Old Seven Mile Bridge, an engineering marvel that was once considered the Eighth Wonder of the World.

PLANNING YOUR TIME

Like Islamorada and the Lower Keys, Marathon and the rest of the Middle Keys are made up of numerous islands, most of which are easily accessible by car via the Overseas Highway. Given the sheer variety of attractions, extending from Long Key at Mile Marker 67 to Pigeon Key near Mile Marker 45, a proper visit may take at least three days—perhaps even a week if you plan to add activities like fishing, kayaking, camping, windsurfing, and golf to your itinerary.

As with other parts of the Florida Keys, be prepared to deal with traffic congestion, crowded restaurants and attractions, and higher lodging rates during late winter and early spring. When planning a trip to the Middle Keys, you should also consider factors like climate, fishing seasons, and annual events. If you're a novice to certain activities, such as scuba diving, you might also want to allow for proper instruction time.

Where you decide to stay, however, is entirely up to you. With a car, it's easy enough to navigate the entire region, so whether you choose a resort near Mile Marker 69 or a campground near Mile Marker 47, you should be able to reach everything you hope to see and experience in the Middle Keys.

For more information about Marathon and the Middle Keys, consult the **Monroe County Tourist Development Council** (1201 White St., Ste. 102, Key West, 305/296-1552 or 800/352-5397, www.fla-keys.com, 9am-5pm Mon.-Fri.) and the **Greater Marathon Chamber of Commerce and Marathon Visitors Center** (MM 53.5, 12222 Overseas Hwy., Marathon, 305/743-5417 or 800/262-7284, www.floridakeysmarathon.com, 9am-5pm daily).

Previous: Sombrero Beach; a bottlenose dolphin at the Dolphin Research Center; a lone mangrove tree at Long Key State Park.

Marathon and the Middle Keys

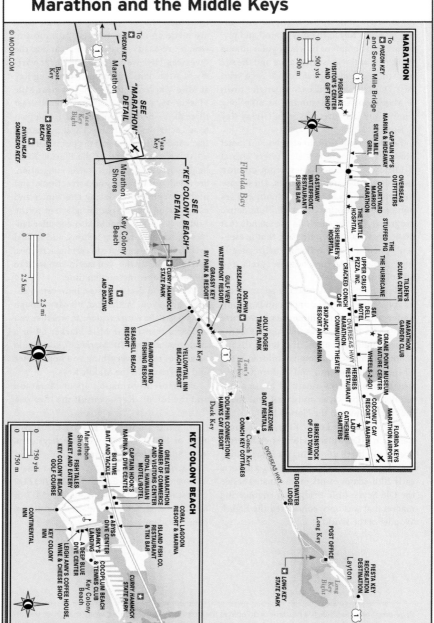

© MOON.COM

MARATHON

To
PIGEON KEY
and Seven Mile Bridge

0   500 yds
0   500 m

PIGEON KEY
VISITOR'S CENTER
AND GIFT SHOP

CAPTAIN PIP'S
MARINA & HIDEAWAY

SEVEN MILE
GRILL

OVERSEAS
OUTFITTERS

CASTAWAY
WATERFRONT
RESTAURANT &
SUSHI BAR

COURTYARD
MARRIOT
MARATHON

THE
STUFFED PIG

THE TURTLE
HOSPITAL

TILDEN'S
SCUBA CENTER

THE HURRICANE

UPPER CRUST
PIZZA, INC.

FISHERMEN'S
HOSPITAL

CRACKED CONCH
CAFE

SEA
DELL
MOTEL

CRANE POINT MUSEUM
AND NATURE CENTER

MARATHON
GARDEN CLUB

OVERSEAS HWY

MARATHON
COMMUNITY THEATER

SKIPJACK
RESORT AND MARINA

WHEELS-2-GO!

HERBIES
RESTAURANT

COCONUT CAY
RESORT & MARINA

LADY
CATHERINE
CHARTERS

FLORIDA KEYS
MARATHON AIRPORT

BIRKENSTOCK
OF OLD TOWN II

To
PIGEON KEY

Marathon

SEE
"MARATHON"
DETAIL

Boot
Key

Vaca
Key
Bight

SOMBRERO
BEACH

DIVING NEAR
SOMBRERO REEF

Marathon
Shores

Vaca
Key

Florida Bay

Key Colony
Beach

SEE
"KEY COLONY BEACH"
DETAIL

0   2.5 km
0   2.5 mi

CURRY HAMMOCK
STATE PARK

GULF VIEW
WATERFRONT
RV PARK & RESORT

GRASSY KEY

DOLPHIN
RESEARCH
CENTER

Grassy Key

SEASHELL BEACH
RESORT

RAINBOW BEND
FISHING RESORT

YELLOWTAIL INN
BEACH RESORT

JOLLY ROGER
TRAVEL PARK

FISHING
AND BOATING

Tom's
Harbor

DOLPHIN CONNECTION/
HAWKS CAY RESORT

Duck Key

WAKEZONE
BOAT RENTALS

CONCH KEY COTTAGES

Conch Key

OVERSEAS HWY

EDGEWATER
LODGE

POST OFFICE

Long Key

FIESTA KEY
RECREATION
DESTINATION

Layton

LONG KEY
STATE PARK

Long
Key
Bight

KEY COLONY BEACH

0   750 yds
0   750 m

Marathon
Shores

KEY COLONY BEACH
GOLF COURSE

FISHTALES
MARKET AND
EATERY

BIG TIME
BAIT AND TACKLE

CAPTAIN HOOK'S
MARINA & DIVE CENTER

GREATER MARATHON
CHAMBER OF COMMERCE
AND VISITORS CENTER

ROYAL HAWAIIAN
MOTEL/BOTEL

CORAL LAGOON
RESORT & MARINA

ISLAND FISH CO.
RESTAURANT
& TIKI BAR

ABYSS
DIVE CENTER

SPARKY'S
LANDING

A DEEP BLUE
DIVE CENTER

COCOPLUM BEACH
& TENNIS CLUB

LEIGH ANN'S COFFEE HOUSE,
WINE & CHEESE SHOP

KEY COLONY
INN

CONTINENTAL
INN

CURRY HAMMOCK
STATE PARK

Key Colony
Beach

Sights

★ LONG KEY STATE PARK

Between the flyspeck community of Layton and the lengthy town of Marathon lies Long Key, a strangely shaped island that appears to resemble the open jaws of a vicious snake. Perhaps that's why Spanish explorers originally called this island *Cayo Vivora*, which means "Rattlesnake Key." In the early 20th century it was the site of a luxurious fishing resort that was favored by the author Zane Grey and other saltwater anglers. The resort was wiped out by the Labor Day Hurricane of 1935, the same terrible tempest that destroyed the Overseas Railroad. Nowadays Long Key often appears on maps of the Upper Keys, but given that it's not technically part of Islamorada and that its upscale past has now been usurped by a quiet, nature-oriented vibe, it seems more suited for the Middle Keys. Just bear in mind that not everyone will agree with such a sentiment.

Today Long Key is home to the aptly named **Long Key State Park** (MM 67.4, 67400 Overseas Hwy., Long Key, 305/664-4815, www.floridastateparks.org, 8am-sunset daily, $4.50 for 1 person, $5 plus $0.50 per additional person for 2 or more people, $2.50 pedestrians and bikers), popular with anglers, swimmers, snorkelers, picnickers, and campers since it was established in 1969. Encompassing roughly 1,000 acres, this pleasant preserve features a variety of foliage, including mangrove forests, lush vegetation, scrubby grass, vibrant wildflowers, and dense inland trees like poisonwood, gumbo limbo, and coconut palm. Hikers may appreciate the two on-site nature trails—the **Golden Orb Trail,** named after a native spider and offering a 1.1-mile stroll through various plant communities; and the **Layton Trail,** a 0.3-mile walk on the bay side of the park. Bird-watchers will relish spying a wide array of vibrant species, from wading egrets to red-bellied woodpeckers, which are particularly prevalent during the winter months.

Canoeists especially favor this tranquil place, which features the leisurely **Long Key Lakes Canoe Trail** through a shallow lagoon. Canoe rentals ($17.50 single, $21.50 double for two hours) and a self-guided tour map make this a relatively easy diversion for novices, too. Another highlight is the narrow, rocky, grass-lined beach on the ocean side of the park, not far from picnic pavilions, public showers, and a canoe/kayak launching area. Only open to those staying in the state park campground, it tends to be more peaceful than the beaches farther south, though it can also be rather muddy at times. Guided two-hour trail walks (10am Wed., free) and interpretive programs (10am Thurs., free), from bird-watching talks to snorkeling excursions, are periodically available. Be aware that leashed, well-behaved pets are ostensibly permitted here, but they are not allowed on the beaches, in the picnic shelters, or in the restrooms. Fireworks and hunting are also prohibited.

DOLPHIN ATTRACTIONS
Dolphin Connection

If you're driving west from Long Key, you'll cross the Long Key Channel and pass through the Conch Keys before encountering the secluded 60-acre island known as Duck Key on the ocean side of the highway. Situated here is the luxurious **Hawks Cay Resort** (61 Hawks Cay Blvd., Duck Key, 888/395-5539, www.hawkscay.com), which offers a slew of diversions, from water sports and spa services to the **Dolphin Connection** (305/289-9975, www.dolphinconnection.com, 9am-5pm daily), which was established in 1990 as a marine mammal education, breeding, and research facility. Like the other interactive dolphin facilities in the Florida Keys, the Dolphin Connection allows visitors to mingle

Dolphins in Captivity

Not all captive animals, such as the dolphins that reside at Dolphin Connection (61 Hawks Cay Blvd., Duck Key, 305/743-7000, www.dolphinconnection.com) and the Dolphin Research Center (MM 58.9, 58901 Overseas Hwy., Grassy Key, 305/289-1121 or 305/289-0002, www. dolphins.org), can or should be released into the wild.

For one thing, reintroducing an animal must be done in a manner that protects wild populations as well as the individual being released. Though the marine mammal community returns hundreds of stranded animals to the wild each year, it can be dangerous to reintroduce one that's been in long-term human care. Such dangers include disease transmission, unwanted genetic exchange, the inability for the released animal to nourish and defend itself, and perhaps most notably, the fact that said animal has lost its natural fear of humans.

Typically, wild animals keep their distance from people, but a marine mammal accustomed to interacting with and being fed by humans can become vulnerable to a variety of problems. Such animals may, for instance, take on some of the following behaviors:

- Spend a lot of time near boats, where they can be struck by hulls and cut by propellers

- Learn to steal fish from fishing lines, thereby ingesting monofilament line and hooks

- Eat inappropriate food, such as spoiled fish, beer, ice cream, or nonedible items

- Get pushy and aggressive when they don't get the handouts they've come to expect

- Encounter people who view them as nuisances, which can get them shot or otherwise injured

In the gulf and ocean waters surrounding the Florida Keys, you'll find plenty of opportunities to see wild dolphins, whether from shore or by boat. Although watching them in their natural habitat can be an amazing experience, it's important that you practice responsible viewing. Approaching such creatures too closely, moving too quickly, or making too much noise can increase the risk of harassment and possibly disrupt natural behaviors like migration, sheltering, breeding, nursing, feeding, and breathing—and is actually against federal law. For more information about the responsible viewing of wild dolphins in Florida Keys National Marine Sanctuary, consult Dolphin SMART (www.dolphinsmart.org), a program that promotes these helpful tips:

- Staying at least 50 yards from dolphins

- Moving away cautiously if dolphins show signs of disturbance

- Always putting your engine in neutral when dolphins are near

- Refraining from feeding, touching, or swimming with wild dolphins

- Teaching others to be Dolphin SMART

with these friendly marine mammals from the dock or within the on-site saltwater lagoon.

Three basic programs are available here. The 30-minute Dockside Dolphins program ($79 pp) allows you to feed, play with, and interact with the dolphins without ever getting in the water, though splashing may still be involved; while all ages are welcome, children under 6 must be accompanied by a paid adult. The 45-minute Dolphin Discovery program ($179 pp) offers you the chance to touch, kiss, hug, splash, and swim with the dolphins; although there are no age restrictions, participants must be at least 4.5 feet tall. Unlike other dolphin facilities in the Florida Keys, the Dolphin Connection does not charge for merely observing the programs.

1: Pigeon Key, west of Marathon **2:** trail at Long Key State Park

★ Dolphin Research Center

On the bay side of Grassy Key, you'll spot the hard-to-miss sign for the Dolphin Research Center (DRC, MM 58.9, 58901 Overseas Hwy., Grassy Key, 305/289-1121 or 305/289-0002, www.dolphins.org, 9am-4:30pm daily, $28 adults, $25 military personnel and veterans, $23 children 4-12, free for children under 3), a nonprofit education, research, and rescue facility that "promises peaceful coexistence, cooperation, and communication between marine mammals, humans, and the environment." Adhering to this mission statement, DRC features a wide array of programs—from brief dolphin dips to daylong research programs—that could easily be classified as "edutainment."

Founded in 1984, the facility that is now DRC has a much longer history. Despite a shift in ownership over the years, this site has been continuously operated as a marine mammal facility since 1956, when fisherman Milton Santini captured several bottlenose dolphins, including one he called "Mitzi," and formed Santini's Porpoise School. In 1963 Mitzi starred in the original *Flipper* movie, along with five other resident dolphins. When Mitzi passed away in 1972, Santini sold the property to an entertainment conglomerate that operated the site as Flipper's Sea School. It wasn't until 1977, however, that the facility began to shift its purpose to the one upheld today—among other things, cultivating environmental ambassadors among the visiting public.

Today visitors can watch a variety of educational shows and demonstrations, during which dolphins get a chance to display their learned behaviors. Trainers offer a bit of insight into caretaking aspects that are rarely seen by the public, such as administering medicine to a sick dolphin. In addition, guests can opt to meet a dolphin from the dock ($30 pp), toss toys to the dolphins ($85 pp), paint with a dolphin ($80 pp), play learning games with the dolphins ($75 pp), experience a group dip with the dolphins ($119 pp, ages 4 and up), or have a shallow-water or deepwater dolphin encounter ($199 adults, $50 children under

5). Truly immersive activities include the trainer-for-a-day ($695 pp, all day), researcher experience ($475 pp, half day), and trainer experience ($475 pp, half day) programs, all of which provide an intensive look into the operation of the DRC. Age restrictions may apply for some of these programs, and almost all require advance reservations. DRC welcomes guests with disabilities, and staff members will do their best to accommodate them.

★ CURRY HAMMOCK STATE PARK

West of Grassy Key is the largest uninhabited parcel of land between Key Largo and Big Pine Key. True, it's composed of several wooded islands, with names like Crawl Key, Little Crawl Key, Long Point Key, Deer Key, and Fat Deer Key, but nonetheless, Curry Hammock State Park (MM 56.2, 56200 Overseas Hwy., Marathon, 305/289-2690, www.floridastateparks.org, 8am-sunset daily, $4.50 for 1 person, $5 plus $0.50 per additional person for 2 or more people, $2.50 pedestrians and bikers) constitutes an impressive, nearly development-free place in the heart of a fairly populated region. Encompassing more than 1,000 acres, Curry Hammock protects sizable seagrass beds, mangrove swamps, and rockland hammocks, including one of the country's largest populations of thatch palms.

Established in 1991 and named after Lamar Louise Curry—a respected Miami teacher whose father, Thomas, purchased large tracts of land in the Upper and Middle Keys—this popular park offers a full-facility campground, picnic tables and pavilions, and easy access to swimming, windsurfing, canoeing, and kayaking opportunities. Visitors can even rent single and double kayaks on-site ($17.20-21.50 for two hours). In addition, hikers can stroll along a 1.5-mile nature trail through a preserved hardwood hammock on Fat Deer Key. Little Crawl Key features a pleasant beach and playground area, which is accessible to overnight campers ($42.70 per day) and day-use visitors alike.

Fishing and beachcombing are popular

activities here, and bird-watchers will also appreciate this park, which lies on a critical bird migration route and hosts the annual Florida Keys Birding and Wildlife Festival. The beaches, hammock, and grass flats are home to a wide array of herons, egrets, plovers, sanderlings, white-crowned pigeons, pelicans, ospreys, and bald eagles. Wildlife lovers might also spot Key Vaca raccoons, nurse sharks, spotted rays, dolphins, and manatees.

Bicyclists are welcome to ride along the park roads as well as a two-mile stretch of the **Florida Keys Overseas Heritage Trail,** which leads to and from Marathon. Just remember to wear a helmet at all times, and be advised that biking is not permitted on the boardwalks, footpaths, or nature trail inside the park. You should be aware, too, that while leashed, well-behaved pets are ostensibly permitted here, they are not allowed along the shoreline, in the water, or in the picnic area and restrooms. Fireworks and hunting are also prohibited.

CRANE POINT MUSEUM AND NATURE CENTER

Near Mile Marker 50, on the bay side of U.S. 1 in the heart of Marathon, lies the **Crane Point Museum and Nature Center** (MM 55.5, 5550 Overseas Hwy., Marathon, 305/743-9100, www.cranepoint.net, 9am-5pm Mon.-Sat., noon-5pm Sun., $14.95 adults, $12.95 seniors 65 and over, $9.95 children 5-13, free for children under 5), a sprawling 63-acre preserve that families with young children especially enjoy. Your first stop is typically the **Museum of Natural History,** where you can learn about the human history of the Florida Keys, including facts about the Calusa native people that once inhabited these islands, the Spanish and British explorers that later visited them, and the Bahamian pioneers that eventually called them home. You'll also discover stories about various shipwrecks and the ill-fated Overseas Railroad. Dioramas and exhibits explore the flora, fauna, and geology that define this diverse region, including mangroves, butterflies, sea turtles, and coral reefs.

From the museum, most visitors venture outside, where you can view a 10-minute orientation video, watch daily fish feedings in the saltwater lagoon, and interact with marine creatures like conch and starfish in the on-site touch tanks. Afterward you can explore ever-changing creature exhibits in a Cracker-style bungalow, venture across a butterfly meadow peppered with aromatic flowers, and stroll among thatch palm trees and mangroves. Additionally, nature trails lead to three interesting destinations, including the historic **Adderley House,** an open, weathered, Bahamian-style structure built in the early 1900s by Bahamian immigrant George Adderley. Formed from tabby, a concrete-like material made of burned conch and other shells, the Adderley House is the oldest house in the Florida Keys north of Key West. Visitors can view old-fashioned beds, chests, and other furnishings reminiscent of those used by George and Olivia Adderley when they lived here between 1902 and 1949.

Other accessible stops along the way include the **Marathon Wild Bird Center,** which aims to rescue, rehabilitate, and release injured gulls, ospreys, and other native birds, and the art deco-style **Crane House,** constructed in the 1950s and once home to Francis and Mary Crane, a Massachusetts couple who purchased the land here in 1949. Passionate conservationists and horticulturists, the Cranes worked hard to preserve and enhance the preserve with flowering trees and shrubs. The family retained the property until the late 1970s, and by 1989, it was purchased by the Florida Keys Land and Sea Trust in order to spare it from impending development. Eventually, this preserve of palm and hardwood hammocks, mangrove forests, tidal lagoons, and wetland ponds was named for the Cranes, whose former home isn't far from **Crane Point** itself, where you can observe pelicans, raptors, and other native bird species along the shore of Florida Bay. If possible, try to visit the nature preserve on a sunny day, when the foliage looks infinitely better than on an overcast one.

Manatee Rescue

While visiting the Florida Keys, you might be fortunate enough to spy an endangered West Indian manatee, also known as a "sea cow," in the warm coastal waters surrounding this archipelago—especially during the winter months, when ocean temperatures drop. A giant yet gentle creature and the state's official marine mammal, the manatee inhabits shallow estuaries and saltwater bays, feeds on aquatic vegetation, and has sadly been diminished by boat collisions, propeller injuries, rope and fishing line entanglements, vandal attacks, poachers, habitat destruction, oil spills, and cold stress.

Although protected from harassment, hunting, capture, or killing by the Marine Mammal Protection Act of 1972 and the Endangered Species Act of 1973, the manatee continues to suffer from human actions—despite the fact that anyone convicted of violating such federal laws may face a fine of up to $100,000 and/or a year in prison. Nonprofit organizations like the Save the Manatee Club (SMC, 500 N. Maitland Ave., Maitland, 407/539-0990 or 800/432-5646, www.savethemanatee.org), begun in 1981 by singer-songwriter Jimmy Buffett and former Florida governor and U.S. senator Bob Graham, are doing what they can to protect these endangered creatures and their habitat for future generations.

The Dolphin Research Center (DRC, MM 58.9, 58901 Overseas Hwy., Grassy Key, 305/289-1121 or 305/289-0002, www.dolphins.org) is actively involved in manatee conservation efforts. The DRC even has a manatee rescue team, nicknamed the Gray Cross, and the efforts of the SMC and DRC are greatly enhanced by assistance from the public. Here are just a few ways that you can protect endangered manatees and aid in conservation efforts:

· Stay in marked deepwater channels, where manatees are less likely to be.

· Obey all signage and speed laws when boating in coastal waters.

· Drive slowly and designate a lookout person who will watch for wildlife, swimmers, boaters, and obstructions.

· Do not enter designated manatee sanctuaries.

· Wear polarized glasses to make it easier to spot the surface swirls that indicate a manatee is near.

· If you see wild manatees, please observe them from the water's surface and at a distance of at least 50 feet.

THE TURTLE HOSPITAL

Situated on the western end of Vaca Key, The Turtle Hospital (MM 23.9, 2396 Overseas Hwy., Marathon, 305/743-2552, www.turtlehospital.org, 9am-6pm daily, $25 adults, $12 children 4-12, free for children under 4) is the only state-certified veterinary hospital of its kind in the world. Featuring up-to-date medical equipment, the nonprofit facility strives to rescue and rehabilitate injured sea turtles with the goal of releasing them back into the wild. The turtle species typically found in the Florida Keys include the threatened loggerhead turtles as well as the endangered green, hawksbill, leatherback, and Kemp's ridley turtles. In recent years, threats to such turtles have come from fishing line and net entanglements; boat strikes; oil spills; coastal development, which damages nesting sites; and intestinal impaction due to the ingestion of floating debris. The hospital can receive as many as 70 turtles yearly—even more during particularly cold winters when hundreds of stunned sea turtles have been found floating in the ocean. To date, the hospital has successfully released more than 1,000 sea turtles.

a West Indian manatee

- Avoid excessive noise and splashing if a manatee appears in your swimming area, and use snorkel gear in lieu of noisier scuba gear when observing the manatees.

- Do not touch, chase, feed, or give water to wild manatees, as such actions can put them on the defensive, alter their natural behavior, and ultimately cause them to vacate warmer areas for fear of being harassed.

- Never isolate an individual or separate a mother and her calf.

- If you spot an injured, entangled, tagged, orphaned, or deceased manatee, call the **Florida Fish and Wildlife Conservation Commission** (FWC, 888/404-3922) or use VHF Channel 16 on your marine radio.

- Do not approach or try to assist such a manatee. This can put you at risk and potentially scare away the injured animal.

- Report any criminal activities committed against these marine mammals.

As part of its educational outreach component, The Turtle Hospital features an education center (plus gift shop) and invites guests to take a guided 1.5-hour tour of the facility. Eight such tours are offered daily (9am, 10am, 11am, noon, 1pm, 2pm, 3pm, and 4pm) and consist of a slideshow presentation, a behind-the-scenes look at the hospital facilities, a visit to the outdoor turtle rehabilitation area, and an opportunity to feed the permanent residents. This tour will require a minimal amount of walking; limited wheelchair access is available. Reservations for these tours are highly recommended, given the space limitations. Poor weather and turtle emergencies may supersede any scheduled tour. All minors under the age of 18 must be accompanied by an adult.

★ PIGEON KEY

To reach the Lower Keys from Marathon, simply head west across the **Seven Mile Bridge.** Along the way, you'll spy an isolated, palm-dotted island tucked beside the **Old Seven Mile Bridge,** an engineering marvel once considered by some to be the Eighth Wonder of the World. This tiny coral island, known as **Pigeon Key,** has been lovingly preserved by the Pigeon Key Foundation (305/743-5999, www.pigeonkey.net) to capture the atmosphere of the early 1900s when it served as a base camp for railroad workers. You can take a self-guided walking tour of the grounds, which include educational facilities, a small museum, and the historic buildings that once housed the more than 400 workers who labored 14 hours a day, six days a week to construct the Overseas Railroad. Besides the history lesson, you might also enjoy picnicking on this lovely little island. Snorkeling is also a possibility; you can either bring your own snorkel and mask or borrow the gear that's available on Pigeon Key.

You can purchase tickets to Pigeon Key at the **Pigeon Key Visitor's Center and Gift Shop** (1 Knight's Key Blvd., Knight's Key, 305/743-5999, 9:30am-4pm daily, $12 adults, $9 students and children 5-12, free for children under 5), housed in a red train car near Mile Marker 47. The admission price grants you all-day access to Pigeon Key and includes a guided ferry ride from Knight's Key to the island (10am, noon, and 2pm daily) and back again (12:20pm, 2:20pm, and 4pm daily). Reservations for the ferry are definitely advised, especially on holidays and weekends. You can also access this historical site by walking or biking down a 2.2-mile segment of the Old Seven Mile Bridge from Knight's Key; you can also reach the island via private boat. If you opt not to use the ferry service and choose to come by foot, bicycle, or private vessel, the admission fees and docking charges will still apply, so be sure to stop by the gift shop to make arrangements for your visit.

BOAT AND AIR TOURS

For a relaxing tour of the surrounding waters, consider heading to the Seascape Resort & Marina (1275 E. 76th St. Ocean, Marathon), where you can hire **Lady Catherine Charters** (305/743-5544 or 305/240-4030, www.diveandfishmarathon. com, hours vary daily, $250 per cruise for up to six people, $20 for each additional person) for a private two-hour sunset cruise. Such cruises can be customized, whether you'd like to toast the occasion with champagne or, as other guests have done, renew your marital vows in the midst of a glorious Florida Keys sunset. The boat can accommodate up to 22 passengers, so bring your friends and loved ones along for the ride. Reservations are a must.

In Layton, near Mile Marker 65.5 on U.S. 1, **Conch Republic Air Force** (305/395-1117, www.keywestbiplanes.com, $249-499 for one or two passengers) offers exciting biplane rides high above the Florida Keys and the shimmering waters of Florida Bay and the Atlantic Ocean. The pristine 1942 WACO UPF-7 open-air biplane is equipped with two cameras to capture your exhilarating experience. They offer history, eco, and photography tours, and it's an incredibly memorable way to see the Keys.

For a unique experience, board one of the three vintage World War II airplanes operated by **History Flight** (MM 54, 5409 Overseas Hwy., Marathon, 888/743-3311, www.historyflight.com, times and rates vary). Under the guidance of a certified flight instructor, you can fly the flagship *Mitchell,* a North American B-25 bomber; the *Texan,* a North American AT-6 trainer; or the *Stearman,* a Boeing N2S biplane. While you're learning to fly, know that you're helping a worthy cause because all flight proceeds fund the nonprofit organization's ongoing research efforts and recovery expeditions dedicated to bringing missing-in-action servicepeople home.

Beaches and Recreation

BEACHES

There is plenty of coastline in Marathon, and if you're staying at a coastal resort you'll probably have easy access to a sandy spot to sunbathe and listen to the waves roll ashore. But if you're staying inland, there are two beaches—Coco Plum Beach and Sombrero Beach—that are easily accessible, and both can become very crowded during the busy tourist season.

Long Key State Park

Long Key State Park (MM 67.4, 67400 Overseas Hwy., Long Key, 305/664-4815, www.floridastateparks.org, 8am-sunset daily, $4.50 for 1 person, $5 plus $0.50 per additional person for 2 or more people, $2.50 pedestrians and bikers) contains narrow, grass-lined beaches on the ocean side of U.S. 1. There are kayak rentals available near the picnic pavilions. The best beach in the park is along the shore of the campground, but only campers staying overnight at the state park have access to it. I'd say a private beach is an excellent reason to camp here.

Curry Hammock State Park

Curry Hammock State Park (MM 56.2, 56200 Overseas Hwy., Marathon, 305/289-2690, www.floridastateparks.org, 8am-sunset daily, $4.50 for 1 person, $5 plus $0.50 per additional person for 2 or more people, $2.50 pedestrians and bikers) has a nice beach at Little Crawl Key where you'll find a playground area. This is an excellent place to fish the flats, kayak, picnic, and explore the beach.

Coco Plum Beach

On the Atlantic side, **Coco Plum Beach** (305/743-0033, 7:30am-sunset, free) offers a long stretch of sandy shore. It's dog friendly and a perfect spot to watch the sun set at the end of the day. Coco Plum is a sea turtle nesting area, and if you're lucky you may have the chance to see them hatching. Like many of the

beaches that are not constantly maintained by a resort or hotel, a large amount of seaweed often builds up along the coast, but this is a natural feature of the beach and is an important part of the marine ecosystem. To get to Coco Plum, turn south at Mile Marker 55 and follow Coco Plum Drive. The entrance to the beach is 1.4 miles on the right, where you'll find restrooms, picnic pavilions, and a good kayak and canoe launch.

★ Sombrero Beach

Located at the end of Sombrero Beach Road, near Mile Marker 50 in Marathon, **Sombrero Beach** (305/743-0033, 7:30am-sunset, free) is one of the more popular beaches in the Florida Keys. Part of a public park that offers picnic pavilions, volleyball courts, public restrooms, and a small playground, this curving, palm-lined expanse of sand is also a preferred spot for nesting turtles from April to October. Popular with swimmers, snorkelers, picnickers, windsurfers, and volleyball enthusiasts, Sombrero Beach is also home to the **Battle in the Bay,** an annual dragon boat race that usually takes place in May. Although there are no concessions, equipment rentals, or camping facilities on-site, families, couples, and active individuals simply adore this place, especially on a sunny, cloudless day—and unlike many beaches in the Keys, Sombrero allows pets, provided they're well behaved.

★ FISHING AND BOATING

Fishing charters and boat rentals are available throughout the Middle Keys. If you're new to the area, your best bet would be to stop by one of the many marinas. Several area resorts feature on-site marinas where guests and nonguests can book offshore and backcountry fishing charters. Some of these include **Hawks Cay Resort** (61 Hawks Cay Blvd., Duck Key, 305/743-7000, www.hawkscay.

com), **Coral Lagoon Resort & Marina** (MM 54, 12399 Overseas Hwy., Marathon, 305/853-5000, www.keyscaribbean.com), and **Captain Pip's Marina & Hideaway** (MM 47.6, 1410 Overseas Hwy., Marathon, 305/743-4403 or 800/707-1692, www.captainpips.com).

Another option is **Burdine's Waterfront Marina** (1200 Oceanview St., Marathon, 305/743-5317, www.burdineswaterfront. com, 6:30am-6pm daily), which not only assists with fishing charters, but also offers a bait and tackle shop, fishing and boating equipment, picnic supplies, and boat dockage that includes bathrooms, showers, water and electric service, cable television, and laundry facilities. As a bonus, you can relax at the **ChikiTiki Bar & Grille** (11am-9pm daily) and choose from cheeseburgers, fresh sandwiches, key lime pie, and cold beer. Return after your fishing trip, and the restaurant will cook your fresh, cleaned catch any way you like it.

The Middle Keys has entirely too many fishing charters to name them all, but there are at least two standouts. **Sweet E'Nuf Fishing Charters** (MM 53, 11601 Overseas Hwy., Marathon, 305/260-6243, www. sweetenufcharters.com, $600-750 per half day, $1,050-1,150 daily) offers reef, wreck, sportfish, and offshore fishing trips, while **Flat Out Sportfishing** (941 E. 75th St. Ocean, Marathon, 305/743-7317 or 305/395-1228, www.floridakeysflats.com, trips and rates vary daily) enables anglers to fish for permit, bonefish, tarpon, and shark in the backcountry.

Lady Catherine Charters (305/743-5544, www.diveandfishmarathon.com, $550 per half day, $800 for three-quarter day, $900 daily), situated at the Seascape Motel and Marina (1275 E. 76th St. OS, Marathon), offers diving excursions and sunset cruises in addition to offshore, reef, and bay fishing, and the *Marathon Lady* (MM 53 OS U.S. 1, 11711 Overseas Hwy., Marathon, 305/743-5580,

www.marathonlady.net, 8:30am-12:30pm and 1:30pm-5:30pm daily in winter, 9:30am-1:30pm and 6:30-midnight in summer Memorial Day to Labor Day, $45 pp, $5 per rod and reel) provides a party boat fishing experience that's ideal for families on a budget. For all fishing charters, reservations are highly recommended—and oftentimes absolutely necessary. Also take note that while the cost for most charters includes a fishing license fee, you should always confirm such details when booking your trip.

If you'd rather venture out on your own, you can rent a boat from **Fish 'n Fun Boat & Watersports Rentals** (1149 Greenbriar Rd., Marathon, 305/743-2275 or 800/471-3440, www.fishnfunrentals.com, 8am-6pm daily), which offers vessels from 20 to 24 feet ($195-310 per half day, $235-350 daily, $1,300-1,995 weekly). You can also try **Wakezone Bay View Inn and Marina** (3 N. Conch Ave., Conch Key, 305/289-1525, 10am-5pm daily), which is based near Mile Marker 63 and has three different vessel types ($85-150 daily plus gas), in addition to reef-fishing charters (starting at $325 per 4-hour trip). Depth finders, swimming ladders, diver-down flags, VHF radios, maps, anchors, and bimini tops are included with every rental. Other options include **Tropical Boat Rentals** (91 Ave. A, Marathon, 305/481-7006, www. tropicalboatrentals.com, 8am-7pm daily, rates vary daily and weekly) and **Boat Rentals in Paradise** (Captain Hook's Marina & Dive Center, MM 53, 11833 Overseas Hwy., Marathon, 305/743-2444 or 800/278-4665, www.captainhooks.com, 6am-6pm daily, $189-369 daily, $910-1,900 weekly), both of which offer a wide array of vessels, plus delivery service. For live, fresh, or frozen bait, plus fuel, apparel, rod and reel rentals, and other supplies, stop by **Big Time Bait and Tackle** (MM 53, 11499 Overseas Hwy., Marathon, 305/289-0199, www.bigtimetackle.com, 6:30am-6pm daily) on Vaca Key before heading out on your fishing trip.

1: Curry Hammock State Park **2:** visitors observing rehabilitating sea turtles at the Turtle Hospital **3:** Sombrero Beach

★ DIVING AND SNORKELING

Whether you're a first-time snorkeler or an experienced scuba diver, you should take some time to explore the waters east of the Middle Keys. Situated in the heart of Vaca Key, **Tilden's Scuba Center** (MM 46.5, 4650 Overseas Hwy., Marathon, 305/743-7255 or 888/728-2235, www.tildensscubacenter.com, 8am-6pm daily), a full-service diving facility and retail store, provides equipment rentals and Snuba diving ($165-250 pp), a patented form of deepwater snorkeling. In addition, you can take scuba-diving classes through Tilden's, including an introduction course ($175 pp), an open-water certification course ($650 pp), a rescue diver course ($350 and up pp), and several other specialty options; some classes have age restrictions. You can also participate in snorkeling ($60 pp) and scuba-diving adventures ($85-150 pp), including wreck and night dives ($115 pp).

Other area operators include **Dive Duck Key** (Hawks Cay Resort, 61 Hawks Cay Blvd., Duck Key, 305/743-9633 or 877/386-3483, www.diveduckkey.com, 8am-6pm daily), **A Deep Blue Scuba Diving and Snorkeling Center** (400 Sadowski Cswy., Key Colony Beach, 305/743-2421, www.adeepbluedive.com, 8am-5pm daily), and **Captain Hook's Marina & Dive Center** (MM 53, 11833 Overseas Hwy., Marathon, 305/743-2444 or 800/278-4665, www.captainhooks.com, 6am-6pm daily). All offer lessons, equipment rentals, and daily snorkeling and diving trips to area reefs. For snorkel-only excursions, consider boarding catamarans like the *Spirit* (MM 47.5 BS U.S. 1, 1480 Overseas Hwy., Marathon, 305/289-0614, www.spiritsnorkeling.net, trips at 9am and 1pm, $29.99 pp) or *Starfish* (MM 47.5 BS U.S. 1, 1480 Overseas Hwy., Marathon, 305/481-0407, www.starfishsnorkeling.com, trips at 9am and 1pm, $37 pp); each offers seasonal sunset cruises (times vary depending on sunset, $35 pp) and specialty trips.

Of the more than 25 underwater sites that you might see on such diving and snorkeling tours, two of the most popular ones are the **Delta Shoals,** a network of coral canyons that nurture star, elkhorn, and brain coral heads, and **Sombrero Reef,** a spur-and-groove reef formation featuring elkhorn coral and designated by a 142-foot tower. Also in these waters lie two curious shipwrecks: the *Adelaide Baker,* the remains of

snorkeling in the Keys

a three-masted, iron-rigged ship now lying in 25 feet of water; and the *Thunderbolt,* a 188-foot ship sunk in 1986 and now encrusted with coral and sponges that lure deepwater fish like jacks and angelfish.

A helpful resource for divers is *Teall's Guide: Marathon Key West,* a detailed nautical map prepared by Keys Charts that indicates water depths throughout the Middle Keys as well as official dive sites. It covers the area from East Turtle Shoal to Sombrero Reef.

CANOEING AND KAYAKING

As with the rest of the Florida Keys, paddling enthusiasts won't be disappointed in the greater Marathon area. There are not only plenty of nooks and crannies for you to explore by kayak, but also several operators and guides to help you navigate these bountiful waters. At **Long Key State Park** (MM 67.4, 67400 Overseas Hwy., Long Key, 305/664-4815, www.floridastateparks.org, 8am-sunset daily, $4.50 for 1 person, $5 plus $0.50 per additional person for 2 or more people, $2.50 pedestrians and bikers), canoeists can enjoy a leisurely trip along the **Long Key Lakes Canoe Trail** through a shallow lagoon. Canoe rentals ($17.50/day for single and $21.50/day for double) and a self-guided brochure make this a relatively easy diversion even for novices. At Hawks Cay Resort, **Sole Watersports** (61 Hawks Cay Blvd., Duck Key, 305/209-9959, www.hawkscay.com, 9am-5pm daily) provides single and double kayak rentals by the hour ($30-35) and half day ($70-75). You can also rent single and double kayaks ($17.20-21.50 per two hours) from the ranger station at **Curry Hammock State Park** (MM 56.2, 56200 Overseas Hwy., Marathon, 305/289-2690, www.floridastateparks.org, 8am-sunset daily, $4.50 for 1 person, $5 plus $0.50 per additional person for 2 or more people, $2.50 pedestrians and bikers), a wonderful place to paddle in the shallow waters that surround several wooded islands.

On Vaca Key, **Wheels-2-Go!** (MM 59.9, 5994 Overseas Hwy., Marathon, 305/289-4279, www.wheels-2-go.com, 9am-5pm daily) offers single and double kayaks, fishing kayaks, paddleboards, and sea sleds, which you can rent by the day ($29-49), for three days ($69-99), or a week ($129-149). Wheels-2-Go! also provides three-hour self-guided kayak tours ($50 pp) through the mangrove islands and backcountry waters.

GOLF

The **Key Colony Beach Golf Course** (460 8th St., Key Colony Beach, 305/289-9859, www.keycolonybeach.net/recreation.html, 7:30am-sunset daily, $13), offers a nine-hole par-three golf course, plus tennis courts that are free to the public. Golf memberships ($150-430 yearly) are available, as are club rentals ($3) and pull carts ($2).

HIKING AND BIKING

Like much of the Florida Keys, the greater Marathon area doesn't typically appeal to long-distance hikers. Nevertheless, you can certainly enjoy a pleasant stroll through places like **Long Key State Park** (MM 67.4, 67400 Overseas Hwy., Long Key, 305/664-4815, www.floridastateparks.org, 8am-sunset daily, $4.50 for 1 person, $5 plus $0.50 per additional person for 2 or more people, $2.50 pedestrians and bikers), which features two nature trails: the 1.2-mile Golden Orb Trail, named after a native spider, and the shorter 0.3-mile Layton Trail, located on the bay side of the park.

Curry Hammock State Park (MM 56.2, 56200 Overseas Hwy., Marathon, 305/289-2690, www.floridastateparks.org, 8am-sunset daily, $4.50 for 1 person, $5 plus $0.50 per additional person for 2 or more people, $2.50 pedestrians and bikers) contains a 1.5-mile nature trail that winds through the hardwood hammock preserved by the park. In the heart of Vaca Key, the **Crane Point Museum and Nature Center** (MM 55.5, 5550 Overseas Hwy., Marathon, 305/743-3900, www.cranepoint.net, 9am-5pm Mon.-Sat., noon-5pm Sun., $14.95 adults, $12.95 seniors 65 and older, $9.95 children 5-13, free

Artificial Reefs

The 2,900-square-mile Florida Keys National Marine Sanctuary encompasses more than just living coral reefs. This incredible preserve also contains several artificial reefs—essentially, artificially constructed underwater structures that have been utilized around the world for a variety of purposes. Centuries ago, ancient Persians and Romans used such reefs to defend waterways or trap enemy ships. In more recent times, the reefs have been employed to improve fishing, control beach erosion, enhance hydrodynamics for surfing, or as is typically the case in the Florida Keys, promote marinelife in areas of featureless bottom.

While artificial reefs can be erected using various materials, including rubble, tires, concrete, and construction debris, those that you'll find in the Florida Keys are usually one of two varieties: actual shipwrecks or vessels intentionally sunk. Once preserved on the seafloor, these structures lure algae, barnacles, oysters, sponges, coral formations, and other invertebrates. The gradual natural accumulation of such diverse marinelife then provides an intricate structure as well as sustenance for a variety of tropical fish, game fish, and other marine creatures.

Naturally, such lively artificial reefs lure both anglers and scuba divers to the Florida Keys. Near Key Largo you'll encounter the USS *Spiegel Grove,* a 510-foot Navy transport ship originally launched in November 1955 and sunk in May 2002 to create an artificial reef. Closer to Key West lies the 522-foot USNS *General Hoyt S. Vandenberg,* a former troop transport ship used during World War II, intentionally sunk in May 2009, and now a marinelife habitat that offers a fascinating look at the developing stages of coral growth. The Marathon area has its share of enticing artificial reefs, including the *Thunderbolt,* a 188-foot steel ship built in 1942, purposely sunk in 1986 four miles south of Key Colony Beach, and now encrusted with coral and sponges that attract deepwater fish like jacks and angelfish.

It's important to remember that artificial reefs provide a necessary service for the ocean environment, offering a home to countless fish and marine creatures. Though the public is welcome to explore and enjoy them, conservation is still a top priority. To that end, scuba divers should avoid defacing or damaging these reefs and refrain from collecting any natural or historical resources found there. Likewise, anglers should avoid anchoring too close to such reefs and, whenever possible, practice catch-and-release fishing in these areas, which helps to protect fisheries from excessive harvest. If you're not familiar with catch-and-release fishing, follow these simple guidelines:

- Use artificial lures, barbless hooks, and fishing line that's strong enough to bring in the fish quickly.

- Wet your hands before handling the fish, and minimize the time that it's out of the water.

for children under 5) features a 1.5-mile nature trail through palm trees and mangroves and alongside historic structures.

Given the Middle Keys' numerous bridges and sprawling nature, bikers will undoubtedly relish the region even more—though care should always be taken on the Overseas Highway, and a proper helmet should be worn at all times. Between Mile Marker 58 and Mile Marker 40, you'll find an 11-mile biking path, part of the Florida Keys Overseas Heritage Trail, plus a wide shoulder along the Seven Mile Bridge. Bicycles can be rented from

Bike Marathon Bike Rental (305/743-3204, www.bikemarathonbikerentals.com, 8am-6pm daily, $45 weekly), Marathon's first and oldest bicycle rental company, which also offers free delivery and free pickup service in Marathon and Key Colony Beach. Each rental includes a free basket and lock.

You can also rent bicycles from Wheels-2-Go! (MM 59.9, 5994 Overseas Hwy., Marathon, 305/289-4279, www.wheels-2-go.com, 10am-6pm daily, $15 daily, $79 weekly), which also supplies free helmets, locks, baskets, and car racks if needed.

the USNS *General Hoyt S. Vandenberg*, an artificial reef near Key West

· Be gentle and keep your fingers away from the gills and eyes.

· Measure and photograph the fish while it's in the water.

· Use long-nosed pliers to back the hook out of its entrance hole, and if possible, remove the hook quickly and gently while keeping the fish in the water.

· Cut the line near the hook if the fish is hooked deeply.

· Move the fish back and forth until it is revived and swims from your hands.

For more information about catch-and-release fishing, consult the Marine Fisheries Management Division of the **Florida Fish and Wildlife Conservation Commission** (FWC, 850/487-0554, www.myfwc.com), and for more information about artificial reefs in this region, consult **Florida Keys National Marine Sanctuary** (305/852-7717 or 305/809-4700, www.floridakeys.noaa.gov).

OTHER ACTIVITIES

At Hawks Cay Resort, **Sole Watersports** (61 Hawks Cay Blvd., Duck Key, 305/743-0145, www.sundancewatersports.net) offers paddleboard rentals ($40 per hour, $90 per half day).

Those hoping to experience a little less activity, or simply relax after a long day in the sun, can make an appointment at the **Calm Waters Spa** (61 Hawks Cay Blvd., Duck Key, 305/289-4810, www.hawkscay.com/amenities/spa-fitness, 9am-7pm daily) at Hawks Cay Resort. Featuring an array of island-inspired manicures and pedicures ($45-95 pp), facials ($150-220 pp), massages ($80-225 pp), body exfoliation treatments ($80-200 pp), and other services, the Calm Waters Spa also offers daily exclusives, such as Sea Stone Saturday when patrons can receive complimentary aromatherapy with every sea stone massage or a complimentary eye treatment with every Sun N' Sea facial. Appointments are highly recommended, and cancellations must be made at least four hours prior to your scheduled treatment time.

Entertainment and Shopping

NIGHTLIFE

If you're looking for a plethora of dance clubs and late-night bars, heading south to Key West might be your best bet. But that doesn't mean that you won't find nighttime diversions in the Middle Keys. As in the Upper and Lower Keys, several area bars and restaurants feature live music throughout the week.

At **The Hurricane** (MM 46.5, 4650 Overseas Hwy., Marathon, 305/743-2220, www.hurricaneblues.com, 11am-midnight daily), patrons can watch televised sports and enjoy nightly entertainment, from blues bands to country-rock performers.

Farther down the road, Barbara and Johnny Maddox invite nighttime revelers to their ever-popular **Porky's Bayside BBQ Restaurant** (MM 47.5, 1410 Overseas Hwy., Marathon, 305/289-2065, www. porkysbaysidebbq.com, 7am-10pm daily), which offers a daily happy hour (3pm-6pm) and live bluegrass, country, or rock 'n' roll nightly (6pm-9pm) in a classic laid-back Keys atmosphere.

In Key Colony Beach, near Mile Marker 53.5, you'll find two winning spots to while away the evening. Owned and operated by Matt and Carolyn Anthony, the rustic **Sparky's Landing** (400 Sadowski Cswy., Key Colony Beach, 305/289-7445, www. sparkyslanding.com, 11am-10pm daily) provides locals and tourists a quintessential Florida Keys experience, featuring a daily happy hour (4pm-6pm) as well as live folk, rock, country, and reggae music Wednesday-Saturday. Not far away, the family-owned **Key Colony Inn Restaurant and Lounge** (700 E. Ocean Dr., Key Colony Beach, 305/743-0100, www.kcinn.com, 10am-2:30pm and 5pm-9pm daily) has been a favorite among residents and visitors for well over 15 years—not just for the delicious cuisine, but also for the live piano music in the on-site lounge every night.

THE ARTS

The Middle Keys offer a few options for those seeking an alternative to outdoor activities. The **Marathon Garden Club** (MM 52.7, 5270 Overseas Hwy., Marathon, 305/743-4971, www.marathongardenclub.org) has been known to host live performances, such as productions by the Island Opera Theatre (showtimes and ticket prices vary). The club also features exhibits, workshops, educational programs, flower shows, and home and garden tours, not to mention an on-site garden and gift shop (10am-2pm Mon.-Sat.).

The **Marathon Community Theater** (MM 51, 5101 Overseas Hwy., Marathon, 305/743-0994, www.marathontheater.org) has presented live theater and other entertainment to the Middle Keys since 1944. They offer dance classes, readings, and screenings, and the theater features live performances (showtimes vary, $9-18 for plays, $24 for musicals), including modern farces, comedies, thrillers, and dramas, plus Broadway musicals. Recent productions have included the musical *Guys and Dolls* and the comedy-thriller *Deathtrap*. Performances are usually held Thursday-Saturday in the winter months, but events occur throughout the year. Student tickets ($9 pp) are available for nonmusical performances, and patrons can purchase annual season passes ($54-70 pp).

Near Mile Marker 49, the **Marathon Community Park** (200 36th St. Ocean, Marathon, 305/743-6598, www.ci.marathon. fl.us, 7:30am-10pm daily) contains an amphitheater for live performances, among other facilities. Call the park for current events. In addition, the **Florida Keys Concert Association** (305/240-1000, www. floridakeysconcerts.com) has been hosting live musical performances, from piano concerts to string quartets, for more than four decades. Seasons usually run from January to March, and most performances take place at the San Pablo Catholic Church (550 122nd St. Ocean, Marathon, 305/289-0636, www.sanpablomarathon.org) near Mile Marker 53.5. For information about other cultural events in the Middle Keys, consult the **Florida Keys Council of the Arts** (1100 Simonton St., Key West, 305/295-4369, www.keysarts.com).

FESTIVALS AND EVENTS
Pigeon Key Art Festival

For over 20 years, art lovers have ventured to Marathon for the **Pigeon Key Art Festival** ($7 pp for two days, free for children under 13), hosted annually by the **Pigeon Key Foundation** (1 Knight's Key Blvd., Knight's Key, 573/680-5468, www.pigeonkeyfestival.com). Established by a gathering of local artists in 1995, this popular art show spent the first decade of its existence on Pigeon Key, the small, isolated island that sits beside the Old Seven Mile Bridge west of Marathon. For logistical reasons, the well-attended art festival, which typically takes place during the first weekend of February, shifted venues in 2005 to the Marathon Community Park on the ocean side of U.S. 1, near Mile Marker 49, where the attendance has continued to rise, even without the ambience of Pigeon Key.

Presented by volunteers, this annual event features live music, art raffles, and the works of roughly 85 artists from around the country—artwork that usually includes photography, jewelry, sculpture, glassware, fine crafts, and graphic arts, as well as watercolor, acrylic, and oil paintings. Food and beverages are often available, and the admission price includes a ferry ride to historic Pigeon Key—an excellent deal, considering ferry tickets usually cost $12 for adults and $9 for children. Pets, except for service animals, are not allowed during the festival.

Battle in the Bay

Each May, visitors flock to Marathon's Sombrero Beach, an oceanside stretch of sand accessible via Sombrero Beach Road near Mile Marker 50, to watch the **Battle in the Bay Dragon Boat Festival** (www.battleinthebaydragonboat.com), an annual race of festively decorated dragon boats. Launched directly from the beach, the colorful boats constitute more than just a heated competition on the water—the dragon boat teams are encouraged to gather pledges for the charities of their choice.

In addition, race organizers typically donate part of the proceeds from this event to local nonprofit organizations, such as Reef Relief. Although it costs a considerable amount to register a team for the race, it's absolutely free to watch the festivities—good news for locals and visitors alike. Parking ($3) is available at Marathon High School, located on Sombrero Beach Road about a mile from the race site. Typically, the one-day event occurs on a Saturday in early or mid-May, and area bars usually host fun-filled parties before and after the race.

There was recently a major shake-up behind the scenes of this beloved event. Following problematic negotiations with the City of Marathon, Battle in the Bay was shifted temporarily to Key West, before being canceled there because of a conflict with the U.S. Navy's harbor regulations; after a public outcry it was relocated to Sombrero Beach. It's wise to check the website for updates before making travel plans.

Florida Keys Birding and Wildlife Festival

In late September, animal lovers head to the Middle Keys for the **Florida Keys Birding and Wildlife Festival** (305/872-0774, www.birdingfestivalofthekeys.org). Typically based out of **Curry Hammock State Park** (56200 Overseas Hwy., Marathon, 305/289-2690, www.floridastateparks.org, 8am-sunset daily, entrance fees apply), the five-day festival, which began in 1999, usually features an environmental fair and a series of field trips. Such educational excursions—some of which are free and several of which range in price—may include a biking tour of the Florida Keys

Dragon Boat Festival

Though Marathon's **Battle in the Bay Dragon Boat Festival** (www.battle inthebaydragonboat.com) epitomizes the spirited vibe of the Florida Keys, dragon boat festivals are certainly not unique to this part of the world. In fact, dragon boat racing is an ancient Chinese tradition. For more than 5,000 years, dragon boats have been used for ceremonial purposes in China, but it wasn't until the death of the beloved scholar, statesman, and poet Qu Yuan roughly 2,300 years ago that the **Duanwu Festival** was born.

As the story goes, Qu Yuan, a loyal minister to the King of Chu, was favored by the Chinese people, but his erudite ways greatly unnerved the other court officials, so much so that he was framed for conspiracy and exiled from his home. During the exile, he wrote numerous poems to express his ire and despair over his king, his country, and his people. Then in the year 278 BC, at the age of 37, he tried to drown himself in a nearby river. Because he was still considered a righteous man by the people, several individuals leaped into their boats and searched the waters for him, but their efforts were futile. Since then the Dragon Boat Festival has commemorated this ill-fated attempt to rescue Qu Yuan.

Celebrated annually in various Asian countries, including Singapore and Malaysia, the festival typically occurs on the fifth day of the fifth month of the lunar calendar and, among other activities, always features dragon boat racing. In the 1970s, Hong Kong was instrumental in the development of dragon boat racing as a modern sport. Today the Duanwu Festival is an official national holiday in China, and the sport, which is governed by the **International Dragon Boat Federation (IDBF)** (www.idbf.org), enthralls more than 50 million people worldwide. So be sure to visit Marathon during its one-day version of this centuries-old celebration, which usually takes place in early or mid-May.

Overseas Heritage Trail, a self-guided stroll through the Florida Keys Wild Bird Center, a snorkeling trip to Looe Key Reef, or an all-day bird-watching journey to Dry Tortugas National Park.

Other Annual Events

Besides community events like the annual **Key Colony Beach Boat Parade** (305/743-7214, free admission, free parking)—a nighttime procession that usually takes place in mid-December and features lighted, decorated vessels on the canals and cuts of Key Colony Beach—the Middle Keys host numerous fishing tournaments throughout the year. In early March, anglers can participate in the three-day **Leon Shell Memorial Sailfish Tournament** (305/289-1310). Champions of the tournament are usually awarded a variety of trophies, prizes, and cash purses at Sparky's Landing in the Key Colony Beach Marina. Other popular fishing events include the three-day **Burdines Waterfront Dolphin & Blackfin Tuna Tournament** (305/432-0046,

www.fishmonstercharters.com) in late June, and the four-day **Marathon International Bonefish Tournament** (305/304-8682, www.mibt59.com) in mid-September.

SHOPPING

Here in the Middle Keys, outdoor diversions, family-friendly attractions, and practical chain stores are definitely more prevalent than unique shopping opportunities. For the most part, you'll find little more than souvenir stores in the Marathon area.

On Vaca Key you'll find a slew of gifts and souvenirs at the **Tropical Island Outlet** (305/289-0250, 10am-5pm daily) and **Marooned in Marathon** (305/289-0250, 10am-5pm daily), which share a building (MM 53, 11528 Overseas Hwy., Marathon). Together they offer T-shirts, beach towels, puzzles and games, tropical art and ornaments, and fine cigars. Also on Vaca Key, you can shop for Birkenstocks, Teva sandals, Crocs, and other footwear at **Birkenstock of Old Town II** (MM 53.5, 8915 Overseas Hwy., Marathon,

305/289-9999, 9:30am-5pm Mon.-Sat.) and stock up on hats, sunglasses, sandals, beach towels, souvenirs, and other island necessities at the **Sandal Factory Outlet/T-Shirt City** (MM 51.9, 5195 Overseas Hwy., Marathon, 305/743-5778, 9am-8pm Mon.-Sat., 9am-6pm Sun.), which also has locations in Key Largo and Islamorada.

191

Food

SEAFOOD

It's probably no surprise that the Middle Keys offer a wealth of seafood options. The laid-back ★ **Island Fish Co. Restaurant & Tiki Bar** (MM 54.5, 12648 Overseas Hwy., Marathon, 305/743-4191, www.islandfishco.com, 8am-10pm daily, $8-32) features one of the largest menus in the Keys, including burgers, sandwiches, fried island platters, and fried key lime pie. The house specialties feature some winning choices, among them a particularly tasty Caribbean dish of seasoned pan-seared grouper served with island rice, black beans, and pineapple salsa. If you favor alcoholic drinks, be sure to try the key lime pie martini, which is served in a glass that's ringed with graham cracker crumbs. The spacious island-style restaurant offers rustic indoor seating as well as outdoor seating along the water.

If you return from a long day of fishing empty-handed, never fear. The family-owned **Fish Tales Market and Eatery** (MM 53, 11711 Overseas Hwy., Marathon, 305/743-9196 or 888/662-4822, 10am-6:30pm Mon.-Fri., 10am-4pm Sat., $4-10) offers plenty of fresh, locally caught seafood, from fish and lobster to shrimp and stone crabs. In addition, the market offers hand-cut steaks, plus a whole slew of spices, spreads, rubs, and hot sauces, not to mention suggested recipes. Before or after making your purchases, be sure to stay for a meal in the cozy, inexpensive eatery; if you're a seafood lover, you surely won't regret sampling everything from the red conch chowder to steamed shrimp to a grilled yellowfin tuna sandwich.

If you have a hankering for conch—indeed a popular item in southern Florida—there's probably no place in the Keys that boasts as many conch dishes as the aptly named **Cracked Conch Cafe** (MM 49.9, 4999 Overseas Hwy., Marathon, 305/743-2233, www.conchcafe.com, 8am-9pm daily, $16-28), just west of the Crane Point nature preserve. Popular with locals for more than three decades, this casual eatery offers delicious conch fritters, both cream-based and tomato-based conch chowders, and several conch specialties, including "conch in the weeds," a conch dish that features spinach and mushrooms. With a relaxing outdoor patio and a simple interior that sports an Old Florida vibe, the Cracked Conch even relies on ceiling fans—in lieu of an air-conditioner—to keep the joint cool during the warm months.

Another popular seafood eatery is the **Keys Fisheries Market & Marina** (3502 Gulfview Ave., Marathon, 305/743-4353 or 866/743-4353, www.keysfisheries.com, 11am-9pm daily, $9-29), which lies roughly half a mile west of the Cracked Conch and features picnic tables overlooking the marina. Try the famous lobster Reuben, the fried scallops, or the blackened mango grouper.

For a more eclectic menu, head to the spacious ★ **Castaway Waterfront Restaurant & Sushi Bar** (1406 Oceanview Ave., Marathon, 305/743-6247, www.castawayfloridakeys.com, 8am-10pm daily, $14-40). Prior to a massive renovation that dramatically expanded and modernized the space, it was the oldest intact building on the island. Owned for the past decade by ever-present husband-and-wife duo John and Arlene, Castaway can get fairly crowded with tourists and locals (including other area restaurant owners) during the high season,

despite its hidden location on a side street in western Marathon. The menu boasts such tasty dishes as the hogfish stuffed with shrimp and scallops, premium queen conch lightly egg-battered and fried, and sautéed alligator tail smothered in mushrooms and scallions—not to mention a full lineup of top-notch sushi. Beyond the incredible food and outdoor seating alongside the adjacent marina, Castaway even offers a casual outer bar where you can listen to live music before or after your meal.

AMERICAN

South of Mile Marker 53.5, you'll spot ★ **Sparky's Landing** (400 Sadowski Cswy., Key Colony Beach, 305/289-7445, www.sparkyslanding.com, 11am-10pm daily, $7-29), a popular local hangout situated beside the Key Colony Beach Marina. This rustic, unassuming eatery offers an extremely eclectic menu, with everything from standard burgers to bacon-wrapped scallops. Even the appetizers are varied, ranging from nachos to shrimp ceviche. For an appetizer, try the blue cheese chips, essentially homemade potato chips covered in blue cheese and drizzled with an herb vinaigrette. The shrimp-and-bacon pizza, fish tacos, and key lime pie are also worth a taste. Like several other restaurants in the Florida Keys, Sparky's promises to cook whatever you catch. As a bonus, the low-key eatery features live music Wednesday-Saturday and hosts the annual Leon Shell Memorial Sailfish Tournament.

While the decor at **Herbie's Restaurant** (MM 50.3, 6350 Overseas Hwy., Marathon, 305/743-6373, 11am-9pm Wed.-Sun., $9-22, cash only) may not win any Vaca Key eatery awards anytime soon, it's the delicious food that ensures return customers. Among the offerings is one of the best conch chowders in the Florida Keys, plus popular dishes like sautéed fish and a burger with onion rings. Herbie's only accepts cash.

The Hurricane (MM 49, 4650 Overseas Hwy., Marathon, 305/743-2220, www.hurricanegrill.com, 11am-midnight daily, $7-19) serves salads, sandwiches, and entrées such as shrimp stuffed with crabmeat. You can enjoy live music here Wednesday-Saturday.

You can relish a dynamite breakfast at ★ **The Stuffed Pig** (MM 49, 3520 Overseas Hwy., Marathon, 305/743-4059, www.thestuffedpig.com, 6am-2pm Mon.-Sat., 6am-noon Sun., $6-18), which also offers lunch. Locals especially favor this casual joint, where you dine indoors, on the side patio, or beneath the enormous tiki hut. Winning items include the blueberry pancakes, the popular Pig's Breakfast, and the seafood Benedict, which is served with two poached eggs, crab, shrimp, and scallops.

Although traditional Florida Keys-style dishes are available at **Porky's Bayside BBQ Restaurant** (MM 47.5, 1410 Overseas Hwy., Marathon, 305/289-2065, www.porkysbaysidebbq.com, 7am-9pm daily, $9-18), it's the exceptional barbecue that separates this popular eatery from other area restaurants. Try the Citrus Mojo Marinade Cuban Pork or the BBQ Dinner, which includes chicken or pork plus your choice of two sides.

If you're planning an afternoon trip to Pigeon Key or the Lower Keys, consider the popular **Seven Mile Grill** (MM 47.5, 1240 Overseas Hwy., Marathon, 305/743-4481, www.7-mile-grill.com, 7am-9pm daily, $4-11), located just east of the bridge that inspired its name. The friendly staff here will make you feel like a regular, and the food is prepared and served with little delay. The extensive menu features everything from three-egg omelets to deluxe cheeseburgers to seafood baskets. Consider trying the excellent conch chowder before heading out on your next adventure.

EUROPEAN

A wonderful place for a romantic meal, the **Hideaway Café** (MM 57.7, 57784 Overseas

---

1: kayakers in front of the Castaway Waterfront Restaurant & Sushi Bar **2:** Hideaway Café upstairs at the Rainbow Bend Fishing Resort **3:** Seven Mile Grill

Hwy., Marathon, 305/289-1554, www. hideawaycafe.com, 4:30pm-10pm daily, $7-19), located at the Rainbow Bend Fishing Resort on Grassy Key, offers both a unique menu and a relaxing atmosphere. Try the escargot appetizer and the Hideaway seafood special, which is the day's catch sautéed with shrimp and scallops in a scampi sauce. As an alternative, try the filet medallions beurre noir, slices of filet mignon flambéed with cognac, garlic, and shrimp. Enjoy your meal while gazing out at the palm-lined ocean.

Head to Key Colony Beach for a tasty espresso martini at the **Key Colony Inn** (700 W. Ocean Dr., 305/743-0100, www.kcinn.com, 10am-2:30pm and 5pm-10pm daily, $12-29), where you'll find plenty of seafood, often merged with French and Italian cuisine. The New Brunswick baked sea scallops dish, for instance, features bacon in a light cream sauce with a hint of rosemary, and the baked lasagna seafood contains layers of noodles, local snapper, scallops, shrimp, cheese, and sauce.

PIZZA

Even in the seafood capital of the world, you might sometimes have a craving for pizza. Luckily, **Upper Crust Pizza** (MM 49, 3740 Overseas Hwy., Marathon, 305/743-7100, www.uppercrustpizzainc.com, 11am-2pm and 5pm-9pm Mon.-Fri., 5pm-9pm Sat., $8-20) can satisfy any such craving. Situated on Vaca Key, this roomy, super-casual joint serves traditional Italian dishes in addition to pizza. Upper Crust offers both take-out and delivery service.

Accommodations

UNDER $100

On Vaca Key, the **Coconut Cay Resort & Marina** (MM 51, 7196 Overseas Hwy., Marathon, 305/289-7672 or 877/354-7356, www.coconutcay.com, $90-170 d) possesses all the charms of a Bahamian resort. The accommodations vary from standard rooms, with one or two double beds and a small refrigerator, to the Coral Cove rental, with three bedrooms and a full kitchen. Pleasantly lined with palm trees, the lovely property features a swimming pool with a 4,000-square-foot sundeck. Kayak and boat rentals are available.

$100-200

The **Edgewater Lodge** (MM 65.5, 65683 Overseas Hwy., Long Key, 305/664-2662, www.edgewaterlodge.com, $100-170 d) offers standard motel rooms, plus efficiencies and two-bedroom cottages with full kitchens. On-site amenities include large sundecks, a freshwater pool, a fishing pier, and a boat ramp.

In Key Colony Beach, the **Continental Inn** (1121 West Ocean Dr., Key Colony Beach, 305/289-0101 or 800/443-7352, www.

marathonresort.com, $168-233 d) invites you to a secluded retreat on the Atlantic Ocean. The one-bedroom and two-bedroom apartments all have full kitchens and cable television. The inn also offers free boat dockage, access to a par-three golf course, and assistance in satisfying all of your water-sports needs.

On U.S. 1, the clean, affordable units at the **Sea Dell Motel** (MM 50, 5000 Overseas Hwy., Marathon, 305/743-5161 or 800/648-3854, www.seadellmotel.com, $119-189 d) include refrigerators and a variety of bed sizes. The pet-friendly "waterview" efficiency features two double beds and a full kitchen and is also available for weekly rentals. Surrounded by palm trees and lush foliage, this family-friendly motel also offers a heated freshwater pool, picnic and barbecue areas, and high-speed Internet access.

Nestled among palm trees and flowering plants on the bay side of Long Key, the intimate **Lime Tree Bay Resort** (MM 68.5 BS U.S. 1, Layton, 305/664-4740, www. limetreebayresort.com, rooms $89-159 d, studios $129-189, mini suites $129-200, suites $159-304, town houses $200-365) features 44 different units, ranging from standard rooms to town houses. Certain lodgings are pet friendly. In addition, guests have free use of the sunning beach, swimming pool and heated spa, boat dockage, wireless Internet, kayaks, hammocks, and barbecue grills.

The secluded ★ **Conch Key Cottages** (MM 62.2, 62250 Overseas Hwy., Walker's Island, 305/289-1377 or 800/330-1577, www.conchkeycottagesfloridakeys.com, $199-570 d) is a small, tranquil boutique resort far enough from the highway to make you feel as though you're on your own private island. Each unit has its own unique ambience, from the stilted two-bedroom cottages to the beachfront bungalows, and each features a well-equipped kitchen and amenities like plush robes, cable television, and free continental breakfast. Guests are welcome to relax in the gated swimming pool or launch complimentary two-seater kayaks from the private beach for a bird-watching excursion among the mangroves. For a fee, you can also launch and dock your own boat during your stay. In addition, the beach and tiki-themed lounge area are ideal places to watch a gorgeous sunrise or sunset.

On Grassy Key, the **Gulf View Waterfront Resort** (MM 58.7, 58743 Overseas Hwy., Marathon, 305/289-1414 or 877/289-0111, www.gulfviewwaterfrontresort.com, $140-295 d) features 11 units, ranging from guest rooms with refrigerators to two-bedroom apartments with full kitchens. This pet-friendly resort also has one of the largest freshwater pools in the Florida Keys, plus complimentary canoes, kayaks, and pedal boats. If you just want to relax, feel free to take advantage of one of the on-site hammocks or tiki huts.

For a no-frills place at a reasonable price, check out the **Yellowtail Inn Beach Resort** (MM 58.1, 58162 Overseas Hwy., Marathon, 305/743-8400 or 800/605-7475, www.yellowtailinn.com, $139-299 d) on Grassy Key. The traditional guest rooms have one queen-size bed or two double beds, a small refrigerator, and a microwave. The efficiencies and cottages feature full kitchens, and some even boast private balconies or porches. Other onsite amenities include a small swimming pool, a private beach, and a fishing pier.

Farther west on Grassy Key, the **Rainbow Bend Fishing Resort** (MM 57.7, 57784 Overseas Hwy., Marathon, 305/289-1505 or 800/929-1505, www.rainbowbend.com,

Rainbow Bend Fishing Resort

$175-290 d) houses one-bedroom and two-bedroom oceanfront suites and one-bedroom patio efficiencies with full kitchens. As a bonus, a full complimentary American breakfast is served at the Hideaway Café each morning. Given that it's a fishing resort, Rainbow Bend also offers free use of the on-site motorboats. In addition, the staff can easily arrange a fishing charter for you.

As the only "botel" in this part of the Florida Keys, the **Royal Hawaiian Motel/Botel** (MM 54, 12020 Overseas Hwy., Marathon, 305/743-7500, www.royalhawaiianmotelbotel.com, $159-199 d) promises easy access to the Gulf of Mexico and Atlantic Ocean through the Vaca Cut. Each standard room contains two double beds and a small refrigerator while each kitchenette comes with two double beds and a full kitchen. Guests receive free boat dockage during their stay.

If you're looking for a one-stop vacation shop, consider the **Skipjack Resort & Marina** (19 Sombrero Blvd., Marathon, 305/289-7662 or 800/433-8660, www.sombreroresortmarina.com, $159-299 d), which offers standard rooms and efficiencies. You can satisfy all of your water-sports needs at slip 53, where you can rent a canoe, kayak, or fishing boat. After playing a few sets on the lighted tennis courts, take a dip in the heated pool, then sip a piña colada while relaxing at the poolside tiki bar. If you get hungry, you're in luck: The on-site Boot Key Bar and Grill serves an array of salads, pizzas, and pasta dishes. In addition, the staff will prepare your day's catch any way you like it.

OVER $200

Just east of the Seven Mile Bridge, the **Courtyard Marriott Marathon** (MM 48.5, 2222 Overseas Hwy., Marathon, 305/289-4411 or 800/222-4832, www.bluewatersmarathon.com, $200-350 d) provides deepwater access to Florida Bay, the Atlantic Ocean, and the only living coral reef in U.S. waters. The property features efficiencies with full kitchens, a freshwater pool, protected boat dockage, and access to area fishing and water sports.

Located on 60-acre Duck Key, ★ **Hawks Cay Resort** (61 Hawks Cay Blvd., 305/743-7000 or 888/395-5539, www.hawkscay.com, $225-450 d) almost lulls you into believing you're on a luxurious Caribbean island. With gorgeous rooms and villas, five unique eateries, five different swimming pools, a world-class spa, a slew of water-related activities, and its own interactive dolphin facility, Hawks Cay promises a unique, all-encompassing experience. Beyond well-appointed West Indies-style hotel rooms and suites, the resort offers luxury villas in four separate areas: Sunset Village, Marina Village, Harbor Village, and Sanctuary Village.

A bit off the beaten path lies the stunning **CocoPlum Beach & Tennis Club** (109 Coco Plum Dr., Marathon, 305/743-0240 or 800/228-1587, www.cocoplum.com, $170-500 d), which features 20 separate two-bedroom villas. Each elevated unit consists of three stories: The ground floor has a washer and dryer, plus storage units; the first floor contains the kitchen and dining room, as well as a large screened porch; and the second floor features two bedrooms, two bathrooms, and a living room. Other on-site amenities include a beachfront swimming pool featuring a zero-edge concept plus a nine-slip docking area that can accommodate boats up to 40 feet in length.

The **Coral Lagoon Resort & Marina** (MM 53, 12399 Overseas Hwy., Marathon, 305/853-5000 or 866/904-1234, www.corallagoonresort.com, $299-399 d) presents Conch-style villas and detached marina homes. All of the two-bedroom villas, three-bedroom villas, and single-family homes feature 2.5 bathrooms, full kitchens, lower and upper porches, and excellent views, in addition to cable television and free wireless Internet access. The on-site water-sports program offers everything you'll need to fish, snorkel, dive, or simply enjoy the water, and their boat slips can accommodate vessels up to 65 feet in length.

Given that most of its guest rooms are named after fish, it's no wonder that ★ **Captain Pip's Marina & Hideaway** (MM 47.6, 1410 Overseas Hwy., Marathon, 305/743-4403 or 800/707-1692, www.captainpips.com, $90-565 d) specializes in arranging the ultimate fishing vacation. This low-key resort near the western end of Vaca Key even offers a few boats that are free for guests to enjoy, and the adjacent marina features a variety of boat rentals, plus fishing guides that can show you the best spots in the bay, ocean, or reefs. Lodgings range from waterfront guest rooms to comfortable efficiencies to spacious apartments. Other on-site amenities include the popular Porky's Bayside BBQ Restaurant.

CAMPING

Campers will find plenty of options in the Middle Keys. Just south of Islamorada is the **Fiesta Key Recreation Destination** (MM 70, 70001 Overseas Hwy., Fiesta Key, 305/249-1035, www.rvonthego.com, $30-80 daily), which offers tent sites, RV sites with water and electricity, and full-hookup RV sites on a day-to-day basis, as well as motel rooms ($140-160 per day), waterfront cottages ($299 per day), and rental travel trailers ($219 per day). The

28-acre property also features an Olympic-size freshwater pool and a complete marina with available slip rentals.

Long Key State Park (MM 67.4, 67400 Overseas Hwy., Long Key, 305/664-4815, www.floridastateparks.org, 8am-sunset daily, $4.50 for 1 person, $5 plus $0.50 per additional person for 2 or more people, $2.50 pedestrians and bikers) presents 60 campsites ($36 daily), each with water and electricity, overlooking the Atlantic Ocean. The park also offers a canoe trail and two land-based nature trails. As a bonus to campers, the beach is only open to those staying in the campground, so you'll surely find this to be one of the more private beaches in the Keys. Reservations can be made up to 11 months in advance through **ReserveAmerica** (800/326-3521, www.reserveamerica.com).

On Grassy Key, the **Jolly Roger Travel Park** (MM 59.2, 59275 Overseas Hwy., Marathon, 305/289-0404, www.jrtp.com, $73-103 daily, $460-662 weekly, $2,397-2,677 monthly) has full-hookup RV sites, van sites with optional water and electrical service, and tent spaces. The park offers daily, weekly, and monthly rates. On-site amenities include high-speed wireless Internet access, cable television hookups, snorkeling and swimming

Hawks Cay Resort

areas, a boat dock with slip rentals, and a free boat ramp for guests.

The **Grassy Key RV Park & Resort** (MM 58.6, 58671 Overseas Hwy., Marathon, 305/289-1606, www.grassykeyrvpark.com, $69-198 daily, $459-1,315 weekly, $1,426-4,077 monthly) accepts RVs of all sizes, including the "big rig" motor coaches. The waterfront, premium, and standard sites are all equipped with water, sewer access, 30/50-amp electricity, and cable television. Other on-site amenities include a freshwater pool, lounging beach, clubhouse, laundry facilities, and boat dockage ($2.25 per foot daily, $10.75 per foot weekly, $15.35 per foot monthly) that allows access to both the Gulf of Mexico and the Atlantic Ocean. Pets are welcome here with some restrictions. Be aware that camping rates can vary greatly depending on the specific site and season. Rates for stays longer than a month are available.

Another state park option is **Curry Hammock State Park** (MM 56.2, 56200 Overseas Hwy., Marathon, 305/289-2690, www.floridastateparks.org, 8am-sunset daily, $4.50 for 1 person, $5 plus $0.50 per additional person for 2 or more people, $2.50 pedestrians and bikers), which has a 28-site campground ($42.70 daily) equipped with picnic tables, charcoal grills, water service, and 20/30/50-amp electricity. A dump station is available at the park. No motorized vessels can be launched here—only kayaks and canoes. Leashed pets are allowed in the campground, but not on the beach. Although bikers, anglers, swimmers, paddlers, and picnickers favor this park, Curry Hammock is especially popular with birding enthusiasts, who will often spot herons, egrets, ibises, plovers, and sanderlings along the shore. Reservations can be made up to 11 months in advance through **ReserveAmerica** (800/326-3521, www.reserveamerica.com).

Information and Services

INFORMATION

For brochures, maps, and other information about Marathon and the Middle Keys, stop by the **Greater Marathon Chamber of Commerce and Visitors Center** (MM 53.5, 12222 Overseas Hwy., Marathon, 305/743-5417 or 800/262-7284, www.floridakeysmarathon.com, 9am-5pm daily), near Mile Marker 53 on the bay side, or consult the **Monroe County Tourist Development Council** (1201 White St., Ste. 102, Key West, 305/296-1552 or 800/352-5397, www.fla-keys.com, 8am-5pm Mon.-Fri.). For government-related issues, contact the **City of Marathon** (MM 52, 9805 Overseas Hwy., Marathon, 305/743-0033, www.ci.marathon. fl.us, 8am-5pm Mon.-Fri.) or the **Monroe County offices** (1100 Simonton St., Key West, 305/292-4459, www.monroecounty-fl. gov, 8am-5pm Mon.-Fri.).

For local news, consult **The Weekly Newspapers** (www.keysweekly.com). The dailies *Miami Herald* (www.miamiherald. com) and *The Key West Citizen* (www. keysnews.com)) are also available throughout the Keys.

Marathon has access to several radio stations, including **WGMX** (94.3 FM) and **WAVK** (97.7 FM), which offer an adult contemporary format, as well as **WFFG** (1300 AM), which provides news and talk radio.

SERVICES
Money

For banking needs, stop by one of the two local branches of **Capital Bank** (800/639-5111, www.capitalbank-us.com). There's one in Marathon Shores (11401 Overseas Hwy., 305/743-7845, 9am-4pm Mon.-Thurs., 9am-6pm Fri., extended drive-through hours) and one in Marathon (2348 Overseas Hwy., 305/743-0072, 9am-5pm Mon.-Thurs., 9am-6pm Fri., 9am-noon Sat., extended drive-through hours). You can also visit the **First State Bank of the Florida Keys** (MM 69, 6900 Overseas Hwy., Marathon, 305/289-4393, www.keysbank.com, 8am-5pm Mon.-Fri., 9am-noon Sat., extended drive-through hours).

Mail

For shipping, faxing, copying, and other business-related services, visit **The UPS Store** (MM 54, 5409 Overseas Hwy., Marathon, 305/743-2005, www.theupsstore. com, 8am-6pm Mon.-Fri., 9am-5pm Sat.). You can also package and ship items at the four area **post offices** (800/275-8777, www. usps.com). There's one on Long Key (MM 68.3, 68340 Overseas Hwy., 305/664-4112, 9:45am-1pm and 2pm-4:15pm Mon.-Fri.), another in Marathon Shores (MM 53, 11400 Overseas Hwy., Ste. 120, 305/743-6050, 9:30am-noon Mon.-Thurs., 9:30am-12:30pm Fri.), one in Key Colony Beach (600 W. Ocean Dr., 305/743-2249, 11am-1pm and 2pm-4pm Mon.-Fri.), and another in Marathon (MM 51.7, 5171 Overseas Hwy., 305/743-5238, 9am-5pm Mon.-Fri., 9am-noon Sat.).

Groceries and Supplies

For groceries, baked goods, and other supplies, head to the **Winn-Dixie** (MM 55.8, 5585 Overseas Hwy., Marathon, 305/743-3636, www.winndixie.com, 7am-11pm daily) or the **Publix** (MM 54, 5407 Overseas Hwy., Marathon, 305/289-2920, www.publix.com, 7am-11pm Mon.-Sat., 7am-10pm Sun.), the latter of which includes an on-site pharmacy (305/289-3192, 9am-9pm Mon.-Fri., 9am-7pm

Sat., 10am-5pm Sun.). There is a **Walgreens** (MM 52.7, 5271 Overseas Hwy., Marathon, 305/359-3634, www.walgreens.com, 7am-10pm daily) that offers limited supplies as well as an on-site pharmacy (9am-7pm Mon.-Fri., 9am-5pm Sat.).

Laundry

You'll find coin-operated machines at **Coyne's Laundry** (MM 52.5, 11201 Overseas Hwy., Marathon, 305/942-9635, 8:30am-4pm daily).

Internet Access

For wireless Internet access, consult your hotel or resort, as many offer free access nowadays, or you can typically use the Internet at the **Marathon Branch Library** (MM 32.5, 3251 Overseas Hwy., Marathon, 305/743-5156, www.keyslibraries.org, 9:30am-6pm Mon.-Tues. and Thurs.-Fri., 9:30am-8pm Wed., 10am-6pm Sat.).

Emergency Services

In case of an emergency that requires police, fire, or ambulance services, dial **911** from any cell or public phone. For nonemergency assistance, contact the **Monroe County Sheriff's Office** (Marathon Substation, MM 31, 3103 Overseas Hwy., Marathon, 305/289-2430, www.keysso.net, 8am-5pm Mon.-Fri.). For medical assistance, consult the **Fishermen's Hospital** (MM 33, 3301 Overseas Hwy., Marathon, 305/743-5533, www.fishermenshospital.org). Foreign visitors seeking help with directions, medical concerns, business issues, law enforcement needs, or other problems can receive **multilingual tourist assistance** (800/771-5397) 24 hours daily.

Transportation

GETTING THERE

Air

Although you can fly small planes directly into **Florida Keys Marathon Airport (MTH)** (MM 52, 9400 Overseas Hwy., Marathon, 305/289-6060), most travelers reach the Middle Keys by first flying into one of the other area airports, including **Fort Lauderdale-Hollywood International Airport (FLL)** (100 Terminal Dr., Fort Lauderdale, 866/435-9355, www.broward.org/airport), **Miami International Airport (MIA)** (2100 NW 42nd Ave., Miami, 305/876-7000 or 800/825-5642, www.miami-airport.com), or **Key West International Airport (EYW)** (3491 S. Roosevelt Blvd., Key West, 305/809-5200 or 305/296-5439, www.keywestinternationalairport.com). From there you can rent a vehicle from agencies like **Avis** (800/331-1212, www.avis.com), **Budget** (800/527-0700, www.budget.com), **Enterprise** (800/325-8007, www.enterprise.com), **Hertz** (800/654-3131, www.hertz.com), or **Thrifty** (800/367-2277, www.thrifty.com) to reach the Marathon area.

Bus or Train

The **Miami-Dade County Metrobus** (305/891-3131, www.miamidade.gov/transit) operates the **301 Dade-Monroe Express** between Florida City and Marathon (5:15am-8:40pm daily, $2.25 per one-way trip), with several stops in between. In addition, the **Key West Department of Transportation (KWDoT)** (305/600-1455, www.kwtransit.com, $4 per ride, $8 per day, $25 weekly, $75 monthly) provides bus service from Key West to Marathon between 5am and 11pm daily. Reduced fares may apply for students under 22 years old, senior citizens over 59 years old, military personnel, and disabled individuals. **Greyhound** (800/231-2222, www.greyhound.com) offers bus service to Marathon

(MM 50, 9400 Overseas Hwy., 305/296-9073). **Amtrak** (800/872-7245, www.amtrak.com) only provides train service as far south as Miami, from where you can always rent a car or hop a shuttle to reach the Florida Keys.

Transport from Airports and Stations

If you arrive in the Fort Lauderdale-Miami area by plane, bus, or train—or Key West by plane or bus—you can either rent a car or hire a shuttle service to reach the Marathon area. Companies include **Keys Shuttle** (305/289-9997 or 888/765-9997, www.keysshuttle.com, $70-80 per shared ride, $300-350 for exclusive service), which provides service from the Miami and Fort Lauderdale airports; and **SuperShuttle** (305/871-2000 or 954/764-1700, www.supershuttle.com, $255 per ride for up to 10 passengers), which only serves visitors flying into Miami.

Car

To reach the Middle Keys from Miami, head south on U.S. 1 (Overseas Hwy.), drive through Key Largo and Islamorada, and continue toward your destination. If you're headed from the Everglades via I-75 (Everglades Pkwy.), drive south on U.S. 27, veer right onto S.R. 997 (Krome Ave.), and follow the signs to U.S. 1. From U.S. 41 (Tamiami Trl.) in the Everglades, head south on S.R. 997 and continue toward U.S. 1. If you arrive during the peak season (Dec.-Apr.), be sure to call **511** for an up-to-the-minute traffic report.

GETTING AROUND

Car

The best way to travel through the Middle Keys is by car, truck, RV, or motorcycle—all of which offer easy access to U.S. 1 as well as the side roads, such as Sombrero Beach Road.

Taxi

Taxicab companies such as **On Time Taxi** (305/289-5656, $4 per pickup, $1 per mile after initial two miles) can help you get around the Middle Keys.

Bicycle or Boat

While you can certainly traverse the Middle Keys by bicycle, the region's sprawling nature and numerous bridges make it challenging for novice riders. Between Mile Marker 58 and Mile Marker 40 is an 11-mile biking path, plus a wide shoulder along the Seven Mile Bridge. Bicycles can be rented from **Bike Marathon Bike Rental** (305/743-3204, www.bikemarathonbikerentals.com, 8am-6pm daily, $45 weekly), Marathon's first and oldest bicycle rental company. They also offer free delivery and free pickup service in Marathon and Key Colony Beach.

You can also experience the Middle Keys by boat. Having your own vessel makes navigating these waters even easier, and you'll find no shortage of boat ramps and marina slips in the Marathon area, a region popular among boating enthusiasts. To rent a boat or kayak for the day, stop by **Fish 'n Fun Boat & Watersports Rentals** (1149 Greenbriar Rd., Marathon, 305/743-2275 or 800/471-3440, www.fishnfunrentals.com, 8am-6pm daily), near Mile Marker 49.5, which offers a range of vessels, including 20- to 24-foot boats ($190-310 per half day, $225-350 daily, $1,295-1,995 weekly).

Big Pine and the Lower Keys

Stretching from Little Duck Key to Boca Chica

Key, the Lower Keys are the largest and least developed part of the archipelago.

Composed of numerous keys and island clusters, the Lower Keys possess a far more sedate vibe than that of Key West to the south. In this region, beaches, campgrounds, and a host of animals—including birds, snakes, alligators, rabbits, and raccoons—take precedence over tourists and museums, making the Lower Keys the ideal place to escape from the world for a while, even in the winter months when snowbirds help to increase the population.

West of the Seven Mile Bridge, the first major stop, Bahia Honda State Park, is one of the most popular parks in the Keys. Its three sandy

Highlights

Look for ★ to find recommended sights, activities, dining, and lodging.

Miami ○

Gulf of Mexico

Snipe Keys

Saddlebunch Keys

Sugarloaf Key

Cudjoe Key

Big Torch Key

National Key Deer Refuge ★

Blue Hole ★

Ramrod Key

Boating and Kayaking ★

Big Pine Key

Bahia Honda State Park ★

Underwater Music Festival ★

Diving and Snorkeling near Looe Key Reef ★

0   5 mi

0   5 km

© MOON.COM

★ **Bahia Honda State Park:** This treasure boasts a range of recreational activities and some of the most photographed beaches in the Keys (pages 206).

★ **National Key Deer Refuge:** This 9,200-acre sanctuary provides habitat for hundreds of native and migratory species, including the diminutive key deer (page 207).

★ **Blue Hole:** This tranquil body of water nurtures an array of creatures, from green herons to turtles to alligators (page 208).

★ **Boating and Kayaking:** Experience the backcountry islands, bountiful waters, and amazing creatures of the Lower Keys by kayak, skiff, powerboat, or glass-bottom catamaran (page 212).

★ **Diving and Snorkeling near Looe Key Reef:** This classic spur-and-groove formation is home to parrotfish, barracuda, moray eels, and varied sharks (page 214).

★ **Underwater Music Festival:** For three decades, this whimsical event has welcomed hundreds of divers and snorkelers to an underwater concert while promoting the preservation of the coral reef ecosystem (page 215).

beaches, with access to the Atlantic Ocean and the Gulf of Mexico, are routinely voted some of the best in the state and are favored by photographers. Soft white sand and calm, shallow waters make this the perfect place for swimmers, snorkelers, and kayakers, though seaweed is often an issue. Fishing, boating, biking, and hiking are also popular.

Among the other islands, Big Pine Key boasts the lion's share of diversions. From here visitors can take biking and diving trips, glass-bottom boat tours, deep-sea fishing charters, full-day kayaking adventures, and island excursions. Also on Big Pine lies part of the 9,200-acre National Key Deer Refuge, established in the late 1950s to preserve the dwindling population of the petite key deer. Nowadays this amazing refuge protects several other threatened plants and animals as well, many of which you might spot at the Blue Hole, the largest freshwater source in the Keys.

While adjacent Little Torch Key offers access to the exclusive Little Palm Island Resort & Spa, it's still a laid-back locale and a terrific jumping-off point for scuba divers and snorkelers. Part of Florida Keys National Marine Sanctuary, the incredible Looe Key Reef—named after a long-ago shipwreck—sits among several historic wreck sites and is home to the fascinating Underwater Music Festival every July. Other keys—such as Ramrod, Summerland, Cudjoe, and Sugarloaf—offer their own diversions, from fishing charters to kayaking excursions. Besides, even though outdoor pursuits are paramount here, you're not so far away from Key West that you can't make a day trip to the bars, museums, and people-watching hot spots there.

PLANNING YOUR TIME

Although many travelers simply pass through this region on their way to Key West, the Lower Keys are definitely worth a look. You might not find museums or historical districts here, but you'll certainly encounter a wealth of outdoor sights and activities, from underwater coral reefs to fishing charters to kayaking excursions. While the attractions and lodgings are spread across numerous islands, it's not terribly difficult to traverse this region by car, as the Overseas Highway links several of the main islands, such as Bahia Honda Key, Big Pine Key, and Sugarloaf Key. Still, some places, like the No Name Pub, can be a bit challenging to find.

Most people only need a day or two to hit the highlights of this region, such as Bahia Honda State Park and the Blue Hole. The length of your stay, however, depends upon your chosen activities. Fishing, kayaking, snorkeling, and diving—all popular activities here—could easily extend your trip to a full week. Such activities might also determine when you choose to visit.

Luckily, you won't often face crowds and congestion in the Lower Keys, unless you head to a Bahia Honda beach on a particularly warm, sunny day—or hope to reach Key West in a timely manner during a popular event. Also, if you're a novice to certain activities, such as scuba diving, you might want to allow for proper instruction time. Regarding other safety issues, crime isn't a major problem in the Lower Keys, but you should still stay alert in the more isolated areas.

For more information about Big Pine Key and the Lower Keys, consult the **Monroe County Tourist Development Council** (1201 White St., Ste. 102, Key West, 305/296-1552 or 800/648-5510, www.fla-keys.com, 9am-5pm Mon.-Fri.) and the **Lower Keys Chamber of Commerce** (MM 31, 31020 Overseas Hwy., Big Pine Key, 305/872-2411 or 800/872-3722, www.lowerkeyschamber.com, 9am-5pm Mon.-Fri., 9am-3pm Sat.).

Previous: Bahia Honda State Park; a white ibis; mangroves in shallow water.

Big Pine and the Lower Keys

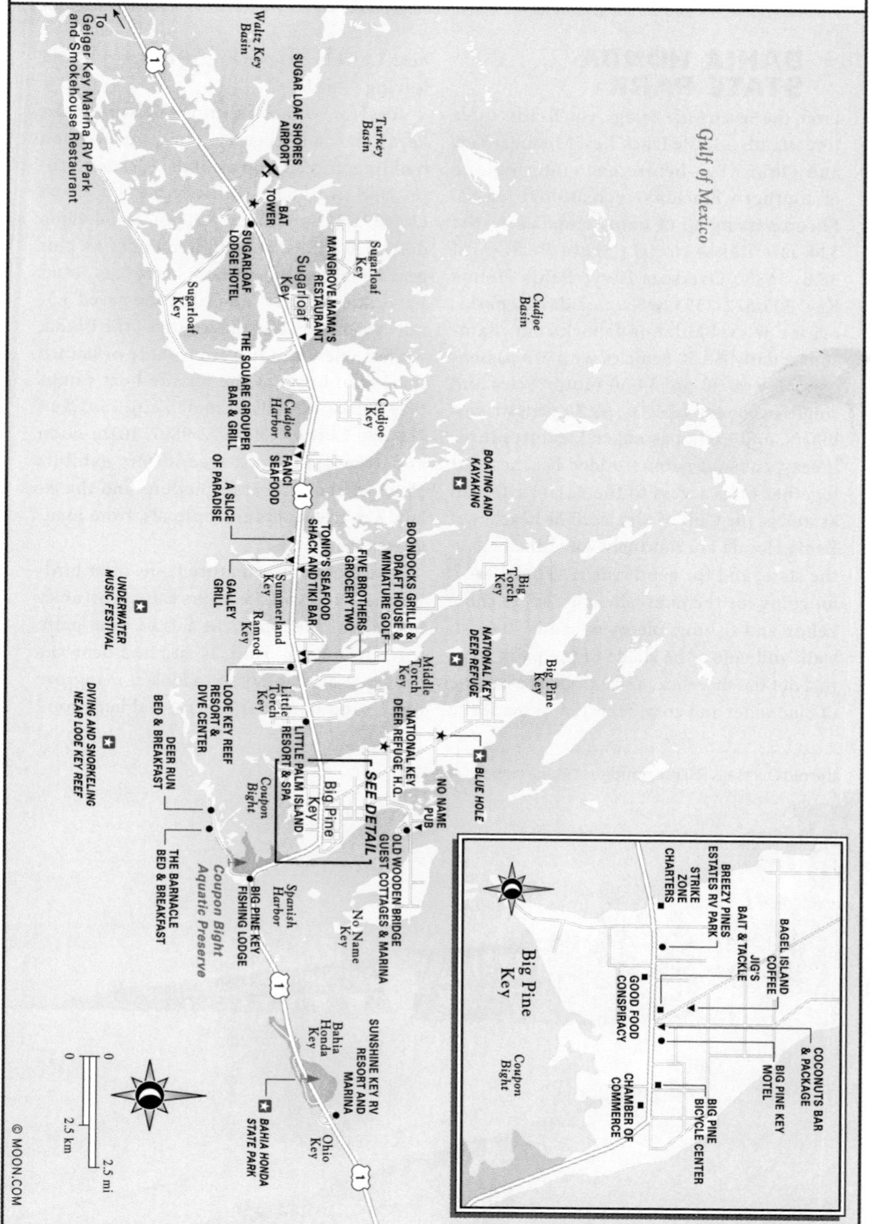

To Geiger Key Marina RV Park
and Smokehouse Restaurant

Waltz Key Basin

SUGAR LOAF SHORES AIRPORT

Turkey Basin

BAT TOWER

SUGARLOAF LODGE HOTEL

MANGROVE MAMA'S RESTAURANT

Sugarloaf Key

Sugarloaf Key

Sugarloaf Basin

Gulf of Mexico

Cudjoe Basin

THE SQUARE GROUPER BAR & GRILL

Cudjoe Harbor

Cudjoe Key

FANCI SEAFOOD

A SLICE OF PARADISE

BOONDOCKS GRILLE & DRAFT HOUSE & MINIATURE GOLF

BOATING AND KAYAKING

FIVE BROTHERS GROCERY TWO

Big Torch Key

TONDO'S SEAFOOD SHACK AND TIKI BAR

Summerland Key

GALLEY GRILL

Ramrod Key

NATIONAL KEY DEER REFUGE

Middle Torch Key

Big Pine Key

UNDERWATER MUSIC FESTIVAL

LOOE KEY REEF RESORT & DIVE CENTER

Little Torch Key

DEER REFUGE, H.Q.

NATIONAL KEY DEER REFUGE

BLUE HOLE

DIVING AND SNORKELING NEAR LOOE KEY REEF

DEER RUN BED & BREAKFAST

LITTLE PALM ISLAND RESORT & SPA

Coupon Bight

Big Pine Key

NO NAME PUB

No Name Key

SEE DETAIL

THE BARNACLE BED & BREAKFAST

BIG PINE KEY FISHING LODGE

Coupon Bight Aquatic Preserve

Spanish Harbor

OLD WOODEN BRIDGE GUEST COTTAGES & MARINA

Coupon Bight

Big Pine Key

SUNSHINE KEY RV RESORT AND MARINA

Bahia Honda Key

BAHIA HONDA STATE PARK

Ohio Key

0   2.5 mi

0   2.5 km

© MOON.COM

Detail — Big Pine Key

Big Pine Key

BREEZY PINES ESTATES RV PARK

STRIKE ZONE CHARTERS

BAIT & TACKLE

JIG'S

BAGEL ISLAND COFFEE

GOOD FOOD CONSPIRACY

COCONUTS BAR & PACKAGE

CHAMBER OF COMMERCE

BIG PINE KEY MOTEL

BIG PINE KEY BICYCLE CENTER

Coupon Bight

Sights

★ BAHIA HONDA STATE PARK

From the Seven Mile Bridge, you'll cross three tiny islands—Little Duck Key, Missouri Key, and Ohio Key—before encountering one of southern Florida's recreational jewels. Encompassing all of Bahia Honda Key, the 524-acre **Bahia Honda State Park** (MM 36.8, 36850 Overseas Hwy., Bahia Honda Key, 305/872-2353, www.floridastateparks. org or www.bahiahondapark.com, 8am-sunset daily, $8.50 vehicles with 2-8 passengers plus $0.50 pp, $4.50 motorcycles and single-occupant vehicles, $2.50 pedestrians, bikers, and extra passengers) features three breezy, coconut palm-studded beaches that together offer access to the Atlantic Ocean as well as the Gulf of Mexico. The beaches of Bahia Honda are routinely voted the best in the state, and for good reason. They have a lot going for them: excellent access to snorkeling and fishing, plenty of sandy shore to walk and enjoy, the shade of the palm trees that dot the shoreline, and a tropical aesthetic of blue water and coral reefs that provide the best Caribbean-esque experience without leaving Florida.

Ideal for swimmers, the park also provides kayak and snorkel gear rentals, a concession building, three campgrounds, vacation cabins, and two-hour **snorkeling excursions** (305/872-3210, 9:30am, 1:30pm, and 4:45pm daily, $30 adults, $25 children under 18, plus gear rentals) to the offshore **Looe Key Reef**. In addition, bikers can utilize the paved 3.5-mile road that runs the length of the island, while anglers can fish from shore or launch their own boats at the on-site boat ramps ($10 per launch). The small **Sand and Sea Nature Center** (305/872-9807, 10am-noon and 1pm-4pm daily, free) offers exhibits about offshore coral formations and the island's native plants and animals, from mangroves to iguanas.

The park's three nature trails offer bird-watchers and wildlife lovers the opportunity to see real specimens in action. One path, the Silver Palm Trail, is situated near the Sandspur area and offers a look at mangrove trees, sand dunes, and a tropical hardwood

the old Overseas Railroad bridge at Bahia Honda State Park

hammock, while another winds through the Wings and Waves Butterfly Garden, which is frequented by vibrant butterflies, including the zebra longwing butterfly and the endangered Miami blue butterfly. The third trail, running beside Calusa Beach, leads to the top of the **Bahia Honda Rail Bridge,** a seemingly unfinished concrete-and-steel structure that once spanned the Bahia Honda Channel as part of the Overseas Railroad. Built in the early 1900s, the bridge was partially destroyed in the infamous Labor Day Hurricane of 1935, and today it affords a panoramic view of the entire island as well as the surrounding waters. From here you may spot fish, eagle rays, sea turtles, bottlenose dolphins, West Indian manatees, and an array of wading birds, shorebirds, and raptors, including great white herons, spotted sandpipers, laughing gulls, mangrove cuckoos, red-bellied woodpeckers, brown pelicans, turkey vultures, and bald eagles.

Other activities here include ranger-led beach walks, various nature and history programs, and, in late January, a reenactment of the first train ride on the former railroad. Reservations are recommended for campgrounds, cabin rentals, boat slips, and snorkeling excursions. Unlike at many places in the Florida Keys, pets are welcome at Bahia Honda, though their access is limited, and they must be well behaved and kept on six-foot handheld leashes at all times.

BIG PINE KEY

As the largest island in the Lower Keys, **Big Pine Key** anchors a region defined by its numerous island clusters and bountiful natural resources—a region that remains the last undeveloped holdout of the Florida Keys. While Big Pine Key, the second-largest island in the entire archipelago, contains the lion's share of attractions, shops, services, and the like, it still represents the laid-back vibe prevalent throughout the Lower Keys, a place where people come to escape the more commercialized—and often more crowded—communities of Key West and Islamorada.

★ National Key Deer Refuge

Founded in 1957, the 9,200-acre **National Key Deer Refuge** (179 Key Deer Blvd., Big Pine Key, 305/872-2239, www.fws.gov/nationalkeydeer, free) encompasses mangrove and pine forests, freshwater and salt-marsh wetlands, and tropical hardwood hammocks on 25 islands in the Lower Keys. The primary purpose of the refuge is to provide critical habitat for hundreds of native and migratory species, including the docile key deer, a miniature version of the white-tailed deer, which only grows to 24-32 inches tall and whose diminishing population inspired the creation of the sanctuary.

Visitors are welcome 24 hours daily in at least part of the refuge, most notably within designated areas of Big Pine Key and No Name Key. Here you'll find the wheelchair-accessible **Fred C. Manillo Wildlife Trail** (0.1 mile) and the **Jack C. Watson Wildlife Trail** (0.7 mile), both of which offer photographers and nature lovers the opportunity to observe many different species of birds, reptiles, and mammals, including great white herons, brown pelicans, various raptors and songbirds, lizards, turtles, alligators, and key deer, which can swim easily between the islands but mainly dwell on Big Pine. Early morning and late afternoon are typically the best times to spot a key deer, especially at the northern end of Key Deer Boulevard.

The wheelchair-accessible **visitors center** (179 Key Deer Blvd., Big Pine Key, 305/872-0774, 9am-4pm Mon.-Fri.) is in the Big Pine Shopping Center near the intersection of U.S. 1 and Key Deer Boulevard. Here you'll also find information about other refuges in the so-called Florida Keys Complex, including **Great White Heron National Wildlife Refuge** (20650 1st Ave. W., Cudjoe Key, www.fws.gov/nationalkeydeer/greatwhiteheron) and **Key West National Wildlife Refuge,** two protected areas that encompass numerous backcountry islands in Florida Bay and the Gulf of Mexico. Unlike the National Key Deer Refuge, these two are only accessible by boat.

Rules of the Refuge

The **National Key Deer Refuge** (179 Key Deer Blvd., Big Pine Key, 305/872-0774 or 305/872-2239, www.fws.gov/nationalkeydeer) was created in 1957 to protect endangered key deer and other precious wildlife resources. Unlike in some national wildlife refuges, however, visitors (and leashed pets) are allowed within its boundaries. Though public access is prohibited in much of the refuge—in order to protect wildlife and critical habitat, as well as visitors—you'll find walking and hiking trails, a visitors center, and opportunities for fishing, biking, wildlife-watching, and noncommercial photography on Big Pine Key and No Name Key. You can even drive in parts of the refuge.

Of course, despite such accessibility, certain activities are prohibited, including the following:

- Bringing weapons onto refuge lands, unless they are unloaded, cased, and secured in vehicles or boats

- Using metal detectors to search for antiquities or treasure

- Bringing horses onto refuge lands, as their manure might carry the seeds of invasive plants

- Camping on refuge lands (there are no sanitary facilities for campers)

- Using poles or pipes, such as beach umbrellas, which might penetrate turtle nests

- Igniting campfires, which can start destructive wildfires

- Storing equipment or property on refuge lands

- Feeding wildlife, which can cause animals to become less wary of humans and potentially increase their exposure to poachers, diseases, parasites, and vehicle collisions

- Injuring or harassing wildlife

- Removing wildlife, plants, or natural items from refuge lands

- Introducing exotic plants or wildlife, which can cause competition with existing native species

In addition, you're expected to drive carefully throughout the refuge—even on the Overseas Highway, which crosses several of the 25 islands contained within the preserve. You must stay alert for key deer at all times, but especially at sunrise and sunset, when they're more likely to emerge. The speed limit, which is 35 miles per hour at night, is strictly enforced, and tickets can be costly. Vehicle collisions are one of the leading threats to these endangered animals, and of course, killing one on purpose can result in steep fines and possible imprisonment.

★ BLUE HOLE

Once an active limestone quarry utilized during the construction of Henry Flagler's ill-fated Overseas Railroad in the early 20th century, **Blue Hole** is a tranquil, much-visited body of water that nurtures an array of creatures, from green herons to turtles to alligators. Situated within the National Key Deer Refuge on Big Pine Key and free to visit, it lures bird-watchers, wildlife lovers, and photographers alike. The observation platform offers an unobstructed view of the water, where if you're lucky, you might spot a key deer stopping for a refreshing drink. To reach the Blue Hole, take U.S. 1 to Mile Marker 30, turn northwest onto Key Deer Boulevard, continue past Watson Boulevard, and look for the sign on the left, near Big Pine Street.

SUGARLOAF KEY

En route to Key West, you'll encounter several quiet residential areas on islands like Little Torch Key and Big Coppitt Key, all the way to the Key West Naval Air Station on Boca Chica Key. Along this route lies **Sugarloaf Key,** a charming residential island that contains its share of friendly eateries, laid-back camp-grounds, and worthwhile attractions—plus a small airport.

Bat Tower

At Mile Marker 17, those headed to the Sugarloaf Key Airport must turn northwest onto Bat Tower Road. En route to the airport, you should stop for an up-close look at the weather-beaten **Bat Tower,** erected in 1929 by entrepreneur Richter Clyde Perky as part of a pesticide-free plan to eliminate mosquitoes from his tourist attractions in the Lower Keys. Based on the theory that bats have a notoriously ravenous appetite for mosquitoes and other insects, the 30-foot-tall pine tower was intended to house a colony of imported bats which would, in turn, solve Perky's pest problem. Despite his creative thinking, however, the bats didn't stay, and the plan subsequently failed. Today the defunct tower, which is listed in the National Register of Historic Places and costs nothing to view, serves as a monument to one man's inability to control nature.

Beaches and Recreation

BEACHES
Little Duck Key

Just past the western end of Seven Mile Bridge lies **Little Duck Key,** a small island that features **Veterans Memorial Park** (MM 40 BS/OS U.S. 1, Little Duck Key, 305/292-4431, 8am-sunset daily, free), formerly known as Little Duck Key County Park. Although most people bypass this key for the well-visited Bahia Honda State Park farther down the Overseas Highway, it's a pleasant stop for those who appreciate a quiet beach, with access to the Gulf of Mexico and the Atlantic Ocean. Amenities here include picnic pavilions, grills, restrooms, a small parking lot, and a paved boat ramp. Dogs must be leashed at all times, and no overnight parking is allowed.

Bahia Honda State Park

Bahia Honda State Park (36850 Overseas Hwy., Bahia Honda Key, 305/872-2353, www.floridastateparks.org or www. bahiahondapark.com, 8am-sunset daily, $8.50 vehicles with 2-8 passengers plus $0.50 pp, $4.50 motorcycles and single-occupant vehicles, $2.50 pedestrians, bikers, and extra passengers) offers three picture-perfect beaches that lure photographers; together the beaches offer access to the Atlantic Ocean as well as the Gulf of Mexico.

The smallest beach, **Calusa Beach,** has several small picnic pavilions and shares a bathhouse and outdoor freshwater showers with **Loggerhead Beach,** considered the shallowest of the three. **Sandspur Beach,** the largest and most popular beach, has three picnic pavilions, plus restrooms with outdoor showers. It's a perfect place to relax, enjoy the warm waters, and watch one of the Keys' famous sunsets.

BIKING

Biking enthusiasts can explore a variety of different bicycle paths on Big Pine Key, No Name Key, the Saddlebunch Keys, and Big Coppitt Key. Many of these short paths connect to county roads, allowing for longer rides and terrific opportunities to view wildlife. Eventually, the **Florida Keys Overseas Heritage Trail** (www.floridastateparks.org/floridakeys) will make it much easier for bikers to traverse the Lower Keys from the Seven Mile Bridge to Stock Island. For now, you must venture along the shoulder of the Overseas Highway, which can be dangerous at times. No matter where you travel, though, always wear a helmet.

If you didn't bring a bicycle of your own, don't fret. The **Big Pine Bicycle Center** (31 County Rd., Big Pine Key, 305/872-0130, www.bigpinebikes.com, 9am-5pm Mon.-Fri., 9am-3pm Sat., $20-25 daily, $80-100 weekly,

Two islands in the Lower Keys—Ramrod Key and the submerged Looe Key Reef—were named after a pair of sunken ships. Originally known as Roberts Island, Ramrod Key derives its modern moniker from a Spanish vessel that wrecked on an offshore coral reef in the early 19th century. Little is generally known about the ship itself or the circumstances of its demise.

Such is not the case, however, for the HMS *Looe*, the 44-gun British frigate that inspired the name of Looe Key Reef. According to Bob "Frogfoot" Weller—the author of such books as *Famous Shipwrecks of the Florida Keys* (1990) and *Galleon Alley: The 1733 Spanish Treasure Fleet* (2001)—the HMS *Looe* was outfitted in Longreach, England, with 190 crewmen and spent the first years of her service patrolling the English Channel and searching for Barbary pirates. After her crew captured four Spanish vessels in Vigo Bay, Spain began attacking Fort Frederick in Georgia and harassing British settlers along America's East Coast. When the governor of South Carolina petitioned to have a warship protect the coastline, Captain Ashby Utting took the *Looe* on its final voyage.

After the ship reached Charleston, a storm damaged the *Looe*. With orders to seek out and destroy enemy ships near Florida, the *Looe* headed to Jamaica for repairs. By December 1743, the ship was again ready to sail, and on February 4, 1744, she was in the Bahama Channel when an enemy ship was sighted. The *Looe* wasted little time in capturing the *Snow*, which upon closer examination, turned out to be a British ship, the *Billander Betty*, which had been taken by the Spanish. The captain decided to escort the ship back to Charleston. Before retiring for the night, he ordered that the lead line be thrown every 30 minutes to sound for depth.

Around 1am, the on-duty crewmen tossed the lead line and found no bottom at 300 feet. Not 15 minutes later, however, the officer of the watch was alarmed to spot breakers directly ahead. A crosswind caught the sails and the stern collided with the reef, and the *Looe* began to fill with water. Utting ordered that his men save as much of the bread and gunpowder as possible. Meanwhile, the *Snow* met a similar fate against a nearby reef.

By morning, Utting and his men found themselves on a small, sandy key, which they rightly assumed would soon be underwater. When they sighted a sloop offshore, Utting armed his small boats and sent them in pursuit. The next morning, the boats returned with the sloop in tow, and by February 8, the entire crews of the two fallen ships—274 men in all—were rescued. Before leaving, Utting set fire to the *Looe*, which exploded into pieces.

Although Utting and his crew arrived in Jamaica on February 13, 1744, the wreck wasn't discovered until 1951, when Art McKee, Mendel Peterson, Dr. Barney Crile, and Crile's wife, Jane Halle Crile, dove down to the wreck site and managed to recover one of the cannons on the *Looe*, plus a number of artifacts. The next year, the group returned and recovered additional artifacts from the *Looe*, including cannonballs, coins, buttons, and a pewter teapot. They also supposedly located one of the anchors from the *Snow* (although there's still some debate as to whether the *Looe* was even towing the *Snow* at the time of its demise). In the early 1970s, Art Hartman and Bobby Jordan explored the site and recovered even more artifacts, from utensils to pewter mugs to silver candlestick holders.

Nowadays, the wreck site—including any remaining artifacts—and living coral reef are protected features of Florida Keys National Marine Sanctuary. As Weller has written, "Salvaging artifacts is illegal, but sightseeing is encouraged."

$200-250 monthly, plus $15 delivery fee) offers beach cruiser, 7-speed, and kids' BMX rentals in addition to repairs, parts, and accessories. All bicycle rentals include helmets and locks.

1: bicycles at Bahia Honda State Park 2: an American alligator at Blue Hole 3: a resident of the National Key Deer Refuge 4: Jack C. Watson Wildlife Trail at the National Key Deer Refuge

FISHING

While anglers tend to favor the bountiful waters of Islamorada, the Lower Keys certainly offer their share of fishing opportunities. **Strike Zone Charters** (MM 29.6, 29675 Overseas Hwy., Big Pine Key, 305/872-9863, www.captainhooks.com, 8am-5pm daily, rates vary) provides deep-sea fishing trips for up to six people, as well as other excursions. Half-day and full-day trips are available, as are backcountry fishing outings. Reservations are highly recommended.

Some area fishing guides have no specific port, but can still be reached to arrange a variety of charters. Two such companies are **Key Flat Charters** (305/304-3152, www. lowerkeysflatsfishing.com, $450-700 per trip), operated by Captain Luke Kelly and covering the flats and backcountry inshore waters, and **Last Cast Charters** (305/744-9796, www.lastcastcharters.net, $450-1,000 per trip), operated by Captain Andrew Tipler and featuring flats, inshore, reef, gulf, and offshore fishing, plus swordfish excursions. Also in the area, you'll find **Sea Boots Charters** (305/745-1530 or 800/238-1746, www. seaboots.com, $700-1,100 per trip), operated from Summerland Key by Captain Jim Sharpe and featuring big-game fishing for everything from wahoo to sharks.

There are also several bait shops in the Lower Keys, including **Jig's Bait & Tackle/ Guns and Ammo** (MM 30.3, 30321 Overseas Hwy., Big Pine Key, 305/872-1040, www. jigsbaitandtackle.com, 7am-7pm Mon.-Sat., 7am-6pm Sun.), a one-stop shop for fishing equipment, bait, tackle, firearms, and charts. Another option is **Fanci Seafood** (MM 22.2, 22290 Overseas Hwy., Cudjoe Key, 305/745-3887, www.fanciseafood.com, 8am-6pm Mon.-Sat.), a wholesale and retail fish market that provides anglers with bait, chum, and ice throughout the day, not to mention fresh seafood for retail customers beginning at 10am each morning.

TOP EXPERIENCE

★ BOATING AND KAYAKING

Given the topography of the Lower Keys, with plenty of open water, beckoning islands, and backcountry channels, this is truly a water lover's playground and an ideal place for boating and kayaking. To help you explore the region, **Strike Zone Charters** (MM 29.6, 29675

Overseas Hwy., Big Pine Key, 305/872-9863, www.strikezonecharter.com, 8am-5pm daily, $59 pp) offers all-inclusive island excursions on glass-bottom catamarans. The five-hour trips combine a breezy boat ride with history and ecology lessons, bird-watching, light-tackle fishing, a fish cookout, and a snorkeling experience amid the offshore coral reefs, part of Florida Keys National Marine Sanctuary. Reservations are recommended.

Boat owners who would prefer to explore this region on their own will find several marinas and public boat ramps at their disposal. If you didn't bring a boat with you, you can rent one from **Big Pine Key Boat Rentals** (MM 33, 33000 Overseas Hwy., Big Pine Key, and MM 24.5, 24500 Overseas Hwy., Summerland Key, 305/849-0130, www. bigpineboatrentals.com, 8am-4:30pm daily, $215-315 daily) and go cruising, fishing, and snorkeling at your own pace. Reservations are a must; typically, the hours of operation are flexible, and help is only available if the staff knows you're coming.

For kayak rentals, guided kayaking nature tours, skiff ecotours, and backcountry catamaran cruises, consult **Big Pine Kayak Adventures** (305/872-7474, www. keyskayaktours.com, 8am-5pm daily, rentals $25 for two hours, $5 for each additional hour, guided tours start at $50 pp), based out of the Old Wooden Bridge Marina (1791 Bogie Dr., Big Pine Key, 305/872-2241) and operated by Captain Bill Keogh, a well-respected naturalist, educator, photographer, and author who has lived in the Lower Keys for more than two decades. In addition, the **Coral Reef Park Company** (305/451-6300) offers kayak rentals at **Bahia Honda State Park** (MM 36.8, 36850 Overseas Hwy., Bahia Honda Key, 305/872-2353, www.floridastateparks.org/ park/bahia-honda or www.bahiahondapark. com, 8am-sunset daily, $8.50 vehicles with 2-8 passengers plus $0.50 pp, $4.50 motorcycles and single-occupant vehicles, $2.50

1: kayaking near Bahia Honda State Park 2: Bahia Honda State Park 3: queen angelfish at Looe Key National Marine Sanctuary

pedestrians, bikers, and extra passengers), including single ($12 hourly, $40 per 4 hours or more) and tandem ($17 hourly, $55 per 4 hours or more) kayaks.

TOP EXPERIENCE

★ DIVING AND SNORKELING

Roughly five nautical miles south of Big Pine Key lies one of the finest and most diverse coral reefs in the Florida Keys. Established in 1981, **Looe Key National Marine Sanctuary,** now part of Florida Keys National Marine Sanctuary, features a 33-acre spur-and-groove network of coral fingers, sand channels, and turtle grass that teems with over 150 species of fish, including parrotfish, angelfish, yellowtail, barracuda, grouper, turtles, eagle rays, whale sharks, and moray eels. Named after the **HMS Looe** (which supposedly ran aground here in February 1744), the U-shaped reef comprises patch reefs as well as outside reefs and has depths that vary from 8 to 40 feet, making it ideal for first-time snorkelers as well as advanced scuba divers. Visitors will get an up-close look at a variety of coral, including elkhorn, staghorn, star, fire, and brain. For most of the year, the water clarity is excellent, and the sea conditions are moderate; January is often the only month during which visibility can be less than ideal. No matter when you visit, however, certain activities are absolutely prohibited, including spearfishing and the collecting of shells and tropical fish.

Several area operators provide tours to this one-of-a-kind reef, including the **Looe Key Reef Resort & Dive Center** (MM 27.3, 27340 Overseas Hwy., Ramrod Key, 305/872-2215 or 877/816-3483, www.diveflakeys.com, 8am-7pm Sun.-Thurs., 8am-8pm Fri.-Sat.), which has offered scuba-diving instruction and half-day diving and snorkeling trips (8am and 12:30pm daily, $70 divers, $38 snorkelers, $26 passengers) to Looe Key Reef since 1978. Through the dive center, you're also able to experience the **Adolphus Busch,** a 210-foot freighter that was intentionally sunk in 1998 to create an artificial reef. Sitting upright in roughly 110 feet of water, the intact shipwreck has become a haven for a wide variety of marine invertebrates and fish, from moray eels to 250-pound goliath grouper often seen in the wheelhouse or cargo holds. Typically, the dive center offers a wreck trip on Tuesday and Saturday; the trip includes a dive on the *Adolphus Busch,* plus one dive on Looe Key Reef ($80-100). All trip prices include tanks, weights, masks, snorkels, and fins; gas fills, equipment rentals, and repair services are also available on-site.

Strike Zone Charters (29675 Overseas Hwy., Big Pine Key, 305/872-9863, www.captainhooks.com, 8am-5pm daily, reservation required) offers both PADI instruction ($210-525 pp) and daily half-day snorkeling and diving trips ($38-89 pp, plus gear rental) to Looe Key Reef on roomy glass-bottom catamarans. **Coral Reef Park Company** (MM 36.8, 36850 Overseas Hwy., Bahia Honda Key, 305/872-3210, www.bahiahondapark.com, 8am-5pm daily) provides thrice-daily 1.5-hour snorkeling trips (9:30am, 1:30pm, and 4:45pm, $30 adults, $25 children under 18, $4 snorkel, $2 mask, $2 fins) from Bahia Honda State Park (where park entrance fees apply) to Looe Key Reef. Even in the waters near Bahia Honda, you're bound to see curious marine creatures, including queen conch, red rock urchin, spiny lobster, sea cucumbers, seahorses, horseshoe crabs, cushion sea stars, tube sponges, moon jellies, and nurse sharks. Snorkel gear rentals ($6 wetsuit, $6 diver-down flag, $5 snorkel, $5 safety vest, $4-5 mask, $4 fins) are available daily in the park.

For more information about snorkeling and diving sites in the Lower Keys, consult the Key West office of **Florida Keys National Marine Sanctuary** (Nancy Foster Florida Keys Environmental Complex, 33 E. Quay Rd., Key West, 305/809-4727, www.floridakeys.noaa.gov).

OTHER OUTDOOR ACTIVITIES

If you're looking for a land-based diversion in this watery playground, stop by **Boondocks Grille & Draft House & Miniature Golf** (MM 27.2, 27205 Overseas Hwy., Ramrod Key, 305/872-4094, www.boondocksus.com, 11am-11pm daily), where you can play an 18-hole round of golf ($10 adults, $8 children) amid the caves and waterfalls of this tropical setting, then enjoy some snacks and libations at the 19th Hole Party Zone. They feature live music every night on a large stage under the largest tiki hut in the Florida Keys. It's an ideal activity for travelers with children.

For a more exhilarating experience, head to the Sugarloaf Key Airport at Mile Marker 17 on Sugarloaf Key, where **Sky Dive Key West** (305/745-4386, www.skydivekeywest. com, by appointment daily, $245-265 pp) offers tandem jumps for an aerial view of the Lower Keys from two miles above the earth. Skydivers must be at least 18 years old, and certain weight restrictions could apply. Reservations are necessary for all jumps.

SPAS AND YOGA

Although outdoor activities are paramount in the Lower Keys, you'll also find more relaxing pursuits like yoga and massage. The **Good Food Conspiracy** (MM 30.2, 30150 Overseas Hwy., Big Pine Key, 305/872-9119, www.goodfoodconspiracy.com, 10am-6pm Mon.-Sat., rates vary) offers massage, reflexology, and facials, as well as light and raindrop therapies.

Entertainment and Shopping

NIGHTLIFE

If you need a place to unwind, the Lower Keys can certainly satisfy you. For more than 30 years, **Coconuts Bar & Package** (MM 30.5, 30535 Overseas Hwy., Big Pine Key, 305/872-3795, 7am-4am daily) has lured night owls with beer, liquor, darts, pool tables, and arcade games—and the fact that it's air-conditioned is a big plus in the summertime. It doesn't hurt either that this casual, late-night lounge now offers wireless Internet access.

The **Looe Key Tiki Bar & Restaurant** (MM 27.3, 27340 Overseas Hwy., Ramrod Key, 305/872-2215 or 877/816-3483, www. looekeytikibar.com or www.diveflakeys. com, 11am-close daily) features a daily happy hour (3pm-7pm) and live entertainment most nights (usually 6pm-10pm Wed.-Thurs. and 7pm-11pm Fri.-Sat.), from acoustic guitarists to funk bands to karaoke. Across the highway, **Boondocks Grille & Draft House & Miniature Golf** (MM 27.2, 27205 Overseas Hwy., Ramrod Key, 305/204-4109, www. boondocksus.com, 11am-close daily) provides an open-air tiki bar where you can enjoy happy hour (4pm-6pm) on weekdays as well as bingo tournaments, trivia contests, and live folk, country, and rock music throughout the week.

Meanwhile, **Mangrove Mama's Restaurant** (MM 20, 19991 Overseas Hwy., Sugarloaf Key, 305/745-3030, www. mangrovemamasrestaurant.com, 8am-10pm daily) offers a daily happy hour (4pm-6pm) plus live blues from local and national musicians on certain nights (6pm-10pm Mon., Tues., and Thurs., 10am-2pm Sun.). Closer to Key West, the **Geiger Key Marina & RV Park** (5 Geiger Rd., Geiger Key, 305/296-3553, www.geigerkeymarina.com, 11am-9:30pm Mon.-Thurs., 11am-10pm Fri., 8am-10pm Sat.-Sun.) also features live music—typically laid-back tunes from the 1970s, '80s, and '90s—on Friday, Saturday, and Sunday nights at the on-site **The Fish Camp** (305/296-3553).

FESTIVALS AND EVENTS

★ **Underwater Music Festival**

For more than three decades, the Lower

Keys have promoted the preservation of the spectacular Looe Key Reef with a unique summertime event: the whimsical daylong **Underwater Music Festival,** which usually takes place in mid-July. This annual underwater concert features an array of seaworthy tunes, from humpback whale songs to ditties by Jimmy Buffett, the Beatles, and other legendary musicians. Every year, hundreds of snorkelers and scuba divers flock to the area for this one-of-a-kind celebration. During the four-hour concert, the music is piped underwater using speakers, and attendees are invited to don costumes and play along on instruments. The concert is also broadcast by a local radio station so that folks on land can enjoy the show as well. For more information, contact the **Lower Keys Chamber of Commerce** (MM 31, 31020 Overseas Hwy., Big Pine Key, 305/872-2411 or 800/872-3722, www.lowerkeyschamber.com).

Big Pine & the Lower Keys Island Art Festival

Typically held in early to mid-December, the **Big Pine & the Lower Keys Island Art Festival** features a full day of arts, crafts, exhibits, raffle drawings, and live music on the grounds of the Lower Keys Chamber of Commerce (MM 31, 31020 Overseas Hwy., Big Pine Key, 305/872-2411 or 800/872-3722, www.lowerkeyschamber.com) near Mile Marker 31, on the ocean side of the Overseas Highway. Food and beverages are available on-site, and admission and parking are free. For more information, contact the chamber of commerce or the Florida Keys Council of the Arts (1100 Simonton St., Key West, 305/295-4369, www.keysarts.com).

Other Annual Events

The Lower Keys host a wide array of other annual events, including the **Big Pine & Lower Keys Nautical Flea Market,** typically held in mid- to late January at the Lower Keys Chamber of Commerce (31020 Overseas Hwy., Big Pine Key, 305/872-2411 or 800/872-3722, www.lowerkeyschamber.com, free admission and parking) and featuring an emporium of boats, motors, and other nautical items, plus live music, food, and beverages. Anglers might also enjoy area fishing tournaments like the three-day **Big Pine & Lower Keys Dolphin Tournament** (305/872-2411 or 800/872-3722, www.lowerkeyschamber.com, entry fees apply) in early June, which has taken place for two decades and typically offers over $35,000 in prizes.

SHOPPING

Although avid shoppers will find a slew of options farther south in Key West, the pickings are much slimmer in this part of the Lower Keys. Still, there are at least a few shops worth mentioning.

Near Mile Marker 30.4, on the gulf side of Big Pine Key, you'll spot the **Artists in Paradise Gallery** (221 Key Deer Blvd., Big Pine Key, 305/872-1828, www.artistsinparadise.com, 10am-6pm daily), a co-op gallery that spotlights the jewelry, photography, sculptures, stained glass, mixed media, watercolor paintings, and other artwork of over 30 local artists. Created in 1994, the gallery also provides framing services and hosts periodic demonstrations, workshops, auctions, and other events, such as an annual Judge Show.

Not far away lies the **Good Food Conspiracy** (MM 30.2, 30150 Overseas Hwy., Big Pine Key, 305/872-3945, www.goodfoodconspiracy.com, 10am-6pm Mon.-Sat.), which sells natural foods, vitamins, herbs, and oils in addition to offering a juice bar, deli, and holistic health center.

Depending on the season, the wholesale and retail fish market known as **Fanci Seafood** (MM 22.2, 22290 Overseas Hwy., Cudjoe Key, 305/745-3887, www.fanciseafood.com, 8am-6pm Mon.-Sat.) can provide seafood lovers with fresh fish, shrimp, lobster, and stone crab.

Food

SEAFOOD

Like the rest of the Florida Keys, the Lower Keys boast several seafood options. On the Overseas Highway, the **Looe Key Tiki Bar & Restaurant** (MM 27.3, 27340 Overseas Hwy., Ramrod Key, 305/872-2215, www.looekeytikibar.com or www.diveflakeys.com, 11am-close daily, $4-22) is part of a resort and dive center on the ocean side of U.S. 1. In addition to a daily happy hour (3pm-7pm) and live entertainment, the restaurant features soups, salads, sandwiches, burgers, and seafood baskets.

It's hard to miss the thatched tiki-style structures of the **Boondocks Grille & Draft House & Miniature Golf** (MM 27.2, 27205 Overseas Hwy., Ramrod Key, 305/872-4094, www.boondocksus.com, 11am-11pm daily, $5-25), which offers a fully stocked open-air bar and a menu of burgers, sandwiches, soups, salads, seafood baskets, and a delicious broiled lobster tail mac-and-cheese. You can also enjoy a weekday happy hour (4pm-6pm) as well as random contests and live musical performances.

On the gulf side of U.S. 1, near Mile Marker 25.5, **Tonio's Seafood Shack and Tiki Bar** (MM 25.2, 25163 Overseas Hwy., Summerland Key, 305/745-3322, 11am-10pm daily, $10-25) is a waterfront seafood restaurant and bar serving fresh fish, sandwiches, steak, pasta, and baskets. Try the lobster rolls, crab cakes, blackened mahimahi, fish tacos, or shrimp scampi.

For innovative cuisine in a contemporary setting, the ★ **The Square Grouper Bar & Grill** (MM 22.5, 22658 Overseas Hwy., Cudjoe Key, 305/745-8880, www.squaregrouperbarandgrill.com, 11am-2:30pm and 5pm-10pm Tues.-Sat., $7-36) is a favorite among residents and tourists alike. Housed in an inconspicuous two-story building beside the highway and jokingly named for the compressed bales of marijuana that used to wash ashore in the Lower Keys, this curious eatery spotlights Floribbean dishes like toasted almond-encrusted grouper with warm Caribbean-style pineapple relish; be sure to save room for the chocolate or turtle fondue.

Besides a daily happy hour (4pm-6pm) and live music on the weekends, **Mangrove Mama's Restaurant** (MM 19.9, 19991 Overseas Hwy., Sugarloaf Key, 305/745-3030, www.mangrovemamasrestaurant.com, 8am-10pm daily, $8-30) offers a wide array of options, including omelets, salads, sandwiches, steaks, seafood dishes, and of course, classic key lime pie.

AMERICAN

The Lower Keys present an array of casual all-American eateries, such as the ★ **No Name Pub** (30813 N. Watson Blvd., Big Pine Key, 305/872-9115, www.nonamepub.com, 11am-10pm daily, $8-15), a friendly, out-of-the-way joint that's been a favorite for locals and tourists alike since 1936. Considered the oldest bar on Big Pine Key, this former bait and tackle shop certainly has a rough-hewn appeal, with its gravel parking lot, shaded patio area, private garden, and no-frills interior, the walls and ceiling of which are plastered with autographed dollar bills (what the owner calls "early and late American clutter"). Besides beer and other libations, you'll find basic vittles like pizza, meatballs, smoked fish dip, and seafood baskets—not to mention some interesting local characters. To reach this long-standing haunt, take U.S. 1 to Mile Marker 30 on the gulf side, turn northwest on Key Deer Boulevard, turn right onto Watson Boulevard, and then veer to the north, toward (but not past) the No Name Key Bridge.

Vegetarians will appreciate the low-key ★ **Good Food Conspiracy** (MM 30.2, 30150 Overseas Hwy., Big Pine Key, 305/872-3945 or 305/872-9119, www.goodfoodconspiracy.com, 10am-6pm Mon.-Sat., $6-15), a health-food store and juice bar that serves smoothies, fresh juices, homemade soups, raw desserts, vegetarian sandwiches, organic salads, and other healthy treats.

You'll find even cheaper vittles at the **Five Brothers Grocery Two** (MM 27, 27023 Overseas Hwy., Ramrod Key, 305/872-0702, 6am-4pm Mon.-Sat., $2-7), which sells breakfast dishes, daily soups, and various sandwiches, including a traditional *cubano*.

Another local favorite is the ★ **Geiger Key Marina Smokehouse Restaurant and Tiki Bar** (5 Geiger Rd., Geiger Key, 305/294-1230, www.geigerkeymarina.com, 11am-9:30pm Mon.-Thurs., 11am-10pm Fri., 8am-10pm Sat.-Sun., $5-19), a family-friendly eatery well off the beaten path. Serving breakfast, lunch, and dinner, this popular joint features southern favorites like fried green tomatoes, fish tacos, and shrimp po'boys. On the weekends, you'll be treated to live music and a Sunday barbecue—a 20-year tradition that includes barbecue chicken, smoked ribs, grilled shrimp, jalapeño corn bread, coleslaw, wild rice, and baked beans ($17 pp).

BREAKFAST AND BRUNCH

On Big Pine Key, **Bagel Island Coffee** (205 Key Deer Blvd., Big Pine Key, 305/872-9912, 7am-3pm Tues.-Sat., $4-8) has you covered with tasty bagel sandwiches, coffee, and pastries at breakfast or lunch. They serve breakfast platters, French toast, and waffles as well. It's a small shop with several tables inside, and it gets packed on weekend mornings; you may want to opt for carryout if you come at this time. At lunch you can build your own sandwich, and they have several vegetarian options and salads. If you need something to cool you down, grab a fruit smoothie or an iced coffee.

On Summerland Key, you can get a classic American breakfast at **The Galley Grill** (MM 24.8, 24862 Overseas Hwy., Summerland Key, 305/745-3440, 7am-2pm daily, $6-12), a casual restaurant that will make you feel at home in your beach attire. The biscuits and gravy is a favorite. The strawberry almond French toast

or pancakes will satisfy a sweet tooth, and the veggie eggs Benedict and omelets are healthier choices.

CUBAN

While you won't find many Latin American options in the Lower Keys, fans of Cuban cuisine might appreciate the long-standing, extremely no-frills **Coco's Kitchen** (283 Key Deer Blvd., Big Pine Key, 305/872-4495, www.cocoskitchen.com, 7am-2pm and 4:30pm-7pm Tues.-Sat., $3-18), one of several businesses in the Big Pine Shopping Center on Big Pine Key. Though the food here is served on disposable plates, hungry visitors will likely care more about the menu options, which range from *huevos rancheros* for breakfast and Cuban mix sandwiches for lunch to nightly dinner specials like Wednesday's *ropa vieja* (shredded beef in tomato sauce), followed by flan for dessert. Of course, diners will also find plenty of American dishes, such as cheeseburgers, fried shrimp, and barbecue spareribs.

EUROPEAN

For an exceptionally exquisite meal, take a boat ride from Little Torch Key to the exclusive ★ **Little Palm Island Resort & Spa** (MM 28.5, 28500 Overseas Hwy., Little Torch Key, 800/343-8567, www.littlepalmisland.com, 8am-10:30am, 11:30am-2:30pm, and 6pm-10pm daily, prices vary depending on the menu), which welcomes the public to its on-site waterfront restaurant for breakfast, lunch, and dinner daily as well as Sunday brunch (11am-2:30pm). Although the French-Latin fusion cuisine is ever evolving, sample dishes might range from shrimp and yellowtail snapper ceviche to duck confit—not to mention the cashew-crusted key lime pie.

The only snag for some Keys vacationers, though, might be that proper "country club" attire is required—that is, men should wear polo shirts with nice shorts for lunch and

1: Geiger Key Marina Smokehouse Restaurant and Tiki Bar **2:** No Name Pub on Big Pine Key **3:** campsite at Big Pine Key Fishing Lodge **4:** Little Palm Island Resort & Spa

collared shirts with long pants for dinner, while women would be okay with a nice sundress at lunch and elegant pants and a blouse at dinner. Also, children under 16 aren't allowed, making it a poor choice for families with kids—but an ideal spot for a romantic meal for two. You can make it even more memorable by requesting the discreet Chef's Table in the kitchen, where executive chef Luis Pous will attend to you personally, preparing and presenting a multicourse tasting menu paired with the perfect wine selection. You can also dine outside on the sandbar, an especially exotic choice for dinner when the romantic atmosphere is enhanced by cool night breezes and flaming tiki torches. Of course, no matter how you choose to enjoy this one-of-a-kind dining experience, advance reservations are required, and while the prices vary from day to day, a couple can expect to pay at least $250 for a multicourse dinner, excluding alcohol.

PIZZA

Situated in the Big Pine Shopping Center, **Pizzaworks** (229 Key Deer Blvd., Big Pine Key, 305/872-1119, 11am-10pm Mon.-Sat., noon-9pm Sun., $8-19) can deliver salads, pizzas, subs, pasta dishes, and key lime pie right to your hotel. **A Slice of Paradise** (MM 24.4, 24458 Overseas Hwy., Summerland Key, 305/744-9718, 11am-9pm Mon.-Thurs., 11am-10:30pm Sat.-Sun., $6-23) offers salads, hot and cold subs, and specialty pizzas. Both of these low-key joints are popular among locals.

Accommodations

The Lower Keys have their share of lodging options. These range from intimate bed-and-breakfasts to affordable campgrounds, almost all of which are privately owned. Just remember that, as with most of the Florida Keys, accommodations are far less expensive in the off-season, which is typically May-November, though it depends on the establishment.

UNDER $100

Snorkelers and scuba divers can pursue their passion at the spacious ★ **Looe Key Reef Resort & Dive Center** (MM 27.3, 27340 Overseas Hwy., Ramrod Key, 305/872-2215 or 877/816-3483, www.diveflakeys.com, $95-150 d). In addition to comfortable air-conditioned rooms, the resort offers a dive shop, a swimming pool, an on-site restaurant and tiki bar, varied scuba-diving courses, plus snorkeling and diving excursions to nearby coral reefs and shipwrecks.

$100-200

Vacations can be expensive in the Florida Keys, but you'll find a handful of bargain-friendly lodgings in the Lower Keys, including the ★ **Big Pine Key Fishing Lodge** (MM 33, 33000 Overseas Hwy., Big Pine Key, 305/872-2351, $134-169 d), a laid-back waterfront establishment on Spanish Harbor that's been family owned and operated since 1972. Besides efficiencies, lodge and loft rooms, and mobile homes, amenities here include a heated pool, a recreation room, a convenience store and gift shop, laundry facilities, wireless Internet access, diving equipment, camping and fishing supplies, a marina with boat dockage and rentals, plus fishing charters and diving excursions.

The no-frills **Big Pine Key Motel** (MM 30.7, 30725 Overseas Hwy., Big Pine Key, 305/872-9090 or 800/897-7103, www.bigpinekeymotel.com, $99-139 d) offers 32 units, including efficiencies and apartments, with cable television, air-conditioning, and access to a swimming pool. Visitors might also appreciate the spacious boat parking area. North of the highway lies the **Old Wooden Bridge Guest Cottages & Marina** (1791 Bogie Dr., Big Pine Key, 305/872-2241, www.

oldwoodenbridge.com, cottages $130-230), a resort and marina facility on five waterfront acres. Situated at the intersection of Watson Boulevard and Bogie Drive, just west of the No Name Key Bridge, this peaceful resort provides 14 efficiency cottages, a boat ramp, a swimming pool, laundry facilities, cable television, and on-site kayak rentals and tours. For the cottages, weekly rates ($775-1,365) are also available.

On adjacent Little Torch Key, near Mile Marker 28.5, you'll find two more laid-back waterfront choices: the pet-friendly **Dolphin Marina and Cottages** (MM 28.5, 28530 Overseas Hwy., Little Torch Key, 305/872-2685, $159-259 d) on the ocean side and **Parmer's Resort** (565 Barry Ave., Little Torch Key, 305/872-2157, www.parmersresort. com, rooms $99-239 d, suites $139-299, cottage $248-459) on the gulf side, both of which are ideally situated for people hoping to explore the National Key Deer Refuge and Looe Key Reef. Dolphin Marina offers a boat ramp, a marina store, boat rentals, and well-landscaped, air-conditioned cottages with cable television, screened porches, and in some cases, full kitchens; Parmer's provides a complimentary breakfast, tiki-style picnic pavilions, hammocks and barbecue grills, a private boat dock, a swimming pool, and a variety of comfortable accommodations.

The pet-friendly **Sugarloaf Lodge Hotel** (17001 Overseas Hwy., Sugarloaf Key, 305/745-3211, www.sugarloaflodge.net, $89-180 d) houses 31 waterfront rooms that are somewhat outdated but are equipped with air-conditioning and cable television. Other amenities include tennis and shuffleboard courts, a miniature golf course, a heated swimming pool, an on-site tiki bar, a restaurant, a fully equipped marina, and a nearby airstrip.

OVER $200

South of the Big Pine Key Fishing Lodge, a long, scenic route winds past mangrove trees and beachfront hideaways, such as **The Barnacle Bed & Breakfast** (1557 Long Beach Dr., Big Pine Key, 305/872-3298 or 800/465-9100, www.thebarnacle.net, $185-265 d). This lush inn offers two relaxing air-conditioned rooms as well as the private Blue Heron Cottage, and all accommodations have satellite TV, wireless Internet access, beach towels, Bahama fans, king-size beds, and private bathrooms. All lodgings come with a full breakfast, and other amenities include a hot tub, a relaxing hammock, a tiki hut, complimentary kayaks, and a private, sandy beach that inspires guests to swim, snorkel, or simply relax. All rooms are smoke-free, and pets and children under 16 are not allowed here.

Along the same route lies the remote, eco-friendly **Deer Run Bed & Breakfast** (1997 Long Beach Dr., Big Pine Key, 305/872-2015, www.deerrunfloridabb.com, $295-455 d), a serene oasis beside the Atlantic Ocean. The four rooms—named Atlantis, Utopia, Heaven, and Eden—are each decorated in a unique way, but all include organic linens, private baths, screened porches, original artwork, and a hot vegan breakfast. Other amenities include a sandy beach, a pool and hot tub, and on-site massage therapy. Guests may also enjoy biking and kayaking. As with The Barnacle, pets, children, and smoking aren't permitted here.

The pinnacle of luxury is the secluded ★ **Little Palm Island Resort & Spa** (MM 28.5, 28500 Overseas Hwy., Little Torch Key, 800/343-8567, www.littlepalmisland.com, bungalows $990-1,790, suites $2,090-2,810), once the site of a family-owned fishing village and now a private, five-acre island getaway south of Little Torch Key only accessible by private yacht, ferry, or seaplane. Filled with swaying Jamaican palm trees, surrounded by aquamarine waters, and favored by presidents, movie stars, pro athletes, and countless other celebrities, Little Palm Island is probably the most gorgeous and certainly one of the most distinctive locales in the entire Florida Keys archipelago.

Here you'll encounter white-sand beaches, a stunning outdoor pool, cushioned lounge chairs, two grand suites, and 28 thatched-roof oceanfront bungalows—many of which have Polynesian-style furnishings, lawn furniture,

Traveling with Fido

In general, it's rather difficult to travel with your pets in the Florida Keys, including the islands that compose the Lower Keys. Only a handful of Big Pine-area hotels—such as the **Sugarloaf Lodge Hotel** (MM 17, 17001 Overseas Hwy., Sugarloaf Key, 305/745-3211 or 800/553-6097, www. sugarloaflodge.net) and the **Old Wooden Bridge Guest Cottages & Marina** (1791 Bogie Dr., Big Pine Key, 305/872-2241, www.oldwoodenbridge.com)—are pet friendly, so it's always best to call ahead if you're considering bringing your cat or dog with you.

Although it's often easier for pet owners to stay in a campground, such as those available at **Bahia Honda State Park** (MM 36.8, 36850 Overseas Hwy., Big Pine Key, 305/872-2353, www. floridastateparks.org or www.bahiahondapark.com), certain restrictions still do apply. While service and guide dogs, with proper identification, are welcome in all areas of the park, pets are typically not allowed in cabins, bathhouses, pavilions, or the concession building. They're also not allowed on the beaches or in the water, which means that you won't be able to swim or snorkel with your pet.

In the limited areas where pets are permitted—such as the campgrounds—they must be well behaved and kept on a six-foot handheld leash at all times. Perhaps it goes without saying, but owners must always pick up and properly dispose of their pets' waste—no matter where they leave it.

and hammocks, as well as private showers, hot tubs, and verandas. Besides the remote location, incredible views, and opportunity to spot key deer frolicking on the lawn, other amenities include free wireless Internet access, complimentary valet parking on Little Torch Key, a boutique and gift shop, a romantic on-site spa (SpaTerre) that provides exotic, spirit-revitalizing massages and treatments, and an on-site restaurant that features gourmet Floribbean cuisine in a candlelit dining room, on the breezy terrace, or, if you're truly daring, directly on a sandbar. Activities range from yoga classes and kayaking to sailing, fishing, and scuba-diving excursions. What you won't find here are phones, televisions, vehicles, and folks under 21. No wonder it's a popular place for weddings.

CAMPING

The Lower Keys contain several laid-back campgrounds, including the ★ **Sunshine Key RV Resort and Marina** (MM 38.8, 38801 Overseas Hwy., Ohio Key, 305/872-2217, www.rvonthego.com/Sunshine-Key-RV-Resort.html, $75-270 daily, $392-807 weekly, $1,950-2,679 monthly), situated on

the gulf side of Ohio Key southwest of the Seven Mile Bridge. A private 75-acre island resort, Sunshine Key offers a wide array of full-hookup campsites with 30/50-amp electric service and cable television. Picnic tables, waterfront views, and pull-through sites are available. Other amenities include a 172-slip marina, a fishing pier and boat ramp, heated 24-hour outdoor pool, sandy volleyball courts, a shuffleboard area, tennis and basketball courts, Ping-Pong tables, an on-site restaurant and a poolside café, a convenience store and gas station, fitness center, coin-op laundry, barbecue and kennel facilities, high-speed Internet access, watercraft rentals, a video game center, a dump station, restrooms, rental cottages, sightseeing tours, and on-site activities, such as weekly potlucks and dances. Leashed pets are welcome, though some restrictions may apply.

The year-round ★ **Bahia Honda State Park** (MM 36.8, 36850 Overseas Hwy., Bahia Honda Key, 305/872-2353, www. floridastateparks.org/park/bahia-honda or www.bahiahondapark.com, 8am-sunset daily, $8.50 vehicles with 2-8 passengers, $4.50 motorcycles and single-occupant vehicles, $2.50 pedestrians, bikers, and extra passengers) offers three budget-friendly campgrounds—Buttonwood, Sandspur, and Bayside—which collectively contain 80 campsites ($36 daily plus a $6.70 reservation fee) for tent and RV campers. Buttonwood has gravel sites, each with electrical and water service, a picnic table, and access to a dump station, restrooms, and hot showers. Some of the sites are beside the water, and all can accommodate a variety of setups, from small tents to 40-foot RVs. Sandspur, located in a hardwood hammock, has much smaller sites, with lower clearance—ideal for tents and RVs less than 14 feet in length. Some of the sites have electricity and waterfront views, and all have a picnic table, grill, and water service. Bayside is the smallest campground, with eight sites and a tiny restroom, but all campers are allowed to use the dump station and restrooms in Buttonwood.

To reach Bayside, your vehicle must be able to travel under the Bahia Honda Bridge, which has a height restriction of six feet, eight inches. Also available for rent near the Bayside campground are three stilted duplex cabins ($120-160 daily) that overlook the bay. Each of the six cabins has a full bath, kitchen/dining room, living room with a sofa bed, one or two bedrooms, and central heating and cooling; five of the cabins accommodate up to six people, and one is wheelchair-accessible. Although pets are prohibited in the cabins, they're permitted in the campgrounds, provided that they're confined, leashed, or otherwise kept under control. In addition to campgrounds and cabins, Bahia Honda provides 19 boat slips for overnight rental ($2 per foot, $30 minimum); these include water, electricity, and the use of park facilities such as restrooms, showers, and trash disposal. For reservations, contact **ReserveAmerica** (800/326-3521, www.reserveamerica.com).

Near Mile Marker 33 on the ocean side of U.S. 1, the family-owned, year-round **Big Pine Key Fishing Lodge** (MM 33, 33000 Overseas Hwy., Big Pine Key, 305/872-2351,

$53-86 daily, $339-541 weekly, $1,272-2,193 monthly) offers a spacious RV and tent-site campground in addition to its cabins and motel-style rooms. Rustic, full-hookup, pull-through, and shaded sites are available. Amenities include 30-amp electric service, cable television, phone access, propane gas, a heated swimming pool, recreation room, convenience store and gift shop, laundry facilities, a marina, boat dockage, boat rentals, and restrooms with showers. Anglers and scuba divers will especially appreciate the easy access to the ocean, as well as the availability of fishing charters and diving excursions to the nearby Looe Key Reef. With its helpful staff and neighborly atmosphere, the campground is popular among families and long-term RVers, many of whom are repeat visitors. Tents are welcome here, but dogs are not allowed due to the presence of key deer.

The **Breezy Pines Estates RV Park** (MM 29.8, 29859 Overseas Hwy., Big Pine Key, 305/872-9041, www.breezypinesrv.com, $33-50 daily, $250-350 weekly, $650-1,000 monthly) is on the gulf side of U.S. 1, not far from the National Key Deer Refuge. The deer are often spotted at Breezy Pines—which despite its name is filled with palm trees, not pines. An ideal base for fishing, kayaking, diving, and snorkeling, this park offers full-hookup gravel sites equipped with 30/50-amp electric service, wireless Internet access, cable television, and phone service. Other amenities include a laundry and an outdoor pool. As with other RV parks in this region, leashed pets are allowed here, and many of the lots are for sale.

Near Mile Marker 20, the beachfront **Sugarloaf Key/Key West KOA** (251 SR-939, Sugarloaf Key, 305/745-3549 or 800/562-7731, www.keywestkoa.com, $100 daily) has been temporarily closed since Hurricane Irma hit the island in 2017. The campground is expected to reopen in 2020, so call or check with them before making reservations. The property contains both RV and tent spaces, some of which offer 30/50-amp electric service, cable television, waterfront views, or pull-through access. This tropical resort provides easy access to a private sandy beach where visitors can savor gorgeous sunsets and warm ocean breezes, as well as snorkeling, fishing, and ecotour excursions. Other amenities include a heated swimming pool and hot tub, air-conditioned trailer rentals ($177 daily), clean restrooms and hot showers, wireless Internet access, propane gas, a pet playground, beach volleyball, a snack bar, an open-air pavilion with a pub and a restaurant, a full-service marina with boat rentals, ramps, and slips, a floating water trampoline and banana bicycle rentals, seasonal activities, and shuttle service to Key West.

On the ocean side of Sugarloaf Key, near Mile Marker 19.8, is the picturesque 28-acre **Lazy Lakes RV Resort** (311 Johnson Rd., Sugarloaf Key, 305/745-1079 or 866/965-2537, www.lazylakesrvresort.com, $50-125 daily, $1,480-2,875 monthly), which offers 99 RV spaces, some of which have full hookups with water, sewer access, 30/50-amp electric service, cable television, and wireless Internet access. Lakefront sites are also available. Other amenities include a clubhouse, camp store, heated pool, laundry facilities and clean restrooms, paddleboats, and complimentary kayaks. In addition, visitors can swim, fish, and snorkel in the seven-acre saltwater lake and participate in on-site activities like bingo, darts, horseshoes, game and movie nights, potluck dinners, and ice-cream socials. A limited number of sites are available for ownership. Both of the Sugarloaf campgrounds allow leashed pets.

Closer to Key West, near Mile Marker 14.5, is the **Bluewater Key RV Resort** (MM 29.5, 2950 Overseas Hwy., 305/745-2494 or 800/237-2266, www.bluewaterkey.com, $112-230 daily), which offers spacious, individually owned lots for rent. Divided into tropical, bay, and canal sites, all are landscaped with shady, tropical foliage and equipped with tiki huts, picnic tables, cable television, wireless Internet access, water, sewage access, and 30/50-amp electric service. Fishing, snorkeling, and sunbathing are popular pastimes here, and amenities include a swimming pool, clubhouse, bathhouse, laundry, and boat dock.

For those who want to be as close to Key West as possible without surrendering the unhurried vibe of the Lower Keys, the pet-friendly ★ **Geiger Key Marina & RV Park** (5 Geiger Rd., Geiger Key, 305/294-1230, www.geigerkeymarina.com, $111-161 daily, $665-965 weekly, $2,110-3,400 monthly) offers the best of both worlds. Founded over five decades ago by two fishermen, Geiger Key still has the vibe of Old Florida. An off-the-beaten-path oasis and a terrific base for snorkeling, scuba diving, and deep-sea fishing, Geiger Key is the sort of place where locals arrive by boat, just to enjoy a relaxing breakfast, lunch, or dinner at the on-site Smokehouse Restaurant and Tiki Bar. Amenities here include waterfront spaces, full-hookup sites, laundry and shower facilities, live music on the weekends, and convenient boat slips ($35 daily, $140 weekly, $300 monthly) for vessels up to 20 feet in length; longer boats will be charged more. If you really enjoy your stay, it's possible to become a permanent resident here.

Information and Services

INFORMATION

For brochures, maps, and other information about Big Pine Key and the Lower Keys, consult the **Lower Keys Chamber of Commerce** (MM 31, 31020 Overseas Hwy., Big Pine Key, 305/872-2411 or 800/872-3722, www.lowerkeyschamber.com, 9am-5pm Mon.-Fri., 9am-3pm Sat.) near Mile Marker 31 or the **Monroe County Tourist Development Council** (1201 White St., Ste. 102, Key West, 305/296-1552 or 800/352-5397, www.fla-keys.com, 8am-5pm Mon.-Fri.). For government-related issues, contact the **Monroe County offices** (1100 Simonton St., Key West, 305/292-4459, www.monroecounty-fl.gov, 8:30am-5pm Mon.-Fri.).

For local news, consult *The Key West Citizen* (www.keysnews.com), **The Weekly Newspapers** (www.keysweekly.com), and www.bigpinekey.com. *The Miami Herald* (www.miamiherald.com) is also available throughout the Keys.

SERVICES

Money

For banking needs, stop by **Capital Bank** (MM 30.4, 30480 Overseas Hwy., Big Pine Key, 305/872-0295 or 800/639-5111, www.capitalbank-us.com, 9am-4pm Mon.-Thurs., 9am-6pm Fri., 9am-1pm Sat.) or the **First State Bank of the Florida Keys** (MM 30.5, 30515 Overseas Hwy., Big Pine Key, 305/872-4778, www.keysbank.com, 8am-5pm Mon.-Thurs., 8am-6pm Fri., 9am-1pm Sat.).

Mail

You'll find two **post offices** (800/275-8777, www.usps.com) in the area: one on Big Pine Key (MM 29.9, 29959 Overseas Hwy., 305/872-2531, 8:30am-4:30pm Mon.-Fri., 9am-noon Sat.) and one on Summerland Key (MM 24.7, 24700 Overseas Hwy., 305/745-3391, 9:30am-4:30pm Mon.-Fri., 9am-noon Sat.).

Groceries and Supplies

For groceries, head to the **Winn-Dixie** (251 Key Deer Blvd., Big Pine Key, 305/872-4124, www.winndixie.com, 6am-11pm daily) in the **Big Pine Shopping Center** (MM 30.4 BS U.S. 1, Big Pine Key), a complex that offers a number of useful services, including hair salons, a laundry, and a **public library** (213 Key Deer Blvd., Big Pine Key, 305/872-0992, www.keyslibraries.org, 9:30am-6pm Mon. and Wed.-Fri., 9:30am-8pm Tues., 10am-6pm Sat.). The Winn-Dixie has an on-site pharmacy (305/872-4850, 8am-8pm Mon.-Fri., 9am-6pm Sat., 10am-5pm Sun.).

Emergency Services

In case of an emergency that requires police, fire, or ambulance services, dial **911** from any cell or public phone. For nonemergency assistance, contact the **Monroe County Sheriff's Office** (Freeman Substation, MM 20.9, 20950 Overseas Hwy., Cudjoe Key, 305/745-3184, www.keysso.net, 8am-5pm Mon.-Fri.). For medical assistance, consult the **Fishermen's Community Hospital** (MM 33, 3301 Overseas Hwy., Marathon, 305/743-5533, www.fishermenshospital.com) or the **Lower Keys Medical Center** (5900 College Rd., Key West, 305/294-5531, www.lkmc.com). Foreign visitors seeking help with directions, medical concerns, business issues, law enforcement needs, or other problems can receive **multilingual tourist assistance** (800/771-5397) 24 hours daily.

Transportation

GETTING THERE

Air

While there are small airports like the **Sugarloaf Shores Airport** (MM 17, 5 Bat Tower Rd., Sugarloaf Key), the Lower Keys have no major airport of their own. To travel here by plane, you'll need to fly into **Fort Lauderdale-Hollywood International Airport** (FLL, 100 Terminal Dr., Fort Lauderdale, 866/435-9355, www.broward. org/airport), **Miami International Airport** (MIA, 2100 NW 42nd Ave., Miami, 305/876-7000, www.miami-airport.com), **Key West International Airport** (EYW, 3491 S. Roosevelt Blvd., Key West, 305/296-5439, www.keywestinternationalairport.com), or **Florida Keys Marathon Airport** (MTH, MM 52, 9400 Overseas Hwy., Marathon, 305/289-6060) and then rent a vehicle from agencies like **Avis** (800/633-3469, www.avis. com), **Budget** (800/218-7992, www.budget. com), **Enterprise** (800/261-7331, www. enterprise.com), **Hertz** (800/654-3131, www. hertz.com), or **Thrifty** (800/847-4389, www. thrifty.com) to reach the Lower Keys.

Bus or Train

To reach the Lower Keys using the regional bus system, you can take the **Miami-Dade County Metrobus** (305/891-3131, www. miamidade.gov/transit), which operates the **301 Dade-Monroe Express** between Florida City and Marathon (5:15am-10:40pm daily, $2.65 per one-way trip). From Marathon, you can then use the **Lower Keys Shuttle** (either the Lime or Pink route, $4 per ride), operated by the **Key West Department of Transportation** (KWDoT, 305/600-1455 or 305/809-3910, www.kwtransit.com), to complete the rest of your journey. The shuttle runs from Marathon to Key West between 5:30am and 10:55pm daily, and from Key West to Marathon between 5:30am and 10:54pm

daily. Other stops include Sunshine Key, Bahia Honda State Park, Big Pine Key, Little Torch Key, Ramrod Key, Sugarloaf Key, and several other Lower Keys. Reduced fares may apply for students under 22 years old, senior citizens over 59 years old, military personnel, and disabled individuals.

Greyhound (214/849-8966 or 800/231-2222, www.greyhound.com) offers bus service to the Lower Keys by making regular stops at the Big Pine Key Motel (30725 Overseas Hwy., Big Pine Key). **Amtrak** (800/872-7245, www. amtrak.com) provides train service only as far south as Miami, from where you can rent a car or hop a shuttle to reach the Lower Keys.

Transport from Airports and Stations

If you arrive in the Fort Lauderdale/Miami area by plane, bus, or train—or Key West by plane or bus—you can either rent a car or, in some cases, hire a shuttle service to reach the Lower Keys. Companies include **Keys Shuttle** (305/289-9997 or 888/765-9997, www.keysshuttle.com, $80-100 per shared ride, $350-450 for exclusive service), which provides service from the Miami and Fort Lauderdale airports.

Car

To reach the Lower Keys from Miami, head south on U.S. 1 (Overseas Hwy.), continue through Key Largo, Islamorada, and Marathon, and cross the Seven Mile Bridge. If you're headed from the Everglades via I-75 (Everglades Pkwy.), drive south on U.S. 27, veer right onto SR-997 (Krome Ave.), and follow the signs to U.S. 1. From U.S. 41 (Tamiami Trl.) in the Everglades, head south on SR-997 and continue toward U.S. 1.

If you are traveling during the high season (Dec.-Apr.), be sure to call **511** for an up-to-the-minute traffic report.

GETTING AROUND

Car

The best way to travel through the Lower Keys is by car, truck, RV, or motorcycle—all of which offer easy access to U.S. 1 and the smaller roads, such as Key Deer Boulevard on Big Pine Key, Watson Boulevard on No Name Key, and Sugarloaf Boulevard on Sugarloaf Key.

Taxi

Taxicab companies such as **Big Pine Taxi** (305/872-2662, $2 per mile, flat rates available) can help you get around the Lower Keys.

Bicycle or Boat

While you can certainly traverse the Lower Keys by bicycle, the sprawling nature of this region makes it challenging for novice riders. Nevertheless, it's a lovely, ecofriendly way to experience the major islands. The **Big Pine Bicycle Center** (31 County Rd., Big Pine Key, 305/872-0130, www.bigpinebikes.com, 9am-5pm Tues.-Fri., 9am-3pm Sat., $20-25 per day, $80-100 weekly, $200-250 monthly), near Mile Marker 30.9 on the gulf side, offers beach cruiser, 7-speed cruiser, and kids' BMX rentals as well as repairs.

Of course, biking will only get you so far. Most of the islands down here stand alone, and without the benefit of roads or bridges, you can only reach them by boat. Having your own boat makes navigating these islands, especially those in the backcountry, even easier, and you'll find no shortage of boat ramps and marina slips in the Lower Keys. It's also possible to explore this marvelous region by kayak. Contact **Big Pine Kayak Adventures** (1791 Bogie Dr., 305/872-7474, www.keyskayaktours.com, 8am-5pm daily, singles $25 for two hours, tandems $35 for two hours, $5 for each additional hour), which is based out of the Old Wooden Bridge Marina (1791 Bogie Dr., Big Pine Key, 305/872-2241) and offers kayak rentals for multiple days.

Key West

At the end of the Overseas Highway lies the

southernmost point in the continental United States—a quirky little island known as Key West.

Residents here are proud to refer to themselves as "Conchs," a remnant from when Bahamian immigrants called this unique place home. To many, the Conch Republic (a term that mainly refers to Key West, though some people also apply it to the entire Florida Keys archipelago) is more than just the inspiration for souvenirs—it's a symbol of the island's distinctive vibe. No wonder such famous visionaries as Ernest Hemingway, Tennessee Williams, and Robert Frost had such an affinity for this town.

These days Key West is home to a blend of varied folks, including

Highlights

Look for ★ to find recommended sights, activities, dining, and lodging.

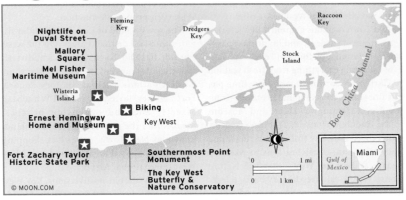

Nightlife on Duval Street
Mallory Square
Mel Fisher Maritime Museum
Wisteria Island
★ Biking
Ernest Hemingway Home and Museum
Fort Zachary Taylor Historic State Park
Southernmost Point Monument
The Key West Butterfly & Nature Conservatory

Fleming Key
Dredgers Key
Stock Island
Raccoon Key
Boca Chica Channel
Key West
Gulf of Mexico
Miami
0   1 mi
0   1 km

© MOON.COM

★ **Southernmost Point Monument:** This large monument is just 90 miles from Cuba and marks the southernmost point in the United States. It's a classic photo op, but be prepared for long lines (page 234).

★ **Mallory Square:** Situated in Key West's Old Town, this waterfront plaza contains several eateries, shops, monuments, and attractions, including the daily Sunset Celebration (page 236).

★ **The Key West Butterfly & Nature Conservatory:** Stroll among hundreds of vibrant flowers, birds, and butterflies in a glass-enclosed habitat (page 238).

★ **Ernest Hemingway Home and Museum:** Surrounded by lush gardens, this 19th-century mansion was once home to the novelist, who wrote *To Have and Have Not* in the backyard studio (page 238).

★ **Mel Fisher Maritime Museum:** Besides educating visitors about marine archaeology, this impressive repository highlights many of the treasures discovered in the famous *Atocha* shipwreck (page 244).

★ **Fort Zachary Taylor Historic State Park:** Centered on an intriguing Civil War fort, Florida's southernmost state park features nature trails, a popular beach, and access to incredible snorkeling (page 248).

★ **Biking:** Bicycling is a great way to see the historic homes, lovely gardens, and scenic beaches of this one-of-a-kind town (page 256).

★ **Nightlife on Duval Street:** Running from the Gulf of Mexico to the Atlantic, this 1.25-mile-long street is the epicenter of shopping, dining, and drinking. Party until late in the evening on the gulf side and stroll amid historic mansions and bungalows on the Atlantic end (page 265).

vacationing families, retired couples, eccentric artists, newlyweds, adventurers, corporate escapees, and hardy natives who can withstand the humidity, isolation, and hurricane season. The island also has a sizable gay population, as evidenced by male-only resorts, gay-themed tours, and events like Fantasy Fest.

Those who have heard of Key West but have never seen it for themselves often liken it to a twenty-four-hour Mardi Gras celebration in New Orleans' French Quarter, but the Southernmost City is not so easy to characterize. In fact, it's as diverse as the rest of the Keys. While there's indeed a party vibe in some of the Old Town bars and restaurants, that's not all that Key West has to offer.

Old Town contains a number of Victorian inns, tropical gardens, and luxurious spas—not to mention a plethora of reliable restaurants, offering everything from fresh seafood to Caribbean cuisine to tangy key lime pie. Historical attractions abound here, too—from the Ernest Hemingway Home and Museum to the Audubon House & Tropical Gardens. Other diversions, like trolley tours, maritime museums, sunset celebrations at Mallory Square, and the Key West Butterfly & Nature Conservatory, can keep history buffs, relentless revelers, and nature lovers busy for days on end.

Shoppers will also find an array of enticing boutiques and emporiums. Cultural enthusiasts will be delighted by the variety of concerts and plays available. Recreationists can play golf, rent a kayak, embark on a fishing excursion, snorkel in the surrounding waters, or venture to the Dry Tortugas—and if that's not enough, Key West also hosts an assortment of festivals and events throughout the year, from the Conch Republic Independence Celebration to the Lighted Boat Parade during the winter holiday season.

Still, while Key West isn't as easy to characterize as some may believe, it is indeed a laid-back locale, where the island time seems to move at a pace all its own. As if to accentuate this easygoing persona, the tunes of Jimmy Buffett—the quintessential mascot for Key West and the Florida Keys—seem to feature prominently in every bar, restaurant, and local performer's repertoire, no matter the time of day or night.

PLANNING YOUR TIME

With its many beaches, museums, nature centers, cultural events, train and trolley tours, sunset cruises, and other outdoor activities, Key West is definitely the most active town in the Florida Keys. It's no surprise that many travelers bypass the other islands to make Key West their primary destination.

The small island of Key West is today divided into two distinct halves. On the western side lies Old Town, a historical district that includes most of the city's major tourist destinations, such as Mallory Square, Fort Zachary Taylor, Duval and Whitehead Streets, and the oceanside beaches. Meanwhile, the eastern side of the island, known as New Town, comprises shopping centers, residential areas, schools, and Key West International Airport.

Ironically, despite its diversions, Key West is also the most compact region in the Florida Keys. Including adjacent Stock Island, the area stretches from Mile Marker 5 to Mile Marker 0 on the Overseas Highway, which makes this an incredibly easy town to navigate. You can walk, bike, or drive around at your own pace. In addition, taxicabs and pedicabs are available day and night—which means you can stay wherever you want, from an Old Town bed-and-breakfast to a coastal resort.

Given all that there is to see and do, you could conceivably stay a long weekend in the Southernmost City, or a week if you plan a trip to Dry Tortugas National Park. Deciding when to visit Key West will depend on several factors, not the least of which is whether or not you hope to catch annual events like

---

Previous: a pier in Key West; an ancient coin at the Mel Fisher Maritime Museum; an aerial view of Key West.

Key West and Stock Island

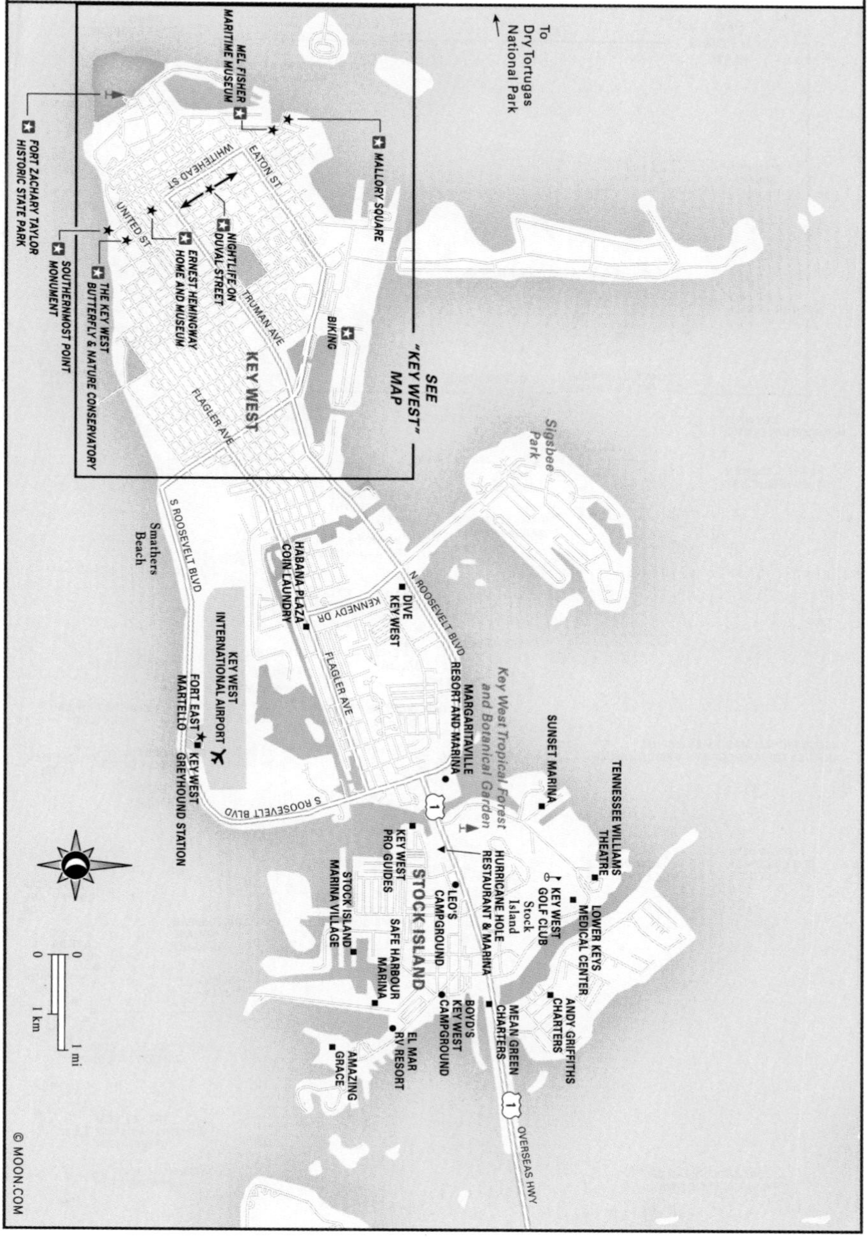

To Dry Tortugas National Park

MEL FISHER MARITIME MUSEUM

MALLORY SQUARE

WHITEHEAD ST

EATON ST

NIGHTLIFE ON DUVAL STREET

ERNEST HEMINGWAY HOME AND MUSEUM

UNITED ST

TRUMAN AVE

FORT ZACHARY TAYLOR HISTORIC STATE PARK

SOUTHERNMOST POINT MONUMENT

THE KEY WEST BUTTERFLY & NATURE CONSERVATORY

KEY WEST

BIKING

FLAGLER AVE

SEE "KEY WEST" MAP

Sigsbee Park

S ROOSEVELT BLVD

Smathers Beach

HABANA PLAZA COIN LAUNDRY

KEY WEST INTERNATIONAL AIRPORT

N KENNEDY DR

FLAGLER AVE

DIVE KEY WEST

S ROOSEVELT BLVD

FORT EAST MARTELLO

KEY WEST GREYHOUND STATION

MARGARITAVILLE RESORT AND MARINA

Key West Tropical Forest and Botanical Garden

HURRICANE HOLE RESTAURANT & MARINA

SUNSET MARINA

Stock Island

KEY WEST GOLF CLUB

TENNESSEE WILLIAMS THEATRE

LOWER KEYS MEDICAL CENTER

LEO'S CAMPGROUND

KEY WEST PRO GUIDES

STOCK ISLAND MARINA VILLAGE

SAFE HARBOUR MARINA

STOCK ISLAND

BOYD'S KEY WEST CAMPGROUND

MEAN GREEN CHARTERS

ANDY GRIFFITHS CHARTERS

EL MAR RV RESORT

AMAZING GRACE

OVERSEAS HWY

0   1 mi
0   1 km

© MOON.COM

Key West

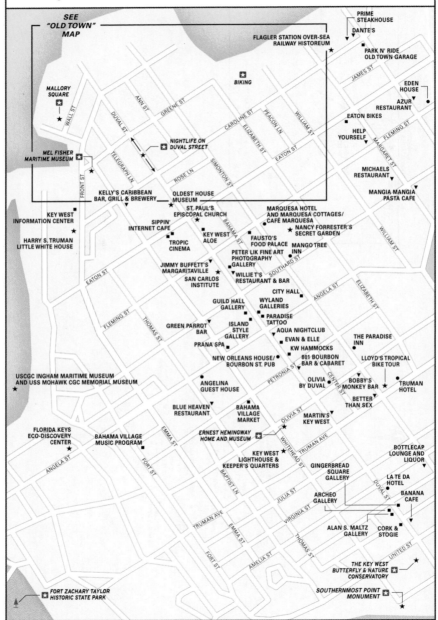

SEE "OLD TOWN" MAP

PRIME STEAKHOUSE
DANTE'S
FLAGLER STATION OVER-SEA RAILWAY HISTOREUM
PARK N' RIDE OLD TOWN GARAGE
BIKING
MALLORY SQUARE
EDEN HOUSE
AZUR RESTAURANT
EATON BIKES
HELP YOURSELF
NIGHTLIFE ON DUVAL STREET
MEL FISHER MARITIME MUSEUM
MICHAELS RESTAURANT
MANGIA MANGIA PASTA CAFE
KELLY'S CARIBBEAN BAR, GRILL & BREWERY
OLDEST HOUSE MUSEUM
KEY WEST INFORMATION CENTER
ST. PAUL'S EPISCOPAL CHURCH
MARQUESA HOTEL AND MARQUESA COTTAGES/ CAFÉ MARQUESA
NANCY FORRESTER'S SECRET GARDEN
SIPPIN' INTERNET CAFE
HARRY S. TRUMAN LITTLE WHITE HOUSE
KEY WEST ALOE
FAUSTO'S FOOD PALACE
MANGO TREE INN
TROPIC CINEMA
PETER LIK FINE ART PHOTOGRAPHY GALLERY
JIMMY BUFFETT'S MARGARITAVILLE
WILLIE T'S RESTAURANT & BAR
SAN CARLOS INSTITUTE
CITY HALL
GUILD HALL GALLERY
WYLAND GALLERIES
GREEN PARROT BAR
PARADISE TATTOO
ISLAND STYLE GALLERY
AQUA NIGHTCLUB
THE PARADISE INN
PRANA SPA
EVAN & ELLE
KW HAMMOCKS
NEW ORLEANS HOUSE/ BOURBON ST. PUB
801 BOURBON BAR & CABARET
LLOYD'S TROPICAL BIKE TOUR
USCGC INGHAM MARITIME MUSEUM AND USS MOHAWK CGC MEMORIAL MUSEUM
ANGELINA GUEST HOUSE
OLIVIA BY DUVAL
BOBBY'S MONKEY BAR
TRUMAN HOTEL
BETTER THAN SEX
BLUE HEAVEN RESTAURANT
BAHAMA VILLAGE MARKET
MARTIN'S KEY WEST
FLORIDA KEYS ECO-DISCOVERY CENTER
BAHAMA VILLAGE MUSIC PROGRAM
ERNEST HEMINGWAY HOME AND MUSEUM
BOTTLECAP LOUNGE AND LIQUOR
KEY WEST LIGHTHOUSE & KEEPER'S QUARTERS
GINGERBREAD SQUARE GALLERY
LA TE DA HOTEL
BANANA CAFE
ARCHEO GALLERY
ALAN S. MALTZ GALLERY
CORK & STOGIE
THE KEY WEST BUTTERFLY & NATURE CONSERVATORY
FORT ZACHARY TAYLOR HISTORIC STATE PARK
SOUTHERNMOST POINT MONUMENT

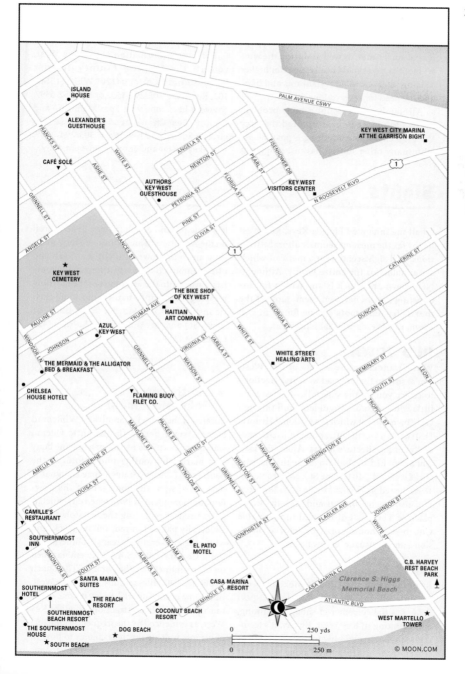

ISLAND HOUSE

ALEXANDER'S GUESTHOUSE

PALM AVENUE CSWY

KEY WEST CITY MARINA AT THE GARRISON BIGHT

FRANCES ST

WHITE ST

ASHE ST

ANGELA ST

NEWTON ST

PEARL ST

EISENHOWER DR

1

CAFÉ SOLÉ

AUTHORS KEY WEST GUESTHOUSE

PETRONIA ST

FLORIDA ST

KEY WEST VISITORS CENTER

GRINNELL ST

PINE ST

N ROOSEVELT BLVD

ANGELA ST

OLIVIA ST

1

FRANCES ST

CATHERINE ST

★ KEY WEST CEMETERY

THE BIKE SHOP OF KEY WEST

DUNCAN ST

PAULINE ST

TRUMAN AVE

HAITIAN ART COMPANY

GEORGIA ST

WINDSOR LN

AZUL KEY WEST

JOHNSON LN

WHITE ST

VIRGINIA ST

VARELA ST

WATSON ST

SEMINARY ST

LEON ST

THE MERMAID & THE ALLIGATOR BED & BREAKFAST

GRINNELL ST

WHITE STREET HEALING ARTS

SOUTH ST

CHELSEA HOUSE HOTELT

▼ FLAMING BUOY FILET CO.

TROPICAL ST

PACKER ST

MARGARET ST

UNITED ST

HAVANA AVE

WASHINGTON ST

AMELIA ST

CATHERINE ST

REYNOLDS ST

WHALTON ST

GRINNELL ST

LOUISA ST

FLAGLER AVE

JOHNSON ST

CAMILLE'S RESTAURANT

VONPHISTER ST

WHITE ST

SOUTHERNMOST INN

SIMONTON ST

C.B. HARVEY REST BEACH PARK

● EL PATIO MOTEL

ALBERTA ST

WILLIAM ST

CASA MARINA CT

SOUTH ST

SANTA MARIA SUITES

CASA MARINA RESORT

Clarence S. Higgs Memorial Beach

SOUTHERNMOST HOTEL

THE REACH RESORT

SEMINOLE ST

ATLANTIC BLVD

SOUTHERNMOST BEACH RESORT

COCONUT BEACH RESORT

WEST MARTELLO TOWER ★

THE SOUTHERNMOST HOUSE

★ SOUTH BEACH

DOG BEACH

0   250 yds

0   250 m

© MOON.COM

Hemingway Days, which usually takes place in mid-July, or Fantasy Fest, which typically occurs in late October. Since Key West is popular at such times, as well as during the winter months, you should be prepared for higher lodging rates, crowded restaurants and bars, and the need for reservations.

Although crime is not a huge problem in the Florida Keys, bear in mind that Key West is a city, where anything is possible. As with many other tourist havens, muggings do occur from time to time, so it's advisable to stay alert and avoid walking on desolate, poorly lit streets at night.

For more information about Key West, consult the **Monroe County Tourist Development Council** (1201 White St., Ste. 102, Key West, 305/296-1552 or 800/352-5397, www.fla-keys.com, 9am-5pm Mon.-Fri.) and the **Key West Chamber of Commerce** (510 Greene St., 1st Fl., Key West, 305/294-2587, www.keywestchamber.org, 8am-6pm daily).

Sights

Of all the inhabited Florida Keys, Key West has by far the most museums, cultural attractions, and sightseeing tours, many of which are suitable for the entire family. Although New Town and Stock Island have a few interesting locales between them, most of the tourist-friendly spots can be found in Old Town, Key West's original settlement.

OLD TOWN

While wandering the streets of Key West, you're sure to find myriad worthy attractions to entice you off the sidewalk—at least for a little while. Just a self-guided stroll through Old Town, part of which is a National Historic District, is a worthy attraction in itself, especially for architecture lovers. Along the way, you'll spot historic buildings like the majestic **Old City Hall** (510 Greene St.), constructed in 1891; the redbrick **Custom House** (281 Front St.), also erected in 1891 and once the workplace of Thomas Edison; and innumerable Conch-style homes, ornate Victorian mansions, and unusual eyebrow houses.

Duval Street

Running from the Gulf of Mexico to the Atlantic, the famous 1.25-mile-long **Duval Street** is the epicenter of shopping, dining, and drinking in Key West. By day, it's teeming with tourists looking for a cold mojito or frozen tropical drink to go along with their key lime pie and conch fritters. Take a stroll on the Atlantic end and admire historic mansions and bungalows. By night, it's a lively and often rambunctious party, where many tourists stay up into the wee hours of the morning hopping from bar to bar. Hit up some classic institutions like **Sloppy Joe's Bar** (201 Duval St.) and **Captain Tony's Saloon** (428 Greene St.).

TOP EXPERIENCE

★ Southernmost Point Monument

Located at the corner of South and Whitehead Streets, right beside the Atlantic Ocean, stands an enormous replica of a marine buoy that marks the southernmost point in the continental United States. Once designated by a mere sign, the spot gained the now-famous monument in 1983, when city officials grew tired of replacing the oft-stolen sign. Colorfully painted in red, yellow, black, and white, the marker simply reads "Southernmost Point Continental U.S.A." Also emblazoned on the monument are the phrases "The Conch Republic," "90 Miles to Cuba," and "Key West, FL, Home of the Sunset." Today it's one of the most photographed attractions in all of Key West, as evidenced by the frequently long line of visitors waiting for their chance to pose in front of the colorful buoy—smaller versions

Old Town

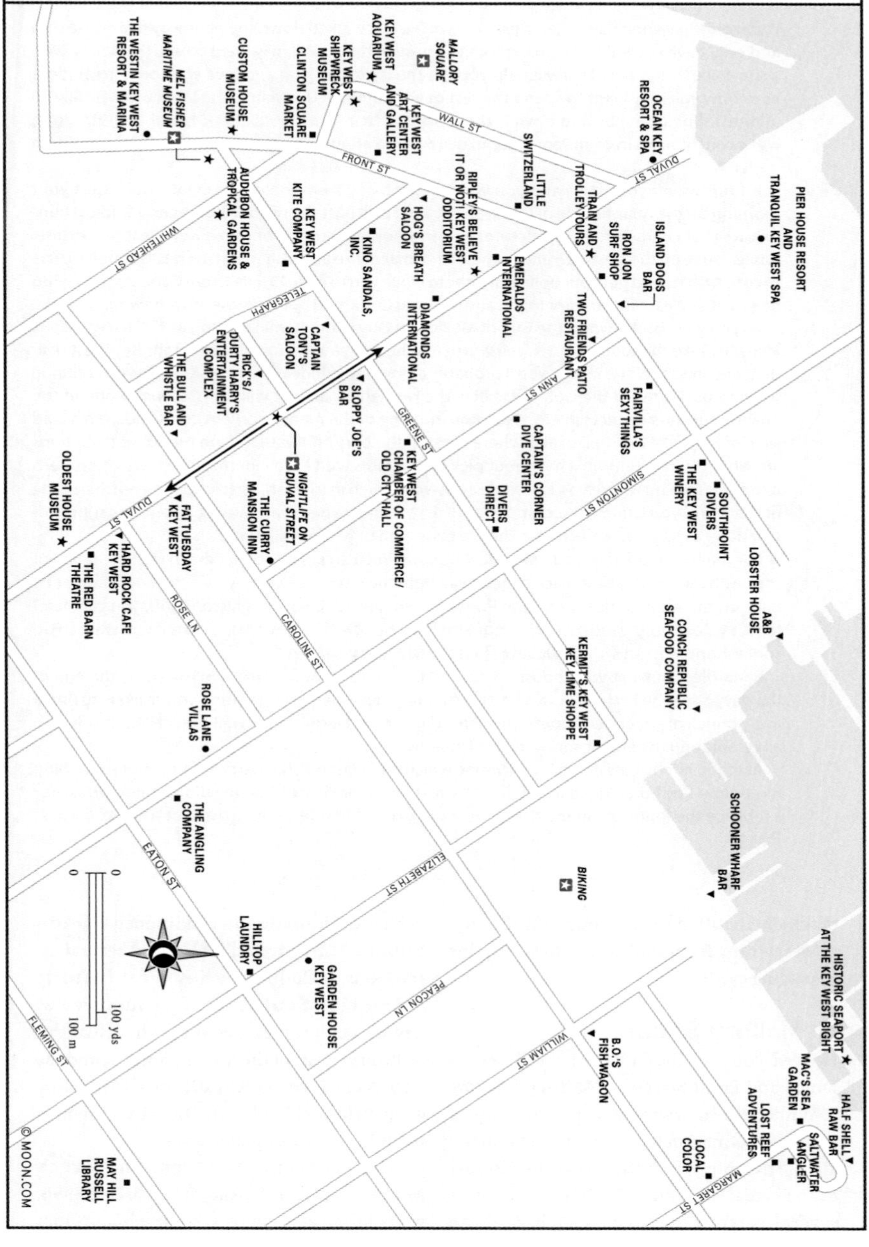

THE WESTIN KEY WEST RESORT & MARINA
MEL FISHER MARITIME MUSEUM
CUSTOM HOUSE MUSEUM
CLINTON SQUARE MARKET
KEY WEST SHIPWRECK MUSEUM
KEY WEST ART CENTER AND GALLERY
KEY WEST AQUARIUM
MALLORY SQUARE
AUDUBON HOUSE & TROPICAL GARDENS
KEY WEST KITE COMPANY
RIPLEY'S BELIEVE IT OR NOT! KEY WEST ODDITORIUM
HOG'S BREATH SALOON
KINO SANDALS, INC.
DIAMONDS INTERNATIONAL
EMERALDS INTERNATIONAL
LITTLE SWITZERLAND
TRAIN AND TROLLEY TOURS
RON JON SURF SHOP
ISLAND DOGS BAR
OCEAN KEY RESORT & SPA
PIER HOUSE RESORT AND TRANQUIL KEY WEST SPA
TWO FRIENDS PATIO RESTAURANT
FAIRVILLA'S SEXY THINGS
CAPTAIN'S CORNER DIVE CENTER
DIVERS DIRECT
THE KEY WEST WINERY
SOUTHPOINT DIVERS
A&B LOBSTER HOUSE
CONCH REPUBLIC SEAFOOD COMPANY
KERMIT'S KEY WEST KEY LIME SHOPPE
SCHOONER WHARF BAR
CAPTAIN TONY'S SALOON
RICK'S/ DURTY HARRY'S ENTERTAINMENT COMPLEX
THE BULL AND WHISTLE BAR
SLOPPY JOE'S BAR
NIGHTLIFE ON DUVAL STREET
THE CURRY MANSION INN
KEY WEST CHAMBER OF COMMERCE/ OLD CITY HALL
OLDEST HOUSE MUSEUM
FAT TUESDAY KEY WEST
HARD ROCK CAFE KEY WEST
THE RED BARN THEATRE
ROSE LANE VILLAS
THE ANGLING COMPANY
HILLTOP LAUNDRY
GARDEN HOUSE KEY WEST
BIKING
HISTORIC SEAPORT AT THE KEY WEST BIGHT
B.O.'S FISH WAGON
HALF SHELL RAW BAR
MAC'S SEA GARDEN
SALTWATER ANGLER
LOST REEF ADVENTURES
LOCAL COLOR
MAY HILL RUSSELL LIBRARY

WALL ST
FRONT ST
DUVAL ST
WHITEHEAD ST
TELEGRAPH
GREENE ST
ANN ST
SIMONTON ST
CAROLINE ST
ROSE LN
EATON ST
ELIZABETH ST
PEACON LN
WILLIAM ST
MARGARET ST
FLEMING ST

0
0
100 yds
100 m

© MOON.COM

One Day in Key West

If you only have one day in Key West, or if you've just walked down the gangway of a cruise ship and only have several hours to explore the best of town, you may want to start your day with a short **trolley tour.** This will help you get the lay of the land and give you some great ideas as to how you may want to spend the rest of your time on the island. The tours are typically 90 minutes. One of the best in town is the **Conch Tour Train** (305/294-5161 or 888/916-8687, www.conchtourtrain.com, 9am-4:30pm daily, $31.45 adults, $15.75 children 4-12, free for children under 4).

If tours aren't your style and you want to get away from the crowds, you could start your morning on the Atlantic side of Duval Street and stroll past the historic homes and tropical bungalows that characterize this picturesque and popular stretch of prime Key West real estate. While you're on the southern end of the island, make sure and visit the **Southernmost Point Monument,** and get your obligatory photo while you're only 90 miles from Cuba. As the saying goes in Key West, "If you want to get any closer to Cuba, you better know how to swim."

As you walk back toward the Gulf of Mexico on Duval Street, make a stop at **Hemingway's House.** Take the tour, which is well worth it. Whether you're a fan of the famous Key West resident and master writer or not, you'll probably enjoy his old hideaway in the Keys. As you continue walking back toward the Gulf of Mexico, the residential district will transform into one of the busiest business districts in Key West. Pop into one of the many excellent cafés and grab a cold slice of **key lime pie.** Duval is where most of the bars on the island are found, so if libations are what you're after, you'll have your pick of barstools with excellent tropical views and superb people-watching where you can while away your lunch in island bliss. Back on the northern side of the island you'll find the iconic **Sloppy Joe's Bar,** where you can get an endless supply of **mojitos and pina coladas.** (They're tasty with or without alcohol.)

For the rest of the day, you have a few options. You can spend some time in the sun at one of the few beaches; the best place to get away from the cruise crowd may be **Smathers Beach,** back on the Atlantic side alongside Roosevelt Boulevard. If you're a history buff, you can head to **Fort Zachary Taylor National Park** or the **Mel Fisher Museum.** If you want to do some shopping, just stay on Duval or head to **Mallory Square.**

Regardless of what you choose to do, you'll want to be at **Mallory Square** by the end of the day to see the **Sunset Celebration.** It happens every evening, and you're likely to find a lively bunch of street performers (think fire-dancers and jugglers), as well as excellent musicians, all celebrating the end of another day in paradise.

At night, hit the bars along Duval Street, which becomes one big party. If you prefer something more "low-Key," then head to **Latitudes** restaurant or **Azur** for a fine dinner; at Azur, ask for a table by the fountain. Spend the night at the **Eden House** or the **Southernmost Beach Resort.**

of which are often seen throughout the city, on everything from shot glasses to key chains to playing cards.

★ Mallory Square

Nestled alongside the Gulf of Mexico between Duval and Front Streets is **Mallory Square** (1 Whitehead St., www.mallorysquare.com), a popular destination for residents and tourists alike. Stretching from the Ocean Key Resort to the cruise ship pier, this district features several eateries and shops, such as those

enclosed within the air-conditioned **Clinton Square Market.** You'll also find several attractions, including the **Key West Historic Memorial Sculpture Garden** (www.keywestsculpturegarden.org), which features 36 bronze busts of the town's pioneers, and the **Key West-Florida Keys Historic Military Memorial,** which honors the city's involvement in America's major wars.

Also here is the **Key West Shipwreck Museum** (1 Whitehead St., 305/292-8990, www.keywestshipwreck.com, 9:40am-5pm

Hemingway's Key West

Perhaps Key West's most popular attraction, the **Ernest Hemingway Home and Museum** (907 Whitehead St., 305/294-1136, www.hemingwayhome.com) lures curious sightseers every day. Built in 1851 by marine architect Asa Tift, this two-story mansion became home to Ernest Hemingway and his second wife, Pauline Pfeiffer, in 1931. Today visitors can see descendants of his six-toed felines, plenty of original artwork and family photographs, and the separate writing studio where the Nobel Prize-winning novelist penned several famous short stories and books, including *To Have and Have Not* (1937), the story of a fishing boat captain who runs contraband between Cuba and Florida.

Captain Tony's Saloon

Naturally, this isn't the sole remnant of Hemingway's time in Key West. Not only does every train, trolley, and walking tour mention his name, but you'll also find some of his former belongings in places like **Ripley's Believe It or Not! Key West Odditorium** (108 Duval St.) and the **Custom House Museum** (281 Front St.). In addition, several hotels and watering holes claim ties to Papa Hemingway. The private Mediterranean Revival-style home known as **Casa Antigua** (314 Simonton St.), for instance, was once a residential hotel above a Ford dealership, and it was here that Hemingway and Pauline stayed during their first visit to Key West. He even finished the initial draft of *A Farewell to Arms* (1929) while awaiting the delivery of his new Model A. Supposedly, Hemingway also stayed at **The Southernmost House** (1400 Duval St.), and he frequented **Captain Tony's Saloon** (428 Greene St.) when it was the original location of Sloppy Joe's; you'll even catch a glimpse of Hemingway's former barstool. Meanwhile, the most recent incarnation of **Sloppy Joe's Bar** (201 Duval St.) features the famous Hemingway Look-Alike Contest, part of the annual **Hemingway Days** celebration in July.

Hemingway first came to Key West in 1928. For the next few years, he and Pauline spent winters in the Florida Keys and summers in Europe and Wyoming. In 1931 they acquired the house at 907 Whitehead Street. During this prolific period, his schedule consisted of writing every morning and relaxing every afternoon and evening with his friends. One particularly close pal was Joe Russell, an irascible fisherman and owner of Sloppy Joe's, a speakeasy. Russell introduced Hemingway to deep-sea fishing; Hemingway repaid the favor by immortalizing his friend as Harry Morgan, captain of the *Queen Conch* in *To Have and Have Not*. The backyard drinking fountain that Hemingway built for his cats is actually a refurbished urinal from Sloppy Joe's, which was also where in 1936 Hemingway met reporter Martha Gellhorn, who would later become his third wife.

Originally, Hemingway's home was surrounded by a chain-link fence, but in 1935 he erected the perimeter wall that exists today, in the hope of providing his family privacy from gawking tourist hordes. Between 1937 and 1938, while Hemingway was serving as a war correspondent during the Spanish Civil War, Pauline supervised the construction of the first residential swimming pool in Key West. When Ernest returned, he was shocked by the final price tag of $20,000, at which point he removed a penny from his pocket and told her that she might as well take his last cent. Today you can see this penny embedded beside the pool.

Hemingway stayed in Key West for well over a decade before divorcing Pauline in 1940, marrying Martha, and heading to Cuba. Pauline, meanwhile, stayed in the Key West home until her death in 1951. Upon Hemingway's death in 1961, the Key West home was sold to local businesswoman Bernice Dickson, who turned it into a museum in 1964. The home, which was designated a National Historic Landmark in 1968, remains the property of Dickson's family, though Hemingway's spirit is alive and well.

daily, $16.11 adults, $13.96 seniors, $9.66 children 4-12, free for children under 4), where live performers, films, and artifacts let visitors experience a 19th-century wrecker's warehouse and learn about the 1856 *Isaac Allerton* shipwreck and its subsequent salvage. You can also discover how Key West once became the richest city in America and even pretend to spot wrecks from the 65-foot lookout tower atop the museum, the last remaining of 20 such towers in Key West.

Just steps from the Shipwreck Museum, the **Key West Aquarium** (1 Whitehead St., 305/296-2051 or 888/544-5927, www.keywestaquarium.com, 9am-6pm daily, $17.19 adults, $15.04 seniors, $10.74 children 4-12, free for children under 4) presents daily shark and turtle feedings as well as hands-on touch tanks featuring starfish, queen conch, and other regional marinelife. Opened in 1934, the aquarium also offers visitors the chance to observe moray eels, barracuda, grouper, tarpon, parrotfish, sea turtles, alligators, and other sea creatures in a 50,000-gallon tank that represents a typical mangrove ecosystem in the Florida Keys.

At least once during your visit to Key West, stroll to Mallory Square in the late afternoon, when artists, musicians, acrobats, and tourists converge to pay homage to Key West's gorgeous sunsets during the daily **Sunset Celebration.** To avoid the crowds along the shore, head to The Westin Key West Resort & Marina at 245 Front Street, where you can watch the sunset while sipping cocktails on the aptly named **Sunset Deck.**

★ The Key West Butterfly & Nature Conservatory

Situated near the southern end of Duval Street, **The Key West Butterfly & Nature Conservatory** (1316 Duval St., 305/296-2988 or 800/839-4647, www.keywestbutterfly.com, 9am-5pm daily, $12 adults, $9 seniors and military personnel, $8.50 children 4-12, free for children under 4) invites visitors to take a stroll through a vibrant glass-enclosed, climate-controlled

habitat filled with waterfalls, trees, flowering plants, and hundreds of colorful birds and butterflies. While here, you can learn about butterfly anatomy, physiology, life cycles, feeding, and migration in the **Learning Center,** which offers a 15-minute orientation film and an up-close view of caterpillars feeding and developing on their host plants. In addition, you can peruse Sam Trophia's kaleidoscopic creations—essentially, a variety of encased butterfly displays—inside the art gallery, **Wings of Imagination** (9am-5:30pm daily). Before leaving the nature center, be sure to browse the wide assortment of butterfly-related items and other souvenirs in the on-site gift shop (9am-5:30pm daily). Visitor parking is available in the lot behind the conservatory, but the gate closes at 6pm every day. Although the conservatory is technically open until 5pm each day, the last tickets are sold at 4:30pm.

TOP EXPERIENCE

★ Ernest Hemingway Home and Museum

Directly across the street from the Key West Lighthouse lies the **Ernest Hemingway Home and Museum** (907 Whitehead St., 305/294-1136, www.hemingwayhome.com, 9am-5pm daily, cash only, $14 adults, $6 children, free for children under 6), one of the most popular attractions in Key West. This island-style domicile once was home to the city's most famous resident, Papa Hemingway himself, and has since become a registered National Historic Landmark. Built in 1851 by Asa Tift, a marine architect and salvage wrecker, the airy two-story structure features white walls and olive-green shutters, wraparound porches on both the lower and upper levels, and arched windows and doors on all sides, which invite a lot of natural light. Surrounded by picturesque palm

1: butterfly at the Key West Butterfly & Nature Conservatory 2: shops lining Duval Street 3: Key West Shipwreck Museum in Mallory Square 4: Ernest Hemingway Home and Museum

trees and blooming foliage, the home invites visitors to retrace the footsteps of Hemingway, an American novelist and short-story writer known all around the world as a big-game hunter, sportfisherman, war veteran, and unabashed adventurer.

Inside the mansion, you'll see a cornucopia of memorabilia, including period furnishings, family photographs, original artwork, and war medals. The lovingly preserved home looks much as it did during the 1930s, when Hemingway and his wife, Pauline, lived here. Some of the docents, while happy to share stories about Hemingway, joke that they wish Hemingway's wife hadn't replaced all of the original ceiling fans with chandeliers—a decision that seems regrettable on the hottest days, when box fans can be found throughout the house.

If you're a first-time visitor to the Hemingway Home, you should definitely opt for a 30-minute **guided tour**, available throughout the day, before exploring the grounds on your own. Beyond the house, you'll encounter a lovely pool, quiet garden nooks, a bookstore and gift shop (305/294-1575), and the Nobel Prize winner's well-preserved studio, where he spent his most productive years. It was here that he wrote and published some of his most enduring novels, nonfiction books, and short-story collections, including *A Farewell to Arms* (1929), *Death in the Afternoon* (1932), *Green Hills of Africa* (1935), and *To Have and Have Not* (1937). While here, you'll also see a plethora of six-toed felines, the descendants of Hemingway's legendary polydactyl cats—many of whom bear the names of famous movie stars, from the calico called Audrey Hepburn to a much-photographed black-and-white cat named after classic film star Charlie Chaplin.

Flagler Station Over-Sea Railway Historeum

Although technically not part of Old Town, the **Historic Seaport at Key West Bight** (www.keywestseaport.com), which lies along the edge of this historical district, beckons many a visitor onto the picturesque harbor walk—especially on sunny days, when it's pleasant just to amble along the waterfront, taking in the majestic schooners, private yachts, and other boats in the harbor. Before completing this stroll, which stretches from Grinnell Street to Simonton, take a short detour inland to the corner of Caroline and Margaret Streets, where you'll spot the **Flagler Station Over-Sea Railway Historeum** (901 Caroline St., 305/293-8716, www.flaglerstation.net, 9am-5pm daily, $5 adults, $2.50 children). Completed in January 1912, the station now serves as a tribute to Henry Flagler's determination to construct a 130-mile extension of the Florida East Coast Railway all the way to Key West.

In spite of his many critics, Flagler achieved his dream, with the help of hundreds of tireless workers. Although the Labor Day Hurricane of 1935 effectively destroyed the Overseas Railroad, this feat is still worthy of exploration. Visitors can browse an assortment of intriguing artifacts, photographs, memorabilia, and eyewitness accounts. After passing through a reconstruction of the original station and a themed mercantile store, you'll step inside an actual railroad car, listen to informative storytellers, and watch various film presentations—including one about the construction of "Flagler's Folly" and another about the celebrations that took place the day Flagler and his wife arrived in Key West after riding the train all the way from New York.

Key West Turtle Museum

At the northern end of Margaret Street, between the Flagler Station Over-Sea Railway Historeum and the Historic Seaport at Key West Bight, is the enlightening **Key West Turtle Museum** (200 Margaret St., 305/294-0209, www.keywestturtlemuseum.org, 11am-4pm Wed.-Sat., donation suggested). Housed in a former cannery and overseen by the lauded Mel Fisher Maritime Museum, this small attraction educates visitors about the long history

Hemingway's Six-Toed Cats

a distinguished resident cat at the Ernest Hemingway Home and Museum

A six-toed cat is *polydactyl*, the technical term for having an extra digit. Seeing such cats is just one more reason why you should stop by the **Ernest Hemingway Home and Museum** (907 Whitehead St., 305/294-1136, www.hemingwayhome.com, 9am-5pm daily, cash only, $14 adults, $6 children, free for children under 6). If you're unfamiliar with feline digits, cats usually have five toes on their front and back paws. The story is that Hemingway was given a six-toed cat by a friend and sea captain who was visiting the island. That cat's name was Snow White. Today there are about 50 six-toed cats living at Papa Hemingway's home, all believed to be descendants of the original cat. Hemingway was purportedly a true cat lover. He apparently preferred to name all of his cats after famous people, and today you may find cats at the house named Marilyn Monroe or Hillary Clinton. Any breed of cat can carry the polydactyl gene, and even the cats on the grounds that don't have six toes are believed to be carrying this extra-toe gene mutation. Some people ask what happens to the cats after the home and museum close. Well, don't worry—these cats are well taken care of. There's even a veterinarian on-site to make sure these pampered kitties get their proper doses of flea medication and top-shelf cat vittles. I would even bet a first-edition copy of Hemingway's *Farewell to Arms* that these are some of the best-cared-for cats in the country. So that's certainly something to clap their little six-toed paws about.

of sea turtles in the Florida Keys. Sea turtles were a main source of sustenance for the Native American tribes that once inhabited these islands, and even the famous explorer Juan Ponce de León noted an abundance of loggerhead turtles in the surrounding waters. He was so impressed that he named the islands *Tortugas,* which means "turtles" in Spanish. Unfortunately, turtle fishing nearly destroyed the local sea turtle population by the early 1900s. Since the 1950s, however, conservation and rescue efforts have helped these endangered creatures by protecting their habitats, tagging them for research purposes, and promoting public awareness of their plight. Besides featuring exhibits that explore Key West's maritime history, including its negative impact on area sea turtles and the subsequent efforts by conservationists like Archie Carr to save them, the museum also presents free lectures and other family-friendly programs, such as educational summer camps.

Key West Lighthouse & Keeper's Quarters

It's difficult to ignore the stately white lighthouse towering above the trees near the intersection of Truman Avenue and Whitehead Street. Here at the **Key West Lighthouse & Keeper's Quarters** (938 Whitehead St., 305/294-0012, www.kwahs.org, 9:30am-4:30pm daily, $12 adults, $9 seniors 62 and over and Key West residents, $5 students and children, free for children under 6) you'll learn about yet another facet of the coastal town's riveting history.

Erected in 1847 on a spot 14 feet above sea level, the 66-foot-tall brick lighthouse effectively replaced the original 46-foot wooden tower on Whitehead Point, which had been built in 1825 to aid ships navigating the dangerous offshore reefs and was destroyed in 1846 by a hurricane. In 1894 the city added a 20-foot extension to the second lighthouse, which was decommissioned by the U.S. Coast Guard in 1969. After an expensive restoration by the Key West Art & Historical Society in 1989—the same year that the lighthouse was featured in a pivotal scene in *Licence to Kill*—it became the tourist attraction it is today.

Visitors can climb the dizzying 88-step spiral staircase to a wraparound observation deck—just beneath the working 175-watt metal halide light—for an incredible 360-degree view of the verdant city. Helpful placards indicate important locales throughout Key West, including the Casa Marina resort in the distance and the grounds of the Ernest Hemingway Home down below. Also on the well-manicured grounds lies a small gift shop, plus the former keeper's quarters, constructed in 1887 to replace the original keeper's dwelling. Today the faithfully restored quarters serve as a museum that offers a look at turn-of-the-20th-century life with period furnishings and old photographs. There's also a collection of lighthouse artifacts, instruments, maps, and photographs within various exhibits that shed some light on the maritime history of the Florida Keys.

Ripley's Believe It or Not! Key West Odditorium

Half a block southeast of Front and Duval Streets is the two-story, 8,000-square-foot **Ripley's Believe It or Not! Key West Odditorium** (108 Duval St., 305/293-9939, www.ripleys.com/keywest, 10am-8pm daily, $13 adults, $8 children 5-12, free for children under 5). While not the most unique place in town, Ripley's is still very popular among visitors, especially children. Boasting over 500 unusual exhibits in 13 themed galleries, this bizarre attraction features everything from a stuffed white buffalo to a portrait fashioned from butterfly wings. Also on display are some of Ernest Hemingway's former belongings, including a typewriter and a shrunken torso.

Custom House Museum

Beside the Clinton Square Market in Mallory Square stands the Custom House, a gorgeous redbrick structure erected in 1891. It was a post office, courthouse, and government center during a time when salvaging cargo from nearby shipwrecks had made Key West the wealthiest city per capita in the United States. By the 1930s, the city had gone bankrupt, and the Custom House was eventually abandoned. Following a nine-year, $9 million restoration project, the Key West Art & Historical Society opened the building to the public in 1999 as the Key West Museum of Art and History at the Custom House, now simply known as the **Custom House Museum** (281 Front St., 305/295-6616, www.kwahs.org, 9:30am-4:30pm daily, $12 adults, $9 seniors 62 and over and Key West residents, $5 children and students, free for children under 6) and listed in the National Register of Historic Places. Among the fascinating exhibits here are Paul Collins's portraits of famous Key West residents, from Henry Flagler to Ernest Hemingway; Mario Sanchez's brightly colored wood paintings of life in Key West during the early 1900s; and various artifacts from Ernest Hemingway's adventurous life before and during his time on the island. You'll also

Key West Historical Tour

You'll find plenty of impressive historical and cultural landmarks in Key West. If you're looking for a quick walking or biking route to see some of the best, consider this quick tour of the island, which starts from the cruise port. If you're walking, plan on spending about five hours to see all of these sights, and budget your time to about fifteen minutes or so at each of the eleven stops. If you're biking, you can see all of the sights in about four hours.

historic Mallory Square

- Start your tour at the **Historic Seaport.** Stroll through the marina and admire the classic seafaring vessels such as Key West's flagship, the impressive schooner *Western Union.*

- Make your way down Greene Street to **Mallory Square,** a historic open-air market. It's the perfect spot to get a few souvenirs of your trip to the Keys.

- Grab lunch on Duval Street at **Sloppy Joe's Bar** or **Captain Tony's Saloon.** These bars are the most famous on Duval. Even if you're not having a drink, go in and walk around.

- Keep walking down Green Street to visit the **Audubon House & Tropical Gardens,** which contains a gorgeous home built in the 1800s by Captain John H. Geiger, a harbor pilot and master wrecker.

- Across the street, see the authentic treasures, coins, and other artifacts recovered from the *Atocha* shipwreck at the **Mel Fisher Museum.** If you don't have time for a tour of the museum, you can see some of the artifacts at the gift shop on the side of the building. It's free to visit the gift shop.

- The amazing redbrick building across from the Mel Fisher Museum on Front Street is the **Custom House Museum,** home to art and history exhibits.

- Walk down Front Street to reach the **Harry S. Truman Little White House,** a breezy structure that once served as the command headquarters for the Key West Naval Station.

- Walk a little bit farther down Front Street and then make a left on Eaton Street. Walk two blocks to Eaton and Duval, where you'll find **St. Paul's Episcopal Church,** a beautiful white building. The church is open to the public.

- Backtrack one block to Whitehead Street and continue for a few blocks until you hit the **Ernest Hemingway Home and Museum,** which was built in 1851 by a marine architect and was once the home of Key West's most famous resident.

- The **Key West Lighthouse** is across the street and on the same block as the Ernest Hemingway Home and Museum. Erected in 1848, it provides stunning views of the city.

- Finally, continue on Whitehead Street until you reach the **Southernmost Point Monument.** You'll usually find a long line of people waiting to take a picture. It's a must-see stop on your Key West trip.

learn about the pirates that once prowled the waters of the Florida Keys and how the U.S. Navy eventually expunged these looters and marauders from the region.

★ Mel Fisher Maritime Museum

Not far from the hard-to-miss Custom House on Front Street stands the massive **Mel Fisher Maritime Museum** (200 Greene St., 305/294-2633, www.melfisher.org, 8:30am-5pm Mon.-Fri., 9:30am-5pm Sat.-Sun., $15 adults, $12.50 students, $5 children), one of the most impressive treasure collections and marine archaeology museums in the world. After passing through the gift shop just beyond the front entrance, you'll encounter an array of fascinating exhibits, the first of which explains Mel Fisher's 16-year search for the *Nuestra Señora de Atocha* and the *Santa Margarita*, two Spanish galleons that shipwrecked off the Florida Keys in 1622. Both vessels were part of a treasure fleet bound for Spain. Loaded with gold, silver, copper, tobacco, indigo, gems, and other valuables, the ships encountered a severe hurricane in early September, driving them onto the coral reefs near the Dry Tortugas and drowning many of those on board. Although Spain managed to recover some of the cargo from the *Santa Margarita,* salvagers were never able to locate the *Atocha,* which had apparently sunk in more than 50 feet of water. The shipwreck attained legendary status when Fisher's determination finally prevailed.

Subsequent museum displays feature a mere fraction of the multimillion-dollar treasures that Fisher and his crew uncovered and preserved after the 1985 discovery. Here you'll see practical items such as daggers, corroded skillets, olive jars, shackles, thimbles, and even an enormous anchor. In the adjacent chamber, it's hard not to be awed by the varied treasures, from gold chains and silver coins to copper chunks and tobacco leaves. Especially intriguing is the 78-carat emerald that seems to glow like plutonium.

After viewing an exhibit about Mel Fisher's life, you'll head upstairs for *La Plata del Mar* exhibit, highlighting the diverse collection of silver artifacts that were carried aboard the 1622 Spanish fleet: enormous silver bars, silver *reales*, goblets, mirror frames, and other intriguing items. In the adjacent rooms, you'll learn about other sunken vessels, including the 1715 Plate Fleet and the *Henrietta Marie* slave ship. After your comprehensive tour, if your yen for treasure hunting has yet to be sated, consider stopping by Mel Fisher's Treasures, a separate jewelry store in the rear of the museum. And if that's not enough, you can be an investor in the ongoing efforts to salvage the *Atocha,* which is still yielding interesting (and often incredibly valuable) finds.

Audubon House & Tropical Gardens

Directly opposite the Mel Fisher Museum on Greene Street is the **Audubon House & Tropical Gardens** (205 Whitehead St., 305/294-2116 or 877/294-2470, www.audubonhouse.com, 9:30am-4:15pm daily, $14 adults, $10 students, $5 children 6-12, free for children under 6), one of several tranquil historic properties in Key West. Built in 1847 by Captain John H. Geiger, a shipwreck salvager and the city's first harbormaster, this gorgeous three-story home is a quintessential example of 19th-century architecture, with a symmetrical tropical-style design that features first-floor porches, second-level balconies, white walls and columns, and dark wooden shutters. Interestingly, John James Audubon never lived here, although the celebrated naturalist presumably visited the property in 1832 during a research trip to the Florida Keys and Dry Tortugas.

Inside the lovely mansion, you'll see plenty of antiques and period furniture, though the most interesting items are the numerous original renditions and reprints of Audubon's ornithological paintings throughout the 2nd and 3rd floors. Among the regional species on display are roseate spoonbills, Florida cormorants, booby gannets, brown pelicans, mangrove cuckoos, blue-headed pigeons, noddy terns, reddish egrets, and mango hummingbirds.

Following your tour of the house, feel free to meander along the brick pathways through the ecofriendly tropical gardens, shaded by palm trees and bursting with vibrant orchids and bromeliads. On your way out, take a moment to peruse the **Audubon House Gallery of Natural History,** a small art gallery near the entrance.

Harry S. Truman Little White House

Just south of Caroline and Front Streets, the Truman Annex features the **Harry S. Truman Little White House** (111 Front St., 305/294-9911, www.trumanlittlewhitehouse. com, 9am-4:30pm daily, $21.45 adults, $19.30 seniors, $10.75 children 5-12, free for children under 5 and Key West residents), another remarkable example of Key West architecture and a fascinating piece of the town's history. This breezy white structure, which was constructed in 1890 and once served as the command headquarters for the Key West Naval Station, became Truman's wintertime White House from 1946 to 1952 and was later a retreat for five other U.S. presidents.

Now serving as Florida's only presidential museum and listed in the National Register of Historic Places, this restored home invites visitors to amble amid original furnishings and learn about President Truman's personal and professional life, the politics of the Cold War, the naval history of Key West, and the origin of the Department of Defense. **Guided tours** are offered every 20 minutes between 9am and 4:30pm daily, and usually last between 45 and 55 minutes; scripts are available for the hearing-impaired. Guests can also take free self-guided tours of the adjacent **botanical gardens,** usually between 7am and 6pm daily, and the gift shop is open 9am-5pm daily. The museum offers wheelchair-accessible restrooms and allows service animals to accompany their owners onto the premises. Parking is only available at Mallory Square or in the Westin's parking garage.

Oldest House Museum

The **Oldest House Museum** (322 Duval St., 305/294-9501, 10am-4pm Mon.-Tues. and Thurs.-Sat., free) is literally the oldest house in southern Florida. Supposedly erected in 1829 by Richard Cussans, a Bahamian builder and merchant, and moved to its current location in the mid-1830s, this white one-story country-style structure was the longtime home of Captain Frances Watlington, a sea captain, shipwreck salvager, and one-time state senator. The historic home remained in the Watlington family until 1972, and soon afterward it was deeded to the Historic Key West Preservation Board.

Over the decades, the stalwart house has survived fires, hurricanes, financial hardships, and occupation by Union troops. Though docents and staff members are available to provide historical information about the property, visitors are free to roam through the tranquil rear garden as well as the house itself, which features many family portraits and original furnishings, plus other period pieces, ship models, and documents that relate to wrecking activities.

St. Paul's Episcopal Church

No matter how you choose to explore Duval, Old Town's main drag, you'll find it hard to miss the imposing white structure on the southeastern corner of Duval and Eaton Streets. Founded in 1831, **St. Paul's Episcopal Church** (401 Duval St., 305/296-5142, www.stpaulskeywest.org, 7:30am-dusk daily, free) is the oldest church community south of St. Augustine, though the building itself is far younger. Originally constructed in 1839, the first church, made of coral rock, was leveled in an 1846 hurricane. Rebuilt in 1848, the second church, a wooden structure, was destroyed by the city's Great Fire of 1886. The third church, also made of wood, was completed in 1887 and taken by a hurricane in 1909.

The fourth incarnation of the church, the concrete structure that exists today, was designed in 1911, completed in 1919, and heavily

renovated in 1993. With a striking frame, gorgeous stained glass windows, and a traditional tin roof, St. Paul's is truly a magnificent building and the widely accepted centerpiece of downtown Key West. No wonder it's often photographed by both residents and out-of-towners. Music lovers will especially appreciate the sanctuary, where the organist offers free lunchtime concerts and musical events are featured throughout the year.

San Carlos Institute

A little more than a block southeast of the prominent St. Paul's Episcopal Church is another fine example of Floridian architecture. Founded in 1871 by Cuban exiles and featuring an ornate Spanish-style facade, the **San Carlos Institute** (516 Duval St., 305/294-3887, www.institutosancarlos.org, noon-5pm daily, free) is one of the state's most historic landmarks. Dubbed *La Casa Cuba* by Cuban poet José Martí, the San Carlos was the site of Martí's 1892 attempt to unite the politically divided Cuban exile community in a bid to win Cuba's independence. Today this venerable institution serves as a nonprofit multipurpose facility featuring a museum, library, school, an art gallery, and a 360-seat theater that often hosts seminars and live concerts. Of particular interest are the permanent exhibits relating to the history of Cuba and Florida's Cuban American community, such as the photographs of Martí and the portraits of Cuba's constitutional presidents.

Nancy Forrester's Secret Garden

Two blocks east of Duval Street is a private tropical oasis that the public can enjoy. Also known as Key West's Exotic Tropical Botanical Garden, **Nancy Forrester's Secret Garden** (518 Elizabeth St., 305/294-0015, www.nancyforrester.com, 10am-3pm daily, $10 adults, $5 children 5-11) is widely celebrated for its gorgeous landscape of ferns,

aroids, shade palms, edible fruits, medicinal plants, and other rare foliage—an ideal home for the macaws who live here. In the center of this enticing sanctuary stands a small cottage that has often served as an inspiring artist's studio, and it can even be rented by those hoping to escape amid nature for a while.

Created by local artist and environmental educator Nancy Forrester, this lush garden is more than just a tourist attraction. It's also meant to represent the artist's wish for humanity to restore balance to the natural world. Unfortunately, this lovely spot—the last undeveloped wooded acre in the heart of Old Town—needs the public's help to remain open, so if you relish this peaceful place, consider contributing to the capital campaign on your next visit.

Key West Cemetery

On the eastern side of Old Town is the palm-lined **Key West Cemetery** (701 Passover Ln., 305/292-8177, www.keywestcity.com, 7am-7pm daily in summer, 7am-6pm daily in winter, free). Established in 1847 following a disastrous 1846 hurricane that unearthed the site's original cemetery, this fenced 19-acre property now contains beautiful statuary, historic gravestones, amusing epitaphs, and the remains of more than 80,000 Bahamian mariners, Cuban cigar makers, Spanish-American War veterans, soldiers and civilians, millionaires and paupers, whites and blacks, Catholics, Protestants, and Jews, and other unique individuals—illustrating Key West's incredibly diverse heritage.

Bordered by Windsor Lane and Angela, Frances, and Olivia Streets, the front entrance is near the intersection of Angela and Margaret, where you can pick up a free self-guided tour map from the office (8:30am-3:30pm Mon.-Fri.). Guided one-hour tours (9:30am Tues. and Thurs., $15 pp donation suggested) are also available through the **Historic Florida Keys Foundation** (Old City Hall, 510 Greene St., 305/292-6718, www.historicfloridakeys.org), though reservations are required. Whether you come alone or as

---

1: Mel Fisher Maritime Museum **2:** Key West Lighthouse **3:** Harry S. Truman Little White House

part of a tour group, remember that the cemetery is still an active place of reflection, so be respectful of mourners when visiting.

SOUTHERN SHORE

Along the Atlantic Ocean side of Key West are several interesting attractions, from military monuments to marine exhibits to fantastic beaches.

★ Fort Zachary Taylor Historic State Park

Accessible via the western end of Southard Street, **Fort Zachary Taylor Historic State Park** (601 Howard England Way, 305/292-6713, www.floridastateparks.org or www.fortzacharytaylor.com, 8am-sunset daily, $7 vehicles with 2 passengers plus $0.50 per additional person, $4.50 motorcycles and single-occupant vehicles, $2.50 pedestrians and bikers) is, in fact, the southernmost state park in Florida—and, for that matter, the continental United States. It's also a popular destination among history buffs and recreationists.

Situated at the convergence of the Gulf of Mexico and the Atlantic Ocean, where the clear, deep waters nurture living coral, yellowtail snapper, tropical fish, lobster, and other marine creatures, the 54-acre park is especially popular with swimmers, snorkelers, scuba divers, sunbathers, and picnickers, not to mention wedding parties. Enhanced by imported sand, the beach here is generally considered the finest in Key West—and an ideal place to watch an incredible Florida Keys sunset. Bikers, hikers, anglers, and bird-watchers also enjoy spending time in this beautiful place. Beyond biking paths and wooded nature trails, amenities include picnic tables, barbecue grills, public restrooms, outdoor showers, and ample parking, as well as beach equipment and water-sports rentals. In addition, the Cayo Hueso Café offers refreshments from 10am to 5pm daily.

But, of course, it's the 19th-century fort that lures many visitors. Completed in 1866, it was designated a National Historic Landmark in 1973. During the American Civil War, Key West remained in Union hands because of the naval base here, even though the rest of Florida joined the Confederate States of America. Fort Zachary Taylor, which was erected and fortified between 1845 and 1866, became a significant outpost during the conflict. Meanwhile, Fort Jefferson, which was constructed in the Dry Tortugas about 68 miles west of the Southernmost City, was a military prison during and after the war.

coastline of Fort Zachary Taylor Historic State Park

Although you're free to wander through the fort on your own, you can also opt for one of the narrated 30-minute tours, which are available daily at noon. You'll especially enjoy visiting Fort Zachary Taylor during annual events, such as Civil War Days in February and the Conch Republic Independence Celebration in April, so plan your visit accordingly.

Florida Keys Eco-Discovery Center

From Southard Street you can head west toward the Truman Waterfront, where you'll spy the **Florida Keys Eco-Discovery Center** (35 E. Quay Rd., 305/809-4750, www.floridakeys. noaa.gov, 9am-4pm Tues.-Sat., free). The 6,000-square-foot nature center features an array of interactive exhibits, dioramas, and displays about the Keys' varied ecosystems, including upland pinelands, hardwood hammocks, beach dunes, mangrove shores, seagrass flats, and coral reefs. Visitors can take a virtual 1,600-foot dive to the deep shelf; learn why a fort was built in the isolated Dry Tortugas; view a 2,500-gallon reef tank filled with living coral and tropical fish; and walk through a mock-up of Aquarius, the world's only underwater ocean laboratory. Free parking is available on-site, and all net proceeds from the gift shop directly fund educational programs at the Eco-Discovery Center.

USCGC *Ingham* Maritime Museum

Military history enthusiasts might enjoy a quick detour to Memorial Park, which holds the **USCGC *Ingham* Maritime Museum** (Truman Waterfront, Old U.S. Navy Pier, 305/292-5072, www.uscgcingham.org, 10am-4pm daily, $10 adults, $5 children 7-17, free for children under 6 and military personnel), a 327-foot U.S. Coast Guard cutter that was built in 1935 and served the nation from 1936 to 1988. Visitors can take a self-guided tour of the ship, which includes authentic artifacts, historical photographs, and interpretive signs outlining the ship's history. While on board, you'll be able to see where the men ate, slept, and played, and for an added fee ($20 pp) you can take a guided tour that includes additional chambers like the boiler room and engine room.

West Martello Tower

On Higgs Beach, where White Street meets the Atlantic Ocean, stands the **West Martello Tower,** a Civil War-era fort whose design was inspired by the round, stalwart fortress at Mortella Point in Corsica, an island in the Mediterranean Sea. Constructed during the 1860s by the U.S. Army Corps of Engineers, the West Martello Tower was never fully completed, and in the late 1940s it was nearly leveled for aesthetic reasons. Luckily, demolition plans were thwarted, and it has since been listed in the National Register of Historic Places.

The property has been home to the **Key West Garden Club** (1100 Atlantic Blvd., 305/294-3210, www.keywestgardenclub. com, 9:30am-5pm daily, free) since 1955, and visitors can stroll along brick pathways amid graceful arches and lush, colorful foliage. There is a rare collection of blooming orchids, bromeliads, and other native and exotic flora. Here you can simply sit beside a water lily pond or butterfly garden, enjoy balmy breezes from an oceanfront gazebo, and temporarily trade the hustle and bustle of places like Mallory Square and Duval Street for tranquil seclusion. The facility is closed during the first two weeks of January.

NEW TOWN AND STOCK ISLAND

Although the bulk of Key West's attractions are spread throughout Old Town, you'll find a few worthy stops in New Town, the eastern half of the island, as well as on adjacent Stock Island.

Fort East Martello

South of Key West International Airport stands **Fort East Martello** (3501 S. Roosevelt Blvd., 305/296-3913, www.kwahs.org, 9:30am-4:30pm daily, $12 adults, $5 seniors 62 and over, children 6 and up, students, and Key West residents, free for children under 6). Modeled after the nearly impenetrable Martello watchtowers of Corsica, Fort East Martello, which was constructed during the Civil War, never witnessed hostile action. A testament to military engineering, the fort now serves as the country's best-preserved example of the Martello style of military architecture. Today its citadel, courtyard, and casemates house a vast array of regional artifacts, historical records, and military memorabilia, in addition to the state's largest collection of drawings and painted wood carvings by artist Mario Sanchez, mainly known for his vivid depictions of life in Key West during the early 1900s. Visitors can also tour an 80-year-old playhouse and enjoy panoramic views from atop the central tower.

The Key West Tropical Forest & Botanical Garden

Nature lovers will find several intriguing attractions throughout Key West, not the least of which is **The Key West Tropical Forest & Botanical Garden** (5210 College Rd., Stock Island, 305/296-1504, www.kwbgs.org, 10am-4pm daily, $10 adults, $7 seniors and military personnel, free for children under 12), the only frost-free botanical garden in the continental United States. Host to various events throughout the year, including Gardenfest Key West, Hot Havana Nights, and the Doo Wop Party, this tropical oasis nurtures rare flora and fauna and serves as a migratory stop for a variety of neotropical birds. After viewing a short orientation film, visitors are welcome to take a self-guided tour of the grounds, featuring a one-acre butterfly habitat, a lush canopy of tropical palms, and two of the last remaining freshwater ponds in the Florida Keys. Parking is free here, and the garden boardwalk is wheelchair-accessible.

ISLAND TOURS

First-time visitors to Key West might benefit from one of the many available sightseeing tours, which will help orient you to the island and its surrounding waters. Before you explore the area on your own, consider any of the array of trolley excursions, guided strolls, sunset cruises, or other informative tours.

Train and Trolley Tours

The 90-minute narrated excursion on the **Conch Tour Train** (305/294-5161 or 888/916-8687, www.conchtourtrain.com, 9am-4:30pm daily, $31.45 adults, $15.75 children 4-12, free for children under 4) offers a look at most of Key West's major attractions, including Mallory Square, the Custom House, and the Ernest Hemingway Home. Since 1958, friendly train "engineers" have been guiding visitors around the Southernmost City and sharing snippets of the town's history—both real and legendary.

Train tours depart every 30 minutes from the Front Street depot (501 Front St.), where you can purchase tickets beforehand. You can also pick up tickets at three other locations: Mallory Square (303 Front St.), Flagler Station (901 Caroline St.), and 3840 North Roosevelt Boulevard. To save money, purchase your tickets online or consider buying packages that also include admission to attractions like the Key West Aquarium and the Harry S. Truman Little White House.

An alternative is the 90-minute **Old Town Trolley Tour** (1 Whitehead St., 305/296-6688 or 888/910-8687, www.trolleytours.com, 9am-4:30pm daily, $41.95 adults, $15.75 children 12 and under), which offers a comprehensive tour of Old Town, fully narrated by expert conductors. Along the route, you'll get an earful of curious anecdotes and well-researched historical tidbits. At no extra charge, you're welcome to get on and off the trolley at a dozen convenient stops, including the Bahama Village Market. The ubiquitous orange-and-green trolleys pick up and drop off passengers every 30 minutes at each location. Tickets can be purchased at four different stops: Mallory Square (No. 1) near Wall and Whitehead Streets, Simonton Row (No. 3) at Greene and Simonton Streets, Truval Village (No. 11) at Truman Avenue and Duval Street, and Angela

Street (No. 12) between Duval and Whitehead Streets. As with the Conch Tour Train, you can save a little money by purchasing tickets online. Ticket packages and wheelchair-accessible vehicles are also available.

Walking Tours

There are several walking tours available in Key West, including the **Historic Key West Walking Tour** (305/292-8990, www.trustedtours.com, 9:30am daily, $16.20 adults, $8.10 children 4-12, free for children under 4), an entertaining tour of Old Town's lush foliage, unique architecture, varied districts, and diverse culture. Guides share stories about the town's early inhabitants, famous and notorious Key West personalities, historical incidents like the Great Fire of 1886, and the island's varied phases, from its wrecking and cigar-making days to its involvement in both World Wars. Tours depart from the Key West Shipwreck Museum in Mallory Square. Given the limited group size, reservations are recommended. Visitors should wear comfortable shoes, bring bottled water, and check in 15 minutes before departure time.

If your interests run toward the paranormal, you may appreciate a nighttime stroll with **Haunted Key West Tours** (423 Fleming St., 305/563-0154, www.hauntedkeywest.com, 9:30pm nightly, and at 10pm also during peak season, $30 pp). Founded in 1996 by David L. Sloan, author of *Ghosts of Key West,* and featured in numerous television programs, this lantern-led walking tour departs nightly from the Crowne Plaza Key West at 430 Duval Street. With a colorful history that includes pirates, smugglers, and wreckers, the town formerly known as Bone Island has its share of curious hauntings, in places as varied as the Banyan Resort, St. Paul's Episcopal Church, the Fort East Martello Museum, and Captain Tony's Saloon—all of which this 90-minute wheelchair-accessible tour encompasses. Reservations are recommended.

Biking Tours

For a more active exploration of the city, consider taking a tour with **Lloyd's Tropical Bike Tour** (601 Truman Ave., 305/428-2578, www.lloydstropicalbiketour.com, $49 adults, $40 children 12 and under, $20 for babies and includes a baby seat), a leisurely ride along Key West's quiet streets and secret lanes amid tropical gardens, historical architecture, and the exotic scents of jasmine and gardenias. Led by a longtime resident of Key West, these one-of-a-kind two-hour tours even enable you

Conch Tour Train

Gay Key West Trolley Tour

With its plethora of gay bars and accommodations, drag shows, and outrageous events like the annual Fantasy Fest, it seems appropriate that the Southernmost City is also home to the Gay Key West Trolley Tour ($25 pp), a fun, interesting, and often hilarious private charter tour that runs every Saturday at 4pm. This 75-minute narrated excursion, which typically leaves from the corner of Angela and Duval Streets, invites visitors to hop aboard a rainbow-hued trolley and learn about the curious history of this spirited town, from its unique architecture to its wreck-salvaging heritage to its famous residents. Of course, given the tour's particular theme, you'll also see gay hot spots, hear about famous gay visitors such as playwright Tennessee Williams and poet Elizabeth Bishop, and hopefully come to understand the impact that the LGBTQ community has had on the culture, politics, and economy of the Florida Keys.

For tour tickets as well as information about other gay-friendly establishments, events, and activities, consult the Key West Business Guild Office & Gay Key West Visitor Center (513 Truman Ave., 305/294-4603 or 800/535-7797, www.gaykeywestfl.com, 10am-4pm Mon.-Sat.), which is one of the oldest LGBTQ chamber of commerce organizations in the United States.

to taste a variety of local fruit, such as mangoes, coconuts, and key limes. The bicycles included on this tour are single-speed beach cruisers, equipped with foot brakes, fat tires, wide seats, and convenient baskets—ideal features for novice riders. Children are welcome if accompanied by at least one adult, and reservations are a must. Be sure to wear comfortable clothes and shoes, and bring your own hat, sunglasses, and sunscreen.

Another option is to pedal around with Key Lime Bike Tours (122 Ann St., 305/340-7834, www.keylimebiketours.com, $45 pp includes a bottle of water and a slice of key lime pie). The 2.5- to 3-hour tour leaves at 10am and follows a roughly four-mile route. You'll start pedaling in Old Town and wheel around the island, visiting most of the Key West highlights. After you spend the morning in the sun and burn a few calories on the bicycle, you can recharge and cool off at the end of the tour when you stop at Kermit's Key Lime Shoppe for a slice of frozen key lime pie.

Boat Tours

Since many of Key West's most memorable attractions actually lie in the waters surrounding the island, you should make some time for one of the many sightseeing cruises available, such as a two-hour glass-bottom boat tour with Fury Water Adventures (305/296-6293 or 888/976-0899, www.furycat.com, noon-2pm, 2pm-4pm, and 6pm-8pm daily, $41.36 adults, $29.66 children 4-10, free for children under 4). From aboard The Pride of Key West, a modern, smooth-sailing catamaran, you'll be able to gaze at dolphins, sharks, and other marine creatures from the comfort of an upper sundeck or, for an even better experience, observe the colorful coral and tropical fish below the boat from the enclosed, air-conditioned viewing area. Other onboard amenities include restrooms and a snack bar. The catamaran leaves twice daily from the marina at 2 Duval Street, between the Ocean Key Resort and the Pier House Resort.

For a more romantic adventure, spend the evening on a sunset cruise. Among those available, Fury offers the two-hour Commotion on the Ocean (305/294-8899 or 877/994-8898, 5:30pm-7:30pm daily late Jan.-mid-Mar., 6pm-8pm daily mid-Mar.-early Nov., 5pm-7pm daily early Nov.-late Jan., $41.36 adults, $29.66 children 4-10, free for children under 4), which, in conjunction with the Hog's Breath Saloon, features appetizers, beer, margaritas, and live music amid the backdrop of a famous Key West sunset. As a bonus, Fury donates a percentage of all sales to coral reef conservation.

Sunset Watersports Key West (201 William St., 305/296-2554, www. sunsetwatersports.info, times vary seasonally, $59 adults, $39 children 5-12, under 5 free) offers a daily two-hour sunset yacht excursion that features a tropical buffet and a variety of libations, from soft drinks to champagne. Couples will especially enjoy watching the sunset together and dancing on the lighted dance floor. Reservations are required for the sunset dinner cruise as well as for the basic two-hour sunset cruise (without dinner: $40 adults, $20 children 6-12, under 6 free). They offer the dinner cruise for free on your birthday.

Other area possibilities include Sebago Watersports (201 William St., 305/292-4768 or 800/507-9955, www.keywestsebago.com, 6:30pm-8:30pm summer, 5pm-7pm winter, $40 adults, $25 children 4-11, children under 4 free), which includes free champagne, margaritas, and other libations on its catamaran champagne sunset sail. They also offer two-hour day sails (1:30pm-3:30pm daily, $35 adults, $22.50 children 4-11, children under 4 free) aboard the Schooner *Appledore V.*

A truly memorable experience awaits you aboard a classic schooner, such as the 80-foot, square-rigged, Caribbean-style Schooner *Jolly II Rover* (305/304-2235, www.schoonerjollyrover.com), which offers two-hour sunset sails (times vary seasonally, $65 adults, $34 children 4-12, children under 4 free) that depart from the Historic Seaport at Key West Bight. The Schooner *Western Union* (305/292-1766, www. schoonerwesternunion.org, times vary daily, $59 adults, $29 children 4-12, free for children under 4) is a historic tall ship and floating maritime museum that also docks at the Historic Seaport. Unlike the *Jolly II Rover,* which invites you to bring your own food and beverages, the *Western Union* (which is listed in the National Register of Historic Places) provides complimentary libations, conch chowder, and live, island-style music with each sail. The *Western Union* is currently undergoing extensive repairs, but the owners vow to bring her back to her glory days and continue offering tours once again; call them before planning any trips to ensure the ship is operational.

Other possible adventures include a daily two-hour Wind and Wine Sunset Sail through Danger Charters (255 Front St., 305/304-7999, www.dangercharters.com, times vary seasonally, $80 adults, $60 children 4-12, free for children under 4), based out of the Margarita Marina, as well as a 4.5-hour day sail and snorkel trips (9:30am and 3:30pm daily, $80-90 adults, $60-70 children 4-12, free for children under 4) and two-hour champagne sunset sails (times vary seasonally, $85 pp, 13 or older only). The Schooner *America 2.0* (305/390-2681, www.sail-keywest.com), based out of the Historic Seaport at Key West Bight and limited to a November-April sailing season, offers day cruises (1:30pm-3:30pm Wed.-Sun., $64 adults, $44 children 4-12, free for children under 4) and sunset cruises (6pm-8pm Wed.-Sun., $96 adults, $55 children 4-17). Most of the sails offered in Key West feature online discounts and recommend advance purchase.

Air Tours

If you'd like to experience an aerial tour of Key West and its surrounding waters, consider taking a biplane ride through Conch Republic Air Force Biplane Rides (3469 S. Roosevelt Blvd., 305/851-8359, www. keywestbiplanes.com, 9am-5pm daily, $249-499 for 1 or 2 passengers). Flying out of the Key West International Airport, each narrated tour invites two passengers (besides the pilot) to view coral reefs, shipwrecks, lighthouses, uninhabited islands, and various marine creatures from aboard an original open-air 1942 World War II Waco biplane, traveling at a smooth, 500-foot cruising altitude. You can choose from three different flights: an 18-minute Island Biplane Ride that offers a look at nearby shipwrecks; a 35-minute Island and Reef Tour that surveys coral reefs as well as Key West attractions; and a romantic 35-minute Sunset Flight, which is essentially the Island and Reef Tour at sunset. Tour times are flexible, and each quoted price includes two passengers. Cloth helmets, headsets, and goggles are provided with all flights—all of which are wheelchair-accessible—and as a bonus, an onboard camera system can record your flight for posterity. Although walk-ins are welcome, reservations will ensure availability.

Beaches and Recreation

BEACHES

Several public beaches, ranging in size and appeal, stretch along the southern shore of Key West. The good news is that all of them are free and open daily, but the bad news is that they're often crowded, especially on a gorgeous weekend during the peak winter season. Just remember that swimming is at your own risk, given the absence of lifeguards. In addition, just because Key West has several clothing-optional resorts doesn't mean that such a flexible policy extends to the beaches down here; topless and nude sunbathing is actually illegal. Alcohol, drugs, campfires, glass containers, and overnight camping are also not allowed on the public beaches of Key West.

At the terminus of Duval Street, you'll first encounter **South Beach** (7am-11pm daily, free), a cute patch of sand that's a far cry from the similarly named one in Miami. While it offers shallow waters, a pleasant pier, and an incredible view of the ocean, it's much smaller—and calmer—than its counterpart a few hours north. Nevertheless, it's a favorite among locals, despite the lack of restrooms and facilities.

East of Simonton, the somewhat rocky **Dog Beach** (7am-11pm daily, free) is obviously popular among pet owners, though it has no restrooms or other facilities.

Farther east, alongside Atlantic Boulevard between Reynolds and White Streets, lies another popular Key West beach, the wide and sandy **Clarence S. Higgs Memorial Beach** (6am-11pm daily, free), where in addition to swimming and sunbathing, sun worshippers can rent water-sports equipment or stroll among pelicans and gulls on the adjacent

Even farther east, near Atlantic Boulevard and White Street, the wheelchair-accessible **C. B. Harvey Rest Beach** (7am-11pm daily, free) offers sandy dunes, picnic tables, public restrooms, a fishing pier, a yoga deck, and a biking path.

On warm, sunny days, crowds flock to lengthy, artificially made **Smathers Beach** (7am-11pm daily, free) alongside Roosevelt Boulevard, a popular spot for spring breakers and an ideal place to watch the sunrise, have a picnic, or play a volleyball game. Watersports and chair rentals, biking paths, concession stands, public restrooms, a boat ramp, and ample parking are available. **Sunset Watersports Key West** (305/296-2554, www.sunsetwatersportskeywest.com, 9am-6pm daily, $45 pp) even offers parasailing excursions from here.

At the southwestern tip of Key West, **Fort Zachary Taylor Historic State Park** (601 Howard England Way, 305/292-6713 or 305/295-0037, www.floridastateparks.org or www.fortzacharytaylor.com, 8am-sunset daily, $7 vehicles with 2 passengers plus $0.50 per additional person, $4.50 motorcycles and single-occupant vehicles, $2.50 pedestrians and bikers) has **Fort Zach Beach,** one of the best beaches in Key West. Located at the southern end of the park, the pebbled beach is large and long and has excellent snorkeling right off the shore. Snorkel equipment

1: sailing on the Schooner *America 2.0* **2:** a boat cruising the turquoise water **3:** South Beach **4:** sunrise on Smathers Beach

is available to rent at the on-site concession stand, which also sells food and drinks. Be advised that there are no lifeguards on duty.

GOLF

While the Florida Keys archipelago isn't the golf mecca that other parts of the Sunshine State purport to be, that doesn't mean that golfers are without options. Besides private golf courses like those at the Ocean Reef Club in Key Largo and the Sombrero Country Club in Marathon, golfers will find a lovely, palm-studded golf course in the Lower Keys. Encompassing at least a third of Stock Island, the 200-acre **Key West Golf Club** (6450 E. College Rd., 305/294-5232, www.keywestgolf. com, 7am-6:30pm daily, $30-99 with a cart) features an 18-hole, 6,500-yard public golf course, set on the gulf side of U.S. 1 amid dense mangroves, tranquil lakes, varied wildlife, and the ever-present trade winds. This year-round full-service facility—incidentally, the southernmost golf course in the continental United States—also offers a driving range ($8/bucket), rental clubs ($45/set), bag storage ($125 yearly), a pro shop and clubhouse, golf instructions ($45-55/lesson), and private parking.

★ BIKING

Whether you're an experienced or novice rider, Key West is a lovely, welcoming place to traverse by bicycle. There are many shaded and quiet tree-lined back roads where you'll find cozy cottages tucked among the tropical plants and trees. When determining a pedaling route, it's hard to go wrong on Key West, but consider choosing roads with less traffic. Duval Street can be difficult to traverse on a bike. The four blocks surrounding the Truman Little White House are especially fantastic for biking; there are many brick-paved paths that are remarkably scenic and well suited for bicycles. Just remember that you'll have to share the streets with cars and other vehicles, so take care while you tour the neighborhoods—and wear a proper helmet at all times.

Bicycles can be rented from several different outfitters, including **Eaton Bikes** (830 Eaton St., 305/294-8188, www.eatonbikes. com, 8am-6pm Mon.-Sat., 8am-noon Sun., $12-50 daily, $55-150 weekly), which offers a range of bicycles from trikes to mountain bikes to tandems, plus free delivery and pickup service throughout Key West. **The Bike Shop of Key West** (1110 Truman Ave., 305/294-1073, www.thebikeshopkeywest.com, 9am-6pm Mon.-Sat., 10am-4pm Sun., $12 daily, $60 weekly, $180 monthly), the oldest in town, also provides a wide array of bicycles, plus accessories, bicycle sales, and a service/repair department. All rentals include locks, lights, baskets, and soft, wide seats.

Another helpful source for bicycle rentals is **JV Rent All** (539 Greene St., 305/293-8883, www.golfcartrentalskeywest.com, 8am-5pm daily, $10 daily, $50 weekly), which also offers scooters ($35-45 for four hours, $55-75 daily) and golf carts ($90-159 for four hours, $169-259 daily). **A&M Rentals** (305/294-4556, www.amscooterskeywest.com, 8am-8pm daily, $10-20 daily) has two spots from which to rent kid-size bicycles, cruisers, and tandems: 523 Truman Avenue and 513 South Street. You can also rent one- and two-seater scooters ($35-60 daily), and multi-seat electric cars ($139-200 daily)—all popular ways to get around town. Free customer pickup and drop-off services are available.

Even Stock Island has a bicycle outfitter: Just north of the Hurricane Hole Marina, **We Cycle** (MM 5.1, 5160 Overseas Hwy., Stock Island, 305/292-3336 or 305/294-7433, www. wecyclekw.com, 9am-6pm Mon.-Sat., 9am-5pm Sun., $15-20 daily) offers a full-service shop and free delivery for its wide array of bicycles.

FISHING AND BOATING

Anglers come from all over the world to explore the waters surrounding Key West, which boasts year-round fishing opportunities. Every month, several different fish species are in season, and anglers can choose from a variety of fishing locales, including deep harbors, backcountry flats, coral reefs, and offshore waters. No wonder Ernest Hemingway found fishing down here so appealing.

Those bringing their own boats to fish the abundant backcountry and offshore waters will find no shortage of boat slips and marine services. For a small city, Key West sure does have an impressive number of marinas, from the **Historic Seaport at Key West Bight** (305/809-3790, www.keywesthistoricseaport. com) near Old Town to the **Hurricane Hole Marina** (MM 4.5, 5130 Overseas Hwy., 305/294-8025, www.hurricaneholekeywest. com) on adjacent Stock Island. In fact, Stock Island features several marinas, including the deepwater **Stock Island Marina Village** (7005 Shrimp Rd., 305/294-2288, www.stockislandmarina.com) and the nostalgic **Safe Harbour Marina** (6810 Front St., 305/294-9797, www.safeharbourmarinakw. com).

Most anglers come to Key West with sportfishing charters in mind, and here, too, you'll find no scarcity of options. At the **Key West City Marina at the Garrison Bight** (1801 N. Roosevelt Blvd., 305/809-3982, www. cityofkeywest-fl.gov), you can hire any number of boats from Charter Boat Row, including offshore fishing services like **Cowgirl Fishing Charter** (305/294-5888, www. keywestfishing-charters.com, $135-750 per half day, $160-900 for six hours, $200-1,100 daily) and **Wild Bill Sportfishing** (305/296-2533 or 305/744-7957, www.wildbillkeywest. com, $165-700 per half day, $200-900 for six hours, $250-1,050 daily), both of which offer individual seats as well as private charters for up to six passengers. Among the other deepsea fishing vessels docked at the City Marina are the *Ramerezi* (305/896-0638, www. keywestfishingboats.com, $450-700 per half day, $1,000 daily) and the **Charter Boat Linda D.** (Slips #19 and #20, 305/304-8102, www.charterboatlindad.com, $600-675 per half day, $900-975 daily), both of which are helmed by longtime local fishing captains and can accommodate up to six anglers at a time.

If you're interested in shallow-water flats fishing, saltwater fly-fishing, or offshore fishing, consider **Key West Pro Guides** (5001 5th Ave., Stock Island, 305/295-9444 or 800/795-9448, www.keywestproguides. com, $500-800 per half day, $700-1,500 daily), Key West's largest charter company, or as an alternative, **Sting Rea Charters** (305/744-0903, www.stingreacharters.com, $500-650 per half day, $750-1,000 daily), which transports its vessel from Sugarloaf Key to various locations and leads anglers to the waters around the Lower Keys and the Marquesas in search of tarpon, barracuda, permit, and bonefish. For reef and wreck fishing, among other fishing styles, consult **Mean Green Charters** (Murray Marina, MM 5, 5710 Overseas Hwy., Stock Island, 305/304-1922, www.meangreenfishing.com, $700 per half day, $1,000 daily), **Cheerio Charters** (Hurricane Hole Marina, MM 4.5, 5130 Overseas Hwy., Stock Island, 305/797-6446, $700 per half day, $1,000 daily), or **Boo-Ya Charters** (Charter Boat Row, 1801 N. Roosevelt Blvd., 305/292-6692, www. booyakeywest.com, $600 for 4 hours, $750 for 6 hours, $900 for 8 hours daily), through which you'll possibly snag grouper, snapper, amberjack, kingfish, tuna, barracuda, permit, yellowtail, cobia, and sharks.

In general, fishing trips are offered daily, and rates, which typically include bait, tackle, ice, and proper fishing licenses, are for the entire trip, not per angler. For most fishing charters, reservations are recommended and deposits are often required. Also, cancellation policies vary between operators, so be sure to check such details well in advance, or else you may lose your deposit.

As an alternative to bringing your own boat or hiring a fishing charter, you can always rent a seaworthy vessel from **Sunset Watersports Key West** (Hurricane Hole Marina, MM 4.5, 5130 Overseas Hwy., Stock Island, 305/294-1500, www.sunsetwatersports.com, 9am-6pm daily), which offers a range of craft, from 16- to 22-foot fishing boats ($300-350 per half day, $375-425 daily) to 22- and 26-foot pontoons ($400-475 per half day, $475-550 daily). Boats

Boating Safety

On especially gorgeous days, you're likely to see a number of powerboats, sailboats, yachts, kayaks, and other vessels in the offshore waters extending from Miami to the Dry Tortugas. With so much action, there's bound to be chaos—unless, of course, boaters obey the following safety guidelines, for the sake of themselves as well as their passengers.

- **Verify Vessel Safety:** Before heading out on the water, make sure that your vessel has been properly maintained, that it meets all local and state regulations, and that your registration numbers are displayed prominently.

- **Equip Yourself:** When planning a boating trip, double-check that you have the following items on board: proper vessel documentation and insurance information, nautical charts, a marine radio, an anchor, a first-aid kit, mounted fire extinguishers, navigation lights, visual distress signals, sound-producing devices, a marine sanitation device, drinking water, extra fuel, and enough personal flotation devices (PFDs) for you and all your passengers.

- **Wear Your Life Jacket:** While it might seem more liberating to ride, fish, or kayak without a PFD, it's imperative that you wear one at all times. Not all boating accidents occur in bad weather and rough seas; many happen in shallow water on deceptively calm, clear days, so be sure to wear a life jacket—even a lightweight inflatable one—whenever you're on the water.

- **Stay Safe and Sober:** Although many boaters will partake of beer and other alcoholic beverages while out on the water, it's simply not advisable to do so. Wind, noise, motion, and sunlight can intensify the effects of alcohol and prescription medications, making it exceedingly dangerous to operate a vessel while under the influence.

come equipped with GPS, fish and depth finders, live bait wells, and bimini tops.

If you need to rent a fishing rod or stock up on essentials like live bait and cold beer, head first to the Historic Seaport district, where **Key West Bait & Tackle** (241 Margaret St., 305/292-1961, www.keywestbaitandtackle. com, 7am-7pm daily) features a wide selection of fishing tackle, rods and reels, frozen bait, lures, hooks, sunglasses, towels, and other necessities. Other helpful fishing stores include **The Angling Company** (333 Simonton St., 305/292-6306, www.theanglingcompany. com, 9:30am-7pm daily) and the **Saltwater Angler** (243 Front St., 305/294-3248 or 800/223-1629, www.saltwaterangler.com, 9am-8pm daily), a one-stop shop for travel gear, fishing apparel, reels, rods, sunglasses, and other fishing accessories.

As a bonus, all three stores can help you arrange fishing charters. Through Saltwater Angler, you can opt for a backcountry flats fishing charter ($600 per half day, $700 for 6 hours, $800 daily) in search of redfish, snook, permit, and bonefish; a deep-sea fishing excursion ($950 per half day, $1,100 for 6 hours, $1,300 daily) to snag tuna, wahoo, mahimahi, and other game fish; and a light-tackle saltwater fishing charter ($950 per half day, $1,100 for 6 hours, $1,300 daily) that allows you to fish for tarpon in the harbor, marlin and swordfish in the offshore waters, and yellowtail near the reefs. Through the Angling Company and Saltwater Angler, you'll also find a slew of professional guides (rates vary) for flats fishing, offshore fishing, and light-tackle fishing.

Long-Term Cruising

If you're a serious sailor, consider renting a sailboat or yacht for a multiday sail through the Keys. Key West is extremely boat friendly, with an abundance of excellent and popular anchorage sites, moorings, and slips for rent. There are several companies in Miami and throughout the Florida Keys that offer long-term bareboat rentals and captained vessels. Whether you plan on starting your sailing

- **Monitor Your Propeller:** Unfortunately, boat propellers are responsible for numerous injuries and fatalities every year. To avoid being yet another statistic, purchase propeller safety devices such as sensors and propeller guards, and don't forget to wear an engine cut-off lanyard at all times—which will ensure that if you and, by extension, your lanyard are thrown from the boat, the engine will immediately power down.

- **Monitor Your Passengers:** To ensure your passengers' safety, never allow them to board or disembark while the engine is running, and insist that they remain seated (in proper seats and not on the bow or transom) while the boat is in motion. In an effort to avoid accidents, assign someone to keep watch around the propeller area whenever other passengers, especially children, are swimming in the surrounding waters. To protect the passengers of other boats, stay alert when operating in congested areas, avoid swimmers altogether, and be aware of boats that are towing skiers or tubers. If someone on your vessel falls overboard, stop immediately, turn the boat around, keep the person in sight as you approach, and shut the engine off before rescuing him or her.

For additional advice or information about boating safety courses, consult the **Boat Owners Association of The United States (Boat U.S.)** (800/395-2628, www.boatus.com) or the **U.S. Coast Guard's Boating Safety Division** (www.uscgboating.org), which aims to prevent fatalities, injuries, and property damage on U.S. waterways by improving the knowledge and skills of recreational boaters.

trip from Miami or anywhere in the Keys, you can rent a sailboat or yacht without a captain for bareboat cruising from **Cruzan Yacht Charters** (18120 SW 88th Ct., Miami, 305/858-2822, www.cruzan.com/sail, $1,200-20,000 per week). They have a jaw-dropping variety of boats for rent, with many of their boats anchored in the Florida Keys and Miami. Their fleet includes smaller sailboats such as the *Nepenthe,* a 31-foot Cheoy Lee with two cabins that can hold up to six guests; the *Nepenthe* has been used for photo shoots by Ralph Lauren, Macy's, Urban Outfitters, Belk, and many others. On the larger-sized end, you can cruise in style and luxury when you rent a 76-foot Lazzara yacht with three staterooms for around $20,000 per week.

Another option is to book a captained multiday charter from **Key West Sailing Academy and Yacht Charter** (207 Simonton St., Key West, 305/394-4266, www.keywestsailingacademy.com, 9am-6pm daily, $1,295-7,995). They offer a wide range of trips aboard the *Sargasso,* their 45-foot Hunter Passage sailboat that features 7-foot headroom (6.5-foot headroom in the cabins) and three cabins. Each private cabin has queen-sized mattresses, 400-thread-count sheets, and down comforters. Sailing trips range from overnighters to a week or more. They offer excellent example itineraries on their website with pricing. An overnight trip costs roughly $1,295 for two people and $1,595 for four. A four-night sailing trip for four costs around $5,195. The prices include all bedding and towels, drinks, bottled water, beer and wine, and meals. During your sail you can fish, snorkel, dive, explore remote islands, and dingy to quiet beaches.

KAYAKING

Paddling enthusiasts will find a number of helpful operators in Key West. Based at the Hurricane Hole Marina, **Lazy Dog** (5114 Overseas Hwy., Stock Island, 305/295-9898, www.lazydog.com, 9am-5pm daily) offers two-hour guided kayaking tours ($50 pp, 10am and 2pm) through backcountry waters and winding mangrove creeks. Lazy Dog also features a 3.5-hour kayaking and snorkeling trip ($70 pp) along the Mosquito Coast, plus single and double kayak rentals ($25 per half day, $45 daily), stand-up paddleboard rentals ($30 each), paddleboard tours ($50 pp), and paddleboard yoga ($30 pp). Reservations are required, and complimentary pickups are available. Area maps are provided with all rentals.

Blue Planet Kayak (305/294-8087 or 800/979-3370, www.blue-planet-kayak.com) offers guided kayaking trips into the fascinating backcountry, such as the 2.5-hour Boca Chica Tour (10am and 12:40pm in winter, 10am in summer, $50 adults, $47.50 military and locals, $45 children 4-12, free for children under 4) and the 2.5-hour Romantic Sunset & Moonlight Tour ($50 adults, $47.50 military and locals, $45 children 4-12, free for children under 4). Beginners and families are welcome, though advance reservations are required. Since tour guides will only lead a maximum of 10 passengers on each personalized trip, slots can fill quickly. Complimentary transportation is available for all tour customers. In addition, Blue Planet rents sit-in single kayaks ($30 per day), tandem kayaks ($40 per day), and fishing kayaks ($30 per day). For the fishing kayaks, only charts, anchors, and advice are included; anglers must bring their own tackle.

For an alternative experience, consider **Key West Eco Tours** (305/294-7245, www.keywestecotours.com), situated in the Historic Seaport at Key West Bight, behind the Turtle Kraals Restaurant and Bar at the end of Margaret Street. As part of a two-hour ecotour ($65 adults, $50 children 12 and under) that includes sailing and coral reef snorkeling, Key West Eco Tours offers kayaking trips amid seagrass beds and winding mangrove creeks, where you'll get an up-close look at tropical fish, aquatic birds, sea turtles, spotted eagle rays, dolphins, crabs, sponges, and other marine wonders. Tours occur four times daily (9am, 11am, 1pm, and 3pm) and allow a maximum of six passengers.

Single- or double-seat, sit-on-top kayaks are provided.

Based out of The Westin Key West Resort & Marina at 245 Front Street, **Danger Charters** (305/304-7999, www.dangercharters.com) operates daily sailing excursions amid pristine coral reefs, deserted mangrove islands, and sponge gardens in the backcountry. These half-day ($80-90 adults, $60-70 children pp) and full-day trips ($120 adults, $95 children pp) also feature kayaking and snorkeling and include snacks, beverages, and gear.

DIVING AND SNORKELING

Key West is surrounded by thriving coral reefs and fascinating shipwrecks. On your own, you can easily dive and snorkel amid the tropical fish and varied coral formations in the bountiful waters near **Fort Zachary Taylor Historic State Park** (western end of Southard St., 305/292-6713 or 305/295-0037, www.floridastateparks.org or www.fortzacharytaylor.com, 8am-sunset daily, $7 vehicles with 2 passengers plus $0.50 per additional person, $4.50 motorcycles and single-occupant vehicles, $2.50 pedestrians and bikers) and **Dry Tortugas National Park** (305/242-7700, www.nps.gov/drto/index.htm or www.dry.tortugas.national-park.com, sunrise-sunset daily, $15 weekly), roughly 68 miles to the west. Still, many of the underwater attractions this far south are only accessible through professional diving charters.

Besides offering scuba-diving instruction and equipment rentals, several local companies, such as **Southpoint Divers** (606 Front St., 305/292-9778, www.southpointdivers.com, 8:30am-noon and 1:30pm-5pm daily), provide trips to two curious wrecks: the 187-foot *Cayman Salvage Master* ($85-120 pp) and the 522-foot USNS *General Hoyt S. Vandenberg* ($85-120 pp). The latter was a troop transport ship during World War II, later served as the backdrop for the 1999 film *Virus,* and is now the foundation for an

1: Jet Ski rentals 2: the freshest lobster

artificial reef. Sunk in May 2009, the ship has since become a habitat for varied fish and offers a unique look at the developing stages of coral growth. Guides are required for all open-water dives on the *Vandenberg*. Varied gear—including tanks, weights, regulators, wetsuits, and nitrox bottles—is available through Southpoint Divers, and classes range from a refresher course ($75 pp) to a PADI divemaster course ($895 pp).

In addition to leading excursions to the *Cayman* and *Vandenberg* wrecks, **Dive Key West** (3128 N. Roosevelt Blvd., 305/296-3823 or 800/426-0707, www.divekeywest.com, 9am-1pm and 2pm-6pm daily, $95-160 pp)—one of the oldest and largest full-service diving facilities in the Florida Keys—offers trips to other wrecks, such as *Joe's Tug,* a storm-battered vessel that sits in 65 feet of water and is now home to assorted coral formations and nosy eels.

Additional diving resources include **Lost Reef Adventures** (261 Margaret St., 305/296-9737, www.lostreefadventures.com, 8:30am-1pm and 1:30pm-5:30pm daily, $75-169 pp) and the **Captain's Corner Dive Center** (125 Ann St., 305/296-8865, 9:30am-1:30pm and 2pm-6pm daily, $45-115 pp), whose 60-foot aluminum diving vessel was used in the film *Licence to Kill.* Some of these operators even offer night dives as well as trips to reef formations like the deep spur-and-groove networks of **Sand Key, Rock Key,** the **Eastern Dry Rocks,** and the **Western Sambo Ecological Reserve.** Other interesting habitats include the **Kedge Ledge,** a patch reef that contains coral-encrusted anchors from 18th-century schooners, and the **Ten-Fathom Ledge,** a series of coral ledges, caves, and outcroppings that nurture grouper, lobster, sharks, and eagle rays.

Like the rest of the Keys, Key West appeals to snorkelers, too. All of the aforementioned diving operators also cater to snorkelers, offering at least two trips daily ($40-50 adults, $35-45 children), with rental equipment usually included in the price. In addition, **Sebago**

Watersports (201 William St., 305/292-4768 or 800/507-9955, www.keywestsebago.com, 9am-12:30pm and 1pm-4:30pm daily, $40-45 adults, $27.50-30 children 4-11, free for children under 4), **Sunset Watersports Key West** (201 William St., 305/296-2554, www.sunsetwatersportskeywest.com, 9am-noon and 1pm-4pm, $40-45 adults, $22 children 6-12, free for children under 6), and **Fury Water Adventures** (1 Duval St. and 245 Front St., 855/831-5997, www.furycat.com, 9:30am-12:30pm and 1pm-4pm daily, $40-47.95 adults, $20.95-23.95 children 6-12) offer snorkeling trips, among other water-related activities. Instruction and necessary equipment are provided with all trips. Based out of the Historic Seaport at Key West Bight, **Sunny Days** (866/878-2223, www.sunnydayskeywest.com), operated by Fury Water Adventures, also features the *Reef Express* (305/296-5556 or 800/236-7937, 9am-noon and 12:30pm-3:30pm daily, $52.16 adults, $35.96 children 4-10, free for children under 4, plus $5 park entrance fee for guests 17 and over), a high-speed catamaran that takes you to two incredible snorkeling locations on a three-hour trip.

Two other noteworthy vessels, the *Echo* catamaran (Historic Seaport at Key West Bight, 305/294-5026, www.dolphinecho.com, 9am-1pm and 1:30pm-5:30pm daily, $89 pp) and the smaller *Amazing Grace* (6000 Peninsular Ave., Stock Island, 305/294-5026 or 800/593-6574, www.wildaboutdolphins.com, 8am-noon and 1pm-5pm daily, $99 pp), combine snorkeling trips with wild dolphin encounters. Both offer private charters as well.

You might also want to visit **Snuba of Key West** (Key West City Marina at the Garrison Bight, 1801 N. Roosevelt Blvd., 305/292-4616, www.snubakeywest.com, 9am, 1pm, and 4pm daily, $109 adults, $89 children 8-12, $60 riders or non-Snuba snorkelers), where you can try an unusual form of deepwater snorkeling that requires no dive certification. On these personal guided tours amid the offshore coral reefs, you'll be able to breathe easily underwater without wearing heavy, restrictive diving gear. Just note that children must be at least eight years old to try Snuba snorkeling.

Though nearly all of the aforementioned diving and snorkeling outfitters should have the equipment and accessories that you need, you can also make a quick stop at **Divers Direct** (535 Greene St., 305/293-5122, www.diversdirect.com, 9am-9pm Mon.-Fri., 9am-8pm Sat., 10am-6pm Sun.), a well-stocked scuba-diving retailer, for any last-minute items.

OTHER OUTDOOR ACTIVITIES

For thrills of a different kind, consider renting a Jet Ski, Sea-Doo, or WaveRunner from the following outfitters: **Barefoot Billy's** (The Reach Resort, 1435 Simonton St., 305/900-3088, www.barefootbillys.com, 10am-6pm daily, $80 per half hour, $120 hourly), **Key West Jet Ski and Parasail** (The Westin Key West Resort & Marina, 245 Front St., 305/797-6423, www.keywest-jetski.com, 9am-sunset daily, $175.95 per Jet Ski for 2-hour tour), or **Key West Water Tours** (Hurricane Hole Marina, 5106 Overseas Hwy., Stock Island, 305/294-6790, www.keywestwatertours.com, $129 per Jet Ski for 2-hour tour).

If you'd rather be *above* the water, three parasailing companies operate out of the Historic Seaport at Key West Bight: **ParaWest Parasailing** (700 Front St., 305/292-5199, www.parawestparasailing. com, 9am-sunset daily, $65 pp), **Sebago Watersports** (201 William St., 305/292-4768 or 800/507-9955, www.keywestsebago.com, 9am-4pm daily in winter, 10am-5pm daily in summer, $60 pp), and **Sunset Watersports Key West** (201 William St., 305/296-2554, www.sunsetwatersportskeywest.com, 9am-5pm daily, $45-49 pp), which also operates out of Smathers Beach. Another operator, **Fury Water Adventures** (305/294-8899 or 877/994-8898, www.furycat.com, 9am-5pm daily, $65 pp), offers parasailing adventures from two locations: the Pier House Resort (1 Duval St.) and The Westin Key West Resort & Marina (245 Front St.). All four offer solo and tandem rides, and all promise smooth takeoffs, gentle landings, breathtaking aerial views, and safe experiences. No matter which you choose, try to book your trip in advance, especially during the peak winter months.

For a combination of such activities, consider opting for Fury's **Ultimate Adventure** (10am-4pm daily, $149.95 adults, $124.95 children 4-10, free for children under 4), an all-inclusive experience that features kayaking, reef snorkeling, Jet Skiing, parasailing, rock climbing, and access to a water trampoline, plus a complimentary meal and unlimited beverages. Sunset Watersports offers a similar package, the **"Do It All!" Watersports Adventure** (10am-4pm daily, $139 adults, $69 children under 12, free for children under 5, and free on your birthday), which includes snorkeling, kayaking, rafting, Sunfish sailing, knee-boarding, waterskiing, windsurfing, and access to various water sports, plus a grilled lunch. Not to be outdone, Sebago Watersports features its own version of this all-day fun with the **Watersports All Day Adventure** (10am-4pm daily, $159 adults, $99 children 4-11, free for children under 4), which encompasses reef snorkeling, a guided kayaking tour, parasailing, and access to personal watercraft, water trampolines, and other water sports—plus free meals, snacks, and beverages. For all three adventures, booking online will typically save you a bit of money.

SPAS AND YOGA

What better way to relax after a hard day of golfing, biking, fishing, kayaking, diving, or parasailing than to experience a soothing massage treatment or beachside yoga lesson? Fortunately, Key West provides an array of such rejuvenating experiences.

Several area resorts feature on-site spas. At the **Pier House Resort** (1 Duval St., 305/296-4600, www.pierhouse.com), the full-service **Tranquil Key West Spa** (9am-6pm daily) offers services such as manicures and pedicures ($35-80 pp) and restorative facials ($50-135 pp). Several massages ($75-180 pp) are also available, including the 75-minute hot stone therapy massage and the 50-minute Thai foot massage ($120 pp), which is as relaxing as it sounds. Guests should make appointments in advance and provide at least four hours' notice for any cancellations.

The **Ocean Key Resort & Spa** (0 Duval St., 305/296-7701 or 800/328-9815, www.oceankey.com) features the waterfront **SpaTerre** (305/295-7017, 9am-6pm Tues.-Sat., 9am-5pm Sun.-Mon.), which provides day spa services as well as spa vacation packages. At SpaTerre, men and women alike can experience various massages ($75-260 pp), refreshing body treatments ($130-260 pp) such as the milk and honey wrap and the incredible Cleopatra's milk bath ritual (110 mins., $230 pp), or the Javanese Royal Spa Treatment, which includes a Balinese spa massage, an herbal exfoliation, a cool yogurt splash, an aromatic shower, and a tub soaking amid rose petals and tropical fragrances (110 mins., $260). Other services include facials ($75-260 pp) and manicures and pedicures ($30-100 pp). The spa also features a fitness center with a hot soaking tub and steam rooms.

At **Southernmost Beach Resort** (508 South St., 305/296-6577, www.southernmostbeachresort.com), the full-service **Spa at Southernmost** (305/293-6136, www.southernmostbeachresort.com, 9am-6pm Mon.-Sat., 9am-5pm Sun.) offers an array of salon and spa services. Hotel guests as well as nonguests can enjoy various manicures and pedicures ($55-135 pp), facials ($70-180 pp), massages ($70-230 pp), and waxing ($15-55 pp). Appointment cancellations must be made 24 hours in advance.

Another top-notch spa can be found at the **Casa Marina Resort** (1500 Reynolds St., 888/303-5717, www.casamarinaresort.com). Only open to hotel guests at the Casa Marina and its sister facility, **The Reach Resort** (1435 Simonton St., 888/318-4316, www.reachresort.com), the **Spa al Mare** presents facials ($80-200 pp), massages ($85-210 pp), aromatherapy treatments ($150-225 pp), and yoga classes ($20-80 pp). Spa packages are also available. Note that all massages are offered either in the studio or on the beach. Guests must notify the spa 24 hours in advance to cancel an appointment.

Beyond luxurious resorts, Key West also contains several stand-alone day spas. The locally owned **Prana Spa** (625 Whitehead St., 305/295-0100, www.pranaspakeywest.com, 10am-7pm Mon.-Sat., 11am-5pm Sun.) lures both residents and tourists with its clinical skin care ($60-210 pp), exotic spa treatments ($35-350 pp), and massage therapy ($105-165 pp). Specialties include the Thai yoga massage ($160 for 1.5 hours, $190 for 2 hours) and the Prana Decadence ($350), a complete three-hour experience that includes a body-polishing scrub, a 75-minute body massage, an ultimate foot treatment, a 60-minute ultimate rejuvenation facial, and a shirodhara warm oil hair and scalp treatment.

White Street Healing Arts (1217 White St., 305/393-4102, 305/296-5997, or 305/304-5891, www.whitestreethealingarts.com, by appointment) is a holistic professional group that provides massage therapy in addition to acupuncture, chiropractic and Chinese medicine, and intuitive healing. Offerings include Swedish, deep tissue, aromatherapy, and reflexology massage ($90 hourly, $110 per 75 minutes, $130 per 90 minutes), plus hot stone massage ($165 per 90 minutes) and couples massage ($180 hourly, $220 per 75 minutes, $260 per 90 minutes). The licensed massage therapists here are often willing to bring their skills directly to you, but a 24-hour cancellation policy applies to all appointments, whether inside or outside the office.

For relaxation of a more active variety, consider **Yoga on the Beach** (305/296-7352, www.yogaonbeach.com), which offers daily, year-round classes on the beach at Fort Zachary Taylor Historic State Park, Marriott Beachside, and the Southernmost Beach Resort property. The hour-long classes cost $18 per person and include the park entrance fee. Mats, blankets, and props are provided for all classes, and instructors will make every effort to accommodate those with disabilities.

Entertainment and Events

TOP EXPERIENCE

★ NIGHTLIFE

If you like to prowl the streets at night, seeking out spirited bars, live music, and the like, then you've come to the right town. With a slew of late-night watering holes, hotel lounges, piano bars, and other entertainment options at your fingertips, Key West promises the most fun you'll have outside of the French Quarter. **Duval Street** offers the largest concentration of nightlife selections—hence the term "Duval crawl," a popular activity whereby locals and visitors alike endeavor to stop by every bar along the street, from the Atlantic Ocean to the Gulf of Mexico.

Beyond the late-night chain establishments on Duval, such as the **Hard Rock Cafe Key West** (313 Duval St., 305/293-0230, www.hardrock.com, 8am-midnight daily) and **Jimmy Buffett's Margaritaville Key West** (500 Duval St., 305/292-1435, www.margaritavillekeywest.com, 11am-10pm daily), you'll spot unique, laid-back establishments like **Willie T's Restaurant & Bar** (525 Duval St., 305/294-7674, www.williets.com, 10am-2am Sun.-Thurs., 10am-4am Fri.-Sat.), a popular watering hole that features an enormous selection of mojitos, a daily happy hour (4pm-7pm), and live acoustic music on the patio at 1pm and 7pm every day.

Farther down Duval stands the inimitable **Sloppy Joe's Bar** (201 Duval St., 305/294-5717, www.sloppyjoes.com, 9am-4am Mon.-Sat., noon-4am Sun.), which has been luring patrons to the corner of Greene and Duval (supposedly even Ernest Hemingway) since 1937 and is now listed in the National Register of Historic Places. Home to the annual Hemingway Look-Alike Contest, Sloppy Joe's offers terrific food, televised sports, plenty of libations, and live rock, country, or funk music all day long, which often entails three different bands or solo artists from noon to 2am.

Across the street from Sloppy Joe's, the **Rick's/Durty Harry's Entertainment Complex** (202-208 Duval St., 305/296-5513, www.ricksbarkeywest.com, 11am-4am daily) encompasses eight separate late-night options, including a Mardi Gras-style daiquiri bar, and Durty Harry's, which features several televisions and live rock music 8pm-4am daily. At Duval and Caroline Streets, you'll encounter the clothing-optional **Garden of Eden** atop **The Bull and Whistle Bar** (305/296-4565, 10am-4am Mon.-Sat., noon-4am Sun.), where body painting is a frequent activity. **Fat Tuesday Key West** (305 Duval St., 305/296-9373, www.fattuesday.com, 10am-2am daily) claims to have the world's best selection of frozen drinks, including rumrunners, piña coladas, and New Orleans-style Hurricanes.

You can also groove the night away at the predominantly gay **Aqua Nightclub** (711 Duval St., 305/294-0555, www.aquakeywest.com, 4pm-2am daily), which features a daily happy hour (2:30pm-8pm) in addition to karaoke, live piano and Caribbean-style music, and drag shows ($15 pp). Not far away lie two more gay hot spots: the **Bourbon St. Pub** (724 Duval St., 305/293-9345, www.bourbonstpub.com, 10am-2am daily), which offers three inner bars, a clothing-optional garden bar, and male dancers; and **801 Bourbon Bar & Cabaret** (801 Duval St., 305/294-4737, www.801bourbon.com, 10am-4am daily), which features multiple bars, happy-hour specials (10am-6pm daily), karaoke (4pm-9pm Sun.), drag queen bingo (5pm Sun.), and a twice-nightly drag show (9pm and 11pm). Both of these lively complexes factor heavily into annual events like Fantasy Fest and New Year's Eve.

Other enticing hotel options include the weekend cabaret show (9pm, dates vary, $32.25 pp) at the **La Te Da Hotel** (1125 Duval St., 305/296-6706, www.lateda.com); the full bar inside **Rambler's** (7am-9pm daily) at the

Casa Marina Resort (1500 Reynolds St., 305/296-3535, www.casamarinaresort.com); and the tropical bar at the Southernmost Inn (525 United St., 888/525-0037, www. thesouthernmostinn.com).

Also off Duval, the Bottlecap Lounge and Liquor (1128 Simonton St., 305/296-2807, www.bottlecaplounge.com, noon-4am daily) lures revelers with pool tables, comfortable lounge chairs, oodles of beer, late-night vittles, and live blues and rock music. Bobby's Monkey Bar (900 Simonton St., 305/294-2655, noon-4am daily) invites patrons to shoot some pool, play some free Wii games, and try their hand at karaoke (9:30pm Sun.-Mon. and Thurs.-Fri.).

Over on Whitehead, the Green Parrot Bar (601 Whitehead St., 305/294-6133, www. greenparrot.com, 10am-4am daily) has been luring night owls since 1890. Today you'll encounter a daily happy hour (4pm-7pm), an awesome jukebox, and of course, live blues, jazz, rock, and acoustic music almost every night.

Closer to the gulf, you can enjoy live rock and country music, plus a raw bar, at the Hog's Breath Saloon (400 Front St., 305/296-4222, www.hogsbreath.com, 10am-1am daily), plus annual events like a bikini contest in October and a Parrot Head tribute party to Jimmy Buffett in November.

Captain Tony's Saloon (428 Greene St., 305/294-1838, www.capttonyssaloon.com, 10am-2am Mon.-Sat., noon-2am Sun.), a Key West tradition since 1851 and the original location of Sloppy Joe's from 1933 to 1937, promises, among other things, live contemporary, classic rock, and country music every day, not to mention a glimpse at Ernest Hemingway's former stool. Typically, you can expect solo acoustic performers on weekdays and a house band on the weekend.

Locals flock to the funky Schooner Wharf Bar (202 William St., 305/292-3302, www.schoonerwharf.com, 7am-4am daily), a weathered, open-air joint beside the Historic Seaport at Key West Bight that offers excellent seafood, tropical drinks, and live acoustic music three times daily (noon, 7pm, and 9pm). If you haven't had your fill of live entertainment yet, stroll over to the open-air B.O.'s Fish Wagon (801 Caroline St., 305/294-9272, www.bosfishwagon.com, 11am-9:30pm daily) for the Friday night jam session. Closer to Grinnell, Dante's (951 Caroline St., 305/293-5123, www.danteskeywest.com, 11am-10pm daily) features a weekday happy hour (4pm-8pm), daily raw bar specials (4pm-8pm), nightly live entertainment, and access to a pool (11am-sunset daily).

For a sensual late-night experience, stop by Better Than Sex (926 Simonton St., 305/296-8102, www.betterthansexkw.com, 6pm-midnight Thurs.-Tues.), an intimate, dimly lit bordello-style lounge and restaurant that features live jazz and acoustic music and focuses exclusively on wine and decadent desserts. Even Stock Island has a nightlife option: the casual Hogfish Bar and Grill (6810 Front St., 305/293-4041, www.hogfishbar.com, 11am-10pm Mon.-Sat., 9am-10pm Sun.), which provides waterfront views and live blues, rock, and country music on Wednesdays.

THE ARTS

While the rest of the Florida Keys host their fair share of plays, concerts, and screenings, most cultural enthusiasts head first to Key West—and with good reason. Despite its small size, America's Southernmost City nurtures a number of winning theatrical venues and musical organizations.

Theater and Cinema

Situated on the Florida Keys Community College (FKCC) campus, the Tennessee Williams Theatre (5901 College Rd., Stock Island, 305/296-1520 or 305/295-7676, www. twstages.com, showtimes and ticket prices vary) was saved from permanent closure in 2002 by the nonprofit Performing Arts Centers for Key West (PACKW). Since then this fantastic venue has featured a variety of

1: Green Parrot Bar 2: Captain Tony's Saloon 3: Key West Songwriters' Festival 4: Sloppy Joe's Bar

nationally recognized performers and productions, from Lily Tomlin's one-woman show to Patti Lupone's musical reviews. To purchase tickets for events at the Tennessee Williams Theatre and other area venues, contact **KeysTix.com** (305/295-7676, http://keystix.ticketforce.com, phone hours 1pm-4pm Mon.-Fri.).

Mallory Square features the nonprofit **Waterfront Playhouse** (310 Wall St., 305/294-5015, www.waterfrontplayhouse.org, showtimes and ticket prices vary), home to the Key West Players. From November to May, theater lovers are treated to a variety of cutting-edge productions, from rowdy musical comedies like *Reefer Madness* to classic dramas such as *Twelve Angry Men.*

The Red Barn Theatre (319 Duval St., 305/296-9911 or 866/870-9911, www.redbarntheatre.com, showtimes and ticket prices vary) has celebrated live theater for more than three decades. From November to May, the theater showcases a wide array of modern comedies, dramas, and musicals, plus the springtime Short Attention Span Theatre, a popular event that features an assortment of 10-minute plays.

Occasional live dance, musical, and theatrical performances take place at the nonprofit **San Carlos Institute** (516 Duval St., 305/294-3887, www.institutosancarlos.org, showtimes and ticket prices vary), a stunning multipurpose facility that was founded by Cuban exiles and now features a museum, a library, an art gallery, a school, and a lovely 360-seat theater. Contact the Institute or **KeysTix.com** (305/295-7676, http://keystix.ticketforce.com) for upcoming events.

Even movie lovers won't be disappointed in Key West. The **Tropic Cinema** (416 Eaton St., 305/396-4944, www.tropiccinema.com, showtimes and ticket prices vary) offers four different screening rooms—the Natella Carper Theater, the Frank Taylor Cinematheque Theater, the George Digital Theater, and the Peggy Dow Theater—and a spacious lobby (dubbed the Sussman Lounge) that have not only played host to the latest independent, alternative, and foreign films, but also community events, from jazz concerts to literary lectures to songwriting festivals. For information about other cultural events in Key West, consult the **Florida Keys Council of the Arts** (1100 Simonton St., 305/295-4369, www.keysarts.com).

Music

If you appreciate live classical music, then you're in luck: For more than 15 years, the **South Florida Symphony Orchestra** (954/522-8445, www.southfloridasymphony.org, showtimes and ticket prices vary) has offered remarkable performances to the small community of Key West. Now composed of about 90 orchestral musicians and soloists from around the world, the orchestra splits its time between several venues, including the **Tennessee Williams Theatre** (5901 College Rd., Stock Island, 305/296-1520, www.twstages.com) and the **Broward Center for the Performing Arts** (201 SW 5th Ave., Fort Lauderdale, 954/522-0222, www.browardcenter.org).

Featured at the Tennessee Williams Theatre is the **FKCC Keys Chorale** (Florida Keys Community College, www.fkcc.edu, showtimes and ticket prices vary), Monroe County's only major vocal ensemble, which has been performing everything from pop songs to show tunes for more than 20 years. To purchase tickets for these musical organizations, consult **KeysTix.com** (305/295-7676, http://keystix.ticketforce.com, phone hours 1pm-4pm Mon.-Fri.).

The **Key West Council on the Arts** has offered **Impromptu Concerts** (www.keywestimpromptu.org, 305/296-1520, showtimes and ticket prices vary) for more than 35 years. These concerts, which can range from solo piano performances to brass quintets to world-renowned operas, usually take place at the Tennessee Williams Theatre or at **St. Paul's Episcopal Church** (401 Duval St., 305/296-5142, www.stpaulschurchkeywest.org). For tickets, contact the Tennessee Williams Theatre (305/295-7676).

Another good option is the **Bahama Village Music Program** (103 Olivia St., 305/504-7664, www.bvmpkw.org), a nonprofit group that offers free musical education to the children of Bahama Village, a historic community of multigenerational Bahamian Conchs. The students, who range in age from 6 to 13 and learn various styles of music from piano to percussion, offer free concerts and recitals throughout the year. For more information about musical events in the Key West area, consult the **Florida Keys Council of the Arts** (1100 Simonton St., 305/295-4369, www.keysarts.com).

FESTIVALS AND EVENTS

Key West may have many facets, but above all, it's still a town that knows how to party. Just consider the numerous festivals and events that lure revelers down here, sometimes even during the hottest months. Beyond fishing tournaments and New Year's Eve bashes, you'll find a number of art and heritage festivals, food events, and other exciting celebrations and competitions throughout the year. Perhaps you can even plan your next trip around such unabashed festivities.

Conch Republic Independence Celebration

On April 23, 1982, the U.S. Border Patrol set up a blockade near Florida City to search for illegal aliens and possible drug runners. Following the subsequent traffic jam on U.S. 1, the people of the Florida Keys briefly declared their secession from the United States by forming the "Conch Republic," a mock micronation, and successfully ended the disruptive blockade. Since then the people of Key West have honored the 1982 ceremonial secession with the 10-day **Conch Republic Independence Celebration** (www.conchrepublicdayskeywest.com).

Every spring, in late April, residents and visitors can enjoy a lineup of varied activities around the city, such as the raising of the Conch Republic flag at Fort Zachary Taylor Historic State Park and the Great Conch Republic Drag Race, featuring competing drag queens, on Duval Street. Throughout the celebration, you can enjoy an array of events at area bars and restaurants, from the conch shell-blowing contest at the Schooner Wharf Bar to a fiddler's contest at the Green Parrot Bar. Other events include bed and dinghy races, car and crafts shows, miniature golf challenges, a pirate's ball, and of course, the Conch Republic Naval Parade and the Great Battle for the Conch Republic—a mock naval confrontation between the Conch Republic's "armed forces" and the "U.S. Border Patrol," a homage to the April 1982 protest. Needless to say, the Conch Republic is always victorious.

Hemingway Days

The spirit of Ernest Hemingway, one of Key West's most beloved former residents, endures in the Southernmost City—and not just through the popular Ernest Hemingway Home and Museum or because of the numerous establishments, such as Sloppy Joe's Bar and Captain Tony's Saloon, that claim to have been the famous novelist's favorite watering hole. Every summer, in late July, residents and visitors alike celebrate this fascinating man with the annual **Hemingway Days** (800/352-5397, www.fla-keys.org), a six-day event that commemorates Hemingway's lust for life; his passion for activities like writing and fishing; his adoration of Key West, where he spent the better part of the 1930s; and of course, his literary works, several of which he wrote while living here.

Scheduled events typically include a literary competition; a Caribbean-style street fair; dramatic performances about Hemingway's life; a museum exhibit of rare Hemingway memorabilia; a three-day marlin tournament; and perhaps most famous, the Hemingway Look-Alike Contest, for which upwards of 150 stocky, white-bearded old men flock to town to demonstrate their uncanny resemblance to this one-of-a-kind American writer. Another not-to-be-missed event is the wacky "Running of the Bulls," a slow-moving parade that

What's in a Conch?

While visiting the Florida Keys, you're likely to hear or see the term "conch" (pronounced CONK) virtually everywhere. From menus that feature conch fritters and conch chowder to stores that offer Conch Republic souvenirs, this multipurpose term typically has one of three meanings in the Keys.

First of all, "conch" can signify a marine gastropod, such as the large queen conch, the feisty Florida fighting conch, or the imported conch that's often found in Keys cuisine. Since the 20th century, however, the term "conch" has also been used to refer to a resident of Key West. Some residents even go so far as to differentiate between "saltwater conchs," or those residents actually born in Key West, and "freshwater conchs," those who, though born elsewhere, have lived in Key West for at least seven years. While "conch" is now a widely used term for a Key West resident, regardless of his or her origin, the original meaning of "conch" solely applied to the Bahamian immigrants that arrived in Key West during the 18th and early 19th centuries and made their living by fishing, logging, and salvaging shipwrecks. Many of these so-called Conchs were descendants of Loyalists who had fled to the Bahamas, the nearest British colony, during the American Revolution. After arriving in Key West, many of these immigrants established a neighborhood in the western part of Old Town that is still known today as Bahama Village.

There are many theories, of course, for why these Bahamian immigrants were called Conchs in the first place. One such theory is that the affluent British Loyalists who settled in the Bahamas looked down upon the native residents, calling them "conchs" because shellfish was an important aspect of their diet. Another theory suggests that Bahamians told British authorities that they'd rather "eat conch" than pay taxes levied by the British Crown. Regardless of the true inspiration, the fact is that the term "conch," while considered a derogatory expression for Bahamian immigrants in other parts of Florida, has become a source of pride for those who live in the Florida Keys. Just consider the events of April 23, 1982, when in protest of a U.S. Border Patrol blockade near Florida City, the Florida Keys collectively declared their tongue-in-cheek secession from the United States,

features the "Papa" Hemingway look-alikes, dressed in Pamplona-style apparel, including khaki shorts and red berets, and riding or strolling beside phony bulls-on-wheels—a silly photo opportunity for residents and tourists alike.

Fantasy Fest

Every October, revelers pour into Key West for Fantasy Fest (922 Caroline St., 305/295-9112, www.fantasyfest.com), a spirited 10-day event that nearly rivals the Big Easy's annual Mardi Gras celebration. With colorful parades, outrageous costumes, and oodles of drag queens, this is surely Key West's grandest—and gayest—party of the year. Initiated in the late 1970s to help the local economy during a traditionally slow period, Fantasy Fest has become such a successful event that it often sustains the hotels, restaurants, and other local establishments until the winter holiday season. Usually held in late October

and culminating with Halloween, this hallowed event features everything from a children's costume contest to a two-day goombay street fair in Bahama Village—essentially, a Bahamian celebration that highlights the calypso-style music and dancing associated with goombay drums. In addition, Fantasy Fest revelers will experience fetish and toga parties, headdress balls, pet masquerades, various costume and wet T-shirt contests, body-painting displays, and plenty of other hedonistic activities. Though not for the faint of heart, Fantasy Fest is a bash you may wish to observe—if not participate in.

Cultural Festivals

With a past that includes pirate legends, Bahamian immigrants, Civil War skirmishes, Cuban refugees, and other colorful facets, it's little surprise that Key West plays host to a number of cultural events throughout the year.

conch shell

forming a micronation called the Conch Republic—an incident that's still celebrated today with such annual events as Key West's Conch Republic Independence Celebration, a zany 10-day festival that typically occurs in late April and features everything from Conch Republic flag raisings to drag queen races to conch shell-blowing contests.

On multiple weekends from late December to mid-March, those interested in Key West's unique architecture and gardens can take a **Key West House and Garden Tour** (www.keywesthometours.com, $45 pp) through the historical Old Town district. Sponsored by the **Old Island Restoration Foundation** (322 Duval St., 305/294-9501, www.oirf.org) for the past five decades, these beloved tours allow both residents and visitors a chance to peer beyond the front porches of some of Key West's one-of-a-kind homes. Each tour features five private domiciles, all of which reflect the varied tastes of their owners and many of which feature authentic restorations, creative renovations, and impressive art and antiques collections.

In late February, **The Key West Tropical Forest & Botanical Garden** (5210 College Rd., Stock Island, 305/296-1504, www.keywestbotanicalgarden.org, 10am-4pm daily) celebrates the island's bountiful flora with **Gardenfest Key West** (prices vary), a three-day event that typically includes raffles, demonstrations, lectures, nature-oriented artwork, and a plant sale featuring fruit trees, exotic palms, orchids, bromeliads, and native plants. Also in late February, the city celebrates a three-day event known as **Civil War Days** (fees apply for some activities) with candlelit tours of Fort Zachary Taylor (western end of Southard St., 305/292-6713, www.floridastateparks.org), artillery demonstrations, a military parade down Duval Street, and reenacted engagements between Union soldiers and Confederate blockade runners in authentic 19th-century schooners.

In early March, the Old Island Restoration Foundation (322 Duval St., 305/294-9501, www.oirf.org) hosts a popular **Conch Shell Blowing Contest** (free), also known as the "Conch Honk," during which children, teenagers, adults, and senior citizens alike demonstrate their shell-blowing skills in order to highlight the significance of the conch in Key West's past.

Typically held in late April, the **Key West Songwriters' Festival** (www. keywestsongwritersfestival.com, showtimes and ticket prices vary) is a five-day event that presents more than 30 live concerts at popular locales throughout the city, from the Ocean Key Resort to the San Carlos Institute to Jimmy Buffett's Margaritaville. In late May, residents and visitors celebrate the influence of Cuban culture on the development of Key West with the three-day **Cuban American Heritage Festival** (5570 3rd Ave., 305/295-9665, www.keywestchamber.org, prices vary), which typically includes activities like a coast-to-coast conga line, a Latin dance party, a Cuban cigar dinner, a domino tournament, and a progressive dinner at various Cuban restaurants.

Besides Hemingway Days, other popular summertime events include the five-day **Key West Pridefest** (305/294-4603, www. gaykeywestfl.com, fees apply for some activities) in mid-June and the four-day **Mel Fisher Days** (Mel Fisher's Treasures, 200 Greene St., 800/434-1399, www.melfisherdays.melfisher. com, fees apply for some activities) in mid-July. In a town that possesses a healthy share of gay-friendly bars and hotels—and whose motto is "one human family"—it's no wonder that Pridefest is a much-anticipated event, filled with contests, shows, tours, dance and cocktail parties, a street fair, and a pride parade along Duval Street. A month later, Mel Fisher Days honors a different aspect of the city's heritage—its lust for treasure hunting. To honor the anniversary of Mel Fisher's discovery of the *Atocha* mother lode, this event features, among other activities, a parade, a poker tournament, and a bikini contest that offers authentic treasure coins as prizes.

In early November, **Parrot Heads in Paradise Inc.** (www.phip.com), the non-profit international organization of Parrot Head Clubs—the official fan clubs of singer-songwriter Jimmy Buffett and the carefree tropical lifestyle he exemplifies—hosts a four-day **Meeting of the Minds** for all members in good standing, whether they be members of the virtual club or one of the more than 200 chapters that exist around the world.

Food Events

In a city that celebrates so many hedonistic pleasures, it's no wonder that food plays a major role in so many annual events. In mid-January, the one-day family-friendly **Florida Keys Seafood Festival** (www. floridakeysseafoodfestival.com, free) highlights the region's commercial fishing industry by offering the freshest local seafood available, from crab to lobster. Later in January, the four-day **Key West Food & Wine Festival** (800/474-4319, www. keywestfoodandwinefestival.com, prices vary) celebrates an assortment of local delicacies, including seafood, Cuban cuisine, tapas dishes, fine wine, and tropical ice cream, at various local bars and restaurants. Other activities may include a coconut bowling tournament and a tea dance at La Te Da.

In mid-April, another annual food extravaganza, the one-day **Taste of Key West** ($1 per food/wine ticket), celebrates the cuisine of more than 100 vineyards and 50 local restaurants while benefiting the efforts of **AIDS Help** (1434 Kennedy Dr., 305/296-6196, www.aidshelp.cc). A few months later, in early August, residents and visitors celebrate one of their favorite crustaceans with the **Key West Lobsterfest** (www.keywestlobsterfest.com, prices vary), a three-day event sponsored by Key West Promotions (305/294-7170, www.keywestpromotions.com) that features live music, cold drinks, and, naturally, fresh lobster.

Art Festivals

The Southernmost City hosts its share of art-related events during the peak tourist season. In late January, the long-standing **Key West Craft Show** (305/294-1241, www. keywestartcenter.com/craft, prices vary), a two-day juried outdoor craft festival, attracts over 100 potters, fabric experts, jewelry makers, glass sculptors, wood craftsmen, and other skilled artists to Key West's Old Town.

Usually held in late February, the nationally recognized **Old Island Days Art Festival** (305/294-1243, www.keywestartcenter. com, prices vary) has celebrated various art forms amid the historical structures of Key West's Old Town for well over four decades. Originally held as a fundraising event for the building that now houses the **Key West Art Center and Gallery (KWAC)** (301 Front St., 305/294-1241, www.keywestartcenter.com, 10am-5pm daily), this two-day juried festival features the work of over 100 painters, photographers, sculptors, and other artists, many of whom favor tropical themes.

Fishing and Racing Events

Outdoor events are popular in Key West, perhaps none more so than the fishing tournaments and racing championships that take place throughout the year. In late January, thousands of sailors from around the world flock to Key West for the **Key West Race Week** (914/834-8857, www.keywestraceweek. com, entry fees apply), a five-day international sailing competition in the waters surrounding the Southernmost City. Beginning in mid-March, men, women, juniors, and young children compete to catch and release more than 40 different fish species in the nine-month-long **Key West Fishing Tournament (KWFT)** (www.keywestfishingtournament. com, entry fees apply).

From mid-September to early November, celebrities and ordinary fishing enthusiasts come together for the **Redbone Celebrity Tournament Series** (305/664-2002, www. redbone.org, entry fees apply), a trio of three-day "Catch the Cure" competitions throughout the Keys that seek out permit, tarpon, bonefish, and redfish—ultimately benefiting cystic fibrosis research. Also in early November, a slew of high-speed powerboats race across the waters of Key West to vie

for the world title in the five-day **Key West World Championship** (www.superboat. com, entry fees apply)—a competition that's equally appealing to spectators.

Holiday Celebrations

A year in Key West wouldn't be complete without experiencing the city's annual holiday celebrations. In early December, residents and visitors, often dressed in shorts and sandals, line up along Duval Street for the **Key West Holiday Parade** (free), a family-friendly event that usually occurs on a Saturday evening and features decorated floats, marching bands, and perhaps a few Santas holding fishing poles. On a Saturday evening in mid-December, locals "deck the hulls" for the **Key West Lighted Boat Parade** (free), a maritime tradition that features a procession of vessels in Key West Bight. All the boats, most of which are owned by Florida Keys residents, are enhanced by bright lights, holiday decorations, and live music, from choirs to steel drums.

For two enchanted evenings in early or mid-December, the self-guided **Holiday Historic Inn Tour** (www.keyslodging.org, $20 pp) highlights some of the city's loveliest properties, all of which are decorated for the holiday season with twinkling lights, poinsettia plants, and festooned palm trees. Often you'll be able to step inside such historic inns as the Cypress House, the Curry Mansion, and The Mermaid & The Alligator B&B. In addition, fine food and beverages are usually available throughout the tour.

Not surprisingly, **New Year's Eve** is a popular holiday in the Southernmost City. Among the various midnight celebrations on December 31, you'll spy a conch shell dropping from the roof of Sloppy Joe's Bar, a pirate wench descending the mast of a schooner at the Historic Seaport, and a local drag queen being lowered from a Duval Street balcony in an enormous high-heeled shoe. Many of the bars are open into the wee hours, so the celebrating doesn't typically stop at midnight.

Shopping

With its cornucopia of art galleries, gift and souvenir shops, clothing boutiques, jewelry stores, and food emporiums, Key West promises you the most engrossing treasure hunt in the Florida Keys—at least on land. Here shoppers will find all manner of items for sale, from hammocks to erotic literature to pendants fashioned from salvaged Spanish coins. While such diverse shopping opportunities exist throughout the city, certain areas such as Mallory Square and the rest of Old Town offer the lion's share of options, especially for tourists.

The suggestions listed here merely scratch the surface of Key West's shopping scene. For even more ideas, consult www.shopkeywest.com—or just take a stroll around the neighborhoods.

BAHAMA VILLAGE

Southwest of Whitehead Street and roughly bordered by Southard, Fort, and Louisa Streets is the historic neighborhood known as Bahama Village. Named for its original inhabitants, many of whom were of Bahamian ancestry, this residential area is a lively place in the daytime and rather quiet at night. Some visitors even find it a little too quiet once the sun goes down. With the occurrence of criminal activities, such as muggings and drug transactions, local police officers often advise outsiders against venturing into this area after dark.

Nevertheless, the presence of several interesting shops and restaurants, such as the dessert-only eatery Better Than Sex, makes Bahama Village an enticing place for tourists. Shoppers might especially appreciate the Bahama Village Market, an open-air flea market near the village entrance on Petronia Street. Here you'll find a collection of colorful stalls featuring typical souvenirs like straw hats, T-shirts, beads, sponges, and Caribbean crafts.

MALLORY SQUARE

Although technically part of Key West's Old Town, Mallory Square (1 Whitehead St., www.mallorysquare.com) operates as its own unique entity. Situated at the northernmost part of Duval and Whitehead Streets, this popular collection of shops, eateries, and attractions is perhaps best known for its daily Sunset Celebration, when hundreds of locals and tourists gather beside the shore to enjoy the antics of musicians, artists, acrobats, jugglers, and other street performers while paying homage to the sun as it seemingly sinks into the Gulf of Mexico.

If you're in search of souvenirs, you're in luck here. Vendor carts present a variety of goods, from coconut pirates to colorful flip-flops. You'll also spot the long-standing Shell Warehouse (305/294-5168, 8:30am-9pm daily), which offers an intriguing assortment of shells, jewelry, artwork, and decorations. Another favorite tourist stop is the Sponge Market (305/294-2555, 8am-9pm daily), which features a variety of local art, model ships, sea sponges, shipwreck treasure jewelry, and other maritime collectibles—not to mention an enormous "sponge man," the subject of many a tourist's photograph, just outside the doorway. Not far away, adjacent to Mallory Square, you'll encounter the Clinton Square Market (291 Front St., 305/296-6825, 9am-9pm daily), an air-conditioned, two-story mall that contains a variety of shops, featuring everything from jewelry and tropical clothing to toys and pet items.

HISTORIC SEAPORT

From Mallory Square, head northeast to the renovated Historic Seaport district at Key West Bight, home to dozens of yachts and

1: Shell Warehouse at Mallory Square 2: coconut pirates, a souvenir of Key West 3: entrance to Bahama Village

The Wyland Walls

Robert Wyland is the most famous marinelife artist in the world. For more than three decades, Wyland—an avid scuba diver, marine conservationist, painter, sculptor, photographer, and world traveler as well as an official artist for the United States Olympic Committee—has used his artwork to spread awareness about the ocean, its inhabitants, and the need to preserve and protect this fragile environment. His oil and watercolor paintings, bronze and Lucite sculptures, and other creations—which typically feature magnificent whales, peaceful manatees, frisky dolphins, giant sea turtles, and kaleidoscopic tropical fish—are on display in galleries throughout the country, most notably in Florida, California, and Hawaii. The flagship store of **Wyland Galleries** (623 Duval St., 305/292-4998, www.wylandgalleriesofthefloridakeys.com) is in Key West.

Nicknamed the "Marine Michelangelo" by *USA Today,* Wyland has been recognized for his conservation efforts by the United Nations, the Sierra Club, and other public and private institutions throughout the world. In fact, he cares so deeply about the environment that in 1993 he established the **Wyland Foundation** (www.wylandfoundation.org), a nonprofit organization that has supported numerous art, education, and conservation programs, including his most famous endeavor: the monumental "Wyland Wall" mural project. Begun in 1981 in Laguna Beach, California, this impressive series of 100 life-size marinelife murals now spans 13 countries on five continents, and captures nearly 1 billion viewers per year. You'll find several of these amazing murals in southern Florida, including *Minke Whales,* which was created in 1990 at Crane Point's Museum of Natural History in Marathon, as well as a more recent offering, which was painted in October 2012 to replace *Florida's Living Reef* (1993) on the exterior wall of the former Waterfront Market in Key West. For more information about Wyland's art and conservation efforts, visit www.wyland.com.

tour operators. Generally, people come here to hire charters, board sailboats, stroll along the boardwalk, or dine at lively places like the Schooner Wharf Bar, but shoppers will also find a couple of interesting stores in the vicinity. Difficult to miss is **Mac's Sea Garden** (208 Margaret St., 305/293-7240, 9am-9pm daily), a rustic gift shop with chimes hanging beneath the porch roof, an old, weathered pickup sitting in the front yard, and the distinct appearance of a Cajun fishing camp. Not far away, at the corner of Elizabeth and Greene Streets, **Kermit's Key West Key Lime Shoppe** (305/296-0806, www.keylimeshop. com, 9am-9:30pm daily) offers a slew of key lime products, from key lime bath soap to key lime barbecue sauce to classic key lime pie, of course.

OLD TOWN

Most of the available shopping opportunities are concentrated on or near **Duval Street,** the main drag of this historical district. Here and on surrounding roads, like Greene and Whitehead Streets, you'll find a ton of places to satisfy your cravings for art, souvenirs, fashion, jewelry, food, and so much more.

Art Galleries

If you're an art lover, then you've come to the right place. Key West boasts well over 30 art galleries—certainly more than any other place in the Florida Keys. Over half of these can be found on Duval Street, in two separate clusters.

On the upscale end of Duval, closer to the Atlantic Ocean, lie nearly a dozen elegant galleries, bunched together amid tropical foliage and historic buildings. At the **Archeo Gallery** (1208 Duval St., 305/294-3771, www.archeogallery.com, 10am-6pm daily) you'll find hand-chosen primitive art from around the world, such as vibrant Gabbeh rugs from Iran, teak furniture from Indonesia, and masks, sculpture, pottery, and metalwork from Africa. Across the street stands the **Gingerbread Square Gallery** (1207 Duval St., 305/296-8900, www.gingerbreadsquaregallery.com, 10am-6pm daily), which was established in 1974 by Key West's former mayor Richard Heyman, making it one of the oldest art galleries in town. Represented here are the paintings, sculptures, and glassware of several different artists, from Sal Salinero's lush rain forest landscapes to George Bucquet's contemporary art glass.

The **Alan S. Maltz Gallery** (1210 Duval St., 305/294-0005, www.alanmaltz.com, 10am-6pm daily) displays the stunning images of Florida's official wildlife photographer.

Several blocks down Duval, closer to the rowdier Gulf of Mexico end, lie nearly 10 more winning galleries, including the **Island Style Gallery** (512 Duval St., 305/292-7800, www.islandstylegalleries.com, 9am-10pm daily), which presents artistic jewelry, handcrafted glass, and colorful, tropical-themed home furnishings. On the same side of the street, you'll find the **Guild Hall Gallery** (614 Duval St., 305/296-6076, www.guildhallgallerykw.com, 10am-8pm daily), which has supported local artists since 1976 and today displays the watercolor and acrylic paintings, contemporary sculpture, and youthful jewelry of more than 20 artists. About a block away, the dramatically lit **Peter Lik Fine Art Photography Gallery** (519 Duval St., 305/292-2550, www.lik.com, 10am-10pm daily) is one of 13 such galleries in the United States. Lik's highly successful landscape photography is known for its beautiful saturated colors and massive mainstream appeal. The Australian photographer achieved stratospheric success when he sold a one-of-a-kind original photograph for $6.5 million in 2015, the highest price ever paid for a photograph to date.

Perhaps the most famous gallery in town, however, is the flagship store of **Wyland Galleries** (623 Duval St., 305/292-4998 or 888/292-4998, www.wylandgalleriesofthefloridakeys.com, 9am-10pm daily), the largest Wyland gallery in the world. Inside this spacious store, you'll see an array of impressive glass creations, bronze sculptures, and vibrant paintings by the prolific muralist and environmentalist, whose work typically focuses on photogenic marinelife like dolphins, manatees, orcas, and sea turtles. In addition, this incredible gallery features the work of Wyland's fellow artists, including David Wight's amazing glass wave sculptures.

There are also plenty of worthwhile art galleries off Duval. Near downtown Key West, the **Audubon House & Tropical Gardens** (205 Whitehead St., 305/294-2116, www.audubonhouse.com, 9:30am-4:15pm daily) includes the **Audubon House Gallery of Natural History**, which offers limited editions of John James Audubon's famous 19th-century ornithological paintings. For more information about these and other art galleries, consult the **Florida Keys Council of the Arts** (1100 Simonton St., 305/295-4369, www.keysarts.com).

Gift and Souvenir Shops

Gift and souvenir shops abound in Old Town. For one thing, there's a plethora of strategically placed museum shops in this part of town. Whether they're situated just beyond the front entrance—as with the **Mel Fisher Maritime Museum** (200 Greene St., 305/294-2633, www.melfisher.org, 8:30am-5pm Mon.-Fri., 9:30am-5pm Sat.-Sun.)—or located at the end of the tour, you're usually forced to pass through an eclectic collection of books, DVDs, jewelry, apparel, and the like. If you're less interested in nautically themed items, consider browsing the gift shop at **The Key West Butterfly & Nature Conservatory** (1316 Duval St., 305/296-2988, www.keywestbutterfly.com, 9am-5:30pm daily), which features a wide selection of butterfly-themed jewelry, ceramics, books, and other souvenirs.

You'll find several other curious gift shops along Duval. **Key West Hammock Company** (717 Duval St., Ste. 2, 305/293-0008, www.kwhammocks.com, hours vary daily) has been distributing hammocks and hammock-style porch swings, chairs, and rockers for over a decade, and while it's

They Sell Conch Shells by the Seashore

So you've come to Key West. You've conquered the Duval Street pub crawl and seen the six-toed cats and climbed the lighthouse, and now you want a souvenir to take home to remember your sunny days in the Conch Republic. And what better than take home a beautiful queen conch, the shell that best symbolizes the Florida Keys? The best place to start is the Shell Warehouse (305/294-5168, 8:30am-9pm daily). Yes, they have conchs…and about a zillion other varieties of shells, as well as starfish, shark teeth, and about everything else sea-related that can legally be sold as a souvenir. Plan on digging deep into your pockets for the perfect conch—just one will probably run you $10-40.

If you're lucky, you can pull a conch shell out of the surrounding waters for free if you keep a keen eye out while snorkeling or diving. However, it is important to know the rules and regulations of conch harvesting. Florida regulations state, "It is not illegal for any person to obtain, or keep queen conch shells from the waters or lands of the State of Florida, as long as the removed shells do not contain a live animal at the time, and so long as a living queen conch is not killed, mutilated, or removed from its shell prior to collection. Possession of conch meat or a queen conch shell having an off-center hole larger than 1/16 inch in diameter through its spire is prohibited." Talk about attention to detail. So make sure and break out that tape measure and fully inspect the shell before you bag it and show it off to the closest Florida wildlife officer. The fines can be hefty—upwards of a thousand dollars or more if you get caught pink-shell-handed.

The queen conch was once plentiful in Florida, but since the fishery's collapse in the 1970s it has been illegal to harvest any live queen conch in Florida waters. So before you buy your next favorite memory of Key West, remember to ask the seashell store manager if the shells are harvested in a sustainable manner. Let's ensure that the Conch Republic lives on in more than name only by protecting its namesake sea creature.

---

true that **Jimmy Buffett's Margaritaville** (500 Duval St., 305/292-1435, www.margaritavillekeywest.com, 11am-10pm daily) is part of a famous bar and restaurant chain, that doesn't mean that the attached store isn't worth browsing. Here you'll find all manner of souvenir hats, T-shirts, flip-flops, lawn chairs, dog collars, and of course, Buffett's novels and CDs. Not far away, you can pick up unique aloe-based fragrances, hair products, and skin creams for women and men at **Key West Aloe** (1075 Duval St., 305/517-6365, www.keywestaloe.com, 10am-6pm daily).

If you've come to Key West with more amorous amusements in mind, consider stopping by **Fairvilla's Sexy Things** (524 Front St., 305/292-0448, www.fairvilla.com, 11am-midnight Sun.-Thurs., 11am-11pm Fri.-Sat.), where you'll find a wide selection of erotic gifts and games, fantasy fashions, and sensual accessories. Just a few blocks away lies a completely different megastore: With a view of Key West Harbor, the 4,000-square-foot **Saltwater Angler** (243 Front St., 305/296-0700 or 800/223-1629, www.saltwaterangler.com, 9am-8pm daily) is a one-stop shop for anyone interested in saltwater fishing in the Florida Keys. Operated by Captain Tony Murphy and situated within The Westin Key West Resort & Marina, the Angler houses an extensive inventory of travel and fishing apparel for men and women, plus luggage, wind chimes, stained glass fish art, rare books, and locally made jewelry. While you're here, you can even ask about fishing guide services.

Clothing and Shoe Boutiques

Most of the clothing and footwear stores in Key West focus on carefree island styles. The **Ron Jon Surf Shop** (503 Front St., 305/293-8880, www.ronjonsurfshop.com, 9am-9pm daily) is no exception. This two-story behemoth offers a wide array of apparel and accessories for the vacationer, from swimsuits to backpacks to sunglasses. In keeping with that laid-back vibe, **Kino Sandals** (107 Fitzpatrick St., 305/294-5044, www.kinosandalfactory. com, 8:30am-5:30pm Mon.-Fri., 9am-5:30pm Sat., 10am-3pm Sun.), established in 1966 by Cuban immigrants, invites visitors to watch the sandals being made by hand before choosing from an array of men's and women's selections.

If you want to match your new outfit with the perfect hat, purse, or necklace, stroll to The Westin Key West Resort & Marina, where the locally owned **Key West Madhatter** (253 Front St., 305/294-1364 or 888/442-4287, www.keywestmadhatter.com, 10am-6:30pm daily) offers, among other accessories, more than 2,000 hats for women, men, and children, from elegant straw hats to goofy holiday fedoras.

Jewelry Stores

You'll certainly find an impressive assortment of shiny, pretty things in Key West, including oodles of gemstones at **Diamonds International** (122 Duval St., 305/293-1111, www.diamondsinternational.com, 10am-8pm daily), the largest duty-free jeweler in the world, as well as emerald, conch pearl, and Australian black opal rings at **Emeralds International** (104 Duval St., 305/294-2060 or 877/689-6647, www.emeraldsinternational. com, 10am-6pm Mon.-Sat., 11am-5pm Sun.). For more precious gemstones—plus Key West's largest supply of Swiss watches—head to **Little Switzerland** (271 Front St., 248/809-5560, ext. 20370, www. littleswitzerland.com, 9am-5pm daily). If your interests run a little less expensive, visit **Local Color** (276 Margaret St., 305/292-3635, www.localcolorkeywest.com, 9am-9pm daily), which since 1988 has offered a wide array of fun jewelry, including locally inspired beads and charms, rings, and silver and gold "KW" hook bracelets. You could also try **Paradise Tattoo** (627 Duval St., 305/292-9110, www. paradisetattoo.com, 10am-10pm daily), which offers basic jewelry in addition to tattoo and body-piercing services.

For valuables that will evoke memories

of your trip to the Florida Keys, head to **Mel Fisher's Treasures** (200 Greene St., 305/296-9936 or 800/434-1399, www.melfisher.com, 9:30am-5pm daily), situated at the rear of the Mel Fisher Maritime Museum. Here you can purchase a piece of the famous *Nuestra Señora de Atocha* shipwreck, including pearls, iron spikes, musket balls, pieces of eight, and pendants and earrings crafted from old Spanish coins. In addition, you can speak with the staff about investing in the site—from which underwater explorers are still recovering hidden coins, artifacts, and other treasures. Just be prepared to spend a bundle. Being an investor isn't cheap, but neither are the goods in the store, where you might spot an authentic *Atocha* silver coin mounted in 14k gold and diamonds for $32,400.

Food and Beverage Emporiums

Key West residents celebrate all aspects of life, not the least of which is fine food. If you're hoping to take a taste of the Conch Republic home with you, look no farther than the **Key West Key Lime Pie Co.** (511 Greene St., 305/517-6720, www.keywestkeylimepieco. com, 10am-9pm daily), which sells award-winning key lime pies in addition to gourmet jellies, marinades, cookies, candies, spices, cookbooks, and other items, including the popular key lime pie bar—a scrumptious treat that features a slice of key lime pie covered in rich chocolate.

Of course, key lime pie isn't all that Key West has to offer. Founded by Cuban immigrant and cigar maker Fausto Castillo, **Fausto's Food Palace** (www.faustos.com) has served the people of Key West with fine wines, gourmet cheeses, and other delicious vittles since 1926. Today Fausto's, which has moved and expanded over the years, offers two locations: 522 Fleming Street (305/296-5663, 7:30am-8pm Mon.-Sat., 7:30am-7pm Sun.) and 1105 White Street (305/294-5221, 7:30am-8pm Mon.-Sat., 7:30am-7pm Sun.). Wine lovers might also appreciate **The Key West Winery** (103 Simonton St.,

305/916-5343, www.thekeywestwinery.com, 10am-6pm Mon.-Sat., noon-5pm Sun.), which features key lime, mango, and other tropical wines, plus a variety of key lime condiments. Another option is the **Cork & Stogie** (1218 Duval St., 305/517-6419, www.corkandstogie. com, 10am-11pm Mon.-Sat., noon-11pm Sun.), which offers a fine selection of wine and cigars, including those produced by **The Original Key West Cigar Factory** (305/517-7273, www.kwcigarfactory.com), whose history stretches back to the 1880s.

Food

Key West has the largest selection of restaurants in the Florida Keys, and the cuisine here runs the gamut from fresh seafood to all-American hamburgers to upscale French and Italian dishes. So whatever your mood, you're sure to find something tasty in the Southernmost City. Of course, only a small percentage of the available eateries are listed here. For more suggestions, consult the **Florida Keys Dining Guide** (www.keysdining.com).

SEAFOOD

Key West boasts a plethora of fresh seafood options, especially near the Historic Seaport at Key West Bight. While meandering around this lively area, be sure to stop by the **Half Shell Raw Bar** (231 Margaret St., 305/294-7496, www.halfshellrawbar.com, 11am-10pm Mon.-Sat., noon-10pm Sun., $7-21), a former shrimp-packing facility that has maintained its charm as an authentic fish house. Though it does offer fried dishes, this laid-back eatery really specializes in raw, steamed, broiled, and grilled seafood. After starting with a bucket of steamed clams, try the stuffed shrimp, prepared with crabmeat and spices and broiled with garlic butter, white wine, and lemon juice.

Along the boardwalk, you can enjoy fresh seafood on the breezy upper deck of the weathered ★ **Schooner Wharf Bar** (202 William St., 305/292-3302, www. schoonerwharf.com, 7:30am-4am daily, $8-18). Here you'll find standard Keys fare like the filling seafood sampler, featuring conch fritters, mahimahi, four kinds of shrimp, and fries. In addition, the Schooner Wharf now serves complete breakfasts, such as the shrimp Benedict Florentine. This casual, open-air watering hole also offers live music, which starts at noon and continues late into the night.

The harborside **Conch Republic Seafood Company** (631 Greene St., 305/294-4403, www.conchrepublicseafood.com, 11am-midnight daily, $15-30) provides a casual atmosphere for seafood lovers. Here you'll enjoy raw oysters and clams, traditional dishes like grilled mahimahi, 80 different varieties of rum, and daily entertainment, with musicians often playing late into the evening.

The **A&B Lobster House** (700 Front St., 305/294-5880, www.aandblobsterhouse. com, 5:30pm-10pm daily, $24-70) is a fancy, white-tablecloth restaurant that offers signature dishes like grouper Oscar and tuna au poivre. It's also the home of **Alonzo's Oyster Bar** (www.alonzosoysterbar.com, 11am-11pm daily, $9-28), a casual eatery that serves key lime garlic oysters, steamed shrimp, roasted mussels, and other tasty treats.

Though not as old or as legendary as some Key West eateries, the family-owned **Two Friends Patio Restaurant** (512 Front St., 305/296-3124, www.twofriendskeywest.com, 8am-close daily, $9-25) is still a lively choice for breakfast, lunch, and dinner. Established in 1967, this open-air eatery prepares filling breakfast dishes like shrimp and crabmeat quiche and crab cake Benedict, as well as terrific chargrilled steaks, fresh seafood dishes, and tropical drinks later in the day. As a bonus, you'll find early-bird specials from 4pm to 6pm daily, plus live karaoke nightly.

Even if you never work up the nerve to take the stage, you'll certainly enjoy the show.

For an alternative experience, head to the **Hurricane Hole Restaurant & Marina** (MM 4.5, 5130 Overseas Hwy., Stock Island, 305/294-0200, www.hurricaneholekeywest.com, 11am-midnight daily, $11-20), where you can enjoy fresh seafood, steak, and chicken while overlooking the marina. Bring in some freshly caught fish, and the cooks will grill, blacken, or fry it for you.

CUBAN

For one of the best cups of Cuban coffee on the island, head toward the cruise ship port to the Cuban Coffee Queen (284 Margaret St., 305/292-4747, www.cubancoffeequeen.com, 6:30am-7pm daily, $6-10), which is also a hot spot for breakfast and lunch. The service has been known to be a little slow, but if you're willing to wait a bit for an excellent Cuban sandwich, then this is the place to go. For breakfast they offer a variety of sandwiches pressed on Cuban bread. If you didn't get enough Cuban pastries in Miami, you can soothe your sweet tooth with their guava and cream cheese on Cuban bread. Try the Havana beans and rice that's served with eggs, or sink into something more American with one of the many deli sandwiches—it's hard to go wrong here. The menu is delicious, and this is also an excellent place to people-watch in the early morning as tourists stumble or crawl in to nurse their Duval hangovers with a few cups of extra-strong Cuban coffee.

For something a bit more eccentric, but just as tasty, head near the center of the island and about a half block west of Duval to **Frita's Cuban Burger Café** (425 Southard St., 305/509-7075, 11am-11pm Mon.-Sat, 11am-10pm Sun., $5-8.95). The prices are very reasonable, and the favorite item on the menu is of course the fabulous Traditional Frita Cuban Burger, a seasoned beef and pork patty smothered with onions, spicy sauce, and a fried potato slice, all served on Cuban bread. If that's not enough you can add a fried egg or cheese for an extra dollar each. The menu is quite large, with a variety of sandwiches, drinks, coffees, and sides. For something sweet, try the churros dusted with cinnamon, sugar, and...bacon. They are truly a slice of Cuban heaven on Earth.

In Mallory Square, you can get your Cuban cuisine at **El Meson de Pepe** (410 Wall St., 305/295-2620, www.elmesondepepe.com, 11am-10pm daily, $10-20). The colorful and charming restaurant has nice touches of

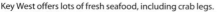

Key West offers lots of fresh seafood, including crab legs.

Make Your Own Key Lime Pie

Of all the regional treats favored in the Florida Keys, perhaps none is as widely known—or as universally celebrated—as key lime pie. While you'll encounter a variety of styles down here—from the deep-fried, cinnamon-encrusted version at **The Island Fish Co. Tiki Bar & Restaurant** in Marathon to the chocolate-covered pie-on-a-stick at the **Key West Key Lime Pie Co.** in Key West's Old Town—most gourmands seek the classic recipe, a creamy, tangy, sweet concoction on a graham cracker crust, the kind you'll find at **Mrs. Mac's Kitchen** in Key Largo.

If you simply can't wait to taste this treat on your next trip to the Florida Keys, never fear. With little fuss, you can easily make your own classic key lime pie, using this simple recipe.

CRUST INGREDIENTS

1½ cups crushed graham crackers
3 Tbsp. sugar
6 Tbsp. salted butter, melted

FILLING INGREDIENTS

4 large egg yolks
1 14-oz. can sweetened condensed milk
½ cup freshly squeezed key lime juice (or bottled, if necessary)

INSTRUCTIONS

· Preheat the oven to 350°F.

· Combine the graham cracker crumbs, sugar, and melted butter in a medium-size bowl.

· Press the mixture evenly into the bottom and sides of a nine-inch pie pan.

· Bake the pie shell at 350°F for 10-15 minutes, or until slightly brown.

· Place the pie shell on a wire rack to cool.

· Beat the egg yolks with an electric mixer until the color turns a pale yellow.

· Add the condensed milk, and mix on low speed.

· Fold in the lime juice.

· Pour the mixture into the pie shell and bake at 350°F for 10-12 minutes.

· Once cooled, refrigerate the pie for at least six hours.

· When you're ready to serve, garnish the pie with whipped cream and lime wedges.

Cuban art, and you might even find a few chickens wandering among the tables. Along with a traditional selection of tapas, soups, salads, and sandwiches, you'll find classic Cuban entrees such as *polla al ajillo* (roasted chicken marinated with mojo sauce and caramelized onions) and *ropa vieja* (shredded beef stewed with tomatoes, green peppers, onions, and red wine). For dessert, try the guava bread pudding or the coconut flan. For

drinks before or after the sunset celebration, have mojitos and tapas at the patio and listen to the excellent salsa band that plays every night as the sun goes down. It's the perfect way to start a Key West evening.

AMERICAN

Seafood isn't the only option for gourmands in Key West. Burgers, steaks, barbecue, and even vegetarian dishes are available, too. If you're looking for a well-prepared steak, head first to the **Prime Steakhouse** (951 Caroline St., 305/296-4000, www.primekeywest.com, 6pm-10pm daily, $20-55), a fine-dining steak house that also offers an excellent selection of complementary wines. Begin with a signature martini before sampling one of the steak specials. Reservations are recommended, especially during the high season.

The **Turtle Kraals Restaurant & Bar** (231 Margaret St., 305/294-2640, www.turtlekraals.com, 11am-10pm daily, $9-25) serves typical Keys-style dishes for breakfast, lunch, and dinner, though it definitely specializes in barbecue. Both the quaint indoor dining area and the covered outdoor patio provide the ideal atmosphere for enjoying a barbecue beef brisket platter or one of several other choice selections.

Just steps from Duval Street is the **Island Dogs Bar** (505 Front St., 305/509-7136, www.islanddogsbar.com, 9am-4am daily, $9-18), one of the few late-night kitchens in town. When most restaurants are closed, this casual bar and eatery continues serving food until 3:30am every night. You'll find all-American favorites like chicken wings, hot dogs, burgers, and sandwiches, not to mention an array of alcoholic libations. Both indoor and outdoor seating are available.

★ **Sloppy Joe's Bar** (201 Duval St., 305/294-5717, www.sloppyjoes.com, 9am-4am Mon.-Sat., noon-4am Sun., $4-13)—a spacious, boxy white building that's hard to miss with its redbrick columns and the bar's name in giant black letters—has been a Key West tradition since 1933. Supposedly one of Ernest Hemingway's favorite Key West watering holes, Sloppy Joe's has run an annual Hemingway Look-Alike Contest since 1980. The menu is fairly extensive, with traditional Key West-style cuisine as well as the famous Original Sloppy Joe Sandwich, which features delicious ground beef in a rich tomato sauce with onions, peppers, and spices. The food isn't the only attraction here; various bands keep you entertained day and night.

If you enjoy listening to good music while noshing on good food, then you're in luck: Sloppy Joe's isn't the only game in town. **Willie T's Restaurant & Bar** (525 Duval St., 305/294-7674, www.williets.com, 10am-2am Sun.-Thurs., 10am-4am Fri.-Sat., $11-17) also offers live music, excellent food, and terrific libations. The menu includes 28 different mojitos, from key lime to ginger to espresso. As for the food, Willie T's provides an assortment of tasty dishes, from the goat cheese and avocado salad to the blackened mahimahi with avocado butter and red pepper jam.

Key West Bight has a variety of dining options. **The Commodore Waterfront Restaurant** (700 Front St., 305/294-9191, www.commodorekeywest.com, 5:30pm-10pm daily, $20-38) features traditional Florida Keys-style dishes, including seafood and steaks, in a fine-dining setting along the waterfront. Farther inland, you'll encounter another winning option, **First Flight Island Restaurant & Brewery** (301 Whitehead St., 305/293-8484, www.kellyskeywest.com, 11am-11pm daily, $16-30). Known as the birthplace of Pan American Airlines and now home to the Southernmost Brewery, First Flight Island presents a menu of island and American flavors with such tasty dishes as Caribbean pork with plantains, as well as burgers, fish tacos, steak quesadillas, and a variety of seafood dishes. The food is excellent, but the real draw is the beer, crafted by the on-site brewer. Be sure to try their flagship beer, the Havana Red Ale.

Only a block off Duval, the classy and often noisy ★ **Café Marquesa** (600 Fleming St., 305/292-1919, www.marquesa.com, 5:30pm-10pm daily, $20-49) feels as though it could be in Manhattan. The 50-seat restaurant offers contemporary American cuisine like pan-seared grouper in tomato beurre blanc or seared duck breast with roasted baby carrots. Whether you're a guest of the adjacent Marquesa Hotel or you're just looking for a fantastic place to start the evening, this small hot spot provides an elegant alternative to Key West's casual waterfront eateries.

The **Blue Heaven Restaurant** (729 Thomas St., 305/296-8666, www.blueheaven kw.com, 8am-4pm and 5pm-10:30pm daily, $9-22) has been serving breakfast, lunch, and dinner since 1992. The full menu features everything from pancakes to Caribbean barbecue shrimp. For dessert, try the Banana Heaven, a banana bread with bananas flambéed in rum, served with vanilla ice cream.

Stroll over to the **Flaming Buoy Filet Co.** (1100 Packer St., 305/295-7970, www. theflamingbuoy.com, 5pm-9:30pm daily, $18-48), where you can savor a New York strip steak with garlic and blue cheese butter, or the chicken and waffles. If you'd prefer to stay in your hotel, take advantage of the Flaming Buoy's delivery option.

BREAKFAST AND BRUNCH

The **Banana Cafe** (1215 Duval St., 305/294-7227, www.bananacafekw.com, 7:30am-10pm daily, $7-30) is a popular French-style eatery that specializes in delectable crepes for breakfast, including the tasty veggie and avocado, which features cooked asparagus, roasted beets, onions, spinach, goat cheese, and avocado. The dinner menu is also divine, offering such winners as seafood risotto or a French-style steak and frites.

On the ocean side of Old Town is **Camille's Restaurant** (1202 Simonton St., 305/296-4811, www.camilleskeywest.com, 8am-10pm daily, $6-28), a fun, exotic eatery that features breakfast, lunch, and dinner. Unique dishes include a three-egg omelet made with fresh lobster, or the tender veal with an Asian panko crust. Camille's specializes in an array of eggs Benedicts and also has creative daily specials at breakfast and brunch, which may include French toast drizzled with Godiva chocolate, or cashew waffles with passion fruit and coconut sauce. Despite the delicious food, the prevalent sexual innuendos in Camille's might not make it the most family-friendly establishment in town.

For an organic vegetarian meal, stroll over to **Date and Thyme Organic Café and Market** (829 Fleming St., 305/296-7766, www.helpyourselffoods.com, 8am-6pm daily, $8-14), which features a fairly extensive menu that includes healthy choices such as black bean burgers at lunch or granola with fresh fruit and coconut milk for breakfast. If you're just looking for a quick snack and need a boost, consider ordering a refreshing smoothie, such as the Chocolate Buzz, made with cacao powder, cacao nibs, and banana. This place is seriously delicious and nutritious, and the food does not taste like chicken.

EUROPEAN

Situated in a garden oasis, ★ **Michaels Restaurant** (532 Margaret St., 305/295-1300, www.michaelskeywest.com, 5:30pm-11pm daily, $20-35) provides one of the most romantic dining opportunities in Key West. The menu features a variety of dishes, from macadamia-encrusted mahimahi to shrimp and grits. There's also a wonderful selection of starters, salads, and wines.

★ **Martin's Key West** (917 Duval St., 305/295-0111, www.martinskeywest.com, 4pm-11pm daily, $27-50) is a stylish German fusion restaurant that offers scrumptious dinner options as well as a terrific weekend brunch, featuring specialties such as Wiener schnitzel as well as a great variety of seafood and steaks. Both the menu and the decor superbly blend classical and tropical attributes with a touch of European sophistication. The space is divided into three unique sections: the elegant dining room, the chic lounge, and the sumptuous garden. Unlike many fine-dining restaurants, Martin's welcomes children, which means that busy parents can enjoy delicious food, but couples without kids may find a quiet, romantic meal less than probable.

FRENCH

Popular with couples in a romantic mood, **Café Solé** (1029 Southard St., 305/294-0230, www.cafesole.com, 6pm-10pm Tues.-Sun., $17-25) combines French sauces with locally caught seafood. Fish dominates the menu, which includes such favorites as a grouper

Romesco served with garlic, tomatoes, and a spicy roasted red pepper and hazelnut sauce, and tuna seared in pistachios with wasabi cream and a hoisin garlic sauce.

MEDITERRANEAN

For authentic Italian cuisine, look no farther than **Mangia Mangia Pasta Cafe** (900 Southard St., 305/294-2469, www.mangia-mangia.com, 5:30pm-10pm daily, $10-28). Situated in the heart of Old Town, this corner restaurant channels the ambience of a small Italian village. You'll find an array of fresh pastas with delicious homemade sauces, such as the New Zealand mussels with spaghetti, prepared in a garlic-based marinara sauce and topped with shaved parmesan cheese.

If you have a craving for various Mediterranean flavors, visit the well-regarded **Azur Restaurant** (425 Grinnell St., 305/292-2987, www.azurkeywest.com, 9am-3pm and 5:30pm-10pm daily, $6-36) beside the Eden House. Serving breakfast, lunch, and dinner on the shaded terrace or in the dining room, Azur features such delicious creations as key lime pie-stuffed French toast; charred octopus marinated with garlic, lemon zest, and Italian parsley; and apple and almond tarts with cardamom ice cream.

DESSERT

Dessert connoisseurs will find a lot of key lime pie in the eateries of Key West, but that's not the only treat that the Southernmost City has to offer. Late in the evening, you can head to **Better Than Sex** (926 Simonton St., 305/296-8102, www.betterthansexkeywest. com, 6pm-midnight Thurs.-Tues., $9-13), a bordello-style lounge that prepares unforgettable desserts, such as Peanut Butter Perversion, the Missionary Crisp, and the Three Way, a dessert combining dark chocolate sorbet, vanilla ice cream, and raspberry sorbet. Enhance your visit to this exotic, infinitely romantic spot with a dark chocolate-rimmed glass of merlot.

Accommodations

Key West has by far the greatest assortment of lodging options in the Florida Keys, from intimate bed-and-breakfasts to sprawling resorts—only some of which are listed here. **The Lodging Association of the Florida Keys and Key West** (818 White St., 305/296-4959, www.keyslodging.org) can help you choose the place that's right for you. No matter where you decide to stay, reservations are highly recommended, especially on weekends during the peak season (Dec.-Apr.).

$100-200

Conceived to honor the many literary masters who have lived and worked in Key West, the **Authors Key West Guesthouse** (725 White St., 305/294-7381 or 800/898-6909, www. authorskeywest.com, $120-240 d) comprises a compound of Conch-style houses, suites, and rooms. Typically named after famous writers or artists, the accommodations range from the John James Audubon Room, which contains a queen-size bed and a private bath, to the Ernest Hemingway Cottage, which contains a queen-size bed, a trundle bed, a living room, and a full kitchen. Whether you choose to swim in the heated pool or sip an evening cocktail in the garden, the Authors Guesthouse may be the perfect place to start that novel you've always wanted to write.

The ecofriendly ★ **Eden House** (1015 Fleming St., 305/296-6868 or 800/533-5397, www.edenhouse.com, $185-355 d) offers the ideal setting for a wide variety of visitors, from couples on a romantic getaway to large family reunions. Composed of an art deco-style main building and several renovated Conch-style houses, the Eden House seems a world away from Duval Street, though it lies within walking distance of the busy thoroughfare.

While not technically a spa resort, this picturesque place—which once served as the backdrop for *CrissCross,* a film starring Goldie Hawn—certainly has the ambience of one. The main focus of the complex is the freshwater pool area, where you'll find shady palm trees, gurgling fountains, numerous tables and chairs, a peaceful gazebo, a sundeck, and a six-person hot tub. Although the rooms and suites vary in size and amenities—from a cozy spot beside the pool to a two-level house with a hot tub of its own—all guests can enjoy the hotel's varied features, including a comfortable library area, relaxing hammocks, wireless Internet access, beach towels that can be used off-site, a daily happy hour beside the pool, a 24-hour staff, and complimentary coffee and tea in the lobby. As a bonus, the Eden House will let you store your luggage even after you check out, so that you can savor a few more hours in Key West.

The motto at the **Garden House Key West** (329 Elizabeth St., 305/296-5368 or 800/797-8787, www.the-garden-house.com, $129-229 d) encourages guests to "leave the grumpy attitude at home." That's pretty easy to do when you spot the sumptuous grounds, which include an upper-level sundeck as well as a heated pool with spa jets and a cascading waterfall, all surrounded by lush tropical gardens. There are 10 uniquely decorated rooms—ranging from the Gecko Grotto, with its queen-size bed and private bath, to the Writer's King, with its Tiffany-style reading lamps and king-size bed.

Not far away, in a quiet area of Old Town, the **Rose Lane Villas** (522-524 Rose Ln., 305/292-2170, www.roselanevillas.com, one-bedroom villas $155-299 d, two-bedroom and three-bedroom villas $402-539) are a tempting haven for those who want to stay within walking distance of the action. Though the one-bedroom, two-bedroom, and three-bedroom villas vary in size, each has a full kitchen, cable television, free wireless Internet access, and an allotted parking space. Before hitting the town, take an early-morning swim in the beautiful pool, accented by a stunning mural of lush gardens. After a long day exploring Key West, finish your evening with a cocktail on one of the peaceful porches or balconies and listen to the murmur of Old Town fading into the night.

The **Mango Tree Inn** (603 Southard St., 305/293-1177, www.mangotree-inn.com, $145-400 d), constructed in 1858, is a gorgeous example of Old Town's historical architecture. Inside, the inn offers comfortable rooms, some with two bedrooms and full kitchens. Relax with a swim in the pool, surrounded by lush gardens and tall palm trees, or chat with the resident celebrities: Jade the parrot and Leilani the cockatoo.

A 1920s bordello and gambling spot has become a simple and affordable place to stay in Key West. At the **Angelina Guest House** (302 Angela St., 305/294-4480 or 888/303-4480, www.angelinaguesthouse.com, $99-234 d), "simple" means having no phones or televisions, allowing you to truly escape your daily existence. Only two blocks from the hustle and bustle of Duval, you'll find infinite tranquility in the verdant garden and heated lagoon-style pool. The accommodations vary from having a shared bathroom and full-size beds to having a king-size bed, a private bathroom, and a refrigerator.

The **Truman Hotel** (611 Truman Ave., 305/296-6700 or 866/487-8626, www.trumanhotel.com, $169-199 d), one of the newer boutique hotels in town, prides itself on being "South Beach hip with a Key West flair." With accommodations that range from a standard room to a suite featuring two king-size beds and a living room, each selection contains swanky touches like zebra-striped rugs, leather chairs, and modern lighting. After a long day wandering around Key West you'll relish a dip in the combination pool and spa.

The adults-only **Azul Key West** (907 Truman Ave., 844/307-9775, www.azulkeywest.com, $189-269 d) features 11 rooms and suites surrounding a beautiful freshwater pool. Each room includes a king-size bed, a flat-screen television, and wireless Internet access. The suites range from those possessing shared balconies, with views of the pool or Truman Avenue, to the Aria Suite, situated at treetop level and offering stunning views of the entire area.

The **El Patio Motel** (800 Washington St., 305/296-6531 or 866/533-5189, www.elpatiomotel.com, $96-169 d), a 30-room motel designed in the art deco style, features a lush tropical garden, a serene fountain, and a freshwater swimming pool. Accommodations here range from a basic room with a refrigerator to an apartment with a full kitchen. In addition, limited wireless Internet access is available, depending on your location on the property.

OVER $200

Just two blocks off Duval, **The Paradise Inn** (819 Simonton St., 305/293-8007 or 800/888-9648, www.theparadiseinn.com, $259-500 d) provides elegant suites, ranging from a mini suite with two queen-size beds to the Royal Poinciana Suite, featuring two bedrooms, two bathrooms with Jacuzzi tubs, and a wraparound porch. The grounds, teeming with tropical flora, include a Jacuzzi and a fountain-fed pool.

In the Old Town section of Key West, the historic ★ **Chelsea House Hotel** (709 Truman Ave., 800/845-8859, www.historickeywestinns.com, $150-279 d) consists of two grand Victorian mansions on an acre of lush tropical gardens. Dating from 1888 and 1906, these two former homes now contain a variety of comfortable guest rooms and suites, with amenities like private bathrooms, cable television, and air-conditioning. Other features include a continental breakfast, a heated pool, on-site parking, free wireless Internet access in the courtyard, and proximity to Key West's most popular restaurants and attractions. With advance arrangements, you might also be able to bring your pet during your stay. After all, the Chelsea House was named for a cat (a British shorthair named Chelsea) that lived here in the 1970s.

On the quieter end of Duval, the **La Te Da Hotel** (1125 Duval St., 305/296-6706 or 877/528-3320, www.lateda.com, $225-475 d) features plenty of activities to distract you from the "Duval crawl." Two bars, a restaurant, and a cabaret add to the charm of this beautiful hotel. The accommodations here range from standard rooms with two queen-size beds, a refrigerator, and cable television to luxury rooms featuring extra touches like British colonial-style furnishings and 800-thread-count linens.

La Te Da Hotel

Given that it's also a respected museum, **The Curry Mansion Inn** (511 Caroline St., 305/294-5349 or 800/253-3466, www.currymansion.com, $195-255 d) is surprisingly accommodating to its guests. The historic 22-room property contains various types of lodgings, from standard deluxe bedrooms with king-size beds and private bathrooms to magnificent master suites featuring large balconies, comfortable sitting rooms, and cable television. Situated within the bustling heart of Old Town, the Curry still allows you a modicum of peace and quiet, whether you're dining on a full breakfast, enjoying an afternoon cocktail party, swimming in the on-site pool, or simply relaxing on the grounds.

Northeast of the Curry, the **Cypress House Hotel** (601 Caroline St., 800/549-4430, www.historickeywestinns.com, $189-300 d) offers comfortable bed-and-breakfast accommodations in a historic Conch-style building that was erected in 1888. Guests can expect spacious, high-ceilinged rooms with air-conditioning, ceiling fans, cable television, refrigerators, bathrobes, and complimentary high-speed wireless Internet access. Other amenities on this gated property include lush tropical gardens, a heated swimming pool, bicycle rentals, a continental breakfast buffet (8am-11am daily), and complimentary cocktails (6pm-7pm daily). On-site parking is $10 daily. Note that minimum stay requirements vary seasonally, and guests must be at least 16 years of age.

Two blocks south of the Cypress House, the casually elegant, Conch-style ★ **Marquesa Hotel and Marquesa 4-1-4** (600 Fleming St., 305/292-1919, www.marquesa.com, $255-550 d), originally built in 1884, provide luxuriously furnished hotel rooms and well-equipped private cottages. All chambers are clean, comfortable, and airy, with tropical-style touches like wooden floors, ceiling fans, and vibrant paintings. Despite its proximity to Duval Street, the Marquesa still offers enough of a buffer to make it feel as though you've found a quiet little nook of your own. That's especially true in the well-landscaped pools

and garden areas of the properties, which feature a waterfall, three freshwater pools, and numerous chaise lounges and shaded tables. Other property amenities include wireless Internet access and an upscale restaurant that is open to both guests and nonguests.

Farther south, **The Mermaid & The Alligator Bed & Breakfast** (729 Truman Ave., 305/294-1894 or 800/773-1894, www.kwmermaid.com, $198-368 d) aspires to be "your home in Key West." This beautiful 1904 Victorian-style home offers eight unique rooms in the main house in addition to a Conch-style cottage on the grounds. Amenities include a full complimentary breakfast, a lush garden, and a heated pool featuring built-in benches and whirlpool jets.

The stylish **Santa Maria Suites** (1401 Simonton St., 305/296-5678 or 866/726-8259, www.santamariasuites.com, $300-500 d) feature accommodations with private balconies and terraces. Only a block from the Atlantic Ocean and not far from Duval, this lovely hotel provides an escape from the craziness of Key West. The accommodations vary from standard one-bedroom suites to luxury two-bedroom bi-level suites. Other amenities include flat-screen televisions and a pair of garden-enclosed heated swimming pools.

The magnificent Spanish-style ★ **Casa Marina Resort** (1500 Reynolds St., 305/296-3535 or 888/303-5717, www.casamarinaresort.com, $270-529 d) beckons an upscale clientele with its cream-colored walls, red roof tiles, and arched entryways. Built in 1920 and now part of the Waldorf Astoria Collection, the largest resort in Key West comprises a wide array of elegantly furnished rooms and suites, from the Island Vista, with two double beds, to the Ocean Vista two-bedroom suite, comprising 900 square feet. All accommodations include a mini refrigerator and wireless Internet access. This grand resort also encompasses two enormous pools, a beautiful 1,100-foot beach with hammocks strung between palm trees, the Sun-Sun Beach Bar & Grill, and the Spa al Mare, where you can opt for massages, facials, aromatherapy, or a

Gay-Friendly Lodging

Key West is definitely a gay-friendly destination, as evidenced by Old Town's numerous gay bars and the city's annual events, from Pridefest to the ultimate bacchanal, Fantasy Fest. There are even several inns and resorts that cater to a gay and/or lesbian clientele.

- The 38-room **Island House** (1129 Fleming St., 305/294-6284 or 800/890-6284, www. islandhousekeywest.com, $99-449 d) is Key West's largest resort catering to gay males—and, as some visitors have claimed, the classiest and most outrageous as well. Within this secure, clothing-optional compound, gay men can relax and be themselves in an accepting environ- ment, where a friendly all-male staff is available day and night. Here you'll find a swimming pool, a health club, a poolside bar and café, and a spa that includes a sauna, a five-man shower, and a Jacuzzi. The accommodations are enclosed within four separate buildings, which were formerly a private residence, a boardinghouse, a laundry, and a cigar factory. The uniquely furnished lodgings range in size, though all have comfortable beds, extra-large bath towels, air-conditioning, and cable television.

- In the same block, **Alexander's Guesthouse** (1118 Fleming St., 305/294-9919 or 800/654- 9919, www.alexanderskeywest.com, $145-290 d) welcomes a gay and lesbian clientele to a tranquil, comfortable setting surrounded by lush tropical gardens. While here, you're free to enjoy the relaxing spa and sumptuous pool, which serves as the property's social center. Three levels of sundecks also allow guests a semiprivate setting to catch some rays and forget daily cares. Evenings at Alexander's begin with poolside cocktails, while mornings include a continental breakfast. No matter how you spend the time in between, you'll be sure to find a room that's right for you, as the inn houses a wide selection of airy accommodations, all individually decorated. You'll find 15 comfortable guest rooms, one well-lit suite ($205-305 d) with a private patio, and a gorgeous apartment ($275-410) with wooden floors, a full kitchen, private sundeck, and front porch with a hammock.

- The **New Orleans House** (724 Duval St., 305/293-9800 or 888/293-9893, www. neworleanshousekw.com, rooms and suites $150-344 d, cottages $224-374) in Key West's Old Town is the only gay, all-male guesthouse on Duval. It puts you just steps away from all the action, including the on-site Bourbon St. Pub. Still, if you're looking to relax, you can do just that on the private sundeck overlooking the pool and hot tub. The accommodations here range from standard rooms with a shared bathroom to an intimate cottage, equipped with a full kitchen and a king-size bed. There are eight rooms, one suite, and three cottages here.

For more gay-friendly establishments, consult the **Key West Business Guild** (513 Truman Ave., 305/294-4603 or 800/535-7797, www.gaykeywestfl.com, 10am-5pm Mon.-Sat.).

---

yoga session. In addition, guests can enjoy live entertainment in the on-site Rambler Lounge and savor a delicious steak at the Strip House, located at the hotel's sister property, The Reach Resort.

Situated on seven waterfront acres on the eastern side of the island, the **Key West Marriott Beachside Hotel** (3841 N. Roosevelt Blvd., 305/296-8100 or 800/546- 0885, www.beachsidekeywest.com, $200-420 d) features luxurious accommodations, a lush tropical garden, a waterfront swimming pool, a sandy tanning beach, complete spa services, and immediate access to the on-site Tavern N'

Town Restaurant. In addition, all guests can enjoy complimentary high-speed Internet ser- vice and flat-panel LCD televisions with cable.

Located on the gulf side of the island, ★ **Margaritaville Key West Resort & Marina** (245 Front St., 305/294-4000 or 866/837-4250, www.westinkeywestresort. com, $329-520 d) provides splendid accom- modations just steps from Mallory Square and the Custom House. This spacious resort fea- tures 178 luxurious guest rooms and suites, all of which include specially designed beds and showers, complimentary wireless Internet access, cable television, air-conditioning, and 24-hour room service. Some rooms and suites include flat-screen televisions, vaulted ceilings, Jacuzzi tubs, balconies, patios, and terrific views of the ocean, pool, courtyard, or gardens.

Also within walking distance of Mallory Square, the ★ **Ocean Key Resort & Spa** (0 Duval St., 800/328-9815, www.oceankey. com, $250-500 d) provides fantastic sunset views and easy access to the heart of Key West. The luxurious, tropical-style accommodations range from a 600-square-foot junior suite with a king-size bed, a spacious living room, plasma television, and a private balcony, to a two-bedroom, 1,200-square-foot suite that's purportedly the largest suite on the island. On-site amenities include a heated outdoor pool, water-sports rentals, sailing and fishing trips arranged through the marina, unbelievable body treatments at SpaTerre, and the waterfront Hot Tin Roof restaurant.

Across the street from Ocean Key, the **Pier House Resort and Caribbean Spa** (1 Duval St., 305/296-4600, www.pierhouse. com, $290-400 d) has been serving guests since 1979. Known as the first true resort on the island, Pier House encompasses a private beach, a heated outdoor pool, and a private dock for charter pickups. While here, relax with a massage at the resort's world-class spa, savor a meal at One Duval or the Beach Bar and Grille, or consider deals like the Romance Package, which includes breakfast, champagne, and welcome strawberries.

You'll be hard-pressed to miss the **Southernmost Hotel Collection** (800/354-4455, www.southernmostresorts.com, $245-650 d), set within Duval, United, and Simonton Streets. Each of the four hotels here offers sophisticated accommodations, sometimes with stunning ocean views: the airy 127-room **Southernmost Hotel** (1319 Duval St.), the tropical 123-room **Southernmost Beach Resort** (508 South St.), and the elegant side-by-side Victorian-style boutique hotels, the 11-room **La Mer Hotel** and the 8-room **Dewey House** (508 South St.). No matter which property you choose, you'll be able to relax on the private beach, enjoy a dip in one of the resort's pools, work out in the on-site fitness center, relish a delicious meal at the Southernmost Beach Café, sip cocktails at the Pineapple Bar, or of course, venture onto nearby Duval. Other amenities include free parking, lush gardens, and complimentary wireless Internet access.

Situated near the quieter end of Duval and built as a private residence in 1896, the colorful, Victorian-style ★ **Southernmost House** (1400 Duval St., 305/296-3141, www. southernmosthouse.com, $260-385 d) has seen its share of dignitaries, from Presidents Truman, Nixon, Kennedy, Eisenhower, and Carter to Key West fixtures like Ernest Hemingway. The accommodations here vary from the Southernmost Point Room, with its private balcony overlooking the Atlantic Ocean, to the Royal Suite, one of Key West's most popular suites, featuring a separate sitting parlor, stunning ocean and island views, and a four-poster king-size bed. While staying at the Southernmost House, refresh with a dip in the oceanside heated pool, then relax with a drink at the poolside bar.

The Reach Key West Resort (1435 Simonton St., 305/296-5000, www. reachresort.com, $329-509 d), part of the Waldorf Astoria Collection, is essentially a tropical playground. This boutique hotel provides the same experience you might receive from a Caribbean resort, with access to a spacious private beach, a variety of sailboats and water-sports gear, and a terrific spa (at its sister property, the Casa Marina Resort) to help renew your focus. Finish your evening with an exquisite meal at the on-site Strip House Steakhouse before retiring to your luxury room or suite.

On the Atlantic Ocean, the **Coconut Beach Resort** (1500 Alberta St., 305/294-0057 or 800/835-0055, www. coconutbeachresort.com, studios $200-315 d, suites $310-550) contains a variety of accommodations, from studios to two-bedroom suites. In addition, the property features an open-deck pool and Jacuzzi, plus a small sandy beach.

Farther inland, the adults-only **Olivia by Duval** (511 Olivia St., 305/296-4275 or 800/880-4275, www.oliviabyduval.com, $144-300 d) offers uniquely decorated rooms and suites, some of which include kitchenettes. Operated by Old Town Suites, this charming inn provides the perfect location for those hoping to experience the action of Duval while still enjoying the serenity of a private guesthouse. Amenities include cable television, air-conditioning, and a clothing-optional pool. For even more solitude, Old Town Suites also operates two lovely cottages on Center and Petronia Streets.

CAMPING

Although most people visiting Key West choose to stay in one of the city's varied inns, hotels, or resorts, campers will also find a few options on nearby Stock Island. South of the Key West Golf Club, **Boyd's Key West Campground** (6401 Maloney Ave., Stock Island, 305/294-1465, www.boydscampground.com, $55-130 daily) offers tent sites as well as RV spaces, many of which are equipped with water service, 30/50-amp electricity, sewer access, and cable television. Both inland and waterfront spots are available. In addition, the property features a heated swimming pool, a lounging beach, free wireless Internet access, and numerous planned activities, including craft and yoga

classes, potluck dinners, movie nights, line dancing, and casino cruises.

The intimate **El Mar RV Resort** (6700 Maloney Ave., Stock Island, 305/294-0857, $80-115 daily) caters to RV enthusiasts only. No tents, pop-ups, or truck campers are allowed. Situated on the ocean, the property offers 10 spaces, half of which have waterfront views. All of the lengthy gravel sites in this park feature patios and full hookups, including 30/50-amp electricity.

Closer to the Overseas Highway and not far from the Hurricane Hole Marina, the family-operated **Leo's Campground** (5236 Suncrest Rd., Stock Island, 305/296-5260, www.leoscampground.com, $54-98 daily) welcomes tent and RV campers alike. Pets, however, are only allowed in the RV portion of the park, at a daily fee of $1 per pet. All rates are based on two people. For more than two people, there is a charge of $8 per person per day. Tent sites are limited to four people; RV sites are limited to 6 people per site. There is also a charge of $8 per day for an additional trailer. The tent sites, most of which have barbecue grills and picnic tables, are situated along a small, quiet lake, surrounded by mangroves, while the RV spaces feature picnic tables, 70-channel cable television, and full hookups with 30/50-amp electricity. Other on-site amenities include a barbecue area for RV campers, a laundry facility, and a bathhouse with hot showers. Monthly rates for RV campers ($1,500-2,620) are also available.

Information and Services

INFORMATION
Tourism and Government Offices

For maps and other information about Key West, plus assistance with hotel and tour reservations, call or visit the website of the **Key West Visitors Center** (855/539-9378, www.keywestvisitorscenter.com) or the **Key West Information Center** (888/222-5590, www.

keywestinfo.com), or contact the **Key West Chamber of Commerce** (510 Greene St., 1st Fl., 305/294-2587, www.keywestchamber.org, 8am-5:30pm daily). In addition, you can consult the **Key West Attractions Association (KWAA)** (www.keywestattractions.org), **Key West's Finest** (www.keywestfinest.com), or the **Monroe County Tourist Development Council** (1201 White St.,

Ste. 102, 305/296-1552 or 800/352-5397, www. fla-keys.com, 8am-5pm Mon.-Fri.). You can even save money on sightseeing adventures through online companies like **Trusted Tours and Attractions** (800/844-7601, www. trustedtours.com).

For government-related issues, contact the **City of Key West** (525 Angela St., 305/809-3700, www.keywestcity.com, 8am-5pm Mon.-Fri.) or the **Monroe County offices** (1100 Simonton St., 305/292-4537, www. monroecounty-fl.gov, 8am-5pm Mon.-Fri.).

Media

For local news, consult the daily *The Key West Citizen* (www.keysnews.com) or **The Weekly Newspapers** (www.keysweekly. com). The daily *Miami Herald* (www. miamiherald.com) is also available throughout the Keys.

In Key West, you'll have access to several radio stations, including the popular **US-1 Radio** (104.1 FM, www.us1radio.com), which offers local news, including up-to-the-minute weather information during hurricane season. In addition, most hotels offer access to the major television stations in the Miami-Fort Lauderdale market.

SERVICES
Money

For banking needs, stop by **Capital Bank** (330 Whitehall St., 305/294-6330 or 800/639-5111, www.capitalbank-us.com, 9am-4pm Mon.-Thurs., 9am-6pm Fri., 9am-1pm Sat., extended drive-through hours). Another option is the **First State Bank of the Florida Keys** (www.keysbank.com), which offers five locations in the Key West area, from Stock Island (5450 MacDonald Ave., 305/296-8535, 8am-5pm Mon.-Thurs., 8am-6pm Fri., extended drive-through hours) to Old Town (444 Whitehead St., 305/296-8535, 9am-4pm Mon.-Thurs., 9am-6pm Fri.).

Mail

For shipping, faxing, copying, and other business-related services, visit **The UPS Store** (2900 N. Roosevelt Blvd., Ste. 1107, 305/292-4177, www.theupsstorelocal.com, 7:30am-6pm Mon.-Fri., 8am-2pm Sat.). You can also package and ship items at the two local **post offices** (800/275-8777, www.usps. com): one on the eastern end of the island (2764 N. Roosevelt Blvd., 305/296-7327, 9am-5pm Mon.-Fri., 9am-noon Sat.) and one in Old Town (400 Whitehead St., 305/294-9539, 8:30am-5pm Mon.-Fri., 9:30am-noon Sat.).

Groceries and Supplies

For groceries, baked goods, and other supplies, head to the nearest **Winn-Dixie** (2778 N. Roosevelt Blvd., 305/294-0491, www. winndixie.com, 24 hours daily), which has an on-site pharmacy (305/294-0658, 8am-8pm Mon.-Fri., 9am-5pm Sat., 10am-5pm Sun.). In Key West, you'll also find a **Publix** (3316 N. Roosevelt Blvd., 305/296-2225, www. publix.com, 7am-11pm daily, 7am-10pm Sun.), which includes an on-site pharmacy (305/296-3225, 9am-9pm Mon.-Fri., 9am-7pm Sat., 11am-6pm Sun.). The area also has a **CVS/pharmacy** (530 Truman Ave., 305/294-2576, www.cvs.com, 24 hours daily), which offers limited supplies as well as an on-site pharmacy (9am-9pm Mon.-Fri., 9am-8pm Sat., 10am-6pm Sun.).

Laundry

There are several coin-operated laundries in the area, including **Hilltop Laundry** (629 Eaton St., 8am-10pm daily) and the **Habana Plaza Coin Laundry** (3124 Flagler Ave., 8am-10pm daily).

Internet Access

You can access high-speed wireless Internet service at any number of hotels and resorts in the Key West area. In addition, there are several charming coffee shops that are favorites for visitors, including the **Coffee Plantation** (713 Caroline St., 305/295-9808, www.coffeeplantationkeywest.com, 7am-6pm Mon.-Sat., 8am-3pm Sun.). You'll also find useful services, including Internet access, at the **Monroe County May Hill Russell Library** (700 Fleming St., 305/292-3595, www.keyslibraries.org, 9:30am-6pm Mon-Tues. and Thurs.-Fri., 9:30am-8pm Wed., 10am-6pm Sat.).

Emergency Services

In case of an emergency that requires police, fire, or ambulance services, dial **911** from any cell or public phone. For nonemergency assistance, contact the **Monroe County Sheriff's Office** (5525 College Rd., 305/292-7000, www.keysso.net, 8am-5pm Mon.-Fri.). For medical assistance, consult the **Lower Keys Medical Center** (5900 College Rd., Stock Island, 305/294-5531, www.lkmc.com). Foreign visitors seeking help with directions, medical concerns, business issues, law enforcement needs, or other problems can receive **multilingual tourist assistance** (800/771-5397) 24 hours daily.

Transportation

GETTING THERE

Air

Travelers can reach Key West directly by flying into the **Key West International Airport (EYW)** (3491 S. Roosevelt Blvd., 305/809-5200 or 305/296-5439, www.keywestinternationalairport.com). Major carriers include **American Airlines** (800/433-7300, www.aa.com), **Delta** (800/221-1212, www.delta.com), **Silver** (801/401-9100, www.silverairways.com), and **United** (800/864-8331, www.united.com).

Other area airports include the **Florida Keys Marathon Airport (MTH)** (MM 52, 9400 Overseas Hwy., Marathon, 305/289-6060), the **Fort Lauderdale-Hollywood International Airport (FLL)** (100 Terminal Dr., Fort Lauderdale, 866/435-9355, www.broward.org/airport), and the **Miami International Airport (MIA)** (2100 NW 42nd Ave., Miami, 305/876-7000 or 800/825-5642, www.miami-airport.com). From each airport, you can rent a vehicle from such agencies as **Avis** (800/331-1212, www.avis.com), **Budget** (800/527-0700, www.budget.com), **Enterprise** (800/325-8007, www.enterprise.com), **Hertz** (800/654-3131, www.hertz.com), or **Thrifty** (800/367-2277, www.thrifty.com) in order to reach your hotel or primary destination in Key West.

Bus

To reach Key West using the regional bus system, you can take the **Miami-Dade County Metrobus** (305/891-3131, www.miamidade.gov/transit), which operates the **301 Dade-Monroe Express** between Florida City and Marathon (5:15am-8:40pm daily). From Marathon, you can then use the **Lower Keys Shuttle,** operated by the **Key West Department of Transportation (KWDoT)** (305/600-1455, www.kwtransit.com, $2-4 per ride, $8-25 weekly, $25-75 monthly), to complete your journey. The shuttle runs from Marathon to Key West between 5:30am and 11:15pm daily. Other stops include Bahia Honda State Park, Big Pine Key, and several other Lower Keys. Reduced fares may apply for students under 22 years old, senior citizens over 59 years old, military personnel, and disabled individuals.

Greyhound (800/231-2222, www.greyhound.com) offers bus service to the **Key West Greyhound Station** (3535 S. Roosevelt Blvd., 305/296-9072, 7:30am-11am and 3pm-6pm daily) near the Key West International Airport.

Train

Amtrak (800/872-7245, www.amtrak.com) only provides train service as far south as

Miami, from where you can rent a car or hop a shuttle to reach the Florida Keys.

Transport from Airports and Stations

If you arrive in the Fort Lauderdale-Miami area by plane, bus, or train—or Key West by plane or bus—you can either rent a car or hire a shuttle service to reach your destination in the Key West area. Companies include **Keys Shuttle** (305/289-9997 or 888/765-9997, www.keysshuttle.com, $90-100 per shared ride, $400-450 for exclusive service), which provides service from the Miami and Fort Lauderdale airports.

Car

To reach Key West from Miami, head south on U.S. 1 (Overseas Hwy.), drive through the Upper, Middle, and Lower Keys—roughly 110 miles from the mainland—and continue toward your destination, likely west of Mile Marker 5. If you're headed from the Everglades via I-75 (Everglades Pkwy.), drive south on U.S. 27, veer right onto SR-997 (Krome Ave.), and follow the signs to U.S. 1. From U.S. 41 (Tamiami Trl.) in the Everglades, head south on SR-997 and continue toward U.S. 1. If you arrive during the peak season (Dec.-Apr.), be sure to call **511** for an up-to-the-minute traffic report.

Boat

You can also reach Key West by boat. The **Key West Express** (888/539-2628, www.keywestexpress.net, $125-155 adults, $125-145 seniors 62 and over, $92 juniors age 5-12, $62 children under 5) offers a fleet of comfortable jet-powered passenger ferries that provide year-round daily service from Fort Myers Beach to Key West—a ride that typically takes 3.5 hours. Passengers can opt for one-way travel, same-day return, or different-day return and, with certain restrictions, may be allowed to bring pets and bicycles on board. All passengers 18 years of age and older must present valid identification in order to ride.

GETTING AROUND

Car

If you're not on foot or a bicycle, the third-best way to travel through Key West is by car or motorcycle—both of which offer easy access to U.S. 1 as well as the residential roads throughout this compact city. The smaller the vehicle, the easier it will be to find street parking when necessary; just remember to watch for parking signs and feed any required meters. Note, too, that Key West offers a few public parking areas in Old Town, including the **Park N' Ride Old Town Garage** (305/809-3910, www.cityofkeywest-fl.gov, $4 hourly, $32 daily) at the corner of Grinnell and Caroline Streets, not far from the Historic Seaport. The garage provides covered overnight parking and convenient access to tourist attractions, and as a bonus, parking here allows you free, same-day access to the city's public transportation.

Taxi

Taxicab companies can also help you get around Key West. These include **Perfect Pedicab** (305/292-0077, www.perfectpedicabkw.com, 9am-4am daily, $1.50 per minute), offering three-wheeled open-air human-operated vehicles, and **Five 6's** (305/296-6666, www.keywesttaxi.com, $2.95 for first 0.2 mile, $0.70 per each additional 0.2 mile), which provides 24-hour service with its pink ecofriendly hybrids that you'll spot seemingly everywhere.

Public Transit and Tours

Key West has public transit options in addition to taxicabs, pedicabs, and vehicle rentals. Upon arriving in town, you might want to opt for the **Conch Tour Train** (305/294-5161 or 888/916-8687, www.conchtourtrain.com, 9am-4:30pm daily, $31.45 adults, $15.75 children 4-12, free for children under 4) or the **Old Town Trolley Tour** (305/296-6688 or 888/910-8687, www.trolleytours.com, 9am-4:30pm daily, $41.95 adults, $15.75 children 4-12, free for children under 4), both of which offer guided excursions through the city—an ideal way to get an overview of all available attractions before exploring them in more depth. The **Key West Department of Transportation (KWDoT)** (305/600-1455, www.kwtransit.com, $2-4 per ride, $4-8 daily, $8-25 weekly, $25-75 monthly) provides bus service around Key West and the Lower Keys between 5am and 11pm daily.

Bicycle

Key West is a lovely, welcoming place to traverse by bicycle, whether you're an experienced rider or a novice. Just remember that you'll have to share the streets with cars and other vehicles, so take care while you tour the neighborhoods.

Bicycles can be rented from several different outfitters, including **Eaton Bikes** (830 Eaton St., 305/294-8188, www.eatonbikes. com, 8am-6pm Mon.-Sat., 8am-noon Sun., $12-50 daily, $55-150 weekly), which offers a range of bicycles from trikes to mountain bikes to tandems, plus free delivery throughout Key West. **The Bike Shop of Key West** (1110 Truman Ave., 305/294-1073, www. thebikeshopkeywest.com, 9am-6pm Mon.-Sat., 10am-4pm Sun.), $12 daily, $60 weekly, $180 monthly), the oldest in town, provides a wide array of bicycles, plus accessories, bicycle sales, and a service/repair department. All rentals include locks, lights, baskets, and wide, soft seats.

Another helpful source is **JV Rent All** (539 Greene St., 305/293-8883, www. golfcartrentalskeywest.com, 8am-5pm daily, $10 daily, $50 weekly), which also rents scooters ($35-75 daily), and golf carts ($90-159 per four hours, $169-259 daily).

A&M Rentals (305/294-4556, www. amscooterskeywest.com, 8am-8pm daily, $10-20 daily) has two spots from which to rent kid-size bicycles, cruisers, and tandems: 523 Truman Avenue and 513 South Street. You can also rent one- and two-seater scooters ($35-60 daily), and multiseat electric cars ($139-200 daily)—all popular ways to get around town. Free customer pickup and drop-off are available. Note that such outfitters typically require that all electric-car operators possess a valid driver's license and be at least 21 or 22 years old.

Boat

You can also experience Key West by boat. Having your own vessel makes navigating these waters even easier, and you'll find no shortage of marinas in the area. If you'd like to rent a boat, stop by **Sunset Watersports Key West** (Hurricane Hole Marina, 5130 Overseas Hwy., Stock Island, 305/294-1500, www.sunsetwatersports.com, 9am-6pm daily), which offers a range of vessels, from 16- to 22-foot fishing boats ($300-350 per half day, $375-425 daily) to 22- and 26-foot pontoons ($400-475 per half day, $475-550 daily). Boats come equipped with GPS, fish and depth finders, live bait wells, and bimini tops.

Also at the Hurricane Hole Marina is **Lazy Dog** (305/295-9898, www.lazydog.com), which offers two-hour guided kayak tours ($50 pp) in addition to kayak rentals ($25 per half day, $45 daily).

Dry Tortugas National Park

Roughly 68 miles west of Key West lies a cluster of seven islands that are collectively known as the Dry Tortugas. Originally named Las Tortugas (The Turtles) by Spanish explorers, the coral-and-sand islands eventually became "Dry Tortugas" on mariners' navigational charts to indicate the lack of freshwater here. Part of the 220-mile-long Florida Keys archipelago, these islands and their surrounding shoals and waters comprise the 64,657-acre **Dry Tortugas National Park** (open 24 hours daily, $15, under 16 free), established in 1992 to preserve this unique area and now one of the most remote parks in the National Park System. In addition, Dry Tortugas has been listed in the National Register of Historic Places.

Celebrated for its diverse wildlife, remarkable coral reefs, enthralling shipwrecks, and pirate legends and military past, Dry Tortugas is a must-see destination, the kind of place that really makes you feel as though you're a world away from the Florida mainland. If you have the time, you should board a ferry or come by private boat to this unique destination—popular with sunbathers, swimmers, snorkelers, kayakers, anglers, bird-watchers, photographers, and overnight campers.

SIGHTS

While visiting the Dry Tortugas, you should take a guided or self-guided tour of **Fort Jefferson** (open sunrise-sunset), the well-preserved Civil War fort on Garden Key, the centerpiece of these remote islands. Nicknamed the "American Gibraltar," the country's largest 19th-century coastal fort was established in 1846 in order to control navigation in the Gulf of Mexico, though its construction was never quite completed. During and after the war, it served as a remote, Union-affiliated military prison for captured deserters. From 1865 to 1869 it was even home to Dr. Samuel Mudd, who was incarcerated here

for setting the broken leg of assassin John Wilkes Booth, an act that authorities determined made him complicit in the assassination of President Abraham Lincoln. By the 1880s the U.S. Army had abandoned the facility, which became a wildlife refuge in 1908 and a national monument in 1935. An interesting tidbit is that in 1847 seven enslaved African Americans fled Garden Key in a dramatic self-emancipation attempt. Although they were ultimately caught, their daring effort has been officially acknowledged by the National Underground Railroad Network to Freedom Program.

Within the fortified walls of this historic citadel are officers' quarters, soldiers' barracks, a cistern, magazines, and cannons. The visitors center and park headquarters are also located here. From November to May, parts of Fort Jefferson are closed to the public while mason crews work on much-needed preservation projects. Such temporary closures are not in effect during the hurricane season (June-Nov.), which might only add to the logistical difficulties of working in this remote marine environment. Note that pets, food, and drinks are not allowed inside the fort. In addition, service and residential areas are closed to the public.

While visiting Fort Jefferson, be sure to take a look at the **Fort Jefferson Harbor Light,** northeast of the boat dock. Established in 1825 and still operational today, the lighthouse, whose present tower was erected in 1876, is a favorite among photographers. In addition, Loggerhead Key, which once housed the Carnegie Institute's Laboratory of Marine Ecology and is only accessible by private boat or charter, features the **Loggerhead Light,** also established in 1825, with an existing tower that was erected in 1858. Just remember that all buildings and structures on Loggerhead Key are closed to visitors, unless accompanied by a park ranger.

There are two visitors centers for Dry Tortugas National Park. At the **Dry Tortugas Visitor Center** (located inside the fort), you can watch a historical movie about the fort and shop for souvenirs. The **Florida Keys Eco Discovery Center** (35 E. Quay Rd., Key West, 305/809-4750, www.floridakeys.noaa. gov, 9am-4pm Tues.-Sat., free) features exhibits on the wildlife and environment of the Dry Tortugas area.

SPORTS AND RECREATION

Although visiting Dry Tortugas National Park is only possible by ferry or private boat, the isolated **Fort Jefferson Beach** is well worth the trip. Besides its proximity to historic Fort Jefferson, it's a terrific locale for swimming, snorkeling, kayaking, fishing, and bird-watching. Certain activities are prohibited, such as spearfishing, lobstering, using personal watercraft, collecting artifacts and marine life, or bartering with commercial fishermen for seafood. Federal law also prohibits firearms in certain facilities in Dry Tortugas National Park; those places are marked with signs at all public entrances.

Bird-Watching and Wildlife-Viewing

Many people come to Garden Key for the bird-watching opportunities, which are truly excellent. More than 200 varieties are spotted annually, especially from March through September, when nearby Bush Key serves as the nesting grounds for migratory birds. During April and May, over 85,000 brown noddies and sooty terns nest on Bush Key. In the spring you might spot herons, raptors, and shorebirds, and in summertime you might observe frigatebirds and mourning doves. The fall and winter months bring such species as hawks, merlins, peregrine falcons, gulls, terns, American kestrels, and belted kingfishers. Other possible sightings include orioles, warblers, cormorants, masked boobies, black noddies, mangrove cuckoos, and white-crowned pigeons. Be sure to pick up an official bird checklist from the visitors center in Fort Jefferson, or consult the **Audubon Society of Florida** (Keys Environmental Restoration Trust, 11399 Overseas Hwy., Ste. 4E, Marathon, 305/289-9988, www.audubon. org) for more information.

While you can spot many bird species during a short visit to Garden or Loggerhead Keys, you might have a better experience on board a bird-watching charter—though admittedly a pricier one as well. **Sea-Clusive Charters** (1107 Key Plaza, Ste. 315, Key West, 305/744-9928, www.seaclusive.com, $2,800-3,475 per trip) features such tailored excursions, led by professional bird guide Larry Manfredi (www.southfloridabirding.com). While on board, you might also spot other wildlife, such as sharks, dolphins, and, if you're lucky, gigantic sea turtles. These cruises can accommodate a minimum of 8 passengers and a maximum of 11.

Boating and Kayaking

Garden Key and Loggerhead Key are both accessible by private boat. The dock on Loggerhead Key is only open to government vessels, but private vessels are allowed to land south of the boathouse. Docking on Garden Key can also be problematic, as the public dock is often occupied by ferries and supply boats. Given that you can only tie up to the dock for two-hour increments between sunrise and 10am and then again between 3pm and sunset, your best bet is to anchor in the harbor and use a dinghy to reach the island, which offers a dinghy beach for that exact purpose. Overnight anchoring between sunset and sunrise is only allowed in the designated anchorage area, which comprises the sand and rubble bottom within one nautical mile of the Fort Jefferson Harbor Light.

All boaters should have self-sufficient, fully equipped vessels. Necessary items include life jackets, nautical charts, a tool kit with spare parts, plenty of fuel and drinking water, and a VHF radio to monitor weather forecasts. In addition, all vessels must conform to U.S. Coast Guard regulations.

Kayaking can also be a wonderful way to experience the islands, though you'll need to take care. The currents here can be very strong, making the area suitable for experienced sea kayakers only. If you do choose to tote kayaks along for the ride, make sure to bring a life vest, an anchor, a bailer, extra paddles, drinking water, and waterproof bags for gear. Other necessary safety equipment includes flares, bow and stern lines, a sound-producing device, a 360-degree light for operating at night, and the NOAA nautical chart #11438.

Fishing

Anglers are welcome to fish from the public dock on Garden Key, as well as the beach west of the dock. With the establishment of the 46-square-mile Research Natural Area (RNA), however, fishing from a boat is only permitted within a one-mile radius of Garden Key. Nevertheless, several local fishing charters operate multiday trips to this area. With proper permits and licenses, these guides are allowed to fish in and around Dry Tortugas National Park. **Andy Griffiths Charters** (40 Key Haven Rd., Key West, 305/296-2639, www.fishandy.com) offers three-day, two-night excursions ($3,800-4,600) to the Dry Tortugas for up to six anglers. These trips typically last from 10am on Friday to 2pm on Sunday, or from noon on Monday to 2pm on Wednesday.

Dream Catcher Charters (5555 College Rd., Stock Island, 888/362-3474, www.chartersofkeywest.com) offers 10-hour trips ($1,600) for up to six passengers as well as overnight excursions (trip times and rates vary). Of course, if you choose instead to fish on your own, remember that Florida state laws, regulations, and licensing requirements apply in these waters. Commercial fishing, spearfishing, taking fish by sling or speargun, dragging a net, casting near sea turtles, collecting shells and artifacts, and possessing

lobster, conch, or ornamental tropical fish are not allowed within the boundaries of Dry Tortugas National Park.

Diving and Snorkeling

With numerous patch reefs and shipwrecks, including the 19th-century Bird Key Wreck and early-20th-century Windjammer Wreck, within the boundaries of Dry Tortugas National Park, it's no wonder that snorkelers, scuba divers, and underwater photographers favor this area. Whether you arrive on Garden Key by ferry or private boat, you'll be able to snorkel directly off the beach in warm, shallow waters that boast a cornucopia of kaleidoscopic tropical fish, conch shells, lobster and sponges, sea fans and sea anemones, staghorn coral clusters, and occasional sea turtles.

For access to even more snorkeling and scuba-diving sites around the Dry Tortugas—part of Florida Keys National Marine Sanctuary—consult **Sea-Clusive Charters** (1107 Key Plaza, Ste. 315, Key West, 305/744-9928, www.seaclusive.com, $2,800-3,475 per trip), which offers multiday diving excursions for 6-11 passengers. With Sea-Clusive, divers will be able to explore the Windjammer wreck site as well as the overhangs, caves, and swim-throughs of these incredible coral reefs, which offer water depths of 45 to 80 feet. Here you'll spot tropical fish, resident jewfish, black grouper, coral formations, and sponges.

If you choose to snorkel or dive on your own, you should be aware of certain offshore protection zones that are closed to the public. In addition, you need to prepare for potentially strong gulf currents. Remember, too, that dive flags are required beyond designated swimming channels at all times.

CAMPING

Since Dry Tortugas National Park has no public lodging, camping is the only option for those who hope to stay overnight on Garden Key. Just a short southwesterly walk from the public dock lies a primitive 10-site campground. Although the group site, which must be reserved in advance, can accommodate

1: frigate birds over Fort Jefferson **2:** aerial view of Dry Tortugas National Park

10-40 people, most of the sites are available on a first-come, first-served basis and will suit up to six people and three tents. The campground is a self-service fee area, charging a nightly fee of $15 per camping site (not including the $15 per person entrance fee), and the sites offer little more than picnic tables and barbecue grills.

Grocery stores, fresh water, ice, and fuel are unavailable here, so plan accordingly. No trash receptacles are present either, which means that all visitors, boaters, and campers must pack out any and all trash. Unless you plan to anchor a private boat in the harbor near Garden Key, you'll probably be reaching the park by a commercial ferry. If so, be aware that most transportation companies have cargo weight restrictions: On the *Yankee Freedom III*, campers are limited to 60 pounds of gear plus water. The ferry does not allow the transport of fuels like propane or lighter fluid, so campers are encouraged to use self-starting charcoal.

In order to make your camping trip as smooth as possible, there are several items you should be sure to pack, including picture identification, a fishing license, camping regulations, and the current weather forecast. To make your stay more comfortable, bring along a tent, a sleeping bag and pad, rain gear, clothing for warm and cold weather, a wide-brimmed hat, and plenty of food, water, and ice. Cooking equipment should include a portable stove or grill, fuel of some kind, waterproof matches and a lighter, cooking utensils, biodegradable soap, and trash bags. Personal gear, such as medications, a first-aid kit, knife, flashlight and spare batteries, sunglasses, sunscreen, and insect repellent, will also prove to be helpful. Although you can bring pets with you, they are only allowed on Garden Key (outside Fort Jefferson), and must be leashed and well behaved at all times. Owners must remove all pet waste from the park. Campers are only allowed to stay for four days and three nights at a time.

INFORMATION

Technically, Dry Tortugas National Park is open all year, though restrictions are in effect on certain islands. Garden Key, which contains Fort Jefferson, is surely the most visited island in the park. Although the island itself is open year-round, Fort Jefferson is only open during daylight hours. Loggerhead is also open year-round during daylight hours. Middle and East Keys, however, are closed from April to mid-October during turtle nesting season, while Bush, Hospital, and Long Keys are closed all year, meaning that visitors should remain 100 feet offshore of these particular islands.

To visit the park, anyone 16 years of age or older must pay an entrance fee of $15. The pass, which is valid for seven days, is typically collected by commercial transportation operators; otherwise, you'll have to remit payment at the Dry Tortugas Visitor Center. Annual passes, which can be purchased or procured at the **Florida Keys Eco-Discovery Center (FKEDC)** (35 E. Quay Rd., Key West, 305/809-4750, www.floridakeys.noaa.gov, 9am-4pm Tues.-Sat., free) with qualifying documentation, are all honored in Dry Tortugas. These include the National Parks and Federal Recreational Annual Pass ($80) and the lifetime versions for senior citizens 62 years of age and older ($80), disabled visitors (free), volunteers (free), and the fourth-grade pass that is available to all fourth-grade students (free)—plus the now-discontinued Golden Eagle, Golden Age, and Golden Access Passports. All such passes are only eligible to legal U.S. citizens and permanent residents.

The 46-square-mile Research Natural Area (RNA)—an ecological preserve that encompasses a little less than half of the park and protects species affected by overfishing and loss of habitat—may eventually limit your fishing access to certain areas and require permits in other areas. For more information about Dry Tortugas National Park, including details about the RNA, contact the **park headquarters** (305/242-7700, www.nps.gov/drto, 8:30am-4:30pm Mon.-Fri.) or the Florida Keys Eco-Discovery Center. You can also consult websites like www.drytortugas.com. In addition, you can download park maps and regulations, plus information about camping, bird-watching, island history, and the RNA, from the official National Park Service website. Books are also helpful resources, such as Thomas Reid's *America's Fortress: A History of Fort Jefferson, Dry Tortugas, Florida* (Gainesville: University Press of Florida, 2006).

TRANSPORTATION

Dry Tortugas National Park, which lies approximately 68 miles west of Key West, is only accessible by ferry or private boat—all of which can be boarded in Key West. To reach Garden Key by ferry, you can schedule a day trip on the 100-foot catamaran **Yankee Freedom III** (240 Margaret St., 305/294-7009 or 800/634-0939, www.drytortugas.com, 8am-5:30pm daily, $180 adults, $170 students, military personnel, and seniors 62 and over, $125 children 4-16, free for children under 4), which is docked in the Historic Seaport at Key West Bight. Reservations are recommended for the ferry, which will charge an additional park entrance fee of $15 per person aged 16 or over. Cancellations must be made the day before your scheduled trip, and all passengers should arrive no later than 7:30am on the day of departure. In addition to day trips, the ferry offers overnight excursions, for which

reservations are absolutely required. The *Yankee Freedom III* charges $200 for adult campers and $145 for children; however, such rates do not include the requisite park entrance and camping fees.

For the ferry, which has comfortable air-conditioned cabins, the day trip from Key West begins at 8am. While you journey past the Marquesas, the famous *Atocha* shipwreck, and various marinelife, you'll be treated to a complimentary continental breakfast. Once you arrive on Garden Key, you can opt for a 45-minute narrated tour of Fort Jefferson with one of the ferries' knowledgeable guides, after which you can relax on the pristine beach, go for a swim, have a picnic, or take a bird-watching nature stroll. In addition, you'll have free use of the onboard snorkeling equipment. It's recommended that you bring a swimsuit and towel, sun protection, a camera and batteries, binoculars, sunglasses, water shoes, a jacket, and a hat. A reliable watch is also necessary, as the ferry will leave around 3pm in order to reach Key West by late afternoon.

If you choose to travel to Garden Key by private vessel, bear in mind the docking restrictions, which limit your use of the public dock between the hours of sunrise and 10am, and between 3pm and sunset. On Loggerhead Key, which is only accessible by private boat or charter, you can only land your vessel south of the dock and boathouse. Once on the island, you can explore the developed trails and shoreline, but remember that the dock and all structures are closed to the public.

Background

The Landscape

GEOGRAPHY

Between 25 million and 70 million years ago, dramatic fluctuations in the sea level gradually formed the limestone upon which southern Florida now exists. Beyond the beaches and urban sprawl of Miami lies a fascinating region for nature lovers, most notably in the Everglades and the Florida Keys.

Shaped by water and fire, the Everglades are essentially **subtropical wetlands,** part of a massive watershed in southern Florida. Termed the "river of grass" by writer Marjory Stoneman Douglas in the late

Average Temperatures

The table below shows average high/low temperatures in degrees Fahrenheit.

Month	Miami	Key West
January	74/61	74/64
February	75/63	76/66
March	76/65	78/68
April	79/69	81/72
May	83/74	85/76
June	87/77	88/79
July	88/78	89/80
August	89/79	90/80
September	87/78	88/79
October	84/75	85/76
November	79/70	80/72
December	76/64	76/67

1940s, the Everglades comprise a complex system of interdependent ecosystems, including sawgrass marshes, cypress swamps, mangrove forests, tropical hardwood hammocks, pine rocklands, coastal prairies, tidal mudflats, sloughs and estuaries, and the marine environment of Florida Bay.

The Florida Keys, meanwhile, are essentially a series of low offshore islands composed of sand and coral. While the Upper and Middle Keys are principally made of Key Largo limestone, once the peaks of living coral forests, the Lower Keys are basically an enormous shoal, made of sand, compacted oolite, and Key Largo limestone and traversed by many channels—hence, the reason why the northernmost islands tend to be larger and longer, while the Lower Keys are smaller and more numerous. In the Keys, you'll also find hardwood hammocks, mangrove swamps, and beaches, though many visitors come to experience the ecosystems that can't be seen above the water. Along the Atlantic side of the 220-mile-long Florida Keys archipelago, which technically stretches from Key Biscayne to the Dry Tortugas, lies a series of living

coral reefs. Filled with tropical fish and varied coral formations, they constitute the third-largest coral reef system in the world—and the only one of its kind in the continental United States. While snorkelers and scuba divers enjoy exploring these offshore coral reefs, anglers appreciate the patch reefs closer to the coast, which are usually teeming with worthy game fish.

CLIMATE

Positioned between the Gulf of Mexico, Florida Bay, and the Atlantic Ocean, southern Florida tends toward a subtropical climate. Typically, the fall, winter, and spring months, from November to April, are mild and pleasant, with temperatures usually ranging from 61°F to 82°F. On occasion, temperatures can reach over 90°F, and cold fronts, though rare, are indeed possible. Although such cold snaps don't normally last too long, they can create near-freezing conditions, sometimes resulting in the loss of tropical fish, sea turtles, and manatees. Nevertheless, while frost is possible in the Everglades, there is no known record of such an occurrence in Key West.

Summers, meanwhile, are hot and humid, with temperatures usually ranging from 74°F to 90°F and humidity well over 90 percent. Unless you're an avid angler, snorkeler, or scuba diver, you might want to avoid the unbearable summer months, when mosquitoes are abundant and afternoon thunderstorms are common. Although prevailing easterly trade winds and sea breezes can suppress the summertime heat, Key West at times reaches 100°F.

Hurricane Season

In southern Florida, the dry season usually runs from November through April. During this time, you'll experience abundant sunshine and roughly 25 percent of the annual rainfall. The wet season, meanwhile, runs from May through October and usually

---

Previous: an alligator in Big Cypress National Preserve.

constitutes about 75 percent of the annual rainfall. Part of this rainfall may include infrequent hurricanes that can occur during the **Atlantic hurricane season,** which typically runs from June through November. Although hurricanes can certainly happen at other times of the year as well, most residents and visitors don't worry about such potentially destructive storms until June 1.

Based on wind speeds, hurricanes are classified on a scale that ranges from a mild Category 1 to a powerful Category 5. While Miami, the Everglades, and the Florida Keys haven't been hit by hurricanes very often, southern Floridians have certainly experienced their share of terrible storms, including the Labor Day Hurricane of 1935, which killed more than 400 people and destroyed the Florida Keys' Overseas Railroad; Hurricane Andrew, which hit the Miami area in 1992 and at the time was considered the costliest hurricane in U.S. history; and Hurricane Wilma, which caused massive damage in the Everglades and some flooding in the Lower Keys during the 2005 season.

ENVIRONMENTAL ISSUES

In general, southern Florida is heavily dependent upon a healthy environment. The effects of water pollution, overdevelopment, overfishing, and overhunting can easily affect at least two of its major industries—agriculture and tourism—not to mention the fragile ecosystems that compose this fascinating region. Of course, it's these very industries that have, at times, overwhelmed the ecosystems down here. This is especially true in the Everglades, where habitat loss and long-term drainage efforts—to satisfy agricultural needs and a growing population—have had long-term negative effects on native flora and fauna. Oftentimes, the welfare of keystone species, such as the American alligator, has helped to reveal the condition of the entire region.

Researchers and conservationists are equally concerned about the health of the Florida Keys. While visiting the area, you'll find several ecofriendly adventure operators, plus animal facilities—such as the Florida Keys Wild Bird Center near Key Largo and The Turtle Hospital in Marathon—that are doing what they can to save marine birds and animals from detriments caused by humans, such as mercury poisoning, fishing line and net entanglements, boat strikes, intestinal impaction due to the ingestion of floating debris, and oil spills. Be sure to visit such facilities to learn more about how you can help minimize your impact on the fragile ecosystems of southern Florida.

Plants and Animals

The varied habitats that extend from the Everglades to the Florida Keys are home to literally thousands of animal, insect, and plant species, more than can possibly be listed here. Nevertheless, consider this section a sampling of what you can expect to encounter while visiting the marshes, forests, beaches, and coral reefs of southern Florida.

TREES

The Everglades, part of a massive watershed and subtropical wilderness north of the Florida Keys, nurture well over 120 different tree species. In Everglades National Park, for instance, you'll spy numerous **wetland tree islands** and **upland hardwood hammocks,** both of which support various mammals and serve as critical rookeries for wading and migratory birds.

The tree islands typically consist of bay, willow, bald cypress, dwarf cypress, or pond apple trees. The **cypress,** perhaps the most recognizable tree in the Everglades, is curious in that it can live either on dry land or in water and, unlike many subtropical trees, tends to shed its leaves every autumn.

The hardwood hammocks, meanwhile, often consist of landlubbing trees, such as slash pine, live oak, royal palm, cabbage palm, saw palmetto, and West Indian mahogany. Another intriguing tree often present in these drier hardwood hammocks, as well as throughout the Florida Keys, is the **gumbo limbo,** a fast-growing, salt-tolerant tropical tree that has featherlike leaves and a shiny red exfoliating bark. Interestingly, it's also called the "tourist tree" due to the bark's resemblance to a peeling sunburn.

Prevalent throughout the marshes and tidal shores of both the Everglades and the Florida Keys is the **mangrove,** a coastal tree noted for its vast interlaced aboveground root system. Mangroves, which constitute many of the smaller keys in this region, are a keystone plant community in southern Florida, where they serve as a buffer along the coast. Together, these interlocked trees protect the land from wind and waves, reduce soil erosion, build the soil through growth and decomposition, and provide a border between saline coastal waters and freshwater marshes. Intolerant of cold weather and typically classified as black, white, or red, mangroves are protected by law, so be sure not to damage or deface any while exploring the backcountry waters.

In the Florida Keys, you might also spy small ornamental trees like the buttonwood, the palmlike coontie, and the coral bean, which has spiny magenta-hued leaves and toxic seeds. Flowering trees also abound here, such as the geiger tree, the locust berry, the poisonwood, and the coco plum, the fruit of which is often used in preserves. Other curious native species include the strangler fig, the wild coffee, and the silver palm. In addition, the Keys are well known for several non-native tree species, such as mango, coconut palm, and key lime.

PLANTS AND FLOWERS

Oases for nature lovers, the Everglades and the Florida Keys boast a wide array of native plants. In the Everglades, you'll encounter more than 100 marsh plant species that live in water for most or all of the year. Perhaps the most prevalent of these is **sawgrass,** a hardy sedge named for its serrated leaf blade, which now constitutes thousands of acres of marshland in the Everglades. Here you'll also spy cattails, algae, and a variety of floating aquatic plants like bladderwort, spatterdock, maidencane, and white water lily.

In addition, this warm, often humid region nurtures an assortment of **epiphytes,** plants that grow on the branches, trunks, and leaves of other trees. Deriving their water and nutrients from the air, epiphytes here include beautiful orchids, bromeliads, tropical ferns, and Spanish moss.

Along the beaches of southern Florida, even in the Florida Keys, you're likely to see sandspur plants, the seeds of which resemble little spiked balls, as well as sea grapes and sea oats, both salt-tolerant plants that help to stabilize sand dunes and prevent erosion. While exploring the Florida Keys, you're also bound to see vibrant tropical flowers, whether you're driving along the Overseas Highway or walking amid the lush gardens of a posh resort. Two of the most common flowering plants down here are the **hibiscus** and the **bougainvillea,** both of which are usually ablaze with white, pink, red, orange, purple, or yellow flowers.

MAMMALS

More than 40 mammal species call the Everglades home, including cotton mice, rice rats, skunks, raccoons, opossums, marsh rabbits, river otters, gray foxes, bobcats, and white-tailed deer. Of course, the most well-known and most elusive mammal in the Everglades is the endangered **Florida panther,** the official state animal and the symbol of this vast, fragile ecosystem. Typically, panthers live in the upland areas, where they feed on deer and other mammals.

Raccoons and opossums dwell in the Florida Keys as well, along with oodles of feral cats. The Lower Keys are also home to

Invasive Plants in the Everglades

In **Everglades National Park,** several invasive plant species are threatening native plant populations, including the Australian pine (*Casuarina equisetifolia*), Brazilian pepper (*Schinus terebinthifolius*), latherleaf (*Colubrina asiatica*), melaleuca (*Melaleuca quinquenervia*), Old World climbing fern (*Lygodium microphyllum*), and seaside mahoe (*Thespesia populnea*).

You can take action to prevent the introduction or spread of all invasive alien plants into natural areas by

- Not disturbing natural areas, such as clearing native vegetation, planting nonnatives, and dumping yard wastes

- Refraining from the use of exotic species in your landscaping, land restoration, or erosion-control projects

- Using ornamentals that are native to your local region

- Consulting a local university, arboretum, nature center, native plant society, or Department of Agriculture office if you have any concerns about a plant that you intend to grow

- Using techniques such as cutting, mowing, pruning, or herbicide to remove or manage any invasive exotics

- Asking local nurseries and garden shops not to sell invasive exotic plants

- Notifying land managers about invasive exotic plant occurrences

- Assisting in exotic-plant removal projects

- Working with your local government to encourage the use of native plants in urban and suburban landscapes

the diminutive **key deer,** an endangered subspecies of the Virginia white-tailed deer. Key deer, which typically weigh 65-80 pounds, tend to stand between 24 and 32 inches high. Researchers believe that the key deer migrated from the Florida mainland to the Florida Keys thousands of years ago. Found nowhere else in the world, the key deer were in danger of extinction in the 1940s, until the establishment of the National Key Deer Refuge in 1957.

Naturally, marine mammals are prevalent in the Florida Keys, too. On sightseeing cruises, you're bound to spot an **Atlantic bottlenose dolphin** or an **Atlantic spotted dolphin.** Rare sightings of the endangered **West Indian manatee,** or "sea cow," are also possible in the Florida Keys as well as the Everglades, especially in warmer waters. A giant yet gentle creature, favoring a vegetarian diet, the manatee is Florida's state marine mammal.

BIRDS

Boasting more than 350 **resident or migratory bird species,** the Everglades and the Florida Keys constitute a bird-watcher's paradise. It's no wonder, then, that the famous ornithologist John James Audubon traveled to southern Florida to paint the region's native birds. Although overhunting and habitat destruction have caused a steep decline in the native bird population since Audubon's time, you'll still encounter plenty of wonderful species during your visit to southern Florida.

In the Everglades, you'll encounter a variety of wading birds, including the white ibis, glossy ibis, wood stork, green-backed heron, great white heron, great blue heron, great egret, snowy egret, reddish egret, and roseate spoonbill. Other commonly seen birds range from cardinals and meadowlarks to blue jays and red-bellied woodpeckers. If you're looking for raptors, you're likely to spot red-shouldered hawks, barred owls, ospreys, and if you're lucky, a bald eagle or two.

To the south, the Florida Keys nurture many of the same bird species that you'll find in the Everglades. In addition, you might spot common sandpipers, double-crested cormorants, laughing gulls, mangrove cuckoos, mourning doves, turkey vultures, and white-crowned pigeons. Also, no matter where you travel in the Keys, you're bound to encounter the **brown pelican,** which you might see floating in a marina, standing on a beach, or coasting above the water.

REPTILES

While exploring the Everglades, keep a lookout for the more than 50 species of reptiles found here. Whether you're traveling by kayak, canoe, airboat, or foot, you're likely to see at least some of the 27 snake species, 16 turtle species, and various lizards that call the Everglades home. **Snakes** can be found in nearly every habitat, from brown water snakes in freshwater ponds to mangrove salt marsh snakes in the saltwater marshes. Of course, you'll also find several venomous varieties here, including the Florida cottonmouth, the multicolored eastern coral snake, and the pygmy rattler, so be aware at all times. Meanwhile, notable **turtle** species in the Everglades include the striped mud turtle, the peninsula cooter, the Florida red-belly turtle, and the yellow-bellied slider, all of which favor freshwater ponds and marshes. In the pinelands and hardwood hammocks, you may also spy tiny camouflaged **lizards,** such as native green anoles, exotic brown anoles, and Florida reef geckos, the smallest lizards in North America.

Naturally, most visitors come to the Everglades hoping to catch a glimpse of an **American alligator**—the official state reptile—which you might spot drifting in a slough, resting in an alligator hole, or sunbathing alongside the Tamiami Trail. You're also likely to see these prehistoric-looking creatures in the Florida Keys, especially near places like the Blue Hole on Big Pine Key.

In Dagny Johnson Key Largo Hammock Botanical State Park, you might even spy an **American crocodile.** Just be advised that crocodiles can be far more aggressive than alligators. Meanwhile, other commonly seen reptiles in the Keys include brown and green anoles, corn snakes, Mediterranean geckos, and the green iguana, which you'll surely encounter everywhere, from Islamorada's Theater of the Sea to the trees of Key West's Old Town.

While exploring the Florida Keys, you might also be lucky enough to spot a **sea turtle,** in either the offshore waters or an onshore facility, such as Theater of the Sea or The Turtle Hospital in Marathon. Some of these species include the Kemp's ridley turtle, hawksbill turtle, leatherback turtle, loggerhead turtle, and green turtle—all of which are either threatened or endangered.

AMPHIBIANS

In addition to numerous birds and reptiles, the Florida Everglades are also home to nearly 20 species of **frogs, toads,** and **salamanders,** including the grass frog, supposedly the tiniest frog in North America, and the Everglades dwarf siren, a salamander that is only found in the Everglades. Of course, most amphibians are nocturnal, well-camouflaged creatures, so you're more likely to hear them than see them. That's certainly the case with pig frogs, whose grunts can be heard in freshwater marshes, and noisy oak toads, which favor pinelands, hardwood hammocks, and wet sawgrass communities.

FISH AND SEALIFE

Given the prevalence of saltwater, freshwater, and brackish water in and around Miami, the Everglades, and the Florida Keys, it comes as no surprise that there are more than 600 species of tropical and game fish in southern Florida, some of which you might spy while snorkeling along an offshore coral reef and some of which you might snag from a fishing boat in the backcountry. Depending on the fishing season, you could encounter redfish

Alligators vs. Crocodiles

Southern Florida is home to a wide variety of reptiles, including snakes, iguanas, and sea turtles. Of course, the most well-known species are the American alligator *(Alligator mississippiensis)* and the American crocodile *(Crocodylus acutus)*. While these two carnivorous crocodilians—which are both members of the Reptilia class and the Crocodylia order—resemble each other greatly, there are a number of differences between them.

Typically, alligators dwell in freshwater habitats throughout the Everglades and the Lower Florida Keys. Their telltale characteristics include black scales; a wide, rounded snout; and a hidden fourth tooth on the lower jaw. Crocodiles, meanwhile, tend to be more elusive—a threatened species within saltwater habitats in the Everglades and places like Dagny Johnson Key Largo Hammock Botanical State Park. Their telltale characteristics include grayish-green scales; a narrow, tapered snout; and a lower fourth tooth that juts out noticeably. As a rule, crocodiles are faster, more active, and more aggressive than alligators, and they tend to spend more time in the water.

an alligator at Blue Hole on Big Pine Key

Alligators can reach up to 15 feet in length, weigh up to 1,000 pounds, and live for up to 60 years. Normally, they reach maturity after 4-7 years and can lay 10-50 eggs, with hatching occurring after a 65-day incubation period. Crocodiles, conversely, can reach up to 20 feet in length, weigh up to 2,200 pounds, and live for up to 75 years. Unlike alligators, they reach maturity after 10-15 years and can lay 20-60 eggs, with hatching occurring after about 90 days.

Of course, alligators and crocodiles have plenty of common traits. For one thing, the location of their eyes, ears, and nostrils on the top of their heads allows them to conceal much of their bodies underwater, making it easier to sneak up on their prey, which consists of fish, reptiles, rodents, birds, insects, and other mammals—some of which can be half their size. In addition, both alligators and crocodiles are ectothermic, meaning that they rely on external sources of heat to regulate their body temperature—hence, the reason that they often bask in the sun or, depending on the season, move to areas with warmer or cooler water. Moreover, all crocodilians lay their eggs on land, well above the water line, where the females guard them from predators that might try to unearth them. Despite such efforts, though, many crocodilian eggs fall prey to other animals.

Other similar traits include webbed feet, powerful jaws, keen eyesight, acute hearing, an excellent sense of smell, an armored exterior made up of overlapping scales, a broad tail that enables them to swim smoothly and quickly, and short legs that can move surprisingly fast on dry land. In fact, although both species tend to float listlessly in the water like drifting logs, they can actually swim up to 20 miles per hour and run up to 11 miles per hour—a fact that you should well remember the next time you venture into the wilderness.

(also known as "red drum"), red grouper, bonefish, permit, common snook, amberjack, Spanish mackerel, wahoo, yellowfin tuna, king mackerel (also known as "kingfish"), tarpon, sailfish, blue marlin, and mahimahi, which are also known as "dorado" or "dolphinfish." While snorkeling or diving, you might see some of these very same species, plus colorful Spanish hogfish and yellowtail snapper, torpedo-shaped barracuda, abundant nurse sharks, southern stingrays, spotted moray eels, and kaleidoscopic queen angelfish. In the Everglades, you might also spy freshwater fish like the Florida gar, the mosquitofish, and the official state freshwater fish, the largemouth bass.

Of course, fish aren't the only entities you'll observe while exploring the coral reefs of Florida Keys National Marine Sanctuary. Here you may also notice banded coral shrimp, stone crabs, fire sponges, sea cucumbers, sea anemones, long-spined urchins, jellyfish, sand dollars, sea fans, sea stars, the Portuguese man-of-war, the spiny lobster, the Florida fighting conch, and a variety of coral, including brain coral, fire coral, elkhorn coral, and staghorn coral. Remember, though: As tempting as it might seem, it is illegal to collect any and all coral formations.

INSECTS AND ARACHNIDS

Between the Everglades and the Florida Keys, there are literally hundreds of insect and arachnid species, ranging in size from the minuscule chigger to the giant diving beetle. In the Everglades, four of the most commonly spotted insects include the large **lubber grasshopper,** which has wings but cannot fly; the **golden orb weaver,** a beautiful spider that weaves intricate webs in the hardwood hammocks; the bloodsucking **mosquito,** which, despite being annoying to humans, is a critical part of the food chain in mangrove estuaries; and the gorgeous **dragonfly,** affectionately known as a "mosquito hawk." Other curious creatures in the Everglades include the apple snail and the Liguus tree snail.

Many of these insects, including the pesky mosquito, can be seen—and, in some cases, felt—in the Florida Keys. Besides the mosquito, other bloodthirsty critters include the **no-see-um,** or "punkie," a tiny biting gnat that thrives in coastal areas, especially during the summer months. Down here you may also spy **woodland cicadas,** crablike **spiny orb weavers,** and **fire ants,** large, aggressive red ants that are prevalent in tropical areas, capable of building large mounds, and inclined to inflict painful stings.

In both the Everglades and the Florida Keys archipelago, some of the most beautiful insects are, of course, **butterflies,** more than 50 species of which can be observed in southern Florida. Some commonly spotted species include the Florida purplewing, the hammock skipper, the mangrove skipper, the sleepy orange, the white peacock, and the zebra longwing, which is the official state butterfly.

the endangered Florida panther

Wild Animal Encounters

Lizards, iguanas, roosters, and feral cats roam freely in the Florida Keys. You'll see them everywhere—in parking lots, on porches, even amid the foliage. Because such creatures are so accustomed to people, it's sometimes easy to forget how to handle an encounter with truly wild animals.

Whether you spot a lounging alligator, a tiny key deer, or something else, you should always adhere to the following rules:

· Observe wildlife from a distance; do not follow or approach the animals.

· Never feed wildlife; feeding wild animals can damage their health, alter their natural behavior, and expose them to predators.

· Never taunt or disturb wildlife.

· Protect wildlife by storing your food and trash securely.

· Control pets at all times, or leave them at home.

· Avoid wildlife during sensitive phases, such as mating or nesting.

For more information about respecting wildlife, consult the recreation and parks division of the **Florida Department of Environmental Protection** (850/245-3029 or 850/245-2043, www.dep.state.fl.us or www.floridastateparks.org) or contact the Colorado-based **Leave No Trace Center for Outdoor Ethics** (303/442-8222 or 800/332-4100, www.lnt.org).

ENDANGERED SPECIES

More than 20 animal species found in the Everglades and the Florida Keys are federally listed as threatened or endangered, largely due to habitat loss, urban development, water flow alteration, overhunting, and in some cases, highway collisions. Some endangered creatures, such as the Florida bonneted bat, Key Largo cotton mouse, Key Largo woodrat, and snail kite (a bird that survives exclusively on the apple snail) are perhaps less well known to outsiders. Others, however, such as the Florida panther, West Indian manatee, and hawksbill turtle (not to mention the threatened American alligator), receive a lot more attention from conservationists, media representatives, and government officials.

The **Florida panther,** a large long-tailed cat of which there are less than 100 left in the wild, is perhaps the most at risk for extinction. Presently, conservation efforts include radio-tracking collared individuals and introducing other panther strains to increase the gene pool.

Meanwhile, the **West Indian manatee,** a gentle creature that feeds on aquatic vegetation and typically inhabits sloughs, shallow estuaries, and saltwater bays, has been systematically diminished by boat collisions, vandal attacks, poachers, habitat destruction, and cold stress. Although it's protected by the Marine Mammal Protection Act of 1972 and the Endangered Species Act of 1973, human actions continue to threaten, harm, or kill the manatee. Luckily, groups like the Save the Manatee Club, which is based in Maitland, Florida, are doing what they can to save these endangered creatures, though individuals can help by obeying speed limits, recording manatee sightings, and reporting criminal activities affecting these gentle marine mammals.

Sea turtles, such as the Kemp's ridley turtle, hawksbill turtle, leatherback turtle, loggerhead turtle, and green turtle, have long been endangered everywhere, though conservation efforts are underway throughout Florida and other parts of the world. Other endangered species in the Everglades include birds: the Cape Sable seaside sparrow,

Bachman's warbler, Kirtland's warbler, and the red-cockaded woodpecker.

REINTRODUCTION PROGRAMS

Following successful efforts to reintroduce the eastern bluebird to the Florida Everglades, the National Park Service is currently overseeing the reintroduction of the Florida wild turkey to Everglades National Park. Such reintroduction programs are critical for habitat restoration efforts. In the case of the Florida wild turkey, for example, this reintroduction program has a twofold benefit: to help restore the pine rocklands of the Everglades and to monitor the progress of said restoration.

Perhaps more well known, though, are the reintroduction programs that involve endangered sea turtles. In the Florida Keys, for instance, The Turtle Hospital, which opened in 1986, has endeavored to rehabilitate injured sea turtles and return them to the wild. The hospital also educates the public about the plight of sea turtles, conducts and assists with relevant research, and strives for environmental legislation that will make beaches and offshore waters safer and cleaner for these endangered creatures.

History

EARLY CIVILIZATION

Even without written records, it's generally accepted among historians that Native American tribes have inhabited the region now known as southern Florida for thousands of years, perhaps as early as 10,000 BC. As evidenced by archaeological finds and the accounts of Spanish explorers in the early 1500s, the predominant tribes in this region were the Tequesta Indians in the Biscayne Bay area near present-day Miami, the Seminole Indians in the Everglades, and the Calusa Indians in the Florida Keys. The first European explorer to encounter these native tribes was allegedly Juan Ponce de León, who traveled to these waters on behalf of Spain in 1513. Although there's no evidence that he actually interacted with these native peoples, the written accounts of his expedition indicate their presence in southern Florida, even amid the twisted islands that de León named *Los Martires* (The Martyrs), later known as the Florida Keys.

Once Spain claimed the Florida territory as its own, European interactions with the native peoples increased—the nature of which varied from tribe to tribe. While the Tequesta, for instance, welcomed the Spanish explorers that took refuge in Biscayne Bay in 1565, the fierce Calusa subjected others to repeated attacks.

COLONIALISM

After Florida was claimed by Spain, life changed drastically for the native peoples here. Over the ensuing decades, many Native Americans died as a result of European diseases and various battles between the Spanish, French, and British. By the mid-1700s, most of the Tequesta and Calusa people had either moved elsewhere or been sold into slavery by the British. Those that remained were relocated to Cuba in 1763, when Spain transferred the Florida territory to Britain. Although the Seminole were also adversely affected by the Europeans' presence, they nonetheless managed to survive in the Everglades.

By the 1780s, the United States had been formed, though Florida was once again under Spanish control. Given incidents like the First and Second Seminole Wars during the first half of the 19th century, it took some time for permanent settlements to take root. In fact, by the late 1830s, Miami was little more than a fort beside the sea.

While Europeans were trying to settle this diverse region, pirates were trolling the waters of the Florida Keys, plundering unsuspecting

The Fort Taylor Timeline

Fort Zachary Taylor was one of the most important fortresses of the mid-19th century.

- **1821:** After the United States acquires the Florida territory, the federal government considers extending the Third System of seacoast defenses to protect the Gulf Coast.

- **1836:** The U.S. Congress allocates funds to begin construction of a fort on Key West.

- **1845:** Construction of the fort begins. The foundation is established in offshore waters on the southwestern side of the island. Construction is a challenge. Materials and workers have to be shipped from the mainland, funding problems often interfere, and yellow fever is common among the workers.

- **1846:** A hurricane hits Key West, but construction of the fort resumes soon after.

- **1850:** The structure is named for President Zachary Taylor.

- **1859:** Much of the fortress is complete, including cannons, tidal flush latrines, and a draw-bridge.

- **1860:** Though unfinished, Fort Taylor is ready for occupancy. Following President Lincoln's election, Florida considers secession. Captain E. B. Hunt, the commander of the fort, meets with other officers to discuss securing Fort Taylor and nearby Fort Jefferson for the Union. U.S. Artillery Captain John Brannan orders 20 men to move into the fort under the guise of a training mission. Hunt arrives on December 2 with another 60 laborers.

- **1861-1865:** In January 1861, Florida secedes from the Union, and Hunt orders Brannan to assume command of Fort Taylor. Engineers strengthen the cover face and mount additional cannons. During the American Civil War, Fort Taylor serves as the headquarters for the U.S. Navy East Gulf Blockading Squadron, which captures about 300 Confederate vessels. After the war ends in April 1865, Army engineers continue construction on the cover face. In October 1865, a hurricane passes west of the fort, destroying part of the seawall and the bridge to Key West.

- **1866:** Technically, the fort is complete, though construction continues.

- **1871:** The secretary of war approves a plan to modify Fort Taylor, with the addition of two barbettes and the fortification of the main magazines.

ships and salvaging cargo. By the 1820s, the U.S. Navy had managed to scare away most of the marauding pirates, and permanent settlers, from places like Cuba, the Bahamas, and the northeastern United States, were beginning to populate the Upper, Middle, and Lower Keys. One of the earliest settlements was that on Indian Key, which in 1836 became the first county seat of Dade County and by 1840 was destroyed by invading Seminole during the Second Seminole War; the harrowing invasion also caused the disbandment of Conch Town, a Bahamian settlement in the Middle Keys. In 1845, while Florida was becoming the 27th U.S. state, four main industries were underway in the Florida Keys:

farming, fishing, salt production, and cargo salvaging. By the mid-1800s it was cargo salvaging that had become the most lucrative enterprise, helping to make Key West one of the richest cities in the country by the late 1800s.

CIVIL WAR

By 1860 the island of Key West had become the largest and richest city in the state, and although Florida joined the Confederate States of America during the American Civil War, the isolated Southernmost City remained in Union hands because of the presence of a naval base. **Fort Zachary Taylor,** constructed between 1845 and 1866, became an important outpost during the Civil War,

- **1875:** Another destructive hurricane halts work on the fort.

- **1885:** Secretary of War William Endicott decides to modernize Fort Taylor. Congress approves the plan, but funds are slow to come.

- **1896:** Given the likelihood of a war with Spain, funding is made available.

- **1897:** Army engineers and civilian contractors begin upgrading the fort.

- **1898:** When the Spanish-American War erupts, soldiers occupy the fort, and construction continues.

- **1903-1945:** The coastal weaponry, operated by the U.S. Army's Coastal Artillery Corps and the Florida National Guard, remains at Fort Taylor until mid-World War II, after which the Army builds new mounts for antiaircraft guns. At the war's end, the Coastal Artillery Corps is abolished.

- **1947:** After assuming control of the property, the U.S. Navy removes the antiaircraft guns.

- **1950:** Fort Taylor is listed as government excess property and relegated to service as a scrap metal yard.

- **1968:** Once the fort is landlocked in the mid-1960s by the Navy, volunteers excavate Civil War guns, cannons, and ammunition from long-abandoned sections.

- **1970:** The Navy transfers the property to the Department of the Interior.

- **1971:** Fort Taylor is listed in the National Register of Historic Places.

- **1973:** The fort becomes a National Historic Landmark.

- **1976:** The Florida Park Service acquires Fort Taylor.

- **1985:** The fort opens as a state park, and soon afterward a moat is dug around the fortress to prevent easy entry into the structure and to create the illusion of its early days.

while **Fort Jefferson** in the Dry Tortugas was used as a military prison during and after the conflict. Also in the 1860s and 1870s, many Cuban refugees escaped to Key West, where they initiated a thriving cigar-making industry, which ultimately helped to replace the dwindling salt and salvaging industries in the late 1800s.

THE 20TH CENTURY

By the 1890s, Miami, which was officially incorporated as a city in 1896, was experiencing a real estate boom and subsequent population growth. Meanwhile, the Florida Keys were thriving because of the sponging and cigar-making industries. By the turn of the 20th century, however, the expansion of this area was due, in large part, to Henry Flagler, who envisioned a 130-mile extension of the Florida East Coast Railway between the mainland and Key West. In 1904 railroad construction began on Key Vaca, now known as Marathon, and by 1908 scheduled daily train service was helping to bring more settlers to Key Largo, the largest and northernmost island in the Florida Keys. By 1912, after the tireless efforts of hundreds of workers, Flagler's costly **Overseas Railroad** had become a reality, and Key West, which became a strategic training base for U.S. Army and Navy forces during World War I, benefited greatly from the new route. Even Prohibition didn't hinder the

Southernmost City, which soon witnessed a rise in rum-running and bootlegging.

During the 1920s, Miami also thrived culturally and financially, earning its nickname "Magic City." Tourism began to expand in the Everglades, largely because of the Seminole, who made their living from homemade crafts and alligator-wrestling spectacles, and thanks to the 1928 opening of the Tamiami Trail between Tampa and Miami, the first official road across the Everglades. At the same time, the state completed a highway and ferry service alongside the Overseas Railroad, which continued to bring settlers, tourists, and cargo to the Florida Keys—until, that is, the **Labor Day Hurricane of 1935** brought an end to Flagler's dream. Without modern detection techniques, the people of the Upper and Middle Florida Keys were caught off-guard by this powerful storm, eventually considered the first recorded Category 5 hurricane to hit the United States. Forming on August 29, 1935, during a relatively quiet season, this legendary hurricane began as a small tropical storm and grew explosively during the Labor Day weekend, eventually making landfall with winds as high as 200 miles per hour. The hurricane was so monstrous that it single-handedly destroyed the Overseas Railroad and claimed at least 400 people in Florida and other eastern states.

Following the death and destruction caused by the hurricane, the Florida Keys experienced a financial downturn during the 1930s—also as a result of the collapse of trade with Cuba, the decline of the cigar industry, and the closing of the Key West Naval Station. Similarly, Miami experienced an economic decline because of the statewide real estate collapse, a devastating hurricane in the 1920s, and of course, the Great Depression. Three factors, however, saved the Florida Keys: the state-funded creation of the Overseas Highway in 1938, the attention of famous residents like Ernest Hemingway and President Harry S. Truman, and the expansion of the U.S. Navy in the Lower Keys.

Miami, too, benefited from World War II, and by the 1950s, tourism became the dominant industry throughout southern Florida.

A growing concern for conservation seemed to go hand in hand with this economic upswing. Everglades National Park was established in 1947 to conserve this fragile ecosystem and prevent further degradation of its habitats, flora, and fauna. In 1957, the same year that the Seminole Tribe of Florida officially formed, the federal government designated the National Key Deer Refuge in the Lower Keys.

During the 1960s, while many Cubans were immigrating to Miami and increasing the city's population, the focus in the Florida Keys began to shift to the offshore coral reefs along the eastern side of southern Florida, which together constitute the third-largest coral reef system in the world. By 1960 John Pennekamp Coral Reef State Park had become America's first undersea park, and in 1968 Biscayne National Monument was established north of Key Largo, eventually to become Biscayne National Park in 1980. In 1974 Big Cypress National Preserve, which has long been home to the Seminole and Miccosukee Tribes, became one of the country's first federally protected preserves, and after Key Largo National Marine Sanctuary was established in 1975 and Looe Key National Marine Sanctuary followed in 1981, the Florida Keys archipelago truly began to secure its niche as a world-class underwater diving destination.

Conservation efforts continued into the 1990s, with the establishment of Florida Keys National Marine Sanctuary in 1990 and Dry Tortugas National Park in 1992. Even remnants of "Flagler's Folly" have become part of the tourism landscape, most notably places like the coral rock quarries of Windley Key Fossil Reef Geological State Park, the early 20th-century worker buildings on Pigeon Key, and the old railroad bridge that's now part of Bahia Honda State Park.

This growing tourism industry experienced a temporary setback in April 1982, when a U.S. Border Patrol blockade near Florida City caused an enormous traffic jam for those leaving the Florida Keys via U.S. 1. In response to this disruptive search for illegal aliens and potential drug runners, Key West and the rest of the Florida Keys briefly declared their secession from the United States, subsequently forming a micronation called the Conch Republic. Today this incident, which successfully ended the Border Patrol blockade, is celebrated with an annual Conch Republic Independence Celebration in Key West and a similar event in Key Largo. Despite this upset, the Florida Keys continued to thrive, and by 1997 several Upper Keys were incorporated into the town of Islamorada.

Meanwhile, the 1980s and 1990s were not as kind to Miami, which experienced drug wars, hurricanes, and increased crime, among other crises.

CONTEMPORARY TIMES

In the 21st century, tourism has continued to be the lifeblood of southern Florida. Despite the impact of other industries, such as international trade in Miami, agriculture in the Everglades, and commercial fishing in the Florida Keys, southern Florida has endured as a popular vacation and recreation destination, making it one of the more financially stable regions in a state that was hit hard by a nationwide economic downturn.

Government and Economy

LOCAL GOVERNMENT

In general, the political climate of southern Florida is heavily Democratic. Given the cultural diversity of this region, it might also come as no surprise that, over the years, several of Miami's mayors and commissioners have been Latinos. The local government of Key West, which also serves as the Monroe County seat, has been equally diverse. The mayors down here have included such colorful characters as Carlos Manuel de Céspedes (1875-1876), father of the Cuban Republic, and Richard A. Heyman (1983-1985 and 1987-1989), one of the country's first openly gay public officials.

ECONOMY

Throughout much of Miami's past, seasonal tourism has been the overriding industry. Nowadays, however, the local economy has diversified to include year-round tourism as well as international trade and international banking.

The economy of the Florida Everglades, meanwhile, has long revolved around agriculture, commercial fishing, recreation, and tourism. While some of these industries have

become the subject of controversy over the years, due to the detrimental impact on the fragile Everglades ecosystem, perhaps no industry has been as controversial or as devastating as the production of drinking water. Over the years, water suppliers in southern Florida have systematically drained the Everglades, to such a degree that the state is now in the midst of a costly restoration effort. As of 2007, the state of Florida refused to issue new water supply permits for the region and instructed water utilities to develop alternative means of water production, such as desalination techniques, for the growing population of southern Florida, which has, in recent years, depended on an estimated daily supply of 300-600 million gallons of water from the Everglades.

The economic history of the Florida Keys has been just as complicated. During the 19th century, the regional economy evolved from a dependence on cargo salvaging to a reliance on sponging, cigar making, and commercial fishing. By the 1930s, the Florida Keys were suffering a financial decline, soon afterward to be remedied by the U.S. Navy, which expanded its presence in the Lower Keys. Following World War II, fishing and tourism became the dominant industries in the Keys, which is still the case today.

Agriculture

Southern Florida is a bountiful place, so it's no surprise that agriculture plays a critical role in the local economy. The Everglades have an abundance of plant nurseries, which line miles of Krome Avenue north of Homestead. The plethora of farmers markets in Miami-Dade County is also an indication of the region's agricultural abundance. The subtropical climate allows for a year-round growing season, resulting in a diverse agricultural industry that, according to county statistics, employs more than 20,000 people and amasses more than $2.7 billion annually.

Shipping and Fishing

Given that the Port of Miami is nicknamed the "cruise capital of the world," it makes sense that commercial shipping is a viable industry in southern Florida. In the Florida Keys, meanwhile, commercial fishing is a major part of the economy. Though plenty of fishing guides and charter services make their living from visiting tourists, several fishing companies rely on the wholesale seafood market for their livelihood. Depending on the season, such fisheries sell a variety of fish, shrimp, Florida lobster, and stone crabs.

Tourism

While agriculture and fishing are important facets of the southern Florida economy, it surely comes as no surprise that Miami, the Everglades, and the Florida Keys rely heavily on the tourism industry for survival. The entire area boasts numerous hotels, resorts, fine restaurants, golf courses, sightseeing tours, fishing charters, diving operators, national and state parks, shopping districts, and annual events—all of which help to fund local communities. In the Florida Keys, the peak tourist season—which essentially runs from late December to early January and from mid-February through April—is often so lucrative that it helps to sustain residents through much leaner times, such as the slow, unbearably hot month of September.

Local Culture

NATIVE PEOPLES

Long before Spanish explorers encountered the land now known as southern Florida, various American Indian tribes called this bountiful region home. Although it's difficult to pinpoint all the native peoples that once lived here, archaeological finds have indicated that three specific tribes once dominated the area.

Along the southeastern Atlantic coast of Florida, in the territories now known as Broward and Miami-Dade Counties, lived the Tequesta Indians. Also called the Tekesta, Chequesta, and Vizcaynos, the Tequesta inhabited this region from at least the 13th century to the mid-18th century—by which time they had all but disappeared. During that time, the Tequesta established towns and camps at the mouths of rivers, streams, and inlets, where they fished, hunted, and gathered fruit and roots. In general, their diet consisted of manatees, sharks, sailfish, porpoises, stingrays, sea turtles, snails, lobster, venison, saw palmettos, sea grapes, prickly pear fruit, and other plants. Given the generally mild climate, clothing was minimal, ranging from loincloths made of deer hide to skirts crafted from Spanish moss, and tools consisted of canoes, nets, spears, bows, arrows, and simple pottery. At the height of the mosquito season, the Tequesta would typically relocate to the Florida Keys or to barrier islands in Biscayne Bay.

The Everglades, meanwhile, constituted the home of the Seminole Indians. While researchers assert that the Seminole's ancestors lived in the area 12,000 years ago, it was in the early 1500s that Europeans first encountered the tribe that would become known as the Seminole, which at that time numbered nearly 200,000 people. Unfortunately, thousands of these native people were killed by European diseases, such as measles and smallpox, as well as in the resulting wars between the Spanish, English, and French. Unlike the Tequesta, however, the Seminole survived such intrusions and subsequently thrived in the virgin forests and grass flats of the Everglades.

In the early 1800s, the Seminole lived in chickee-style domiciles, essentially palmetto thatch over cypress log frames, and their clothing tended to be more complicated and more colorful than that of the Tequesta. Like the Tequesta, however, the Seminole relied on the bountiful flora and fauna of southern Florida for sustenance, including native stone crabs. Although their customs have evolved over the years, some of their traditions still remain, such as an affinity for beadwork, the fashioning of palmetto fiber husk dolls, and the sacred springtime gatherings known as the Green Corn Dance.

Although the Tequesta sometimes inhabited the Florida Keys, it was the **Calusa Indians** that dominated the region between the southwestern coast of mainland Florida and the Florida Keys. As with the Tequesta, most of the Calusa tribe died out in the mid-1700s, and any remaining native people were sold as slaves or sent to Cuba. Before that time, however, the Calusa thrived in this part of Florida. Known as the "Shell Indians," the Calusa allegedly numbered 50,000 people at one time.

In the early 1500s, when Spanish explorers first discovered them, the Calusa were known to be a fierce, warmongering people. Like other native people in southern Florida, the Calusa lived along the coast and inner waterways, relying on fish, eels, turtles, conch, crabs, clams, lobster, oysters, and deer for sustenance. Their homes were typically built on stilts, with palmetto thatch roofs and no walls, and their tools consisted of nets, spears, dugout canoes, and arrowheads made of fish bones. In addition, archaeological finds indicate that the Calusa collected shells, which they used as tools, utensils, jewelry, and shrine ornaments—hence the nickname "Shell Indians." They were also known to salvage the wealth from shipwrecks along the coast, much as Key West residents did in later centuries.

THE IMMIGRANTS

Of course, native peoples were not the only inhabitants of southern Florida. Immigrants from Europe, Cuba, Haiti, and the Bahamas helped to establish the communities that exist today. Miami, for instance, is a mosaic of various cultures and cuisines, as evidenced by neighborhoods like Little Havana and Little Haiti. The Florida Keys were also settled in part by immigrants. In the early 1800s, Bahamian nationals came to these islands seeking autonomy. Evidence of their presence remains today in the form of specific buildings, such as the Adderley House in Marathon and the Oldest House Museum in Key West, as well as neighborhoods like Bahama Village, adjacent to Key West's Old Town.

MODERN DEMOGRAPHICS

Today the influence of native peoples and varied immigrants is evident in the demographics of southern Florida. In the three-county metropolitan area (Miami-Dade, Broward, and Palm Beach Counties), Latinos comprise roughly 42 percent of the total population, which numbers around 5.7 million people. The Jewish community makes up around 10 percent of the population, and other factions include Muslims, Canadians, Europeans, and Caribbean immigrants, plus former snowbirds from the Northeast who tend to be of Jewish, Muslim, Italian, Irish, African, Dominican, or Puerto Rican descent.

Although the population of the Florida Everglades is harder to assess, the people are predominantly Caucasian, Latino, and

Native American, most notably Seminole or Miccosukee. The Florida Keys, meanwhile, encompass all of Monroe County; the county seat is Key West. The archipelago has a population of about 77,400, 68 percent of which is Caucasian and 22 percent of which is Latino, with even smaller percentages of Asian and African American. Curiously, many of the residents here aren't native to the area. You'll find that a lot of the locals are actually transplants from other parts of the United States, such as Midwestern snowbirds who decided to stay permanently in this subtropical paradise.

RELIGION

Given the ethnic diversity of southern Florida, it's no surprise that residents tend to practice a variety of religions, or none at all. While you'll find large Jewish and Catholic factions in Miami, you'll also encounter, as with any other multicultural American city, Methodists, Lutherans, Presbyterians, Buddhists, and Muslims. The same can be said for the Florida Keys, where you'll spot everything from the Key Largo Baptist Church to the Southernmost Unitarian Universalist Congregation in Key West to the iconic St. Paul's Episcopal Church on Duval Street in Old Town.

LANGUAGE

While English is the predominant language in most of Miami, the Everglades, and the Florida Keys, Spanish often seems to be a close second, reflecting the influence of Cuban, Mexican, and other Latino immigrants on the region. In places like Miami's Little Havana, the prevalence of Cuban exiles and Cuban Americans means you're likely to hear more Spanish than English. Miami's Little Haiti, meanwhile, contains a mixture of English, French, and Spanish speakers, plus a Creole dialect that combines French, African, Arabic, Spanish, and Portuguese. In Miami, you might also hear German, Italian, Russian, and Yiddish. Although many Miami residents are fluent in both English and Spanish—or at least a form of "Spanglish"—the Florida Keys are a different story. Here you'll do more than survive with just a solid command of the English language, even though Spanish, French, Italian, and German can be heard on occasion.

The Arts

LITERATURE

Writers have long favored the inspiring landscapes and diverse communities of southern Florida. Miami, called the Magic City by some and a dangerous metropolis by others, has nurtured several contemporary crime and mystery novelists, including John Katzenbach, a *Miami Herald* crime reporter whose debut novel, *In the Heat of the Summer* (1982), focuses on a dangerous cat-and-mouse game between a clever serial killer and an ambitious Miami journalist. Other popular novelists include Carl Hiaasen, a Florida native and *Miami Herald* columnist whose various madcap novels take place throughout southern Florida, and Charles Willeford, whose well-known crime series about an unorthodox Miami homicide detective began with *Miami Blues* in 1984.

The Florida Everglades have also inspired their share of modern literature, from Hiaasen's novel *Nature Girl* (2006) to Susan Orlean's *The Orchid Thief: A True Story of Beauty and Obsession* (1998), a quirky tale of orchid fanatics in the Fakahatchee swamp. But, of course, it's the isolated Florida Keys archipelago that has sparked the creativity of countless writers, including Pulitzer Prize winners like the playwright Tennessee Williams and the poets Robert Frost, Wallace Stevens, and Elizabeth Bishop— all of whom once called Key West home.

Naturally, the most famous writer to have been touched by the Southernmost City was Ernest Hemingway, who lived in Key West with his second wife, Pauline, during most of the 1930s. It was here that the Nobel Prize-winning novelist wrote and published *To Have and Have Not* (1937), the story of a fishing boat captain who runs contraband between Cuba and Florida—no doubt inspired by Hemingway's own fishing experiences in the Florida Keys, not to mention his interactions with the eccentric locals of Key West.

VISUAL ARTS

The varied landscapes and diverse cultures of southern Florida have influenced not only writers but visual artists as well, as evidenced by the variety of art galleries and museums throughout Miami and the Florida Keys. In Miami, home to a thriving community of artists, designers, and collectors, you'll find such engaging sights as the Wynwood Arts District, an entire area devoted to visual arts, boasting well over 70 galleries, studios, stores, bars, and antiques shops all within walking distance. Art lovers might also appreciate the Bass Museum of Art in Miami Beach, which contains a vast accumulation of European paintings, sculptures, and textiles from the 15th to the 20th centuries.

The Florida Keys also present enticements for art aficionados, from Key Largo's Bluewater Potters to The Rain Barrel, a working village of artists in Islamorada. Of course, it's Key West that houses the greatest number of art galleries and museum exhibits, including the flagship store of Wyland Galleries, the Custom House Museum, and the Audubon House, which presents numerous originals and reprints of John James Audubon's famous ornithological paintings.

Southern Florida also features several annual art events, especially during the winter months. In Miami you'll find celebrations like the Coconut Grove Arts Festival and Art Basel Miami Beach. Key West stages events like the Key West Craft Show and the Old Island Days Art Festival, both of which attract numerous artists and artisans to historic Old Town.

PERFORMING ARTS

In addition to visual arts, the communities of southern Florida boast a variety of performing arts. The Adrienne Arsht Center for the Performing Arts of Miami-Dade County, for instance, presents everything from opera productions to jazz concerts to contemporary dance performances. You'll find a similar array of entertainment options throughout the Florida Keys, such as theater troupes like The Key Players and music organizations like the Florida Keys Concert Association. As with art galleries, Key West naturally offers the widest array of performance venues, including the Tennessee Williams Theatre on Stock Island, where you can see regular performances of the South Florida Symphony Orchestra, the Key West Pops Orchestra, and the FKCC Keys Chorale.

CINEMA

For more than seven decades, southern Florida has been a favored spot for filmmakers. Miami is an integral part of high-energy dramas like *Scarface* (1983), *Miami Blues* (1990), *Bad Boys* (1995), *Any Given Sunday* (1999), *Transporter 2* (2005), and *Miami Vice* (2006), and Miami Beach's Art Deco District and luxurious Fontainebleau hotel have been featured in many films.

Likewise, the Everglades have served as a key backdrop for films like *The Mean Season* (1985), inspired by John Katzenbach's debut novel and partially filmed in Everglades National Park, and *Adaptation.* (2002), a bizarre interpretation of Susan Orlean's book *The Orchid Thief. The Glades* (2010-2013), a TV crime drama, was filmed in the Everglades.

Reap the Wild Wind (1942), *Key Largo* (1948), *Flipper* (1963), and *True Lies* (1994) all had filming done in the Florida Keys. Even in Key West, you may recognize former cinematic backdrops, from the Ernest Hemingway Home, which appears at a pivotal moment in the James Bond flick *Licence to Kill* (1989), to the Eden House, where Goldie Hawn's character and her son live in the movie *CrissCross* (1992). Of course, many real-life people have escaped to Key West over the years, a fact that's embraced in the action comedy *Running Scared* (1986).

ARCHITECTURE

Those who appreciate alluring architecture will also enjoy a trip to southern Florida. Listed in the National Register of Historic Places, the vibrant Art Deco District in Miami Beach comprises several sub-styles, such as the less decorative depression moderne, evident in governmental buildings, and the more whimsical tropical deco, which employs relief ornamentation depicting local flora and fauna as well as ocean-liner motifs to reinforce the city's reputation as a seaside resort. Of course, Miami Beach also boasts examples of Mediterranean Revival, an old-world style that features decorative columns, bell towers, arched windows, spindle gates, and picturesque courtyards, and MiMo (Miami Modernism), a post-World War II style that embraces such elements as sunshades, tiled mosaic walls, and open balconies.

The Florida Keys also harbor their share of unique architecture. In Key West's Old Town are a cornucopia of architectural gems, from Caribbean-style bungalows to Victorian-era gingerbread mansions, such as the colorful Southernmost House, built in 1896 and now a popular inn. Another curious style is the eyebrow house, so named because it has an overhanging porch roof that conceals the upper front windows. While you're free to wander amid Key West's historic buildings on your own, you can also experience the architecture of Old Town on one of several guided excursions, including those that feature the city's most haunted structures.

Essentials

Transportation

GETTING THERE

While international tourists will most likely arrive in Miami or the Florida Keys by plane or cruise ship, domestic travelers can reach southern Florida by air, water, rail, or road. Consider your budget, destination, and intended activities before choosing the method that's right for your trip.

Air

With at least five different airports in the region, southern Florida

is an easy place to access by airplane. The two biggest airports are **Fort Lauderdale-Hollywood International Airport (FLL)** (100 Terminal Dr., Fort Lauderdale, 866/435-9355, www.broward.org/airport) and **Miami International Airport (MIA)** (2100 NW 42nd Ave., Miami, 305/876-7000, www.miami-airport.com), both of which accommodate major air carriers, including **American Airlines** (800/433-7300, www.aa.com), **Air Canada** (888/247-2262, www.aircanada.com), **Caribbean Airlines** (800/920-4225, www.caribbean-airlines.com), **Avianca** (800/284-2622, www.avianca.com), and many more. To reach Key West, travelers can fly directly into **Key West International Airport (EYW)** (3491 S. Roosevelt Blvd., Key West, 305/809-5200 or 305/809-5200, www.keywestinternationalairport.com), where you'll find major airlines like **Delta Air Lines** (800/221-1212, www.delta.com), as well as smaller air carriers such as **Silver Airways** (801/401-9100 or 954/509-7495, www.silverairways.com), which offers daily service between Fort Myers and Key West, and **Air Key West** (305/923-4033, www.airkeywest.com), which features quick flights in a five-passenger plane to and from places like Orlando, Miami, Naples, and Nassau in the Bahamas.

Other area airports include **Naples Municipal Airport (APF)** (160 N. Aviation Dr., Naples, 239/643-0733, www.flynaples.com) and **Florida Keys Marathon Airport (MTH)** (9400 Overseas Hwy., Marathon, 305/289-6060), both of which can accommodate commuter flights.

Train

Amtrak (800/872-7245, www.amtrak.com) offers train service to this region via the Silver Service/Palmetto route. The three southernmost stations are **Fort Lauderdale (FTL)** (200 SW 21st Terr., Fort Lauderdale),

Hollywood (HOL) (3001 Hollywood Blvd., Hollywood), and **Miami (MIA)** (8303 NW 37th Ave., Miami). Unfortunately, Miami is as far as Amtrak goes, so to reach the Everglades and the Florida Keys, you'll have to rent a car or find alternative transportation.

Bus

For those traveling from elsewhere in the country, **Greyhound** (800/231-2222, www.greyhound.com) offers bus service to locations throughout southern Florida. These include the **Miami Greyhound Station** (4111 NW 27th St., Miami, 305/871-1810), the **Central Park Bus Terminal** (2669 Davis Blvd., Naples, 239/774-5660), and the **Key West Greyhound Station** (3535 S. Roosevelt Blvd., Key West, 305/296-9072) near Key West International Airport.

Transport from Airports and Stations

If you arrive in Naples, Key West, or the Fort Lauderdale-Miami area by plane, train, or bus, you can either rent a car or hire a shuttle service to reach your destination in southern Florida. Shuttle companies include **Keys Shuttle** (305/289-9997 or 888/765-9997, www.keysshuttle.com) and **SuperShuttle** (305/871-2000 or 954/764-1700, www.supershuttle.com).

Car

DRIVING TO MIAMI AND THE EVERGLADES

If you're driving to southern Florida, Miami is accessible via several major roads, including I-75 from Tampa, Florida's Turnpike from Orlando, and I-95 from Jacksonville. To reach the Everglades from the west, take I-75 through Fort Myers or U.S. 41 through Naples. Alternatively, to reach the Everglades from the east, take I-595 and I-75 from Fort Lauderdale or U.S. 41 from Miami.

DRIVING TO THE FLORIDA KEYS

If you're headed to the Florida Keys from Miami, simply drive south on U.S. 1 (Overseas Hwy.), pass through Homestead and Florida City, cross Barnes Sound to Key Largo, and keep a lookout for the telltale mile markers (MM) that indicate your position along the 110-mile-long Overseas Highway.

To reach the Florida Keys from the Everglades, you can take I-75 (Everglades Pkwy.) and then drive south on U.S. 27, veer right onto SR-997 (Krome Ave.), and follow the signs to U.S. 1. From U.S. 41 (Tamiami Trl.) in the Everglades, head south on SR-997 and continue toward U.S. 1.

After arriving in the Keys, be sure to call 511 or visit www.fl511.com for an up-to-the-minute traffic report. This free statewide service is especially helpful during special events, holiday weekends, and the high tourist season (late Dec.-Apr.).

Boat

Given that southern Florida has miles and miles of shoreline, plus a variety of marinas, it's no surprise that many visitors arrive by boat—whether by cruise ship, ferry, or private vessel. The **PortMiami** (1015 N. America Way, Miami, 305/347-4800, www. miamidade.gov/portmiami) is, after all, the "cruise capital of the world." In addition, the Florida Keys offer their share of deepwater marinas, including the **Key West Bight Marina** (201 William St., Key West, 305/809-3984, www. keywestbightmarina. gov) at the northwest end of Grinnell Street in Key West, where the **Key West Express** (888/539-2628, www.keywestexpress.net) arrives from Fort Myers Beach almost every day and from Marco Island on certain days during December-April.

GETTING AROUND

While a private vehicle is probably the most convenient mode of transportation in southern Florida, it's by no means the only way to get around this diverse region.

Air

Several operators invite visitors to tour southern Florida by airplane. **Everglades Area Tours** (239/695-3633 or 800/860-1472, www. evergladesareatours.com, Nov.-May) offers flights on an Alaskan bush plane from Everglades Airpark and across various destinations, including Everglades National Park, Big Cypress National Preserve, Key West, and the Dry Tortugas. You can also hop aboard sightseeing flights in the Florida Keys—an ideal way to survey the islands, coral reefs, and lighthouses that compose this unique region. One such operator is **Conch Republic Air Force Biplane Rides** (3469 S. Roosevelt Blvd., 305/851-8359 or 305/294-8687, www. keywestbiplanes.com), which operates out of Key West International Airport.

Car

Southern Florida is probably best navigated by vehicle, and it's possible to rent cars, RVs, and motorcycles throughout the region. Once you've secured a vehicle, it's a snap to traverse the area's major roads and highways, such as I-75 and U.S. 41, which link the Everglades to Miami, and U.S. 1, which connects Homestead to the Florida Keys.

MILE MARKERS

Throughout the Florida Keys, you'll encounter **mile markers (MM)** that help you navigate where you are on the islands—they're little green signs that indicate your position along the **Overseas Highway (U.S. 1)**, the main road that traverses the Keys. The first mile marker is found in Florida City at MM 127.5. The last mile marker, MM 0, is in Jackson Square in Key West.

Key Largo lies roughly between Mile Marker 110 and Mile Marker 91, while the islands of **Islamorada** lie between Mile Marker 91 and Mile Marker 72. From Mile Marker 70 to Mile Marker 45, you'll find the **Middle Keys,** and after crossing the Seven Mile Bridge, you'll encounter the **Lower Keys** between Mile Marker 40 and Mile Marker

Driving the Keys

Basic mileage from northern Key Largo and Key West's Old Town to several regional destinations is listed below, though bear in mind that distances between towns in the Florida Keys can vary greatly depending upon your specific origin and destination. For example, the distance between Key Largo and Marathon can range between 30 and 60 miles.

DISTANCE FROM KEY LARGO TO

- Homestead: 24 miles
- Miami: 52 miles
- Fort Lauderdale: 85 miles
- Everglades City: 106 miles
- Naples: 134 miles
- Islamorada: 16 miles
- Marathon: 47 miles
- Big Pine Key: 73 miles
- Key West: 105 miles

DISTANCE FROM KEY WEST TO

- Homestead: 129 miles
- Miami: 157 miles

0—an area that includes **Key West** and adjacent Stock Island, which lie between Mile Marker 5 and Mile Marker 0 and are the most compact areas in the Keys.

If you're looking for a particular destination, be advised that most people in the Keys use mile markers to denote addresses, and that places are often indicated as being on the **bay side (BS)** or **ocean side (OS)** of the highway. From the western end of Marathon to Key West, where Florida Bay gives way to the Gulf of Mexico, some residents use the term "gulf side" instead of "bay side."

The mile markers often (but not always) correspond with the addresses on the Overseas Highway. For example, 100000 Overseas Highway will be located at MM 100, where you'll find a Wells Fargo Bank on Key Largo.

RENTAL CARS AND TAXIS

If you've arrived in southern Florida without a vehicle of your own, you'll easily be able to rent one at the airports in Naples, Fort Lauderdale, Miami, Marathon, and Key West. Depending on the location, the agencies available may include **Advantage** (800/777-5500, www.advantage.com), **Alamo** (888/826-6893, www.alamo.com), **Avis** (800/633-3469, www.avis.com), **Budget** (800/218-7992, www.budget.com), **Dollar** (800/800-4000, www.dollar.com), **Enterprise** (800/261-7331, www.enterprise.com), **Hertz** (800/654-3131, www.hertz.com), **National** (877/222-9058, www.nationalcar.com), or **Thrifty** (800/847-4389, www.thrifty.com). In addition, you can rely on various taxi services, such as Key West's **Five 6's** (305/296-6666, www.keywesttaxi.com), to help you navigate the region.

- Fort Lauderdale: 190 miles

- Everglades City: 211 miles

- Naples: 239 miles

- Big Pine Key: 29 miles

- Marathon: 47 miles

- Islamorada: 72 miles

- Dry Tortugas: 68 miles

ESTIMATED DRIVING TIMES

Assuming that you adhere to posted speed limits—and barring any accidents, parades, or popular events (like Hemingway Days or Fantasy Fest)—it takes 3.5-4 hours to drive from Miami to Key West during the mid- and low seasons (May-mid-Dec.). Below are the estimated driving times during these slower seasons. In high season (late Dec.-Apr.) set aside 5 hours or more to drive from Miami to Key West.

- Miami to Key Largo: 1 hour

- Key Largo to Islamorada: 30 minutes

- Islamorada to Marathon: 45 minutes

- Marathon to Big Pine Key: 30 minutes

- Big Pine Key to Key West: 45 minutes

RV RENTALS

Given the plethora of RV campgrounds in southern Florida, it's no wonder that it's a popular region to traverse by motorhome, travel trailer, or pop-up camper. If you don't have an RV of your own, you can rent one from companies like **Cruise America** (800/671-8042, www.cruiseamerica.com), which operates more than a dozen locations in Florida, including Fort Myers, Fort Lauderdale, and southern Miami. As with rental cars, age restrictions may apply.

MOTORCYCLES AND SCOOTERS

Traveling through southern Florida by motorcycle or scooter is also a viable option. In some places, you can even rent them. Key West's **JV Rentals** (305/204-4830, www.keywest-scooter.com), for instance, provides scooters and golf carts.

Train or Trolley

If you visit Key West without a car, you'll have no problem getting around town. This fairly compact city is easy to navigate on foot. You can also opt for a train or trolley ride. The **Conch Tour Train** (888/916-8687, www.conchtourtrain.com) offers a look at most of Key West's major attractions, while the **Old Town Trolley Tour** (855/623-8289, www.trolleytours.com), which provides a comprehensive tour of Old Town, allows you to get on and off the trolley at a dozen convenient stops.

Bus or Rail

Southern Florida features a convenient public transit system for those traveling by bus. In addition to offering routes throughout Miami, the **Miami-Dade County Metrobus** (305/891-3131, www.miamidade.gov/transit) provides service to the Florida

Keys with the **301 Dade-Monroe Express** between Florida City, Key Largo, Tavernier, Islamorada, and Marathon. From Marathon you can then use the **Lower Keys Shuttle** (either the Lime or Pink route), which is operated by the **Key West Department of Transportation (KWDoT)** (305/809-3910, www.kwtransit.com), to access Bahia Honda State Park, Big Pine Key, Key West, and other Lower Keys.

As an alternative, you can travel through Miami on the light-rail system. The **Miami-Dade County Metrorail** (305/891-3131, www.miamidade.gov/transit) features 23 stations, offering convenient access to stops such as the Civic Center and Coral Gables.

Bicycle

Miami, the Everglades, and the Florida Keys are all terrific areas for biking enthusiasts to explore. While having your own bicycle might make it more convenient to travel this way, you can easily rent one from several outfitters in the region.

Although the **Florida Keys Overseas Heritage Trail (FKOHT)**, a planned 106-mile scenic corridor for bikers, pedestrians, and other recreationists, isn't yet complete, you can travel from Key Largo to Key West using a combination of biking trails, highway stretches, and bridges. Just remember that you'll have to share the road with motor vehicles, so take care while navigating the highway—and always wear a proper bicycle helmet. For more information about the Heritage Trail, contact the **Florida Department of Environmental Protection's Office of Greenways & Trails (OGT)** (850/245-2065, www.floridadep.gov/parks/ogt).

Boat

You can easily travel southern Florida by boat. Those with private vessels will find plenty of available marinas, such as the **Key Largo Resorts Marina** (305/451-4107, www.keylargomarina.com), a full-service facility in the Upper Florida Keys. If you don't have a vessel of your own, you can rent one at places like **Robbie's of Islamorada** (305/664-8070, www.robbies.com) or from independent companies such as **Sunset Watersports Key West** (855/378-6386, www.sunsetwatersportskeywest.com) on Stock Island, which offers a range of vessels, from 15-foot speedboats to 24-foot pontoons, for half-day or full-day rentals.

Tour boat operators are plentiful in these waters, too. In the Everglades, you'll find about a dozen airboat operators, including **The Original Coopertown Airboats** (305/226-6048, www.coopertownairboats.com), which guides numerous trips through the "river of grass." Down in the Florida Keys, you can even take a glass-bottom boat ride amid the offshore coral reefs with operators like the **Coral Reef Park Company** (305/451-6300, www.pennekamppark.com), based out of John Pennekamp Coral Reef State Park, or Key West's **Fury Water Adventures** (866/878-2223, www.furycat.com). Sunset cruises, such as those offered by **Sebago Watersports** (305/507-9955, www.keywestsebago.com) in Key West, are prevalent here, too.

Top Spots for Bird-Watching

There are plenty of spots in the Keys offering excellent bird-watching. If you want to know where to find your feathered friends, here's the short list of the best places in this region:

· **Turner River Road:** Located three miles from the Big Cypress Preserve Welcome Center, this gravel road cuts through the heart of the Everglades and lets you spot a wide variety of birds from the comfort of your air-conditioned car. You'll also see plenty of gators in the adjacent waterways and swamps that border the road.

· **Fakahatchee Strand Preserve State Park:** This linear swamp is one of the region's best spots for bird lovers. Best experienced by canoe or kayak, you'll see an amazing number of wading birds and catch glimpses of colorful orchids among the trees.

· **Dagny Johnson Key Largo Hammock Botanical State Park:** This beautiful park in northern Key Largo is home to 84 protected species of plants and animals. Six miles of nature trails are available to bird-watchers.

· **Key Deer National Wildlife Refuge:** This 9,200-acre preserve may be named after the key deer, but you'll find a great wealth of birds along the refuge's nature trails.

Birding enthusiasts might also enjoy tailored excursions like those offered by professional bird guide Larry Manfredi (www.southfloridabirding.com), or a visit to the **Florida Keys Wild Bird Center** in Tavernier (305/852-4486, www.keepthemflying.org), which is almost entirely operated by volunteers and interns. And if you're in the Keys in late September, consider heading to the Middle Keys for the **Florida Keys Birding and Wildlife Festival** (305/304-9625, www.keysbirdingfest.org). It's usually based out of **Curry Hammock State Park** (56200 Overseas Hwy., Marathon, 305/289-2690, www.floridastateparks.org/curryhammock, 8am-sunset daily, entrance fees apply).

Sports and Recreation

Although Miami and the Florida Keys boast a number of museums, art galleries, and other cultural attractions, it's the outdoor diversions and athletic endeavors that tantalize most visitors. One thing to keep in mind when making plans is that many activities, such as fishing and snorkeling excursions, are cheaper if you book them online or utilize brochure coupons, which are often available in area visitors centers and chambers of commerce. In addition, you should take safety precautions before embarking on any water-related adventure. If you're a first-timer to activities like kayaking and snorkeling, be sure to ask for instruction before venturing into the water, and no matter what your level of experience, you should always have a personal flotation device (PFD) handy.

NATIONAL AND STATE PARKS

There are three national parks, one national preserve, and five national wildlife refuges in the region between Naples, Miami, and the Dry Tortugas. If you enjoy escaping into untamed places, consider taking a kayaking trip through **Everglades National Park,** diving amid the coral reefs of **Biscayne National Park,** or exploring the remote islands that compose the 9,200-acre **National Key Deer Refuge**—all of which are accessible to visitors every day. For more information about southern Florida's national parks, contact the **U.S. National Park Service** (Southeast Region, 100 SW Alabama St., 1924 Bldg., Atlanta, GA 30303, 404/507-5600, www.nps.gov), and for more information about the region's wildlife

Southernmost State Parks

While southern Florida's national parks, especially the Everglades, receive the lion's share of media attention, the vibrant region between Miami and Key West also nurtures 14 state parks that are worth a look.

- **The Barnacle Historic State Park:** Located beside Biscayne Bay, this lovely locale preserves the former home and grounds of Ralph Middleton Munroe, a yacht designer and one of Coconut Grove's most influential pioneers.

- **Bill Baggs Cape Florida State Park:** Home to a historic lighthouse—the oldest standing structure in Miami-Dade County—this park is popular among picnickers, bikers, swimmers, kayakers, anglers, and overnight boat campers.

- **Fakahatchee Strand Preserve State Park:** Often called "the Amazon of North America," this linear swamp forest beckons wildlife lovers, who can take guided canoe trips amid bald cypress trees, royal palm groves, and colorful orchids, while it serves as home to alligators, varied birds and snakes, Florida panthers, white-tailed deer, and other engaging creatures.

- **Collier-Seminole State Park:** Situated along the Tamiami Trail in the Everglades, this 7,271-acre park invites visitors to canoe through mangrove swamps, hike or bike amid pine flatwoods, camp beneath majestic royal palm trees, and fish in the Blackwater River.

- **Dagny Johnson Key Largo Hammock Botanical State Park:** Hikers, bikers, birdwatchers, and photographers enjoy the more than six miles of nature trails within this wooded park, situated in northern Key Largo and featuring 84 protected species of plants and animals, from semaphore cactus to American crocodiles.

- **John Pennekamp Coral Reef State Park:** People flock daily to America's first undersea park, where visitors can snorkel amid offshore coral reefs, kayak through mangrove swamps, fish or swim in the warm waters, and view tropical fish and other sea creatures in the on-site aquarium.

- **Windley Key Fossil Reef Geological State Park:** Located near Islamorada, this historical park offers self-guided trails through the former coral quarry, plus educational exhibits

refuges, contact the **U.S. Fish & Wildlife Service** (Southeast Region, 1875 Century Blvd., Ste. 400, Atlanta, GA 30345, 404/679-7319, www.fws.gov/southeast).

Southern Florida also boasts 14 unique state parks, from outdoor oases like **Collier-Seminole State Park** in the Everglades to cultural landmarks like Key West's **Fort Zachary Taylor Historic State Park.** For more information about the incredible state parks in this region, consult the **Florida State Parks Information Center** (3900 Commonwealth Blvd., Tallahassee, 850/245-2157, www.floridastateparks.org), part of the Florida Department of Environmental Protection's Division of Recreation and Parks.

BEACHES AND SWIMMING

Between Miami and the Florida Keys are plenty of sandy beaches ideal for sunbathing, picnicking, and general relaxation. Given the typically warm, shallow waters of southern Florida, swimming is also a favored pastime down here.

Where you decide to go, though, will depend on your interests. If people-watching is your prime objective, you should head to the beaches of **Miami Beach** or even

about the connection between the quarry and Henry Flagler's Overseas Railroad in the early 1900s.

- **Lignumvitae Key Botanical State Park:** Not far from Islamorada and only accessible by boat, canoe, or kayak, this wooded offshore island features the kind of virgin tropical hardwood hammock that once thrived in the Upper Keys.

- **Indian Key Historic State Park:** Once the site of a lucrative shipwreck-salvaging business and only accessible by boat, canoe, or kayak, this lovely island near Islamorada lures hikers, swimmers, and anglers alike.

- **San Pedro Underwater Archaeological Preserve State Park:** South of Indian Key Historic State Park is where snorkelers and scuba divers will find this underwater preserve, which features the remains of a Spanish ship that sank in a 1733 hurricane.

- **Long Key State Park:** Between Layton and Marathon, this peaceful park was once the site of a luxurious fishing resort that was destroyed in a 1935 hurricane. It's now a popular place for canoeists, hikers, anglers, swimmers, snorkelers, and overnight campers.

- **Curry Hammock State Park:** Composed of several islands near Marathon, this park offers a campground, picnic tables and pavilions, playground equipment, and easy access to swimming and kayaking, not to mention a 1.5-mile nature trail through a preserved hardwood hammock.

- **Bahia Honda State Park:** Considered one of southern Florida's finest state parks, this gorgeous, breezy locale features three stunning beaches, a boat ramp, kayak rentals, snorkeling excursions, a small nature center, cabins and campgrounds, and hiking trails, among other diversions.

- **Fort Zachary Taylor Historic State Park:** History buffs and recreationists alike appreciate Florida's southernmost park, which offers access to the finest beach in town, plus guided tours of the 19th-century fort that was designated a National Historic Landmark in 1973.

For more information about these and other state parks, consult the **Florida State Parks Information Center** (850/245-2157, www.floridastateparks.org).

Smathers Beach down in Key West. If you're looking for a bit more peace and quiet, consider stopping by **Sombrero Beach** in Marathon, near Mile Marker 50 on the Overseas Highway.

No matter where you go, however, make sure that you understand the rules of that particular beach. For instance, most beaches in this part of Florida have no on-duty lifeguards, which means that you'll be swimming at your own risk, so be aware of undertows, riptides, and other potential dangers. Remember, too, that nude sunbathing, overnight camping, alcohol, drugs, and campfires are illegal on all public beaches.

HIKING AND BIKING

While long-distance hikers might find fewer options in southern Florida than in other parts of the country, this bountiful region certainly offers a lot of opportunities for hiking enthusiasts to enjoy a range of unique landscapes. In **Big Cypress National Preserve,** for instance, hikers can either use designated trails—part of the **Florida National Scenic Trail (FNST)**—or venture into unmarked territory. Just be advised that, during the dry season (Nov.-Apr.), you'll have to carry all necessary drinking water with you. Conversely, during the wet season (May-Oct.), you may find yourself tromping through waist-deep water, so be prepared for such problematic conditions. For more information about the Florida National Scenic Trail, contact the **Florida Trail Association** (1050 NW 2nd St., Suite A, Gainesville, 352/378-8823, www.floridatrail.org).

Bikers, too, will enjoy exploring southern Florida. Besides biking through Miami and the Everglades, recreationists can also explore the Florida Keys by bicycle. Even though the planned, 106-mile **Florida Keys Overseas Heritage Trail** isn't yet complete, you can travel from Key Largo to Key West using a combination of biking trails, highway stretches, and bridges. Just remember that you'll have to share the road with motor vehicles, so take care while navigating the highway—and always wear a proper bicycle helmet. For more information about the Heritage Trail, contact the **Florida Department of Environmental Protection's Office of Greenways & Trails (OGT)** (850/245-2065, www.dep.state.fl.us/gwt).

BIRD-WATCHING AND WILDLIFE-VIEWING

The varied landscapes and waters of southern Florida nurture a wide array of bird species, fish, reptiles, mammals, and other wildlife. Between terns in the Dry Tortugas, alligators in the Everglades, sea turtles in the ocean, and key deer on Big Pine Key, bird-watchers and wildlife lovers will find no shortage of sightings in this part of the state. While you can easily spot such creatures on self-guided excursions through the marshes, in the hammocks, among the mangrove islands, and along the beaches of the Sunshine State, you might see even more on guided adventures, such as airboat rides through the Everglades with companies like **Billie Swamp Safari** (863/983-6101, www.billieswamp.com), located on the Big Cypress Seminole Indian Reservation. Birding enthusiasts might also enjoy tailored excursions like those offered by professional bird guide **Larry Manfredi** (www.southfloridabirding.com). Just remember to be respectful of all wildlife that you see. For their safety as well as yours, you should not feed, approach, or disturb them at any time.

HUNTING

Even hunters will find opportunities in southern Florida. In **Big Cypress National Preserve,** which hunters were instrumental in protecting, you'll find various seasons for archery, muzzleloaders, and general firearms. Although alligator hunting is not allowed within the preserve, hunters can, depending on the time of year, pursue white-tailed deer, turkeys, and hogs. For more information about hunting regulations, including proper licenses, contact the **Florida Fish and Wildlife Conservation Commission (FWC)** (Farris Bryant Bldg., 620 S. Meridian St., Tallahassee, 850/488-3831 or 850/488-4676, www.myfwc.com); call 888/486-8356 for round-the-clock licensing information.

FISHING AND BOATING

Anglers and boaters flock to southern Florida, most notably the Florida Keys, year-round to explore the offshore and backcountry waters of this abundant region. Considering the variety of game fish in these waters, not to mention the incredible views and gorgeous sunsets, it's easy to see why it's such a popular place. From Key Largo to Key West, you'll find more party boats, private fishing charters, boat rentals, sunset cruises, and full-service marinas than you can probably count—especially in Islamorada, the self-proclaimed "sportfishing capital of the world." In addition, most of the hotels and resorts along the Overseas Highway (U.S. 1), many of which are situated beside marinas, are more than willing to help arrange fishing and boating excursions for you.

For safety tips and necessary regulations that apply to both anglers and boaters in the Florida Keys, as well as up-to-date fishing information, consult the **Florida Fish and Wildlife Conservation Commission (FWC)** (850/487-0554 or 850/488-4676, www.myfwc.com); call 888/347-4356 for

Fishing Tournaments

While fishing opportunities abound throughout the year, many anglers plan their trips around the region's varied fishing tournaments. Every month, at least one highly prized fishing tournament is happening somewhere in the Florida Keys. Here are some suggestions:

- **January:** the **Islamorada Fishing Club Sailfish Tournament** (305/664-4735, www.theislamoradafishingclub.com) and the **Cheeca Lodge Presidential Sailfish Tournament** (800/327-2888, www.cheeca.com/experience/fishing) in Islamorada

- **February:** the **Cuda Bowl Flats Fishing Tournament** (305/360-6969, www.cudabowl. com), an artificial, fly-, and spin-fishing competition that usually takes place near Hurricane Hole Marina in late January or early February

- **March:** the eight-month-long **Key West Fishing Tournament (KWFT)** (305/923-5934, www.keywestfishingtournament.com), during which anglers compete to catch and release more than 40 different fish species

- **April:** the prestigious **World Sailfish Championship** (866/550-5580, www.worldsailfish. com), which occurs near Key West and typically awards cash prizes totaling about $1 million

- **May:** the **Marathon International Tarpon Tournament** (305/289-2248, tarpontournaments@yahoo.com) and the **Lower Keys Dolphin Tournament** (305/872-2411, www.lowerkeyschamber.com), which usually offers over $40,000 in prizes

- **June:** the **Burdines Waterfront Dolphin & Blackfin Tuna Tournament** (305/743-5317, www.burdineswaterfront.com) near Marathon

- **July:** the **Conch Republic Ladies' Dolphin Tournament** (305/304-7674), which, despite being a women-only competition near Key West, does allow male captains and mates

- **September-November:** the **Marathon International Bonefish Tournament** (305/304-8682) in September and the **Redbone Celebrity Tournament Series** (305/664-2002, www.redbone.org), a trio of competitions from September to November that seek out permit, tarpon, bonefish, and redfish

- **December:** the **Islamorada Sailfish Tournament** (305/852-2102, www. islamoradasailfishtournament.com)

For more information about annual fishing tournaments and area fishing guides, consult the following websites: www.fla-keys.com/fishing, www.fishingfloridakeys.com, and www. fishfloridakeys.com.

---

around-the-clock licensing information. In addition, you'll find helpful resources through **The Florida Keys Fishing Directory** (www.fishfloridakeys.com), **Florida Keys Boating** (www.floridakeysboating.com), the **U.S. Coast Guard's Boating Safety Division** (www.uscgboating.org), and *Florida Sportsman* (www.floridasportsman.com).

Also, whether you plan to bring your own properly registered boat to the Florida Keys, rent a vessel, or even charter a fishing trip, you might want to consider joining **Sea Tow** (800/473-2869, www.seatow.com),

a nationwide provider of marine assistance for recreational boaters. Membership assures you such services as towing, prop disentanglements, fuel drops, and jump-starts—useful assistance to have when you're stranded in the backcountry.

CANOEING AND KAYAKING

Given its cornucopia of freshwater swamps, mangrove creeks, backcountry waters, and offshore islands, southern Florida is indeed a paddler's dream. Luckily, you don't even have

Tips for the Paddler

Paddling through the Keys can be a rewarding experience, but it can also be dangerous if you're ill-prepared. High winds and waves can make paddling conditions challenging; while beginners are welcome to give paddling a try, it's helpful if you've had at least some experience before attempting it here. No matter what your experience level, however, follow these guidelines:

- Ensure that you've had proper instruction for the vessel that you plan to use.

- Check the daily weather forecast, especially predicted wind speeds, beforehand.

- Be aware of tidal conditions, currents, and water levels; under normal circumstances, you should allow for a minimum paddling time of two miles per hour.

- Inform someone on shore of your plans, especially your intended destination and expected return time; leave a float plan with a responsible individual, place a copy of the plan in a visible spot in your vehicle, and contact the onshore person when you do, in fact, return.

- Arrange to have a vehicle (if not yours) and dry clothes waiting at your take-out point.

- Secure a spare paddle to your vessel.

- Place your keys, identification, money, and other valuables in a waterproof bag and secure the bag to the vessel.

- Apply sunscreen and insect repellent, even on cloudy days.

- Wear appropriate clothing for weather and water conditions.

- Have a readily accessible personal flotation device (PFD) with attached whistle for each occupant; children under six must wear PFDs at all times.

- Bring plenty of food and drinking water (one gallon per person per day) in nonbreakable, watertight containers.

- Bring a cell phone in case of an emergency, but don't rely solely on said phone; reception can be sporadic in the backcountry and offshore waters.

- Pack up all trash and store it on board until you can dispose of it properly at your trip's end.

- Leave all historical resources, plants, birds, and marine creatures as you find them.

- Respect all wildlife; do not approach, harass, or feed any animals that you see.

- Be considerate of anglers and other paddlers, avoid crossing fishing lines, and stay to the right of motorboats.

- If you're taking an overnight paddling trip and plan to camp somewhere, be sure to camp on durable surfaces away from the water, and minimize the impact from campfires (if they're even allowed where you're staying).

to bring your own canoe or kayak to explore this fascinating region, as you'll find plenty of helpful outfitters between Miami and Key West. In Everglades City, for instance, **Everglades Adventures** (877/567-0679, www.evergladesadventures.com) provides canoe and kayak rentals from November to April.

You'll find even more outfitters in the Florida Keys, some of which also offer guided tours. **Florida Bay Outfitters** (305/451-3018, www.paddlefloridakeys.com) in Key

Besides the items already mentioned, you should bring the following essentials with you:

- anchor (if you plan to snorkel or camp) and some rope

- area maps and NOAA nautical charts

- bilge pump and sponge

- binoculars

- camera and extra batteries

- compass or GPS

- duct tape

- extra waterproof bags

- first-aid kit

- insect repellent

- lip balm with SPF

- long-sleeve shirt for extra protection

- pocketknife or multipurpose tool

- repair kit

- signaling devices such as a flashlight, flare, mirror, or air horn

- sunglasses

- sunscreen

- 360-degree light for operating your vessel at night

- towels, extra clothing, and extra shoes in a waterproof bag

- VHF or weather radio to monitor weather forecasts

- wide-brimmed hat

For more information about canoeing and kayaking in the Florida Keys, consult the **Florida Department of Environmental Protection's Office of Greenways & Trails (OGT)** (3 La Croix Ct., Key Largo, 305/853-3571, www.dep.state.fl.us/gwt), the **Florida State Parks Information Center** (850/245-2157, www.floridastateparks.org/thingstodo/activities.cfm), and the **Florida Professional Paddlesports Association (FPPA)** (P.O. Box 1764, Arcadia, 800/268-0083, www.paddleflausa.com).

Largo, for instance, provides an array of canoe and kayak rentals, in addition to three-hour instructional sessions and several guided kayaking trips, from three-hour tours to nine-day excursions. Free pickups and drop-offs at participating resorts are offered for most trips, and reservations are necessary for all of them. No matter where you rent your vessel, however, you should make sure that personal flotation devices (PFDs) are included with each rental or at least available on-site.

DIVING AND SNORKELING

Within the ocean waters east of southern Florida stretches the third-largest coral reef system in the world. With **Biscayne National Park** southeast of Miami and the 220-mile-long series of coral reefs that constitute **Florida Keys National Marine Sanctuary,** scuba divers and snorkelers will find no shortage of underwater delights, from brain coral formations to historic shipwrecks to oodles of tropical fish. While you can certainly bring or rent a vessel to dive or snorkel on your own, you'll also have access to a wide array of operators offering snorkeling and diving excursions in addition to equipment rentals and instruction.

In the Miami area, the **South Beach Dive and Surf Center** (305/531-6110, www.southbeachdivers.com), a PADI Five Star facility, provides a variety of courses, including an introduction class, a divemaster class, and a digital underwater photography class—plus snorkeling and diving trips in the waters near Key Largo. Of course, you'll find an assortment of similar operators throughout the Florida Keys, from **Amy Slate's Amoray Dive Resort** (305/451-3595, www.amoray.com) in Key Largo, which provides accommodations in addition to classes and trips, to **Sea-Clusive Charters** (305/744-9928, www.drytortugasdiving.com) in Key West, which offers multiday diving excursions to the Dry Tortugas.

Typically, reservations are required—or at least recommended—for all snorkeling and diving trips in Miami and the Florida Keys, and most of the time, operators include necessary equipment, such as tanks, weights, and snorkels, within their quoted prices. For more information about area wrecks and reefs, consult **Florida Keys National Marine Sanctuary** (305/852-7717 or 305/809-4700, www.floridakeys.noaa.gov); if you're interested in helping to preserve and protect the living coral reef ecosystems in Florida and elsewhere in the world, contact the **Reef Relief Headquarters &** **Environmental Center** (631 Greene St., Key West, 305/294-3100, www.reefrelief.org). Lastly, if a diving emergency occurs, such as decompression sickness (i.e., the bends), dial **911** or contact a nearby hospital without delay.

OTHER WATER SPORTS

Some local outfitters, especially in the Florida Keys, make it easy for visitors to embrace a wide array of water sports, from windsurfing to parasailing; some even offer WaveRunner and Jet Ski rentals, plus access to water trampolines and jet boat rides. Key West boasts the lion's share of such companies, including Sebago Watersports, Sunset Watersports Key West, and Fury Water Adventures. In addition, several outfitters between Key Largo and Key West invite outdoors enthusiasts to try stand-up paddleboarding (SUP), an ancient form of surfing used by Hawaiians and now a fast-growing sport that allows paddlers to stand above the water and get a bird's-eye view of the fish and other marine creatures below them.

GOLF

Although southern Florida is a recreationist's paradise, golf is less prevalent here than water-related activities like fishing and diving. Nevertheless, you'll find several golf courses in the region, including the **Biltmore Golf Course** (305/460-5364, www.biltmorehotel.com), a well-landscaped, 18-hole course adjacent to the legendary Biltmore Hotel in the Miami area. Even the Florida Keys have a few options, from the exclusive **Ocean Reef Club** (305/367-2611, www.oceanreef.com), which features two championship 18-hole courses on the northern end of Key Largo, to the 200-acre **Key West Golf Club** (305/294-5232, www.keywestgolf.com), which offers an 18-hole public golf course on the gulf side of U.S. 1. Many of these courses also provide golf club rentals, so there's usually no need to lug your own equipment with you—which is good news for those traveling by plane, bus, cruise ship, or any method with luggage restrictions.

SPECTATOR SPORTS

If you favor spectator sports, then you can't go wrong in Miami, where you'll find an array of professional teams. From September to December, football fans can watch the **Miami Dolphins** (305/943-8000, www.miamidolphins.com) take on other NFL teams at Hard Rock Stadium, while from April

to September, baseball lovers can flock to Marlins Park to cheer on the **Miami Marlins** (305/480-1300, http://miami.marlins.mlb.com). Meanwhile, from October to April, basketball fans can catch the **Miami Heat** (786/777-1000, www.nba.com/heat) at the AmericanAirlines Arena. Even hockey fans will be happy in Miami, where the **Florida Panthers** (954/835-7000, http://panthers.nhl.com) play between October and April at the BB&T Center.

Festivals and Events

Given the favorable climate, cultural diversity, and carefree vibe of southern Florida, it's no wonder that the region hosts numerous festivals and events throughout the year. In Miami, you'll learn firsthand about the varied cultures that shaped the city by attending such engaging events as the **Miami Fort Lauderdale LGBT Film Festival** (www.mifofilm.com) in late April; Coconut Grove's **Miami/Bahamas Goombay Festival** in early June; and **Calle Ocho** (www.carnavalmiami.com), which usually occurs in mid-March and is one of the largest Latino block parties in the country. The Everglades, meanwhile, have their own unique history, informed by the Native American tribes that have called this mysterious region home. At the **Miccosukee Indian Arts Festival** (www.miccosukee.com) in late December, for example, visitors can watch Native American dances and browse genuine arts and crafts in the Miccosukee Indian Village.

Naturally, the fun-loving Florida Keys offer

their own share of annual festivals and events. In the Upper Keys, history is honored with zany happenings like the **Key Largo Conch Republic Days,** a late-April event that honors the 1982 ceremonial secession of the Florida Keys from the United States. The Middle and Lower Keys celebrate the great outdoors with the **Underwater Music Festival** (www.lowerkeyschamber.com) near Looe Key Reef in early or mid-July and the **Florida Keys Birding & Wildlife Festival,** which typically occurs in September and features field trips throughout the region. Key West hosts the lion's share of annual celebrations, including the **Conch Republic Independence Celebration** (www.conchrepublic.com) in late April; **Hemingway Days** (www.fla-keys.com), which typically happens in late July and celebrates the life of Key West's most famous former resident; and **Fantasy Fest** (www.fantasyfest.com), a rowdy late-October event that features colorful parades, outrageous parties, and drag queens galore.

Annual Art Celebrations

Southern Florida hosts a number of annual cultural events that appeal to art and architecture aficionados, primarily from December to March.

Every January, the **Art Deco Weekend** lures visitors to Miami Beach's Art Deco District, and the **Key West Craft Show** attracts more than 100 skilled artists to Key West's Old Town.

In February, art lovers venture south to the **Pigeon Key Art Show,** an annual event featuring live music, art raffles, and the artwork of over 70 fine artists from around the country. Also in February, the **Coconut Grove Arts Festival** lures even more paintings, jewelry, photography, and glass sculptures to the Miami area while the **Old Island Days Art Festival** celebrates various art forms in Key West's Old Town.

Early December brings two more art festivals to this vibrant region: **Art Basel Miami Beach,** an enormous show featuring an exclusive selection from more than 250 art galleries in North America, Latin America, Europe, Asia, and Africa, and the **Big Pine & the Lower Keys Island Art Festival,** a smaller art and music event ideal for families. Typically taking place from late December to early January, the **Miccosukee Indian Arts Festival** welcomes visitors to the Miccosukee Indian Village, where you can watch Native American dances and browse genuine arts and crafts. At multiple times from late December to mid-March, those interested in Key West's unique architecture can take a **Key West House Tour,** sponsored by the Old Island Restoration Foundation. For a more unusual experience, consider visiting during **Sculpture Key West,** an annual wintertime exhibition (Dec.-Mar.) of contemporary outdoor sculpture throughout the city.

Food and Accommodations

FOOD AND DRINK

Eating and drinking are popular pastimes in southern Florida, and luckily for visitors, there are a lot of choices available. Given the varied cultural influences in the region, you'll find that the cuisine ranges from Creole dishes in Miami's Little Haiti to *cubanos* (Cuban sandwiches) in Little Havana to seafood galore in the Florida Keys. Depending on the season, you're likely to spot fried catfish, grilled snapper or grouper, Caribbean-style mahimahi, gulf and rock shrimp, stone crab claws, and Florida lobster in the assorted seafood restaurants between Key Largo and Key West. Throughout the year, you'll be able to sample local delicacies like conch fritters, conch chowder, and key lime pie, and of course, given that it's the South, you'll often see grits and hush puppies on the menu, too. In the region's finer restaurants, you'll also encounter "Floribbean" cuisine, which consists of fresh Florida produce and seafood prepared with American, European, Caribbean, and Latin American influences. For more information about available eateries between Miami and Key West, consult the **Miami Dining Guide** (www.miami.diningguide.com) and the **Florida Keys Dining Guide** (www.keysdining.com).

Although you won't find too many microbreweries and wineries in southern Florida, Key West presents a couple of notable options: the **Southernmost Brewery** (305/293-8484, www.firstflightkw.com), which features such local favorites as Havana Red Ale, Key West Golden Ale, and Southern Clipper Wheat Beer; and **The Key West Winery** (305/916-5343, www.thekeywestwinery.com), which prepares unusual tropical wines, enhanced by flavors like key lime, pineapple, coconut, and jalapeño. In addition, if you choose to stay in self-sufficient lodgings, such as a cottage with a well-equipped kitchen, you'll fortunately find numerous groceries throughout southern Florida, including several branches of **Publix** (800/242-1227, www.publix.com), each of which typically features a pharmacy, bakery, deli, fresh sushi and produce, meat and seafood departments, and wine and beer—as well as other services, such as automated teller machines (ATMs). You'll also find specialty stores throughout the region.

ACCOMMODATIONS

Southern Florida contains a wide array of accommodations, from major hotel and motel chains to luxurious resorts to primitive campgrounds. Naturally, where you plan to stay depends on your interests, budget, and ultimate destination. Though spontaneity can be fun on a vacation, be aware that you might have to make reservations far in advance of your trip. Inns, bed-and-breakfasts, cottages, and campgrounds can fill up quickly, especially during the high winter season, from late December through April.

For more information about southern Florida's accommodations, consult organizations like **Miami Beach 411** (1521 Alton Rd., Ste. 233, Miami Beach, 305/754-2206, www.miamibeach411.com) or **The Lodging Association of the Florida Keys and Key West** (818 White St., Ste. 8, Key West, 305/296-4959, www.keyslodging.org). If you're interested in budget-friendly camping options, consult the **Florida Association of RV Parks and Campgrounds (FARVC)** (1340 Vickers Rd., Tallahassee, 850/562-7151, www.campflorida.com), or contact **ReserveAmerica** (800/326-3521, www.reserveamerica.com) to reserve a spot at one of southern Florida's state park campgrounds.

Travel Tips

FOREIGN TRAVELERS

International travelers should become familiar with current American policies before heading here.

Passports and Visas

While international travelers are required to show a valid passport upon entering the United States, most citizens from Canada, Bermuda, and the 37 countries that are part of the **Visa Waiver Program (VWP)**—such as France, Italy, Germany, Australia, New Zealand, Japan, Ireland, and the United Kingdom—are allowed to travel to Florida without a visa. They will, however, still need to apply to the **Electronic System for Travel Authorization (ESTA)**. All other temporary international travelers are required to secure a nonimmigrant visa before entering Florida. For more information, consult the **U.S. Department of State's Bureau of Consular Affairs** (202/663-1225, www.travel.state.gov).

Customs

Upon entering Florida, international travelers must declare any dollar amount over $10,000 as well as the value of any articles that will remain in the country, including gifts. A duty will be assessed for all imported goods; visitors are usually granted a $200 exemption for items intended for personal or household use. Illegal drugs, Cuban cigars, toxic substances, and unapproved prescription drugs are generally prohibited. In order to protect American agriculture, customs officials will also confiscate certain produce, plants, seeds, nuts, meats, and other potentially dangerous biological products. For more information, consult the **U.S. Customs and Border Protection** (877/227-5511, www.cbp.gov).

Embassies and Consulates

While the embassies for most countries are located in Washington, DC, some nations have consular offices in Miami. Such helpful European resources include the **Austrian**

Consulate Miami (2445 Hollywood Blvd., Hollywood, 954/925-1100, www.austrianconsulatemiami.com, 9am-5pm Mon.-Fri.), the **British Consulate-General Miami** (1001 Brickell Bay Dr., Miami, 305/400-6400, www.gov.uk, 9am-4:30pm Mon.-Fri.), the **Consulate General of the Federal Republic of Germany** (100 N. Biscayne Blvd., Ste. 2200, Miami, 305/358-0290, www.germany.info, 8:30am-4:30pm Mon.-Thurs., 8:30am-1pm Fri.), and the **Consulate General of Italy** (4000 Ponce de León Blvd., Ste. 590, Coral Gables, 305/374-6322, www.consmiami.esteri.it, 9am-noon Mon.-Tues. and Thurs.-Fri., 9am-noon and 3pm-5:30pm Wed.). Other helpful consular offices include the **Consulate General of Canada** (200 S. Biscayne Blvd., Ste. 1600, Miami, 305/579-1600, www.miami.gc.ca or www.canadainternational.gc.ca, 8:30am-4pm Mon.-Fri.), the **Consulate General of Costa Rica** (2730 SW 3rd Ave., Ste. 401, Miami, 786/655-0990, www.costarica-embassy.org, 9am-1pm Mon.-Fri.), the **Consulate General of Mexico** (1399 SW 1st Ave., Miami, 786/268-4900, 8am-5pm Mon.-Fri.), and the **Consulate-General of Japan** (80 SW 8th St., Ste. 3200, Miami, 305/530-9090, www.miami.us.emb-japan.go.jp, 9am-12:30pm and 1:30pm-5pm Mon.-Fri.).

OPPORTUNITIES FOR STUDY AND EMPLOYMENT

With the many colleges and businesses in southern Florida, there are plenty of educational and work-related opportunities for residents and travelers. If you're interested in such a long-term stay, your best bet would be to research the schools and companies that interest you, consider details like transportation and accommodations, and, for foreign travelers, look into U.S. visa policies *before* making travel or relocation plans. Of course, some facilities, such as the **Dolphin Research Center (DRC)** (305/289-1121, www.dolphins.org) on Grassy Key, offer short-term educational opportunities, such as trainer-for-a-day

programs ($695 pp), that you might find enriching—without having to uproot your entire life.

VOLUNTEER VACATIONS

Sometimes, being a tourist isn't enough. If you want to explore southern Florida *and* lend a helping hand, then perhaps a volunteer vacation is right up your alley. National and state parks can especially use some extra assistance, and working in such diverse environments can be a truly rewarding experience. For more information about volunteering in Florida's national parks, consult the **National Park Service** (www.nps.gov/volunteer). For more information about volunteer opportunities at southern Florida's state parks, contact the **Florida State Parks Information Center** (3900 Commonwealth Blvd., Tallahassee, 850/245-2157, www.floridastateparks.org/getinvolved).

Of course, parks aren't the only places that need help. **Theater of the Sea** (305/664-2431, www.theaterofthesea.com) in Islamorada, for instance, invites volunteer interns to assist the animal care staff in feeding and attending to the dolphins, sea lions, sea turtles, and other marine creatures on the premises during the spring, summer, and fall months. Other places, such as the nonprofit **Florida Keys Wild Bird Center** in Tavernier (305/852-4486, www.missionwildbird.org), are almost entirely operated by volunteers and interns.

ACCESS FOR TRAVELERS WITH DISABILITIES

Southern Florida offers limited accessibility for those with disabilities. Major store and hotel chains, such as Publix and Holiday Inn, are often wheelchair-accessible, as are attractions like the glass-bottom boat tours of John Pennekamp Coral Reef State Park in Key Largo and the Mel Fisher Maritime Museum in Key West.

As with most federal lands, Everglades National Park, which is open 24 hours daily, provides wheelchair-accessible visitors centers, featuring designated parking spaces, curb ramps, and automatic doors. In addition, vision-impaired and hearing-impaired visitors can utilize audio recordings, Braille signage, and assistive listening devices (ALDs) for use in the park's interpretive programs. Also, the **National Park Service** (www.nps.gov/planyourvisit/passes.htm) offers a special lifetime pass (free) for U.S. citizens and permanent residents with permanent disabilities, allowing them free access to any federal recreation site that charges an entrance fee, including Everglades National Park and Dry Tortugas National Park.

Nevertheless, plenty of establishments, such as independently owned inns and cottages in the Florida Keys, cannot accommodate wheelchairs. When in doubt about the possibility of access, contact the establishment in question.

TRAVELING WITH CHILDREN

With its multitude of beaches, state parks, museums, boat tours, and other amusements, southern Florida is clearly a kid-friendly place. If you're traveling here with children, you'll surely find something for them to do. Just remember to supervise them at all times, both to keep them safe from harm and to minimize the possibility of disturbing others. Be advised, too, that while plenty of hotels and resorts welcome children, some lodgings, such as the Azul del Mar in Key Largo, are adults-only establishments.

TRAVELING WITH PETS

Although pets aren't allowed on most of southern Florida's beaches and within many hotels, restaurants, and stores, several places do welcome them, including state park campgrounds. In locations where dogs, cats, and other pets are allowed, it's crucial that you understand and follow any relevant rules. Typically, you are asked to keep your pets on a leash at all times, walk them in designated areas, control their behavior so as not to disturb or endanger others, and always pick up after them. Barking or aggressive dogs are usually forbidden everywhere. When in doubt, call ahead to verify the pet policies of a particular park, attraction, or establishment.

WOMEN TRAVELING ALONE

Although southern Florida, especially the Keys, is a relatively safe place for women, things can still go wrong—on the road, in a campground, even in a crowd—so it's important for solo female travelers to take precautions, especially in urban centers like Miami and Key West. If possible, tell someone back home about your intended travel plans, stick to daytime driving, and stay close to busy attractions, streets, and campgrounds. In Miami, for instance, your best bet is to stay in tourist-friendly neighborhoods like Miami Beach, Coconut Grove, and Coral Gables. Just be advised that some resorts in Miami and Key West are clothing-optional, so if public nudity makes you uncomfortable, be sure to choose your accommodations carefully.

No matter where you go, though, try to stow your money, credit cards, and identification close to your person, as big purses make easy targets. If you feel that someone is stalking you, find a public place (such as a store, hotel, or bar), and don't hesitate to alert the police. In addition, you should keep the doors to your lodging and vehicle locked at all times.

Before heading out on your trip, you should also invest in a canister of pepper spray as well as a cell phone, which can be useful in an emergency. Just remember that cellular reception is limited in the region's more remote areas, such as the backcountry of the Everglades and the Florida Keys.

SENIOR TRAVELERS

Southern Florida is an exceptionally helpful place, and senior travelers should have little trouble finding assistance here. For help with directions, there are several visitors centers and tourism bureaus throughout the region, not to mention plenty of locals able to point you in the right direction. In addition, many attractions offer discounts to senior travelers. The **National Park Service** (www.nps.gov/planyourvisit/passes.htm) even offers a special lifetime pass ($80) for U.S. citizens and permanent residents aged 62 or older, allowing them free access to any federal recreation site that charges an entrance fee, including Everglades National Park and Dry Tortugas National Park.

GAY AND LESBIAN TRAVELERS

Parts of southern Florida, namely South Beach and Key West, are openly friendly to gay and lesbian travelers. Besides annual events like Key West Pride and Fantasy Fest, Key West even has exclusively gay and/or lesbian accommodations and a variety of gay bars. For more information about gay-related events and establishments in Key West, contact the **Key West Business Guild** (513 Truman Ave., Key West, 305/294-4603 or 800/535-7797, www.gaykeywestfl.com). Those traveling to Miami, meanwhile, can consult www.miami.gaycities.com.

CONDUCT AND CUSTOMS

Florida is similar to other Southern states in temperament and traditions. While a major city like Miami might not follow the general rule, most areas of southern Florida, especially the Florida Keys, have a laid-back, friendly vibe. Many residents seem to embrace the value of having a good time while treating others with respect, though it's good to remember that a lot of the locals weren't necessarily born here. In fact, plenty of them have escaped colder climates in New England and the Midwest, giving them a sense of appreciation for the benefits of living in a bountiful, comfortable landscape like southern Florida.

Given the region's multiethnic history, reliance on tourism, and proximity to Cuba, foreigners and tourists are generally welcome here. Overall, the residents are helpful, hospitable, and gregarious. So while in Florida, do as the natives do. Be kind and considerate, ask for help when you need it, thank others for their time, and as a courtesy, ask permission before taking a photo.

Health and Safety

Despite the best-laid plans, trouble can occur at any time. Before hitting the road or boarding a bus, plane, boat, or train, it's critical that you pack a well-stocked first-aid kit and prepare yourself for the common pitfalls of traveling in southern Florida.

HEALTH RISKS

Given that outdoor diversions reign in Miami, the Everglades, and the Florida Keys, most of the possible health risks that you may face will probably involve the great outdoors.

Contaminated Water

Most of the water you'll encounter in southern Florida will be saltwater in the ocean or brackish water in the backcountry, neither of which you should ever drink, due to the high probability of dehydration. Nevertheless, you may encounter freshwater in the Everglades and a few spots in the Florida Keys. At such times, the water may look inviting, but don't take a chance. Many of Florida's inland bodies of water may be tainted with *Giardia lamblia,* a nasty little parasite that is most commonly transmitted through mammal feces. The resulting illness, **giardiasis,** can result in severe stomach cramps, vomiting, and diarrhea. While Halazone tablets, bleach, and other chemical purifiers may be effective against such organisms, your best bet will be to use an adequate water filter (which filters down to 0.4 micron or less) or boil the water for at least five minutes.

Insects

With the prevalence of marshes and beaches in southern Florida, you'll find a wide array of insects in this region, from harmless ones like dragonflies to more bothersome critters. Perhaps the biggest concerns are **mosquitoes** and **fire ants,** whose stings can cause itchy red welts, or worse.

Mosquitoes are typically more prevalent during the wet season (May-Oct.), especially during the summer months when the humidity is at its worst. To protect against these relentless creatures, you should use a combination of defenses, including light-colored clothing, long-sleeved shirts, long pants, closed shoes, scent-free deodorant, and insect repellents containing DEET. In addition, you should avoid grassy areas and shady places. Instead, seek open, breezy locales, especially out on the water, and avoid peak hours for mosquito activity, namely sunrise and sunset. Also, try to open and close your car doors quickly, and keep your car windows rolled up, as it's no fun being stuck in a vehicle with a roving, bloodthirsty mosquito.

Of course, if you are stung by a mosquito, you should be fine—unless you have an unforeseen allergy or the mosquito is a carrier for a disease like the West Nile virus. Beyond cleaning the affected area and treating it with calamine lotion, hydrocortisone cream, or aloe vera gel, all you can do is take some anti-inflammatory or antihistamine medication for the pain and swelling and wait for the skin to heal.

Fire ants, meanwhile, are large, aggressive red ants prevalent in tropical areas, such as southern Florida. Often nesting in moist soil near riverbanks, ponds, highways, and watered lawns, these ants are capable of building large, dome-shaped mounds. They are also inclined to inflict painful stings, whose aftereffects can be deadly to small animals and sensitive humans. To protect yourself and your pets, try to avoid fire ant colonies. However, if you are stung by an ant—or several—avoid scratching the affected area and

instead treat any bumps with a hydrocortisone cream or aloe vera gel. In addition, you can take an antihistamine medication to reduce the itching. Individuals who experience severe reactions, such as chest pain, nausea, sweating, loss of breath, serious swelling, and slurred speech, should consult a doctor or hospital immediately upon contact.

Plants

While hiking amid southern Florida's forests, marshes, and beaches, be careful where you step. It's easier than you think to trip on a root or other obstruction. In addition, unless you're certain that you've found a patch of recognizable fruit, you should refrain from digesting any tempting berries, flowers, plants, and the like without first consulting local residents or expert field guides.

Wild Animals

Since much of southern Florida comprises undeveloped marshes and forests, not to mention the surrounding waters, you're bound to encounter wild animals at times. While many of these, such as the iguanas and roosters that roam the streets of Key West, are fairly harmless, more dangerous creatures, such as alligators and Florida panthers, live here too. To avoid perilous encounters with such animals, don't venture into places like the Everglades by yourself and try to observe all wildlife from a distance. Although it should go without saying, you should also never taunt, disturb, or feed any of the wildlife that you see.

Heatstroke

Hot, sunny days are common in southern Florida, and it's crucial that you prepare for them. Although sunscreen will help to prevent sunburn (which, if experienced often, can cause long-term problems for your skin), you must apply it frequently and liberally. Prolonged sun exposure, high temperatures, and insufficient water consumption can also cause dehydration, which can lead to heat exhaustion—a harmful condition whereby your internal cooling system begins to shut down. Symptoms may include clammy skin, weakness, vomiting, and abnormal body temperature. In such instances, you must lie down in the shade, remove restrictive clothing, and drink some water.

If you do not treat heat exhaustion promptly, your condition can worsen quickly, leading to heatstroke (or sunstroke)—a dangerous condition whereby your internal body temperature starts to rise to a potentially fatal level. Symptoms can include dizziness, vomiting, diarrhea, abnormal breathing and blood pressure, cessation of sweating, headache, and confusion. If any of these occur, you must be taken to a hospital as soon as possible. In the meantime, your companions should move you into the shade; remove your clothing; lower your body temperature with cool water, damp sheets, or fans; and try to give you some water to drink, if you're able.

Hurricanes

One of the biggest concerns for travelers to southern Florida is the possibility of facing a hurricane, especially in an isolated place like the Florida Keys. Some out-of-towners are apprehensive about visiting the Florida Keys during the Atlantic hurricane season, which usually runs from June through November. The truth is, however, that hurricanes are infrequent in this region, and many of the most popular events, such as Hemingway Days and Fantasy Fest, occur during this half of the year.

The best advice is to stock up on extra water, flashlights, batteries, and other supplies during the season, develop a possible exit strategy, and stay apprised of the weather at all times. Although most radio and television stations provide weather updates, it's also possible to contact the National Weather Service (NWS) directly; there are offices in Key West (1315 White St., 305/295-1316, www.weather.gov/key) as well as Miami (11691 SW 17th St., 305/229-4522, www.srh.noaa.gov/mfl).

MEDICAL SERVICES

While southern Florida might feel a bit isolated at times, especially deep in the Everglades and down in the Florida Keys, expert medical services are never too far away. Although you can utilize free services like www.mayoclinic.org to learn about infectious diseases and illness prevention in the United States, it's good to know that in-person care is available throughout southern Florida.

Emergency Care

All of Florida is tied into the 911 emergency system. Dial 911 free from any telephone (including pay phones) to reach an operator who can quickly dispatch local police, fire, or ambulance services. While this service also works from cell phones, be aware that you may find it difficult to make calls from the Everglades, Florida Keys backcountry, or offshore waters, where reliable cellular service isn't always guaranteed.

Hospitals and Pharmacies

If you experience an illness or injury while traveling through southern Florida, rest assured that, as with other U.S. states, hospitals abound here, even in the Florida Keys. Some of these area hospitals include Mercy Hospital (3641 S. Miami Ave., Miami, 305/854-4400, www.mercymiami.com), Mariners Hospital (91500 Overseas Hwy., Tavernier, 305/434-3000, www.baptisthealth.net), Fishermen's Community Hospital (3301 Overseas Hwy., Marathon, 305/743-5533, www.baptisthealth.net), and the Lower Keys Medical Center (5900 College Rd., Key West, 305/294-5531, www.lkmc.com). Just be advised that most medical facilities will require you to have insurance or make a partial payment before admitting you for treatment or dispensing medication.

If you need to fill a prescription, you can do so at various pharmacies throughout southern Florida. Besides pharmacies like Walgreens (800/925-4733, www.walgreens.com), you'll find that several area grocery stores, such as

Winn-Dixie (866/946-6349, www.winndixie. com) and **Publix** (800/242-1227, www.publix. com), also have on-site pharmacies. If you're a foreign visitor with medical concerns, you may take advantage of the region's 24-hour, multilingual tourist assistance by phoning 800/771-5397.

Insurance

Although you might be the sort of traveler who likes to live dangerously, insurance is highly recommended while traveling in southern Florida. Whether you're a U.S. citizen driving your own car or an international traveler in a rented RV, you should invest in medical, travel, and automotive insurance before embarking upon your trip—to protect yourself as well as your assets. Research your insurance options and choose the policies that best suit your needs and budget.

CRIME AND POLICE

Despite the crime-ridden reputation of Miami, most of southern Florida is a relatively safe, laid-back place. People here are, for the most part, friendly and helpful. Still, whether you're visiting Miami's South Beach, Everglades City, Big Pine Key, or Key West, it's important to take precautions.

Never leave valuables in plain view on a car seat; secure them in the trunk, where they're less tempting to thieves. Similarly, in case of an accident on the highway, do not abandon your vehicle, as this might also invite thieves.

When sightseeing, keep your money, credit cards, identification, and other important items hidden on your person; purses and backpacks are much easier to steal. Bicycles should be secured properly whenever they're left unattended, and just to be on the safe side, lock your hotel and car doors at all times.

Although the Florida Keys are definitely safer than most urban areas in the United States, it's still prudent to be aware of your surroundings. For instance, you should always stay alert when walking alone at night, especially on poorly lit residential streets in Key West. As in other tourist hot spots in America, muggings have been known to happen here.

If you're traveling by RV, do not boondock alone in an isolated place. Try to stay in an RV park, a campground, or at the very least, a well-lit parking lot. When venturing into the Everglades, for instance, try to camp with others. If you do find yourself in trouble, don't hesitate to find a phone and dial **911**. Of course, the time it takes police and emergency vehicles to reach you will depend upon your location.

While in the Keys, if you witness a crime of any kind, feel free to contact **Crime Stoppers of the Keys** (305/471-8477) to offer an anonymous tip. Likewise, you can always consult the **Monroe County Sheriff's Office** (www. keysso.net) in the Upper Keys (305/853-7021), Middle Keys (305/289-2430), or Lower Keys (305/745-3184).

Information and Services

Although southern Florida—especially the Everglades and the Florida Keys—often feels isolated from the rest of the country, you're not as secluded as you might think. You'll find plenty of necessary resources here, from helpful chambers of commerce to well-stocked post offices.

MAPS AND TOURIST INFORMATION

For general information on traveling in southern Florida, your best source is the state-run **Visit Florida** (888/735-2872, www. visitflorida.com). Your call will be answered by a live person who can send you brochures and field your questions about festivals, activities, lodgings, and more. You may find it even more convenient to surf the website, which offers a comprehensive database of communities, accommodations, activities, golf courses, beaches, parks, attractions, shops, events, restaurants, and other aspects of southern Florida. You'll even find free maps and the latest deals here. Just be aware that some of the information can be out-of-date, so always call ahead when making travel plans.

Suggested Maps

In a state known for its tourism industry, you'll find no shortage of helpful maps, including Florida's official transportation map (www.thefloridamap.com). For more detailed information, you should consider purchasing a map from **AAA** (800/222-4357, www.aaa.com) or **Rand McNally** (800/275-7263, www.randmcnally.com).

For more detail, **DeLorme** (800/511-2459, www.garmin.com) produces the *Florida Atlas & Gazetteer,* which divides the state into 145 large-scale maps, complete with GPS coordinates. Though the 15-inch-long format is unwieldy for hikers, it's a great resource for planning your trip; it even identifies historical sites, state parks, public beaches, and other points of interest throughout southern Florida. You can find it at many regional bookstores and gas stations for $24.95.

If you'll be exploring the backcountry, you should order an official topographical (topo) map produced by the **U.S. Geological Survey** (888/275-8747, www.usgs.gov). Florida's national parks have topo maps for sale at their visitors centers or ranger stations. Anglers will especially appreciate nautical charts produced by the **National Oceanic and Atmospheric Administration (NOAA)** (800/638-8972, www.noaa.gov). Charts of the Florida Keys are also available at many local marine businesses.

Tourism Bureaus and Visitors Centers

In addition to **Visit Florida** (888/735-2872, www.visitflorida.com), you'll find several helpful convention and visitors bureaus (CVBs) or chambers of commerce in southern Florida. To reach local tourism offices, consult the **Florida Association of Destination Marketing Organizations** (www.fadmo.org) or simply contact the tourism bureaus directly.

On the Florida mainland, helpful resources include the **Naples, Marco Island, Everglades Convention & Visitors Bureau** (2800 N. Horseshoe Dr., Naples, 800/688-3600, www.paradisecoast.com), the **Everglades Area Chamber of Commerce** (32016 E. Tamiami Trl., Everglades City, 239/695-3941, www.evergladeschamber.org), and the **Greater Miami Convention & Visitors Bureau (GMCVB)** (701 Brickell Ave., Ste. 2700, Miami, 305/539-3000 or 800/933-8448, www.miamiandbeaches.com).

For information about the Florida Keys, contact the **Monroe County Tourist Development Council** (1201 White St., Ste. 102, Key West, 305/296-1552 or 800/352-5397, www.fla-keys.com). To learn more about the Upper Keys, consult the **Key Largo Chamber of Commerce and Florida Keys Visitor Center** (106000 Overseas Hwy., Key Largo, 305/451-1414 or 800/822-1088, www.keylargochamber.org) or the **Islamorada Chamber of Commerce** (P.O. Box 915, Islamorada, 305/664-4503 or 800/322-5397, www.islamoradachamber.com) on the bay side of Upper Matecumbe Key, near Mile Marker 83.2. For information about the Middle Keys, contact the **Greater Marathon Chamber of Commerce and Marathon Visitors Center** (12222 Overseas Hwy., Marathon, 305/743-5417 or 800/262-7284, www.floridakeysmarathon.com). To learn more about the Lower Keys and Key West, consult the **Lower Keys Chamber of Commerce** (P.O. Box 430511, Big Pine Key, 305/872-2411 or 800/872-3722, www.lowerkeyschamber.com), which is situated near Mile Marker 31 on the Overseas Highway, or the **Key West Chamber of Commerce** (510 Greene St., 1st Fl., Key West,

COMMUNICATIONS AND MEDIA
Postal and Shipping Services

In southern Florida, a post office is never terribly far away, especially by car, so it's easy to purchase stamps, receive mail (via "General Delivery" for temporary visitors), and send letters and packages all around the world. To locate a post office in Miami, the Everglades, and the Florida Keys, consult the **United States Postal Service** (800/275-8777, www. usps.com). Of course, if you need to send a package quickly (and cost isn't an issue), you'll also find plenty of shipping stores throughout southern Florida, including **The UPS Store** (101425 Overseas Hwy., Key Largo, 305/453-4877, www.theupsstore.com) and **PostNet** (88005 Overseas Hwy., Ste. 10, Islamorada, 305/853-1101, www.postnet.com).

Phones and Internet Access

Public pay phones can be found throughout southern Florida—at airports, gas stations, stores, bars, restaurants, hotels, and so forth. To place a call, listen for a dial tone, deposit the necessary coins, and dial the desired number (including 1 and the area code, if you're making a long-distance call). In the case of an emergency, you can dial 911 at no charge. For international calls, it's probably best to use a prepaid phone card, which you can often purchase in gas stations or convenience stores. To figure out the correct international calling code, visit www.countrycode.org.

Nowadays, a cell phone is a necessary tool for travelers. It can make it easier to get roadside assistance, call an establishment for directions, and seek help in an emergency situation. Just be advised that cellular reception might be unreliable when you're traveling through the backcountry or in offshore waters.

As for the Internet, it's hard to imagine the days when travel was possible without it. With the help of a computer and a modem, you can research the Everglades' native flora, book a fishing charter, monitor the day's weather, view the menu of a Key West restaurant, and perform a host of other duties. Access to your own laptop can make such tasks even more convenient, especially since several of Florida's hotels, restaurants, and other establishments offer wireless Internet access. Internet cafés also make it difficult to stay out of touch for long—especially down in Key West. Just remember that not all websites are updated regularly. Consult local residents or contact businesses directly before making any firm travel plans.

Publications and TV/Radio

Southern Florida news publications include daily newspapers like *The Miami Herald* (www.miamiherald.com) and *The Key West Citizen* (www.keysnews.com), the twice-weekly *Florida Keys News* (www.flkeysnews.com), plus magazines like *Florida Monthly* (www.floridamagazine.com), and the bimonthly *Florida Travel + Life* (www.floridatravellife.com). Such periodicals are terrific sources of information for festivals, restaurants, sporting events, outdoor activities, and other diversions.

Local television and radio stations, such as Key West's popular **US-1 Radio** (104.1 FM, www.us1radio.com), are also excellent sources for regional information, including up-to-the-minute weather details during hurricane season.

MONEY
Currency and Credit Cards

Bank debit cards and major credit cards (like Visa and MasterCard) are accepted throughout southern Florida, even in the smallest towns. In addition, automated teller machines (ATMs) have become more prevalent, allowing travelers to withdraw cash whenever they need it. If you're uncomfortable using ATMs, you're sure to find a bank open during regular business hours (9am-4pm daily) and sometimes on the weekend. That said, you'll need cash at self-registration campgrounds, and many independent motels, eateries, and stores will accept only cash or traveler's checks. As any wise traveler knows, you should never rely exclusively on plastic.

Foreign currency can be exchanged at all branches of the **First State Bank of the Florida Keys** (305/296-8535, www.keysbank. com). For up-to-date exchange rates, consult www.xe.com.

Banks and ATMs

Throughout southern Florida, you'll find numerous automated teller machines (ATMs) at restaurants, stores, and other establishments, offering convenient access to your money. In addition, most regional banks provide access to ATMs inside and outside their branches. In Miami, there are several different banks available, including the **First Bank of Miami** (877/662-3872, www.firstbankmiami. com), which has five branches in the Miami area. **Capital Bank** (800/639-5111, www. capitalbank-us.com), meanwhile, has branches throughout southern Florida, including two in Naples, two in Homestead, a handful in Miami, and several in the Upper, Middle, and Lower Florida Keys. Also in the Florida Keys are several branches of the **First State Bank of the Florida Keys** (305/296-8535, www.keysbank.com), from Key Largo to Key West.

Sales Tax

In southern Florida, most goods and services, save for perhaps movie tickets, often cost more than their listed price. That's due, of course, to state taxes—specifically, the 6 percent sales tax on taxable retail items and services, such as clothing and sightseeing tours. The tax rates on hotel rooms range from 7 to 13 percent, depending on the county.

Tipping

Although the amount of a gratuity depends on the level of service received, general tipping guidelines exist in Florida (and throughout the United States). Typically, restaurant servers should receive 15-20 percent of the entire bill, while pizza delivery drivers should receive at least 10 percent. In addition, taxi and limousine drivers should receive at least 15 percent of the entire fare, while valets, porters, and skycaps should expect around $2 per vehicle or piece of luggage. The housekeeping staff members of your hotel, inn, or resort also deserve a tip; a generally accepted amount is $2 per night.

Remember that tour guides, fishing guides, boat captains, and other excursion operators should be tipped as well; no matter how much such tours or trips cost, the gratuity is never included in the quoted price. Of course, how much you choose to tip is entirely up to you. While the exact amount of a tip will depend on the cost, length, and nature of the trip in question—not to mention your satisfaction with the services received—it's generally accepted to tip between 10 and 20 percent of the overall cost of the trip. If a guide or operator makes an exceptional effort, such as unexpectedly extending the length of a trip, then it's highly recommended that you increase the size of your tip accordingly. Tipping badly in a close-knit place like the Florida Keys can harm your reputation among other guides and operators, while tipping well could ensure even better service the next time.

Lastly, tourists often overlook the need to tip street performers, such as magicians, dancers, musicians, acrobats, jugglers, caricaturists, fortune tellers, and living statues. On many occasions, spectators have watched an entire performance, only to walk away without even dropping a dollar in the performers' upturned hat, cardboard box, open instrument case, or other tip receptacle. So if you stay long enough to observe a trick, enjoy a song, or take a photograph, be sure to leave a tip behind. After all, many performers depend upon gratuities for part, if not all, of their livelihood.

WEIGHTS AND MEASURES

For the most part, Floridians employ U.S. standard units to measure temperatures, distances, vehicle speeds, cooking volumes, clothing sizes, and everything in between. So if you've come from a foreign country that relies instead on the metric system, visit www.onlineconversion.com to convert almost any measurement.

Electricity

In southern Florida, most standard electrical outlets operate at 120 volts. If you're traveling from Europe, Asia, or a country that operates at 220-240 volts, you'll need to bring an adapter in order to use your hair dryer, laptop, or other small appliance. Outlets here vary between the two-pronged and three-pronged variety, for which you might also need an adapter—which can easily be purchased in any decent hardware or building supply store. You'll find several locations of **The Home Depot** (www.homedepot.com) in the Miami area, including one just north of the Florida Keys (33001 S. Dixie Hwy., Florida City, 786/243-9370, 6am-10pm Mon.-Sat., 7am-8pm Sun.).

Time Zone

Miami, the Everglades, and the Florida Keys are all located in the eastern standard time (EST) zone. Florida also observes daylight saving time (DST), so adjust your watches and alarm clocks accordingly.

Resources

Glossary

These regional terms and abbreviations will help you navigate Miami, the Everglades, and the Florida Keys—and perhaps better understand the region's unique people, culture, and ecology:

airboat: a small, open boat driven by a caged rear-mounted airplane propeller and capable of traveling at relatively high speeds through marshes and shallow water; also called a swamp boat

Alligator Alley: a nickname for the stretch of I-75 that runs through the Everglades between Naples and Fort Lauderdale; also called Everglades Parkway

backcountry: areas within the Everglades and the Florida Keys that consist of shallow water and islands close to shore, ideal for fishing and kayaking

bight: a body of water bounded by a bend in the shore

bougainvillea: a tropical vine that flourishes throughout the Florida Keys, usually ablaze with white, fuchsia, or vermilion flowers; also known as paper flowers

brackish water: a mixture of freshwater and saltwater

BS: a commonly used abbreviation for addresses on the bay side of U.S. 1 in the Florida Keys

cafecito: Cuban coffee without milk

chum: a foul mixture of fish blood and diced fish parts, usually tossed into open water to lure fish to the area

coastal prairie: a region of vegetation that lies between the tidal mud flats of Florida Bay and dry land

coconut telegraph: the laid-back, word-of-mouth method by which news travels in the Florida Keys

conch: a multipurpose term used to describe a marine gastropod, a Bahamian immigrant, or a native inhabitant of the Florida Keys

conch fritter: a fried ball made with spices and ground conch meat, popular as an appetizer in the Florida Keys

Conch Republic: a micronation declared after the Florida Keys' symbolic secession from the United States in April 1982

cortadito: Cuban coffee with steamed milk

CR: a commonly used abbreviation for a county road

cracker: a term that refers to the state's early settlers, who cracked long whips to herd cattle and oxen; now, informally used to designate a native-born Floridian

Creole: a language infused with French, African, Arabic, Spanish, and Portuguese, often heard in Miami's Little Haiti

cubano: a flattened, grilled sandwich made with sliced ham, slow-roasted pork, Swiss cheese, and pickles, popularized by Cuban immigrants who settled in Miami in the early 1900s

cypress dome: a dense cluster of cypress trees in water-filled depressions, found in the Everglades and Big Cypress National Preserve

Duval crawl: the local expression for stopping by each bar along Key West's Duval Street, which stretches from the Atlantic Ocean to the Gulf of Mexico

epiphyte: a plant, such as an orchid, moss, or fern, that grows on the branches, trunks, and leaves of trees and derives its water and nutrients from the air

estuary: a partially enclosed body of water along the coast, where the freshwater from a river mixes with the saltwater of the ocean

eyebrow house: a type of Key West domicile that has an overhanging porch roof that conceals the upper front windows

fire ants: large, aggressive red ants, prevalent in tropical and subtropical areas, capable of building large mounds, and inclined to inflict painful stings

fishing guide: a person who is knowledgeable enough to lead a hired charter and teach the passengers how to catch fish in a given region

flats: shallow-water areas that compose most of the backcountry in the Everglades and the Florida Keys; often covered by sand, rocks, or grass

"Floribbean" cuisine: Florida's hybrid cuisine, consisting of fresh Florida produce and seafood prepared with American, European, Caribbean, and Latin American influences

Florida fighting conch: a feisty mollusk found in the southeastern United States, known for its tendency to fight with potential collectors and predators

Florida lobster: a warm-water crustacean that has no claws, unlike its New England counterpart; also called a rock lobster or spiny lobster

gingerbread architecture: an elaborate Victorian-era style of construction, prevalent throughout Key West

Gold Coast: the area that extends from Fort Lauderdale to Miami, popular among movie stars, musicians, and other wealthy celebrities

goombay: a form of calypso music and dancing popular in the Bahamas; also refers to a type of Bahamian drum, held between the legs and played with the hands or sticks

grass flats: shallow-water areas covered in grass

grits: dried, ground corn kernels, typically boiled and served with a southern-style breakfast

grouper: a firm white fish, popular in the Florida Keys

Gulf Stream: a swift, warm ocean current that originates off the coast of southern Florida in the Gulf of Mexico and continues along the East Coast toward the North Atlantic Current

gumbo limbo: a fast-growing, salt-tolerant tropical tree, which flourishes in the Everglades and has featherlike leaves and a shiny red exfoliating bark; also called the tourist tree for its resemblance to a sunburn

hardwood hammock: a dense growth of trees on a slightly elevated area above a marshy region, present in the Everglades and the Florida Keys

hush puppy: a crunchy cornmeal fritter popular in the South and typically served with fried seafood

Intracoastal Waterway (ICW): a 3,000-mile-long waterway, partly natural and partly artificial, along the Atlantic and Gulf Coasts of America, meant to protect small boats from the dangers of the open sea

island time: the perception of a slower, more relaxed way of life on islands like Key West

key: a low, offshore island composed of sand or coral, the name of which is derived from the Spanish word *cayo*, meaning "little island"

mahimahi: a sweet, lean fish also known as a dorado or dolphinfish

manatee: the endangered state marine mammal, a giant yet gentle vegetarian preferring warm waters; also called a sea cow

mangrove swamp: a coastal marine swamp prevalent in southern Florida and dominated by tight thickets of red, black, and white mangrove trees

marsh: a flat, flooded, treeless area in the Everglades, containing plants such as sawgrass and cattails

MM: the abbreviation for "mile marker," how

most Floridians designate addresses along U.S. 1 in the Florida Keys

no-see-um: a tiny biting gnat that thrives in coastal areas, especially in the summer; also known as a punkie

Old Florida: a term used to describe Florida prior to theme parks and other commercial developments; now refers to the state parks, sleepy villages, and vast wildlands that still exist

OS: a commonly used abbreviation for addresses on the ocean side of U.S. 1 in the Florida Keys

Overseas Highway: the popular term for the stretch of U.S. 1 that links many of the keys between Key Largo and Key West

patch reef: an isolated coral formation closer to the coast than the main offshore reef and usually filled with fish

pineland: a type of terrain in the Everglades that contains slash pine forest, saw palmettos, and a wide array of tropical plant varieties

red tide: a periodic massive bloom of toxin-producing marine algae that causes waters to appear brownish red, suffocates fish, contaminates shellfish, and affects the respiration of susceptible individuals

riptide: a potentially life-threatening tide that opposes other tides, causing a violent disturbance in the ocean

sandspur: the seed of the sandspur plant, prevalent in grassy or sandy areas and resembling a little spiked ball; also called a sandbur

sawgrass: any of several sedges that have spiny, serrated leaf blades and are prevalent in the Everglades

saw palmetto: a hardy fan palm that has spiny leafstalks and can grow in large clumps, present in places as varied as hammocks and coastal sand dunes

sea grape: a native, salt-tolerant plant that grows on Florida's beaches and helps to stabilize sand dunes

sea oat: a wispy, salt-tolerant plant found along the Atlantic and Gulf Coasts, where it helps to protect the state's beach dunes from erosion

skunked: an unfortunate condition whereby one returns to the dock after a fishing trip without having caught any fish

slough: a channel of slow-moving water in a marshland

snook: a tropical inshore fish found in the Florida Keys and notoriously difficult to catch

snowbird: anyone who vacations or lives in Florida during the winter months, usually from November to April, to escape the cold and snow in other parts of the country

Snuba: an underwater breathing system, patented by Snuba International, that combines features of snorkeling and scuba diving

Spanglish: a mix of Spanish and English, spoken by many Miami residents

Spanish moss: a specific epiphyte that resembles a grayish, lacy cluster and typically hangs from oak trees

SR: a commonly used abbreviation for a state road

stingray shuffle: the method by which people shift their feet as they venture into gulf waters to avoid inadvertently stepping on a camouflaged stingray

Tamiami Trail: the alternative name for U.S. 41, which connects Tampa to Miami and traverses the Everglades

trolling: a type of fishing by which baited lines or lures are towed slowly through the water behind the boat

Turtle Walk: a state-organized nighttime event, usually held in June or July, when the public can view sea turtles nesting and hatching on Florida's shores

watershed: a region drained by a river, a river system, or another body of water

wetland: a lowland area saturated by surface or ground water, with vegetation adapted to such conditions, prevalent throughout the Everglades

Suggested Reading

While not an exhaustive list of titles, the following books will shed some light on the singular geography, history, culture, and offerings of Miami, the Everglades, and the Florida Keys. Peruse them before your trip, and bring a few along for the ride.

CUISINE

Whether planning to dine out for every meal or rent a place with a kitchen, you'll find several books dedicated to this region's unique cuisine.

Gassenheimer, Linda. *The Flavors of the Florida Keys*. New York: Atlantic Monthly Press, 2010. From mojitos to conch chowder to key lime pie, this cookbook contains many of the classic recipes popularized in bars, restaurants, and resorts throughout the Florida Keys—some of which would be hard to recreate if not for the author's suggested substitutions for regional ingredients.

Herbenick, Fran. *Appetizing Appetizers from The Florida Keys*. Bloomington, IN: AuthorHouse, 2008. Compiled by a longtime resident of the Florida Keys, this collection features many of the treats found in this flavorful region, from crab fritters to Blackbeard's clam pie.

Raichlen, Steven. *Miami Spice: The New Florida Cuisine*. New York: Workman, 1993. Penned by a cooking teacher and cookbook author, this collection of lively recipes illustrates the Cuban, Caribbean, and Latin American influences on Miami's culinary arts.

Shearer, Victoria. *The Florida Keys Cookbook: Recipes & Foodways of Paradise*. Guilford, CT: Globe Pequot Press, 2013. Written by an experienced travel and food journalist, this multicultural cookbook presents nearly 200 regional recipes, from lobster ravioli to guava custard pie.

Sloan, David L. *The Ultimate Key Lime Pie Cookbook*. Key West: Phantom Press, 2012. Boasting a slew of tips, tricks, and historical tidbits, not to mention easy-to-follow recipes for an assortment of mix-and-match crusts, fillings, toppings, and sauces, this specialized cookbook enables readers to create more than 150,000 varieties of Key West's signature dessert.

Van Aken, Norman, and Justin Van Aken. *My Key West Kitchen: Recipes and Stories*. London: Kyle Books, 2012. In this unabashed love letter to Key West, two chefs share recipes from their past and present and reveal how Florida's Southernmost City has influenced their multicultural cuisine.

Voltz, Jeanne, and Caroline Stuart. *The Florida Cookbook: From Gulf Coast Gumbo to Key Lime Pie*. New York: Knopf, 1996. Dividing the Sunshine State into six distinct regions, this collection includes southern Florida recipes like frog legs and conch salad.

FICTION AND PROSE

Fictional tales, personal essays, and travel memoirs—though no substitute for practical guidebooks—can definitely give travelers a tantalizing sense of the cultural and natural diversity of Miami, the Everglades, and the Florida Keys.

Breakfield, Jon. *Key West: Tequila, a Pinch of Salt and a Quirky Slice of America*. Key West: Key West Press, 2012. In this true account of a semipermanent vacation, a U.K. man and his wife impulsively decide to move to Key West, where their once-in-a-lifetime adventure includes wacky locals, a bit of corruption, and unfortunately, a hurricane.

Cerulean, Susan, ed. *The Book of the Everglades*. Minneapolis: Milkweed Editions, 2002. Separating the Everglades into five regions, this lively anthology presents environmental, historical, and human-interest essays from a variety of authors, including Carl Hiaasen and Susan Orlean.

Corcoran, Tom. *The Mango Opera*. New York: St. Martin's Press, 1998. This Key West-based mystery is the first in a series featuring photographer-turned-detective Alex Rutledge. Other titles include *Gumbo Limbo* (1999), *Bone Island Mambo* (2001), *Octopus Alibi* (2003), *Air Dance Iguana* (2005), *Hawk Channel Chase* (2010), and *The Quick Adiós (Times Six)* (2012).

Hemingway, Ernest. *To Have and Have Not*. New York: Scribner Classics, 1999. Originally published in 1937, this novel, which was partially inspired by the eccentric people that Hemingway met in Key West, focuses on a fishing boat captain who runs contraband between Cuba and Florida. Other books written during Hemingway's prolific Key West period include *A Farewell to Arms* (1929), *Death in the Afternoon* (1932), *Winner Take Nothing* (1933), *Green Hills of Africa* (1935), and *For Whom the Bell Tolls* (1940).

Hersey, John. *Key West Tales*. New York: Vintage, 1996. Published posthumously, these short stories offer a snapshot of ordinary Key West residents facing momentous events in their lives.

Hiaasen, Carl. *Tourist Season*. New York: G. P. Putnam's Sons, 1986. This madcap Miami mystery is one of several Florida-based capers written by popular *Miami Herald* columnist Carl Hiaasen, whose extensive bibliography includes *Native Tongue* (1991), which takes place in Key Largo, and *Chomp* (2012), a madcap adventure through the Everglades.

Katzenbach, John. *In the Heat of the Summer*. New York: Ballantine Books, 1982. Adapted for the screen as *The Mean Season,* this debut novel by a *Miami Herald* crime reporter features a dangerous cat-and-mouse game between a clever serial killer who's terrorizing Miami and the journalist who's captured his attention.

Molloy, Johnny. *Hiking the Florida Trail: 1,100 Miles, 78 Days, Two Pairs of Boots, and One Heck of an Adventure*. Gainesville: University Press of Florida, 2008. A veteran hiker experiences Big Cypress National Preserve firsthand during an incredible three-month journey.

Murphy, George, ed. *The Key West Reader: The Best of Key West's Writers, 1830-1990*. Key West: Tortugas, 1989. This impressive collection features the work of some of Key West's most celebrated writers, from Ernest Hemingway to Hunter S. Thompson.

Murrell, Muriel V. *Miami: A Backward Glance*. Sarasota, FL: Pineapple Press, 2003. In this engrossing memoir, the author shares vignettes about her life in Miami, from the glitzy 1920s through the postwar 1950s.

Orlean, Susan. *The Orchid Thief: A True Story of Beauty and Obsession*. New York: Ballantine Books, 1998. This quirky tale of orchid fanatics in the Fakahatchee swamp inspired the film *Adaptation*.

Reisig, Michael. *The Road to Key West*. Mena, AR: Clear Creek Press, 2010. Set in the 1970s, this novel features two fearless divers on a madcap adventure through the Florida Keys, Cuba, and other Caribbean locales.

Willeford, Charles. *Miami Blues*. New York: Ballantine Books, 1984. In the first of

Willeford's well-known crime series, Hoke Moseley, a chronically depressed, unorthodox homicide detective, must pursue an ex-convict who has recently relocated to Miami and stolen Moseley's gun, badge, and dentures.

GEOGRAPHY AND ECOLOGY

Many books aim to familiarize visitors with southern Florida's unique flora, fauna, and topography.

Alden, Peter, Rick Cech, and Gil Nelson. *National Audubon Society Field Guide to Florida*. New York: Knopf, 1998. This comprehensive guide unravels the state's natural history, teaches visitors how to identify varied habitats and organisms, and explores some of Florida's finest parks and preserves.

Alderson, Doug. *Encounters with Florida's Endangered Wildlife*. Gainesville: University Press of Florida, 2010. Blending adventure with cultural and natural history, this book features the state's rare, threatened, and endangered wildlife, from panthers to manatees.

Bartlett, Richard D., and Patricia P. Bartlett. *Florida's Snakes: A Guide to Their Identification and Habits*. Gainesville: University Press of Florida, 2003. A color photograph accompanies the description of each snake in this guide, which covers more than 85 species and subspecies.

Bartlett, Richard D., and Patricia P. Bartlett. *Florida's Turtles, Lizards, and Crocodilians: A Guide to Their Identification and Habits*. Gainesville: University Press of Florida, 2011. This comprehensive guide features helpful range maps, color photographs, and detailed descriptions of roughly 125 different reptiles.

Daniels, Jaret C. *Butterflies of Florida Field Guide*. Cambridge, MN: Adventure Publications, 2003. Containing large color photographs, this easy-to-use field guide helps travelers identify butterflies in the wild.

Hammer, Roger L. *Everglades Wildflowers: A Field Guide to Wildflowers of the Historic Everglades, Including Big Cypress, Corkscrew, and Fakahatchee Swamps*. Guilford, CT: FalconGuides, 2003. This guide offers detailed plant descriptions, drawings, and photographs of roughly 300 common wildflowers in this fertile region.

Hammer, Roger L. *Florida Keys Wildflowers: A Field Guide to the Wildflowers, Trees, Shrubs, and Woody Vines of the Florida Keys*. Guilford, CT: FalconGuides, 2004. Featuring color photographs and detailed descriptions of more than 300 plants, this guide is ideal for botanists and amateurs alike.

Kaplan, Eugene H. *Coral Reefs: Caribbean and Florida*. New York: Peterson Field Guides, 1999. Visitors can use this guide to identify the fishes, sponges, mollusks, corals, and other sea creatures of southern Florida.

Landau, Matthew, and Larry Gates. *Eco-Touring the Florida Keys*. Flagstaff, AZ: Best Publishing Company, 2005. This guide offers travelers an introduction to the ecosystems, plants, and marine mammals that define the Florida Keys.

Levin, Ted. *Liquid Land: A Journey Through the Florida Everglades*. Athens, GA: The University of Georgia Press, 2004. Based on extensive research, this book recounts the negative impacts of draining the Everglades and describes the controversial restoration plan that could revitalize these fragile wetlands.

Lodge, Thomas E. *The Everglades Handbook: Understanding the Ecosystem*. Boca Raton, FL: CRC Press, 2010. This work provides a comprehensive understanding of the Everglades, including the history of human influence.

Myers, Ronald L., and John J. Ewel, eds. *Ecosystems of Florida.* Gainesville: University Press of Florida, 1990. This book offers a comprehensive examination of Florida's habitats, from pine flatwoods to salt marshes to coral reefs.

Nellis, David W. *Poisonous Plants and Animals of Florida and the Caribbean.* Sarasota, FL: Pineapple Press, 1997. Filled with illustrated information about poisonous organisms, toxins, symptoms, and treatments, this guide is essential for any outdoor enthusiast.

Renz, Mark. *Fossiling in Florida: A Guide for Diggers and Divers.* Gainesville: University Press of Florida, 1999. This book offers help in finding, identifying, and preserving fossils.

Ripple, Jeff. *The Florida Keys: The Natural Wonders of an Island Paradise.* Stillwater, MN: Voyageur Press, 1995. With this gorgeous book, travelers can learn about the island chain's natural history, from its formation as a living coral reef to the ways in which climate, storms, ocean currents, and other factors have shaped the Keys and their inhabitants.

Taylor, Walter Kingsley. *A Guide to Florida Grasses.* Gainesville: University Press of Florida, 2009. With over 500 color images, this guide will assist hikers, plant enthusiasts, and professional botanists in identifying the varied grasses of the Sunshine State.

Tekiela, Stan. *Birds of Florida Field Guide.* Cambridge, MN: Adventure Publications, 2005. Birding enthusiasts will find this easy-to-use guide helpful for exploring the Sunshine State.

Winsberg, Morton D. *Florida Weather.* Gainesville: University Press of Florida, 2003. This book explains the forces that control the state's climate and offers advice for dealing with seasonal hazards.

Witherington, Blair, and Dawn Witherington. *Florida's Living Beaches: A Guide for the Curious Beachcomber.* Sarasota, FL: Pineapple Press, 2007. Focusing on the natural history of Florida's beaches, this guide features a variety of animals, plants, minerals, and human-made objects.

Witherington, Blair, and Dawn Witherington. *Florida's Seashells: A Beachcomber's Guide.* Sarasota, FL: Pineapple Press, 2007. Color photographs and clear descriptions help beachcombers to identify 252 different seashells.

HISTORY AND CULTURE

History buffs, amateur sociologists, and curiosity seekers will find a varied selection of books about southern Florida's intriguing past—and the people that have made Miami, the Everglades, and the Florida Keys what they are today.

Biondi, Joann. *Miami Beach Memories: A Nostalgic Chronicle of Days Gone By.* Guilford, CT: Globe Pequot Press, 2006. Enhanced by hundreds of archival photographs, this oral history features the memories of criminals, taxi drivers, strippers, actors, and others who experienced this colorful area between the 1920s and 1960s.

Bramson, Seth H. *Miami: The Magic City.* Charleston, SC: Arcadia Publishing, 2007. Written by a Miami native and respected historian, this book celebrates the colorful history of southern Florida's megalopolis.

Burke, J. Wills. *The Streets of Key West: A History Through Street Names.* Sarasota, FL: Pineapple Press, 2004. In this unique take on Key West's history, the author explores the people whose names now grace the city grid, from Truman to Whitehead.

Caemmerer, Alex. *The Houses of Key West.* Sarasota, FL: Pineapple Press, 1992. This full-color photographic survey of Key West's architectural treasures celebrates the city's varied building styles, from eyebrow houses to Conch Victorians.

Carter, W. Hodding. *Stolen Water: Saving the Everglades from Its Friends, Foes, and Florida.* New York: Atria Books, 2005. In this exploration of the Everglades and its complicated existence, the author includes encounters with native flora and fauna—plus naturalists, farmers, politicians, and swamp inhabitants.

Cox, Christopher. *A Key West Companion.* New York: St. Martin's Press, 1983. Numerous photographs and several essays illustrate this curious history of the Conch Republic.

Douglas, Marjory Stoneman. *The Everglades: River of Grass.* Sarasota, FL: Pineapple Press, 2007. Originally published in 1947, this book helped to draw much-needed public attention to the area's rich flora, fauna, and history and to muster support for the creation of Everglades National Park.

Frawley-Holler, Janis. *Key West Gardens and Their Stories.* Sarasota, FL: Pineapple Press, 2000. Full of color photographs, this book explores the history and features of Key West's lovely gardens.

Fuson, Robert H. *Juan Ponce de León and the Spanish Discovery of Puerto Rico and Florida.* Blacksburg, VA: McDonald & Woodward, 2000. Filled with critical documents, original maps, and historical illustrations, this extensive biography chronicles the life of the infamous explorer, who might have been the first Spaniard to set foot on Floridian soil.

Grunwald, Michael. *The Swamp: The Everglades, Florida, and the Politics of Paradise.* New York: Simon & Schuster, 2006. Written by an award-winning *Washington Post* reporter, this well-researched book explores the modern history of the Everglades, from drainage attempts to restoration.

Gutelius, Scott, Marshall Stone, and Marcus Varner. *True Secrets of Key West Revealed!* Key West: Eden Entertainment Limited, 2011. Intended for trivia lovers, this reference guide offers bizarre facts about the Southernmost City, such as pirate rules, building oddities, and questions that visitors should never ask.

Hiaasen, Carl, and Diane Stevenson, ed. *Kick Ass.* Gainesville: University Press of Florida, 2009. Originally published in 1999, Hiaasen's first collection of selected *Miami Herald* columns explores development, corruption, and other facets of southern Florida.

Hiaasen, Carl, and Diane Stevenson, ed. *Paradise Screwed.* Gainesville: University Press of Florida, 2009. Originally published in 2001, Hiaasen's second collection of selected *Miami Herald* columns chronicles life in southern Florida over a 15-year period.

Homan, Lynn M., and Thomas Reilly. *Key West and the Florida Keys.* Charleston, SC: Arcadia Publishing, 2006. This collection of historical postcards illuminates the intriguing history of the Florida Keys.

Jinbo, Susan. *Diary of a Key West Innkeeper.* Key West: Phantom Press, 2007. This book chronicles the zany adventures of a Chicago couple who moved to Key West, purchased a guesthouse, and eventually opted for a quieter life.

Kerstein, Robert. *Key West on the Edge: Inventing the Conch Republic.* Gainesville: University Press of Florida, 2012. This engrossing urban history details the evolution of Key West, from its wrecking and cigar-making days through the war years to its tumultuous modern times, during which tourism and development have taken their toll on the city's uniqueness.

King, Gregory. *The Conch That Roared.* Lexington, KY: Weston & Wright, 1997. This spirited book explores the bizarre true story of Key West's 1982 secession from the United States and the subsequent formation of the Conch Republic.

Linsley, Leslie. *Key West: A Tropical Lifestyle.* New York: The Monacelli Press, 2007. Filled with full-color photographs and anecdotes about homeowners, designers, and architects, this book illustrates the unique character of several Key West residences.

McCally, David. *The Everglades: An Environmental History.* Gainesville: University Press of Florida, 2000. In exploring the formation, development, and history of the Everglades, the author crafts an argument for abandoning agriculture in order to save this fragile ecosystem.

McIver, Stuart B. *Hemingway's Key West.* Sarasota, FL: Pineapple Press, 2002. For Hemingway fans, this book offers intriguing biographical information about one of Key West's most famous residents, plus a two-hour walking tour of the city.

McKeen, William. *Mile Marker Zero: The Moveable Feast of Key West.* New York: Crown Publishers, 2011. Cultural enthusiasts might appreciate these crazy but true tales of the writers, painters, musicians, pirates, and potheads that have inhabited Key West, an artistic haven and subtropical refuge like no other.

Ogle, Maureen. *Key West: History of an Island of Dreams.* Gainesville: University Press of Florida, 2006. This well-researched book covers the colorful, controversial history

of the place formerly known as Bone Key—from its 19th-century days as a pirate haven to its modern incarnation as a tourist hot spot.

Oppel, Frank, and Tony Meisel, eds. *Tales of Old Florida.* Secaucus, NJ: Book Sales, Inc., 1987. This collection of essays from 1870 to 1911 includes stories about boat rides through the Everglades and John James Audubon's birding adventures in the Florida Keys.

Posner, Gerald. *Miami Babylon: Crime, Wealth, and Power—A Dispatch from the Beach.* New York: Simon & Schuster, 2009. Penned by an investigative journalist, this fresh, forceful narrative shows how Miami Beach evolved from a quiet resort into the convergence of crime, finance, politics, and hedonism.

Raymer, Dorothy, and Tom Corcoran, ed. *Key West Collection.* Lakeland, FL: The Ketch & Yawl Press, 1999. Illustrated with photographs by the mystery writer Tom Corcoran, this colorful collection features three decades' worth of newspaper articles by Raymer, a columnist of *The Key West Citizen* from the late 1940s to the early 1980s.

Reid, Thomas. *America's Fortress: A History of Fort Jefferson, Dry Tortugas, Florida.* Gainesville: University Press of Florida, 2006. A compelling narrative about the history of the "American Gibraltar," once the most heavily armed coastal defense fort in the United States.

Shultz, Christopher, and David L. Sloan. *Key West 101: Discovering Paradise.* Key West: Phantom Press, 2005. This humorous book describes plenty of intriguing facets about Key West, from drag queens to the coconut telegraph.

Shultz, Christopher, and David L. Sloan. *Quit Your Job and Move to Key West: The*

Complete Guide. Key West: Phantom Press, 2003. An amusing look at life in Key West, with advice for relocating to this crazy town.

Sloan, David L. *Ghosts of Key West.* Key West: Phantom Press, 1998. Written by the founder of The Original Ghost Tours of Key West, this book contains 13 chilling stories about the spirits that supposedly haunt the Southernmost City.

Standiford, Les. *Last Train to Paradise: Henry Flagler and the Spectacular Rise and Fall of the Railroad That Crossed an Ocean.* New York: Three Rivers Press, 2002. History buffs will appreciate the incredible, ill-fated tale of Flagler's efforts to connect the Florida Keys to the mainland.

Suib, Michael, and Nancy Butler-Ross, ed. *Confessions of a Key West Cabby.* Key West: SeaStory Press, 2003. In this entertaining compilation, a taxi driver shares his quirky columns from *The Key West Citizen* and *The Miami Herald.*

Viele, John. *The Florida Keys: A History of the Pioneers.* Sarasota, FL: Pineapple Press, 1996. Though slightly outdated, this loving account offers a glimpse into the curious history of these legendary islands.

PARKS AND RECREATION

Outdoor enthusiasts will find several books geared toward exploring and camping amid the beaches, swamps, rivers, and islands of Miami, the Everglades, and the Florida Keys.

Bertelli, Brad. *Snorkeling the Florida Keys.* Gainesville: University Press of Florida, 2013. Offering practical travel advice, GPS coordinates, and historical facts, this guide explores more than 40 coral reefs, shipwrecks, and beaches in the Florida Keys.

Burnham, Bill, and Mary Burnham. *Florida Keys Paddling Atlas.* Guilford, CT: Falcon-Guides, 2007. From Key Largo to Key West, this detailed color atlas provides helpful information for kayakers and other shallow-water explorers.

Clement, Skip, and Andrew Derr. *Fly Fishing the Florida Keys: The Guides' Guide.* Portland, OR: Frank Amato Publications, 2005. Beyond colorful maps and hundreds of images, this how-to guide offers plenty of helpful information, from fly-fishing techniques to game fish descriptions.

Conway, David. *Fishing Key West and the Lower Keys.* Gainesville: University Press of Florida, 2009. Filled with local knowledge, tips, and techniques, this guide will help even first-time anglers navigate these bountiful waters.

Friend, Sandra. *50 Hikes in South Florida: Walks, Hikes, and Backpacking Trips in the Southern Florida Peninsula.* Woodstock, VT: The Countryman Press, 2003. This guide features hikes throughout southern Florida, including the Everglades and the Florida Keys.

Hammer, Roger L. *A FalconGuide to Everglades National Park and the Surrounding Area.* Guilford, CT: FalconGuides, 2005. Containing historical facts, detailed maps, trail descriptions, and other useful information, this guide helps hikers, bikers, kayakers, canoeists, and wildlife lovers explore this remarkable region.

Harrigan, William. *Lonely Planet Diving & Snorkeling Florida Keys.* Footscray, Victoria, Australia: Lonely Planet Publications, 2006. Filled with maps and color images, this guide offers detailed diving information about 64 underwater sites, including shipwrecks and coral reefs.

Horn, Bill. *Seasons on the Flats: An Angler's Year in the Florida Keys*. Mechanicsburg, PA: Stackpole Books, 2012. Written by a veteran fly-fisherman and Marathon resident, this book details all four fishing seasons in the Keys, offers handy tips and techniques for saltwater anglers, and includes advice from some of the region's top fishing guides.

Jewell, Susan D. *Exploring Wild South Florida: A Guide to Finding the Natural Areas and Wildlife*. Sarasota, FL: Pineapple Press, 2011. This comprehensive guidebook contains information about southern Florida's habitats, wildlife, parks, and recreational opportunities.

Keogh, Bill. *Florida Keys Paddling Guide: From Key Largo to Key West*. Woodstock, VT: The Countryman Press, 2004. Written by the owner of Big Pine Kayak Adventures, this guide offers route suggestions through this paddler's paradise, plus safety tips and information about regional wildlife and habitats.

Molloy, Johnny. *A Paddler's Guide to Everglades National Park*. Gainesville: University Press of Florida, 2009. Filled with detailed maps and information about campsites, dangerous routes, wind challenges, and packing requirements, this guide reveals the pleasures and pitfalls of canoeing and kayaking through the Everglades.

Moore, Marilyn. *Moon Florida Camping: The Complete Guide to Tent and RV Camping*. Emeryville, CA: Avalon Travel Publishing, 2007. This comprehensive campground directory also contains advice on hiking trails, fishing spots, and other nearby attractions.

O'Keefe, M. Timothy. *Hiking South Florida and the Keys: A Guide to 39 Great Walking and Hiking Adventures*. Guilford, CT: FalconGuides, 2009. Containing detailed information about a wide range of hikes, this user-friendly guide includes excursions through Everglades National Park, John Pennekamp Coral Reef State Park, the National Key Deer Refuge, and other intriguing sanctuaries.

Patton, Kathleen. *Kayaking the Keys: 50 Great Paddling Adventures in Florida's Southernmost Archipelago*. Gainesville: University Press of Florida, 2002. Packed with detailed maps and concise descriptions, this guide features a range of trips, from short paddles to overnight excursions.

Ripple, Jeff. *Day Paddling Florida's 10,000 Islands and Big Cypress Swamp*. Woodstock, VT: The Countryman Press, 2004. In addition to featuring trips for canoeists and kayakers, this guide includes information about equipment, outfitters, low-impact paddling, and the area's history and ecology.

Strutin, Michal. *Florida State Parks: A Complete Recreation Guide*. Seattle: The Mountaineers Books, 2000. Featuring Florida's entire state park system, this illustrated guide covers a wide array of activities, from canoeing in Fakahatchee Strand State Preserve to snorkeling in John Pennekamp Coral Reef State Park.

Valentine, James, and D. Bruce Means. *Florida Magnificent Wilderness: State Lands, Parks, and Natural Areas*. Sarasota, FL: Pineapple Press, 2006. Divided into six sections and filled with full-color images, this book provides a stunning journey through Florida's most precious wild areas.

Young, Claiborne S., and Morgan Stinemetz. *Cruising the Florida Keys*. Gretna, LA: Pelican, 2006. Offering reliable advice about traveling from the Port of Miami to the Dry Tortugas, this book includes information about marinas, anchorages, restaurants, attractions, and other facilities.

REGIONAL TRAVEL

Mainstream travel guides typically offer details about southern Florida's towns, attractions, restaurants, and shops.

Goodwin-Nguyen, Sarah. *Key West: A Guide to Florida's Southernmost City.* New York: Channel Lake, 2011. Part of the Tourist Town Guides series, this revised third edition contains information about the city's beaches, restaurants, hotels, and attractions.

Keith, June. *June Keith's Key West & The Florida Keys.* Key West: Palm Island Press, 2005. Though a bit outdated, this fourth edition offers an insider's look at the subtropical islands that stretch from Key Largo to the Dry Tortugas, including tips about notable events, bars, restaurants, and activities, plus a few hidden gems.

Kinser, Joshua Lawrence. *Moon Florida Gulf Coast.* Berkeley, CA: Avalon Travel, 2016. Among other Gulf Coast destinations, this revised fifth edition includes information about Everglades City and its environs.

Muirhead, Marsh. *Key West Explained: A Guide for the Traveler.* Bemidji, MN: The Island Journal Press, 2008. This guidebook offers a little of everything, from historical facts to romantic tips to details about transportation, hotels, restaurants, and bars.

Williams, Joy. *The Florida Keys: A History & Guide.* New York: Random House, 2003. Illustrated by Robert Carawan and written by a part-time resident of Key West, this guide provides details about the Upper, Middle, and Lower Keys, including little-known spots.

Internet Resources

CUISINE AND TRAVEL

Everglades Area Chamber of Commerce
www.evergladesonline.com
Use this website to find information about airboat tours, fishing guides, campgrounds, attractions, restaurants, and other businesses in the Everglades.

The Florida Keys
www.floridakeys.com
This helpful website offers lodging, dining, and sightseeing advice for those traveling to Key Largo, Islamorada, Marathon, Big Pine Key, and Key West.

Florida Keys Dining Guide
www.keysdining.com
This directory contains a wealth of bar and restaurant information for Key Largo, Islamorada, Marathon, the Lower Keys, and Key West—places that especially favor

conch, key lime pie, and seasonal seafood like Florida lobster and stone crab claws.

The Florida Keys & Key West
www.fla-keys.com
The official website for the Monroe County Tourist Development Council, this portal provides information about the region's accommodations, attractions, events, and recreational opportunities, plus interactive maps and advice about weather, transportation, weddings, and other aspects of traveling in the Keys.

Florida Monthly
www.floridamagazine.com
The official website of *Florida Monthly* magazine contains plenty of information regarding the state's restaurants, festivals, and other facets.

Florida Travel + Life
www.floridatravellife.com
Here you can check out the latest issue of *Florida Travel + Life* and even purchase past issues.

Gay Key West
www.gaykeywestfl.com
Operated by the Key West Business Guild, this website supports gay-friendly accommodations, events, and businesses.

Greater Miami and the Beaches
www.miamiandbeaches.com
The official website of the Greater Miami Convention & Visitors Bureau features a wealth of information about accommodations, attractions, events, dining options, and special offers in the Miami area.

Islamorada Chamber of Commerce
www.islamoradachamber.com
Visitors will find listings of events, shops, restaurants, activities, accommodations, and water sports in and around the "sportfishing capital of the world."

The Islands of Marathon
www.floridakeysmarathon.com
Operated by the Greater Marathon Chamber of Commerce, this website features places to stay and things to do on the islands that compose Marathon.

Key Largo Chamber of Commerce
www.keylargochamber.org
Visitors can check this website for lodging, dining, shopping, and activity suggestions in the Key Largo area.

Key West Chamber of Commerce
www.keywestchamber.org
Here travelers will find information about accommodations, restaurants, activities, events, and festivals in Key West.

Lower Keys Chamber of Commerce
www.lowerkeyschamber.com
This website provides information about activities, events, restaurants, and accommodations on and around Big Pine Key.

Visit Florida
www.visitflorida.com
You'll find a wealth of dining, lodging, and recreational information through this website, the official source for travel planning in the Sunshine State.

ECOLOGY AND RECREATION

Boating Safety Resource Center
www.uscgboating.org
The official website of the U.S. Coast Guard's Boating Safety Division has information to prevent accidents and fatalities while boating in southern Florida.

Florida Department of Environmental Protection
www.dep.state.fl.us
The official DEP website includes information about Florida's state parks, greenways, and trails.

Florida Fish and Wildlife Conservation Commission
www.myfwc.com
Boaters, anglers, and hunters can find a slew of helpful information—from safety tips to wildlife facts to necessary regulations—on this comprehensive website.

Florida Keys Boating
www.floridakeysboating.com
This directory features a wide array of information for those interested in boating, fishing, diving, sailing, and other water sports in the Florida Keys.

The Florida Keys Fishing Directory
www.fishfloridakeys.com

This directory will assist anglers in finding fishing guides, charters, and boat rentals throughout the Florida Keys; included here are articles about specific fish, a fishing calendar, and information regarding weather, tides, lodging, and dining.

Florida Keys National Marine Sanctuary
www.floridakeys.noaa.gov

Snorkelers and scuba divers will find helpful information about the underwater features that compose this sanctuary, from the waters beside Biscayne National Park to the area around the Dry Tortugas.

Florida Sportsman
www.floridasportsman.com

Check this website for gear advice, relevant recipes, boating and diving tips, and local fishing reports in the waters around Miami, the Everglades, and the Florida Keys.

Florida State Parks
www.floridastateparks.org

From this recreational portal, you'll learn everything you need to know about hiking, biking, boating, fishing, snorkeling, camping, horseback riding, and other activities in Florida's state parks and preserves. Also included here are maps, directions, and information regarding lodging, visitors centers, ecology, history, and accessibility.

National Park Service
www.nps.gov

The National Park Service provides detailed maps, brochures, and contact information for each of its roughly 400 parks, monuments, recreation areas, trails, and other natural and cultural sites throughout the United States. Use the state-by-state search function to learn more about southern Florida's protected places, including Biscayne National Park, Big Cypress National Preserve, Everglades National Park, and Dry Tortugas National Park.

Save-A-Turtle
www.save-a-turtle.org

This nonprofit organization educates the public about preserving rare and endangered marine turtles in the Florida Keys.

Save the Manatee Club
www.savethemanatee.org

This nonprofit organization teaches residents and visitors ways to protect the endangered manatee, the state's official marine mammal.

U.S. Fish & Wildlife Service
www.fws.gov

Here you can find useful information about southern Florida's endangered species, such as the Florida panther and West Indian manatee, as well as details regarding national wildlife refuges like Crocodile Lake and Key Deer, both in the Florida Keys.

GENERAL INFORMATION

MyFlorida.com
www.myflorida.com

Through Florida's official website, you can look up state government agencies, research attractions and professional sports, locate highway construction, check campground availability, purchase fishing and hunting licenses, and even learn more about the state's history and landmarks.

U.S. Department of State
www.travel.state.gov

U.S. citizens can use this website to get information on traveling safely, by cruise or flight, to other countries; international travelers will find guidelines for flying into and out of Florida.

HISTORY AND CULTURE

**Florida Department of State's
Division of Historical Resources
www.dos.myflorida.com/historical**
Here history buffs will find information about the state's archaeological sites, historical markers, and past events.

**Miccosukee Seminole Nation
www.miccosukeeseminolenation.com**
This website offers historical information about the Miccosukee Seminole Indians, who now dwell in the Florida Everglades and operate one of the area's few casino resorts.

**University Press of Florida
www.upf.com**
Peruse this website for a wealth of Florida-related books—from biographies to field guides—that shed some light on the state's history and culture.

Index

E

M

NO

List of Maps

Acknowledgments

I'd like to thank everyone at Avalon Travel for all their help in making this project possible, as well as Laura Martone, author of the first and second editions of *Moon Florida Keys*.

I'd also like to thank the following people for their time and expertise during the researching of this guide: Sandee Harraden at North American Canoe Tours and the Ivey House in Everglades City; Marco Island & Everglades City CVB; Kelly Robinson of Visit Florida; the Florida Keys Tourism Council; Greater Marathon Chamber of Commerce; Key West Chamber of Commerce; Monroe County Tourist Development Council; Holly Zawyer at Cheryl Andrews Marketing Communications; Key Largo Chamber of Commerce; Biscayne National Park; Islamorada Chamber of Commerce & Visitors Center; the Lower Keys Chamber of Commerce; and all the wonderful people I've met while traveling across the Florida Keys.

Photo Credits

Title page photo: Meinzahn | Dreamstime.com;

All interior photos © Joshua Kinser, except page 2 © Sean Pavone | Dreamstime.com; page 3 © Michael Gordon | Dreamstime.com; page 6 © (top left) Damien Verrier | Dreamstime.com; (bottom) Robert Zehetmayer | Dreamstime.com; page 7 © (top) timgimages | Dreamstime.com; (bottom left) Prochasson Frederic | Dreamstime.com; (bottom right) Michael Gordon | Dreamstime.com; page 9 © (top) Sergey Chernyaev | Dreamstime.com; (bottom left) Benkrut | Dreamstime.com; pages 10–11 © Shutterstock / Rich Carey; page 12 © (top) Tea | Dreamstime.com; page 13 © Beatrice Preve | Dreamstime.com; page 14 © Francisco Blanco | Dreamstime.com; page 15 © (top) Daniel Korzeniewski | Dreamstime.com; (bottom) Meinzahn | Dreamstime.com; page 16 © Buurserstraat386 | Dreamstime.com; page 18 © Juan Moyano | Dreamstime.com; page 20 © Bisogni | Dreamstime.com; page 23 © Sandra Foyt | Dreamstime.com; page 26 © Romrodinka | Dreamstime.com; page 27 © Poladamonte | Dreamstime.com; page 28 (right) © Lunamarina | Dreamstime.com; page 30 © Offaxisproductions | Dreamstime.com; page 33 © Maisna | Dreamstime.com; page 34 © Photosvit | Dreamstime.com; page 35 © (left) Sergey Chernyaev | Dreamstime. com; (right) Kevin Barry | Dreamstime.com; page 40 © Meunierd | Dreamstime.com; page 44 © Giovanni Gagliardi | Dreamstime.com; page 45 © Coralimages2020 | Dreamstime.com; page 47 © (bottom) Dennizn | Dreamstime.com; page 50 © (top) Viocara | Dreamstime.com; (right middle) Karel Miragaya | Dreamstime. com; (bottom) Meunierd | Dreamstime.com; page 55 © (top) Francisco Blanco | Dreamstime.com; page 57 © Felix Miizioznikov | Dreamstime.com; page 61 © (top) Galinasavina | Dreamstime.com; (right middle) Din Lapidot | Dreamstime.com; page 68 © Ruth Peterkin | Dreamstime.com; page 72 © Sergey Chernyaev | Dreamstime.com; page 74 © Dreamstime.com; page 78 © Brian Lasenby | Dreamstime.com; page 81 © (top left) Marynag | Dreamstime.com; (bottom) Dimitrios Timpilis | Dreamstime.com; page 88 © (top) Sandra Foyt | Dreamstime.com; (left middle) Francisco Blanco | Dreamstime.com; (right middle) Gordon Logue | Dreamstime.com; (bottom) Simon Dannhauer | Dreamstime.com; page 92 © Fotoluminate | Dreamstime. com; page 96 © Smitty Smitty | Dreamstime.com; page 99 © Fotoluminate | Dreamstime.com; page 100 © (left) timgimages | Dreamstime.com; (right) Fotoluminate | Dreamstime.com; page 105 © (bottom) Michael Wood | Dreamstime.com; page 107 © Rafael Ben Ari | Dreamstime.com; page 110 © Andrew Jalbert | Dreamstime.com; page 113 © Sergio Llaguno | Dreamstime.com; page 116 © (bottom) Luminouslens | Dreamstime.com; page 132 © TasFoto | Dreamstime.com; page 134 © Kevin Ruck | Dreamstime.com; page 139 © (top) Wilsilver77 | Dreamstime.com; (bottom) Romrodinka | Dreamstime.com; page 144 © (top) Idania Le Vexier | Dreamstime.com; (left middle) Fotoluminate | Dreamstime.com; (right middle) Tony Bosse | Dreamstime.com; (bottom) Steveheap | Dreamstime.com; page 147 © Sandy Andreoletti | Dreamstime. com; page 154 © (bottom) Kevin Cable | Dreamstime.com; page 161 © (left middle) Mmorell | Dreamstime. com; (bottom) Kevin Ruck | Dreamstime.com; page 169 © SimonDannhauer | Dreamstime.com; page 170 © (top left) Pawel Mazur | Dreamstime.com; (top right) Fapnature | Dreamstime.com; page 174 © (top) Felix Mizioznikov | Dreamstime.com; page 179 © Shutterstock / Jeff Stamer; page 182 © (top left) Tony Bosse | Dreamstime.com; (top right) Sandra Foyt | Dreamstime.com; page 184 © Michael Wood | Dreamstime.com; page 187 © Peter Leahy | Dreamstime.com; page 202 © Edytamlaw | Dreamstime.com; page 203 © (top left) Hakoar | Dreamstime.com; (top right) Michael Rosebrock | Dreamstime.com; page 210 © (top) Sandra Foyt | Dreamstime.com; (left middle) Sally Siko | Dreamstime.com; (right middle) Hakoar | Dreamstime. com; (bottom) Steven Prorak | Dreamstime.com; page 214 © (bottom) Peterclark1985 | Dreamstime. com; page 219 © (top right) Wilsilver77 | Dreamstime.com; page 228 © Beatrice Preve | Dreamstime. com; page 229 © (top right) Maisna | Dreamstime.com; page 239 © (top) Kaye E | Dreamstime.com; (left middle) Wangkun Jia | Dreamstime.com; (right middle) Fotoluminate | Dreamstime.com; page 241 © Joe Sohm | Dreamstime.com; page 246 © (top left) Sandra Foyt | Dreamstime.com; page 248 © Giovanni Gagliardi | Dreamstime.com; page 255 © (top) Tim Armstrong | Dreamstime.com; (left middle) Roman Stetsyk | Dreamstime.com; (bottom) Aiisha | Dreamstime.com; page 261 © (bottom) Charles Wagner, Jr. | Dreamstime.com; page 267 © (top) Smitty Smitty | Dreamstime.com; (bottom) Daniel Korzeniewski | Dreamstime.com; page 271 © Marilyn Gould | Dreamstime.com; page 275 © (top left) Wangkun Jia | Dreamstime.com; (top right) Worachat Sodsri | Dreamstime.com; (bottom) Meinzahn | Dreamstime.com; page 281 © Romrodinka | Dreamstime.com; page 298 © (top) Tony Bosse | Dreamstime.com; (bottom) Anirav | Dreamstime.com; page 309 © Svetlana Foote | Dreamstime.com; page 321 © Giovanni Gagliardi | Dreamstime.com

Moon Travel Guides to the Caribbean

ARUBA

BAHAMAS

MARIAN JAINE HOYLE

BERMUDA

ROSEMARY JONES

CUBA

CHRISTOPHER P. BAKER

DOMINICAN REPUBLIC

LEBAWIT LILY GIRMA

JAMAICA

Central & South America Travel Guides

BELIZE

LEBAWIT LILY GIRMA

CARTAGENA & COLOMBIA'S CARIBBEAN COAST

COSTA RICA

ECUADOR & THE GALÁPAGOS ISLANDS

BETHANY PITTS

TRIP OF A LIFETIME

GALÁPAGOS ISLANDS

TRIP OF A LIFETIME

MACHU PICCHU

RYAN DUBE

TRIP OF A LIFETIME

PATAGONIA

WAYNE BERNHARDSON

PERU

RYAN DUBE

MOON FLORIDA KEYS

Avalon Travel
Hachette Book Group
1700 Fourth Street
Berkeley, CA 94710, USA
www.moon.com

Editor and Series Manager: Kathryn Ettinger
Acquiring Editor: Nikki Ioakimedes
Copy Editor: Brett Keener
Graphics and Production Coordinator:
  Lucie Ericksen
Cover Design: Faceout Studios, Charles Brock
Interior Design: Domini Dragoone
Moon Logo: Tim McGrath
Map Editor: Albert Angulo
Cartographers: Andrew Dolan, Brian Shotwell,
  and Albert Angulo
Indexer: Greg Jewett

ISBN-13: 978-1-64049-860-0

Printing History
1st Edition — 2011
4th Edition — April 2020
5 4 3 2 1

Front cover photo: boats at Islamorada © Water
  Frame / Alamy Stock Photo
Back cover photo: great egret in the Everglades ©
  Ivan Cholakov | Dreamstime.com

Printed in China by RR Donnelley

Avalon Travel is a division of Hachette Book Group,
Inc. Moon and the Moon logo are trademarks of
Hachette Book Group, Inc. All other marks and logos
depicted are the property of the original owners.

MAP SYMBOLS

═══	Expressway	○	City/Town	✈	Airport	⚲	Golf Course
═══	Primary Road	◉	State Capital	✗	Airfield	🅿	Parking Area
═══	Secondary Road	✸	National Capital	▲	Mountain	🏛	Archaeological Site
┄┄┄	Unpaved Road	★	Point of Interest	✛	Unique Natural Feature	⛪	Church
───	Feature Trail	•	Accommodation		Waterfall	⛽	Gas Station
------	Other Trail	▼	Restaurant/Bar	⚑	Park		Glacier
··········	Ferry	■	Other Location	🚩	Trailhead		Mangrove
═══	Pedestrian Walkway						Reef
▨▨▨	Stairs	Λ	Campground	⛷	Skiing Area		Swamp

CONVERSION TABLES

$$°C = (°F - 32) / 1.8$$
$$°F = (°C \times 1.8) + 32$$

1 inch = 2.54 centimeters (cm)
1 foot = 0.304 meters (m)
1 yard = 0.914 meters
1 mile = 1.6093 kilometers (km)
1 km = 0.6214 miles
1 fathom = 1.8288 m
1 chain = 20.1168 m
1 furlong = 201.168 m
1 acre = 0.4047 hectares
1 sq km = 100 hectares
1 sq mile = 2.59 square km
1 ounce = 28.35 grams
1 pound = 0.4536 kilograms
1 short ton = 0.90718 metric ton
1 short ton = 2,000 pounds
1 long ton = 1.016 metric tons
1 long ton = 2,240 pounds
1 metric ton = 1,000 kilograms
1 quart = 0.94635 liters
1 US gallon = 3.7854 liters
1 Imperial gallon = 4.5459 liters
1 nautical mile = 1.852 km

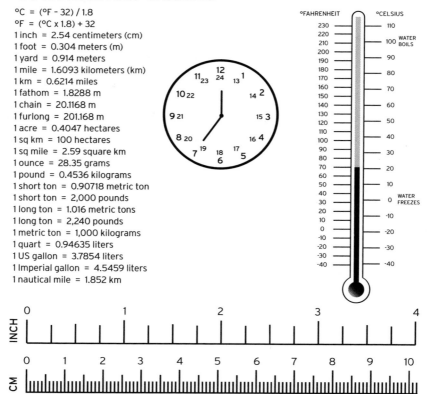